REFUSENIK

REFUSENIK

Trapped in the Soviet Union

MARK YA. AZBEL

Edited by Grace Pierce Forbes

Boston

HOUGHTON MIFFLIN COMPANY

1981

Library of Congress Cataloging in Publication Data

Azbel', Mark IAkovlevich.
Refusenik, trapped in the Soviet Union.

Includes index.
1. Azbel', Mark IAkovlevich. 2. Jews in Russia—
Biography. 3. Israel—Emigration and immigration—
Biography. 4. Physicists—Russia—Biography.
5. Russia—Emigration and immigration—Biography.
I. Forbes, Grace Pierce. II. Title.
DS135.R95A937   323.1'1924'047 [B]   80-22081
ISBN 0-395-30226-9

Printed in the United States of America

V 10 9 8 7 6 5 4 3 2 1

Contents

BOOK II

Illustrations

Foreword

by Freeman J. Dyson

MARK AZBEL is one of the genuine heroes of our time, worthy to stand on the stage of history with Andrei Sakharov and Aleksandr Solzhenitsyn. I met him first in Moscow in 1956 when he was shy and thin, a brilliant young physicist rising rapidly through the ranks of the Soviet scientific establishment. He and I had worked independently on the same problem in solid-state physics. His solution was more general and more powerful than mine. I knew then that he would become an important scientist. I had no inkling that he would become a famous dissident. His book describes the human background of his life: the hardships of childhood in wartime Siberia, the joys and sorrows of becoming a full member of the privileged Soviet intelligentsia, the gradual growth of awareness of his Jewish roots, the transfer of his loyalties from Russia to Israel, the decision to emigrate, the drama of his five-year leadership of the group of Jewish dissidents in Moscow, and the final safe arrival in the promised land with wife and daughter and cat.

Two aspects of the book make it unique as a historical document. In Book I, Azbel gives us an authoritative record of the vicissitudes of Soviet science during the post-Stalin era. The record is based primarily on his first-hand knowledge of the leading physicists and of the Party hacks with whom they had to struggle. But his interests and his knowledge extend far beyond physics, into all areas of Soviet intellectual life. And his understanding of the hidden sources of power and influence give his record a depth that is lacking in accounts written by outsiders.

In Book II we have a record of the duel that was fought, in the secret chambers of the KGB, between Azbel and the various KGB interrogators who tried to break down his resistance. This duel is similar in many ways to the duel described in Arthur Koestler's novel *Darkness at Noon*, forty years earlier. Koestler's hero, Rubashov, is one of the old Bolshevik leaders of the 1917 revolution. Stalin's policemen succeed in breaking his spirit and persuade him to incriminate himself and his friends before they execute him. Azbel was given the same treatment. He tells me that he has never read *Darkness at Noon,* and I therefore accept as accurate his memory of the many details of his interrogations, which faithfully echo the interrogations of Rubashov. There is only one essential difference between Rubashov's duel and Azbel's. Rubashov lost and Azbel won.

How could it have happened that Azbel won? There are two main reasons. In the first place, Azbel is gifted with superhuman courage and presence of mind. When, in the course of his interrogations, he is brought before a group including a full general of the KGB and the Prosecutor-General of Moscow, his immediate reaction is to think: "I suppose it was not until this confrontation with such a formidable array of top-ranking authorities that I fully realized what a threat we posed to them." Which of us ordinary mortals would entertain such a thought at such a time? The final turning point of his duel comes when he is interrogated by an official of even higher rank, Sergei Ivanovitch Gavrilov, the liaison man between the KGB and the Central Committee. Here Azbel takes the offensive. "You'll encounter some new troubles, which, I assure you, you don't anticipate. Either you'll have to let me go, or you'll have to imprison me for a long term; you won't have any other choice. You seem to know a lot about me, Sergei Ivanovitch. You probably realize that I'm not lying . . . So there are the alternatives for you. Which do you prefer: simply to let me go, or to create another martyr to arouse the sympa hies of the scientific community? It seems to me that in this case our interests coincide."

The second reason Azbel won is that the Soviet establishment has in some sense lost its nerve. Forty years ago, the interrogators of Rubashov would not have been intimidated by Azbel's defiance. They would not have hesitated to add one more martyr to the millions they had already made. They would have replied to his recalcitrance by sending him down to be shot in the cellar or sending him away to rot in a labor camp. Now, forty years later, things have changed. The Soviet regime, even in the innermost recesses of the KGB, is unsure of itself. Azbel prevailed over his enemies because he was prepared to die and they were unprepared to kill. This is a historical development of profound importance, not only for the future of Soviet society but for the future of all mankind.

We in the West have a double responsibility, which we cannot evade. In the first place, as Azbel's story makes clear, we have a responsibility to give practical and moral support to individuals who are fighting for their lives and their freedom within the Soviet system and who call to us for help. In the second place, we have an even greater responsibility to avoid doing harm to the millions of loyal Soviet citizens who do not ask for our help and can only be endangered by it. In particular, we must think of the plight of the multitude of Jews who are striving to build a future for themselves and their children in the Soviet Union and for whom any action tending to identify Jews in general as Western protégés represents a deadly threat. Above all, we must avoid repeating the mistakes of 1918–1920, when the well-meaning but blundering attempts of the United States and other Western countries to help the opponents of the Soviet regime ended in the strengthening of our enemies and the massacre of our friends.

Confronted with this double responsibility, what should we do? Whether we decide to involve ourselves or not to involve ourselves in the struggle for human rights in the Soviet Union, we are gambling with other people's lives. I have generally believed that it is wise for us to avoid involvement, remembering the words of Solzhenitsyn: "I put no hopes in the West — indeed, no Russian ever should. If we ever become free it will only be by our own efforts." But now Mark Azbel has convinced me that there are occasions when Western involvement is practically effective and morally justifiable. I regret now that I gave no help to Azbel during his years of struggle. I still am afraid that our impatient attempts to force the Soviet regime to adopt our alien standards may result in halting the slow internal evolution of the regime toward more humane patterns of behavior. We must weigh the consequences of intervention in each case as best we can, never acting in a spirit of self-righteous ignorance, giving help only when we can clearly see that the people we help are like Mark Azbel, people who have the strength and the courage to become free by their own efforts.

BOOK I

Prologue

I⊤ ɪѕ a relatively comfortable Soviet prison, located in a former monastery near the ancient little town of Serpukhov. There are supposed to be four of us to a cell: a tiny cramped space; two double-deck iron beds bolted to the floor. A fixed iron table, a fixed iron bench six inches wide. A window, twelve inches by six, ten feet above the floor, with some sort of awning over it on the outside so that even if you sat on an upper bunk to look out you could not catch a glimpse of the sky. Only a few square inches of floor space for four men to walk upon. A small spy-hole through which we can be observed day and night. Day and night, electric light in the cell. Built into the cell door is a narrow hatchway through which our food is shoved. The food, according to regulation, costs thirty kopeks per person; but half of this money is regularly stolen by the prison guards, so there remains something around twenty cents' worth of food a day for each prisoner.

Every other day, we are taken out for a short interval of exercise, a "walk" in a cramped stone box with a cement floor. The walls are twelve feet high and topped by a section of curved wire. Not a blade of grass underfoot. When we are led out for this fresh air, we are ordered to keep our hands clasped behind our backs, and we pass through a dozen doors, each locked with its own key.

A prisoner who defies any regulation, or fails to obey any order of a guard, is liable to hours, or days, in the punishment cell. This is a stone box one square meter in size, totally dark throughout the twenty-four hours. One can stand in it, crouched, or sit on a small bench, but then one's back and knees hurt because the walls are of rough-plastered stone. Only cold water and bread. That is punishment.

That was our "easy" prison, near the medieval city of Serpukhov. The monastery is surrounded by high walls, four feet thick. We were supervised at all times, even during our walks, because above all these boxes was a sentry's platform. An armed guard watched us, oversaw our every movement, and was ready to fire if he felt the slightest suspicion about our intentions.

Inmates had not a minute to themselves. The regulations forbade books; forbade any occupation; everything was forbidden. Forbidden to lie down between six A.M. and eleven P.M.; forbidden to come close to the guard's one-inch spy-hole; forbidden to turn one's back to the guard; forbidden even to sit quietly and think, because there was a radio loudspeaker in the cell, switched on from the outside.

No charges had been made against us; there had been no trial. We had been brought in simply on orders "from above." This was unconstitutional — but who cared? We had not committed any crime. All we had done was to apply for permission to leave the Soviet Union for Israel.

Several years have passed since my imprisonment in Serpukhov, but not long ago I had a nightmare about it. In the dream, it seems that someone is working on plans for an escape. Help might be coming from friends on the outside. We would assume the identities of prisoners who had died, and use their passports * once we were free. (In real life, this would be something that could never happen — but everything is possible in dreams.) For myself, I decide against the plan. If I escape, I'll lose access forever to the documents I need in order to obtain a visa to get out of the country, and I'll spend the rest of my life a fugitive under a false name within the enormous prison called the Soviet Union. If I stay here, maybe I'll be killed. But as long as I am alive, I can always believe that some day I may get the chance to leave the Soviets.

Without warning, the door opens, and two guards are standing in the doorway. They take me to the cellar; lock me in a tiny pitch-dark cell. Through the thick walls I can hear shots in the cells to one side of me. The sounds come closer and closer. Then my turn comes. I hear "my" shot — and then I wake up: a free man, in Israel. Thank God! it was a dream; but a very real dream. The cell, the other prisoners, the stone steps, were exactly those I had known in real life.

I have left the Soviet Union. But many of my friends are still there. Some of them may be arrested at any time; some of them are already imprisoned; and one of them, Anatoly Shcharansky, was sentenced in June, 1978, to thirteen years of imprisonment.

That is why I feel committed to write this book: for all of my friends who are still in the U.S.S.R.; both for those who have risked their freedom and perhaps their lives by applying for their visas; and for those

---

* Soviet citizens are issued internal passports; without them, one cannot travel at all within the country. Also, they are indispensable for obtaining an apartment, for performing any sort of financial transaction, etc.

who make no protest against Soviet oppression and who are not trying to leave — they have their reasons. I can only write about what is happening to them. I feel I have no right to recount anything but facts here. Obviously I will be unable to mention the names of some of my colleagues and friends, out of consideration for their safety. Otherwise, I am trying to tell everything I have observed with my own eyes.

Thirty-five Centuries

MY FAMILY NAME is mentioned in the Bible. The family of Ashbel (Azbel is the Russian version of this name) was among the sixty families who came to Israel with Moses. Apparently I can trace my ancestry back to Adam.

But I never learned about this until I was forty-two years old. In the U.S.S.R., to own or read a Bible is almost impossible. When I tried to get hold of a Bible in the largest library in the Soviet Union, the Lenin Library, I was refused, and was told that you have to have special permission to read it.

Although my name is mentioned in the history of Israel, I didn't know a single Hebrew letter until I reached the age of forty. I knew very little about Jewish history, Jewish religion, Jewish culture. If I had tried to learn more — that would have been the end of my job; practically everything Jewish is forbidden in the Soviet Union. The standard history textbook studied in the schools of that country doesn't mention Judaea. There is Ancient Greece, China, India, Ancient Egypt — but no Judaea, no Israel. This whole area simply does not exist for a Soviet person. There is no mention of Jews in any of the school and high-school textbooks in the Soviet Union, until Jews appear in the nineteenth century — completely without antecedents — as ruthless exploiters, the original creators of evil Capitalism.

Impossible though it may seem to the Western reader, there is no mention of the Holocaust in history books used in the schools today.

Of course, it is not only the Jews who are repressed in the Soviets. Quite recently, it was only due to angry demonstrations by Georgians that the Georgian language was mentioned in the constitution of that republic: the *"Independent* Soviet Socialist Republic of Georgia," as it is described! Not all of the minorities are as fortunate as the Georgians: most of the national constitutions of the U.S.S.R. do not indicate the national language as the official language of the republics, "indepen-dent" though they may be.

But Jews do not have their republic; * therefore there is not one school in the Soviet Union where they can study Hebrew, and just a couple in Birobidjan where they can learn Yiddish. And that is why, al-though I eventually learned about my long-ago forefathers, I was brought up knowing nothing about my ancestors closer in time. It was impossible for me to find out anything about them. Alex Haley, author of the popular *Roots,* was able to trace his ancestry. I cannot.

These enormous lacunae in the history taught in Russia are in accord with a deliberate aim on the part of the Soviet officials: to hinder Jews from learning their own past. Significant history starts with the Great October Revolution, and that is why until recently I knew absolutely nothing about my people. I knew only the story of my own father and mother — a story very representative in its way of their time and place.

* * *

My father, Yakov Aronovitch Azbel, was born in Novgorod-Seversky, a little city that was once the capital of an independent princedom. By the early years of this century, Novgorod-Seversky had become a kind of *shtetl.*

By the time Father reached the age of fifteen he had become aware of the terribly poor, confined, and hopeless prospects facing him in that town, and he realized that if he were to have any sort of future he would have to leave home.

He went to Kharkov, which was at that time still the capital of the Ukraine,† possessing nothing by way of property but a few roubles and the homemade (actually even homespun) clothes on his back.

In 1925, when he arrived there, Kharkov, formerly a prosperous and flourishing city, was in the grip of the tragic economic depression that would worsen over all of the Russias in the wake of Soviet attempts to collectivize and industrialize the nation.

It looked as though Father's dream — to join a trade union, to get a job at no matter how low a level, and apply to the Kharkov Medical In-stitute to be trained as a physician — was impossible. People were starving, the lines of men looking for jobs were endless, and the work-ers who had priority at that time (this was only eight years after the

---

* An "Autonomous Region," Birobidjan, is officially designated for Jews; but very few of them have settled in that cold, inhospitable, and infertile land (part of Siberia). The population there at present is only 6.6 percent Jewish. There is not a single *shul,* not even a single Hebrew book, in this entire region.

† In 1934 Kiev was restored as the capital, which it had been for centuries before 1917.

Revolution) were those from peasant or working-class backgrounds. Anyone applying for a job, then as now, had to fill out a long and elaborate questionnaire, and no one with "bourgeois" connections was eligible for work.

Grandfather, a very poor man who rented a tiny grocery stall in the Novgorod-Seversky marketplace, sparsely stocked with the produce of his own small truck garden, was a member of the "wealthy merchant" class in the eyes of Soviet officials. When filling out these innumerable forms, Father had to conceal his affluent background!

However, he possessed one great advantage when it came to finding work: although not above medium height, he was — and still is — one of the strongest men I have ever seen. His muscular build was a great asset in the hiring line, and before it was too late, he got a job as a loader on a factory building then under construction. Other job-seekers were not so fortunate: by the end of the decade it was an everyday experience for him to see corpses lying in the road — the remains of people who had died of starvation.

Kharkov is a big sprawling town, and the factory was ten miles outside the center. As always in the Soviet Union, the job was planned without any thought as to where the workers would live. They still manage construction the same way: I have seen many "tent cities," even in Siberia, where laborers have to live. The building comes first, and accommodations for the construction workers and other employees are taken care of later — if ever. Father had to walk to work ten miles, and ten miles back: on the wage he was paid, he could not afford the three-kopek street-car ride.

Now that he could earn a living, he applied at the pre-medical high school, where he studied for a year, and then to the Medical Institute. He had little trouble being accepted: he performed extremely well in the entrance examinations, and moreover the school was far from over-crowded. Very few people at that time had the strength or ambition to concern themselves with education.

I should mention that in the U.S.S.R. one doesn't go to "college" and then to graduate school. You start out from the very beginning studying intensively in your field. In those days it took five years to become qualified as a physician; further study was required to achieve a doctorate. Father's specialty was roentgenology. For the entire five years, he attended the institute by day and worked on the late shift at night.

I have always been impressed by the single-minded dedication my father must have had in order to survive those very hard years and fulfill his aim; and even more so by that of my mother, who had more obstacles to contend with.

She was Cecilia Ysayevna Slobodkina, a medical student herself when they met. She had much the same experiences Father did during those hard days. She came to Kharkov from Poltava, with no job, no food, no money. In 1928 she was living in such extreme poverty that she had to go through the entire Russian winter without a coat. She fell very ill, almost died (and certainly would have without the devoted care of the sister with whom she lived, sharing one corner of a crowded unheated flat), and never recovered her health completely. She had frequent attacks of bronchial asthma, and was subject to bouts of fever throughout the rest of her life. I remember her as tall, dark-haired, good-looking, but with something unmistakably fragile about her appearance.

My mother had much more reason than Father did for anxiety when the inevitable questionnaires had to be filled out. Her father had been a factory manager before the Revolution, and therefore belonged to the class of "ruthless exploiters." A very dangerous background; something to be carefully covered up.

I knew all four of my grandparents and one great-grandmother, but have only the most shadowy memories of them. They simply didn't talk much in the presence of a small child. I never heard reminiscences of their past lives, nor the faintest hint of their political views. Anything of importance they may have wanted to say, they said in Yiddish (that was one language nobody in the family encouraged me to learn: no Jews wanted to emphasize their Jewish identity at that time). A great many unfortunates who had been people of means before 1917 were reported and shot because a child had innocently mentioned in the wrong company that his family had once had a servant or owned one or two cattle. All these bourgeois were supposed to be "liquidated." So Mother and her parents concealed their origins, not only from the officials, but from me.

In 1931, my parents graduated from the Medical Institute and married. Almost immediately, my father was drafted into the army and sent to the far east of Russia, to Vladivostok, where he spent three years. My mother had to go home to Poltava and stay with her parents when I was born.

The standard food for babies in Russia is milk and a pabulum made of fine-ground *kasha*. This kasha was sold at that time for fantastic prices; it was actually and literally worth its weight in gold.

Everything my maternal grandparents had left of gold and silver they hocked at the notorious Torgsin, the government-operated pawnshop, through which the State came into possession of all the precious metal in the country, and of everything else of value. By the time I was one year old, the family belongings were gone, down to the last little silver saltspoon.

All this happened at a time when Soviet officials had so much food, they didn't know what to do with it. A woman who had been a housemaid for one of the Party leaders told me not long ago that these people had everything they wanted during the famine — including caviar, including cognac. They were throwing a lot of it away. But when she tried to smuggle leftovers to people outside the house — friends of hers who were dying of hunger — she was warned that if she tried that once again, she would be immediately fired, which meant that she would die of starvation herself. Nobody was supposed to know what was happening behind the high fences that separated this elite from the rest of the world.

My parents considered themselves fortunate. They were not imprisoned, as many were; they didn't die of hunger, as many did; and their child survived, unlike the children of many of the people they knew.

The famine was not an act of God: the brutal, irrational removal of the most productive element of the peasantry from the land — whole villages were emptied — wiped out the harvests. Farm workers who were reluctant to join the collective were exiled or killed.

That is why when I mentally compare Stalin and Hitler, it strikes me that those who say, "They were both incredible monsters; there's no difference between them" are mistaken. Hitler was a monster mainly toward other peoples; but Stalin was a monster toward his own people. He destroyed his loyal friends, his allies, his benefactors, as ruthlessly as he did his enemies; laid waste to the wealth and sustenance of the nation he ruled.

*   *   *

Stalin was not the first such in the history of Russia. In fact, this has happened over and over throughout the centuries. It was probably Peter the Great who was the worst of the monsters. The second Russian capital, Leningrad, the former St. Petersburg, was literally built on top of human bones among the swamps. Starving, freezing workers, actually slaves, were expendable. If they died for lack of food or shelter, there were many to replace them. St. Petersburg cost about a million human lives, and another million died similarly in other parts of Russia, and in that Czar's wars. Two million dead out of approximately fourteen million — that was one of the most notable contributions of Peter the Great to Russian history. Russians remember him as the great conqueror who wrested the shores of the Baltic Sea from Sweden; who brought Western culture to Russia; who set an example to his people by mastering science, carpentry, and the shipwright's craft. But in the course of his labors, he killed off perhaps a higher percentage of his countrymen than even Stalin did.

People in search of freedom have been fleeing Russia in waves for centuries. Prince Kurbsky was one of the first political émigrés, and that was under Ivan the Terrible, who condemned him as a traitor for his escape. Emigration was prevented for long decades; in the intervals when the barriers were lifted, thousands of people poured out. Nothing has really changed in Russia for hundreds of years. The borders of that vast country are closed; except for brief time-spans Russians have been unable to cross them, and foreigners coming in have been greeted with heavy suspicion.

Not long ago I picked up the Marquis de Custine's *Nicholas' Russia*, published in 1825. I was simply amazed: I could have sworn it was written yesterday. Everything he described is only too similar to what happens at the present time. When de Custine plans to go to Russia, friends give him names and addresses of Russians whom he should call upon; but they warn him that when he is asked at the border whether there is anyone in Russia whom he is planning to meet, he should answer no — otherwise the people in question will be in real jeopardy.

Visiting foreigners who have looked me up in Moscow had been given the same warning by their friends who had been there before, and for the same good reason.

When the Marquis de Custine arrives at the Polish-Russian border, he is interrogated by the Russian officer there: "What are you coming to Russia for? Do you plan to trade there?" and de Custine answers, No. "Do you have some kind of political mission?" No. "Well, why are you coming to Russia?" "I am a traveler." "Oh, come on! Can't you tell me the real reason you are here?"

When he finally manages to obtain his entry permit, de Custine goes into the *traktir* (a sort of tavern), where the tavernkeeper issues him a warning. "Sir, don't go to Russia. It's a bad country."

"Why? Have you been there?" asks de Custine.

"No, but I've lived here for twenty-five years. And I've never seen a person go into Russia smiling. And I never saw a person leaving Russia — without a smile."

Fifty years later the Russian journalist Bartholomé Zaitsev writes: "Why do we aim at conquering the whole world? . . . With so much misfortune in our own land, why do we want everyone else to be under the Czar? Why do we aim at conquest? Why do we criticize the whole world? Why do we bark at the whole world?"

This same "barking" has gone on throughout the centuries. And always, a Russian has been presented with only two alternatives: to obey dumbly, or to be killed. To be intelligent, to think for oneself, can be fatal. "One should be very wary of being bright," Pushkin writes. "It was the Devil who fated me, with my talent, to be born in Russia."

Even the great heroes in Russia became victims of the destructive forces that have always reigned there. The commander who saved Moscow from the Tatars, when Ivan the Terrible fled the city to escape the invasion, was tortured to death between two slowly burning logs because the Czar could not forgive him for displaying more courage than he himself possessed. Those familiar with the behavior of Stalin toward his lieutenants, heroes of the Revolution, and later toward heroes of the Great Patriotic War (World War II) will note the similarity.

In the course of the last thousand years, the process of natural selection has operated upon the population, ensuring survival for the most obedient, the least independent of mind. Such centuries do not pass by without results. I wish Russia everything good, but I am skeptical about her future, because I doubt that what has been created over a millennium can change in some dozens of years.

Of course, it is for Russians themselves to think of their history. For Soviet non-Russians, I think, there is no point in trying to introduce concepts of a fairer, freer life into the nation: "outsiders" will never be thanked no matter how much good will they may feel toward the citizens of that unhappy country. I am positive that only the Russian people themselves can change their fate; one can learn only from his own experience.

Indeed, Russia is one of the most unhappy countries in the world. But it is not for Jews to try to change it. That is why I left it, with little hope and much grief for my native land.

Who I Am

NINETEEN THIRTY-SIX. I am four years old. As far as I can remember, I have never been outside the vicinity of our tenement building at Pletnovsky Lane, in Kharkov. Our apartment is one room, twenty-five square feet. Most of this space is taken up by the furniture: a bed, a folding cot, a wooden table, and two straight chairs, all of them old and scarred. This leaves me with about four square feet to move around in. There is no running water in the building: all of the residents get water from a tap in the courtyard; and also in the court is the outhouse, shared by all. There is no stove, no gas. I heat my meals (a saucer of kasha, or a potato) on a Primus stove. There is a low-watt light bulb hanging from the ceiling, but I am not supposed to pull the cord that switches it on until nightfall. It is always twilight in the room, because the only window looks out into the corridor. Many other rooms in this building also have just one window, facing the corridor.

I play with my only toys: scissors and paper. I cut out of the paper different animals, and I invent adventures for them. I am alone. My parents are physicians, and the medical profession is one of the worst paid in the Soviet Union. That is natural — physicians don't produce anything. So Mother and Father work at several jobs, and they leave home at the same time every morning. They have gone to work by the time I wake up, and by the time they get back I am often asleep again.

But tomorrow is Sunday. This is their day off. Tomorrow I'll have a chance to ask my mother a question that has given me no peace for many hours today.

Tomorrow comes, and I ask my mother: "Mama, is it true that I am a Jew?" And my mother answers yes.

"And Father too?"

"Yes."

"And you too?"

"Yes."

"And how about our cat? Is he a Jew?"

This is not a joke. Many years later, when I was growing up, I read Chukovsky's very good study of the minds of children, which includes a collection of the sayings, conversations, and questions he heard from children between the ages of two and five; here I found exactly that same question I had asked my mother.

The incident that put it into my mind had occurred the previous morning. I was playing by the window in the corridor with another boy. Like myself, he was left alone all day — hungry, unsupervised, with nothing to do. There were a great many of us in the building who had to take care of ourselves while our parents were out at work, and we very small kids had devised for ourselves one outdoor sport, to play if the weather was good, and one indoor game. The sport consisted of kicking — not a ball; that would have been an unheard-of luxury to us — but a small piece of lead with a cheap fur covering, obviously once a decoration on a chair or sofa, which somebody had found in the courtyard. The indoor game was as follows: having collected candy wrappers after a birthday party or some such celebration, we folded them into neat squares, and snapped them onto the broad windowsill, using a special style of throwing we had evolved. Once your wrapper landed on the sill, your opponent threw his, and if it fell on top of the first paper, then that paper became his property.

On the morning in question I had won almost all of the other boy's candy wrappers.

"Why do you always win?" he asked furiously. "It must be because you're a *zhid*. All you zhids are tricky."

"What do you mean, zhid? What's a zhid?"

"Jew. Zhid means Jew. You're a Jew."

I repeat: the question about the cat is not a joke. It illustrates the brutal amputation of a Jew's heritage. As I mentioned before, in the Soviet Union a Jew can know nothing about his own religion, history, or culture. The Jewish child is faced with a dilemma: he doesn't see any difference between himself and others, but he is not for a minute allowed to forget that he is a Jew.

Years ago, I read a study of the distribution of minority groups in Europe, written at the turn of the century by the German scholar Runge, in which he states that within fifty years no one will know what a Jew is, since fewer and fewer Jews practice Judaism, and there is no other way of distinguishing Jews from the rest of the population.

How strange this perfectly rational, intelligent statement looked to me, reading it at a time when the half-century and more had passed. Considerations of the Nazi Holocaust aside (a horror far too vast to analyze here), what of the Soviet Union? Here I was, a citizen of a country where *officially* there was no religion; *officially* no distinctions made among the various ethnic groups and nationalities that made up the population. In fact, anti-Semitism was outlawed, and all the propaganda sent abroad maintained that not a trace of it remained. But on one's passport there is a space where one's nationality is indicated, "Georgian," "Estonian," "Russian," and so on, and — perfectly irrationally, since the Soviets do not accord recognition to the Jewish nation — "Jew." Lenin inveighed against anti-Semitism, which is one prime reason that Russian Jews were so naïvely hopeful when the Revolution came. But this is one tenet of the revolutionary faith that has almost always been ignored, and it is a dangerous liability to be Jewish — or half-Jewish, or a quarter.

Children are very perceptive; they understand early that Jews are "second-class" people, and that to call someone a Jew is the worst of insults. The best of compliments is to say "Oh, you're a Jew? But you're nothing like other Jews!"

It is as if this hatred of Jews is actually built into many, many Russians. A Russian could go through an entire lifetime without seeing a single Jew — but it wouldn't matter. One of my friends, after she graduated from the university, was a teacher at a village school. She had a way with children, and they were very fond of her. Once she overheard one of her pupils saying, "God-damned zhids!" She asked him: "Did you ever see a zhid?" "No," he said, "but I know they're evil!" "Well," she said, "take a look at me. I am Jewish." The boy promptly had a fit of real hysterics. Everything clashed in his head; there was no escape from this contradiction.

A Jewish child understands almost from the start that he is a cripple. But he can't understand exactly what his handicap is; he can't figure out wherein he is defective. What is the matter with him? And he tries to pinpoint where his shortcoming is; what it is related to. Maybe animals, too, fall into two categories, sound and cripples; of the first class, and of the second class. Who knows?

This idea is but natural to a mentality brought up in the Soviet style, starting with nursery school, where everybody is told how good the Soviets are and how bad everyone in the capitalist countries is, except maybe for genuine workers and genuine poor peasants. I remember quite well that the whole world, when I was a child, was divided into Red — that is, Soviet, good; and White — non-Soviet, bad. I thought this principle applied to the whole world. I had no doubt that an elephant, or a nightingale, was "red"; that wolves were "white"; and I plagued my mother with questions such as "What about rabbits? They're not bad, but they're cowards; so should we consider them Red or White?"

In the Soviet Union, one's whole consciousness is twisted, one's whole life is warped; and especially the life of a Jew. There is a joke among Russian Jews: a Jew goes to see God, and asks, "Is it true, that you are *our* God?" and God says, "Yes, my son." "And is it true that we are your Chosen People?" and God says, "Yes, my son." "Well — couldn't you choose somebody else for a while?"

That incident by the corridor window with a playmate was my first experience with anti-Semitism. It was a late experience because I was delayed in going to nursery school; the school was overcrowded, and I was over five before a place came free. Had I left the relative shelter of our building and courtyard and entered the tough competitive world of nursery school as an infant, I would have found out what it meant to be a zhid at a much earlier age.

But a child is a child, and I was soon distracted from my anxiety by excitement over plans that were being made for the summer. We were going to the Crimea! Of course my parents were in no position to take a vacation at any of the resorts there. But they were very fond of me, and they were willing to do anything to provide me with the benefits of a holiday by the warm Black Sea. My father had to remain in Kharkov, but my mother planned to get a position at a resort for officials. There was almost always a summer opening at one of these places for a physician.

I remember that ghastly trip in 1937 very well. The train is horribly overcrowded. We are in a car of the "hard" class, what Europeans would call Third Class. One side of the car contains a long wooden bench; on the other side, at right angles, are separate benches supposed to accommodate three people each; and overhead are folding shelves that you pull down at night for sleeping. On our trip to the Crimea, all this space and the aisles are taken up by at least four times as many passengers as the car was designed to hold. No one lay down for twenty-four hours except the small children, who were able to sleep on their mothers' laps. My mother was dismayed when she realized what we were in for, but I was still in a state of wild enthusiasm: "Don't worry! Tomorrow we'll be in the Crimea!"

Unluckily, the only provisions we had brought along were two hard-boiled eggs (incidentally, eggs were absolute treasures at that time). My mother gave me one. Somehow it got stuck in my throat. I couldn't swallow it; I started choking; it was hard to breathe. In the entire train there was not a drop of water with which I could have washed it down. Just when I thought I would die, the egg went down; but for the next twenty years I could not even look at a hardboiled egg!

But everything comes to an end, and finally we arrived at the house in which we were assigned a room by the sanitarium in Yevpatoria, very close to the seashore.

To me it was a fantastic room. It had three windows! They looked out on the street! And there was enough space here so that I could walk around. Not run, of course; but take a few steps in any direction. And ten minutes' walk away — there was the sea!

In a very short time I had made friends with the other children, and we spent hours making sand castles and chasing the waves, which turned around and chased us back.

I made friends also with our neighbor, a lady who lived in a very small house next to ours. I can't really call it a house; it consisted of only one tiny room. From the outside one would have assumed it was a kennel or a woodshed. What was most astonishing to me were the tablecloths and curtains in this house. The place was very neat; it was very clean; but the tablecloth and curtains were made of newspapers. They were very beautifully cut out, with elaborate borders: almost works of art. But these works of art had to be replaced all the time, being made of paper. I hated to see anything so marvelous thrown away.

I became very fond of Sofya Dmitrievna and spent time with her every day. Once or twice I was present when she was having lunch: an onion and a piece of bread; no butter. She ate even worse than we did, and I couldn't understand why, in this great country of ours, she would live so very, very poorly. Here she was, almost next door to the sanitorium where a great many people — I'd seen it with my own eyes — were being served with extraordinarily good food. I couldn't see why, when each of them had a room to himself even better than our luxurious room, they couldn't give her something better to live in than this weatherbeaten shed.

Some time later I found out that our room, and all the other rooms in the whole house, had once belonged to Sofya Dmitrievna. Inconceivable! to own a whole house. But why had she moved to this little lean-to? I couldn't understand it. I asked her why, over and over, but she didn't answer anything that I could understand.

One day when I came to visit her and knocked on the door, expecting the usual warm welcome, she didn't answer. I knew she was there because the door wasn't locked. Downcast, I went back to our house. In the hallway a woman who had the room next to ours asked me what was the matter, and I told her about my friend not having asked me in.

"She can't see anyone, she has just heard very bad news," the neighbor told me. "Her son is dead. Only eighteen years old, and he's dead." I had never known she had a son; she'd never mentioned a husband or family at all.

I stayed away for a few days to respect her mourning and then, after my mother and I had encountered her on the sidewalk one evening, decided the next day to call on her again. She wasn't there. And she never appeared again. I wondered: Why hadn't she said goodbye?

It was not until many years later that I thought it all out and realized that, very probably, her son had been executed and that she had been arrested herself. Unexplained deaths and departures in those worst days of the Great Purge — 1937 — occurred very frequently. One had to assume that the missing people had been swept away by the flood that was cleansing our society of "bourgeois" and "enemies of the people." Sofya Dmitrievna was the first friend I ever had who disappeared that way.

Of course, it was not all the time that I was so unhappy. But I cannot refrain from mentioning a memory such as this, which has always remained with me.

*   *   *

Most of the time I spent by the sea. It was such an astonishing pleasure to see little fish in the water, to see crabs, to see so many living creatures. I loved them and was not afraid of any of them, not even of the spiders and frogs I saw on my way back from the shore. Very often the women in our house were horrified when I ran happily into the entrance hall carrying a frog in each hand. It was during that stay on the Black Sea, too, that I discovered I had been misinformed about butterflies' living for only a single day, because I observed some of them who lived in our house, and they flew around for many days.

I was very close at that time to a familiar dream. Often I had dreamed that I was in the woods with wild animals — and we were friends. I was convinced that if you are kind to an animal, then it won't do you any harm. And of course in the dream it was possible to talk to animals; all I had to do was to learn their language.

It was at the time of this vacation too that I learned to fish, using a net; and almost immediately decided never to go fishing again. The first fish I caught I wanted to adopt. I kept her in a bowl; I brought her water from the sea; I changed the water; I fed her with seaweed and bits of bread. But when after four or five days I found her floating on her back and realized that despite all my care she could not live in captivity,

I decided never to attempt to domesticate another one. I mourned that fish for weeks.

I wandered about alone a great deal and, despite all my mother's cautions, inevitably ran into some near-disasters. The one I remember best was when I encountered a clump of beautiful trees with lovely fuzzy yellow flowers on them, and tasted one of them. It turned out to be very sweet. To a child who had so seldom had the treat of eating any candy or sugar, these flowers were irresistible; I ate a handful of them. When I got home to our room, although I was late and had been very hungry, I found I could not eat. I put my supper — a slice of bread and butter — on a chair, sat down unexpectedly on the floor, threw up, and a minute later lost consciousness.

The blossoms were sweet acacias, quite as deadly as hemlock or toadstools. My mother ran as she had never run before in her life, and was able to get an ambulance to the rescue barely in time to save me. I woke up in the clinic where she worked. They had pumped my stomach.

While I was convalescing, we moved to another room in Yevpatoria, two or three miles from our original place. I remember lying on my back in the horse-drawn wagon, watching the tree branches pass by overhead and the sun's rays playing through the leaves. It was a very strong, grateful feeling; I have never been so glad to be alive.

Probably the life of every child is a sequence of miracles. Every child is prepared for happiness and is awaiting it.

One of the marvels that I saw and loved at that time was a magic show which was put on at the resort; I was privileged to attend it because my mother worked there. There was a magician who changed a sofa into a white horse! He was even good enough to explain the process; how one could do it; what the magic words were that should be pronounced to achieve this transformation. So that very same evening I asked my mother, "Mama, which is better, a sofa or a horse?" She answered, "Well, that depends!" But I immediately set about persuading her that a horse is much better, because there's nothing you can do with a sofa except sleep on it, whereas you can not only ride a horse but at night you could sleep on him, with your back propped up on his soft warm belly. Finally I succeeded, I thought, in convincing my mother, who undoubtedly had guessed what I had in mind and didn't want me to be disappointed, but found it impossible to distract me from the approaching disillusionment. After half an hour of trying and trying to transform our sofa into a horse, it began to dawn on me that something was wrong. Probably I had mixed up some of the magic words!

But the very idea of such beautiful metamorphoses remained with me. I wanted to change our life for the better. I had all kinds of good ideas.

For example, I decided that we shouldn't prepare tea in the regular way; we should rather warm it as we warm ourselves in winter, by wrapping ourselves in a warm coat, in wool. So I took a bottle of water, corked it tightly, and started to heat it up in a coat. It took me quite a while to realize that it is not the coat which gives us our heat, but we who give our heat to the coat.

Another discovery was more real — because the world really is full of magic things. Playing around in our room one day, I found a broken thermometer, and I watched a live liquid slide out of it. It was marvelous: the drops of mercury were quite alive. They could be separated or, again, they were very happy to unite in one large drop. Wonderful! Then I remembered that among my treasures was a piece of aluminum wire, and I decided that these two marvels should make friends. So I put one end of the wire into the mercury, and then I observed a new phenomenon. Before my eyes, both the wire and the mercury disappeared, and where they had been nothing remained except a little heap of white powder. Thus I discovered that aluminum can burn without flame; but I didn't know then that it's surrounded by a thin layer of pure oxide. Aluminum spends all its existence in an invisible prison of oxide, which prevents this very volatile metal from quickly oxidating.

This was a very happy summer, and only the thought of seeing my father again kept me from being too sad at the prospect of going back home to Kharkov.

Shortly after our return to the city, an opening came up in the nursery school, and after that I spent my days there — long, long days. Now I had to wake up in the morning at the same time my parents did, which for six months of the year was long before sunrise. My mother and I emerged onto the dark street and spent an hour on the jam-packed street car. No one who has not seen these conveyances can imagine the terrible overcrowding. Many commuters, unable to squeeze into the car, cling on precariously outside: there is always a cluster of people riding with only a toe-hold on the platform. The majority of early-morning passengers were people like ourselves, children going to school accompanied by their mothers, who were on their way to work (in the Soviet Union very nearly 100 percent of women work). The endless ride was bad enough in winter, but perfectly unbearable in the heat of summer, when you spent that hour, standing of course, wedged in among hundreds of other miserable sweating bodies.

The school taught nothing but obedience to routines of senseless regimentation. The teachers were incompetent and cruelly overworked. They offered us little but discipline and punishments. And actually, how could they have been attentive, how could they even have remembered our first names (they didn't), when each group of forty of us had only one teacher? And this teacher was paid for her enormous task even less than a physician's salary; something around sixty* roubles a month. Whatever she made, the money was of little use to her, because of the food shortage. In the 'thirties this shortage was still extremely acute; it was almost impossible to find anything to eat. These poor women were not only tired to death, but were suffering from malnutrition.

Of course, no small child could understand how hard their lives were; it is only now, in retrospect, that I can summon some sympathy for their constant irritability.

The first day in nursery school was all I needed to be completely disenchanted as to my optimistic expectations about it. "Another zhid!" exclaimed one of the two teachers who stood at the entrance when my mother brought me in to enroll. "Where do they all come from?"

Mealtimes were particular hell in school. None of us had seen any real food before, save for the scraps on which we somehow managed to survive, and there were near-riots when the dinner appeared (an austere collation of cabbage soup, a potato, an occasional beet, and at rare intervals perhaps a tiny bit of sausage). To us this sparse, rough meal was worth fighting for. Everyone battled wildly for his share, and for more. "Dirty zhids — they're grabbing it all!" the others yelled. A belated but telling lesson in what it meant to be a Jew in Russia.

Some time between five and seven in the evening Mother would reappear, thank God, and then back to the ordeal of the street car, and finally home to bed. I suppose I was better off than some of the children I knew in our apartment house: their parents' working hours were so long, or their jobs were such a distant commute from their homes, that

---

* Here and elsewhere, unless otherwise indicated, I am expressing monetary values in today's roubles, taking into account the two currency devaluations that occurred during my time, when 1 new rouble was assigned the value of 10 old ones. The buying power of the dollar and of the rouble differ so widely that it is impossible to use a single index to compare them. The mean income in the Soviet Union is 100 roubles per month. Food in the Soviet Union is "cheap" if one considers the official exchange — 1 rouble to about $1.15 — but not if one takes into account the average wage. Ordinary meat (very inferior grade, mostly bone and gristle) costs from 50 to 70 kopeks per pound. Eggs are ten for a rouble. Milk is 16 kopeks a half-liter; soft drinks, 12. Bread is 5 kopeks a pound. (Without the artificial depression of the price of bread, there might be starvation in the country. There are millions of Russians for whom it is the basic essential staple.) Subways and buses cost 5 kopeks, irrespective of the distance one travels; trolley cars, 4. Movies are 30 to 70 kopeks. A hotel room, 2 or 3 roubles a night (though a foreigner will be charged 40). Dinner in a restaurant, 2 to 4 roubles. A suit of men's clothes, 100 roubles. To buy a State-owned apartment costs between 5 and 10 thousand roubles, depending upon its size; charges thereafter are 20 to 25 roubles per month. A good apartment in a co-operative costs 30 thousand. As one can imagine, I knew very few people in the Soviet Union who were able to accumulate any savings at all.

the children had to live in a boarding kindergarten, and never got home at all except for Saturday night and Sunday. But knowing that some of my friends were having an even worse time than I, did nothing to relieve the bleakness of that year and a half of nursery school.

However, nothing can keep a child from thinking, and from being happy. So I continued to investigate life and to profit by the occasional school holiday and by the cherished Sundays. I had learned to read when I was quite small, around five; and one of the first books I read was on airplane design. I was fascinated, and immediately began to draft plans for what I considered to be improved and superior models of aircraft. For better or worse, this zeal to excel, to produce, to perfect, is a typical ambition in a Russian-Jewish child, constantly aware that he is looked down upon, that he is regarded as defective in some mysterious way. He becomes anxious to do his best, to redress the balance, to overcome the handicap and prove his worth. So of course, I had to invent something new. At that time the great vogue in aeronautical design was the plane called "flying wings," with body and tail almost eliminated. I designed a modification of this aircraft, including a more substantial tail with maneuverable fins. Also, I dreamed up a motor that worked on the principle of a pump, using air, pumped from the rear-mounted engine, by way of motive power! I sent my inventions to the Central Aero-Hydrodynamic Institute, about which I had read a piece in a children's science magazine. How incredibly happy I was when I received from them a booklet about airplane models and a letter suggesting that I work on models! As a matter of fact, I already had this booklet — but who could compare *my* booklet to the one received from the famous Aero-Hydrodynamic Institute?

Naturally, I immediately made plans to join the model-makers' club, whose rooms were situated very near my school. This sort of club is operated, like the Pioneers (the Boy and Girl Scouts), under the auspices of the State. When I applied I learned that no one under the age of ten, that is, third-graders, could be admitted to this club. I was so disappointed that the young man who ran the club took pity on me and suggested that I make a certain model, of which he gave me the plans, and promised that if I succeeded he would make an exception to the age rule and let me into the group. I worked very hard for two weeks, with cardboard, glue, and cellophane, and finally produced the model. But when I took it to the club, the leader told me again that children as young as myself could not become members.

I was very angry. No one had ever deceived me that way before. But it was only the first of a series of similar rejections: for years, I was "too young" for whatever step I wanted to take. I dreamed about the time when I would finally become a third-grader; I knew that a new life would open up before me.

I had to wait a long time before I could start school. I was all ready to go when we discovered that, since my birthday was in May and you had to pass the seventh birthday to enter first grade, I had to wait another year, spending the time in a state of dreadful suspense and impatience.

Let me mention here a diversion I discovered during the summer of that suspended time — 'thirty-nine. One of the boys in my building, a perfect Rothschild in my eyes, had been given a set of dominoes, and he and I, with several others, played the game every chance we got. The unlucky double six we called the "double-Hitler." We had just enough idea of what "Fascist," "Nazi," or "Hitler" meant so that the words conveyed anathema.

The grownups, passing by us in the yard or in the corridor, usually paid no attention to our games; but one evening when three or four of us were playing dominoes at the entrance to the building, the father of the boy who owned the set came up the steps and stopped to watch us.

"Double-Hitler!" someone shouted.

"Don't say that again!" the father commanded. "You can't say anything bad about Hitler any more. Don't let me hear that again." We stared at each other. We had picked up the expression from overhearing the grown peoples' games; now suddenly it was forbidden. No one had ever bothered to listen to our play before, much less to interfere with it.

Like so many other mysteries of my childhood, this one made sense only years later, when I realized what had been going on in the world at that time. Stalin and Hitler had just signed the nonaggression pact, and the constant barrage of anti-German propaganda I had been absorbing all my life was abruptly — of course only temporarily — cut off. Overnight, it was a criminal offense to malign Hitler.

This was a trifling event to me then, and it was a long time before these sudden changes in official policy, these freezes and thaws, began to fall into a pattern of inconsistency, if one may use such an expression.

I thought nothing of that man's injunction when I heard it. My mind was taken up with my own child's world, particularly with great expectations of starting "real" school.

At last my long wait was over, and I was in the first grade. But what could I do there? I could already read and write without any trouble; I knew arithmetic. This time I had better luck than I had with the club; in those days it was possible to skip a year. I took exams for the first time in my life, passed, and was entered into the second grade.

One baffling experience in school, even in those early years, was to encounter history textbooks with whole passages blacked out. This was never explained. Sometimes we were given a black pencil and assigned to go through a chapter, crossing out a particular name. Some of the illustrations, pictures of historical figures, were stamped across with the words ENEMIES OF THE PEOPLE.

My best friend in the second grade was a dark, thin little boy, Yuri Dorakhov; he and I used to speculate about the reasons for these odd lessons. By that time we were both losing the conviction, common to small children, that our own families, our own surroundings, our own country, were just as they should be, and that anything unpleasant in our lives was pure accident. Yuri and I got together at every opportunity to plan the organization of our own "Central Committee," dedicated to the creation of a truly just, honest, and happy society. Our schemes were evolved under an oath of utmost secrecy: "A to Z" secrecy, as we said: not one word of our ideas from A to Z could be mentioned to a living soul. But one day we would astound the world with a master plan for universal happiness.

In the middle of that same winter, a very welcome change occurred in the life of my family. My father was now working at three jobs — literally day and night — (spending twelve to fifteen hours, instead of the regulation five, under X-rays; practically unprotected, the only security being lead gloves and apron). Owing to this reckless overwork, he was able to save enough money so that we could move from our small apartment to a new one, very nearly twice the size of the one we had, and much brighter. There was a large window that looked out not onto a corridor but onto the tree-lined street, Kaplunovskaya. (I can cite the area of any room or apartment in which I have ever lived, because the dimensions of living space are covered by law — so many square meters per resident, with extra space allocated to those whose work requires it. In our cramped living conditions, people felt very strongly about their rights in this regard, and there were constant feuds and lawsuits when someone was awarded more room than his neighbors thought he was entitled to.)

My father bought the apartment from the man who owned the two adjoining rooms, in an under-the-table transaction. Because of the tremendous amount of red tape and the innumerable regulations covering housing in the U.S.S.R., everyone you know is involved in some such extra-legal arrangement. Even my strict and law-abiding father had to evade the rules unless we were to resign ourselves to our dark corner in Pletnovsky Lane forever.

Even more exciting to me than the change of apartments was the news that in June, when I finished the second grade, my mother would take a vacation — the first real holiday she ever had in her entire career. She and I were to go to Novgorod-Seversky to visit Father's family, and — incredible! — Father too planned to take a few weeks off, and would join us there around the middle of the month.

That was a delightful time. Grandfather's home was a small four-room wooden house, stuffed to bursting with Azbels — my father was one of an enormous family. Actually, there were many more people than usual staying there during our visit; this was something of a family reunion. The grandparents and my great-grandmother and the countless uncles and aunts made an absolute festival of our arrival — as did the entire village — but I have to admit that I paid almost no attention to the grown people and can now hardly single them out in my memory. I do remember that everyone talked a great deal, but often in Yiddish, so I didn't really seek out their company, as I couldn't follow the conversations. I was constantly busy with my own nine-year-old concerns, absolutely fascinated by observing ducks, geese, and pigs — creatures I had never encountered before outside books. There was a pond not far from the house, and a pasture with two or three cows, one of them ours.

I can't say that my mother was quite as happy in Novgorod-Seversky as I was: the pigs, the dirt, the manure piles here and there — she couldn't get used to all that. Her own background was much more middle-class and urban than Father's: she was born and brought up in the city, and village existence struck her as more than a little squalid. But of course she concealed her squeamishness from Grandmother and Grandfather; and, too, she was very grateful for the chance to rest from the harsh routine of her working life. Moreover, the opportunity to eat enough for the first time in years, or perhaps more exactly to see me get enough to eat, was a pleasure for her.

Father joined us after a few days. I couldn't ever remember having had the company of both parents, day and night, before. By great good luck I was able to preserve photographs of that memorable time, and I include a few of them in the book. Being in his native village put Father into a nostalgic mood. He showed me the hill where he and his brothers had gone sledding when he was a boy; described how they had made the sleds themselves, out of boards; took me down to the river — almost a mile from Grandfather's house — and told of how he and his next older brother, Uncle Boris, had carried water home in pails hung on a yoke over their shoulders; that was the sole water supply for the household. (Now there was a faucet in the center of the village, used by the whole neighborhood, but pails and yoke remained in use.) He talked about the endless hoeing, weeding, and digging they had worked

at in summer, and the woodchopping, which had been the most essential of his chores in winter.

In our wanderings Father also showed me the *cheder,* now boarded
up and abandoned, where he had studied until the age of twelve. At
that age he had quit outward religious observance altogether, and to all
appearances joined the great Soviet majority, as far as his beliefs were
concerned.

Nearer the center of town was the Seven-Year School, where he had
received his secular education.

We had been in Novgorod-Seversky for about two weeks when one
morning, as I ran into the room where my parents and I slept to ask
why Father hadn't come out yet to go on our daily excursion, I found
him picking up all the clothes and books we had brought with us and
handing them to my mother, who was hastily wrapping everything into
bundles.

"What's going on, Papa? Aren't we going out to see the cows? Please
let's go! Let's go now!" But they went on packing; embraced the old
people and the brothers and sisters in farewell; and we caught the train
to Kharkov — all within the hour.

It was June 22nd, 1941. The War had begun.

War

AT THE BEGINNING of the fall, shortly before school was to start, Mother and her sister Fanya and I, with Aunt Fanya's two boys and her mother- and father-in-law, and another elderly couple related to them, went aboard a *teplushka*. This is a railway car that is supposed to carry horses or, if necessary, troops for very short hauls. A wooden boxcar, with no heating system, no seats, no washroom, with very small windows. Over the big sliding-door entrance there is a sign reading "8 Horses or 40 Men."

These wagons are intended for side trips of not more than a few hours, but we, with about fifty-five other refugees from Kharkov, were in one of them for three months on our way to Eastern Siberia. There were no men of military age aboard: we children left our fathers behind us, knowing nothing about what was happening to them. We would hear nothing about their fates for an entire year. Less than a month after we left, Kharkov fell.*

I was in a state of the wildest excitement as we boarded this boxcar, and so were all the other children. We had been waiting ever since we could remember for war against the hated Fascists.

There was one thing about it, however, that I could not understand: How could the Germans have been so insane as to attack us first? We

---

* Many of us Kharkovchans were Jewish. A great number of Ukrainians, like the people in the Baltic regions, would not leave their homes even when it was still possible to get out. Those who remained out of loyalty to their home ground, who formed partisan groups and kept on fighting, received scant reward for their patriotism: when captured by the enemy, they had no hope of release. There was no prisoner exchange, as the Soviet Union had never signed the Geneva Accords. The few who survived the German prisoner-of-war camps were sent to Soviet concentration camps when the War ended; anyone who was still alive was assumed to have been a collaborationist. Also, almost everyone else who remained in occupied territory was regarded as a traitor, and was punished accordingly.

But we never could have foreseen all this in 1941, nor could we possibly have guessed that thousands of Ukrainians had, in actual fact, welcomed the Germans and joined forces with them.

had always heard that when the conflict occurred, the battle would be on the enemy's territory; no one could have anticipated an invasion across our borders. Didn't the Germans realize that technologically we were the most advanced nation in the world, with such sophisticated aircraft, tanks, and weaponry that no aggressor had a chance of defeating us? Wasn't the staunchly patriotic Red Army absolutely invincible? And didn't every schoolchild know that Germany had been so crushed by the last war that of all industrialized nations she was still the weakest and the most backward? It was strange, but — no matter! The War had started at last, and victory would follow soon.

Aboard the train were my cousins Victor, a boy a little younger than myself and my closest friend, and his brother, Yuri, only four, too young to really appreciate what a great adventure we were having. Victor and I weren't the only ones who viewed this trip as the most wonderful excursion: almost all the children on the train were delighted to be there. None of us had traveled any real distance before; we had had very little excitement of any kind. And now we were off! Living dangerously! I kept a diary at the time, starting out with the words: "We are fleeing the Germans for our very lives, escaping we know not where!"

This was true; we had not been told where we were going, nor our route. We zigzagged across half of the nation; I don't believe even the engineer knew where we were going next until he got his orders at each station. The train stopped at frequent unpredictable intervals, and many of us would pour out of the teplushka, the grown people in hopes of finding a food vendor, and the children wanting to run and play. But we were afraid to go more than twenty paces away from the train, because there was no way of knowing when it would start up again. A stop at a siding or at a station might last for hours, perhaps even days; or the train might start moving after a two-minute halt. It was frightening to think of what might happen if one of us failed to get back aboard when the train went off: there you would be, in a completely foreign place, while your family disappeared to an unknown destination. God knows how you would find each other again. Even if the person left behind discovered the location of his companions, which would be very difficult, owing to the regulations pertaining to secrecy in wartime, how would he get to them? Passenger service had come to a halt almost the minute the War began; all the rolling stock was now troop trains and freight trains.

My Aunt Fanya very nearly was left behind once. We had stopped in a strange, flat, desertlike landscape, somewhere in Central Asia I believe, and she had the tremendous luck to be offered a huge water-

melon, maybe twenty-five pounds in weight, by one of the native ven-
dors who materialized at the little station. (We rather stared at these
people; to us, who had never seen Oriental faces before, they appeared
strikingly similar one to another, and very foreign. But there was nothing exotic about their dress: most of them wore the same drab clothes
worn in rural areas all over the Soviet Union.)

While Aunt Fanya was negotiating with the man, a loud hiss of steam
arose from the engine. Everyone else who had disembarked hurried
aboard the car before we realized that she was not with us. We crowded
in the doorway, watching in horrible suspense as Aunt Fanya paid for
the enormous fruit and then struggled to pick it up. It was not only
heavy but slippery, almost impossible to grasp. Slowly, the train wheels
began to turn. She was desperate — how could she possibly leave this
treasure behind? Finally, with a supreme effort, she got hold of the
melon and ran along the cinder track until she was opposite the doorway, when fifteen pairs of hands grabbed it away from her and carried
it in. Others caught hold of her and hauled her aboard.

After about six weeks of pretty stifling travel, we began to feel, not
the heat, but the cold. Snow flew past the tiny windows, and we became
almost grateful for the overcrowding, since practically the only warmth
we obtained was from each other. We did have a small stove, a *bourzhuika* (so called after the bourgeois, who had used this type of stove
during the Civil War), vented by a pipe that ran out a window. But it
was a dangerous object: you couldn't get near it when it was lit. The
metal was thin, and the stove would get red-hot; it glowed like a live
coal after dark. The track was rough, and we were jolted no matter
how slowly the train moved, so the mothers were very careful to keep
small children well away from the stove.

Fuel was woodchips and coal dust. (Solid coal was unobtainable as of
the start of the war; it all went to the munitions factories and such, and
there was not a chunk left over for civilian use.) It's impossible simply
to pour this dust over the lighted kindling: we had to water it down
until it was the consistency of clay, shape it into manageable bricks, and
drop it onto the wood fire, where it dried out and burned.

But the vexing problems of housekeeping in a freight wagon caused
us children no concern at all. We were sure that fuel and food would
come from somewhere; and it didn't bother us to go without bathing
for long intervals, or to use a pail instead of a water closet — that was
all part of the fun. There were plenty of people to play with, and we
never ran out of ideas for games, songs, and jokes. We made so much
noise that it scared some of the women aboard: on the single occasion
when an enemy plane was sighted overhead some of the mothers pan-

icked and commanded: "Hush! The Germans will hear us!" — innocently believing that our uproar really was audible to the pilot. But
we kids simply did not worry about being bombed; the "flight for our
lives" was — to me, at least — only a literary concept, even while I was
in the midst of it. The German airplane was just a stage prop in our exciting drama.

By sheer chance, the train that we were in made the trip to Siberia
successfully. A great number of trains carrying evacuees on that route
were bombed; but for us there was only that one scare during the entire
three months, and nothing came of it.

In November we arrived at Krivoshchokovo, a suburb of the Eastern
Siberian city of Novosibirsk. This town had always been terribly overcrowded; now it was jammed with refugees. My mother and I, my aunt,
Victor and Yuri, the grandparents and their in-laws, were allocated one
room to live in. One room, twenty square meters — nine people in this
one room.

For three months the four old people and Victor and Yuri and I spent
almost all of our time there. We did not have the very warm coats and
the special *valenki* — extremely thick boots that come up over your
knees — without which you cannot spend more than a minute or two
outside in the Siberian winter. It was terribly hard to find clothing during the War (it is far from easy even now), and the coat I eventually got
was made by my mother herself. I have no idea how she managed to
find the time to make it. Both she and Aunt Fanya were out at work all
day and half the night. We hardly ever saw them. My mother worked at
the Krivoshchokovo Hospital for the Wounded.

When at last we were equipped for the very severe climate, Victor
and I started school. The one we attended was not the school nearest to
our apartment, where there was no room for us, but another, situated
about two miles beyond the outskirts of town. Getting there entailed a
long, long walk on a flat stretch of treeless vacant land, snow-covered,
windy, incredibly cold.

We were greeted in this school with blank hostility. As evacuees, we
were occupying precious space and consuming precious food; we were
undesirables. Moreover, we were Jews.

The Sibiryaki in the Krivoshchokovo school were bigger, tougher,
and more independent of mind than the children in my Kharkov school.
Some were descendants of exiles and pioneers — rugged stock. But of
course they inherited their ancestors' prejudices: again we were the
"bloody zhids," as we had been in the Kharkov school.

We newcomers were lucky only in one respect: despite the months of
lost school time, we were not much behind our classmates.

Having looked around a little in the West, I get the impression that the general level of education provided in urban Soviet schools is quite high; my guess is that it is considerably higher than the level in comparable Western schools. But on the other hand, I believe that 30 to 40 percent of Russians are just about illiterate. (Actual statistics are unavailable.) There is a vicious cycle that ensures that the farther away from the metropolitan centers you are, the worse the education you receive. Like everything else in the Soviet Union, production and consumption, grain harvests, population growth — everything — the success of pupils is predicted according to the Five-Year Plan, including the number who will graduate into a higher class every year. If a pupil is not good enough, it is officially considered that it is not the pupil who is letting the Plan down, but his teacher, so the teachers are simply forced to give passing grades to almost everyone. By the time a pupil is in the higher grades he has caught on to this system, and presents his teachers with the attitude: "I don't give a damn about studying — it's your business; you'd better pass me or you'll be in trouble." And he is right.

In the village schools, it frequently happens that the teachers are recruited from exactly this group of high-school graduates — the very worst students, who could not get a position in the better schools. Having drifted into the bottom of this low-paying profession for lack of training in any other, these are people who cannot even correct their pupils' math papers and other exams themselves, so they collect the answers from colleagues in the city schools. Hardly bothering to conceal the deception, they hand out the answers to those pupils who would otherwise fail. The rural population is thus defrauded of an education, and since they have so little desire to acquire one in the first place, they are doubly cheated.

Villagers have absolutely no motivation to learn anything, because for all practical purposes it is impossible to leave a village. I said before that all Soviet citizens are issued passports; this is not quite true. Peasants do not own passports, and so are unable to travel or move.

One of the primary aims of the Plan is to keep the population stable. Knowledge of languages, science, geography, or history would be useless to a person who will spend his life on a kolkhoz or in a village. If by accident a good teacher does find himself in a village school, it is rare for him to find a pupil with a glimmering of ambition. The result is near-illiteracy among the rural people; I have met many who can hardly read or write a word beyond their own names.

As to the almost insuperable problem of leaving the village and moving to a city: it would not be hyperbole to say that the entire Soviet

Union is a concentration camp, with many divisions separated into individual cells, arranged in a hierarchy. All cities are divided into certain groups, and one cannot leave a small city for a larger one, or a larger city for a real metropolis. Without a compelling officially sanctioned reason, without miles of bureaucratic red tape, a Soviet person cannot change his place of residence. This includes even a move from one apartment to another in the same building — it cannot be made without permission. The rationale behind these regulations has to do with the shortage of apartments, which, although the State has made every effort to increase the rate of construction in the last two decades, is still acute. But obviously the authorities have another motive as well for locking the population in place in this way, which is that the system facilitates the close surveillance of all those millions of people. A Soviet citizen is "tracked" from the day he is born until the day he dies. There is almost no such thing as a "missing person" in Russia.

It is easy to guess what a number of tragedies result from this system. There are sometimes conditions in one's life that make a change of residence imperative. You might be divorced, for example, and permanently trapped in the same tiny living space as your former spouse. Or you might suffer the death of a child or a parent, or husband or wife, and be unable to escape the scene of such intolerably sad associations. This caging of human beings gives rise to untold sufferings and may be the cause of many suicides — perhaps of murders, too, when people who hate each other are forced to live together.

When it comes to the lack of educational opportunities, one can imagine how often a person of real potential is simply born in the wrong place, and finds himself stuck forever in some outpost of the U.S.S.R. where he will strangle intellectually. Only the extraordinarily talented have a chance of fighting their way out of the provinces.

This immobility is principally in the "upward" direction. A resident of Moscow or Leningrad — the meccas for anyone who is trying to achieve anything of importance — would have no trouble getting a permit to *leave* his city. But to move to those cities from anywhere else involves overcoming tremendous obstacles. Thus, villagers stay in their villages; provincials in their small towns.

I think this problem of education in the Soviet Union is very special. There are two extremes: a certain level of very well-educated people, almost all of them in the great cities, and then the absolutely stationary population of the farming districts, many of whom are almost analphabetic.

Victor and I and our other fellow-refugees in Krivoshchokovo were lucky: among our teachers were a few exiles from Czarist days, people of considerable cultivation and dedication to their work. So the time we spent in Siberian schools was not wasted.

But our life there was not easy. The cold we could stand — in fact, I think I may say that Russians love the winter. But it was tough to be hungry so much of the time. Not only were meat, "butter," and sugar rationed, but also the commonest vegetables, such as beets or onions. Everyone was issued *kartochki,* ration cards, but the shortages were such that one very seldom received even the tiny ration officially allowed. Let's say you had points sufficient for a quarter-pound of butter: you would be extremely fortunate to receive an eighth of a pound of the worst possible margarine. Even so, the kartochki were the most precious objects in our lives, and to lose them would have been a serious disaster. You couldn't just advise the authorities that you had lost them by accident, or that they had been stolen, and hope to be issued a new set; there were no regulations to cover such a loss, since the officials were so afraid of people cheating. If the ration points were gone, you actually could die of starvation.

About four or five times during the entire course of the War, we had the rare treat of obtaining one of the food parcels sent to the U.S.S.R. by American relief agencies. Canned compressed pork or beef; "Tushonka" on the label. Powdered eggs. Jam. These were real feasts for us; I remember them very well.

Novosibirsk

MOTHER AND I spent the first half of 1942 in a state of near-mourning for Father. She could not conceal from me the news about Kharkov: that the city had been horribly bombarded and had fallen to the enemy soon after we left. We never got a letter or any word from Father, nor from anyone else in Kharkov.

When, one hot evening in July, we heard a knock at the door and Father walked in, alive, unhurt, much thinner than when we had last seen him but otherwise, as my mother said, exactly as she had seen him in so many of her dreams, we were struck dumb with joy. I can't describe it. No one in the place slept that night; we all stayed up, talking, laughing, and weeping, until dawn.

It turned out that Father had stayed at his hospital right up until the last hours before Kharkov fell; then had remained with it during a long retreat, until it was set up as a field hospital. He attempted for almost eight months to discover where Mother and I had been moved; it was not until a few days before his transfer to the hospital for the wounded in Novosibirsk that the authorities let him know we were near there.

Almost immediately after his return, we moved to Novosibirsk and my mother obtained a post as general practitioner in the same hospital to which Father was now attached.

In Novosibirsk, we were only three. We lived in a kitchen. All the other rooms in the apartment were already occupied; there was no space left for us except this very small kitchen. We had a stove, fueled with coal dust, which was lit once a day.

It was quite a test of endurance to live in this unheated room. In Siberia the temperature in winter is quite often forty degrees below zero Fahrenheit. All day, except for the brief hour when you were cooking and the stove warmed the kitchen, you wore your overcoat and your heavy valenki indoors. When we woke up in the morning the windows were covered on the inside with frost, half an inch thick. I always enjoyed my first chore of the day, which was to scrape it off. Naturally, there was no running water in our kitchen; there was just a pail of water. This was also deep in ice.

I remember at that time occasionally waking up in the night and seeing Father sitting at the table wearing coat and valenki, writing his doctoral thesis; this after a twelve- or fourteen-hour stint at the hospital. The only time he could find to write was at night.

Krivoshchokovo is only about an hour's train ride from Novosibirsk, so every few weeks Aunt Fanya and Victor and Yuri came into town to visit us, or we went out there. We saved what we could of our rations and gathered for Sunday "dinner." Victor and I were always impatient to see each other: we had to talk about everything we had read since we last met; everything we had been thinking. I had to describe to him the mechanical and electrical experiments I was always devising at that time. (Terribly frustrating, because I couldn't carry them out. You couldn't buy so much as a flashlight battery during those years.) Or we pored over his tiny stamp collection. If one of us by extraordinary good luck had seen a movie, he had to give the other a reel-by-reel description. The plots were always the same: evil inhuman Germans outwitted by heroic Russians.

The War proceeded. Great battles were fought and lost; cities were bombed to rubble; huge sections of our nation fell to the enemy; hundreds of thousands, then millions, of Russians died. But we in this remote part of the Soviet Union received only a watered-down, heavily censored version of what was happening. At the beginning of the War all privately owned radios were confiscated by the authorities, and in their place one could rent for a few kopeks a speaker that broadcast only programs controlled by Radio Moscow. To listen to a short-wave program from abroad was a capital crime. We heard nothing but official news, which played down Russian losses as much as possible and emphasized sagas of individual heroism. Our parents were anxious and serious — most intelligent Soviet people know how to interpret the official news — but for us kids, victory was certain.

To give my reader an idea of how thoroughly one-sided these programs were: on February 1st, 1943, the victory of Stalingrad was announced. And it was not until that date that we had any idea the city had been under siege — which it had been for a year and a half. As for the millions who died there under fire or of hunger — the War had long been over before people in other regions apprehended the scope of that enormous tragedy.

As a result of these filtered reports, I did not worry much about the War. Like most parents, my mother and father wanted to spare me any misery they could, and they never described any of the cases they were tending in the military hospital nor any of the other horrors of war. Even when, in the space of two years, 'forty-two and 'forty-three, Father lost three of his brothers — two were pilots, shot down in action, and the third was at the front in the regular army — they suppressed the bad news from me, and I never knew about those deaths until after the victory. Also, one of my aunts on Mother's side was wounded.

At the time, I was in ignorance of most of this. I remember the start of the 'forties as a period of reading a lot, and trying to understand what was happening around me. Unfortunately, the more I tried to understand, the more I was baffled and disillusioned by our Soviet life.

When I first came to Novosibirsk, I had just read *Timur and His Team,* a children's book by the very talented writer Arkady Gaidar. Gaidar was an honest and idealistic man. A fighter in the Civil War, he was a colonel in command of a regiment at the age of only sixteen. The contrast between Soviet reality and the ideal state this author envisioned may have been what killed him. He died in the first few days of World War II, and it is widely believed that he was a suicide.

I was much impressed by his book about the Pioneers — the Pioneers that existed in his imagination. I was inflamed by the idea of becoming a Pioneer, of doing good deeds in secret like the characters in his book, helping people in trouble.

Having been ill at the time the Pioneers were being recruited — you join this organization when you are in the second grade — I wasn't a member, and was told that it was impossible now to repair this omission.

I was outraged. I decided to protest in my own way: to make what seemed to me like a significant gesture of civil disobedience. After saving up ten kopeks, I bought myself a red Pioneer kerchief, the most conspicuous emblem of membership. I was sure that everybody would pay attention to this defiant action, and that I would constitute a "test case" as to the requirements for joining. I imagined a protest, an uproar, an attempt to force me to relinquish this insignia, which would result in the vindication of the rights of anyone to become a Pioneer, no matter what his age.

Nobody noticed. Nobody cared. I became a Pioneer without creating any stir at all. There had been thirty-nine Pioneers from my class; now there were forty. Who counted?

The real disappointment was that nothing changed for me. I found out that the life of a Pioneer is no more chivalrous, no more uplifting, than the life of a non-Pioneer. I had imagined an existence dedicated to benefiting suffering humanity. But such a career was nonexistent, outside of Gaidar's novels, radio plays, and fanciful newspaper stories.

I again decided that something was very wrong, and planned to make a protest against the meaningless routinized activities of the Pioneers. So this time I took *off* the kerchief, to demonstrate publicly my opinion of the Pioneers. But this outrage was exactly as invisible, and went just as unnoticed, as my unauthorized assumption of the tie had been.

And that was the end of my stint in the Pioneers. I went back to my reading.

Just at that time I took out of the library a copy of *Don Quixote*. I read the uncut edition, straight through, in a single day. I was so absolutely struck by that great work and by what seemed to me the parallels between the hero's delusions and some of the delusions I saw around me — not to mention several of my own — that I literally could not put it down. I didn't go to school; actually did not stop reading for more than a minute before I finished it. *Don Quixote* sank into my spirit and made an ineradicable impression.

There was nobody to stop me from cutting school, or from reading all day and all evening, because, as almost always throughout my childhood, I didn't see my parents except on Sundays; and these days even the Sundays were often solitary. Both Mother and Father were in the hospital from early morning till late at night. They left while I was still asleep. They left me my breakfast and a little note. I knew what I was supposed to do: I had to haul in the water, drawn from the courtyard pipe; clean the room; prepare something for my parents to eat when they got back from the hospital; and, before I went to bed, add one or two small coal bricks to the stove so that it wouldn't go out. I was almost always sleeping by the time they got home to their supper — usually just kasha and bread.

Recalling the meager meals of that time brings to mind an incident that I suppose is rather revealing of the very strong interests I began to display then, and that one way or another have stayed with me ever since.

One day I heard from a boy in school that in one of the midtown shops, miraculously, microscopes had appeared — pocket microscopes, with a forty-to-sixty-power magnification. This was something I had dreamed about all my life. The price (I remember it exactly) was 195 roubles.* No one could imagine how such instruments came onto the market: probably some optical factory was getting rid of all its civilian supplies to provide space for military productions.

When I heard the news, I ran all the way home from school in a per-

---

* This was before the currency reform of 1947.

fect fever. I performed all my jobs with unusual care, cut the bread and boiled the kasha for my parents' supper, and set myself to stay awake for their arrival. It seemed an eternity before they came home. When the door finally opened, I hurled myself upon them before they could open their mouths to ask what I was doing still up at that hour, told them about the microscope, and urgently begged for the 195 roubles.

"Why, you must be crazy, Mara!" was the answer. "Where in the world would we find a hundred and ninety-five roubles? Get that idea out of your head right now! And go to sleep."

I was shattered.

The next morning, when I woke up, I started to evolve an idea. From that day on I began saving my breakfast — a small piece of sour brown bread, now and then covered with a thin film of margarine — and stored it away in a summer shirt. I went without breakfast for weeks and weeks. The bread dried out, turned into a sort of hardtack — not much of a change, because even when it is fresh this bread is very hard.

Some time in May, when I considered that I had accumulated enough of this dried bread, I wrapped it up and went down to the Novosibirsk bazaar, which was at the time almost entirely a black-market affair. I didn't know — and didn't ask — the going rate for black-market food, but I have heard since that bread went for the astronomical price of 700 to 1000 in 1940s' roubles — close to the average person's monthly salary — per kilogram in that lean year. My hoard of about four kilograms sold in no time for the exact price I specified: 195 roubles. The buyer thought he was getting a terrific bargain; considering the times, he was.

I ran to the optical store, bought the microscope, and spent the rest of the day in a state of absolute rapture, looking at everything through it. A drop of dirty water — I couldn't believe my eyes — turned out to be a jungle of various-shaped animals, fighting with each other. A crumb became a crater-pocked boulder. Everything in sight I had to look at through the microscope, and, very happily, I spent every minute of my spare daylight hours from that time on making observations. One particularly rewarding source of material was the rain barrel in our courtyard, in which I found interesting little dark gray rod-shaped fish. Where could they possibly have come from? I examined them for several days in succession, mystified as to their origin and identity. After a while I noticed with alarm that, one after another, they seemed to be dying. The dead ones were simply empty shells. What a strange death! — leaving not an entire corpse, but only the exterior of the body, a hollow "skin." I had to look into this further; I decided to observe them for a longer time at a stretch to discover what this perplexing phenomenon really was. My patience was finally rewarded when I saw what happened: a mosquito emerged from one end of this tiny fish and came out from the water, and wings appeared. It was very exciting. Once dried out, he flew off, and shortly would become a giant among insects, one of the swarms that are the plague of the Siberian spring.

I could go on and on about what I saw through the microscope, but I have to mention the dark side of that episode. At first I told my parents that I had just found the instrument in the street, and because I had never lied to them before in my life they believed the story, unlikely though it was. In the end I couldn't stand it any more; I felt too guilty about the lie, so I told them how I had managed to buy it.

They reacted as if I had committed the worst of crimes. I knew I had done something furtive, something unauthorized, but I was astonished by the pitiless scolding I received. Only now I look back and realize how hard it was for my parents, during that eternal fast, to sacrifice even those small slices of bread they left on the table for my breakfast, and what a shock it was to them — on the edge of starvation, as we all were — to learn that this precious staff of life had been exchanged for what was in their view little better than a toy.

I cannot say that I am sorry. I still have the microscope, at this very day. It came out of Russia with me; it got to Israel; and now my daughter Yulia uses it sometimes. I have always thought of it as the most valuable acquisition I ever made.

Another occupation during those three years in Novosibirsk was the study of languages.

It was frustrating for my mother and father, both people of wide interests and intellectual curiosity, to have to work such long hours that they never had a moment to study or to read, not even the medical journals, or to learn anything at all outside their specialties. I can't remember them ever going to a theater or to a concert, much as they longed to. The only music they heard was what we got on the radio. (Incidentally, we were offered some very good music over the air on occasion: we had two of the greatest symphony orchestras in the world, the Moscow and the Leningrad.) They felt the confinement of their intellectual lives and wanted to make sure that I should not be limited as they had been. They insisted upon taking every opportunity that offered to help me acquire as broad a background as possible: a liberal education.

When it appeared that one of the women who lived on the floor above us in the apartment house knew German, my mother persuaded her to tutor me in that language. This was not a success. My teacher methodically followed the schedules in a very dry lesson-book, and I finally refused to continue memorizing grammatical rules and boring vocabulary lists. I just couldn't stand it. (Being of German ancestry, the poor woman was exiled even farther than Novosibirsk, not long after the tutoring stopped. The Volga Germans, unassimilated after two centuries of residence in Russia, were "enemy aliens" during the War, and they still constitute a markedly oppressed minority.)

My parents then found out that the mother of one of their colleagues at the hospital, also a very near neighbor, had spent twenty years in America and knew English perfectly. This lady, Yekaterina Alexeyevna, was at first reluctant to attempt teaching me, protesting that she had no idea how one was supposed to set about it. But she finally consented to try. The method she used was simply to speak English, not a word of Russian, throughout the tutoring hour. No one who has been involved with the teaching of languages will be surprised to hear that this system worked.

Yekaterina Alexeyevna was about sixty years of age when I knew her. I believe she was the daughter of people who had been in the consular service in Czarist times, which accounts for her long stay in America. Now that I think of it, it is perfectly amazing that she escaped arrest during the later 'thirties. People with antecedents and connections such as hers were among the very first victims. Any contact, past or present, with a foreign country was suspect to a highly dangerous degree. I happened to be visiting an uncle of mine in Kharkov once when he received a letter with a foreign stamp on the envelope. He became terribly agitated and threw the letter into the stove almost before he had finished reading it. Caution was so thoroughly ingrained in me by that time, though I was still very young, that it never occurred to me to ask where it had come from. You might say that when it came to forbidden subjects, we Soviet children were trained not only to keep silent, but almost to silence our thoughts.

So I didn't ask Yekaterina Alexeyevna anything about her life in America, and of course she didn't bring the subject up. I knew nothing about that country and was not even curious. It was run by wicked capitalists; that I knew. Also, I was aware that they were sending food parcels to Russia — but this was solely for reasons of self-interest so that they themselves would not be conquered by the Fascists. Like everyone else, I had read *Tom Sawyer* and *Huckleberry Finn,* extremely popular classics in Russia; but, childishly, I made no connection between the country where these boys had lived and the cynical allies who gave us powdered milk.

This enormous blank in my picture of the world proves the effec-

tiveness of the Soviet teaching of history. The fact that about two million Jews had emigrated to America at the turn of the century was unknown to me. And I learned only yesterday, through correspondence
with my father, that my great-grandfather Azbel had been a member of
this great exodus. But he could not stay in America: he was one of the
small number of very, very devout people who, finding it impossible to
live as an observant Jew in the United States, came back to the shtetl.
His wife and his son, my grandfather, came back with him, but he left
four grown-up married daughters in Kansas City.

(My father wrote me also that his own father, Aron, died after the
most acute phase of the wartime food shortage because the only food
available was *treyf*, nonkosher, and he could hardly touch it. I only
learned of this thirty-two years after the fact.)

                              *   *   *

During the War years I spent most of my time, aside from schoolwork,
with my books, with my thoughts, with my microscope. I tried to teach
myself to draw, and also wrote a great deal of poetry.

I fell in love. There was something mysterious in this feeling: I wondered if it was common for a boy of my age — not quite ten at that
time — to fall in love; but was cheered by reading Lermontov's observation that early passion is characteristic of a soul which is destined to
love the arts.

I worried terribly about the difference in age between myself and the
girl, because when we met, which was when we first came to Novosibirsk — her family lived in the same building we did — she was only
five years old. The distance between us seemed enormous — but on this
point too, my books reassured me.

It was one of the strongest feelings of my life. I still remember her:
Lili Orlova. She was a very pretty and intelligent little person. I think of
her every time I hear the song "My dear Moscow." It's not a particularly good tune, but it has inescapable associations for me: you heard it
very often in the 'forties, and Lili and I, with the other children who had
made friends and played together in our apartment house, sang it all the
time.

I never saw her again after 1944, when I was twelve.

                              *   *   *

I am not writing much about the War, because I am trying to present
here only my own impressions; only my own experience, and I was too
young to understand much more than that, finally, just as was to be expected, the fortunes of war turned and we started to push the Germans

back. But my story will be incomplete if I don't mention some observations of the life around me that I made even at that age.

Of course I was carried away by the accounts of heroism that poured out of the radio and were splashed over the newspapers. I didn't know at the time that some of these heroes were selected for qualities quite different from heroic ones, and that they came in for such loud publicity, not because of their great deeds, but for the aims of propaganda. I will expand on that theme later.

But there was one national Soviet hero, not a soldier but someone whose courage and patriotism were constantly invoked, whom even I, young as I was, found disgusting.

This was Pavlik Morozov, a boy whose heroism consisted in betraying his own father. The father was a *kulak,* a wealthy peasant, "exploiter" of the poor. When wheat was confiscated, he had held back a small supply to save his family and neighbors from actual starvation. Pavlik Morozov reported him to the secret police. The father was arrested and shot. Subsequently, the boy was caught by friends of his father, also kulaks, who avenged the elder Morozov's death by killing Pavlik in his turn. The child was not only a shining national hero, but a martyr. He was held up to Russian children as a model, an exemplary person who had sacrificed his life in a higher cause. We heard lectures about him in school and in the Pioneers — paeans of praise for this brave child. I absolutely could not understand the story. Could anyone at such an early age decide who is right and who is wrong? The father had not done any wrong that could be obvious to a small child; he hadn't killed anybody; he hadn't done anyone any harm. And if this child was so anxious to bring about the ideal Socialist state, why, I wondered, didn't he talk to his father? How could it be possible for a boy to be a traitor to his own family? How could such a child be described as a hero?

When I expressed to my parents my indignation at this story, Mother put her hands on my shoulders and said: "Look, Mara. Just ask no questions about Pavlik Morozov at school or anywhere. Don't say anything about him. Keep your thoughts to yourself; otherwise your father and I will suffer."

I had no idea why, but I could tell it was important to obey such an injunction, and I kept quiet thereafter on the subject.

It was not until many years later that I discovered the reason Mother, in particular, was fearful that I might make myself conspicuous by asking the wrong questions in the wrong places. Her family on the distaff side were members of the *haute bourgeoise* Jewish intelligentsia in Chernigov. Their name was Schwartz. My grandfather, Mark Isayavitch Schwartz, was a scholar; perhaps something of a dilettante; well-read in the classics — he was particularly fond of Ovid — and in Russian, English, and French poetry. In 1913 when my mother, his eldest granddaughter, was five years old, the family had to move to Poltava. The geographical line behind which Jews might live was reinforced in that year of pogroms. In Poltava, however, one might still cultivate the arts and sciences, and my mother studied at the gymnasium there until 1919, when she entered what was called the Labor School. She became a teacher for a while; also, she was good at painting and acquired the very special art of painting playing cards. These cards were in great demand, and her earnings saved her family from starvation. When her family moved to Kharkov she entered the Art Institute there. Later, having decided that she would probably never become an artist of real stature, she enrolled at the Medical Institute. (In Russia for almost a century the medical profession has attracted a great many women, and at the present time a considerable majority of physicians are women.)

This sort of background was, as I say, a dangerous one to have and had to be kept carefully concealed. To learn how to keep silent was an important aspect of one's education. Very often, in recent years, people I have met outside the Soviet Union have asked me, "How does a person know what he *can* say, and what he *can't*, in Russia?" This awareness starts in very early childhood. Not to keep your thoughts to yourself is not only folly, but one of the major sins, since the freedom of friends and relatives may be in jeopardy, as well as one's own.

That is why Solzhenitsyn considers that simply not to lie is of tremendous importance. He says that in Russia one's ambition should be not to tell the truth — obviously it is impossible to demand of everybody to take such risks — but merely to avoid telling lies. Even this is real heroism.

Another thing put doubts and confusion into my mind, about which I couldn't ask anyone. During the War, people gave a high proportion of their very poor salaries to the so-called State Loans. Actually, these were not loans; they were taxes, or, more accurately, outright gifts to the State, in the guise of "Victory Bonds." We were told these loans would be repaid in twenty years. When I first heard about the loans I took the idea for granted: during a war everyone must sacrifice everything he has. But it did seem strange that this money could not have been raised as voluntary contributions. In such a vital cause, the patriotic Russian people would gladly impoverish themselves; we would gladly work even harder, move even closer to the borderline of starvation, to promote the victory over Fascism. Why was this loan — this donation — raised by force? It was impossible not to contribute to this fund; even I, at the age of eleven, realized that to refuse constituted a crime. It didn't make any sense! I was sure that the great majority of people would purchase these bonds if they possibly could. Why should such a sacred duty be compulsory?

The bond certificates were guaranteed at face value, pending the time of their redemption, when they would have appreciated by a factor of 3 percent. Everybody had thousands of these fictitious roubles. By the second or third year of the War, people were actually starving, and those who badly needed real money were eventually happy to sell a hundred-rouble bond for five, maybe for three, roubles. For them the money was a matter of life or death. And somehow, as happens everywhere in every era, there were people who had plenty of money. They were *speku-lyants;* not only rich but looking far ahead and making plans to get richer. They assumed the time would come when, even if the bonds were not redeemed, at least the interest would be paid; and the interest by that time might be much more substantial than this tiny present outlay. So there was a market for these notes, the going rate but a fraction of the original cost.

No sooner had trade in these securities started to move briskly than a law was passed against negotiating them. They were frozen;* could not change hands. The penalty for infringing this law was extremely severe: buyers or sellers were sent to prison camps for ten years.

I was bewildered by this new regulation. Why was it forbidden for hungry people to improve their situation, at least a little bit? Again, there was no explanation.

This sort of occurrence sank in on me. I began to absorb the tremendous difference between Soviet ideals about which one heard in school, and the realities of our life.

---

* Twenty years later, when the bonds reached maturity, Khrushchev canceled payment on them; by that time such an outcome was no surprise.

Alien Home

In 1944 Kharkov was liberated. The entire military hospital in Novosibirsk was moved there, so all of us who had been evacuated found ourselves at home again.

I couldn't recognize Kharkov. I had left it when I was barely nine years old, and even if I had had a better memory than most children, there was nothing left to recognize. The city was almost entirely in ruins. Imagine: walking down any once-familiar street you see on either side almost no buildings at all; nothing but rubble. Those few houses that are still standing are horribly damaged.

Our former place, in the large apartment building on Kaplunovskaya Street, was all right; that particular building had escaped the bombs. But just because of this fact our former apartment was occupied by a petty KGBst and his family, so we had no hope of getting our room back.

Mother's sister Sara, a doctor, had also owned a room in that building. Not everyone would have fought as stubbornly as Aunt Sara did when she returned from the front and found her apartment occupied by officials' families, but she was something of an eccentric.

She had been very beautiful as a young woman; had attracted a crowd of beaux, but was not interested in any of them. One suitor in particular was so desperately in love with her that when she rejected his proposal of marriage, the man committed suicide. This tragedy pushed Aunt Sara into a nervous breakdown, and she was always very highstrung afterward. Then during the War, almost all of which she spent at the front, she suffered from a concussion blast when a shell exploded near her — this was a severe shock to her system, serious enough to qualify her for a disability pension — and she became more irascible than ever. When she was angry, most people did what she told them to do. After a battle with the family who had pre-empted her room, and another one with the city authorities, she regained the room she had originally owned, and moved back in. The occupants of the adjoining rooms subjected Aunt Sara to every annoyance they could think of in hopes of getting her out, but she wouldn't move, and spent the rest of her life (she died in 1970) at swords' points with these neighbors.

My father managed to find us a place on Garshina Street, in a house that had been partly destroyed by a bomb. (On our entry door was scratched the word *Ostdeutsch;* the previous tenants had been collaborationists and this was how they had advertised their loyalty.) One of our walls had originally been an interior wall of the house, but now none of the apartments beyond that point was still in existence. But it was quite luxurious, to us. It consisted of one and a half rooms, plus a corridor (created by the installation of a beaverboard partition cutting off a little space from the two rooms beyond it), which led to the communal kitchen, shared by six people. Off the kitchen there was actually a bathroom with all the facilities. This was not quite as splendid as it sounds, however, because Kharkov has always suffered from a chronic water shortage, and there was water in the pipes during only two hours of the day. Needless to say, the "hot" tap produced only cold. One of the tenants had built a huge box-shaped shelf into the bathroom, on which stood a twelve-gallon bucket; this was filled up whenever the water went on. That way we had a supply for cooking, for washing the dishes, and for flushing the toilet; but I certainly can't remember ever taking a bath in that tub. One couldn't have heated that much water. We had to use the public baths.

These were nothing like the large beautifully equipped baths you see in Moscow; but still it was fun to make a family excursion of the trip to the big warm building, bringing soap, towels, and also any laundry that had to be done, and spend an hour pouring an unlimited amount of hot water over oneself (there are few tubs or showers; they give you a basin) and then, feeling very clean and wearing the fresh linen you had brought with you, to sit for a while in the warming-room to store up heat before the plunge back into the cold street.

There was no heat in our apartment, but after Siberia this did not seem to us a terrible inconvenience: we installed a small bourzhuika, and rigged up a stovepipe leading out a window.

I will never understand how my mother managed to housekeep and cook so beautifully under the circumstances in which we lived. Our room was always perfectly neat: the folding cots stored away inconspicuously by day, the bedding out of sight, and our clothes hung in an orderly row. Our shirts were ironed: Mother used flatirons heated on the stove. The table — used for eating, for study, for reading and writing,

and around which my friends and my parents were often gathered —
was always covered with a clean cloth. There was not a speck of dust
anywhere. Moreover, my mother was a marvelous cook. She could
make a cake, for example, that was the envy of the other women who
shared the stove, out of almost nothing.

I can't exaggerate how long her working hours were. There was no
definite time at which she could expect to leave the hospital: it was just
a matter of when her last patient had been attended to, however late at
night that might be. When Father began to be a little more secure financially — he got his Ph.D. (which was quite rare at that time; hardly 1
percent of physicians had it) and became Deputy Director at the Scientific Research Institute — he constantly urged Mother to stop working.
He worried about her health. But she never even thought of retiring.
Taking into consideration the heavy demands of her work at home, she
really held down two jobs during her whole lifetime, as most Soviet
women do.

*   *   *

We arrived in Kharkov just in time for me to attend the last quarter of
the fifth grade. The Kharkov school was better than the one in Novosibirsk. Not only were the pupils held to a higher standard of perform-
ance so that we were aware of accomplishing considerably more, but
it was warmer! You still had to wear your overcoat in class, but at least
the ink didn't freeze in the inkwells.

The school I had originally attended through the second grade had
been bombed, and the new building was still lacking in almost all
equipment. There were no desks or chairs; we each had to bring a chair
from home. Boys and girls were in separate schools, although segregation of the sexes in educational institutions had been denounced as a
bourgeois custom after the Revolution and for a decade or more they
had studied together. Boys' and girls' schools have merged and separated alternately ever since. (The universities and institutes, however,
have never been segregated.) With each change, the State has labeled the
previous system "inadequate to the present increased level of culture
and education."

All the courses were easy for me except for the Ukrainian language.
One doesn't hear it much in the cities, and even in the villages a strange
mixture of Ukrainian and Russian is spoken; I could understand it but
not speak it. Some of the letters of the alphabet are different from the
Russian. But I had never in my life had any trouble with Russian spelling, owing, I suppose, to having been such an inveterate reader. (By this
time I had really read a great deal — everything I could lay my hands

on — and had memorized reams of poetry.) So I assumed that I would do well in Ukrainian. Pride goeth before a fall! I remember that in the first dictation I ever took in school, I was doubtful about the spelling of only one word. I thought maybe if worse came to worst, I would get a mark not of 5 (an A in Russia) but a 4 (a B). In two days, our teacher brought in the dictations and handed them around to us, announcing the grades. First of all the 5's were distributed — I was not among them. Well, I had been prepared for that possibility. When I wasn't among those who received a 4, I was astonished. When I realized I wasn't in the 3's, I began seriously to worry. When the papers that had gotten a mark of only 2 were passed out, the obvious solution occurred to me — my paper must have been lost. This view was confirmed in my mind when I wasn't among the 1's, either. But then the teacher announced: "The remaining dictations were so dreadful, I couldn't grade them at all!"

I was not the only failure; Kharkov having just been liberated, there were other children who were also ex-refugees and who had been in Siberia, or other regions outside the Ukraine, where this language was not studied in school. I asked to see my dictation, but the teacher had been so horrified by finding mistakes in every word that she had thrown away mine and the others that were in the same hopeless condition. Those of us who were newcomers to the school finished the year with no rating in Ukrainian.

This was a very short school year, since I had come in at the end of March. The vacation started on June 31st.

During that summer I had a stroke of luck for which I will never cease to be thankful to the fates: I had access to the best library that I could possibly have found. Thousands of books had been collected more or less at random in the Kharkov Regional Young People's Library, among them English, French, and German books. God knows where they all came from; many may even have turned up in the ruins left by air raids; others may have been confiscated from private libraries, decades before my time. There was some mistake here: among them were many books that were not supposed to be read in the Soviet Union. It must have been the wartime confusion and disorganization that permitted these forbidden works to remain in the collection. When, years later, I came to the same library to renew my acquaintance with these beloved books, I found that most of them were now unavailable, and nobody could tell me how they had disappeared. In the Soviet Union there is a clearly defined "Index," and no one reads anything that is forbidden.

At the time, however, I reveled in these books. I was very happy. All of Pushkin, Lermontov, Dostoievski, Tolstoi, Turgenyev, Goncharov, Chekhov, Gorki, Blok, Babel, Bulgakov, Akhmatova — everyone. And the English classics: Shakespeare, in the Oxford edition, complete; Milton, Pope, Shelley, Keats, Byron! The Byron was a wonderful volume, bound in red leather. I had never seen anything so beautiful. Swift, Sterne, Trollope, Dickens, Thackeray, Scott — I would hardly know where to begin or end my catalogue. The Americans: Mark Twain, Jack London of course; O. Henry, Dreiser, even Hemingway, Faulkner. I had chanced upon a treasure trove; spent that summer tunneling into it, and would do the same for several years to come.

There was also a great deal of science fiction, in Ukrainian translation, which I simply devoured. These readings proved to be a great advantage, as when I entered the sixth grade I no longer had any trouble writing the language.

*   *   *

In the sixth grade, I was initiated into the mysteries of officially approved literature, with its astonishing limitations. In this literature, Dostoievski was nonexistent, except to be condemned. Tolstoi was a very doubtful writer; we were given almost nothing of his to read. Homer was unknown. The great Russian writers Nabokov, Bunin, Kuprin, Bulgakov, were not even mentioned. They simply did not exist. Even Gogol, even Chekhov, were heavily cut. In essays and examinations, when we had to answer questions about any author frowned upon by the authorities, our answers were supposed to consist of a derogatory opinion of this author, mentioning specific works of his and explaining what was wrong with them. There were a number of authors whose names we learned only in relation to negative commentary. We had to condemn them — but we were not allowed to read them! We were simply supposed to repeat what we had heard about these authors.

In other words, we had absolutely no right to think; our education consisted in memorizing what we were *supposed* to think. For me, there was a serious problem: it was naturally very hard not to mention what I had already read and to remember — my brain simply did not want to retain it — which literary pundit disapproved of *Crime and Punishment,* for example, and why. And I had to suppress from my consciousness the fact that there were such poets as Blok, Akhmatova, Pasternak, and many others.

Another stumbling block was that the policies — the viewpoints of the educational Establishment — were changeable. Once we were assigned to study the Ukrainian poet Rylsky. But shortly after we had learned to appreciate him and had written laudatory essays and favorable criticisms of him, Rylsky was abruptly denounced as a Ukrainian nationalist, and his poems simply vanished. He was just a blank. A little later we were told to write an essay, our "own" thoughts on some patriotic topic, I can't remember exactly what, and we were supposed to start off the paper with an epigraph. I had a perfect couplet in mind; very good, very pro-Soviet — but the problem was that the author was Rylsky. I asked the teacher, "Can I use these two lines?" She thought it over and said, "All right, you can write that down, but don't cite the author. Just say 'Ukrainian Folk-Song.' "

That was our literary education. At the same time it was dinned into us that literature was very important and marvelous; that books are very important things. Actually, despite everything, a lot of good books were available in the school library, and were also very cheap to buy. A big thick hard-bound novel might cost seventy-five kopeks or a rouble, something around there. In any case, educated Russians seem to read absolutely all the time. On park benches, on the Metro, lying on a riverbank, standing in one of the eternal queues — many of the people you see are reading, and not only the newspapers but books. When I came to the West, it was a surprise to me to find that this habit is not universal.

Peacetime

I IMAGINE there has never been a national celebration in the history of Russia half so joyous as the one that took place when the war ended. Hardly anyone was still unaware of how narrow the margin of victory was, and the feeling of miraculous relief and release was universal. People celebrated in the streets all night. Oddly enough, Stalin postponed the announcement of the peace for twenty-four hours after the hostilities ceased, and the holiday that marks the occasion is still observed on May 9th rather than on the 8th, when the Germans actually surrendered.

Like everyone else I was swept away by this happy mass delirium, and it was not until several months later that I really assimilated the shock of my cousin Victor's death. He died just before the War was over. He had always suffered from spells of extreme fatigue, and while we were still in Siberia had been diagnosed as suffering from a cardiac valvular lesion.

In March, he had gone to the hospital. I had been to see him there two or three times. These were pleasant visits; as always, we had a thousand things to talk about. It never occurred to me that he might not get better.

Victor's coffin was loaded onto a truck; the mourners followed it on foot; and we made our way to the cemetery, where after a few farewell words Victor was buried, surrounded by Aunt Fanya and Yuri and the rest of us. There are people who hire a band to play funeral marches on these occasions, but in our family this custom was regarded as more or less pompous.

No music and few words. A grim farewell.

*   *   *

September 1st, and back to school again.

I was very quick at studies and, having already read so much, got rather bored in the eighth grade. In the autumn I decided that at the end of the year I would try to pass not only the eighth-grade exams but the ninth-grade ones as well; then I would qualify to go into the senior year. Schools in Russia go through ten grades rather than twelve, which is more common in the Western world; but I would guess that the number of classroom hours is about the same, since our summer holidays were almost a month shorter than the American or English ones, for example. Also — regrettably — there are few sports to take up time that might be devoted to study. Only the most gifted athletes receive any training in sports after the sixth grade. Children put in a staggering number of hours at homework, and, in the good city schools, such as the one I attended, receive a very thorough grounding at least in mathematics and science.

I managed to obtain the ninth-grade books and, after finishing my daily assignments, studied an extra hour or two from the texts assigned to the class ahead of me. I didn't mention my plan to anyone.

In the spring, a mathematical Olympiad was conducted, with entries from all the schools in the Kharkov Region. I was reluctant to compete in it — I had friends who I was sure were superior to me as mathematicians, and felt it would be a wasted effort — but everyone persuaded me to take my chances. When I was told that I had been awarded the first prize in the Olympiad, I assumed it was some kind of joke; I didn't even go to the session where the prizes were handed out. So they sent someone around to deliver it to me.

Achieving this distinction turned out to be a liability rather than an asset when it came to my attempt to skip a grade. When I asked one of my teachers, the "class leader," if I might take exams for the ninth grade as well as the eighth, the answer was "Absolutely not! There are new regulations about that — nobody can do it." She was furious with me, because the class in which I was stuck really was a weak one, and she wanted to keep me there in order to bring up the average of achievement in that group.

But I was very persistent. I went to see the school principal, and made my request to him — again without results. In the end I called on the Chairman of the Kharkov City Department for People's Education. He appeared to be interested in my case, and gave me a *viva voce* examination in mathematics, in physics, in history, and so on. The fact that he was a man of broad culture did not surprise me at the time, but the high officials in the school system whom I subsequently encountered were usually people of minimal background in any field; and, looking back, I realize how lucky I was to have been interviewed by this particular man. I remember his name to this day: Babitch.

After I had answered all his questions, he gave me permission to take the ninth-grade finals; and I passed them without trouble.

My new class turned out to be a very good one, very strong, with many brilliant pupils. An extraordinary number of people in my grade or the one above me eventually earned national and even international reputations in the sciences, perhaps the best known being the biophysicist Maleev and the mathematician Lubitsch.

A word about the teachers of that class. They were rather interesting personalities, somehow gathered in that one school; fairly representative of good Soviet teachers.

Our mathematician, Alexander Petrovitch Multanowski, was very devoted to his subject. He tried to do everything to involve us in mathematics. He devised specific problems for individual students who were gifted in the subject. His career took an unfortunate turn. Some ten years after I graduated from the school, Alexander Petrovitch, then in late middle age, fell in love with a teacher of geography, a woman a great deal younger than himself and married her. It was considered an absolute scandal, something highly immoral, for a Soviet teacher to behave in such a frivolous manner. Soviet officialdom is more strait-laced than the Victorian, which I suppose could have tolerated such a romance even if it originated within the prim premises of a school. Despite the fact that Multanowski was rightly considered to be an excellent teacher, he was fired. After that he was almost unemployable. The only post he could obtain eventually was in one of those benighted village schools on the outskirts of Kharkov. He had no pupils there worth struggling with, and his only gratification was to follow with pride the careers of those he had taught in our school. He and I used to run across each other on the streets of Kharkov occasionally for years after I left school and university, and every time we met he expressed warm interest in what I was doing. I've always felt much indebted to this man.

The physics instructor, Mikhail Mikhailovitch Truskevitch, was the director of the school. He was a very good administrator and organizer; I have to give him a lot of credit for setting up a well-equipped laboratory — extremely rare in the Soviet Union, where even government-operated university laboratories were so short of supplies that technicians had to fight over every test tube, every scrap of wire. But his teaching of physics was so poor that I, for one, turned to mathematics at that time, and later it was almost an accident that I became a physicist.

The teacher of chemistry, Mikhail Alexandrovitch, was very good; enthusiastic about his field and remarkably well informed. He had us doing university-level chemistry while we were still in the tenth grade. Those who studied under him did extremely well in the university examinations; when I took them, the examiners were delighted with my results and urged me to go into the Chemistry Department.

The literature teacher, Sara Samoilovna, tiny, lame, gray-haired, typically Jewish in appearance, really appreciated books and conducted a very interesting Reading Circle at the school. She was one of those personalities about whom nobody feels neutral. The class was divided into two camps: those who loved her and those who hated her. I have to admit that while I felt I was getting a lot from her course I didn't like her indiscriminate enthusiasm, and also I believed that her system of marking reflected her preferences among the pupils more than it did their capacities.

The history teacher was Vera Moiseyevna, a tall and rather handsome woman but chilly in her manner. She was a Party member, a good Communist of long standing; fond of history and of Marxism-Leninism. She made us study this subject far beyond the requirements set by the school board. We all had to read a great deal of Lenin, Marx, Engels, and Stalin; and for my part I am very glad I did, as these readings hastened the crystallizing of my thoughts about them.

Reading Engels, who occasionally expounds his philosophy on mathematics and physics, I was amazed at the extremely low level of his comprehension of those sciences. His exposition is very naïve and frequently absolutely wrong. It was pretty obvious even to a tenth-grader that Engels' grasp of mathematics and physics was shaky, but he refers to these subjects with the greatest conviction. I wondered: How can one study, and learn, on the basis of a book that is full of errors and is patently obsolete? How can one discuss any subject, using as an authority someone who — even for his time — didn't understand it himself? How can a correct philosophy arise from an incorrect foundation? Can the corollaries of erroneous statements be true and important?

Another work of the same kind is Lenin's *Materialism and Empiriocriticism,* in which the revolution in physics at the beginning of the century is discussed. Here the author dismisses the work of Ostwald and Mach — certainly among the greatest minds of their time; indeed Einstein credits Mach with a profound influence on his own thinking. It dawned on me that Lenin understood neither physics nor the philosophers he was criticizing. His ideas on science are simply those of a layman.

Lenin was not bothered by contradictory theories of his own nor by evidence of disagreement among his adherents. In one publication he writes that since the aims of the proletariat are identical the world over, the independence and self-determination of nations is a reactionary and outmoded idea. Then later, when revolution was approaching — specifically in Russia, which is a multinational country — Lenin didn't hesitate to change his views to the exact opposite. Now he declared that only capitalists held that nations should be kept compulsorily in the same state. Now the true proletarian approach *supports* the idea of national self-determination.

After Lenin came to power he changed tack again, and he oscillated on this point throughout his lifetime, depending on which way the political wind was blowing. For instance: after the Revolution he allayed the fears of Finland with regard to the plans the Soviet Union might have in respect to that country by allowing for its separation from Russia, but almost simultaneously tried to reconquer the newly born state of Poland.

As to Marx — what can one say? Here is a tough, brilliant personality. His work must have been interesting in its time, but once again we are dealing with conclusions that are patently obsolete. Theories and predictions drawn from observation of British working-class life in the last century have completely lost their relevance by now.

Despite the patent shortcomings in logic and science, and the hopelessly dated character of their thinking, Marx and Lenin have won. Their ideas capture ever new countries and people. Political genius proves to be far more important than knowledge or intellectual honesty.

I owe to Vera Moiseyevna, with her excessive zeal for enforcing Soviet studies upon us tenth-graders, my early awakening to the fallacies and contradictions of the very gospel she was trying to spread. I wonder if she herself was ultimately satisfied with Communism, with the Soviet system. We kids were unaware of it at that time, but Vera Moiseyevna was a heavy drinker, and she died of alcoholism some years after I graduated from the school.

The conclusions I came to about Communism at that time have stayed with me ever since. That goes for any kind of Communism, even the new "liberal" varieties that are gaining popularity in Europe and America. If Euro-Communism is so independent, why have these parties not denounced Stalin's Communism and the concentration camps of the Soviet Union? Why is it considered a great achievement if they offer one cautious word of criticism when the problems of dissent and of emigration from Russia are discussed? Have they not adopted Lenin's logic and credo?

In my senior year I became a member of the Literary Circle at the library. This was again a very worthwhile activity. Here we discussed

Soviet literature, which of course comprises quite a few seriously idealistic works; much of the "allowed" Russian and Western literature
includes a great many authors worth talking about.

At the library we formed ourselves into two groups, the Literary Organization of Perfectionists, the "L.O.P.'s," and the "Anti-L.O.P.'s."
The nicknames that evolved for these two organizations were, naturally,
the "Lopes" and "Antelopes." I was one of the latter. In due course I
will relate the consequences of our having innocently created these
groups.

I continued to be constantly absorbed in science. I was a "bad little
duck" — a maverick. I didn't like to read the standard texts on
mathematics; I preferred to figure things out for myself. And of course I
aimed at the most difficult, arcane problems. I was fascinated, for example, by the famous Fermat's Great Theorem. At first glance it looks
perfectly simple, the kind of formula any schoolboy could solve. It
states that there is no solution for $x^n + y^n = z^n$ in nonzero integers x, y,
and z if n is an integer greater than 2. Upon study, it turns out to be a
puzzle, an enigma in mathematical theory, and it has been a bone of
contention to mathematicians for over three centuries. Everything about
this mystery intrigued me, even including the fact that Fermat wrote the
equation in the margin of one of Diofant's books and added: "I have
solved it but I have not the space here to prove it." Fermat was known
as a mathematical genius, and a very modest man. There was not the
slightest possibility that he could falsify anything in his scientific work;
but he could have been mistaken, as many scholars believed, so generations of mathematicians have tried to prove or disprove this theorem,
and a whole science has been created in relation to it. Naturally, I was
tempted also.

I struggled too with other problems that were considered insoluble.
Some of them had actually been proven to be insoluble, but I just didn't
know the literature on them.

Looking back upon my attempts in this field, I think they were definitely the most useful way I could have been spending my time. It was
the very best training for my mind, to take up challenges of this kind.

All this experimentation led to results that were most rewarding.
When I was in my senior year, another mathematical Olympiad was
announced. This competition had been devised by the brilliant new
crop of mathematicians at Kharkov, enthusiastic young professors, including Pogorelov, who was to contribute so much to the luster of that
university.

When we heard the problems they would present were to be so difficult and innovative that even some professors had not solved all of

them, very few of us wanted to compete in the final trials. But we got our reward when it was announced that those who took first prize would be accepted to the Physics or Mathematics division of any of the Kharkov institutes, or of the university, without taking the entrance exams in math.

Again, I won this prize. For a while, I was quite a celebrity!

New Thoughts

THAT YEAR, 1948, was filled with a series of events that meant a lot to me. The most important was the creation of an independent State of Israel.

At that time eruptions of the ever-present anti-Semitism had become more frequent, more ominous. The kind of thing you heard was: that the Jews had dodged the draft during the War; that they had fled to Tashkent and hidden until it was all over.

This was a painful offense to me, for one, since so many members of my own family had been killed or wounded fighting the Germans. But it was not with reference to them in particular that I reacted with such shock and indignation to these defamations. It was the overall injustice that infuriated me.

I came to realize after the War that there had been vicious anti-Semitism at the front and among the partisans. I was told that in the Baltic Republics and in the Ukraine, Jews who tried to join the partisans were simply turned away — which meant they were sent to their deaths. And most of Russia shut its eyes to the massacres of tens of thousands at the Kharkov Tractor Works and, in Kiev, at Babi Yar.

But at the same time, the Soviets were very eager to make a good impression on the West during the War, and in 1944 a book was published about the contributions being made by Jews, which included statistics on the number of Jews awarded the most coveted military decoration of all, the Hero of the Soviet Union. The Jews came out in third place among the most-decorated nationalities in the Soviet Union. If one takes into account that according to their absolute numbers they were in *ninth* place among the Soviet nationalities, this statistic is impressive.

Jews contributed disproportionately to the war effort, not only on the battlefield but in science and technology. The Great Soviet Encyclopedia does not break down its entries on scientists according to which ethnic group they may belong to, but among the dozens of names of prominent engineers, technicians, designers, and inventors who were credited with the improvement of Russian weaponry, tanks, aircraft, and other war matériel, Jewish names are numerically equal to, and in some cases preponderant over, those of the other nationalities.

This doesn't mean of course that Jews are brighter than other Russians. The number of Jewish composers or artists, for instance, is rather low. Obviously this top-heavy representation of Jews in the sciences is related, first, to the Jewish reaction to Nazism. No matter how much the other Russian peoples may have hated Hitler, the Jews had reason to hate him a thousandfold more. Second, when it came to scientific work, Jews had the advantage of a centuries-old tradition of absorption in abstract studies.

The Jews of the Diaspora in the Slavic world had faced two choices: to abandon their faith and embrace Christianity, or to remain literally enclosed by a fence, on the gate of which was nailed the ultimate symbol of degradation: the head of a pig. There is no way of knowing what number took the first course, but obviously it was a hard core left in the ghetto: those who valued Torah over any possible rewards, material or social, that might accrue to them through baptism. And so, despite inescapable poverty, despite the loathing of neighbors in their host countries, these Jews remained Jews. There were no satisfactions to be found in the external world, nor accomplishments to be made there. They turned inward, to a life of study.

It doesn't matter that these studies were in the area of religious problems; what matters is that the Jews were products of a culture that held scholarship in far higher esteem than any other occupation. Men who spent their entire lives studying the Scriptures and writing finely wrought analyses and commentaries upon them, had been revered in their society for countless generations. Those without some foundation of scholarship could not survive — spiritually, psychologically — in Czarist Russia. After the Revolution, which put an end to religion, the only self-identity Jews could still cling to was in that same sphere, the acquisition of knowledge, to which they were by long tradition so well accustomed.

But the point I am making is that the notable contribution by Jews to the victory and to various kinds of progress was something nobody in the Soviet Union wanted to acknowledge. The Jewish population had never received any credit for its patriotism and achievements aside from the hastily assembled propaganda tract published for export during the War (it was practically unavailable in Russia), and by the late 'forties even that was almost forgotten.

One incident that happened right after the War will provide a clue to the mood of the nation. A much-decorated veteran returned home to Kiev after his years at the front. Walking in the street, he was stopped by a passerby, who sneered, "Jew, where did you buy your medals?" and struck him. The veteran, shocked to the breaking point, pulled out his pistol and shot the man. Most Soviet people are very patriotic, and — particularly at that time, when the War was barely over — had an almost religious reverence for combat heroes. But not if they were Jews. The soldier received the full penalty of the law: the firing squad.

A non-Russian could hardly understand what tragic and terrifying possibilities such an event stirred up. Every Soviet person over forty could remember the last wave of pogroms. This memory, however, was one of the facts of recent history that were never discussed. Fear was in the air; but for my generation it was a nameless fear, and perhaps even more intense for that reason than if we had known exactly what could happen in this country. We were aware only that it was a bad time for Jews. One was conscious of it every waking hour; there was a feeling of menace that never went away.

When the State of Israel was created, I rejoiced. To see Jews for the first time in two thousand years responsible for their own fate, and in a position to defend themselves, was an immense source of gratification to me and to all my friends. I exuberantly wrote a series of poems about Israel. (I might note that, although the Soviet position toward that country was such that to write or read pro-Israeli literature was a serious crime, not one of the friends who read the poems betrayed me. Some were Ukrainians and Russians. In the ocean of fear and distrust in the Soviet Union, there are little islands of loyalty that cannot be submerged.)

But recognition of Israel gave rise to a new upsurge of official anti-Semitism. Russian Jews were not to consider themselves full members of the Soviet nation, but still less should they be allowed to feel loyalty or sympathy toward Israel.

That same year, a crippling blow was dealt to Soviet science, a blow that affected the entire academic world and spread consternation throughout the community of educated people.

The prime victim was the science of genetics, but all other sciences, and the arts and humanities as well, felt the shock waves of this attack.

The liquidation of genetics was the achievement of Academician Trofim Lysenko. Lysenko had Stalin's trust, and therefore even the Soviet Academy of Sciences, the staunchest and most independent body in the nation, could not hold out against him: they had been forced to elect him a member, and they were forced to support him.

Stalin gave Lysenko credit for originating the idea of planting the eyes of potatoes when the supply of seed-potatoes ran out, and thereby increasing the size of the potato crop during the War. To earn approval from this all-powerful source was all Lysenko needed: from that time forward he was czar of Soviet agriculture and he could make or break the science of his betters. He chose to do the latter, throwing out experimental work that had been years in the making (much creative and pioneering work had been initiated in Russia in the field of genetics), promoting his theory of the heritability of acquired characteristics and other ideas too confused and absurd to describe. He impressed top Party members, who had always been bored by the incomprehensible lectures of other geneticists and suspicious of "time-wasting" experiments with drosophila and various laboratory specimens. He could show officials the splendid plants and animals he raised on the model farm Stalin permitted him to operate. Most of these productions were culled from the cream of the crop, wherever he could find them. The second generation of his livestock sometimes displayed hybrid vigor but — according to rumor, which it is hard not to believe — when it came to his failures, he simply buried them. Lysenko's entire career was like a series of sleight-of-hand tricks. The illusions could not last forever, but when one fell through he replaced it with another. Meanwhile, with Stalin's blessing, he presided over tragically sparse harvests, and smashed the entire science of genetics.

In Stalin's Russia, this meant Lysenko destroyed the scientists as well as the science: many of the most distinguished geneticists were imprisoned, and of them many died. There was nothing gradual about this disaster. It occurred at the notorious spring, 1948, session of the All-Union Academy of Agriculture. *Pravda* and *Izvestia,* usually four to six pages in length, expanded that day to sixteen pages: the record of the entire session was published. For weeks afterward you read in the paper almost every day a eulogium to the new science and a retraction, by some well-known scientist, of the "bourgeois" views he had previously held in regard to genetic laws. At seminars of the Academy of Agriculture speeches were made to Stalin, thanking him for showing the scientists the error of their ways and opening up the new enlightened agronomy originated by Michurin and improved by Lysenko. The florid Oriental language of these addresses, the bouquets to the Dear Leader, the obsequious homages to the Great Scholar, might have seemed excessive to a Mongol Khan.

The news reports in which scientific heresies were recanted always concluded: "Ten minutes of applause." If you heard them on the radio, you had to hear all ten minutes of clapping. (At one time, people were buying phonograph records of Stalin's speeches, huge albums of 78 rpm recordings. Six or eight of the sides consisted of nothing but applause.) It began to look as though nothing could suit the Russian national mood better than the annihilation of scientists. A precedent for such a move had been set: during the Great Purge of the previous decade many distinguished scientists, including the great Lev Landau, had been imprisoned. Not all of them by any means had survived and returned to freedom.

Stalin's antipathy toward modern science reflected, moreover, a feeling widely shared by Russians. One of the tenets of the Revolutionary faith was that human possibilities are limitless. There is absolutely nothing Man cannot do; no achievement is beyond his reach. Man and his science are infinite in their potential. Nineteenth-century science, which opened so many avenues for exploration and suggested such vast new areas for the improvement, even the perfectibility, of every aspect of life, supported this thinking. Science and the Revolutionary philosophy that had captured Russia's intelligentsia complemented each other. But contemporary science announces impossibilities, limitations. The Einstein universe may turn out to be finite in space and time. Einstein proves also that nothing can exceed the speed of light. Quantum mechanics discovers that it is essentially impossible to measure precisely the coordinate of the particle. All these barriers, all these outside limits, are a profound disappointment. People were reluctant to acknowledge them.

I am not trying to say that the reasons for opposition to science are all on a conscious level; but I believe that basically, it is just this concept of impassable boundaries that made Einstein's physics so uncongenial to the generality of Russians. Even as late as the 'fifties there was much discussion in literary journals on this point: Could it not be possible, at least for Communists, to achieve velocity faster than light? So quite a few people were in sympathy with the policy of purging Soviet universities of those who had brought these foreign, destructive influences into the country.

Without explaining his real reasons — he didn't have to — my father was always urging me to stay out of the exact sciences and go into medicine. "You'd be a very good doctor," he kept saying. "There's a desperate need for physicians in Kharkov. If you went into roentgenology, I could teach you a great deal myself."

Decisions and Discoveries

I CAN'T SAY I was very happy during most of my sixteenth year. This was owing not only to external events but to my interior thoughts. I became aware of the problem that I suppose every adolescent has to grapple with, and that will recur throughout his life, but never again with the same poignancy: What is the point of life, if it has to end with death?

Constant pondering on the subject almost tore me to pieces. I wrote a long poem, thinking it over. Like practically all Soviet youths of my time, I was positive that there was no God; so there is no escape from death. And if that is the case, what is the point of human consciousness — or of anything? I went through a long period of thoughtfulness and unhappiness.

Actually, I consider that this is about the time when I left my childhood behind. I already had very clear political ideas. And my tastes and appreciation in literature, if not yet in any of the other arts, had matured.

But there were not many people in my life at that time with whom I could sound out these ideas. I had early become aware of how small a circle of one's acquaintances one could trust, and I am ashamed to say that in political discussions with all but my closest friends, when anyone broached a dangerous topic I spoke up in a very demagogic way and, I believe, persuasive — because I was already quite strong in logic and pseudo-logic. But any thinking person incapable of some measure of dissimulation is not likely to keep his head above water very long in that society.

Also much on my mind was science. I had become completely engrossed in it, an enthusiasm that has never left me since.

What deflected me from mathematics into physics was that at this time I chanced upon the Smythe Report, *Atomic Energy for Military Purposes,* which became available in translation soon after it was published in America. I was absolutely struck — not, of course, by the military aspects — but by the possibilities which Henry Smythe's thesis opened up for physics, by the atomic nuclei.

I decided that this would be my field. I immediately started to work on the problem that presented itself here, the separation of isotopes. I thought it over, and after some time deduced a method for the separation of isotopes by electrochemical means. I sent a description of my method to the Bureau of Inventions and Discoveries. The answer I received was evidently written by someone who either could not decipher my handwritten scrawl, or who understood even less than I did about the whole area. I realized I would have to wait until I got into an institute or into the university before I could find people who would understand what I wanted to say.

The time had come to decide in which institute to study. I went from one to another of them and asked the admissions officials only one question: "Do you work on atomic energy?" When I received the answer "No — *but* we have many important problems here in physics," and so forth and so on, I lost interest. At the Polytechnical Institute I was told that they probably would have a Faculty of Atomic Physics within three years; but of course three years seemed as long to me then as thirty years do now.

Finally, at Kharkov University they said to me: "We cannot tell you specifically, but we have a division under Academician Valter, and we think that is the department that will suit your purposes." And so I applied to the university.

I ran into the familiar obstacle of being too young: I was sixteen and you are supposed to be at least seventeen before they will admit you to an institution of higher education. But having won the Olympiad, which meant I had already passed the math, I was permitted to take the other exams as well. When I had no trouble with them, the regulations were waived, and I was admitted a year early.

That was 1948. It was not yet forbidden to accept Jews into the university; and physics and mathematics were at that time very unpopular fields. When I was asked what I wished to concentrate in and answered "Physics," any layman automatically asked, "Do you intend to be a teacher of physics?" According to the view generally held in those days, teaching was the sole future for a physicist. Therefore the number of applicants was not great; there were fewer students applying for this department than there were places available. So being Jewish was not too much of a liability.

But a problem arose with the Deputy Chairman of the Physics Department, a former KGB colonel and now a very poor physicist, Kri-

vetz, who, one can guess why, had been assigned to work in this department at the university. He was deputy chairman even though he did not
have a Ph.D. in physics, or in anything else. He was very clever in politics, however, and in everything concerned with Soviet relations.

Deputy Krivetz — short, bald, with eyes like two pins — was someone I disliked at first meeting, and I would say the feeling was mutual.
He did everything he could to keep me out of the field I had chosen. He
gave me a 3 (a C) on the physics exam, and sent me to the Mathematics
Department. When I repeatedly attempted to enroll in the Physics Department, he reiterated in his soft inquisitor's voice: "But you have excellent results in mathematics. You'll be an excellent mathematician." It
took me two exasperating months before I managed to register myself
in the department that, according to all the regulations, I was perfectly
free to choose.

Now I had two weeks to wait before classes at the university would
start.

I had tried not to waste the summer months; studied and read, and
spent hours talking with my friends, quite a few of whom were planning to attend the university as well. Also of course I had to perform my
usual domestic chores and do the shopping for the household.

So much has been written about the difficulties of shopping in the Soviet Union that I will not weary the reader with a detailed description of
that frustrating occupation. But I would say that a Soviet person spends
almost as much time and strength in search of food as a member of
some primitive desert tribe. That is hardly an exaggeration. To join a
long, miserable, irritable queue; to inch along for an hour or more in
hopes of a one-day supply of potatoes; to reach the end only to discover
that the last potato is gone — this is too ordinary an experience to warrant comment. Not only food is in short supply, but anything else you
can mention. You have to keep your eyes open and grab anything that
might come on to the market which you might need at some time,
whether or not you want it right now. My mother would have been dismayed if I had seen a whiskbroom, let's say, or tinned fish, and failed
to snatch it up.

I had to go to the shops almost every day. If the ordinary markets
were empty, there was nothing to do except go down to the bazaar.
Here you will find just about the only free enterprise in the Soviet
Union. In these markets, people are allowed to sell small amounts of the
food they raise themselves, on their very tiny plots of land.

Only 3 percent of the land in Russia is in private hands; even this
property cannot be sold or exchanged and is constantly under the threat
of confiscation by the State. (Under Khrushchev, people had to surren-

der their livestock to the communes. When that happened, there was no meat or milk available anywhere for months.) This 3 percent produces what is officially estimated to be *30* percent of all the food in the country; in all likelihood closer to 40, since the government is not anxious to reveal the extent of the incompetence prevailing on the State-run kolkhozes.

But the prices in the bazaars are higher than those in the sparsely stocked food stores — being pegged to the laws of supply and demand, rather than to the completely unrealistic computations extrapolated from the Plan — so you don't go there unless you have to.

It was a pleasant, bustling, lively place to be. I remember threading my way through the bazaar, hearing the seductive cry of kids hawking cigarettes: *"Papirosi Kazbek! Ekstra! Zakurivai!"* (Kazbek "Extra" Cigarettes. Smoke!) These cigarettes, small but with a long paper holder (so designed so that the smoker will not catch his beard on fire) cost ten times more here than anywhere else — but usually you simply couldn't get them anywhere else.

My frequent visits to this part of town gave me an education in something more than the shortcomings of the Soviet economic system; it was here that I made a discovery that will haunt me for the rest of my life.

After a few weeks of almost daily excursions to the bazaar, it occurred to me suddenly that something had changed in this crowded section of the city. Something was different; something was missing. I can't pin down the exact date of this strange impression.

During the War, twenty million people were killed in Russia. I mean, killed in the War — I am not counting those who died in concentration camps. There were many more who were wounded and who were permanently maimed. Nobody knows the precise figure of these cripples, but certainly it must have been way up in the tens of millions. A large proportion of the population was handicapped, missing arms or legs, or blind. At the bazaar you would always see a lot of these unfortunates; also at the railway station, going through the cars. Their pensions were minuscule; without occasional alms, they could not survive. They were often drunk — but how could people be so callous as to condemn them for it? There was nothing left of their lives. They went off to war at a young age; most were much too young to have been trained for any job or profession; and now almost no work was available to them. The multiply handicapped, having lost both arms or both legs, were in some cases taken care of in veterans' hospitals (very poor ones); but those who could get around were everywhere in Kharkov.

It dawned on me one day only in retrospect — I had been somehow trying not to realize it — that the cripples were gone. What a strange phenomenon! It seemed that only a few days ago, maybe yesterday, there had been hundreds of them at the bazaar, around the cathedral, all over; and then suddenly, today — not a crutch in sight, not a one- or two-fingered hand held out for a donation.

I shuddered when I realized they were gone. Later that evening when some of our neighbors were coming home from work, I asked one of them if he had noticed the disappearance of the beggars.

"I have no idea what's happened to them," he said.

His wife joined the conversation. "Oh, I think I heard they've all been moved to a wonderful resort somewhere in the Crimea," she said. "They were always supposed to be rewarded for their heroism; it's about time."

I was doubtful. If this story about the resort were true, all the newspapers would have been filled with articles about the veterans' happiness and the generosity of the Soviet government. I could hardly help realizing that if such an event was not mentioned in the papers, something very bad had occurred.

It was not until I read what Solzhenitsyn wrote about the cripples' fate that I learned my own horrible surmise was true.

They had been exiled to islands in the North Sea, and deprived of the right of correspondence.

The State policy toward heroes and patriots was irrational beyond belief. Many underground fighters against the Germans were imprisoned after the war. Soldiers who were *ordered* to the enemy rear, for purposes of reconnaissance, were later condemned for "fraternizing" with the Germans, and imprisoned also. The great pilot Bondarenko, in his book about the astounding wartime exploit that made him famous, makes no mention of what happened to him upon his return to Russia in the plane that he, a fugitive from a prisoner-of-war camp, had single-handedly captured from an enemy aerodrome. Like many other authors of war memoirs, he simply provides his reader with a long vague blank, covering the next twenty years, and then ends abruptly with a chapter on how happy he is now, resting on his laurels, decorated with the highest honors his country can award.

Soviet readers acquire the knack of decoding, not only what is written, but what is left out. Obviously Bondarenko's superiors had felt there was room for doubt as to the truth of this fantastic story, and to be on the safe side had decided to discredit it. That twenty-year interval was spent in labor camp, undoubtedly under conviction of an attempt to spy for the Germans.

Bondarenko was not the only one. In the 'sixties there was a rash of belated awards announced, the delay having been caused for similar reasons. These people had served their terms and, unlike many of their less fortunate comrades-in-arms, survived until the Khrushchev amnesty.

People were thus punished for their heroism. But who among these victims was treated more cruelly than the cripples who disappeared from Kharkov — and, of course, at the same time, from all the other great Russian metropolises?

* * *

That is the sort of thing that sank in on me.

That is how I grew.

I had to grow by myself. My parents were too afraid for me to express agreement with my views concerning our life. When I spoke about my reaction to the horrors I mention here, my father would try to convince me that everything that was going wrong was some mistake, some natural accident. He used to say "If you carve a piece of wood, you have to expect woodchips — you can't save the wood entire." He was trying to ensure my survival.

He did his best. Very few people had the courage to talk honestly to a youngster.

But I do remember very vividly one man, a friend of Father's, whom I met only once when he dropped in with some other people for a Sunday evening gathering. For some reason I got talking with him, and his ideas had a real influence on mine. I can't even recall his name, our encounter was so brief, and I never saw him again. But I haven't forgotten what he said, guarded though his language was. Had I read Pasternak? Why was Dostoievski not studied at school? Did I have any thoughts about the suicide of Mayakovsky, the most respected of Soviet poets? Would I be surprised by the suicide of Akhmatova or Zoshchenko?

Mayakovsky's life is an absolute paradigm of the career of a dedicated idealist of his time, a man who hoped to see justice and equality on this earth. Before the Revolution, he had made a name for himself as a poet of extraordinary lyric power. Later, caught up by Revolutionary fervor, he made a deliberate decision to subordinate his genius to the cause of social progress, and he descended to the level of writing "inspiring" rhymed slogans, which all the schoolchildren of my time were required to read, and which I naturally considered to be trash. Mayakovsky's continued popularity during the time he was producing this inferior stuff was a result of Stalin's patronage: Stalin declared him to be the greatest poet of our era, so his success was assured.

In the early 'twenties Mayakovsky wrote a long poem entitled *Good!* in which he enumerated the marvels and benefits of the Soviet system.

In those days honest criticism was still possible, and the critic Kogan wrote a piece on the naïveté of that poem. Mayakovsky, stung, went to see Kogan, and the two argued at length. The critic challenged Mayakovsky: "Are you blind? You've seen people starving, people imprisoned, people shot. How can you write about the marvelous new Soviet life?" Mayakovsky answered: "If these tragedies are a step toward our great future, then I am right. If things go on the way they are now, then it doesn't matter — since nothing will matter in that case."

Years went by. Mayakovsky began to see the truth. Finally, in 1930, he started a poem entitled *Bad*. Before completing it, he killed himself.

When at school I found titles by Mayakovsky on the summer reading list. I was vexed. Who needed to read more slogans and pro-Soviet doggerel? But when I discovered his early work, I suddenly saw what a fantastically gifted artist he was. After reading *A Cloud in Trousers,* I took everything he ever wrote out of the library and couldn't stop reading until I had absorbed it all.

Mayakovsky is a tragic figure. He was the foremost among Russian artists of his time whose art was to be distorted, deformed, by Soviet pressure.

A lot of things fell into place.

I started to do my own thinking; and by the time I entered the university, my understanding of what was really going on in the U.S.S.R. was practically the same as it is now. This time I regard as the end of my gropings for a basis of thought, and the beginning of the history of a grown-up person.

Kharkov State University

I ought to thank God that I happened to live in Kharkov, and also that I went into the field of physics.

Kharkov State University was the cradle of Soviet physics. The Physical-Technical Institute there was one of the first specialized research institutes in the Soviet Union, and perhaps in the whole world.

The first leader of Kharkov theoretical physics was Lev Davidovitch Landau, most distinguished of Soviet theoreticians and among the most brilliant physicists of his time. He had been a disciple of the great Niels Bohr, with whom he studied in Copenhagen as a very young man. Landau's school of physics was one of the most fruitful and successful in the world.

His career at Kharkov was meteoric but brief. He was unpopular with the officials, even with those in his own field, because of his outspoken, undiplomatic, blunt personality. He never hesitated to tell a scientist that he had no talent, if the man in question didn't have any. He didn't care about official scientific degrees; could be delighted with a student and could despise a professor. He was very free and liberated in all his attitudes. He would come to a lecture carrying a kitten, and stand at the desk patting it as he spoke.

Typically, Soviet professors are very remote from students and very rigid and formal in their behavior. The fact that Landau was incapable of observing artificial conventions, of appearing *comme il faut*, created problems for him all during his life. He was not elected a member of the Soviet Academy* until years after he should have been. His individuality, his independence, made him many enemies.

* The Soviet Academy of Sciences is the direct descendant of the Academy of Sciences founded by Peter the Great, and its charter remains as originally written. Its membership is limited to approximately fifty Academicians in each discipline, with the same number of Corresponding Members. Ideally — and in most periods of history, actually — it comprises only the most indisputably brilliant scholars in the country. But in recent times, its standard was violated by the inclusion of Lysenko and by the non-election of two mathematicians of world repute, Israel Gelfand and Mark Krein.

In the disastrous year of 1937 one of the physicists at Kharkov, a man of very meager talent who had probably been offended by Landau's too-honest comments on his work, wrote to the NKVD (the Secret Police, successor to the OGPU and forerunner of the KGB) charging Landau with anti-Soviet activity. (At that time people were often arrested on the strength of a single anonymous letter.) Landau was imprisoned. He was forced to testify that he had worked below his capacity, had made only very minor contributions to physics, and that his purpose in concentrating on such trivia was the destruction of Soviet science. (I may mention that the "minor contributions" under discussion were among his most famous achievements, the Landau Levels and Landau Diamagnetism, as they will be found described in any physics textbook.)

Landau, although at that time only twenty-nine years old, was not physically very strong. He would never have survived much more than a year in a Soviet jail.

Fortunately, he was rescued through the good offices of another great physicist, Academician (now Nobel Laureate) Pyotr Leonidovitch Kapitza. Kapitza, when he heard of his colleague's fate, risked his own career and freedom by going over the heads of the officials and protesting furiously to still higher authorities, who arranged for Landau's release. Kapitza then invited Landau to work at his own institute in Moscow. Landau, still pale and very thin after his ordeal, accepted immediately and went straight to Moscow. He never worked in Kharkov again.*

His prison term had no effect upon Lev Davidovitch's attitudes; he emerged no more in awe of officialdom, and no more willing to observe Soviet conventions, than when he went in. He demonstrated his contempt for the petty regulations controlling scientific secrecy, for example, by carrying the permit that gave him access to classified institutes in the seat of his pants!

The same forces that had threatened to destroy Landau actually did crush the careers of many other distinguished scientists at Kharkov. One of them was Professor Yuri Rumer, a brilliant physicist, a disciple of

---

*I remember very well that once, years later, at a break in a seminar at the Institute for Physical Problems, Landau was asked by someone, in an aside, "Well, Dau," (no one among his close colleagues called him Landau or Lev Davidovitch) "let me ask you something: we've all noticed that you're not half as tough with Kapitza as you are with the others. You never tell him that he's talking nonsense, the way you tell the rest of us — and he sometimes is. Now of course he's the Centaur here" (that was his nickname, because of his being very talented as a man but very tough, and quite liable to kick like a horse when the occasion arose) "but you're never intimidated by anyone." Landau became serious and answered: "I'll tell you. I can never forget even for a minute that this is the person who saved my life."

Landau. He too was imprisoned — guilty by association — but there was no one to rescue him. He spent years in a labor camp and then was exiled to Novoyeniseisk, where he worked at a very small pedagogical institute. I remember the fight his fellow scientists put up in Moscow in order to get Rumer's papers published; I remember reading his papers — published under the imprint of this little institute in Novoyeniseisk. It was not until the later 'fifties that he was allowed to move to Novosibirsk and work at the institute there, by which time he was quite an elderly man.

The Director of the Physical-Technical Institute at Kharkov, Academician Ivan Vassilyevitch Obreimov, was also arrested in 'thirty-eight. Academician Obreimov was a fascinating personality: not only an excellent scientist, but a man of broad cultivation. He knew several languages, including Hebrew, classical Greek, and Latin. He had read absolutely everything from Homer to Conan Doyle.

In Russian prison camps, regular criminals — murderers, rapists, and thieves — are the aristocracy, and political prisoners are people of no account whatsoever. These distinctions obtain not only in the eyes of the criminals, who will beat and rob an incoming political without a second thought, but in the eyes of the authorities as well. The warden of a prison camp, if he knows what is good for him, extends privileges and favors to the members of this very tough class, and ignores most of the violations of the rules that they may commit. He would not have the nerve to attempt to protect the politicals, even if he could. Russian criminals form a powerful and cohesive minority both in and out of the State prisons.

Academician Obreimov, when he arrived in camp, found himself completely without the sort of "capital" that a prisoner needs to survive: he had no money, expected no food parcels, had no tobacco, and no clothes except the shabby summer outfit he was wearing when he was arrested. He couldn't have been more helpless. But it developed that he did possess one asset: he was very good at telling stories.

The criminals are more than likely to be illiterate, so books would be of no use to them; and there is no entertainment or recreation of any kind to be found in a prison camp. There was no radio; almost no one had a musical instrument. Ivan Vassilyevitch remembered the plots of hundreds of novels, detective stories, and plays, and had a marvelous talent for recounting them, full of color and detail. Once this gift had come to light, he became the protégé rather than the slave of the gang that was running the section of the camp in which he found himself. His stories were much in demand; his barrack-mates demanded one at every opportunity, and sat or lay around him entranced, listening attentively to that night's installment of *The Hound of the Baskervilles* or *The Man in the Iron Mask.*

Ivan Vassilyevitch's life became much easier. Someone was assigned to provide him with food; someone else managed to produce a coat for him, and a pair of boots. But more than that: when the inmate bosses learned that he was a professor of physics and that he was anxious to continue his work, they "scrounged" writing materials for him and made a point of allowing him space and uninterrupted time in which to think and write. The administration, in order not to alienate the powerful elements that had made this arrangement, shut their eyes to it, although for a prisoner to have paper and pen was strictly against the regulations.

Professor Obreimov was able to do a considerable amount of work and before too long made a very important technical discovery: he invented an express-method of determining the optical characteristics of glass before it has solidified. It turned out to be a perfectly practicable method and highly important in its military applications. Obreimov's prisoner patrons, who had ways of getting around all the restrictions, helped him smuggle his papers out of the camp. The papers reached Kharkov. The physicists there read them, realized their significance almost at once, and brought them to the attention of the scientists in Moscow. The result was unexpected: Stalin liberated Obreimov.

Stalin was fond of playing such jokes with the lives of others. He enjoyed raising people to a pinnacle of power and success and then plunging them into the abyss; or, occasionally, performing the same act in reverse. He saw to it that Obreimov was awarded the Stalin Prize of the First Order.

Ivan Vassilyevitch came back to science just in time: the war with Germany began shortly after his release. The labor camp in which he had been imprisoned was in Karelia, close to the border, and there was no time to evacuate it when the war started. Everyone in that camp was killed. There were many scientists there from the Physical-Technical Institute, including Academician Shubnikov, after whom the Shubnikov-DeHaas Effect is named. He died. Obreimov, like Landau and Korolev, barely escaped this fate. The two latter became the most important scientists of their time.

Owing to the foundation laid by Landau, Obreimov, Rumer, and the founder of the Kharkov school of mathematics Mark Krein, Kharkov was one of the centers of the exact sciences that could compete with any other in the U.S.S.R. And in 1948, when I entered the university, there were still famous physicists there, including Professor Ilya Lifshitz, brother of Landau's eminent collaborator Yevgeny Lifshitz, and considered by many to be an even superior mind. Also teaching physics were Professors Alexander Akhiezer, Yakov Fainberg, Lipa Rosentzweig, and Veniamin German, author of many interesting theoretical works. Among the mathematicians were not only Pogorelov but Naum Ilyitch Akhiezer and Alexander Yakovlevitch Povzner. I could hardly have been more fortunate: with only a few exceptions, the faculty was made up of men whose capabilities ranged from highly competent to absolutely brilliant.

At present, regrettably, there remain only a few scientific centers in the U.S.S.R., by far the most important being Moscow. Although it is hard even to visit Moscow, much less get a permit to live there, people are willing to contend with almost insuperable odds and defy any number of legal restrictions to become residents of that city. Moscow is too tempting; it has become the magnet for everybody. There has been a "drain" from all the other scientific loci, and the latter are now left to stagnate. If you attended the once-great University of Kharkov now, you would come out with rather indifferent grounding in almost any field you can mention. There are a few men of international reputation still there, notably the mathematician Pogorelov, but, in the main, the most brilliant of the professors are gone.

However, the luster shed by Lev Davidovitch Landau and the others was still bright on that September 1st, when I was a keen, enthusiastic sixteen and I walked up the steps of the Physics and Mathematics Building with a feeling of hope and optimism.

The vast majority of us who were entering the field of physics at Kharkov University at that time were Jews; 85 or 90 percent of us. It's an interesting phenomenon, and I suppose deserves some sort of explanation.

The attractions of becoming a student in any field were certainly not patent. A university student received a stipend of just twelve roubles a month; if he achieved the highest marks it went up by 25 percent. The prospect of spending five years on such a small pittance (call it about $40 a month) did not appeal to many people of my age. (In my own case, I took on only occasional tutoring work; but among my friends few were supported by their families during their student years.)

Once graduated from the university, the rewards we might anticipate were very slight. Science at that time was not yet a prestigious field, and not even great scientific luminaries made good salaries. We could look forward to pay no better than the wages of a manual laborer, not much over 100 roubles a month. (The same rule obtained for physicians, for engineers, for almost all professionals.) There was little or no material advantage to becoming an ordinary scientist. And who could rely upon becoming one of the rare few who attained to distinction and fame?

Moreover, mathematics and physics are known to be extremely difficult studies; my sparse group of classmates and I had these fields to ourselves. The arts, history, philology, languages, and philosophy were not overcrowded either; but the science faculties had smaller enrollment than, say, the engineering or medical departments, and we were almost all Jews. Why were we there?

I think the reason had to do with the same response to centuries of imprisonment beyond the Pale of Settlement that I mentioned earlier. Our ancestors, forbidden to engage in any occupations respectable in the eyes of the Gentiles, had plunged deep into Torah and Talmud; into Gemara and Cabala; had written vast tomes of commentary on all the classic and very difficult Hebrew texts. Thus they survived.

We were similarly attracted by a serious intellectual challenge, and for much the same reasons. We immersed ourselves in the abstract sciences, which were for us exactly what Holy Writ had been for our grandfathers: a mental shelter from intolerable pressures that impinge upon an alien in a would-be homogeneous world. We were perhaps in a position to feel, before anyone else, almost subconsciously, that physics was a most interesting field, and would be pre-eminent among the sciences for the next few decades.

One can imagine the upheaval when the time came to throw Jews out of the universities. But, owing again to the chance element of timing, it was still just possible in 1948 for a Jew to gain admission and to complete the courses.

*   *   *

Now that I had overcome the obstacles put in my path by Deputy Krivetz, and was finally enrolled in the Physics Department, I was in haste to show my discovery in isotope separation to the professors. The most logical person to approach, I thought, would be the Dean of the Physics Department. He must be the best person there. So I made an appointment to see him.

Dr. Abram Solomonovitch Milner had once been a scientist of great promise, but — I didn't know this until much later — he had the very bad luck to fall ill with encephalitis contracted while on a trip to the far east of the U.S.S.R. just before the War. As is well known, this disease can cause brain damage. When Milner recovered, he was no longer capable of any very creative science. He remained dean, because the position is basically an administrative one, and bright scientists try to avoid the job. I hadn't heard at the time about his misfortune; none of his students knew about it; and I am sorry to say that when I took one of his courses I joined everyone else in making a lot of trouble during his lectures. We despised the poor man, and we ridiculed him.

In any case, he was obviously a very kindly and honest person. He listened to me, let me describe the idea I had in mind for the separation of isotopes, and then said: "Well, I'm not qualified to comment on your idea. I'll ask Dr. Piatigorsky to talk to you."

Dr. Piatigorsky was also a theoretical physicist; but evidently after a conversation with Dr. Milner he too felt uncertain as to whether this idea fell within his area of competence, and when I came to the interview with him I found another man present: dark, balding, with penetrating black eyes. This was Professor Ilya Lifshitz. I can say without hesitation that Professor Lifshitz is one of the most brilliant scientists I've ever known.

It didn't take him very long to understand that my proposal was based on incomplete knowledge. He suggested that I read a book which would help me see that my method wouldn't be nearly as effective as I imagined. (It took me the next two years to get through this book — *Statistical Physics,* by Landau and Lifshitz — and to understand wherein the method lost its efficiency.) But it was almost an aesthetic pleasure to talk to this man, even when the conversation consisted principally of the dissection and refutation of my ideas.

I was glad then and ever afterward to have had the privilege of knowing Professor Lifshitz. We became good friends.

Another experience I had that winter was very different from this one. You might call it an object lesson.

The faculty had organized an Experimental Circle so that the students in the beginning course could study and participate in experimental work on real physics. I found this really interesting, to investigate phenomena that had never been investigated before, however small the phenomena might be.

But my enthusiasm for the work was much dampened by the extreme scarcity of laboratory equipment. There were no tools: it was even a problem to get hold of an ordinary hammer — there was just one hammer! — and everybody needed it. Naturally the researchers and the more advanced students, those who had obligatory work for their studies, had priority when it came to the acquisition of materials, and the turn of the first-year students almost never came.

I was planning an interesting experiment. I had collected all the necessary devices; I had made everything that it was within my own power to make. All I needed was an AC-DC mercury converter; a compensator, which can measure resistance with accuracy; a powerful magnet;

and a high-precision galvanometer, for the measurement of weak current. So for almost half a year I waited for the chance to assemble all these instruments. Just when I had got three of them together, someone would walk off with the fourth.

When I finished the first entire year of my studies without getting a single chance to perform the measurements I was planning, I decided that for the rest of my life I could not depend upon anybody or anything except myself. So I made up my mind to become a theoretician.

I think it was one of the wisest decisions of my whole life. It meant that I did not need access to a laboratory. It meant that despite all changes in Soviet policy (and I could already see that Jews were in an increasingly insecure situation, and the more independent one could be of official approval and support, the better), I was able to proceed in science.

*   *   *

Indeed, changes were imminent. Life was becoming more dangerous for everybody. The handwriting on the wall was clearer every day, in our department.

I witnessed the first disappearance of one of my fellow-students. He had been arrested, and would spend years behind bars or behind barbed wire, without any public trial. None of the victims happened to be a close friend of mine, nor even in my group, but like everyone else I heard about them: the KGB had arrested So-and-so the night before. We knew that his only crime was listening to the BBC or the Voice of America or some other Western broadcast (which we all did, but most of us had enough sense not to be caught) or making some chance remark about how badly the regional collective farms were run, or asking the wrong questions in our political education class.

The study of Marxism-Leninism, throughout one's university career, is absolutely compulsory. It takes up quite a large proportion of your study time; perhaps 20 percent of it. I think it is not the knowledge the student gains that counts nowadays; it is his training during all those years in how to say what he is supposed to say. This is a course in obedience. You learn how to study without asking questions. People who read more than they are assigned may get into great trouble.

At this time I remember a special meeting of the Komsomol, the Young Communist group. (If you were a student, you had to join this group. After graduation it was possible to stay outside the Communist Party, but it was almost impossible to avoid being a member of the Komsomol. When it came to being assigned a post after graduation, you had no future at all if you had not participated in it.) This meeting was called in order to criticize a student, Smelyansky, for a question he had asked in a seminar on Marxism-Leninism.

Smelyansky, a man a class or two ahead of myself, was curious enough to read Stalin's *Problems of Leninism.* In the first edition there is a passage in which Stalin mentions the "Testament" of Lenin, one of Lenin's last letters before his death, wherein he suggests that Stalin should not become General Secretary of the Party because he is "too rude." * Stalin answers, saying, "Yes, I am rude, I am tough — to the enemies of the Revolution." Smelyansky asked the instructor: "What exactly was Lenin's 'Testament'? What was the problem with Stalin? What was that all about?"

The question simply terrified the lecturer. Certainly he was familiar with the first edition (later editions had eliminated this entire section), but he also knew that the subject was explosively dangerous. The time when one could venture to ask such a question had long since passed. He was so frightened that he actually ran out of the seminar room; he hurried off to the officials to tell them what had happened.

The appropriate officials in such a case constitute what is called the First Department, which exists in every institution and place of work. It is a department of the KGB.

Without delay, a special meeting of the Komsomol of the whole department was called. It was moved unanimously to exclude Smelyansky from the Komsomol, and to ask the rector to expel him from the university, which was done.

Smelyansky was lucky not to be imprisoned. The question did arise as to whether he should be subjected to criminal prosecution, but it was not quite clear to the authorities if the fact that he had quoted Stalin's comment was grounds for arrest or not. Even the KGBsts were somewhat doubtful, because it could happen that they might be considered insufficiently pro-Soviet themselves if they drew attention to this passage. It was a touchy situation.

The most notable aspect of this meeting was that it was never once mentioned what the student had done! No one outside Smelyansky's own small seminar group knew what his crime was; nobody explained it to the rest of the department. Nor did anyone ask. At the start of the meeting, it was simply announced that Smelyansky had performed an anti-Soviet action; and we were told we should condemn him for it — just condemn! — but certainly not discuss the definition of an anti-Soviet act, or what specific one Smelyansky had committed.

* Stalin had indeed been worse than rude, subjecting Lenin's wife, Krupskaya, to threats and invective when she reported his unauthorized activities to Lenin as the latter was ill and dying.

This was a model case (similar ones cropped up all the time throughout my university years). We got a lesson in how to pass judgment on a
malefactor without the slightest knowledge of what he was accused of.
Such is the training of *Homo sovieticus.*

To be punished for an attempt to achieve a more profound knowledge of Marxism-Leninism was not particularly unusual. My second
year at the university, I made friends with Alexander Voronel, a first-
year student from Makhach-Kala. (These many years later, he is still my
closest friend.) When we had come to know each other well enough to
establish a mutual trust, he gave me an account of his own harrowing
experience as an overzealous seeker for Marxist-Leninist truth.

While Voronel was still in the ninth grade, he had been very eager to
encourage his classmates, to fire them with his own idealistic Communist zeal, to combat the indifference of the Komsomol to anything of
importance. As a result he was arrested. He was sentenced to three
years in prison, and only his extreme youth — he was sixteen — saved
him from serving out that term. As it was, he spent some weeks in
prison camp: the remainder of the sentence was suspended. "When the
whole thing was over," he told me, "a KGB colonel who had been involved in my case — not a bad guy — told my mother: 'Your son is
very intelligent, but if he goes on in this direction, sooner or later he'll
go to prison; and next time he won't be so lucky. He'll be there for
years.' He advised my mother to urge me to go into the exact sciences."
Voronel had the good judgment to believe the colonel. He went into
physics, in which field he proved to be very gifted.

But despite having to devote so much time to what you might call the
courses on survival in Stalin's Russia, we did learn a great deal of physics and mathematics.

*　　*　　*

During the spring and fall, the students had to go out to the collective
farms, the kolkhozes, and help the kolkhozniks with their planting and
harvesting. As the kolkhozniks were indifferent to their crops, which
were not their property and which brought them no income whatsoever, someone had to assist with the work in the fields. So engineers,
scientists, students, commuted out to the kolkhozes in the countryside
at the edge of town, and thus learned what life was like on those farms.

At that time — and still today, to a large extent — the farming population was actually tied to the land. Peasants, as I mentioned, had no
passports. In 1961, when the hundredth anniversary of the Emancipa-
tion of the serfs occurred, there was no celebration; this was a very ap-

propriate omission, because these people were still in the same condition of servitude as their ancestors a century ago. They were paid next
to nothing, and received no old-age pensions. In those days I hardly
ever saw a kolkhoznik working in the fields, either on his own behalf
or the State's. There was a joke current at the time: a slogan is put up
in the collective farm reading, "Kolkhozniks! Let us help the students
with the crops!" This went straight to the point. They simply had no
incentive to work. Owing to haphazard methods of storage and inefficiency of transport, a staggering percentage of what was raised simply
rotted and went to waste.

But if one of the "volunteer" helpers was foolish enough to discuss
what he had seen on the farms, to express indignation at the miserable
and desperate lot of the kolkhozniks — he could easily be arrested. The
subject was taboo.

(In the next few decades conditions improved a little for peasants on
the collective farms, but the lot of the tiny percentage of "free" villagers
worsened. They were ruined when Khrushchev collectivized privately
owned cows.)

All students at the university took compulsory courses in military tactics; when we graduated we had the rank of lieutenant junior grade (the
lowest officer's rank) in the army reserves. Twice during our university
careers we had to put in a two-month stretch in an army camp, performing military exercises. My camp was near Odessa.

I must say living in that bleak steppe-like plain was quite an experience. We were crowded into tiny tents, row upon row of them on the
flat barren earth, six to eight men to a tent. We were issued ill-fitting
khaki uniforms that had already been worn by generations of trainees.
Our hats were *pilotki* — garrison caps — which had to be worn at a
very particular angle, one finger above the left eyebrow, two fingers
above the right. Footgear were *sapoghi,* oversize high boots: you had to
learn a special technique for wrapping the cloths worn inside them.

All of our training consisted basically in wasting time, in becoming
accustomed to discipline. We marched, attended stultifying lectures on
obsolete military tactics, and were taught to shoot weapons antiquated
decades before. University students were officers only temporarily: to
teach us modern warfare might be dangerous!

The Korean War was in progress at the time, and we were subjected
to "political hours," during which we absorbed propaganda about the
American imperialists. The officers told us quite bluntly that we were to
be prepared to go on the attack against the Americans.

No controversial reading matter — such as the relatively liberal journal *Novy Mir,* for example — was permitted in camp. There was next

to nothing to read. We never had a leave, of course, and the only entertainment we were ever provided during the training period, as far as I
can remember, was to be driven in trucks once to Odessa, where we attended the opera — sitting in the last rows of the top balcony. We still
had only enlisted men's rank, and seating for army personnel in a Soviet
theater is strictly hierarchical.

Every other day we were marched two miles to the Black Sea and ordered to swim. Ordinarily this was perfectly pleasant, but on the occasion I have in mind there was a gale with winds of force nine. The
order was not suspended; we were forced to go into the water. The
waves were mountainous, overwhelming. One of our number, Alik So-
kolov, drowned. On our way back from the shore, we were supposed to
march with song; this was a regular part of our routine. On this day,
we would not sing.

That was the first strike in which I ever took part. It was our only
means of protesting the officers' refusal to take responsibility for the disaster, which by any ordinary standards could be considered nothing
less than the result of criminal negligence.

We were punished for our silent rebellion. They didn't allow us to
sleep; they didn't allow us to eat; they forced us to run, to do all kinds
of exercises. But this time we won. We absolutely would not sing. They
couldn't imprison us all.

This was a very profound experience.

We tried to complain, to write letters to people in authority; but we
learned that justice simply does not apply in such a situation. The duty
officer in question was never punished in any way. We eventually realized that there was no use thinking of redressing wrongs in this sort of
case. There is a lawyer's joke: "Justice is blind — but keeps one eye
open toward the Regional Party Committee."

Over and over, we discovered anew that our primary duty as good
citizens was to do what we were told, and not to ask questions.

By way of a postscript to this point I might observe that the unquestioning obedience demanded of Soviet people, the rigid system of authority, provides marvelous scope for pranksters. At Kharkov, there
was a very famous practical joker, Dr. Davidov, a professor of chemistry, whose lectures were so amusing that he always had a crowd of
auditors from other fields, in addition to his regular students, at all his
classes.

Professor Davidov was related to the rector of the university, Professor Bulankin, and was very good at imitating the rector's speech. He
once telephoned the Komsomol Committee and said, in Bulankin's
voice, "Quick! Take the university banner down to the railway station

to meet ————!" and hung up. The student leaders didn't dare call back and ask *whom* they were to meet, and *when;* so they took the university banner, hastily assembled the university brass band, and hurried down to the station. Each of the trains that came in, they greeted with the banner, the band blaring. The day wore by; this happened in winter, and everybody was freezing. Finally, in the late afternoon, they decided to check on what was happening; so one of the students summoned up the nerve to call the rector. "Excuse me, sir, but could you tell us who we are supposed to meet at the station?" As the rector had no idea what the student was talking about, he just told the caller to go to hell and slammed down the receiver. The poor standard-bearer and the musicians spent several more hours greeting all the trains, until Davidov finally sent a boy down to the station to tell them they could go home.

Davidov was incorrigible. One day he ran across an old professor, Semenov-Zusser, and said to him, "You know that soon they're going to hold the jubilee of Kharkov University?"

"Yes."

"And they're going to award decorations?"

"Yes, so I understand," said the old professor.

"Well, I just heard that Professor Lifshitz will receive the Order of the Red Banner, and Professor Slutzkin will receive the Order of Lenin, and I hear *you're* going to receive a pair of valenki [the high felt winter boots]."

"*What?*" asked Semenov-Zusser. "My God, why? I'd look like a perfect ass, being given valenki!"

"Well, you're an elderly person. They thought it was a good idea. That was the decision."

Semenov-Zusser had no doubt that this could happen, so he rushed to the Trade Union Committee.

"What's going on here? Why are they going to give me valenki?"

The Chiefs of the Trade Union, who had no idea this was Davidov's invention, were astonished that an elderly professor should have any objection to receiving so useful an award, so they did something very irregular: they sent him on to the university Party officials. In this way, Professor Semenov-Zusser was sent higher and higher, until he arrived at the District Party Committee: that is, the governors. They could hardly refer him higher still — to the Central Party Committee — so the District Committee started to make inquiries as to what had happened. Only then did the joke come to the surface.

Fear

THERE IS a very expressive modern fable in Russia: a little bird, flying around on a very cold day, gets frozen and falls to the ground. Along comes a cow, and on her rambles happens to let a cow-pat fall on the bird. The bird is revived by the warmth, emerges from the mess, and lets out a few cheeps. Now along comes a fox, attracted by the chirping. The fox picks up the bird, cleans it off, and then eats it. Moral: Not everyone who covers you with shit is your enemy, and not everyone who cleans you off is your friend. And more important: if you're deep in the shit, don't make a sound.

Learning to keep silent turned out to be an essential part of our education.

By the time I entered the university, a campaign had been mounted against a new crime: "Cosmopolitanism." Cosmopolitanism referred formally to literature, to the theater, to the cinema; "cosmopolites" introduced undue foreign influence into these areas. This meant that now not only the sciences were under attack, but also the arts. It turned out that almost all who were condemned — that is, all who didn't care about patriotism, about nationality, about Soviet pride — were Jews; and everybody understood it.

After 1948, each year, and sometimes each month, brought some new terror. Writers and critics were not just silenced: some were exiled or imprisoned. People suspected of being interested in or influenced by cultures outside the Soviet were linked to Fascism, to imperialism. They were saboteurs.

The purge was not confined to the great and famous; these criminals were sought out everywhere. Two of my classmates were threatened because simply the Jewish origin of one, and the interest in European history of the other, brought them dangerously close to "Cosmopolitanism." As a result, the entire course of their lives was changed;

you might say, derailed. One was Vladlen* Klyot. He had a profound grasp of history and was considered a very promising scholar by the professors in his department. But upon leaving the university he found himself barred from continuing his studies, and almost unemployable. He was forced to take a job teaching in one of the poorest village schools, and it was ten years before the barriers against studying non-Soviet culture, and the ban on Jews, lifted sufficiently so that he could resume work toward his candidate's degree and doctorate.

The second was a Russian, a handsome, attractive person named Podmarkov. His field was literature. At the time when we really knew each other his ideas were not at all pro-Soviet; moreover he considered himself to be a man with the courage of his convictions. But when the campaign against Cosmopolitanism started, and he came under suspicion, he very quickly changed his ideas. He jettisoned his principles, joined the Communist Party, and became very cynical in all his thinking. I came to dislike him heartily.

So for the students of my generation, to have one's career hamstrung, or even one's character warped, by the repressive forces of the State, was not a fate reserved solely for scientists: the entire intelligentsia was under attack, particularly those in the arts and humanities, and many many people ensured their survival through intellectual and moral compromises.

During this time of constant apprehension, we kept thinking of the Terror of only the previous decade. People recalled Landau's "confession," Obreimov's arrest, and the attempted suicide of the Director of the Physical-Technical Institute. (He had jumped from a window, but, to his misfortune, survived the fall. Horribly injured, he was taken not to the hospital but to the NKVD.) As a matter of fact, in 1938–39, only one of the Kharkov professors was sure of his safety. When he had seen one after another of his colleagues taken, he devised a scheme to get out of the trap. As I said before, you cannot "fade" into the population in Russia; the most ordinary of citizens is under surveillance too close to permit it. So the professor simply boarded a street car, stood in the middle of a crowded aisle, and, with no attempt at concealment, picked the pocket of the man standing next to him, taking his wallet. There were a great many witnesses. In no time, the police arrested him, and he was arraigned. He pleaded guilty and was sentenced to a year in jail. By

* This name, Vladimir Lenin abbreviated, is one of the many such ridiculous names inflicted on children born in the 'twenties and 'thirties. A girl's name in the same category is Ninel — Lenin spelled backward! Perhaps the most incredible of all is the name Rem — from the initials for *Revolutzia i Elektrifikatsia Mira,* "Revolution and Electrification of the World," which Lenin promised.

the time of his release from the Kharkov Regional Jail, very nearly all the professors in his department — as he had foreseen — were serving long sentences in labor camps, many in the far north. These events had occurred within very recent memory; and now, when the sciences and, even more, the humanities were coming under the axe, it was increasingly clear that history was about to repeat itself. Academics hastened to comply with the new guidelines.

Not only were genetics, linguistics, psychiatry, psychology (except for Pavlovian psychology) annihilated, but new and "better" sciences took their places. I remember interminable seminars during which we had to repeat the naïve and uninformed linguistic theory of Stalin. We also had to discuss the foundations of economics according to Stalin. We simply had to learn to talk nonsense: to decide where to lay the bricks in the castle in the air, and what would be the best style for the Emperor's new clothes.

Theoretical chemistry was toppled. World-famous scientists were forced to announce that quantum mechanics, and the resonance theory in chemistry, were nonsense. Cybernetics was pronounced a "pseudo-science."

Some of these crazy things happened right before my eyes. I was there when the brilliant mathematician Povzner took the floor at a meeting and explained that cybernetics is in fact a Fascist science; that the very concept of cybernetics is a Fascist idea. It was terribly humiliating when, after cybernetics had again long since been restored to the status of a science, the very slow government-operated presses published the proceedings of this so-called conference. Incredibly, they were even translated, and abstracts appeared in a widely read international scientific journal. I have never seen anyone as frustrated as Professor Povzner when this publication came to his attention.

The Lysenko catastrophe had repercussions all over the Soviet Union, affecting biologists in even the smallest, most remote institutes, obscure little places of minor importance. Now the laws against Cosmopolitanism were threatening artists, composers, writers. Russians were not wholly exempt from these attacks; but nine out of ten of the criminals were Jews.

*   *   *

Because during that frightful time bravery, decency, and kindness were qualities that became increasingly hard to find among people in positions of responsibility, I feel very strongly that here I have to mention Professor Bulankin, Rector of Kharkov University.

Professor Bulankin was a biologist. He was not a particularly brilliant man, nor was he in an invulnerable position. He was Corresponding Member only of the Ukrainian (not of the Soviet) Academy of Sciences. (Members of the Soviet Academy enjoy extraordinary privileges and immunities, but for a mere regional Academician to defy authority is extremely risky.) But he was a man of integrity and courage.

Bulankin knew perfectly well that he could not retain on his faculty biologists who failed to reject their science. But he took it upon himself to confer with each one of them privately; explained what was happening; and persuaded them to act the part of converts to the new genetics. Those who accepted his advice were safe.

Very few others in a position such as Bulankin's at other Soviet universities had the bravery or consideration to devise this way out for their staffs. Professor Bulankin stubbornly refused to understand any official hints as to the advisability of getting rid of certain Kharkov University lecturers. (These directives are always conveyed merely as proposals, as suggestions; there are no written orders. Everyone knows how to interpret the telephone call "from above" — no memorandum is needed.) All over the nation, institute and university officials responded in haste: they got rid of all the Jews on their staffs the minute the faintest rumor spread that this policy was indicated.

This man was not a Jew himself; he was a Ukrainian. I am positive that if there had been a few more people of his caliber in authority, the whole situation in the late 'forties and early 'fifties would have been different. His quiet success reveals that the local officials were not yet prepared for a show-down.

*   *   *

Among the sciences, physics almost alone was exempt from Stalin's destructive hand. But only a short time before I entered the university, a new Soviet system of physics was waiting in the wings. Ivanenko, who would have been the Lysenko of physics, was about to take charge of the field. Landau, Tamm, Pomerenchuk, and many other famous scientists were about to be condemned. The science in which I was soon to immerse myself, which I found so totally absorbing and significant, was on the brink of dismemberment, and transformation into a laughingstock in the eyes of the world.

It didn't happen. In 1945, the atomic bomb was dropped on Hiroshima, and Stalin came to realize that physics might have a practical application of interest to him. Here were waters he had best not muddy. Ivanenko sank back into obscurity, and real physicists were out of danger. These men, who had been on the edge of the abyss, were pulled back; their prestige soared; the material rewards they were offered increased ten- or twentyfold; and they were accorded a measure of freedom allowed in no other profession.

There is something horribly ironic in the fact that the weapon that brought death and suffering to so many thousands, that initiated a terrifying new threat for the entire future of humanity, was actually a blessing to a great number of scientists in Russia. I find it hard even to contemplate this ghastly contradiction.

But while physics was liberated, fantastic obstacles to teaching and learning in other fields were still being erected, and the ridiculous fight for "primacy" in Soviet science began. Everything that was done had to be attributed to Russian genius — the invention of airplanes, automobiles, engines of all kinds, telephones, locomotives — everything. Two of the most prominent professors at Kharkov were condemned by a special decision of the Ukrainian Central Committee because one of them, a physicist, had mentioned Einstein in a lecture, and the other, a mathematician, had mentioned Newton!

The concept of Russian superiority in science died hard. Even after Stalin's death when I was teaching in an evening school, I was trying once to give my pupils an idea of Newton's First Law, the Second, the Third, and the Law of Gravity (by this time it was again permissible to mention Newton), and one of my pupils asked me, absolutely sincerely: "Well, Mark Yakovlevitch, does this mean that Newton made a contribution as important as that of the Russian *'samo-uchki'*?" (The samo-uchki are the illiterate self-taught scientists and inventors, Russian "Edisons," "Fords," even "Einsteins," who were credited with all the modern technology and science.)!

I heard a story about that time from Professor Povzner, who taught a course at the Military Academy for Engineers. He walked into class one day, ready to start his lecture with a routine little spiel about Russian primacy in mathematics, and then settle down to a serious session of really teaching mathematics. But to his alarm, the minute he got up in front of the class he saw that among the audience was the general, the chief of the Academy. He pulled himself up short and decided that he had better devote the whole lecture to the subject of early Russian genius in mathematics. Luckily, he was a very talented man, good at thinking on his feet, so on the spur of the moment he invented a wonderful lecture on Russian mathematics in the twelfth century. He engaged in flights of fancy for the entire hour, stopping only five minutes before the end to ask, as was customary, "Are there any questions?" He saw that one of the students had raised his hand.

"Yes?"

"This is so interesting, about medieval Russian mathematics. Could

you tell us, please, where we could get more information about it —
what the reference books would be? I would like to learn more." Having no time to think, the professor immediately answered: "Well, that's
impossible! All the archives were burned during the Tatar invasion!"

When the class was over, the general came up to the lecturer and
said, "So, Professor . . . all the archives were burned?" Only then did
poor Povzner realize what he had said. The unspoken question hung in
the air: If all this evidence of Russian primacy in this science was
burned, how in the world did the professor *himself* know the history of
pre-invasion mathematics? He was ready to panic when, unexpectedly,
the general smiled at him sympathetically, turned around, and left. This
high-ranking commander was a clever and decent person; otherwise
Professor Povzner would have been in deep trouble.

This tense situation did not lighten even after Stalin's death. You
heard a great deal less about "primacy," but secrecy and censorship in
scientific and technical fields are still a handicap to anyone writing in
those areas, and at that time so much information was under lock and
key that research was incredibly hampered and crippled. Among my
few souvenirs from the Soviet Union is a document giving me permission to read an issue of the *Physical Review*. This journal is purely scientific; it is published by the American Physical Society, and it contains
nothing except physics — not even advertising. But it was a *foreign*
journal! Underneath my application the Chairman of the Department of
Theoretical Physics wrote: "I attest that the above-mentioned volume of
the *Physical Review* is required for the preparation of a talk at the
Science Seminar, and I herewith request that student Azbel be permitted
access to it." With his signature. And then, "I endorse this application,"
signed by the dean of the faculty. Then: "I also support this application," signed by the deputy director of the university. Finally: "I hereby
permit student Azbel access to this journal, to be read only on the library premises — Director of the Library!"

As time went by there were more and more arrests. There were more
and more things that one couldn't talk about.

By the time I was close to graduation, Jews were being fired from almost every kind of job; first by the hundreds, then by the thousands.
Students who were enrolled in the universities or institutes could complete their courses, but no more Jews were allowed to enter these institutions. The whole atmosphere in the country began to be absolutely intolerable.

When my father spoke his mind to the director of the Roentgenology
Department at his hospital about some promising junior colleagues who
had been fired, he too was fired. Although by that time he had his doc-

torate, he had to take a job as a sort of itinerant general practitioner, serving in the villages and outlying districts at the edge of Kharkov.

* * *

Anti-Semitism has ancient roots in the Ukraine. Before the seventeenth century, when the Ukraine was still under the domination of Poland, the Polish landowners, unwilling to reside in such a faraway part of the world, deputed the stewardship of their estates to Jews. These overseers moved in, occupied the manors, operated the mills, oversaw the farms, and collected tithes from the peasants. They were the objects of loathing. The absentee landlord, indifferent to the poverty and suffering of these subject people, was too far off to be hated: his agent received the brunt.

At the same time in Great Russia, no Jews at all were permitted entry. When one of her advisers suggested to Catherine the Great that she invite Jewish traders and merchants into the country, she replied that she had no intention of allowing the "enemies of mankind" onto the sacred soil of Russia. Under the Czars this ban was never really lifted. When the borders of Russia expanded to include Polish territory, Jews were confined, as is well known, to the clearly demarcated areas beyond the Pale of Settlement.

Anti-Semitism was a fact of life taken for granted by everybody, including some of the greatest Russian writers. For example, in *Taras Bulba,* Gogol (who was a Ukrainian) describes with relish the brutalities of a pogrom; he presents the event as nothing but good fun. Russian critics and historians of literature have no comment to make on this attitude. They too see it as perfectly natural. No part of the Soviet Union was more amenable to the adoption of measures toward the suppression of Jews than the Ukraine. Constitutional prohibitions against discrimination had never sunk below a lip-service level in this part of the U.S.S.R., and the majority considered the ever-increasing dismissals and arrests of Jews in the late 'forties and early 'fifties a matter of indifference, if not a welcome change in policy.

The mounting tension was inescapable. It was not easy for any of us to ignore it, when one after another of our fellow-students disappeared, when our fathers and mothers were losing their jobs, and the newspapers were filled with increasingly unambiguous threats. There was a wartime spirit abroad; only this time the educated classes, the intelligentsia, and particularly the Jews among them, were the enemy.

How could one survive in this atmosphere? I don't mean if you fell into the hands of the KGB; once that happened the problem of survival was little dependent upon what you did or what you didn't do. I mean what you might call moral survival.

There were several possibilities. One was to try to forget everything and simply concentrate on one's own personal life. In other words, to be like a caged rabbit, who has no alternative save merely to exist from day to day, never knowing when he may become a rabbit stew.

Then there were people who decided to devote themselves to a struggle with the system. Unfortunately, they had no positive program. Their principal idea was to study, to search for the truth and analyze the problem of where our society had gone astray, through the works of Marx. They devoutly hoped to find that the leading idea behind Marxism was correct; that it was only its application that was vicious.

For my part I did not, and I do not, believe in that theory. I was convinced that the political climate in the country depended upon its people: that the KGB was the consequence of history, not that present Russian history was the consequence of the KGB.

Another possibility for people like myself was to escape into pure science; and if this science was outlawed, just to try to think for oneself, to create and invent if only for one's own satisfaction, *pour le tiroir*. This means of survival was not open to everyone; but as far as I was concerned there was not a moment in my life when I regretted having become a theoretician. It meant that I was independent of every external factor.

Still, I had no intention of shutting my eyes to the life around me, of avoiding everything outside of science. I knew people who did that. They made no friends outside scientific circles; they dared venture no interest in art, in literature, in political theory. Having decided that science was a safe haven, they found shelter in it, and refused to look out. They made a point of drifting away from acquaintances whose fields of endeavor — particularly now, when the campaign against Cosmopolitanism was so virulent — might lead to serious trouble.

I could not make any of those choices. I felt that my own way of life was to be in science, but as to friends: it seemed to me that it would be crippling, demeaning, to choose my friends on the basis of which friendships would be safe and which would not. To confine my loyalties to science, and to my fellow-scientists, for reasons of security; to cultivate indifference to everything and everyone else — I knew I couldn't do that.

In a word, I simply made up my mind at that time that I would try to be a decent human being.

* * *

Of course, young people are inclined to seek out fun, to have a good time, and even under pressure of the most serious of threats manage to entertain themselves when they can.

Although university life in the Soviet Union is nothing like the casual lighthearted routine I later saw in the West, we did amuse ourselves quite a bit. There was a great deal of visiting back and forth among students; there were plenty of friendships and flirtations; on holidays we had our dances (although to the dismay of everyone, particularly of the girls, we were confined to mazurkas and so forth, and were not allowed to learn up-to-date dances — fox trots or tangos). In Kharkov there were no cafés or restaurants that anyone on a student's allowance could possibly afford, but movies were very cheap, or we could visit the museums. We did a great deal of walking, both summer and winter, in the many pleasant wooded parks of the city.

But the principal pastime of almost everybody I knew in Russia was — talking. We never stopped. Perhaps there is another nation where people talk as inexhaustibly as Russians do, but I have yet to see it. We were constantly thrashing out our ideas — political, religious, psychological, philosophical, scientific. Moreover, since the news media were so rigidly limited, we constituted a news exchange among ourselves. (As for outside news: anyone with a short-wave radio, particularly if he had the good luck to obtain the services of a technician who could cut out the jamming, was consulted and visited all the time.) We discussed everything under the sun.

When it comes to relations between the men and women undergraduates — the reader can well imagine that our circumstances were not conducive to anything much more serious than an occasional kiss, and then only if you were fortunate. The housing situation, with several people occupying every room of every apartment, meant that we were heavily chaperoned. And chaperonage aside, Soviet people of my generation were brought up with a straitlaced outlook that would strike their European or American counterparts as distinctly antiquated. I must have been eleven or twelve before anyone told me how conception occurs and how children appear — it was one of the boys in our apartment house in Novosibirsk who mentioned it, not my parents — and I was so shocked by his blunt description that for a month afterward I couldn't look a member of the opposite sex in the eye.

Boys didn't even know what the female form looked like: not only were old-fashioned conventions adhered to with regard to dress and undress, but there were no nude statues or paintings in any of the museums we saw. Sex was looked upon as something inappropriate, almost bad. No cinema, no Soviet book, revealed anything more than kisses — very light kisses.

I believe that things are a little different nowadays, except in villages and small towns, where everybody knows everybody, and even the most discreet affair gives rise to a storm of gossip. Moscow University of late years has the reputation of being a very uninhibited place. Despite terribly strict parietal rules and high walls and many locks between the men's and women's dormitories, one hears that there is an increasing number of abortions. (In Stalin's time, abortions were illegal, and bastardy was a calamitous disgrace. Neither mother nor child had any legal rights whatsoever; there was no such thing as a paternity suit, nor any provisions for the support of a child born out of wedlock.)

In my day, I would say that an absolute majority of the girls went into marriage as maidens. Women and quite a few of the men were almost completely uninformed about marital relations and about modern birth control. They knew very little about any aspect of marriage, except that they were in love, which meant that everything would be wonderful.

It may be due to these nineteenth-century attitudes that there is such an enormous number of unhappy marriages in the Soviet Union. Offhand, I would say that one out of four of the couples in my own circle of acquaintance is divorced. Who could estimate how many other marriages would terminate if either of the partners had any chance of obtaining a permit to move to another residence? It became a source of repeated depression and disappointment to me, by the time I was in my mid-twenties, to visit friends whose wedding parties I had attended only two or three years before, and whose happiness had been so infectious then, to find a drab, defeated pair imprisoned in one small room, usually with a squalling baby or, worse still, with two of them; husband and wife equally irritated by each other's constant company. Many who had planned to obtain advanced degrees, to make something of themselves in the world, simply had to give up and settle for a career of mere endurance. I saw it often. There was no religious tradition to hold these couples together, and the popular idea of marching shoulder to shoulder to create a great Soviet future was hardly sustaining.

Of course none of us had a crystal ball, and we students fell in love as optimistically as young people the world over!

The group of theoreticians with whom I studied was without exception bright. All of the people in my class became scientists of very high caliber in later years. At the tenth jubilee of this class, Professor Ilya Lifshitz spoke of our group as the strongest one in the history of Kharkov University and expressed a real regret at the delay that had prevented us from continuing directly on after graduation with our doctoral studies. (The ban on Jews in universities and institutes held almost all of us up for years in starting graduate work.)

It was a piece of good fortune to find myself in courses that, for the most part, were of real significance and taught by brilliant people. By the second year we were studying under the best mathematicians and physicists at Kharkov, and at that time the faculty was still a remarkably distinguished one.

But I certainly can't say the same for the university administration. By 1950, Abram Solomonovitch Milner was no longer dean. His replacement, Slastyonov, was a very special case, perfectly capable of handling the delicate political situation in which he found himself; and he got along very well with the deputy dean, Krivetz.

Slastyonov was supposed to be an astronomer, but the only publication of his that I ever heard of was on the history of the Kharkov Observatory. It was an extraordinary document. For this history he provided forms, regular questionnaires such as those presented to everybody who applied for a position at the university, and he filled them in with biographies of the men who had been directors of the observatory for the last hundred and forty years. A novel literary device! He presented all the data in the appropriate spaces: who the director's parents were; what his status was — noble, merchant, whatever — his nationality, place of birth, where he had been educated, and so on. He investigated the histories of his subjects exactly as it would be done by the KGB.

Slastyonov was a fool. But he was just right for dean at that time: he was totally lacking in the scruples that would have hindered his career.

Slastyonov and Krivetz formed a partnership and became invincible, whatever the times might bring. Slastyonov stayed on at the university, even after Stalin's death had resulted in the elimination of such people at most institutions of higher learning, and was still lecturer up to the time of his retirement. These men had powerful control over our lives not only when we were students, but afterward, for reasons that will appear. Both of them contributed heavily to the diminution of the great reputation once held by Kharkov University.

*   *   *

In the late fall of 1951, my mother had an attack of bronchial asthma more severe than any she had ever suffered before, and she was forced to go to the hospital.

In November, she died.

It was a heavy blow to my father and myself. We had been a very close family.

I hardly remember those days at all. They were in a mist. I just remember the night of November 14th through 15th, running to the hospital and, for the first and last time in my life, seeing my father cry.

I remember the funeral. My entire class was present; everybody tried to support and console me.

I can still see in my mind's eye the tombstone on my mother's grave, on which are the words my father had had inscribed:

Farewell, Our Dearest
We will remember thee as long as we live.

And it was true.

* * *

The following spring, during the semester break, my father gave me the present of a trip to Moscow. (I was by then just nineteen, and completing my third year at the university.) Father could ill afford it, but he wanted me to have a change of scene after the sorrows of the preceding winter, and moreover he felt it was essential to my education to have the experience of visiting the great capital.

It was an overnight trip, and I had the novel experience of traveling in a coupé, a compartment that accommodates four people and becomes a sleeping compartment at night when they pull down and make up the berths. (Though I was totally unaccustomed to a luxurious style of life, I did think it a little inelegant when the stewardess roused the passengers an hour before we reached Moscow so as to have time to remove the bedding, fold up the berths, and, for fear we might have stolen them, *count* the sheets and pillowcases before she took them away! This turned out to be routine procedure on trains, and also in hotels.) In any event, I loved the trip. I like being on a train, and this route takes you through hundreds of miles of beautiful woods and fields.

I stayed with an aunt, Father's sister. She lived about a five-minute walk from the Arbat, occupying, with my uncle and their three sons, a room about twelve square meters in floor-span, in an apartment shared by half a dozen other families. Among Soviet people of all sorts and classes, to extend hospitality — to find "room for one more," even under the most crowded circumstances — is absolutely commonplace. One takes it completely for granted either as guest or host, and I wouldn't comment on it except that since I came to the West I have heard so many expressions of astonishment that people living at such close quarters should think nothing of taking in a visitor. Another mat on the floor or perhaps a folding cot — and that's it. You are welcome.

I didn't really like Moscow at first, though of course it was exciting to be there. Everybody was in such a hurry; streets and sidewalks were impossibly crowded. The shops were incomparably better than those in Kharkov, but there were so many people! The queues were endless.

I had to spend a couple of days just learning my way around. There are no city maps of Moscow. They had those schema on the Metro so that you could find your stop, but the distances represented are not even the roughest approximations. There was nothing at that time by way of a published city guide; it was exactly as though Moscow were under strict wartime regulations, with everything except the most conspicuous parts of town kept secret from a possible spy.

But after my initial explorations, I discovered what I had come for. I spent the entire remainder of my two weeks in the art galleries: the Tretyakovsky and the Pushkin Museum of Fine Arts. I went around by myself. I often spent an entire day in just one room, marveling at the first Titians, the first Michelangelos, the first Rembrandts, that I had ever seen.

Despite the fact that many of the great pictures in Moscow museums were hidden away in storage — in fact, almost anything painted in the West since the 1850s and in Russia since the turn of the century was no longer on display because so much of it was considered insufficiently realist or lacking in content edifying to Soviet viewers — the museums of the capital were and are perfect treasure houses. To an eye disappointed by the work of such "masters" as Brodsky (who in any other civilized country would have been relegated to the rank of commercial artist), the Renaissance masters, the Dutch school and the Venetian school came as a revelation; also the beautiful early icons. I fell in love at first sight. I had never before seen so much as a lithograph of a Leonardo, a Rubens, a Rembrandt. Paintings became an obsession, and I have haunted the galleries at every opportunity since.

Poison and Antidote

IN VIEW of the long-established and deeply ingrained anti-Semitism in Russia, the State encountered no resistance at all when the fuse was lit on an explosive charge prepared against Jews. I remember the shock when I found out what had happened.

It was in January of 1953, my last year at the university, and I was getting onto the street car for my usual morning commute to the Physics and Mathematics Building. The tram had barely started moving before I became aware of an ominous atmosphere in the air, an angry hum of conversation. Discussions were springing up around me among the other passengers on subjects that only yesterday would have been impossible to broach in public. Loud voices were exclaiming about some outrage, some criminal conspiracy in which Jews had just been discovered to be involved — I couldn't make out exactly what the story was supposed to be. Right next to me a man had gathered quite a knot of listeners, to whom he was loudly announcing that the three notorious traitors whom Stalin had eliminated — Trotsky and Zinoviev and Kamenev — were Jews. Until today, no one had dared even to whisper the names of these condemned men; now they were being publicly denounced, and identified as Jews.

Another speaker was saying that the Jews were plotting the destruction of the Soviet regime; his listeners agreed vociferously. The unspoken menace that had been gathering force around us for the last five years and more had surfaced.

Just before I got off at my stop I heard more than one person express the opinion that it was too bad Hitler had not succeeded in killing all the Jews; since he had not, now was the time to do it.

This was horrible, chilling — and perfectly extraordinary. It was obvious that the sudden outbursts of hostile conversation were not simply spontaneous; there were some on that tram, and undoubtedly everywhere else in the city, who were under instructions to foment this terror. This would not be the first time in Soviet history that the tinderbox of public opinion had been ignited by such means, but it was the first time I had encountered it myself.

I bought a newspaper after classes. On the front page was an article about a recently discovered terrorist group, physicians, who had for a long time been poisoning prominent Soviet officials. The conspirators were listed; almost every single name was Jewish. This vicious calumny was, of course, what has since become known as the "Doctors' Plot."

Jewish doctors were condemned everywhere. If a hospital patient died — his doctor had poisoned him. Sick people stayed away from the polyclinics, terrified that they — or worse still, their children — might be killed by the doctors there, many of whom were Jewish.

The country was ready for murders, for pogroms. It was no secret. And shortly, word got around that an open letter by the most eminent Jewish writers and scientists was to appear in the papers, saying they understood the guilt of their people, that this guilt had to be somehow expiated. They "knew the harm that Jews had done to the Soviet nation," and they themselves would request, nay, urge the government to send the Jews to the far northeast of Siberia, where they might atone for their crimes, at least in part, by their labor.

Rumors arose that new labor camps were already in the making in Siberia.

The peril came closer and closer. Every week, every day, it became harder to lead a normal life, to do one's work, to ignore the panic that filled the air.

*   *   *

On the evening of March 4th, Father and I had a quarrel. At this late date I can't remember what it was about — probably some difficulties with our domestic arrangements, or perhaps I had been having too many of my friends in and he had reached the end of his patience on that score. Any two people cooped up together in such close confinement inevitably explode now and then, and this was one of those occasions. I grabbed my books and coat, shouted that I was getting out, and slammed the door behind me.

Once out on Garshina Street, walking fast to wear my temper out, I began to consider the problem of where to spend the night. Needless to say, in Kharkov, in March, it is still very cold and the city is deep in snow — I couldn't stay outside indefinitely. There was not the remotest possibility of anyone in my position getting a hotel room. Even if I could have afforded it, the hotels were always so packed that there was not a spare chair in the lobbies at night, much less a bed. But in any case, under no circumstances could I have stayed in a hotel in Kharkov. A resident of any particular city is not authorized to put up in a hotel in that same city. Officially, he has a place to stay, and he must stay there.

For fifty kopeks, I might have rented a mat in an *ugol* — a "corner" — a section of one room owned by some near-destitute landlord who let out space for those even poorer than himself. The customers in ugols are usually students; but some are members of the substratum of the populace whose existence the authorities ignore: beggars, tramps, streetwalkers, odd-job workers, and so forth — the same people about whom Gorki wrote in *The Lower Depths*. Perhaps a little less lousy and a little less hungry than Gorki's characters — but perhaps not. However, it might have taken me a week to find an ugol.

As I approached Dzerzhinskaya Street, it crossed my mind that I might find a bench at the railway station; but the problem there is that loiterers and would-be sleepers are constantly being prodded with nightsticks and ordered to "move along" by the police. That would be very unpleasant.

It was late. There are no places in Kharkov where one can just step in and get out of the cold and order a drink or a cup of coffee. My situation was getting rather tough. I didn't want to land on any of my friends and have to explain that I was at odds with my father.

Finally the obvious solution occurred. I would find shelter at the Central Telegraph Office. This office stays open throughout the twenty-four hours: they handle not only wires and cables but long-distance calls; also there are banks of telephones for local calls if the customer has no telephone of his own. (To have a telephone in those days was a rare luxury, except for officials.) There are always dozens of people waiting around inside for their calls to be put through. In the 'fifties there was no direct dialing, and anyone making a trunk call had a long wait ahead of him. To accommodate all these customers there were quite a few benches and chairs, and I realized there was little chance of my being questioned or bothered if I joined the crowd of dozing people sprawled on these seats awaiting their connections.

I went in and found a vacant bench where I could sit down. The room was large, fairly light, and full of people; there was never a lull between the noises of ringing telephones and loud voices in conversation. It didn't take me long to see that I wouldn't really be able to sleep in this room, so resignedly I started to read one of the books I had brought with me.

Around four or five A.M., I can't remember the exact time but I do know that dawn had not yet broken, everyone in the office suddenly became aware of an extraordinary commotion at the switchboard. The entire board was lit, and the operators appeared to be in some kind of frenzy. Bells rang incessantly. Several of the operators started to scream; others hushed them saying: "Don't alarm everyone! Don't say anything! It couldn't be true." "Call Moscow back—we have to check." The screaming got louder; a few of the women burst into tears.

At first by ones and twos but finally in a cluster, everyone in the office surrounded the switchboard.

"What's happened, girls?"

"What's going on?"

"Not — *war?*"

"Stalin is dead!" one of the women managed to announce, between sobs.

If a bomb had exploded in our midst, no one present could have been more astounded. We were quite a big crowd — forty or fifty of us — and I turned curiously to stare at my sobbing, weeping companions.

The impossible had happened. Although Stalin was over seventy, it had no more occurred to most of the population in all of Russia that he might die than it would occur to the devout that God might die. He was a constant in our lives; no one under middle age could remember a Russia without his vast shadow looming over it, and the younger people could not imagine that such a Russia had ever been.

These stricken people astonished me. Though, like everyone else, I had never contemplated the end of Stalin's reign, had I thought much about it I certainly couldn't have foreseen this reaction. This was deep, overwhelming, heartfelt mourning. Among the crowd were five or six Jews — they looked as bereaved and smitten as everyone else.

I decided to leave the place at once. It was a strange sensation to be the only person in a roomful of mourners who did not share the obviously spontaneous and sincere feelings of all the others there. As I left I heard voices crying: "What will happen to us now? How can we go on without him? Now times will get worse, and worse, and worse!"

I will never understand the tidal wave of sorrow that poured over the Soviet Union in the weeks and months that followed.

Of course, most of those who had suffered personally at Stalin's hands had long since vanished from our midst, dead or forgotten in labor camps. But even many of the witnesses of these tragedies — and actually some of the victims themselves — cast no blame upon Stalin. "He doesn't know what's happening to us. Bad people are preventing him from learning about our fate. If only he knew, we would be rescued." The cruelest of the Czars, too, got the benefit of this same childish belief.

For a long time I and my friends who felt the same way I did had to check ourselves at every moment. When we went to the university (and we could not stay away; we were supposed to be at our lectures and conferences, and this was no time to make oneself conspicuous) and saw people everywhere, genuinely weeping; when we encountered clusters of students and members of the faculty standing almost as if at prayer around the huge bust of Stalin at the entrance hall of the Physics and Mathematics Building, high up on a pedestal like an idol, with a four-man honor guard around it — naturally we had to join them. Everybody had to. Moreover, we students had to take turns donning the black armband and standing guard.

It was very difficult for me to remain serious during this long-drawn-out orgy of mass hysteria. Many meetings condemning those who were not mourning sincerely enough were still taking place months after Stalin's death; people were thrown out of the Party for absentmindedly smiling during that time.

Of course problems arose immediately for the faculty at Kharkov. What views were they supposed to hold? What policies were they supposed to pursue, now that Stalin was dead and there was no way of knowing what the Party line would be on any issue that might come up? There were no Party lectures. A friend of mine observed, joking (of course in strictest privacy), that the Marxist-Leninist cathedras were "closed for revisions."

A few very clever people could see what was going to happen now. One of my friends was smart enough to predict that it would be Khrushchev who came to power next because, he said, it was inevitable that Stalin's present heirs could not make peace among themselves. They would have to choose somebody who was not at the top level, who was not very bright or influential. But once he came to nominal power, according to this friend, whatever his shortcomings, he would shortly find himself the real ruler.

I certainly had no desire to go to Moscow, as many did, to see Stalin for the last time. Thousands of Kharkov people, many of them students, swarmed to the railway station and fought for space on the Moscow train. Not all of them came back. Many of the mourners died, actually crushed to death in the crowds. Stalin's funeral was very similar to the last rites of those ancient Viking rulers who took slaves and horses with them into the next world.

The funeral procession was organized in brutally inefficient style. Enormous crowds were forced to pass through small, narrow streets; all other thoroughfares were closed off. Even these narrow lanes were obstructed by army and militia trucks, and of the masses of people struggling through those passageways hundreds, perhaps thousands, were killed. They were swept up by the inexorably moving mob and simply smashed by the press of people around them.

The corpses left in the wake of that procession constitute an only too-appropriate memorial to the Stalin era.

Steps

LIFE went on.

In 1952 I had started studying under Professor Veniamin Grigorievitch German. He was a brilliant scientist, but at that time he was having a great many troubles. He had been widowed not long before and had too much on his mind to be able to organize his work. He never had time to discuss my papers, certainly not to submit any of them to a scientific journal. This was true not only with regard to his students; it even applied to his own work — he himself hardly ever published then. So when it came time for me to write my dissertation I decided to choose another adviser, a decision a student could make for himself in those days.

I wanted to work with Professor Lifshitz, who was the best physicist at Kharkov and I think one of the best in the Soviet Union. But a conflict arose. It happened that another student wanted to work on the problem Lifshitz proposed (it concerned the thermodynamics of liquid helium). There was nothing to do except toss a coin, and when it came down in the other man's favor I was much disappointed.

But in this case, Fate was wiser than I. As it turned out, the problem the other student had pre-empted turned out to have a negative solution, whereas the one that I had to settle for (an aspect of the Theory of Metals) turned out to be extremely interesting and led to important results. The major applications became clear before too long, and in the course of my investigations in this area, several of my preliminary conclusions were published in the *Journal of Experimental and Theoretical Physics*.

Once our theses were accepted, the central question in the minds of all my classmates and myself was: Where would we be appointed? Where would our jobs be?

The Ministry of Education appoints all university graduates to positions where they will have to work for at least three years after graduation; to leave this post is a criminal offense. Of course, the ministry's decision is guided by the recommendations provided by the university officials. So all of us in the graduating class were in a state of suspense for quite a while, and would have given a great deal to see our character references. I was not optimistic about the assignment I would receive, nor were many of the others. Although after Stalin's death the menace of an approaching pogrom had faded and the doctors accused of the Plot were quietly exonerated, the thousands of Jews who had been fired were not rehired, and official policy remained strictly anti-Semitic.

I had other reasons besides my nationality to believe that the administration was not likely to give me a favorable report. I had had several run-ins with Vipiralenko, the Chairman of the Department Trade Union Bureau (this somewhat corresponds to a student union in a Western university but is not nearly as independent of the authorities). Vipiralenko was a real bastard, an inferior student, and the only one of us on the bureau who was a Party member. He had made it clear from the start of his chairmanship what the function of a trade union in the Soviet Union is: to support the official policy in all cases, without any regard for the members' interests. Time and again I had been stopped when I tried to act on behalf of a student, usually when someone was being suspended or expelled on grounds that were patently unfair. "The Trade Union recognizes no special cases," he would say in his quiet, irritating voice. He was hated for his dirty methods by the whole Trade Union Bureau. I knew that between Vipiralenko, Slastyonov, and Krivetz, the commentary on myself was bound to be negative.

I was not mistaken: the appointment I received was a disaster. I was to be stationed at the Uralmachzavod (Ural Machine Factory) at Sverdlovsk. Obviously, a theoretical physicist would be hopelessly ill suited in a heavy-machinery works.

I was absolutely flattened. I knew I would just rust away at this job. On a factory-worker's schedule I certainly would have no time for my own work in physics. The papers I was already writing in my mind would never be written. I had no future at all.

So I couldn't have been more delighted when I heard that the management of the Uralmachzavod felt that their important and famous factory was no place for a Jew. I took the first train for Moscow and rushed over to the Ministry of Education to find out where I would be going, what sort of appointment I would get instead.

It was summer, vacation time, very hot; and the officials in the ministry were not in the mood for any extra work or thinking. The man who dealt with me shuffled through his files and said: "Oh . . . Azbel; now let's see what's going on in your case. Here we are; yes. As a mat-

ter of fact we were planning to get you an appointment at a small factory in Kamchatka." (This is the remotest inhabited place in the northeast of the Soviet Union.) "But the appointment isn't settled yet; we
have to do a lot of paper work on this one. So look here: Would you
mind if we gave you a free diploma?" A free diploma means you are
allowed to find your own job rather than be posted to one.

That was one of the happiest moments of my life. I've never relinquished money with so much enthusiasm before or since — I had been
issued 100 roubles to finance the trip to Sverdlovsk and to cover the expenses of getting settled there. In return I was handed a paper I have
preserved among my most treasured possessions: a document emancipating me from this serfdom. It meant I was on my own: I could look
for a job that I could fit in with my work on physics.

I returned to Kharkov.

Several possibilities lay before me. One was to apply for a position at
some very remote university. But, as I mentioned before, an absolute
majority of the universities in the Soviet Union outside the great centers
are at the lowest level; so I would make no progress in my own work
there. I would see no science, and I would be kept so busy with various
minor jobs that I would have no time for anything important. Whereas
if I remained here I would have access to a good scientific library and
would not lose touch with Professor Lifshitz and other Kharkov scientists. One cannot pursue science indefinitely in solitude. You have to be
able to give and receive ideas at least occasionally to keep your own
creativity at pitch.

I dismissed the thought of going afield, and started to look for a job
in Kharkov. By that time physicists were very much in demand. A lot of
positions were open, with no one to fill them. Physics was now supposed to be taught in every university; the State saw a great need for
physicists; and this "boom" had mushroomed only in the last five years.
When I appeared at the institutes with my diploma in physics and with
the highest recommendations from the professors under whom I had
studied, the deans were extremely eager to offer me a position. They
could tell at a glance that I was a Jew, but there was always the hope
that maybe one of my parents might not have been. *Maybe* my passport
would declare me to be Russian; in that case they would gladly over-
look the wrong side of my lineage.

As a matter of fact, at the time I obtained my passport, which one
does at the age of sixteen, it was still possible for me to register myself
officially as a Russian, or whatever other Soviet nationality I might
choose. This was a matter of chance: my birth certificate was issued
during a very short interval when there was no nationality indi-

cated on these documents. For me "assimilation" would not bring half
the advantages that baptism did in Czarist times, but in case of urgent
need the officials were willing to observe the convention that, despite
any evidence to the contrary, the bearer of a Russian passport was a
Russian. My parents had refused to influence me — in fact had mentioned the advantages of Russian or Ukrainian papers — but I could not
bring myself to make the change.

So when the officials at the various institutes asked me to fill out the
questionnaire, and when I saw their expressions as they read it over, I
anticipated their answers. Every time, I was told to "come back tomorrow"; and when tomorrow came — it turned out that *just* after I left,
another physicist had applied for the position, someone of more experience, whom they had naturally had to accept. "Sorry." They knew that
I knew this was a lie, but they didn't care too much. To whom could I
complain?

I finally had to take a position at an evening school that offered several courses in theoretical physics. The majority of my students were on
such tough schedules that they had no time at all for study; it was not
love of learning that had driven them to the school but the hope of obtaining credits that would mean they were entitled to a slight raise in
salary, or to a small increase in their pensions when they retired. Seeing
a person in his fifties or sixties sitting there with hands trembling when I
called upon him in an exam, obviously feeling exactly like an ill-
prepared schoolboy in the same position — I tried not to listen to the
answers. He would either have to get his grade or flunk out; there was
no third possibility, no "tutoring" available to him, no teacher for any
"special attention." The poor man had probably been teaching obsolete
physics for decades and would be teaching it until he died. I could
change nothing; all I could do was provide him with a bit of paper that
might increase his salary just a fraction.

This job paid only forty roubles a month, so I had to work at others
at the same time. During the next three years I switched from one
school to another. At one time I taught physics at the Girls' High
School; at another mathematics for the Pedagogical Institute. I liked
teaching and tried my best at these various jobs, but this was stop-gap
employment, merely a means of survival while I pursued my own research. I had absolutely no security because some institutions, to avoid
increasing the percentage of Jewish names on their records, hired me on
a temporary basis: I was paid by the hour, and was never officially on
the rolls of their teaching staffs.

*   *   *

At best, the teaching profession is one of the most vulnerable of all, in Russia. Those in the exact sciences have a hard enough time, but teachers in the humanities are more helpless still. By the 'fifties the humanities was an overcrowded field, with more applicants for jobs than there were positions. Since anyone who had a job could easily be replaced if he or she fell into disfavor with the authorities, teachers were forced to do almost anything in order to hang on to their posts. I later came to know young unmarried women, grade-school instructors in the villages, who had no other choice but to yield to all the demands, including the sexual advances, of any representative of the Regional Committee for School Education who came along. He could assign them so few courses that their salary would fall below subsistence level; he could fire them, leaving them with character references that would ensure they would never be hired again anywhere. The situation of these women was really horrible.

The director of the school where I was teaching in 'fifty-four was an elderly woman, tough, willful, and cruel. She took a special pleasure in treating the teachers badly, mocking them, openly despising and humiliating them. She understood that I was writing scientific papers and that I had already published in my field; that my friends were the university scientists; that I would soon have my C.Sc., or candidate's degree, and go on to a career in physics. As far as I was concerned, she kept hands off. She gave me absolute freedom, even the freedom to absent myself from the official meetings.

However, when I became aware of the insults and injustices some of my colleagues were enduring, I was very uncomfortable. I couldn't shut my eyes to what was happening, and finally I called upon the director and let her know what I thought of her. But nothing changed. Thereupon, I started attending the teachers' meetings and formally protested the high-handed treatment to which my colleagues were being subjected. For most of them, teaching at this school was the top rung of their careers: if they lost their jobs, there was nowhere else to go, so they were very timid about standing up for their rights. Once their grievances had been aired, they too began, however cautiously, to criticize the director.

The result was predictable: I was fired.

Introduction to the KGB

HERE LET ME backtrack a little and mention what I was working on.

Because in a Soviet university the student specializes in his chosen field — physics, mathematics, history, whatever — from the very start, and concentrates upon it almost exclusively for five or five and a half years, a graduate has approximately the status of a Master of Sciences (or Arts) in the West, and his senior dissertation is about the equivalent of a master's thesis. The next step, also usually a matter of some years, is to produce his thesis for the Candidate of Science degree, approximately at the level of a doctor's thesis in the West. (A doctorate — and this degree is an uncommon distinction in Russia — is something you ordinarily would hope to achieve only somewhat later in life, after publishing a great deal. The author of a doctoral dissertation works independently, with no adviser.)

In their comments on my senior dissertation, referees had written that my paper very nearly constituted a candidate's thesis. I was flattered but surprised, because I considered it only the opening wedge in the evolution of the idea I was contemplating. The problem I saw fascinated me very much, and I regarded it as really important. In the event, I turned out to be right. Its solution is now in every textbook on the subject.

The problem was of the high-frequency magnetoresistance of various metals, in different magnetic fields, under very low temperatures. Metals differ in their behavior when subjected to a strong magnetic field: one group of metals almost refuses to react, after a certain point, to an increase in the strength of the magnetic field; another, including bismuth, increases its resistance in correspondence with the magnetic field.

Electrons in metals are in a very special situation. There are hundreds of billions of billions of electrons. All of them interact with each other and with the ions that form the crystal lattice of metal. The interaction of such a number of particles poses an almost insoluble problem. But Landau had an idea that one might introduce a very special kind of ensemble that resembles common particles, which have a charge but which behave quite differently, as to mechanics of motion, from common particles. To investigate this situation, complicated by the presence both of a high-frequency electric field and of a strong magnetic field, was very intriguing but very difficult. Nobody knew how to do it effectively.

I challenged the problem. I worked on it constantly. The solution seemed to be absolutely out of reach; however, the idea that this solution *had* to exist gave me the impetus to pursue my research. It took me a relatively short time to find it: about two years.

At that point my situation became rather peculiar. On the one hand, everybody — Professor Lifshitz and all the other physicists who saw the paper — agreed that this was a very interesting solution, and that certainly it not only met but exceeded the requirements for a candidate's thesis. But at the same time, the experiments were considered too difficult for the cases that I investigated. No experimental researcher was willing to change the direction of his regular work in favor of this very difficult research; moreover, it entailed so many novel elements that there were doubts as to my predictions.

I was very disappointed, and decided that I would have to switch over to a different aspect of the problem, more interesting to experimenters, so that this theoretical work would not all have been in vain.

I told Professor Lifshitz my thought, which was also related to a "common" metal magnetoresistance. He just smiled.

"Drop that problem before you start," he advised. "Landau himself considers it insoluble." But this dismissal of the idea brought out a stubborn streak in me, and I made definite plans to attack it. "What you ought to be doing now," Lifshitz went on, "is to try for your candidate's degree. That will make it easier for us to fight for your being taken on at the institute."

One of the things that I had to do before applying to the Scientific Council was to pass the candidates' oral examination. However, my being no longer affiliated with the university presented a difficulty. In another era, this fact would have proven no obstacle — they would simply have extended me the courtesy of permitting me to take the exams under university auspices. But this was 'fifty-five, and the spirit of Stalin still walked abroad. Kharkov University did not want to accord a candidacy to a Jew.

The person in charge of arrangements for the orals was Professor Khotkevitch. His father was a Ukrainian writer, well known in the 'twenties, who had served a term in prison, having been convicted of the crime of Ukrainian nationalism; Khotkevitch the younger, the man with whom I was dealing, had the inherited reputation of being quite a liberal. In my opinion, however, he was "liberal" only with professors of very high standing. He made every effort to prevent me from taking the exams, using an arsenal of minor obstacles, and it was not until Bulankin himself, at the urging of Professor Lifshitz, interfered on my behalf that I finally received permission to take the orals. (I wasn't mistaken about Khotkevitch: when he became rector, after Bulankin's death, he showed himself in his true colors, and quite a few people at Kharkov besides myself began to see him as an anti-Semite and reactionary.)

Even this minor problem was blown up out of all proportion. But the permission to take the orals was not the end of my troubles. Passing the physics would, of course, present no difficulty; but one had also to pass an exam in Marxist philosophy. Although throughout my undergraduate years I had read a great deal of Marx, Engels, and Lenin, now I plunged into study night and day. I read every book of philosophy, went through all the literature in the Kharkov University Library that might possibly be used in the exam. I had a feeling the exam might be used as a trap, a barrier to prevent one more Jew from obtaining his degree.

The day of the orals came. Counting myself, there were eleven candidates, seven of us Jews. When I was summoned to the committee that was conducting the examination — four people — I guessed from the expressions on their faces that they were well armed for this contest.

My examination lasted two solid hours. I was asked innumerable questions, including many that bore only the remotest relation to the program. But the committee made a mistake that, I understand, they avoided in future years. However difficult this inquisition was, they did adhere to questions about books and problems in philosophy, and I did know the answers. Therefore, after two hours, during which I replied correctly to even the most minute questions and expounded on them within a much wider scope than was expected or demanded, they were in no position to withhold the highest mark. I was the only one of the seven Jews who passed.

Even a single Jew was one too many. This event taught the examiners a lesson. Subsequently, as I learned from friends who underwent this ordeal in the years immediately after I did, the committee did not try to ask examinees whom they wished to exclude any profound philosophical questions. They came up with actually unanswerable questions, such as, "Tell us: how many hogs will there be in the Ukraine at the end of the Five-Year Plan?" Who could remember all the figures, row upon row of them, thousands, included in the Five-Year Plan? That became their tactic.

Once I passed philosophy, that was the end of the candidate's exams. Then a new hurdle appeared: I had to produce a recommendation from my place of work. My school gave me this reference; but it had to be countersigned not only by the director of the school and the Trade Union chief, but by the Party leader. My evening school was too small to have a separate Party organization, and the higher organization refused to sign on behalf of a person who was not a Party member. So it took quite a while, again, before the Physics Department at Kharkov managed to arrange the validation of this recommendation, overriding the missing signature of the Party leader. This was a very serious exception to the rules.

All this took a great deal of time. Since my dissertation and candidates' exams were completed at the beginning of 'fifty-five, I had hoped to have my degree before summer. But there were continual delays in the scheduling of my presentation at the Scientific Council.

Taking into account the atmosphere of the early to mid-'fifties, I don't believe I was wrong to assume that last-ditch attempts were still being made to prevent my ever receiving the degree. I didn't have a single Jewish friend who graduated from the university around the same year I did whose career was not brought to a halt at this time. Due to the new admissions policies, the Jewish student body at Kharkov had been much reduced now, particularly in the science departments. Bulankin had been able to hold on to his staff, but he could not influence the admissions policy.

The postponement of the candidate's degree affected me hardly at all. I could not pay attention to this setback, any more than I could to the poor salaries paid me for teaching, or to being fired from the school. I was already completely absorbed by the problem that I was challenging. My science has always been a medicine for all the ills in my life; when I am caught up in it, I have no room in my brain for other concerns.

When the summer vacation of 1955 was over, I came to Professor Lifshitz with the solution to the problem. It created a sensation, which soon became known not only in Kharkov but in Moscow as well. The paper was presented to Landau.

For the last year or more, Professor German, an extremely kindly and selfless person, had been trying to get me taken onto the staff of the Institute of Radiotechnology and Electronics, where he was director of a department. He did everything he could, but the First Department opposed my appointment, and I couldn't get this job. To be in the bad books of the First Department — and you may not have the slightest idea why; I didn't — is ordinarily the kiss of death. That fact was one of the few things that really worried me. It might easily mean that never in my life would I be able to find employment at a research institute. Even a theoretical physicist cannot work forever in a vacuum; to create in this area you absolutely have to have contact with other minds in the same or related fields.

There were other difficulties. Professor Lifshitz told me that the Physical-Technical Institute would have trouble if they offered me a position. Even if the Physics Department at the institute was able to overcome the possible objections of the KGB, there was another type of opposition to contend with: many of the young people who worked at this institute, men of no particular talent, were outraged by the possibility that I might be taken onto the staff. They considered that my appointment was due only to the support of Lifshitz and others in the department who were influenced, not by the value of the contribution I was making, but were operating according to the well-known principle of solidarity among Jews — "They always hang together." This line of reasoning had been effective for years: no Jew had received a post at the institute since 1948.

At this point word came from Moscow: Kurchatov, Director of the all-important Institute for Atomic Physics, suggested I join his staff. This changed things for me completely. Professor Lifschitz told the Director of the Kharkov Physical-Technical Institute, Academician Sinelnikov, that it would be ridiculous to lose a talented physicist, a native of Kharkov, and to have him immediately go off to an even better post in Moscow. So I was accepted at the institute.

There have been few people in my entire life to whom I owe a greater debt of gratitude than to Professor Lifshitz.

He took up cudgels for me once more before the appointment was made official.

On November 11th, after many months of delay, I finally presented my thesis to the Scientific Council of the Physics and Mathematical Department. The comments on it were marvelous; but the vote on my dissertation was cautious: nineteen in favor, five against, and one abstention. I shouldn't have been surprised in view of what was happening to other Jews who were trying to move ahead in the academic world.

Professor Lifshitz could not sit back and let this happen without any comment. When the time came for the final votes, cast by the Scientific Council of the entire university, he took the floor and openly criticized the decisions of those in the department council who had voted against the thesis. He maintained that this was perhaps the very best of all the dissertations that had been presented at the university since the War and said, moreover, that the unfavorable votes had nothing to do with any scientific reasons.

I will always remember that.

The negative votes cast by members of the faculty who wanted to be absolutely sure of their political safety did not prevent my receiving the candidate's degree.

Within less than two weeks, on November 23rd, I became a researcher at the Physical-Technical Institute. To me this was a kind of miracle. During my entire scientific life, I had done my research without receiving any money for it. On the contrary, I had paid out money, to have my papers typed and to get everything that was necessary for my work. I had paid with more than money. I had paid with my pride, because to have my papers published I had had to join with collaborators. Grateful though I was to them, I would have vastly preferred to work on my own, but no Soviet journal can publish anything without a certification from a research institute or university, stating that the paper contains no classified information. To obtain this imprimatur I absolutely had to have a co-author associated with such an institution.

Here I was, being paid a perfect fortune (according to my lights): over 170 roubles a month, and for nothing! Because even without a salary, I had always done and always would do this research.

I was absolutely happy. I was living in a dream. Everybody understood it, everybody — including the KGB.

* * *

In December, less than a month after I had settled in at the institute, I received a telephone call from someone who asked me to come and meet him in Room 105 of the Polytechnical Institute, only a step away from the Physical-Technical Institute. I didn't happen to recognize the caller's name, but I was by now accustomed to the fact that many physicists wanted to discuss their problems with me, and of course I was very glad to be consulted. I went right over.

When I arrived at Room 105 I found three men there. There was something about them that gave me a feeling they were not physicists. I can't put my finger on it: they were dressed like everyone else you saw around at the institutes, but there was something in their faces that differentiated them from the people I worked with. Maybe it was a deliberate absence of expression: so conscious an attempt to appear inconspicuous that it produced a masklike effect.

This was my first meeting with the KGB.

Later I found that all KGBsts are very much alike; they all have this sort of stamp on them. Not long ago I discovered that this identifiable aura surrounding plainclothesmen is not confined to Soviet members of the profession. When the scientific adviser to the President of the United States took me to the White House and showed me around, I was astonished to see among the visitors faces of that very same type.

"Won't you sit down?" suggested the man who apparently was the senior of the three. I took a chair at the opposite end of the table.

The men introduced themselves, providing me only with their first names and patronymics. (This convention later became familiar to me — it would be very rare for a KGBst to give you his full name.) "We're from the KGB."

I'll have to admit I was on edge.

"Well, now, Mark Yakovlevitch," the chief among them began, "how do you like it at the Physical-Technical Institute?"

"I like it very much."

"Everything there suits you all right? Salary adequate?"

"Yes, everything is all right."

"Is there anything you need?"

"Oh, no." There was a little more of such chitchat, and then a pause. I lit a cigarette.

"Let me ask you something, Mark Yakovlevitch," the chief resumed in a new tone. "Have you ever heard of two organizations called the 'Lopes' and the 'Antelopes'?"

No Soviet person with his wits about him, no matter how inexperienced he might be with the methods of the KGB, could fail to realize that such a question could only be a trap. Operating on an automatic instinct that warned me not to provide them with the slightest material from which they could fashion this teen-agers' intellectual toy into a weapon, I calmly answered, "No."

"At the Kharkov Library? A discussion group?" I didn't answer. "In nineteen forty-seven and nineteen forty-eight, didn't you belong to a group, a circle that called itself the 'Antelopes'?"

"I can hardly remember everything I was doing when I was in high school; that's quite a while ago. I don't recall much about my school days."

My interlocutor prodded my memory for at least twenty minutes before he gave up this line of inquiry. In the course of this questioning I realized what the point was: that, if necessary, they could prove that I had belonged to that circle, and again, if necessary, they could by means of their peculiar and clumsy sleight-of-hand transform that long-extinct group into a subversive organization. One often heard of such grotesque inventions. Thus they would manufacture a blot on my copybook.

When I had repeatedly mentioned how little I recalled from my schooldays, how vague my recollections were, the KGBst finally changed the subject. (This one man did most of the talking; the others only occasionally asked questions of their own. I believe that the principal reason these people seldom conduct interviews alone is that they have to check on each other.) He had never lost his temper with me, despite my uncooperative stance, and now he became positively friendly.

"What we wanted to tell you," he began, "is that we need your help. You are working at a very important technical institute. You can easily understand that this institute may be of great interest to the enemies of this country. Enemies may be everywhere — including in the very institute itself. You can see how essential it is for us to have information about the people here. Even about people at the very top."

This was undoubtedly a vexing problem for the KGB. It was difficult for them to recruit informers from among the senior scientists — they could hardly have summoned one of them over to this room for a talk like the one we were having now — and the junior members of the institute staff would be of little use in the capacity of observers. Most of them were only on formal terms with their superiors.

"We are not asking very much of you. We just want you to give us a little information about what's going on in the institute. You know, if you hear any anti-Soviet talk . . . Just the general picture of how things are running. We want to be of help here. You understand, that's what we're here for."

I would have given anything to be able to tell them how much I loathed them. But of course I had to swallow my bile. I answered that certainly, I understood how essential their work was; certainly I understood how important the institute was; and that if I saw anything I felt to be dangerous to our national security I would inform them about it at once.

"Oh, no, Mark Yakovlevitch," the chief answered. "It doesn't work that way. *You* can't judge. You see, we are trained to judge this kind of thing; we can tell what is dangerous and what is not — you'd have no way of knowing."

"I wonder if you realize," one of the others added, "that if you're not willing to help us, we feel that means you're against us. A person who

does not care to assist in the work of the Soviet regime . . . well, people like that simply can't be employed in an institute of this caliber.
There are classified laboratories here, you know."

"My own particular work is not classified."

The KGBsts stared at me, as if I had said something unanswerably
stupid.

I proceeded, explaining that I was very bad in human relations; that I
never really did make contact with people. I said I was so immersed in
my work that I never noticed what anyone was doing around me. I
poured out a lot of nonsense; anything I could think of. My only aim
was to get rid of these men. I was definitely frightened; I knew this was
no joke. But I had found out once or twice before that it was under conditions of real danger that my mind worked fastest.

It never once crossed my mind that I might ally myself with the KGB.
Afraid though I was of them, I was more afraid of losing my self-
respect; of losing my life as a decent person. Had I decided to cooperate
with them just for the time being, or to affect to cooperate, there would
have been no escape from them. Such an association would be a burden
to me under which I knew I would not be able to live. The fear I had of
them was much less than the fear I had had all my life of betraying my
own conscience.

"I'm very sorry," I said. "I feel I really can't be of any help to you. I
am just not the sort of person you need in this capacity."

"Well, now," said one of the men who had not spoken before. "Why
don't you think it over for a few days? We'll meet again."

The next several days I spent in a state of nerve-wracking suspense. I
didn't "think it over," needless to say, but passed the time under a constant strain. It was increased by my poor memory for faces. I never
remember anyone very well from a first meeting, so every time someone
approached me on the street or on the institute grounds in those days I
would think, Is that one of "them"? On the following Thursday, it really was one of the agents who met me as I was leaving the building. He
fell into step beside me.

"Have you considered what we were discussing last week, Mark
Yakovlevitch?" he asked.

I realized the situation would never come to an end unless I myself
put an end to it. I told the agent that I had given a great deal of thought
to their proposal. I told him that I could not work on my research
because of all these thoughts; that I had come to the institute in order to
do research; and that if I could not perform it because of being distracted by their demands, I would not be an asset to the institute.

"This is our last meeting," I said. "I have not the kind of character that would be useful to you for the investigations you have in mind. I am perfectly aware that you can have me fired, and if you do not consider me good enough for the work I am presently engaged in, then of course you will demand that I be removed from the staff. But nothing else can be changed."

I knew well that, by committing myself to that statement, I had become their enemy. I was prepared to be fired without much delay. Days passed; then weeks. I heard nothing from anybody about plans to dismiss me. After a long interval, it occurred to me that since Kurchatov had expressed an interest in my work, and Sinelnikov had arranged for me to be hired, the KGB was probably reluctant to have a run-in with those powerful men.

That was the end of those meetings. I thought at the time that I would never see those gray people again.

Landau and Kapitza

I REMAINED at the institute and pursued my research. That year, 1955, was one of the most fruitful in my scientific life. I was full of ideas, and within a short time made two new discoveries concerning what are called resonance phenomena. I had the luck to predict a new kind of resonance, a prediction that followed from the further development of the ideas which were the foundation of my candidate's thesis.

At the beginning of 1956, Landau came for a visit to Kharkov — his first visit since 1937. This was naturally a triumphant event among the scientists there, to become hosts to this great man. It was decided that the most interesting research being done at the Physical-Technical Institute should be presented to Landau, and one of those scheduled to describe his work to Landau was myself. I was told that I would have a chance to speak, and that I would have fifteen minutes in which to elucidate my discovery.

The day came. It was tremendously exciting. We were all assembled in a large conference room; the audience consisted of all the leading scientists of the institute; and there, in the center, was Landau himself, with Lifshitz at his side.

Landau was a tall thin man in his mid-forties with a thick shock of black hair; he looked much younger than his years and seemed to radiate a field of energy. His black piercing eyes noticed everything. He spoke very fast and gesticulated expressively to make a point.

When my talk came onto the agenda, I got up and started to describe my theory. I was barely launched when Landau, who had been listening very attentively, interrupted and voiced an objection to what I was saying. He was famous for the speed and bluntness with which he dismissed ideas that struck him as mistaken. Now he was evidently under the impression that mine was just a surface approach, a very unsophisticated approach, and almost certainly the results would be in error.

I was very young at that time; highly impulsive and emotional. Immediately, I was in a perfect fury. I forgot that this was the famous Landau, and started shouting. A friend of mine described the scene to me afterward: "I wish you could have seen yourself. You went bright red — under all that red hair — while Lifshitz" (who was my sponsor) "went perfectly white with alarm. Everyone was aghast." It certainly was lucky for me that it was Landau, and not some other great man more concerned with the offense to his own status than with the subject under discussion. He paid no attention whatsoever to the style of my replies to his objection. Only the essence of them mattered to him. Very attentive, very perceptive, he instantly understood everything I was saying.

Landau was one of the best physicists I ever knew; one of the best in the world. I'm afraid I'm repeating myself, but, having spent seven years of my working life under the spell of this extraordinary mind, it is hard not to.

Instead of the fifteen minutes allocated for my presentation, two hours went by. At the end, Landau declared himself to be almost persuaded. He said he was very glad to have heard about this work. "Let's continue the discussion tomorrow."

The following day I again took the floor, and again we talked for half the morning. At the conclusion, Landau declared himself to be absolutely convinced by my arguments and said that he considered the theory extraordinarily interesting and profound. He invited me to his seminar in Moscow and asked me to give a talk there.

I don't have to say how happy I was.

Nineteen fifty-six seemed to open with a clear sky for me, and for the whole country. For the first time in my life, I had been requested to go on *kommandierovka* (a professional or business trip sponsored by one's institute or office). This was to Moscow, to the most important seminar in the Soviet Union. It was all like something I might have dreamed. I didn't have to bear the expenses of the trip; the money was granted to me by the institute. The administration made all the travel arrangements. I went in style, in a coupé, a luxury I had enjoyed only once before.

After one night of travel (I must say I wasted no time in sleeping; I was too filled with excitement), here I was in Moscow. On previous visits I had stayed either with my aunt or with one of Father's brothers, who lived on the edge of the city occupying with his large family two rooms, in a little wooden house so dilapidated that it eventually collapsed. This time, being in the capital on behalf of the institute, I was put up in the unaccustomed splendor of a room reserved for me at the Academy hotel.

Having checked in there, I hurried over to the Institute for Physical Problems, founded by the legendary Pyotr Leonidovitch Kapitza. Kapitza himself was no longer young at the time of its founding, and already had accomplishments in physics to his name that had won the admiration of scientists all over the world. Soon after the Revolution, he had left Russia for England (in the 1920s, the Soviet authorities were eager to have their talented people go abroad to learn Western science and technology). It was the famous Ioffe who insisted upon Kapitza's being sent away from home, which was a very good thing. It may have saved Pyotr Leonidovitch's sanity — perhaps his life. Both of his parents, his young wife, and small children had been carried off by the epidemic during the First World War. He was in a state of shock; it would have been really hard for him to go on living where all this happened.

Upon his arrival in Cambridge he went to see Ernest Rutherford, the most eminent of all English physicists, and asked if he might be taken on as his student. Rutherford answered: "I already have twelve students. I'm sorry to have to turn you away, but I can't accept anyone else."

"I've read that you maintain the accuracy of your experiments is usually around ten percent," answered Kapitza. "Whatever happens, it would not alter your usual accuracy if you took on one more student." On the basis of that answer — not only witty but knowledgeable — he was accepted. Rutherford early realized that he might well have the most potential of all.

In the 'twenties Kapitza started to make devices with some industrial application. His magnets were so big and powerful that it was a matter for discussion at one time as to whether they might not be extremely dangerous and trigger some natural catastrophe. Kapitza had made the leap from the laboratories of the nineteenth century, using very simple devices, to modern science. These early magnets may be the "grandfathers" of the famous Tokamak magnetic confinement system, presently in use in fusion energy experiments.

One can imagine Kapitza's feelings, when he came back to Russia for what he assumed would be a short visit, upon realizing that he was in a police state unexampled even in the time of Nicholas I. It was explained to him shortly after his return that he would not be allowed to leave. Prayerfully, he wrote to Rutherford, hoping that the latter would read between the lines and insist that he come back to England; that there was much more for him to learn. But Rutherford wrote back, saying that despite his desire to have Kapitza in his laboratory, he considered the decision of the Soviet authorities justified: of course in such an undeveloped country, they had a right to demand the services of so valuable a scientist. Kapitza was forced into the gilded cage, and never left the Soviet Union again, until, when he was very old, he was permitted a few visits abroad.

He was offered every possible compensation for his detention in Russia. Everything he requested to have done for him was done. He got his own institute, planned just as he wanted; even the apartments that were to house himself and his colleagues just opposite the institute were designed according to his specifications. These are duplex apartments, to be found at that time nowhere else in the country. The buildings are located in a park, as in England. Kapitza himself had a two-story, multi-room house in the institute park, with a fireplace and other luxuries unheard of in Russia.

In a sense, Kapitza was one of the most powerful men in the U.S.S.R. Few other scientists would have had the influence — and none would have had the courage — to protest Landau's imprisonment and achieve the miracle of his release at the time of the Purge.

It is interesting to follow the lives of these two outstanding personalities, Kapitza and Landau. The reason I am so anxious to write about those aspects of their careers which are not generally known is that within a few decades those who knew these great men will no longer be among the living, and no one in Russia will ever have a chance to write anything about them outside the standard official biographies.

Kapitza, after being undisputed dean of Soviet science from the time of his return from Cambridge onward, went under a cloud during the 'forties. Even after he and I came to know each other quite well, I never ventured to ask him what happened at that time, but it is widely believed in the international scientific community that Beria requested him to work on the atomic bomb, that he refused, and this was the cause for his long house arrest. (There was even a rumor that Beria attempted to punish Kapitza for his insubordination with the death sentence, but that Stalin would not sign the order for execution.) It was not a very strict arrest — it meant only that he was denied access to the institutes and laboratories — but even so it cramped his work considerably, and until Beria's death his research was very much confined.

Once released, Kapitza was immediately restored to his former eminence. Again, any demands he might make were met. He insisted that there be no Otdyel Kadrov (the department that chooses the collaborators or assistants for the scientists; it consists mostly of KGB officials) at his institute. He himself would appoint the scientists. Furthermore, he firmly requested that he should not have to have any dealings with the man who had gladly accepted the directorship of the institute during his house arrest, Academician Alexandrov (now President of the Soviet Academy of Sciences). He refused to meet Alexandrov under any circumstances. Finally, he wanted the right to allocate funds where he thought they were needed, without interference from anywhere.

Even in minor details Kapitza followed his own line. Once, returning to the institute after an absence, he was surprised to see how dirty and untidy the courtyard was. He asked to see the yard man, the *dvornik*. Along came not one dvornik but three. All of them were supposed to keep the walks and grass plots clean. They earned absolutely miserable salaries, so none of them was afraid of Kapitza. The institute needed them, but they certainly didn't need the institute; it would be easy enough to get another job paying the same slave wage. Kapitza looked at them, singled out one, and said to the other two: "All right, you two men are fired, and you" — indicating the man he had chosen — "you'll be paid the wage of all three. But the courtyard must be clean." It was a terrible violation of the prevailing economic discipline, but Kapitza was Kapitza.

The dvornik began to take pride in his unique position, and thereafter the institute grounds were beautifully kept.

* * *

I entered the famous gates of the Institute for Physical Problems at least an hour early; passed by a long complex of splendid apartments, in one of which Landau lived; and walked up the broad steps of the institute building. I came into a large hall and stood there for a moment. I cannot convey how deeply impressed I was. It seemed to me that in this marvelous building I breathed the very air of Science. This was indeed the clearest, freshest air of science in the whole country, Kapitza having fought so stubbornly against the restrictions and supervisions that hamstring other Soviet institutes and universities.

Landau's seminar was supposed to start at eleven A.M.; but when I had waited and looked around for almost an hour, I was still the only person in the hall, and I began to be nervous. Maybe I hadn't understood; maybe I had got the wrong time? I didn't know then that the seminar started at eleven sharp — just on the dot; not a minute before the hour nor a minute later. This very un-Russian promptness was due to Kapitza's influence; in England he had picked up the concept of the "courtesy of kings," and had never drifted back into the less precise habits of his native land.

Just before the clock struck, a crowd of scientists, all of them men whose work I had known and admired for years, appeared, almost simultaneously, as if by magic. Here was Landau himself, the great

"Dau." One of my lifetime treasures is a copy of his famous textbook, *Theoretical Physics,* with an inscription to me on the flyleaf — this is about the most valuable object I own — and his signature in bold characteristic handwriting, just *Dau.*

Then came Academician Igor Tamm, a short man, with a face like a boiled potato. He was a great and good man. He was the first to fight for the restoration of the science of genetics, at a time when it was still hardly safe to discredit Lysenko.

Next came Academician Alexander Leontovitch, as tall as Landau; a genial-looking man, who, when he saw me and asked who I was, came over to greet me very warmly. "I've heard a lot about you," he said; I was tremendously gratified. Academician Leontovitch was not only a highly gifted physicist but was known as "the conscience of the Soviet Academy"; a man of extraordinary principle and integrity.

With him was Academician Zeldorovitch, three times recipient of the Hero of Socialist Labor Award, the supreme decoration in the Soviet Union.

I was introduced next to Ivan Vassilyevitch Obreimov: short, with a huge black walking stick, his "trademark." Having spent some years making up for starvation in the prison camp, he was rather fat. Accompanying him was Academician Vitali Ginsburg, a prolific contributor to the scientific journals — Landau jokingly accused him of being a "graphomaniac" — very brilliant, and familiar with many areas of science.

There was a group of Landau's junior colleagues: Yevgeny Lifshitz, brother of Professor Ilya Lifshitz and collaborator with Landau on the great series of textbooks. He was an editor of the *Journal of Experimental and Theoretical Physics;* brilliant and decisive. He talked so fast it was often hard to keep up with what he was saying. He introduced me to Khalatnikov.

Khalatnikov's appointment to the institute was somewhat accidental. Not long before, Landau had been criticized for the preponderance of Jews on his staff. When this man was recommended to him, a recent and promising graduate of the doctoral program at one of the provincial universities, Landau invited him to Moscow in the hope of providing himself with what you might call a "token" Gentile. The Russian name notwithstanding, Khalatnikov turned out to be Jewish too! Of course, under the circumstances, Isaak Khalatnikov stayed on, and eventually became Director of the Landau Institute for Theoretical Physics.

This was unusual: in all of Russia there were very, very few Jewish directors of institutes. The ace that Khalatnikov held was his wife. She was the daughter of one of the most publicized heroes of the Civil War, Nikolai Shchors. In actual fact, Shchors, Khalatnikov's father-in-law, had been the commander only of a platoon. He was killed at the front. Other famous commanders, including victorious generals, who had not had the good luck to be killed in action, were later stripped of all their honors, charged with treason, and executed by Stalin — I can think of only two who escaped this fate. But Shchors, safely dead, was posthumously a great national hero. Khalatnikov had Shchors's Golden Sable hanging on his living-room wall — he never let anyone forget whom he was related to — and he had the respect of the Party officials.

Another at that seminar was stout, round Alexei Abrikosov. A diplomat, he always knew what to say, where to say it, and in what manner. He was the son of an Academician and was descended from a famous Russian merchant family who for generations ran a huge fruit-importing business until the Revolution; despite the passage of time you could still see the faded remnants of their advertisements on old buildings in Moscow.

And here was Igor Dzyaloshinsky. He had a severe stutter; he talked slowly, with long painful pauses, so his rare lectures were something of an ordeal to listen to. But his knowledge of physics was very profound. All of these men were still young; they were all Landau's disciples.

We were joined by one of the other really famous luminaries of Soviet science: Isaak Pomerenchuk, then still Corresponding Member of the Academy of Sciences but soon to be full Academician. He turned out to be a tiny little man, wearing an old coat with a large ink stain on it, of which he was sublimely unaware. Later, when I met his wife, I was struck by the contrast they provided one to the other: she was one of the most beautiful women in Moscow, and always elegantly turned out.

Among the last to arrive was Lev Gorkov, a man of aristocratic appearance: thin, tall, with straight neat hair; very reserved in his behavior. When he and the excitable Landau talked together, a stranger to the scene would have been confused as to which of the two was the senior in authority: Gorkov, always calm and assured; Lev Davidovitch, talking with his hands, as he always did, and vociferously ringing every possible change to prove the point he was making.

Finally I met Leonid Keldysh, nephew of the President of the Academy of Sciences, a bright scientist with a brilliant future ahead of him.

Everyone was here. Aside from the Moscow scholars, there were about two hundred physicists from all over the country.

I would have been somewhat daunted by the prospect of speaking before this extraordinarily distinguished assemblage if I had not been aware of Landau's firm support. Even the equipment, the "props," in the conference room were formidable. There was a platform, much like a theatrical stage. The speaker had the use of three huge blackboards, the central one of which, at the touch of a button, expanded to three times its original size — a very unusual device at that time. There was a spotlight. There were curtains that opened and closed mechanically. There was a long table and a single chair on stage — Kapitza's chair. He was the only one who ever occupied this chair during those famous seminars; if he was not present, it remained empty. Landau always sat in the front row.

When I found myself on this platform, I was a little tense for a minute or two; but after the first question from the floor I became absorbed in my subject, the behavior of electrons in metals, and forgot everything except what I was talking about. I had been accorded two hours, rather than the regular one. Landau was on my side throughout the presentation — he always appreciated quick and precise answers, which I had the faculty of giving — and he was warm in his congratulations when the proceedings were over.

After the seminar, I was invited to give a talk at Kapitza's seminar the following week. I was perfectly happy.

The second occasion was very similar to the first one, and there I met Kapitza for the first time. The honor of speaking before this great man — stoutish, graying, completely unselfconscious as he settled himself into his conspicuous seat, hitching up the knees of his trousers and revealing an expanse of long blue winter underwear as he did so — was something that until recently I would never have anticipated.

Thereafter my appearances at the Institute for Physical Problems became regular. I was invited to keep them abreast of the discoveries on which I was working. About once a month or once every six weeks I journeyed to Moscow for this purpose. Of course one cannot see oneself from the outside, but there must have been something a little flamboyant about my style of lecturing; it amused Landau, who called me "the traveling road show from Kharkov."

While I am on the subject of the Landau seminars, I have to mention the one I attended some years later at which Niels Bohr spoke.

Bohr was at that time a very old man, and no greater accolade could have been paid Landau than for his great teacher to travel all the way from Copenhagen in order to make what was actually a ceremonial appearance at his most famous pupil's institute. The crowd that attended was almost the biggest of any in the institute's history, and the most impressive. Even members of the Supreme Soviet were present to pay respects to Niels Bohr. It was there that I first met Academician Sakharov.

Bohr spoke in English (which has replaced German for some decades as the lingua franca of science), and Yevgeny Lifshitz, who served as permanent interpreter at the Landau seminars, translated for him. Lifshitz was a brilliant interpreter. He didn't provide a word-for-word translation, but waited for the end of a statement, several minutes of talk, and then produced a brief, succinct, very concentrated précis of what had been said. He was famous for one funny lapse: he was once at a seminar where the speaker was Russian and spoke in Russian; but Yevgeny Lifshitz was so accustomed to being interpreter that after a while he interrupted the lecturer and "translated" — gave a short but perfectly comprehensive summary of what the man had said. He expressed himself much better than the original speaker had — and got a round of applause!

On this present occasion, Lifshitz was concentrating very seriously and, like anyone who is thinking too hard, was apt to make minor mistakes. One of the questions addressed to Bohr was: "How do you account for the incredibly high productivity that has emerged from your school? How do you account for the fact that almost all of your students have gone on to become Nobel laureates?" Modestly, speaking slowly, Niels Bohr replied: "Well . . . I think it happened because we were never cautious. We were never afraid to look like fools before our students." Yevgeny Lifshitz quickly pronounced his translation: "It happened because we were never afraid to let our students know they were fools." We all roared with laughter.

As a matter of fact, this was the main difference between the Bohr and the Landau schools of physics. Landau's seminar was a very tough school. When a lecturer (and this may have been a famous professor who had traveled thousands of miles to appear) took the podium, the a priori assumption was that he was going to make mistakes; that he was probably a fool. If he did not succeed within fifteen minutes in disproving the challenges posed by the audience — mainly by the first row — he had to yield to the next lecturer. This situation created the widely held view that Landau was egregiously tactless.

There is an explanation for that. In the Soviet Union it was too important never to make mistakes. So much depended on it; and although Landau certainly could not be considered in the least "Soviet" in his thinking, nevertheless I believe he was unwittingly the product of the Soviet system in his own behavior. This was advantageous in some ways, but at the same time had its drawbacks. There is a saying to the effect that Soviet physicists solve those problems which can be solved in a way they *should* be solved; whereas Western scientists solve those that should be solved any way they *can* be solved. It is significant, I think, that not one single fundamental breakthrough has been made in Russia. It's not owing to an absence of talent — Landau was definitely among the most talented physicists of his time. His critical mind enabled him to find mistakes that were unnoticeable to others. Literally hundreds of scientists came from all over the world to hear his opinions and advice; the weekly seminars were always as crowded as that first one I attended. The check-rein on Soviet science was an excess of caution in the solution of problems.

But Landau's strict perfectionism enabled him to sponsor hundreds of physicists; there was never any doubt about the caliber of anyone whom he was willing to back. At his seminars, if a scientist failed to field the challenges Landau and his disciples threw at him, the speaker was simply ignored when he melted back into the crowd and was left to ponder his mistake. But if he returned to a later session armed with proof that he had corrected his error, Landau was very kind to him and most appreciative. Still, it took a strong person to be willing to subject himself to this trial, particularly more than once.

Thaw and Frost

To CELEBRATE, and to relax after my first taxing appearance at Kapitza's seminar, I hurried off to what was my favorite recreation in Moscow: seeing the museums. I looked forward to visiting the by now familiar and well-loved exhibits at the Tretyakovsky and at the Pushkin Museum of Fine Arts. This time, however, I was astonished to see something completely new to me. Incredibly — there were Impressionist paintings in the Fine Arts, a loan exhibition from Dresden.

To my generation, which had never seen or even heard of the long-since-discarded works of Van Gogh, Renoir, and Degas (not to mention those of Chagall and Kandinsky), nothing could have been more astounding, more daring, than these paintings. People were fascinated: there was an endless waiting line outside the museum.

In 1956, there was an almost millennial atmosphere in the air. Khrushchev had delivered his famous talk about the real Stalin, the talk that was nowhere published but everywhere known, and we moved into what felt like a new era. It was a time of great hope. Books, for example, that could never have been published before, were emerging from the presses. One of them in particular became very popular: Dudintsev's *Not by Bread Alone*. Not remarkably great as literature, but it was an honest book: simply the story of an inventor, in which all the tortures he goes through in his fight with the bureaucracy are described. This was the first book published since the 'thirties in which a Soviet citizen could read about the bureaucracy that he met in real life at every step. Dudintsev created a tremendous sensation; subsequently, when the false dawn of intellectual freedom had darkened again, he was never forgiven for his book and has never published a word in the Soviet Union since that time.

But in 'fifty-six, few people could have anticipated a renewal of our national Dark Age.

Another book published at that time was Ehrenburg's *People, Years,*

Life. This is autobiographical. Of course, Ehrenburg could not say everything he wanted to, but the names that were mentioned in the book were those of writers, painters, sculptors, who had been condemned — or, rather, simply erased from the roster of artists who could be mentioned in our country. Moreover, Akhmatova's work began to appear again.

The same loosening of bonds was true for painting. Not everybody knows that Russia was one of the first countries to accept Impressionism and to start a modern school. Two Russians of enormous wealth had, just before the turn of the century, collected a great many paintings by Van Gogh, Matisse, Degas, Manet, and others who were not recognized by their own countrymen at that time. Many years ago there was in Moscow a Museum of Modern Art, but under Stalin all its treasures were removed. Ironically enough, it became a place of display for the gifts that poured in to Stalin from all over the world: automobiles, Chinese ivories, tapestries — thousands of votaries' offerings. This was now a shrine to the god, and the paintings were hidden in the cellar.

Even before Stalin came to power, Lenin got rid of priceless works of art. It was Lenin who sold Velázquez' *Venus with a Mirror* for a paltry three million roubles, which shortly, at that time of disastrous inflation, were hardly worth the paper they were printed on. He built with the proceeds a small brick factory that became obsolete almost before it was finished. Under Stalin there was an actual crusade against art, and, like everyone else of my generation, I knew absolutely nothing about it.

There were not a great many paintings in these new exhibitions, and there was nothing dating from later than 1900; yet I was amazed. To my eyes, these pictures appeared to be done in colors that didn't exist in the real world. Here was a landscape with trees — but where were the individual leaves? The artists were so careless that you could distinctly see daubs of color, splashed on with an overcharged brush, and simply left there. I couldn't accept these paintings.

In the entry hall of the Pushkin Museum was a visitor's book in which one could write his opinion of the show. It was full of negative criticisms. Most of the comments were completely sincere. During the entire Soviet regime, people had been taught that any art is supposed to be easily accessible. "Art serves the people" was the motto. Painting, sculpture, or music should be understood at first glance or at first hearing. If one failed to appreciate it without the least concentration or attention, then it was not art. Several generations of Soviet people, brought up on this idea, were forcibly made illiterate. And I was among them.

I was accustomed to studying paintings very close up and admiring the fine details: the distinctly wrought branches, the very veins and the shading from tone to tone in a single leaf, the exact color, shape, and size of a pearl, the tracery of a lace collar. Just by chance, before I left, I happened to be standing in the center of one of the exhibition halls, idly scanning the pictures from a distance to see if there might possibly be anything worthwhile that I had overlooked.

But standing, as I was, at a distance from a Monet, I received a novel view. All the spots of color in the painting disappeared. Suddenly there were trees and people — very vivid. I was astonished.

It was only in the train, on my way back to Kharkov, that I started thinking over everything I had seen. The route from Moscow to Kharkov is very green in spring; and all of a sudden I realized that what I was seeing from the window was the very same as what I had seen that afternoon at the museum. There were trees bent by the wind, and I observed for the first time that you don't see the separate leaves when they are moving. From that distance the foliage had become like green moss, marvelous in its color and varied shapes. I discovered for myself that every generation sees with the eyes of its great painters. We had been artificially kept generations behind.

On my return to Kharkov I made inquiries among my older acquaintances as to whether any of them might still have reproductions of paintings dating from this strange era. Finally I found someone on the university faculty who owned a book on Impressionist painting: it was Dr. Rosentzweig, who had had the courage to preserve this book throughout the waves of persecution, searches, and purges. He gave it to me, and I mention his name here with gratitude. He died not long afterward.

After studying the survey of Impressionist painting, I went back to the museums with a new appreciation for these artists. It was funny to realize that we Soviet viewers had reacted to them exactly as their French contemporaries had, almost a century before.

*   *   *

Everything appeared to be opening up; horizons were expanding. I can't exaggerate the sensation when the first Westerners to visit the country in years arrived: members of the International Youth Congress, performers in the Tchaikovsky Competition, and other musical figures. The queues outside the concert halls and theaters began to form twenty-four hours before tickets went on sale; people brought blankets and spent the night in the streets. Russians were starved for contacts outside the Soviet Union. Just to feel themselves a part of the modern world, a few young people, even in Kharkov, started wearing berets and narrow trousers. (This departure from the sartorial norm gave rise to tremendous indignation on the part of such publications as *Komsomolskaya Pravda.* With the tacit approval of the authorities, roaming gangs armed with scissors attacked the *stilyagi* — the "fashion plates" — on the streets, slashing their modish pants and ripping off their caps. I myself, although I had never given a moment's thought to clothes, was so angry at this barbarity that I too got a beret and a pair of Western-style trousers, to throw down a challenge to the hooligans. Fortunately or unfortunately, they never did approach me.)

Notwithstanding stubborn attempts to stem it, foreign influence continued to expand. Under special circumstances, one could now see fragments of European or American movies. With very few exceptions, Soviet films were excruciatingly dull, so this was a much-sought-after treat.

Somewhat further along during the "thaw," really contemporary art was briefly on display. It must be hard for the Western reader to imagine the excitement this caused. When at the exhibition Nikita Khrushchev loudly voiced his opinion that abstract painting was "dog shit," and the great sculptor Ernst Neizvestny who was present, took the fantastic risk of telling the General Secretary to his face that "the cobbler should stick to his last"; that Khrushchev had better confine his comments to politics — shock waves of astonishment and admiration went through the entire literate community. Neizvestny, though a much-decorated war hero, never displayed more courage than he did on that occasion. It was only by a fluke that Khrushchev did not retaliate as one would expect a Russian autocrat to do: he confined himself to shouting that Neizvestny should be thrown out of the country, but he never followed up this threat. There is something almost touching in the fact that Khrushchev left instructions in his will that the designer of his tombstone should be Neizvestny.*

Not only literature and painting, but the theater came to new life, and this too was exciting after decades of boring plays on the theme of the excellence of Soviet life. Everyone in Moscow flocked for tickets

* Khrushchev was always apt to make blunders when he ventured into the realm of the arts. Once President Tito and his wife came on a state visit to Moscow, and the General Secretary showed them around the Hermitage Museum. When Madame Tito expressed enthusiastic admiration for a diadem of Scythian gold, Khrushchev took it out of its case and pressed it upon her: "Please accept it, Madame!" The museum curator, who told me the story, almost fainted and had to summon every ounce of his nerve in order to say: "I beg your pardon, Nikita Sergeyevitch — but the diadem belongs to the people; you cannot give it away." "Oh, I suppose that's true," said Khrushchev and reluctantly returned the object to its place.

to the Sovremennik or Taganka theaters, where works were being produced in which at least a glimmering of our reality was reflected. People held their breath, wondering what new risks playwrights and producers would take with the censors (it was very much *de bon ton* among the intelligentsia to know the "inside stories" of dangerous battles between authors and the censors). Shvartz's play *Dragon* actually ran for a month before the authorities closed it down — a play that, despite the décor heavy with swastikas so as to specify *which* tyranny was being condemned, would have meant exile or death to anyone associated with it in Stalin's time.

So new things appeared; and at the same time, very inconspicuously, some familiar landmarks disappeared. Walking through Dzerzhinsky Park in Kharkov one day, I noticed there was something empty about it. It took me a few seconds to focus on the reason for this bareness: the statues of Stalin were gone. Then, not long afterward, the huge pedestaled bust in the hall of the Physics and Mathematics Building, around which the honor guard had stood for so long in 1953, was gone. Stalina Prospect, near Teveleva Square, was suddenly Moscovsky Prospect. Stalin's portrait vanished from office walls. All these changes must have been made by night; neither I nor anyone I knew ever once saw the jobs in progress.

*　　*　　*

Having become a regular speaker at the Institute for Physical Problems meant inclusion for me in the freemasonry of science. There was no snobbery among the physicists here. Nobody cared that only yesterday I had been a student; nobody cared that I was very young, that my manners were not particularly polished, that I had never worn a tie.

By the time of which I am writing, physicists constituted a privileged caste, an aristocracy. There were fewer controls on our freedom than on those of any other member of Soviet civilian society. The only laws we felt restricted by were those relating to the conventions of scientific work. Relatively speaking, we were free people.

The new wind blowing through the country influenced even the scientific conferences. It was still 'fifty-six when it was announced that there would be an international scientific conference.

The Soviet Union had never before opened its doors to scientists from abroad this way, and there was a tremendous stir. A foreigner was still distinctly a *rara avis*. Everyone, even directors of the institutes, had an incredibly glorified concept of life in the West. We all assumed that Americans, at least, must live as luxuriously or better than the Russian nobles in Czarist days. The authorities were desperate to create a good impression, and suddenly a storm broke: a hurricane of pruning and clipping and raking all over the institute grounds, and cleaning and polishing inside the buildings. I have never seen so much bustle and scurrying around. Floors were waxed and gleaming. Tablecloths appeared in the institute dining rooms — something no one had ever thought of before. Most incredible of all — where were the blackbeetles and roaches? They disappeared from the kitchen and dining areas. No one could believe it; people had been complaining about them for years, but the kitchen staff always assured us that it was beyond mortal powers to get rid of them. By the time the visitors arrived, perfection had been achieved.

I was very glad to be present at two of these international conferences and to meet scientists from abroad whose work I had so much admired. It was here that I met for the first time Professor Freeman Dyson, one of the founders of modern science. He was a small man, dark, silent — much more inclined to listen than to talk. He astonished us all with his Western freedom of behavior: he arrived late once at one of the conferences and, noting that all the seats near him were taken, just sat on the floor. Everyone was very upset: anyone present would have gladly ceded Professor Dyson his chair, but he refused to disturb anybody. We were constantly surprised by the informality and approachability of these scientists.

When the presentations were over, we had a chance to talk a little. Professor Dyson had a fresh scar on one side of his nose, and mentioned that he had acquired it diving into a lake in Norway; he hadn't realized the water was already half-frozen, and he had been cut by the ice. This evidence of a far-ranging and sporting life was a revelation to us. We ourselves may have been considered in the Soviet Union a privileged caste, but, even more than the privileged castes under former Russian regimes, we were hobbled when it came to travel abroad. The very thought that Soviet physicists might be permitted to leave the country for purposes of broadening their science was still a novel one. Our guests were talking about freedoms that were absolutely impossible to us. They went all over Europe; some were right now on their way to Japan. Unbelievable.

Still, in many respects this was a relatively liberated and pleasant time in the Soviet Union.

Eventually, inevitably, something happened that made me understand that not much had really changed; that it could be dangerous to believe we were now freer to think and read what we liked. People had become less cautious, and this could lead to trouble.

Among the authors newly published during the next few years was

Ivan Bunin. Bunin was the first Russian writer to receive the Nobel Prize. He lived in France for years, having left the U.S.S.R. right after the Revolution. In the West, he was widely published both in Russian and in translation, but never after 1919 did his works appear in the Soviet Union, until the time of Khrushchev. As a very old man, he came home to see Russia for the last time in 1953 and died soon afterward.

When some of Bunin's books became available, a friend of mine in Kharkov (I am not giving his name here) read them, loved them, and wrote to the author's widow — a really beautiful letter in which he expressed his deep appreciation of Bunin. Madame Bunin, touched, sent him as a present a few of the later works of her husband, which naturally included some that had not as yet been published in the Soviet Union. These writings were not anti-Soviet; Bunin was not a politician — he was an artist. Nothing could be said against them, except that they were printed in the West, in Paris.

My friend was overwhelmed with gratitude at receiving such a gift. He read all the books and lent them to me. Unfortunately, not only to me; another of his acquaintances borrowed them before I did.

A week or two passed. Then one day, as I was arriving in the morning at the institute, I was met at the entrance by a short stout man in a brown suit who stopped me as I passed him on my way into the building.

He addressed me politely. "Mark Yakovlevitch. Would you be so good as to accompany me to this car?"

It was obvious to me at once who he was: one of "them." (In Russia everybody knows who "they" are.)

"KGB," he said. "Don't worry, please. Just step this way."

Nobody can decline this sort of invitation. It is not against the law to decline it, but the results are sure to be disastrous. So I went along with him, got into the car, and we drove off.

"Where are we going?"

"You'll see shortly."

Within a few minutes we were at the headquarters of the Kharkov KGB (the "Big House," as this place is always called in every city). It was a tall concrete building with very small windows, none of them lower than twelve feet from the ground. A uniformed man appeared at the door and handed me an entry pass, and, still escorted by the man in brown, I went inside.

I was led to a small office with high wire-grilled windows, furnished only with two chairs, a desk, and a safe. The man sitting at the desk was nondescript, perfectly ordinary looking — interchangeable with the

KGBsts who had interviewed me at the institute when I was first taken onto the staff there. He rose politely as I was ushered in.

"Sit down, Mark Yakovlevitch." He straightened out the documents on his desk and pushed himself back a little. "You know, of course, why you've been summoned."

"No, I don't."

"Oh, come on!"

"I haven't the slightest idea."

"Just think a bit."

"No. I don't know." Later, when I became more sophisticated in the ways of the KGB, I learned that this was a rather ordinary opening for an interrogation. The person being questioned, assuming he must be under close observation, will blurt out an account of yesterday's accidental encounter with a Western tourist or some other "crime" unknown to the KGB until that moment.

"I am in charge of conducting interrogations concerning crimes against the State," he finally said. "I have a few questions I want to ask you."

My mind raced, but I could not guess what might be coming.

The interrogator started with questions about the man who had lent me the Bunin books. I described him as a person of very good character, very honest and patriotic. The official wrote down this testimony and had me sign it. Then he provided himself with a fresh piece of paper and started a new line of questioning.

"Have you read Ivan Bunin's *On Chekhov*?"

"No, I haven't."

"Have you read the uncut version of *Dark Avenues* by the same author?"

"No, I haven't."

"Have you read *Memories and Days*?"

"No." The list of titles lengthened. These books were at that very moment on the table in my apartment. I hardly have to explain that if I had answered yes, the next question would have been "And where did you get them?" I was in danger, but the friend who had lent me the books was in still greater danger. I could only answer no, and again I was forced to sign an affidavit attesting to my denials.

Once the transcribing and signing was over, the interrogator leaned back, assumed the comfortable position of a man who is settling down for a good long talk, and said with a sigh: "And now — why don't you tell me the truth?"

I sat there, silent.

"We know that you've read these books. And we know that they are in your apartment."

I gathered my forces. "I don't know anything about it. I know very little about this author."

The interrogator got up and walked over to the safe. Inside was a stack of Bunin's books, which I recognized as my friend's collection — minus the copies he had lent me. My first reaction was to feel sick. How loathsome, how crazy, to see the works of this great man, acclaimed among the glories of Russian literature — books that had been translated into every European language and that everyone in the West may read and admire; works of pure art untainted by any politics — locked up here like illegal seditious propaganda or dirty pornography.

My second reaction was fear. I understood that there had been a search. They really knew the missing books were at my place, and they knew whence they had come. Where was my friend right now? What was happening to him?

"Mark Yakovlevitch," the KGBst said in a friendly tone, "it will be much better for you if you tell us the truth. Otherwise we will be obliged to go over to your apartment to round up some witnesses from your building, make a search of your rooms, find the books, and verify with the witnesses that you've been lying." (This is the standard method mandated by law: one's neighbors are dragooned into the role of witnesses for these staged searches and arrests so that no allegations of brutality or illegal activities can later be brought against the KGB.) "You can easily guess all the consequences."

I tried to think. I have never thought so hard in my life. Was there any way out of this? After they found the books, how could I avoid being forced to explain how they had come to be in my place?

"Well," I said, "presumably you have found these books. Presumably you know better than I do what books I have in my house. What does that prove? I have a lot of friends, a lot of visitors; there are people going in and out all the time. I don't keep track of what they bring with them, or what they might leave behind. It's perfectly possible that somebody forgot some of his things in my place — it happens all the time. That could be what occurred in this instance — if you're so sure those books are on my premises."

It was almost noon before he understood that I would not change my story on this point; such a statement, however unlikely, was impossible to disprove. Actually, the fact that he permitted me to reiterate my protestations suggested to me that he might not be planning to have me imprisoned. Something else was in the wind.

"All right," he said at last. "You just go home. Right now. Look around. You'll find those books." I got out of my chair, cramped from tension and from having been trapped so long in one place. I hesitated a moment. Rightly interpreting my unspoken query, he said: "Oh no; don't worry. No one will accompany you. We know you'll be back."

I left. My street was a twenty-minute tram ride from the KGB building. On the way to my apartment I realized that, of course, there were two men shadowing me all the time. I had to think fast on the way. I had to make a decision: I could burn those books, or I could bring them back to headquarters. It was a difficult decision to make. If I burned them, nobody would be able to prove that I had ever had them; I would be absolutely "clean." But I couldn't know what fate might have befallen my friend. I had no way of deducing whether he had been forced to admit he gave the books to me. If he had, my insistence that I had never seen them would complicate his situation, and the question would remain: Where are the Bunin works? What happened to them?

That is why within forty minutes after I came home I was again at the KGB building, with the books. The interrogator appeared to be delighted by my acquiescence, and he tried everything in his power to convince me that I should put it in writing that the books had been given to me, and to mention the name of the donor.

Not until nine P.M. was I allowed to leave his office, having refused over and over again to say where the books had come from. By the end of this session the KGBst had thrown off all pretense of civility, and as I left he said nastily: "Ach! If this were only a few years ago — we could have got you to testify that your grandmother had balls!" (Since Stalin's death, new regulations concerning the practice of torture had modified the methods of the KGB.) He ordered me to sit down in the corridor and wait.

In ten minutes a guard came and accompanied me to another room. It was obvious that the KGBst whose office this was, was much superior in rank to my original interrogator. Here was a huge room with two tables, one great long one and a smaller one set at right angles to it; many chairs around the larger one; and an impressive armchair at the other. (During the years that followed, these furnishings became only too familiar; it was the standard arrangement in such offices.)

The man in charge greeted me cordially. He got up and ushered me in, as hospitable as a friend of long standing. He offered me his hand. I hate to admit it, but I shook hands with him — I was a Soviet citizen, and I knew there were some offenses I couldn't afford to commit if I didn't want to be deprived of my science and my freedom.

"Let's sit down and talk, Mark Yakovlevitch," he urged. "I don't want to waste too much of your time; I'll come straight to the point.

I've been hearing about your conversation with my colleague here, and I am rather upset on your behalf. You've evidently been playing host to some of the wrong element in Kharkov, and you've been taking risks with the law, which can't do you any good. What is the sense of a man in your position behaving in such a way?" I made no answer. "You know, it's unreasonable for you to spoil your career at this juncture. All of us here consider you a most promising young scientist. You have quite a future ahead of you — I suppose you know that.

"Let me tell you something, Mark Yakovlevitch. It would be a real mistake for you to spoil relations with the KGB. We are behind you. We have your interests in mind." In a very smooth, fatherly manner he suggested that I admit the real facts about the books. But he didn't insist. He just criticized me mildly for not understanding which side my bread was buttered on; told me that I was just too young to realize what would be the most prudent course for me to take.

When I remained stubbornly silent, he said with an air of resignation: "Well — all right. These are petty things. I believe in you; I believe in your work. Here is what concerns me. Undoubtedly, it's going to be very important for you to go on missions abroad." Of course he knew only too well how much any scientist longed to go abroad. "Things are opening up these days; some scientists will be permitted to travel. You'll certainly want to have contacts with Western science; to keep in touch with what's going on outside of this country. I believe that's very important to physicists; isn't that right? You want to talk to Western scientists . . . Don't you?" I could not see any particular advantage to telling a lie in answer to this one; it would have been strange.

"Yes. I do."

He smiled. "Of course you do! And I understand it's a very good thing for people in your field to see what they're doing in other countries. I suppose you know that if you are a little bit reasonable, you may find yourself free to travel abroad at will." He leaned toward me; assumed a genial, confidential posture. "We don't want you to become a spy!" he said. "We don't want you to be distracted from your science. We are well aware of how dedicated you are to your work . . ." This was an obvious allusion to the conversations I had had previously with the KGB. "Here is what we are suggesting: something that will be no problem for you — nothing to divert you from your own interests. You have the reputation of being very perceptive to new things. The only thing we ask of you is — to be attentive. To be observant. To keep an eye on all the new scientific developments you encounter when you're abroad. To check on everything. You may not be fully aware of it yourself, but quite a lot of the research that's going on is of military importance. Naturally, your foreign colleagues, meeting such an eminent scientist as yourself, will probably be willing to be perfectly frank and open with you. What I mean is this: just be interested in everything. You already are. And when you come back, just give us a report. A detailed report. On everything you've seen."

It was not until I was offered this suggestion that I realized my friend who owned the Bunin collection was not the only target of this attack. The contraband books, in themselves, meant nothing to the KGB. Their aim was also to pin the commission of an illegal act on me and, once my guilt had been established, to use the record of my "anti-Soviet" behavior as a lever, or better, a goad with which to steer me into cooperation with them.

I had to start repeating what a solitary character I had and how impossible it was for me to think about different things at the same time. My interest was purely in science; I was unobservant, even blind, when it came to anything else.

Our conversation was prolonged until late into the night. I arrived home close to midnight. Throughout the rest of my life as a Soviet citizen, I was never once permitted to go beyond the Iron Curtain.

A Breath of Air

I DIDN'T forget this meeting. But certainly, I didn't live with it all the time. I had my science. I had my freedom — at least for the time being — and I made the best use of it I could.

That very summer of 'fifty-six, I had my first real vacation: thirty-six days with full salary.* I was still not accustomed to my new standard of living: incredible! To have a holiday, and to be royally paid for it! Moreover, in the fall I would have a lectureship at the Polytechnical Institute, a part-time position that added another 120 roubles to my earnings; so I would soon be making almost 400 roubles a month. I have earned a higher salary since but never felt so rich again: having no dependents at that time and few expenses, I could afford to be a little careless if I wanted — to take taxis, eat in restaurants, and so forth.

I packed a briefcase with little more than a toothbrush and left for a trip to the Baltic Republics, at the northwest corner of the U.S.S.R. I went alone. I wanted to see everything with my own eyes and not be either hindered or rushed by a companion; also, I didn't care about comfort, about what sort of accommodation I would find — I was perfectly willing to put up in hostels where a dozen people sleep in one room, or, if even that was unavailable, to spend a night in a railway station.

I visited all the places I thought would interest me. Two of them left the most pronounced impression: one very somber, but the other marvelous and uplifting.

The first was Kaliningrad (formerly Königsberg, in what had been Eastern Prussia). This city had been completely destroyed in the War. Not a single building over one story in height was left intact. There was almost nothing to be seen except for long brick walls. Every other per-

---

* In the Soviet Union absolutely everybody, regardless of rank, is paid in cash. Cash is the only medium of exchange: there are no checking accounts, no credit cards. One's taxes — in my case 10 percent of my earnings — are withheld automatically, at the source. I was very nearly in the top tax bracket. No one pays over 13 percent.

son you saw on the street was in Red Army uniform. It was a grim, defeated place. There were jungles of weeds and vines everywhere you looked. I learned that an elaborate old system of drainage and irrigation, which had been the engineering pride of Königsberg for a very long time, had been destroyed when the city was bombarded. No efforts had been made to restore it. The city was becoming a swamp: it had originally been built on a huge marsh, and now the water was seeping back. It was horrible to walk on the ruins amidst trees and greenery that were growing up where fine buildings had stood. You could see only bare traces of what had formerly been a prosperous city. I couldn't stand it for long, and took the train out of the city on the same evening of the day I arrived.

In the Baltic states nobody, aside from the personnel in cafés and restaurants and shops, who were accustomed to being polite to tourists, attempted to hide their hatred for Russians. This hostility was so virulent, you could actually feel it in the air. If you were lost and asked a passerby the way to Such-and-such Street, in Russian, the answer was typically "I don't speak Russian" — spoken in perfect Russian. People hated them; but it turned out they made a distinction between Jews and Russians. It was not long before I realized this, and it improved my chances of getting an answer if I prefaced my inquiries by saying right off: "Look, I'm not a Russian, I'm a Jew." They didn't like Jews, but at least they would speak to one.

Jews lived among them. Some had come here on vacation; others were survivors of the Holocaust. This was the only part of the world where I had ever heard Yiddish spoken on the streets. In Russia or in the Ukraine or in Siberia, people would be afraid to speak this language in public.

In Vilnius, I heard that there was a synagogue; so naturally I decided to visit it. When I arrived at the building, which had survived the Germans God knows how, I realized there was a service in progress; it was Saturday. I was most anxious to go inside — it would be the first occasion of religious worship I had ever observed in my life — but a ridiculous obstacle halted me. I remembered hearing that one is not allowed to enter a synagogue without some sort of head covering. And, of course, I didn't have a hat. There was no time to walk around and try to find a shop where I could buy a hat; the service might soon be over. Something had to be done.

First I tried to make a hat out of a newspaper. But I didn't succeed. Then I reconsidered the design and thought I would try to make a paper boat that, inverted, ought to make a perfectly good cap; as a child I had mastered the trick of making paper boats. But unfortunately, I had forgotten how it was done. Finally, in desperation, I looked through my briefcase, found a handkerchief, folded it as neatly as I could, and put it on my head. I went into the synagogue.

This was the first synagogue I had ever been in; all the synagogues in Kharkov were closed. Moreover, when some elderly Jews there tried to pray together according to their law, which entails gathering a *minyan* — at least ten men together — the police broke up the group and threatened the worshippers with charges of unlawfully conducting a religious service.

I observed the service with deep interest. The congregants repeated prayers that, even though I could not understand the words, were spoken with a fervor one could not fail to respond to.

For a while no one noticed my presence in the company, but eventually a few people became aware that there was a stranger among them and after the worship was over, a white-haired man approached to talk to me.

"Du bist ein Yid?" he asked. Because I had heard Yiddish spoken between my grandparents when I was little, I had picked up enough of the language to follow that simple phrase.

"Avade [Certainly]," I answered. But this just about exhausted my stock of Yiddish, and after a couple of further questions we started to speak Russian. When I told him where I was from, everybody else in the synagogue flocked around us to see a genuine Jew from the frightful Ukraine.

The event was a turning point in my life; I had never imagined anything like it. Suddenly I was among friends; friends unknown to me until that time. These people who had never laid eyes on me before crowded around, invited me to stay in their homes, offered me money to help with my travel expenses, extended the warmest possible hospitality. I had spent twenty-four years deprived of the right to belong to my own people. Here I was, warmly, unquestioningly, accepted among them.

I've never forgotten.

*   *   *

Back in Kharkov in September, I was ready to go on with my research and to embark upon my lectures at the Polytechnical Institute — the very same institute that had turned me down before. I enjoyed lecturing and always seemed to have a very attentive and responsive audience. I remember the only criticism I received for my teaching methods there: the director and several senior members of the faculty attended one of my classes once, as they routinely do to check upon an instructor's per-

formance, and at the cathedra following this class they were all generous in their praise for my lecture. "But you made one serious mistake,
Mark Yakovlevitch!" warned the director. "When the student asked
you the question about different types of semiconductors, you *never*
should have said you didn't know the answer." Most of my students
were experienced technicians and sometimes knew more than I, a theoretical physicist, about the practical aspects of their particular fields of
expertise. That day one of the men had asked me which of two sorts of
semiconductors was better, and, as I didn't have the faintest idea, I said
so.

"That's the one thing you should never do, to say 'I don't know,' "
the director emphasized. "You should tell your students they are supposed to know the answer and assign them the duty of finding the answer themselves."

A Soviet teacher not only always has to be right and cannot make
mistakes but has to be omniscient.

I didn't take this advice, either when I was teaching at the Polytechnical Institute or later. I believe my students have always given me
credit for this honesty. When I was a student myself I always sensed it
when an instructor tried to convey an impression that he knew something when he didn't.

*   *   *

The first renascence in Soviet history could be seen in everything. Not
only were there more international conferences in this country, but (as
the KGB chief had predicted in the course of my interrogation), Soviet
scientists began to travel abroad and attend conferences in the West,
something that had seemed completely impossible as recently as 1955.

Of course, specifically Soviet problems arose. The Geneva Conference
on Peaceful Uses of Atomic Energy meant that papers on nuclear physics had to be presented to Western scientists. There was a crisis. Which
of these papers could be declassified? It was an extremely important and
responsible task to make this decision. When the papers were considered for inclusion in the proceedings of the conference, it became clear
that most of them did not pass all five stages of declassification, which
they were supposed to before they were submitted for publication. But
it was impossible simply to cancel almost all the papers. Therefore a
decision was handed down from the very top: all papers that could be
cleared through the first *three* stages were to be O.K.'d for publication.

The papers were presented, were read, and were published in the
West. But when the conference was over, the papers still went through
the remaining two stages, and some of them didn't pass! This meant

they could not be published in the Soviet Union, even though they had already been circulated in the West. In other words, the Soviet scientific establishment was supposed to keep "secrets" from *itself,* although the information was in the public domain in the rest of the world. This is not a joke; it really happened.

* * *

So the renascence existed, but it was severely handicapped by the Soviet style of doing things.

Another sign of the times was that the first tourists left for the West. These people were hand-picked; and those who had the best chance of being permitted to travel were the party elite — and the poor and uneducated: peasants and workers. The officials knew that the latter class of Soviet citizen would not speak the language of any of the countries they visited, would have very little idea of what they were seeing, and would have a healthy fear of the international bourgeoisie, which would prevent them from the contamination of foreign ideas. But the tours would provide the Soviet Union with impressive statistics as to the number of people allowed to travel outside of the country and would counteract the "Iron Curtain" image in the minds of Westerners.

Some pretty funny stories went the rounds concerning these innocents abroad. One was about the starving crowd who besieged the Soviet Embassy in Vienna the minute they arrived there, desperately pleading for food. They had declined all the meals offered them on the plane in the belief that they would be charged for them. Another was about a venturesome few who left their hotel rooms in Paris and sought an audience with the mayor to ask permission to take pictures of the city. The experience of the majority was summed up by Yevtushenko in a poem describing the Russian villagers in Paris, hiding in their hotel room — playing dominoes!

Travel literature, purportedly written by these pioneer observers of the foreign scene, began to appear in the press. But you never saw a travel page that couldn't have been composed by a writer who had never taken a step into the West. The content of each and every one of these articles was absolutely identical. "London is a big city. Big Ben is in London. Parliament is in London. There are many very poor people there. When we were in London, we were terribly homesick." Nonetheless, the very fact of this tourism was important. People started to understand that there was actually a world beyond the Soviet Union. (Enough word-of-mouth reports came back to us, describing the technical efficiency and the affluence of the West, so among the intelligentsia it became habitual to read Soviet propaganda concerning America and Europe in reverse. We hardly believed any of it: news of horrible unemployment, poverty, crime, race problems — all that was invention.)

Suppressed longings for freedom began to appear in print. Poems were published that astounded people by their audacity. One related a dream the author had about a sword, and the poet's thoughts on how wonderful it would be if everyone had a sword and, instead of succumbing to a Soviet bureaucrat unarmed, could take him on in honest combat. This was amazingly daring. The fare we had been offered in the public press for decades had been so heavily censored, so thoroughly screened, as to be unreadable.

Of course, I won't say that *Pravda* and *Izvestia* loosened up at this time. *Pravda* is the principal paper; it carries the "official" news; and most of the material in all the other papers consists almost solely of reprints from it.

About eighty years ago a humorist wrote a mocking suggestion for the Czarist press: to establish a newspaper that would present the opinion of the government, so that every citizen would know without any doubt what his own views ought to be on every subject; and to make it compulsory for all other papers to publish nothing but copies of this opinion. This made everybody laugh at the time. What was a joke in 1900 became reality after the Revolution. If you read *Pravda,* you don't have to read any other paper. This is the way to learn what you should know, what you should say, about Soviet domestic and foreign policy.

The first page contains editorials and national news on agriculture, industry, and such. The director of a kolkhoz in Byelorussia has achieved a bumper crop of alfalfa; everybody is urged to follow his example. A metal works in the Ukraine has overfulfilled its production plan. And so on. Nobody, literally nobody, reads these articles, but they do read the editorials. People in official positions have to read them carefully to find out where they should stand on every issue and what policies they are currently supposed to be endorsing. To use an example that would affect people in my own sphere: if an editorial says that science is becoming too abstract, what that means is that there will be less government money for fundamental science — no matter how effective this science may be. The opinion of *Pravda* is final and cannot be challenged. If three months later an editorial appears maintaining the opposite viewpoint and urging that new ground be broken in fundamental science, you will not find a single person who will discuss this about-face. Nobody tries to make sense out of any contradictions; everyone knows that this is an area which cannot be discussed at all.

So that's the front page of *Pravda* (which has, I believe, the largest circulation of any paper in the world). The second page is "human interest" news — for example, the biography of the collective-farm director praised in the headline. Next, we get the foreign news. This news has to be figured out like a cryptogram; once you learn the knack, you can pick up almost as much from this section as from the short-wave Western newscasts. What appears here in print is not very significant; what matters is what is left out. Let's say that suddenly there is absolutely nothing about China. It makes you think. China exists; there must be something happening there. The fact that you don't see a word about it strongly suggests that our relations with China are hostile. On the other side of the coin: if there should be a very small article, just a few lines, saying that a new Soviet-designed poultry battery is built in the Hangchow Province, this is an indication — not about chickens; nobody cares about chickens — but about certain negotiations with the Chinese.

Lastly, we get all the news about literature, sport, the theater, and so forth. (Not only is there no crime reporting, but also missing are fires, earthquakes, hurricanes, train derailments, airplane crashes, and similar disasters — unless they have occurred outside of the U.S.S.R., where such misfortunes happen absolutely uninterruptedly. The newsreels, too, specialize in cataclysms beyond the Soviet borders. Within, everything is wonderful.)

The international sports news — and Russians are wildly enthusiastic sports fans — consists of a succession of victories. Not too long ago there was an international basketball competition. *Pravda* was full of advance buildup before the game, but after it took place you had to use deductive reasoning to find out who had won. The papers forgot about the game for days on end. When it was finally mentioned again you could read about who had won second place, who had won third — everything, except for the fact that Israel had beaten the Soviet Union.

Nothing is a more accurate barometer of official opinion, however, than the obituary column. I need cite no other example than the item on Khrushchev's death. It occupied just one line, and designated the former General Secretary simply as *"Pensioner* Nikita Sergeyevitch Khrushchev."

The *Literaturnaya Gazeta,* a weekly, is different in content from the two other big papers, and is somewhat less directly under the thumb of officialdom, but is sufficiently sacrosanct so that when during the thaw a poem appeared deriding it, people were amazed. The *Gazeta* has a section on social problems, of which the poet gives a sample in a piece about a husband estranged from his wife:

Some members of my mother's family, about 1930. Seated: my aunt Fanya Slobodkina (each of my parents had a sister named Fanya); my grandmother; my uncle Mark Slobodkin. Standing: Mother's younger brother, Dmitri; her sister, Sara; Mother.

My mother, Cecilia Ysayevna Slobodkina, and my father, Yakov Aronovitch Azbel, at the time of their marriage in 1931.

Both of my parents were physicians, and in the summer of 1933 they had posts at the Sviatogorsk Sanitarium. This shows them on one of their rare holidays, in the company of friends, also members of the sanitarium staff. In the background is the ancient Sviatogorsk monastery.

Mother, Father, and I in Sviatogorsk, September 1933.

In a Kharkov park, 1936. Myself, my aunt Sara Slobodkina, and Mother.

In Novgorod-Seversky, about 1940. Front row, seated: my Azbel grandparents, flanked by my Aunts Irina and Fanya. Standing: my uncle Lev Azbel, Father, and two of his brothers, who were killed in the Great Patriotic War, Mikhail and Grigori.

Novgorod-Seversky, 1941. Interior of my paternal grandparents' house. At the table: Father's sister Irina, Mother, my grandmother; and much shaded in right foreground, Father. On the wall: studio photographs of my Azbel grandparents, taken at the turn of the century.

June 1941, a week or two before the German invasion. My aunt Irina Azbel, myself, Father, and a young cousin in Novgorod-Seversky.

Above left: "Evidence of Crime" from a 1953 issue of *Krokodil,* at the time of the "Doctor's Plot." The benevolent-appearing doctor has been unmasked. In the background, a top hat full of other villains. The dollar sign indicates the source of their support. *Above:* Not twenty years after Stalin's death, this sort of vicious propaganda appeared with increasing frequency. From *Sovietskaya Moldavia,* August 1971. Superscript: "Zionist Spiderweb." The spider is Zionism; the struts of the web read: "Slander, lies, provocation, anti-Sovietism, Jewish problem, anti-Communism." Title: "At His Favorite Work." *Left:* From *Sovietskaya Moldavia,* January 22nd, 1972, "Shadow and Substance." The Israeli, with his bloodstained axe, casts Hitler's shadow.

1975. Ernst Neizvestny speaks at our Seminar. The meetings were always crowded—few more than this one—and there were often visitors whom I didn't know, so I cannot identify everyone in the picture. The bearded man whose photo is half cut off is Yuli Kosharovsky. In the doorway are Professor Ilya Piatetsky-Shapiro; behind him a Mrs. Rais from Vilnius; and, standing in front of them, wearing a beard, Felix Dechster. In the front row, left to right, the second woman is Rachel Levitanaite; the third, Mrs. Gildengorn. Next is Professor Naum Meiman; then my wife. At the blackboard is Neizvestny.

B. J. and Jeremy Stone. Jeremy is Director of the Federation of American Scientists. This picture, a present made to my wife and me in 1976, bears an inscription praising my "activism in the defense of so many scientific lives." It is among our greatest treasures.

The People must decide:
Should he embrace his wife
Or not?

This is hardly a lampoon. Marriage, private relations between husband and wife or among any other members of families or groups who live under the same roof, may at any time become the subject of discussion at a Party meeting or in print. Next to nothing is excluded from this process of dissection.

Next, the poet examines the subject of literature as handled by the *Gazeta.* He writes of the literary critic who

. . . flatters you, he loves you —
And suddenly —
He hauls you to the dump.

And this is true too. Critical approval or disapproval depends on politics, and condemnation means actual burial for the work in question; it will simply become unavailable. More than that: any Russian author you can think of, contemporary or classic, has undergone the same alternation between enthusiastic acceptance and total rejection mentioned in the poem. Solzhenitsyn's *One Day in the Life of Ivan Denisovitch* was at first highly appreciated everywhere. The book received kind words from Khrushchev himself; in fact it was the General Secretary's approval that ensured its publication. Solzhenitsyn came very close to receiving the Lenin Prize, and with a little more caution and self-interest would certainly have received it. And everyone knows his subsequent fate; while the fate of his books — including *Ivan Denisovitch* — was to be relegated into the "dangerous" category. Only highly privileged members of Soviet society can afford to display them on their library shelves. (However, they delight in doing so in order to provide evidence that they are too secure, too important, to have to adhere to the taboos that govern lesser citizens.)

Electron Theory of Metals

ALTHOUGH it was pleasant to warm oneself in the welcome new atmosphere of the later 'fifties, few of the people I knew felt sure it would turn out to be permanent. For my own part, I was never sorry that my gifts and inclinations had led me into physics rather than into literature or the arts.

At this time I was involved in the further advance of the problems that had interested me before; but now I was considering the effects in these problems arising from quantum mechanics.

Quantum mechanics is a very interesting physical discipline. For the first time in physics, there appeared a situation one can only describe as "freedom of will" of particles. If before, physics could precisely describe the position of any particle, now, since Bohr, we realized that the position of a particle is not inevitably precisely determined; that, in fact, the position of particles is just as unpredictable as human behavior. This situation obtains with regard to the whole world of small elementary particles. It was fascinating to observe how such "social" phenomena act on the properties of metals.

But, however paradoxically, this freedom results in very definite limitations. The energy of an elementary particle in certain cases may be *not* an arbitrary one but equal to absolutely definite values. I should compare it, of course very loosely, with the situation when trade, and freedom of trade, gave rise to the invention of currency, which is coined in definite portions — there is no .02 cent — and the relatively fixed price of various goods.

It was on observations in this area that I was lecturing at the Moscow seminars, and I was publishing frequently in the *Journal of Experimental and Theoretical Physics* and elsewhere. (Also, by this time, much of what I produced was translated into English and appeared in such publications as *Journal of Physics* and *Chemistry of Solids* and *Progress in Low-Temperature Physics*.)

It occurred to me at the beginning of 'fifty-seven that the body of my work added up to a doctoral thesis. I asked Dr. Rosentzweig if he thought I ought to submit my dissertation. He urged me not to. "It's not a good idea — not good university politics — to obtain your doctorate ahead of so many men who are older than you are," he said. So I resigned myself to wait for years. But not long afterward, at one of the Moscow seminars, Landau approached me after I had spoken, saying, "Mark, it's high time you took steps toward your doctorate." This was definitely a green light, so with little more urging I started the machinery in motion.

From the point of view of drudgery alone, submitting a thesis in the Soviet Union is quite an overwhelming job. The paper — around 300 pages — has to be submitted in septuplicate; entailing countless hours of hand work, because, in my day at least, typewriters that would handle formulas and the Latin notations were simply unavailable. One copy to the institute; one to the Lenin Library; one for the Glavlit (the censor); and three for one's referees; one for my own institute — and one for myself. There were no mimeograph or Xerox machines; you had to make all the copies yourself. An incredibly boring chore! Also, you have to produce an abstract of the paper, a précis.

Once the institute receives the dissertation (mine was submitted not at Kharkov, but in Moscow at the Institute for Physical Problems), they provide you with the names of your referees. If the referees decide the abstract is adequate for the thesis, then you are to oversee the printing of the abstract. This takes a while; you need various official permissions, for example from the Glavlit and from your institute, to have it printed. Access to a press, or to any sort of duplicating machine, is a very special matter in the Soviet Union; printing is closely supervised by the State. You receive a hundred copies of the abstract; fifty of them must be sent to a list provided you by your institute, the others to colleagues in your field, whose names you must provide. Not until all this has been done is a date set for the oral presentation of the thesis.

I was desperately impatient, spending hour after hour laboriously making copies of the paper. I resented my time being taken up. I had fallen in love.

Naya Shteinman was a teacher of German in a technicum, a special school of technology. We had many friends in common, had heard about each other, but had never met until just at this time.

We were married within two weeks of the day we met.

* * *

I suppose I ought to mention right here that our marriage did not last. Although we had long intervals of happiness together, some differences eventually emerged that we could never resolve. But we were still good friends.

I look back on those days — the winter of 1957–58 — as a halcyon time. Naya and I went to Moscow for a holiday before I was to present my thesis; went to all my favorite galleries, to a concert, and for endless walks through the city and — though Moscow provides rather less by way of nightlife and "bright lights" than the drabbest provincial cities in the United States or England — had a wonderful few days' honeymoon.

When the day of my presentation came, I arrived, breathless, at the Institute for Physical Problems, having been delayed by a dozen things, not the least of which was putting on a necktie for the first time in my life. When I finally walked into the large entrance hall I found my father waiting for me there, pale with anxiety.

"Listen, Mark," he said, "are you positive everything is all right? You didn't make a mistake about the day you're supposed to speak? Here it is, almost eleven o'clock, and I've checked — nobody is here except ourselves." I remembered having had the same worry the first time I arrived at Kapitza's institute.

"It's all right — everyone will be here in two more minutes." I was nervous too, but not about the hour: I knew the rigid promptness customary here. I was suffering from the unfamiliar and incredibly uncomfortable sensation of wearing a tie. As the minute hand of my watch approached the hour, I reached the breaking point. Either I would present the dissertation badly, wearing the tie, or do it well, without the tie. An instant before it was too late, I dashed into the washroom and ripped the damn thing off, shoved it in my pocket, and, vastly relieved, rejoined my poor father, who was shocked by my informal appearance but knew there was no time to protest.

When I returned, the hall was already filled with people. The elite of Soviet physics was there. I saw with relief that there was already a quorum present; that is, there was more than 75 percent of all the members of the Scientific Council, which meant that the conditions necessary for presenting the thesis had already been met. I also saw that in the crowd were a few of my Kharkov friends, including Sasha Voronel and his wife. I was very much touched; I had no idea they would be here.

At eleven sharp, Kapitza took the floor. From the very start, I felt a sensation of relief and joy. This was a far cry from the circumstances that prevailed when I obtained my candidacy, when a hostile, reluctant panel of examiners had begrudgingly conceded the degree only when every opportunity to withhold it had been tested.

Pyotr Leonidovitch opened the proceedings with some very kind words, saying how impressed the Scientific Council already was by my scientific results, and what a pleasure it would be to hear the thesis. Throughout my presentation I could feel the friendliness of the audience; the informal, genial atmosphere. The whole occasion was more like a warm family festival than a strict procedure in conformance with official convention.

Afterward there were the usual questions. Then the referees took the floor and made their comments. Finally, I was permitted to say my "last words," which in this case consisted principally of grateful acknowledgments.

Everything that happens during the presentation of a thesis to the Scientific Council is taken down verbatim by stenographers so that there can never be any dispute over what has been said. The candidate's talk, the questions, the answers, and the referees' opinions are all scrupulously recorded — there are no vague areas that could be changed or misconstrued upon review. The candidate, and anyone else present, may read over the record.

At last the members of the Scientific Council cast ballots. Unlike the votes cast in the national elections, these are secret ballots. In fact, this is the only truly democratic process I have ever witnessed in Russia. Then three independent members — they themselves have been elected — count the votes, which are thereupon sealed and sent, with the dissertation and the transcript of the candidate's defense of his thesis, to the Highest Attestation Committee. The committee appoints two more referees, unknown to anybody except itself, who present their separate comments. Not until it has read these does the committee make its final decision as to granting the doctorate. Quite a lengthy procedure; academics from other parts of the world are always astounded to hear of the tortuous route a Soviet doctoral dissertation must take. But I think this thoroughness has its advantages. It could happen that arbitrary elements or undue influence might creep even into this rigid screening process, but it certainly doesn't occur very often. (Or I should say — it *didn't* occur very often at that time.)

At any rate, it would be months before I could be perfectly sure that the doctorate was mine, but it seemed highly unlikely that anything would go wrong, and the congratulations started pouring over me. Landau stood up and made a few most complimentary comments. "It would be impossible to miss the talent and ingenuity displayed in this work," he said. "The dissertant has just one fault, which is his extreme youth! But he is certain to overcome this defect without help from anyone."

Naya and I returned to Kharkov on the crest of the wave. We were met at the station by all of our friends, who a few days later gave an enormous party for us to celebrate both our marriage and my new degree.

Trouble

IN THE EARLY SPRING, events occurred that made us realize the Stalin era was not over, and maybe never would be.

The time for the elections to the Supreme Soviet and to local office was drawing near, and Naya was appointed the so-called Agitator for her technicum.

One hundred percent of the population is supposed to vote. To get out the vote is considered a highly important task and much propaganda is devoted toward this end several months prior to the elections. There is always only one candidate for each post; therefore, there is really no choice in the matter from the very beginning. This candidate is proposed at the general meeting by a spokesman for the Party officials, and each member of the meeting — unless he is crazy — endorses him.

To vote, all you do is drop the ballot, already imprinted with the candidate's name, into the ballot box. A write-in ballot does not exist. Technically, it is possible to cast a negative vote by crossing out the candidate's name, which you would have to do in a special booth designated for that purpose. You would then have to march past the official observers and publicly cast the altered ballot into the box. Very, very few people have the nerve to endanger themselves in this way.

On rare occasions, even in the Soviet Union, the worm turns. One cannot hope for total conformity in a country of two hundred millions. There always may be a remote village somewhere on which a candidate so unpopular and unsuitable is imposed that the electorate actually get together and, hoping for safety in numbers, all cross out the would-be office-holder's name. The State does not deliberately permit the candidacy of such an unpopular person — Moscow tries to avoid that kind of catastrophe. That it happens now and then is owing to defects in the Plan.

A candidate of a certain description is wanted, let's say, to fulfill specific requirements as to nationality, age, and sex — whatever the Party Conference has computed to be the fair and correct amalgamation of qualifications for that particular district. The person who turns up may be someone who simply infuriates the voters. I was told once by a man who lived in the region of the Petrozavodsk that the candidate for city deputy representative was a prostitute, notorious around the entire region. A delegation of citizens went to the City Party Committee to ask for a change of candidate. The Party Committee's answer was: "Look: we know this is not an appropriate person, and we have already written to the Central Committee. But what can we do? You know that the percentage of workers, of peasants, of technicians, and so forth, who are supposed to hold office, is determined in advance. In our case, we had to find for deputy representative a woman between thirty-five and forty years of age, with two children, single, and working in a factory. We combed through the entire region — we couldn't find anyone else who falls into all those categories. If you find us someone else who fits the same description, we will immediately replace this candidate."

Such a situation is very rare and would occur only in the case of a minor office in a remote region. But no matter what, every effort is made to have everyone vote, vote for the right person, and vote early. In Stalin's time they tried to get everyone to the polls before twelve noon, to demonstrate the people's enthusiasm. That is where the Agitator comes in. He or she must call on all the families in a specified district, make sure that all of them are going to appear at the polls, make arrangements for absentee ballots if someone is going to be out of town, and so forth.

Naya was appointed Agitator for a district that included quite a few very poor working families. They greeted her visits with apathy. "We're not planning to vote," she was informed. "Every four years we've been promised they would run the water lines through here. We still don't have running water, and it looks as though we never will."

When Naya reported these conversations at the Agitatory Point, her chairman was furious. He assumed that an Agitator would know enough to assure the people that their needs would be met; would have done everything in her power to get them to the polls, whatever the validity of their protests.

"I didn't know I was supposed to lie to them," Naya said.

The results of her altercation with the chairman were predictable: when the school year ended, Naya was fired from the technicum. We were still naïve and optimistic enough in those days to contemplate bringing suit against the chairman. Looking back on it, I realize what months we would have waited before our case came on the docket and how wildly unlikely it would have been that it could be decided in Naya's favor.

However, we were still thinking over the idea of going to court when this plan — and all our other plans — came to a halt. Naya was stricken with a high fever and unexplained intestinal pains. When the condition persisted for days on end, it became obvious that, dread it as we might, she would have to go to the hospital.

Health services in the Soviet Union are free of charge. But what this means is that nobody actually cares about the hospitals.

When you fall ill in the Soviet Union you have to go first of all to the polyclinic; unless your illness is serious enough to warrant a house call (or, of course, an ambulance). At the clinic there is a very long queue waiting to see the physician. When your turn comes, you have to take into account the fact that this one physician has — literally — from two to five minutes to spend with you. He or she (most physicians are women) has to see a specified number of patients each day, dozens. Under such conditions she cannot pay close attention to any of them. There is no time for tests. Very little testing equipment is available, in any case. This rushed and harried physician is naturally in no position to study, to keep up with any one field; she is simply a mechanism for signing permits to allow the sick person to stay home from work or, if necessary, to go to the hospital. (Of course in a critical emergency you can be rushed to the hospital by ambulance, and these preliminaries will not obtain.) Most consultation time is taken up by paperwork.

We couldn't face this prospect. One alternative, if one has *blat* (pull, or influence), is to engage the services of a doctor privately, who may charge anything from ten to twenty-five roubles per consultation. And that is naturally what we did — with the result that, without the dangerous delay that would have been almost inevitable had we gone through the polyclinic, my wife was admitted to the hospital.

I had been around hospitals as a child, since both of my parents were physicians, so I shouldn't have been surprised by how dreadful this one was (it was supposed to be one of the best in the Ukraine). But it had been years since I had observed a hospital from close up.

The room in which Naya had to spend several weeks was twenty square meters in size. In this room there were twelve iron beds — twelve patients; this allocation of space is typical in an ordinary hospital. No privacy, no telephone, no radio. There was not even a bell or light to summon assistance. Perhaps worst of all, there were no fans, and therefore no air — all this happened in the summer. There was nothing to breathe. Naya couldn't open the window, because the other patients were afraid of drafts.

It is almost impossible to exist in such a room. The patients live very nearly the same lives as prisoners in a jail. Those who are able to move around may go outside to the courtyard only for a short time each day and then only in summer. The doctors are afraid of infection, so nobody is allowed to keep his own clothes. Everyone is issued hospital clothing, inadequate for the Russian climate except during the warmest season. These are old, ill-fitting, shapeless pajamas that have been worn by innumerable patients over the years and have gone through the laundry so many times that the original color is completely bleached out. They may be torn, with missing fastenings. Illness aside, my wife's spirits were completely crushed by having to wear these horrible clothes.

Only sixty-five kopeks per day may be spent by the State on an individual for food, medicine, and all other expenses. I actually don't believe a person could survive on hospital rations without a friend or relative who is able to bring food parcels to him. It seems unlikely that a patient otherwise could ever leave the hospital alive.

The most serious shortage of all is of medicines. The State considers the sixty-five kopeks an extravagance, and the institution's walls are covered with slogans urging doctors and nurses to cut down on costs, to economize everywhere possible. The only medications used are those which are cheap and easily available. Occasions often arise when a doctor knows the patient needs a special medicine not to be found in the hospital supplies. Since in principle the State does provide everything a sick person may need, he faces a serious conflict when it comes to prescribing anything the hospital does not have on hand.

In my wife's case, the doctors trusted me not to get them in trouble and told me that Aureomycin was badly needed; but they begged me not to make a fuss about the problem. They felt that a man in my position would undoubtedly have the blat or the money to obtain it myself. While they were explaining this to me, an uproar was in progress in another ward: one patient overheard a doctor prescribing a drug, expensive and hard to get, for the man in the bed next to him. Knowing that he himself was suffering from the same disease, he demanded of the authorities the same prescription (his ward-mate had acquired it through an under-the-counter deal with a pharmacist friend). The hospital got it for him. But the doctor who had suggested this medicine for the first man lost his job.

The appropriate drugs, in this nation that boasts its medicine is accessible to everyone, are often almost impossible to obtain, and cost a great deal of money. Another expense came as a sort of shock to us. My wife made the discovery early in her hospital stay that every single service performed on behalf of a patient by a *sanitarka* — a ward maid — has to be paid for: changing the bed, bringing an aspirin, turning the patient — everything. It was senseless to complain about this violation of medical ethics. A sanitarka was paid fifty roubles a month; without the tips she simply could not survive, particularly if she had a family. She had dozens of patients; if many of them were bedfast, she was faced with a truly grueling job. Typically, people in this work are not in it for humanitarian reasons. They are a tough lot, perfectly capable of ignoring for an entire shift any of their charges who are unable to pay.

Hospitals have no trouble finding professors or doctors or *meditsinskie sestra* (trained nurses) for their staffs, but to find these attendants is much more difficult. There is no type of employment — even street-cleaner — that isn't better paid and easier. Therefore, the sanitarki are not afraid of anybody, including the Party officials and the director of the hospital. They know that they are almost irreplaceable. It is hard to imagine circumstances under which a sanitarka would be fired.

I won't say that in every hospital in the Soviet Union it is necessary to pay these people for their services; I will say only that in my own experience there has always been a charge for nursing care. You usually pay a rouble for each service performed.

I may note here that, because everything is predicted by the Plan — you are out of luck if you contract an illness that is not included in its computations. Officially, diphtheria and cholera have been eliminated in the U.S.S.R.; therefore a person or community struck by either of these diseases will be misdiagnosed, either deliberately or because the doctor, whose training did not include recognition of those particular symptoms, honestly makes a mistake. The treatment may be inappropriate. The death certificate will read "Inflammation of the lungs."

Some time after Naya's ordeal in that frightful place was over, I described it to a physician friend of mine in Moscow, who scoffed at my indignation. "The conditions you're complaining about are simply wonderful, compared to what I have to face," he said, and persuaded me to visit the hospital where he worked. "More people should know what's going on; then maybe someday something will be done about it."

I never forgot that nightmare institution, particularly the ward for paralytics. There was only one nursing attendant for several wards filled to capacity. Patients lay for hours in their own waste before she got around to attending to them, and they were punished for their incontinence; she beat them with the wet rags she had removed from their beds. The woman was drunk, illiterate, completely callous to the sufferings of the helpless prisoners in her care. But, unable to offer more than fifty or sixty roubles per month to the person who performed this service, whom else could the hospital find?

On the other hand, the relations of doctors themselves with their patients is warmer and more trusting in the Soviet Union than I have observed it to be elsewhere. An ordinary general practitioner leads a life so sacrificial and hard-working that members of any other profession can hardly believe it. A doctor may easily pay twenty or thirty house calls in one day; and of course it must be remembered that almost none of them has a car, so this means miles by public transportation or on foot in all kinds of weather. During epidemics of flu or grippe there are even signs up in the street cars and public places urging people not to leave their houses so as not to spread the infection; no one goes to the polyclinic or the doctor's office, and the house calls multiply to a staggering number. Whatever the level of competence — and it can be abysmal — the dedication of these people cannot be faulted.

The hospitals I saw are those for ordinary people; but of course everyone knew there were special ones for the elite classes. In Moscow there is the Academic Hospital, for the exclusive use of members of the Academy of Sciences and of top-level scientists. There is no overcrowding here; the rooms are spacious and airy, many of them private. Three and a half roubles per day per person is spent on food alone. More elegant still is the Kremlin Hospital, for the Party elite. This is better than a really good hotel. All the rooms are private and are equipped with telephones, TV, and so on. I am not inventing it when I say that caviar is no rarity there. Over thirteen roubles a day is spent on each patient's meals.

Even at the Kremlin Hospital there are problems. Many of the doctors are more notable for their trustworthiness and dedication as Party members than for their medical skills, for they are actually chosen on the basis of these former qualifications. The physicians are terrified of any responsibility, and the effects of this fear can be fatal. To cite one case history: the famous Korolev, the pioneer of Soviet space research, dead — because of hemorrhoids. In a panic at having so important a patient, eminent surgeons called in other eminent surgeons; each one was afraid to operate, and in the end the whole procedure was tragically bungled.

And that is Soviet medicine.

*   *   *

My wife's imprisonment in the hospital finally came to an end, and she was advised by her doctor to go to a resort, Zheleznovodsk in the

North Caucasus, to take the mineral waters. So, although we could not get a permit to stay in one of the sanitaria (reserved as always by Party officials and their families), we went. The mineral waters may have done Naya some good, but our stay there was hardly a vacation. We rented a small dingy room, the only place available, and my most vivid memory of that time is hour-long queues at the restaurant, where we were rewarded by slow service and terrible food.

Vacations in the Soviet Union, like every other aspect of Soviet life, are very rigidly stratified. The middle elite have access to wonderful resorts; the real elite have their own *dachas* (villas), and the absolute top elite have, in some cases, palaces — I mean that literally; palaces that in former times were occupied by the Czar and the Russian princes. Urban-dwelling Russians of all sorts and conditions take some sort of vacation. The State provides a paid holiday for everyone, and since in that tight economy it is almost impossible to save money, there is no point not to take advantage of it. People go to the mountains or the seaside, or to the rivers for boating excursions. If you haven't the blat to stay in a resort sanitarium, you rent a room. If you can't afford that, you take a bedroll to the beach or mountains. Virtually everybody who can go somewhere, goes.

Changes

ONE of my memories from early 1958 is of the great jubilee that was conducted to celebrate Landau's fiftieth birthday. It was a landmark festival for Soviet physicists.

The function took place in the same great hall where Kapitza's and Landau's seminars were held; but even that enormous room was hardly big enough for the huge crowd that attended. Except at the time of Academician Tamm's first lectures on modern genetics, the hall had never been so packed in its history.

The chairman stood up before us and announced: "This celebration is to be conducted under the following rules: any official congratulations are strictly forbidden. Anyone who refers to Landau as the founder of Soviet theoretical physics, as the creator of a great school, as a famous and outstanding scientist — will be prosecuted and condemned to exile outside of this hall." Everyone laughed and applauded. "We had to solve the problem of how to handle the guest of honor himself," he continued. "This person — at all jubilees — is usually the most pitiable object under the sun. He doesn't know where to look, what to do with his hands, how to behave in the glare of so much publicity. So we decided to give him something to do.

"We couldn't simply ply him with drinks; everyone knows that Landau doesn't drink." More laughter. "So we had to invite a *vipivala* [a heavy drinker]. Here are his accessories." And he produced a red false nose and a huge black cardboard mustache. One of the guests, on cue, joined the chairman on the platform and put them on. "He'll do the drinking for Landau! — But Lev Davidovitch can't just sit idle," he went on. "He has to have something to do." At this point a waiter made his way up the aisle, carrying two washbasins, which he deposited under the lecturer's table. "He will wash the glasses for the speakers." And during the whole jubilee, Landau was the person who washed the glasses for the vipivala (about five or six men assumed this role in turn) and for those who presented him with gifts and toasts.

The presents and congratulations were all very varied, but none of them struck a serious note. Knowing Landau, his hosts did not want to burden him with the pomp and tedium that usually accompany these occasions.

First, one of his colleagues ran up to the platform and announced: "We all know Landau is Lev." (*Lev* is Russian for "lion.") "So he's got to have a tail!" and he produced a marvelous tufted lion's tail. Landau immediately got into the spirit of the thing, put on the tail, which had a clip so that it could be attached to his belt, leaped up on the table, and cracked the tail, like a whip, over the audience in the front row.

Then he was presented with two copper plates engraved with "Landau's Ten Commandments," the formulations of his ten principal discoveries in physics.

Next, someone presented him with an icon, in which he was represented as God, surrounded by a litter of blind kittens — his students. Also, there was a very well-done painting of Landau as Don Quixote, with Yevgeny Lifshitz, his lifelong collaborator, as Sancho Panza.

One of the best of all the contributions was a deck of playing cards especially designed for the birthday. The Joker was Landau himself. Next were the other scientists, according to their ranking. I can't cite them all, but I remember that Academician Zeldovitch was the Ace of Spades, with a picture of his face only, the body invisible under a black mantle. There was an inscription: "A secret person, therefore he has no body." (This was an allusion to Timyanov's story *Porutchik Kizhé,* about a phantom army officer created accidentally, on paper, by a slip of a clerk's pen. Because the paper was signed by the Czar Paul himself, no one will admit the clerical mistake and deny the officer's existence; so, on paper, the nonexistent Kizhé is paid, promoted to the rank of general, decorated by the military authorities, and finally, when the Czar wishes to see this incorporeal patriot, he is "killed off" and provided a splendid military funeral.) Zeldovitch was involved in highly classified work; no one knew just what it was; but he was three times decorated a Hero of Socialist Labor.

Another Ace was Academician Migdal, who was represented wearing an octopus by way of bathing trunks. Academician Migdal was famous for aqualung diving, and was one of the first people in the Soviet Union to take up this sport: he spent his vacations in the far east, diving in the ocean.

Khalatnikov and Abrikosov were represented together on one card as the Brothers Highwaymen, an allusion to the Pushkin poem. All four Queens were Landau's wife, Kora, in different dress. I won't describe all the other cards — this kind of humor is by definition "in-house," and

much funnier to the initiates of the institution in question than to anyone else — but they were all extremely clever. I myself was in the
deck — a Knave of Diamonds — I was delighted to find myself in this
distinguished company.

Then there was an album of cartoons, one of which showed Landau
tied to a chair, bound and gagged. The man who has trapped him in
this way is his teacher Niels Bohr, who is saying, "Maybe now, Dau, I'll
be able to get a word in edgewise." Landau was noted for talking very
fast and being impossible to interrupt; the picture struck home to everyone who saw it, and no one laughed harder than Lev Davidovitch himself when he came to this one.

In another of those cartoons Landau appeared again as God, in the
process of creating Adam, "after Michelangelo," and astonished at his
own creation. The Adam was myself. The last offering was a stamp by
the hand of a master engraver, gift of the University of Kharkov. It
depicted Landau's head over a beautifully designed "50." After all the
presentations, everyone connected with the Institute moved over to Kapitza's study, where we were served wine and carbonated drinks. We
celebrated almost all night.

Nothing could have been better than this sort of party for a man like
Lev Landau. He was spared all the awkwardness and ceremony that
usually attend these occasions, but he couldn't help enjoying the demonstration of affection and warmth felt by all of us who came under his
influence.

Only one thing annoyed me on that festive evening, and that was a
self-satisfied comment made by one of my colleagues on the preponderance of Jews at the gathering. He evidently was among those who
believed that Jews were more intelligent than other people, and that the
proof was here.

The naïveté of the idea that physics outranks all the other arts and
sciences aside — as though to be a painter or a jazz composer, let's say,
were patently an inferior gift — this viewpoint always irritated me exactly as much as the stance of anti-Semites. To me, the excellence of
Jews in the exact sciences has roots in easily discernible historical influences, as I explained before. And, then, who knows when the time is
ripe for the flourishing of any particular gift in any particular person or
nationality? Jews for centuries had the reputation of being bad soldiers
and great businessmen. At the present time, the State of Israel is recognized as having produced excellent soldiers, while no one — certainly
no one in Israel, of which I am now a citizen — thinks very highly of
the Israelis' business capabilities. Economically, the country is in poor
shape. Similarly, Jews were for a long time considered to be brilliant

statesmen and diplomats, and this is hardly true in Israel today.

In a sense, the whole problem of ethnic discrimination was summed up once by a friend of Kapitza, when someone asked him if Kapitza was an anti-Semite. "No, why should he be?" was the answer. "I don't believe he feels inferior to Jews in any way."

I feel this reply expressed a profound truth: that a person with real self-respect has no reason to withhold respect from other human beings. The need to raise oneself in one's own esteem by means of humiliating someone else is the basis of the complex inherited by the most unhappy and most oppressed peoples and nations. The disappearance of racism in any given society is, it seems to me, a prime index to the improvement of that society, proving an advance in its self-esteem.

It is an unofficial but widespread view among those in Russia who bemoan the Revolution and its consequences that it was Jews who were responsible for the Revolution. I don't think it's unfair to say that this view can be discerned even in some of the writings of Solzhenitsyn, of Shafarevich, and others. One would think that the very idea of such a tiny minority changing the history of vast Russia — some million people causing such a cataclysmic social upheaval against the will of a hundred and forty million — would be a most humiliating belief on the part of a member of that overwhelming majority. It would be shameful for an elephant to believe that a mouse could lead him in any direction it might choose. Are the Russians so helpless that they could have allowed a small alien ethnic group to direct their history away from their own goals? It would be hard to imagine an Englishman or an American claiming that one or another central aspect of his country's history was not determined by Britons, or Americans, themselves.

*   *   *

When Naya and I returned to Kharkov, we were confronted by that most seriously vexing problem in the life of a Soviet person: we had to find a place to live. It is almost true to say that in Russia someone has to die or go to prison before an apartment becomes available. A top Party boss or an Academician would have no trouble being allocated an apartment. At the other extreme, a very poor person living in dangerously substandard conditions, a damp cellar or a shack in danger of falling apart, may have a chance of being moved. But people anywhere on the intermediate rungs of Soviet society have almost no hope of a change of dwelling.

Naya and I had been staying with my father and his wife (he remarried that year). It was certainly not an ideal arrangement; we had always felt ourselves to be very much in their way, but now my step-mother was expecting a child. The four of us (soon to be six), with our one and a half rooms plus corridor, our kitchen and bathroom shared with many other people, did not qualify for another apartment. There are regulations to the effect that a scholar or scientist is entitled to an extra twenty square meters for his study; but the authorities paid little attention to this point and refused us a *propiska* (residence permit) at any other address.

When people on the staff of the institute heard about our plight, they moved heaven and earth to obtain a place for us in a new building on the institute grounds, and we were moved, initially without a propiska. This meant, of course, that we might be thrown out at any time; but though the officials knew about it they didn't interfere, since it was done under the auspices of the prestigious institute.

The new house was a flimsy postwar structure: one story, four absolutely tiny apartments. We had two miniature adjoining rooms, a slot of a kitchen, no shower, and a water closet so small that one of our friends, a rather stout man, claimed it was almost impossible for him to wedge himself into it! The whole area was twenty square meters.

Nevertheless, Naya and I were delighted to be settled in our first real home. All our friends poured in to visit. In the circles to which we belonged, everyone dropped in constantly, with little regard to time of day or night, and was perfectly sure of a welcome. Nobody could call up and say he was coming, or wait for an invitation, because almost nobody had a telephone. People simply appeared, always unexpectedly, and we were always glad to see them. All our friends lived the same way.

So our new life began, very cheerfully. The walls were absolutely transparent to sound, and our neighbors had to hear this gregarious life all the time, as well as hours of Beethoven (my first purchase, when a real salary started coming in, had been a gramophone and albums of my favorite symphonies). They were very nice people and never complained. In our turn, we never took note of any noise they made. We all simply observed a convention of privacy as the Japanese do in their paper houses. By 1960 my status was such that I was able to get the propiska, and we moved to a considerably better place, on Nikitina Street. There we even had a telephone.

That year I continued with my lectures and with further research in solid state physics. I began to receive invitations for lectures and consultations around the Soviet Union at various institutes; I always accepted, and enjoyed, not only the work, but the opportunity to see different parts of the country. The summer of 1960 my wife and I spent in Latvia, in a little seaside resort, Polanga. By now completely recovered, she was awaiting a child, and we were in that state of long-drawn-out suspense familiar to every couple at such a time.

The Baltic, in the few years since I had been there, had changed considerably. There were more Russians around, and there was less food. But we enjoyed ourselves; life there was still much better than in the Ukraine, and we spent peaceful hours by the water with no very serious concerns on our minds. The summers were always a very good time for me, when I could do my own thinking on work which I had evolved myself. And aside from pure science, I did a little writing; eventually I began to publish, in the *Literaturnaya Gazeta* and elsewhere, articles on such subjects as science in literature, the relation between scientific language and popular language, and similar topics.

* * *

On January 20th, 1961, our son, Vadim, was born. We were happy beyond anything we could have foreseen. But I won't say we had an easy time.

Taking care of a small infant must be difficult anywhere, but customs and conditions in the Soviet Union make it a formidable task. Soviet people are much afraid of germs, so, like all other babies, Vadim spent his first few months in a sort of quarantine, which meant that Naya was isolated too. All visitors, even I, were excluded from the lying-in hospital where Naya had to stay for nine days after the child's birth. From the moment of her return home, there was no relief from the endless nursing, the eternal hand-laundering and boiling of diapers. Needless to say, diapers and other infant's clothing are terribly hard to obtain, and no one could accumulate enough of them to be able to postpone the laundry for a while. And the fact that in Kharkov we had running water for only two hours a day made this a horrendous job.

It was hard to attend to all the chores before the baby was weaned, but even tougher afterward. I would never be able to compute the hours that I, or Naya with the baby in her arms, had to spend during Vadim's first years, scouring the bazaar for some sort of fresh fruit or vegetables. And then the preparation! Of course there was no kitchen machinery; to make carrot juice, for example, one had to grate the carrots and then squeeze them through a cloth. It was a lengthy process. Again: I doubt that there are many societies, primitive or industrialized, where people have to spend more time simply obtaining food than they do in Russia; and when it came to feeding a baby, the problem seemed to take up every waking hour.

Somehow we muddled through. And when Vadim was older and turned out to be one of those children who never feel fear — if you relaxed your vigilance for a minute you would find him balanced on top of an armoire, or teetering on a window ledge three stories over a street — we looked back on those hard early days with nostalgia!

* * *

In 1962 a dreadful blow fell upon the scientific fraternity. On a Sunday early in the year I received a call from a friend at the Institute for Physical Problems. Landau had been in an automobile accident that morning; was badly hurt and not expected to live. I was completely stunned. It was one of those freak accidents, so unlikely that, as a matter of fact, the KGB thought for a while that it might have been an attempt on Landau's life. But it was just fantastic bad luck.

The day of the accident had dawned fair, cold, and sunny. As not infrequently happened, Landau had been asked to visit the International Nuclear Institute at Dubna, some hundred miles outside of Moscow. The weather was perfect for such a trip; road conditions were reasonably good; it was the kind of winter day most people consider ideal for motoring. True, that morning the Academy chauffeur had declined to make the trip because of icy roads — but this man never liked to have his one free day taken up by a trip, and he often had very good reasons not to go anywhere on a Sunday.

The man who took the chauffeur's place was Sudakov, a physicist who wrote his candidate's thesis under Landau, later well known for his solution to the so-called Parquet Problem. In the back seat were Sudakov's wife, who sat on the left — the traffic side — and Landau on the right. On the back seat also, between them, was a basket of fresh eggs, which they were bringing along for a present to the people at the Nuclear Institute (eggs were still a hard-to-find delicacy in most of Russia).

They were just outside Moscow. Somewhat ahead of their car was a bus, waiting for passengers to board at a stop. Sudakov moved into the left lane in order to pass. At that moment he saw a heavy truck approaching. Being a careful driver, he had allowed plenty of room for such a contingency; he turned the steering wheel back to the right, intending to return to the right lane. But he had hit a patch of glare ice; the car failed to respond and continued leftward, making a U-turn. The two vehicles collided, the truck running square into the right-hand rear passenger's door. Landau was literally crushed. The collision left Sudakov absolutely unharmed, and his wife suffered only from shock. The eggs in the back seat were not even cracked.

Landau was to all appearances lifeless. His entire body was broken. Sudakov rushed him to the nearest hospital, and there he was told that many of Landau's bones were fractured; that he had sustained heavy internal injuries and a severe fracture of the base of the skull. Without delay, the best physicians in Moscow were called. Professor Vasilievsky, the first to arrive, examined Landau and wrote the verdict: "Injuries inconsistent with survival." He left, absolutely sure that nothing could be done.

But there were others who refused to see Landau go without a battle. These were the physicists.

A phenomenon unique in the history of Soviet medicine took place: a twenty-four-hour vigil in the hospital, kept by a number of Landau's eminent colleagues and disciples. Two or three were constantly there, around the clock. A special telephone was installed, which rang night and day with anxious inquiries from all over the world.

It was impossible to move Landau, and therefore the best medicine, the most modern life-sustaining devices, were conveyed to this small suburban hospital. Physicists from everywhere in the country and from abroad united in efforts to save Landau. Russian drugs and equipment being so inferior to imported ones, scientists at the institute exerted all their influence to bring in foreign supplies. More than once, planes at takeoff from Europe delayed scheduled flights for an hour or two until medicines for Landau could be brought aboard. The institute obtained an order to expedite or eliminate the customs proceedings when all these things arrived. Foreign doctors, too, were flown in, among them a brain surgeon and two orthopedic surgeons. At one point one of the Russian doctors inquired ironically: "Now Professor Landau needs oxygen; is it all right if we administer Russian oxygen?" — because everything else used for treating Landau came from abroad. It was a disgrace, how defective the Russian equipment was: even catheters, intravenous tubing, the simplest items, were undependable. Hence the desperate need for Western-made equipment.

Four times, Landau was clinically dead. Four times he was saved. This battle with death lasted not a week, not a month, but almost half a year. When Landau was awarded the Nobel Prize in Physics, he received it lying in his hospital bed.

When he was well enough to be moved, he was taken to the Academic Hospital. I remember visiting him there: we walked together in the hospital yard. He moved very slowly. His hands, which had always moved so quickly, so precisely, trembled. He spoke with difficulty. He recognized me, but this was no longer the former Landau.

He lived several more years, but he never returned to active science. His recovery was a miracle but, tragically, an incomplete miracle. Now and then he would appear at the seminars, but he was unable to follow the discussions or to participate in them, and after a few minutes he always left.

Landau had ideas for improving the teaching of physics, and planned to write school and university textbooks incorporating these changes; but he did not have the strength or mental organization for it. To see this brilliant person reduced to such helplessness was unbearable.

New Ties

In 1962 our friends the Gitermans went touring for the summer, and they offered us the use of their apartment in the Moscow suburb of Mendeleyevo, where my closest friend, Alexander Voronel, was working at the Institute for Physical-Technical and Radiotechnical Measurements.

Sasha Voronel and I had spent a great deal of our time together when we were both in Kharkov. He married Nina Abramovna Roginkina, a classmate, when they were both still under twenty years of age. Upon graduation he was assigned to work in the very provincial city of Saransk, at the Pedagogical Institute there.

Sasha's situation was incomparably more difficult than mine. Being a theoretician, I had found it possible to stay in Kharkov and proceed with my science. I needed nothing more than paper, a pen, and access to a library. But to Voronel, the use of a laboratory was essential; even if he had been freed from the obligation to go where he was posted, as I was, he would have had to take some such position as this one. From his letters I could tell what a hard time he was having. It was almost impossible for him to gain experience in science at Saransk; there was only one other real scientist there, Moishe Giterman; but Moishe too was a recent graduate — he had just left Sverdlovsk University — and their seniors were men of very indifferent caliber. This is about what one would expect in a provincial institute: as with the educational institutions, the farther you are from the great cities, the lower are the standards. Voronel and Giterman had to fall back upon their own resources, without any guidance or advice.

Being in such an out-of-the-way place was no easier for Nina than for Sasha. Nina, who had studied in the Physics Department at Kharkov University, over the years found herself much more interested in literature than in science (eventually she was to graduate from the Moscow Literary Institute), and Sasha, who appreciated her talent, pushed her to

go on with it. Here in Saransk, where there was no intellectual stimula-
tion of any kind, she was afraid she would simply vegetate. But with
Sasha's encouragement, she became part of a lecture program that sent
speakers into the remote villages of that region, to give talks on various
popular subjects to small crowds of rural people. Her appearances were
quite an event in these hamlets, which are almost entirely cut off from
the outside world, particularly in winter. It took considerable strength
and courage for Nina to take on this job — to ride in a truck long
miles, or walk, in the dead of winter or, worse still, in the spring, the
"roadless" season, when you sank into mud over your knees if you
were on foot, and when any vehicle, no matter how big, no matter how
stout the chains on the tires, got stuck every few miles. It was neither
easy nor safe, particularly at night, to make these arduous treks; but
Sasha sympathized with Nina's wish not to lose interest in books and in
life, not to become simply a housewife, interested in nothing. So he
urged her on. Nina not only lectured but also wrote literary criticism,
poems, and translations from the English.

Voronel did what he could in Saransk, performing the few experiments that were possible with the primitive equipment provided there,
and also working on theory. His gifts were such as to enable him to rise
above the limitations imposed by his cramped circumstances, and he
managed to publish some of his scientific papers, even then.

By the time Sasha's stint at Saransk was up, it had become a little easier for a Jew to enter a scientific institute. It looked to him as though
there might now be a chance of getting into serious science, and he
applied to the Radio-Technical Institute in Mendeleyevo, outside Moscow. Because of his very interesting papers, and because this institute
had important technical problems to solve, they overlooked his nationality and accepted him. The Voronels left Saransk in 1957 for Moscow.

Literally day and night, Voronel worked at his laboratory. He immersed himself in his experimental work, making up for lost time; and
professionally, this was a very good period for him. But the Voronels'
life as a couple was frightful. They had nowhere to live in Moscow —
no propiska — so they led an itinerant existence, staying every night
with different friends. Quite frequently they were separated, Voronel at
one friend's flat and Nina at another's; often in the crammed Moscow
conditions neither host had room for two people at once. Because of
regulations (it is impossible for a nonresident to stay at any one apartment for more than three days) and also because of their unwillingness
to burden their friends, they never spent more than one night in any one
flat. Sometimes they were reduced to sleeping in places little better than

ugols. They never had an address. They had almost no money, and were hungry all the time. Nevertheless, the sacrifice of any kind of security was one that Sasha Voronel was willing to make in order to be able to work in science. And Nina was willing to stick by him in this vagrant and comfortless life. Perhaps the hardest part for them was to be without their little son, Volodya. It was impossible to keep a baby with them under these circumstances, and they had to leave him with Nina's parents in Kharkov.

It was a change for the better when Sasha finally got the job in Mendeleyevo, at the Institute for Physical-Technical and Radiotechnical Measurements. At first, even there, the Voronels' living conditions were miserable: they were assigned only one room, part of an apartment already occupied by two other families. The original residents were furious at having to accept a couple with a child in one of the rooms they had considered their own, and were further enraged by the fact that when Sasha returned from the laboratory, however late at night, he had to pass through their quarters to the kitchen to cook the next day's meals for Volodya, who was diabetic and had to have special food.

Their life was far from easy, and it was two years before they received a small two-room flat, one of the rooms twelve square meters and the other ten, in another house. It was there that they were living when we joined them on our vacation.

Mendeleyevo is a very pretty place, heavily wooded. Sasha and I spent marvelous hours walking along its trails, endlessly talking, exploring each other's ideas.

Voronel is one of the brightest people I have ever met. He is a true polymath, profoundly knowledgeable in science and philosophy, in religion and literature, in art and history. In his company, I always thought of Pushkin's words about his gifted friend Chaadayev: * "In Rome, he would be Brutus; in Athens, Pericles." It must have been in the course of our many discussions at that time that many of my own ideas, until then in suspension, finally crystallized.

Sasha and I naturally gave a lot of thought to the two great political systems that dominate our world in the twentieth century. I had a feeling that one element was lacking in all the studies related to history and the progress of nations. It seemed to me, as a physicist, that there was a

---

* Chaadayev was probably the first person in Russia to be punished for his political views by being declared insane. Of course, in the nineteenth century there were no KGB psychiatrists like the present-day Snezhnevsky; and no such diagnosis as "political delusions," the affliction modern Russian psychology has discovered. It was simply the will of the Czar to pronounce Chaadayev insane when the latter expressed the opinion that Russia was a country without a history, a nation that contributed nothing to progress.

blank area here: no one cared to find out what the laws restricting the development of society actually are. Social reformers promulgate schemes for the betterment of man, which, however desirable, may be no more possible than those magical inventions like *perpetuum mobile* machines, whose one defect is that they ignore a physical law. For example, it would be wonderful to add economic equality to the realities of democracy. Very good. But the question is: If this equality is added, what will be subtracted? Is it possible to combine Socialist ideas with universal welfare? One might answer: Yes, it is possible, and the signal failure of Russian Socialism — the poverty of Russia and all the misfortunes she has endured — is related only to the specific shortcomings of Russia herself, not to basic defects in Socialism. That may be true —but is it? Who can prove that this continuing disaster is not an inevitable concomitant of Socialism? Who can prove — to focus on one crippled aspect of the Soviet system — that, given human fallibility, the profit motive is not essential to a viable economy?

I feel that the experiment made in Russia proves that good intentions are not a sufficient foundation on which to build a successful society. The admirably idealistic principles on which Russian Communism are based, and the realities of Soviet life, provide a painful and instructive contrast.

One observes in history time and again that rapid change, revolution, gives rise to shock waves just as it does in physics. A charge of dynamite not only destroys its target, but may destroy and will definitely affect everything within atmospheric range of the explosion. There is a law in nature which dictates that every action must have a reaction; a counter-force always appears in opposition to the force that is applied. These effects are little controllable; they do not depend upon our will. The next position of equilibrium in a society thrown off balance by attempts at radical reform may well be one that is overwhelmed by demagoguery, by totalitarianism.

The Terror that followed the Revolution — and, before that, the Terror that succeeded the French Revolution — were in my opinion not accidents but the inevitable consequence of these upheavals. Those who eventually come to power are not the ones who created the ideas that constitute the basis of the revolution, but those who are strong and cynical and who are ready to preserve their power by any means. The new leaders struggle in vain: one shock wave follows another, and in their turn they are wiped out, until a new equilibrium obtains.

The study of world history is very instructive, if one does not insist upon believing that one's own time, or one's own country, is absolutely unique. We have to contend constantly with the fact that we are likely to see every new mistake in a new light, without reference to the familiar cycles of which it is a part. We invest emotion into our social programs; quite a few of us are willing fervently to pursue millennialist schemes that, viewed objectively, are clearly impossible.

I used to quote Churchill's view that "no system of government could be worse than democracy — unless you compare it to all the others."

Mendeleyevo, only an hour from Moscow by train, had become a favorite retreat of a few artists and writers who in summer provided a leavening for the predominantly scientific society. There were informal gatherings all the time among the summer residents, and early on during that vacation I met the writer Yuli Daniel.

Daniel, a poet, translator, and novelist, was a tall slender man a few years older than I, with a thatch of dark wavy hair and a narrow, handsome, very expressive face. One of his arms was stiff and caused him occasional bouts of pain. As a very young man he had been wounded at the front, and he was left with this permanent souvenir of the War.

Yuli Daniel had that rare quick wit which is the hardest thing in the world to describe — all you can remember of his talk is how amused you were, but it's hard to single out a quotation. Very few people with that elusive gift can convey it in writing, but Yuli is an exception to that rule. His stories are full of unpredictable humor.

His wife, Larisa Bogoraz-Bruchman, was a talented scholar in the humanities, and a very interesting personality.

That was a pleasant summer for all of us. Naya and I became very close to the Daniels and thereafter exchanged visits — we would come to them in Moscow, and they to us in Kharkov. Yuli's apartment was on Leninsky Prospect: two rooms crammed with books in bookshelves he had made himself; a comfortable sofa in one of the rooms, also made by him. It was a very cosy place.

Here I have to anticipate and tell about an evening we spent there some time in August of 1962. We were the only guests at the time, and the neighbor, who lived in an adjoining room and shared the Daniels' kitchen, happened to be out. Yuli was lying on the sofa — his favorite place — surrounded by manuscripts, describing to us his writing plans, and as always chain-smoking papirosi.

"Since there's nobody around, let me read you something," he said. "But keep this to yourselves." He began to read aloud.

This was only the second of Yuli's stories I had ever heard or read, very different from the first, which was a historical piece. He hadn't got very far before I realized that here was an authentic talent, a voice with something very new to say. It was his novella *Moscow Speaking*.

On the surface, the story falls into the category of "black" humor. It

is set in the near future. The narrative begins with the Soviet government having decided that its citizenry is now so responsible, so evolved
morally, that it may use its own judgment in decisions of life and death.
The State declares a national "day of open murders"; or, you might say,
"open season on human beings." There will be no penalty for homicide.
I won't outline the plot — and in a sense there is no plot, but the reactions of his characters to this sudden suspension of the Sixth Command-
ment are alternately so narrowly Soviet and so universally human that
the reader is wrenched between laughter and very serious thought. I
won't say the story is perfect — there are awkward spots — but it is
original and very telling. However, even as I followed the twists and
turns of the narrative, I could not be unaware of what having written
this book might portend for Daniel. Absorbed though I was by the
reading, there was room in my mind for apprehension.

This piece was beyond a doubt dangerous, by Soviet standards. It was
a measure of Yuli's trust in Naya and me that he was willing to put his
safety in our hands by letting us hear it. No Russian could fail to understand the danger involved: if this story fell into the wrong hands, the
outcome would be inevitable — the author would be liable to charges
of anti-Soviet activity. I don't mean, of course, that there actually was
one word in the book that violated any Soviet laws, or violated anything in the Constitution covering what is permissible to publish — but
when have these laws mattered in Russia?

Yuli read on for several hours. When he had finished we congratu-
lated him, and I asked what he was planning to do with the piece.

"I don't know yet," he said. "It looks as though there might be some
possibility of getting it out to France or England. Who knows, someone
might publish it there."

My fears for Yuli redoubled. Soviet authors had occasionally published abroad without official approval but never with impunity. Not
long before, Pasternak, whose prestige seemed to be unassailable, was
threatened with exile, harassed by the KGB, and forced to decline the
Nobel Prize when his novel *Dr. Zhivago* made an unauthorized appearance in America and England. If even Pasternak was not immune to
reprisals, what could a relatively unknown writer expect? "I'll use a
pseudonym," Yuli added.

I had a lot of thinking to do that night. I could hardly ignore the
danger Daniel was in. And as his friend, I would be in an extremely vulnerable position myself. The concept of guilt by association is taken absolutely for granted in the Soviet Union. In a sense, I had joined his venture into dangerous waters. To write this book exposed Yuli to the
possibility of criminal charges; to read it meant complicity with his

crime. I didn't know what I might be risking; but I had made up my mind years before that the guiding principle by which I had to live was, very simply, loyalty to my friends. It would be impossible to let caution affect my association with Yuli — to lock myself in a moral prison for fear of a future prison. If it came to that, my family would be better off ashamed of me as a criminal than as a coward.

This decision to live, to seek, to grow, to battle with limitations, is one that I think human beings make repeatedly throughout their lives.

It may have been about two years later that Yuli told me the book had been published in England and in France, under the pseudonym "Nikolai Arzhak." Shortly afterward I read a book that was circulating "underground," the English translation of a Russian novel by one "Abram Tertz," entitled (prophetically) *The Trial Begins*. I guessed that the author was the critic Andrei Sinyavsky, whom I had met at the Daniels', and that he as well as Yuli had found this way of making his voice heard.

Moscow

So MUCH intense conversation and so many late nights in Mendeleyevo proved to be too strenuous for Naya, and when we got back to Kharkov she fell ill again. Once more she urged me not to worry. We had a "guest-maid" (a not uncommon arrangement: the maid's wages are very low, since she is compensated in part by having a place to stay and by being provided her meals. She slept in the room that served us as living room, dining room, and study). "I'll do nothing but rest for a while; Tanya can do the shopping and take care of the baby. I'll be all right," Naya said. By the end of November, she was in the hospital.

We had a very kind and attentive surgeon, who took a real interest in Naya's case, but he was too unsure of himself to take any effective steps toward a cure; in fact, he could not even make a definitive diagnosis. When in December Naya was moved into a semiprivate room, shared by only one other patient, I was terribly alarmed. In the Soviet Union this is an indication that the invalid is in grave danger. I realized that a real specialist was needed.

I knew of a very great Moscow physician, Professor Yosif Kassirsky, in Moscow, probably the most famous hematologist in the country. But the hierarchical divisions in Soviet society are such that even someone like myself, a physicist already represented in the international literature and quite well known, would have no hope of obtaining a consultation with so eminent a personage without going through "channels." I fled to Moscow, and asked Kapitza if he could manage to arrange an introduction for me. Academician Kapitza (whose many kindnesses to me during this crisis I will never forget) immediately made an appointment with Kassirsky.

Distracted though I was by worry at that time, I still remember the strong impression — strange and contradictory — I received from Kassirsky's personality and surroundings. I was stunned when I was ushered into his huge reception room. On one of the walls were two portraits, side by side. One was literally mural size, a full-length, larger-than-life oil of Kassirsky himself, wearing his best suit and holding a stethoscope in his hands. The figure in the portrait was a faithful copy of the one in a widely reproduced picture of Stalin! The only differences were the face and the stethoscope. The other painting, smaller but equally handsome, was of Kassirsky's wife. On the huge mahogany desk was a lot of modern office equipment, including a speaking tube connected with the outer office — a total novelty in the Soviet Union — and a typewriter with two fonts, Cyrillic and Roman. There was an entire wall of bookshelves, and conspicuously displayed were Kassirsky's own works, accompanied by translations into five or six languages.

In all my previous experience, which was principally among physicists, it had struck me that the greater a man's gifts, the more modest he was likely to be. I felt I had made a mistake in coming here. My doubts were reinforced when Professor Kassirsky appeared. He spent at least a half-hour making it clear to me how extremely important he was in his profession in a naïvely vainglorious self-introduction that astonished me and that I found hard to reconcile with my knowledge of him as a talented and dedicated specialist. All this splendor, combined with Kassirsky's assurances to me that it was only the fact of his being Jewish that had prevented him from receiving the Star of a Hero of Socialist Labor (as it was, he had numerous decorations); that it was he who had saved Landau, and on and on, shook my confidence. (I learned later that this sort of display is not at all uncommon for high-ranking Soviet medical specialists.)

When the subject finally turned to my wife's illness, Kassirsky became, without transition, another person. He listened with attention to all the details of the varying diagnoses and suggestions for treatment that I had brought with me. He was very perceptive, very quiet. He gave a brief but very informative lecture on the use and misuse of antibiotics — of which I have remembered every word; he must have been an extremely good teacher — then asked me several questions. Finally he said: "Your wife really should be under the care of Dr. Rizhik here in Moscow; but if that's impossible, there's nothing I can do but give you *zaochnie* advice." (There is no English word for zaochnie; "sight unseen" expresses it best.) He sat down at his typewriter and rapidly wrote three or four pages of a carefully thought-out diagnosis and his recommendations for treatment.

I returned to Kharkov with all Kassirsky's proposals and prescriptions. The treatments he recommended were highly effective, and Naya began to rally.

However, after a few weeks our Kharkov doctor decided that Naya's improvement had nothing to do with Kassirsky's instructions but was the result of his own regimen. He recommenced putting into practice his own ideas, and the results were disastrous. It was soon clear that my wife's condition was worsening.

This time I could see there was really no hope unless I could somehow get Naya to the hospital in Moscow that Kassirsky had mentioned, which had a floor specifically dedicated to patients with her disease.

To attempt a transfer to Moscow was, on the face of it, impossible. We were living in the Ukrainian S.R. The special Moscow hospital was, of course, in the Russian S.R. One is not entitled to utilize public benefits such as medical services of a republic other than the one where one is a legal resident. There is a constitutional fiction that maintains that those services in each of the republics are of the same standard, which they are certainly not. This means one cannot provide the authorities with a reason they will recognize as valid for preferring to be treated in one region rather than in another.

I determined to overcome these problems. Naya was in critical condition now, no longer permitted visitors except for members of the immediate family. I went back to the capital.

Kapitza listened with concern to my account of what had happened, and rushed me immediately over to his office. "We'll find a solution," he said. "I'll have to get to the *vertushka*."

The vertushka, a special red telephone available to only a few members of the very top Soviet elite, is a "hot line" to the powers that be. If you have the privilege of operating a vertushka and you have to contact Brezhnev, for example, you dial his number and Brezhnev himself answers. Kapitza had once told me how he was punished for being absent-minded about putting the vertushka away. When not in use, this telephone is supposed to be locked in a special safe, but one evening when he went home from the office he accidentally left it out on his desk. The cleaning woman, arriving soon after Kapitza's departure, was much interested to see it sitting there, unlocked, and examined it curiously. Attached to the phone was a list of names and numbers that simply astounded her. Thinking fast, she dialed Kosygin direct and, when a voice answered, briskly introduced herself.

"I've called to tell you about my apartment," she announced. "I've been promised a bigger one for years now. The place is simply a closet — fourteen meters square, and we are a family of six! What do you think of that?" she demanded. "Is this fairness, is this the correct Soviet way of doing things?"

"Excuse me," came the answer, "are you aware with whom you are speaking?"

"Why, yes, of course, Comrade Kosygin!"

The result was that the cleaning woman received a bigger apartment, and Kapitza received a severe dressing-down. After that, he never forgot the vertushka again, and it was always locked in the safe in his absence.

"Professor Kassirsky told me that Dr. Rizhik is the best specialist in Moscow," I told Kapitza.

"Rizhik — Rizhik — I don't know his name," he answered. "I can't call a Dr. Rizhik; I don't know him." "But he knows you," I silently prayed. "Please, please call him!"

Kapitza looked through his telephone numbers. "Ah! Here we are!" he exclaimed. "Balashoff, the Minister of Health! Luckily, he owes me a favor." This comment gave me a glimpse into the inner workings of blat among the higher-ups: even in the world where Kapitza moved, an element of quid pro quo was an advantage.

All obstacles to Naya's transfer were removed. The next day an ambulance awaited the plane; the driver was allowed to pass the airport barrier and take the vehicle directly out onto the runway when the plane got in. Everything went off all right, but I was frightened. My wife looked even frailer than when I had seen her twenty-four hours before. It seemed very possible that all these extraordinary efforts were being made in vain.

After two months, just prior to an operation she was to undergo, Naya was moved into a private room completely by herself. I was told to expect the worst.

I myself had been able to spend all this time in Moscow, as had Naya's mother. She is a very self-sacrificing person. She refused to leave Naya's bedside, and we obtained special permission for her to stay in the hospital, day and night. She slept on a sofa in the corridor and herself prepared the special diet that had been prescribed for Naya; I spent hours almost every day combing Moscow for the ingredients necessary to this diet. Due to the eternal scarcity, this was not too easy. I often had to spend half a day going from shop to shop all over the city to find most of the items requested, such as caviar and salmon, in small quantities, and a specific brand of mineral water. Today, you couldn't find them at all.

It was to Kapitza that I owed the privilege of staying in Moscow. He requested permission of my institute in Kharkov to let me work temporarily at the Institute for Physical Problems, and the director at Kharkov gave me a leave of absence. I was given the room reserved for visiting scientists in the building that housed the senior collaborators.

I was young then, and while living in a constant state of fear for the life of my wife, while running through the stores in search of the rare foods we were told were essential if she was to have a chance of recovery, I still had enough strength to think about science, to work, and to write papers, which were published under the imprint of the Institute for Physical Problems.

Those days, those months, were dreadful. I never knew when I arrived at the hospital for the visiting hours if I would find my wife alive.

This medical treatment cost us a fortune. Just to keep the nurses doing their jobs could add up to 200 roubles a month — half of my entire salary in those days. Father helped us out, and Naya's parents gave us what they could. But Dr. Rizhik lived up to his reputation, and we were overjoyed when the operations turned out to be successful. By late spring, Naya was well enough to come home to Kharkov. Her return was a real festival. All of our friends came to the station to meet her. At last our family was together again. Life very gradually came back to normal.

*   *   *

It was around this time, the early 'sixties, that I began to think of moving to Moscow, where there were more physicists, more possibilities to learn new things, and a much wider audience for scientific discussion. The decision struck everybody I knew as absolutely unrealistic. All my colleagues told me that unless I was willing to accept a recent invitation to join the Laser Institute (I had always avoided classified military work), I had no chance at all of making this move. This was the worst possible time to try to obtain a propiska in Moscow. Khrushchev had just declared that the city's population already exceeded all possible limits, and not a single additional person should be allowed to move there. Stalin, before Khrushchev, had also tried to hold down the population of Moscow: the siege of the city by those who want to live there, and its desperate defense by the authorities, is an ongoing battle. But because Academician Petrovsky, Rector of Moscow State University, had more than once mentioned that he would like to offer me a post in the Physics Department, I had hopes.

Petrovsky's career provides a classic example of what can happen to a gifted, dedicated, brilliant academic under the Soviet system. He had been rector of the university since 1949. He was a highly talented mathematician and a very honest person. He was versed in every aspect of science and was one of the few Academicians to whom the integrity of Russian science took priority over every other consideration. The minute it was possible, he got rid of as many of Stalin's "scientist" protégés — Lysenkoists and others — as he could. He tried to sweep out the influence of these petty minds, and addressed himself to the task of creating a really great center of learning.

Moscow University had always been one of the citadels of reaction. The most renowned Russian scholars, among them the great physicist Lebedyev, were fired from the university in the days of the Czar; and in our own time, fifty eminent physicists, including Landau himself, were fired all in one day, when an idiotic ruling went through, restricting professors who were attached to one of the institutes from working anywhere else. (No university is a politically and socially independent body in Russia.) It made no sense to withhold from students of the university the advantages they could receive from lectures by the staff of these institutes, which are the breeding ground of science, both fundamental and applied; this ruling only lowered the already somewhat shaky academic standards at Moscow University.

Petrovsky's central ambition was to repair the damage done over the years to the caliber of this great institution; to attract the best scientists there and to make it the best school in the nation. Petrovsky's zeal, his dream of making this seat of learning into one that rivaled in stature the best English and American universities, was based upon his extraordinarily ardent patriotism. He wanted to make a truly significant contribution to Russia, to erase the blunders made in the past.

The result was that what he sought among the lecturers and students there was simply intellectual superiority. Though Russian through and through himself — he was of peasant origin — he was completely indifferent to considerations of national or social background when it came to choosing his staff; also to political influence, inasfar as he could be. Employing no other criterion, then, in the selection of his staff save that of scientific ability, he created a very beautiful Mathematics Department, of which he was a member himself. I said before that mathematics, more than other sciences, is a field dominated in Russia by anti-Semites. Petrovsky's Mathematics Department provided an exception to this rule: there were many Jewish mathematicians at Moscow University at the time when he had a relatively free hand in choosing his faculty.

Now he intended to organize a distinguished and creative Physics Department; once again he intended to hire people of whose abilities he had a high opinion; Russians, Jews, or whatever.

Such auspicious conditions cannot last long in the Soviet Union. Not many years after I received Petrovsky's invitation, the Central Committee decided that Moscow University should not be run solely by the rector himself; he should share the administration with the university

Party chairman. This change was the thin end of the wedge undermining Petrovsky's authority. But in 'sixty-four, Academician Petrovsky was still a force to be reckoned with.

When I went to see him in Moscow in May, he informed me that the professorship was mine. I asked what I should do about a propiska. (It must be hard for a non-Russian reader to really appreciate this problem. Can one imagine a man being offered a professorship at the University of London, say, or at Columbia, and knowing he might have to decline it because it may be impossible for him to move to London or New York?) By August, Petrovsky obtained permission for me to make Moscow my legal residence: amazingly, he had to apply to Kosygin himself to get it. I was accorded a propiska for a two-room apartment on Lomonovsky Prospect, convenient to the university and also to the Institute for Physical Problems. My family joined me, and we started settling in. I began to plan my lectures.

At this same time, I was invited to be chairman of a department of the Landau Institute for Theoretical Physics. Such a part-time position was strictly forbidden, but the director, Khalatnikov, had this regulation suspended on my behalf.

After Landau could no longer participate in the activities at the Institute for Physical Problems, his colleagues had lost interest in it, and founded this Institute for Theoretical Physics, in a very pleasant country settlement, Chernogolovka, about an hour's drive from Moscow; and I went out twice a week or so to the Scientific Council there and to the seminars. There is bus and taxi service to Chernogolovka, but I and the four other scientists who regularly attended these meetings usually availed ourselves of the chauffeur-driven institute car — quite a luxury!

I now became a member also of the Scientific Council at Moscow University. This wasn't easy — there was considerable opposition to my inclusion — but this was one instance when professional considerations overrode political ones.

Despite Petrovsky's backing, I had been lecturing for six months before the Physics Department formally took me in. Even then I was never given the opportunity to pass the so-called Concourse, the procedure by which one is given five years' tenure. There were very few Jews in my section, and the department was reluctant to add to their numbers. Although they could not reject me out of hand, they managed to keep my position a somewhat insecure one.

Such problems notwithstanding, my life at the university was rewarding. The cathedra into which I was accepted was that of Academician Leontovitch, with whom I always had the most cordial relations. I liked many of my colleagues, and was pleased by the number of them, particularly the younger men, who asked me for help with their work.

During the previous decade, anti-Semitic policies in educational institutions hadn't been pursued so relentlessly as to cause the near-elimination of Jews from Moscow University. But by the mid-'sixties, the line had hardened. At the university, the duty of conducting the entrance examinations is divided among the professors; it was in the course of performing this job that I saw how the quota system really works.

At the time I was appointed to the Examination Committee, I hadn't heard a word contrary to my own convictions. Everyone was apparently agreed that each student should be selected according to a single criterion: ability. No other factors were to influence our decisions. Also, we were urged to make every effort to discover the potential of applicants who might be hampered by shortcomings in their previous training. We were to pay special attention to pupils who had come from poor villages and who, whatever their native talents, were bound to be handicapped by inferior grounding.

So far, so good. I participated in the examinations throughout the entire month during which they were held. I must have read and heard the exams of a couple of thousand students during that time. But all of the applicants assigned to me had two features in common: not one of them was a Jew, and not one was from an intellectual or educated background. All came from villages or were the children of working families.

It could hardly happen by chance. The questionnaires the students have to fill out when they apply are nothing if not thorough: they include occupation of parents and nationality as a matter of course. More than half of those applying to the university are children of the intelligentsia, and at least 30 percent of these are Jews. This is perfectly predictable, because, first, in the Soviet Union it is fairly customary for children to take up the occupations of their parents; and, second, in every generation there will be an increment of Jews, since they are inclined toward intellectual pursuits whatever their origins. The homogeneity of the great crowd of applicants in my particular examination room meant that they had been carefully screened before I ever saw them. If a Jew did manage to get as far as the entrance examinations, his testing was taken care of by one of the professors who understood what the minority representation in the student body was really supposed to be.

Of course, to visit other examiners' rooms was strictly forbidden; so I never heard the specific questions that were used to eliminate candidates the university did not want. However, the system for keeping them out was hardly a secret. Undesirables could be confronted with material completely unconnected with the subject, or, in mathematics, they could be posed questions that have no answers. I knew this device had been used at Kharkov to eliminate Jews; now I saw the same thing happening at Moscow.

The reason for the particular bias against Jewish mathematicians is well known in the Soviet scientific world. Those who rule over Soviet mathematics consist of Academicians Vinogradov, Pontryagin, and — to a lesser degree — Bogoliubov. It was they who locked the gates of the Academy against mathematicians of international repute. I have mentioned that at least two men of undoubted genius, Mark Krein and Israel Gelfand, were never accorded membership even though the British Royal Academy, the American National Academy, and many others, were honored to accept them. The work of these men went unrecognized in Russia. Among the rising generation of mathematicians, extraordinarily gifted scholars are denied degrees — simply stopped in their tracks.

Academician Bogoliubov had a perfectly remarkable career. The son of a priest who was killed during the Civil War, he spent his earliest childhood among the *bezprizorni,* the war orphans who somehow survived the early 'twenties, living in alleys, in doorways, even in forests, roving in packs, raiding and begging. Owing to circumstances with which I am not familiar, Bogoliubov was rescued from this life and adopted by the great mathematician Krilov, and he was still a very young boy when his own prodigious gifts emerged. He published his first paper at the age of thirteen.

At the start of his career, Bogoliubov was most kind and helpful to those who were coming up in the field behind him. But during the Great Purge, when it became a matter of survival to stay in favor with the Party, he changed. By the time I was launched in the scientific world myself, it had long been known that when it came to Jewish scholars, many promising mathematical careers had been brought to a halt by this man. Moreover, he had assisted second-rate talents — people with the right connections — into positions far beyond their merits; had even written D.Sc. and Ph.D. theses for them. (These beneficiaries of his favor were certainly not ungrateful; I once saw Bogoliubov at an international scientific meeting in Kanev, where he was surrounded by a group of high-level scientists who waited on him like slaves, bringing him trays of caviar and other delicacies. Strange to say, I couldn't hate him. His face, deeply seamed with heavy thought, was certainly not that of a self-satisfied man.)

Vinogradov and Pontryagin espoused the same policies as Bogoliubov and were much more ruthless than he when it came to keeping Jews out of their field.

There was a case of a Jewish student who had won the Moscow State University Mathematical Olympiad against contestants from all over the U.S.S.R., but "flunked" the math oral when he was applying to the university. Luckily, one of those who had been among the judges at the Olympiad and had certified the boy as winner was Academician Kikoin, who complained to Petrovsky himself. Petrovsky demanded to see the written record of the oral exam. In reply, he was informed that by some mischance the records (which have to be kept on file for a long time) had been lost! Petrovsky gave orders for the appointment of a committee that would conduct the examination over; the student got a 5.

But this was an extraordinary case, and one can imagine how often the unwanted elements are successfully kept out. At present, Jews constitute less than 1 percent of the student body at Moscow University. By the end of his rectorship, Petrovsky was practically helpless to prevent all this. Once the Party element was entrenched in the university, the rector had to stand by and watch his best mathematicians being treated disrespectfully, and the best students being refused admission to the university. Furthermore, there were quite a few cases, including those of Petrovsky's own doctoral students, in which brilliant theses were turned down because their authors were Jewish. The Party officials in the administration hardly bothered to conceal what they were doing. Nothing could influence them less than the pious provisions against discrimination contained in the Soviet Constitution; they simply followed orders "from above."

But given talent and luck, it was still just possible for a Jew of my generation, educated before the filtration processes were all devised, to achieve a successful career. In 1965, and again in 1968, I was awarded the Lomonosov Prize for my work in solid state physics. And in 1965, I found that I was being considered for the Lenin Prize, the highest scientific award in the Soviet Union.

At this same time Alexander Voronel, too, was attaining recognition; his research into the characteristics of liquids when at what is called the critical point, when the difference between gas and liquid disappears, was to earn him an international reputation. After the New Year he was invited to serve as director of a large laboratory at Dubna.

The institute at Dubna is a very rich one, situated in beautiful wooded countryside outside Moscow. For an experimental physicist, a change of place is very difficult: he has to reorganize his entire laboratory from the bottom up and may spend years at this task before he can even start working again. Because Voronel had experiments in progress at Mendeleyevo, he decided to move the laboratory piecemeal. He accepted only a half-time position at Dubna: he would organize the laboratory, appoint his collaborators, get the research started, and, only when everything was ready and a replacement had been found for him at Mendeleyevo, would he make the move final.

In the meanwhile, the institute at Dubna provided the Voronels with a huge apartment, one whole floor of a separate villa, with a large garden shaded by trees. Sasha and Nina were naturally delighted at having such a marvelous flat — it was the first attractive place they had ever lived in — and they invited us to stay with them every chance we got. We spent a great deal of my summer's leave in Dubna, and were often there on weekends in the fall. It was a joy to see them so happily settled after their many miserable early years.

Lefortovo

NAYA AND I spent the first weekend in September of 1965 with the Voronels in Dubna. Late on Saturday evening we were gathered around the living-room table, drinking tea and talking with Sasha's mother, Faina Lazarevna, when we heard the sound of a car pulling up the drive — something rather unusual, particularly at that hour. There was a knock at the door, and I answered it.

"Voronel?" The man standing at the entrance was no one we knew.

"No."

"Is he here?"

"Just a minute." Sasha rose from the table, went to the door, and, after a word with the stranger, stepped outside. The rest of us couldn't hear their conversation, but we fell silent and exchanged anxious glances. Abruptly, Sasha came back in, disappeared for a moment into the adjoining room, and returned with his briefcase. "They want me to go to Moscow," He said. No one had to ask whom he meant by "they." "I'll be back." The door slammed behind him, and we could hear the car drive off.

We were left bewildered, trying to guess what was going on.

I was one of the few people among Voronel's friends who knew about his having been in prison camp in his youth, which meant that his mother, who was naturally extremely upset, could talk freely with me. She and I knew that such things are never forgotten. And she knew — none better — what the results of such a summons could be.

The minutes passed very slowly. I tried to reassure Faina Lazarevna, suggesting that this might be a mere routine inquiry; but we both understood that it was very unlikely.

It was hard for me to conceal the fact that I was much more alarmed than she was. Voronel knew about Daniel's and Sinyavsky's books; I was worried not so much on his behalf as on theirs. The only reason I could think of for this sudden appearance by the KGB was that Andrei's and Yuli's identities might have been traced: someone could have deduced who was behind their *noms de plume.*

It was not until late in the night that Voronel returned; his mother almost wept with relief when he walked in.

"It was nothing — everything's all right," he assured her. "But I'm stiff after riding in a car for such a long time. Mark, let's go for a walk."

When we were outside he told me what had happened. My fears had been correct. He had been subjected to an interrogation; it was Sinyavsky and Daniel whom the KGB were investigating. Voronel was almost sure that Andrei had already been arrested.

Realizing that Yuli might not yet know that he had been exposed, we had to catch the early train to Moscow the next morning, hoping to get there in time to warn him. We were in a fever of impatience, so anxious we could hardly think; but I do remember our brief speculations as to who the *stukatch* — the informer — might have been.

It didn't take much guesswork. Daniel and Sinyavsky had a young friend, an archaeologist and historian by profession, but also a poet; a man named Chmielnitsky, whom we used to see fairly often at the apartment of one or the other of them. He was a great admirer of both.

Some time ago, two of Chmielnitsky's former classmates, men he had known while they were all still in high school, had been released from labor camp, where they had served ten years for anti-Soviet activity. In the course of the interrogations that preceded their trials, the convicted men had learned it was Chmielnitsky who had accused them. There was no way they could let anyone know who the stukatch was — they had no contact with the outside world during their imprisonment — but once released they revealed his identity.

No criminal in Soviet Russia is considered by decent people to be as degraded as a stukatch. To inform on one's friends is the one unforgivable sin. When people heard what had happened, they shunned Chmielnitsky as a leper. When he delivered his doctoral thesis, one of these former friends rose and denounced him for what he had done, saying that a man who would stoop so low was not worthy to receive a doctorate. (This was an unprecedented event; no one had ever heard of such a denunciation at the presentation of a thesis.) He received the doctorate anyway, but he could not stay in Moscow. He had not a single friend left; not a soul would speak to him. He moved to Central Asia, and none of us ever saw him again — except once, on an occasion that I will come to in due course.

It seemed very likely to us that Chmielnitsky had repeated his treachery. Once a person becomes an informer, there is no way back. Even though we were no longer in Stalin's time, when the pressures and threats under which he had committed his original betrayal may have been too cruel to withstand (under Khrushchev the KGB's powers were weakened), the hold the secret police had established over him at that earlier day would be unbreakable.

Arrived in Moscow, Sasha and I hastened to get in touch with Maria Sinyavsky. She confirmed Sasha's guess: Sinyavsky had been arrested, on September 8th. Daniel was at that moment visiting friends in Novosibirsk with his wife. We spent hours on the telephone trying to make contact with him there, but all we could find out was that Yuli was expected back in Moscow on September 12th, the next day but one, and that he had already heard of the situation.

We spent more than half the day of the 12th waiting for him at Leninsky Prospect. But when Larisa arrived she was alone. She told us that two KGBsts had accompanied them on the plane from Novosibirsk. At the airport, Yuli had to leave immediately with these men; they told Larisa to wait; that her husband would be home later that evening. We waited with Larisa. Around eleven at night, one of the KGBsts arrived and told us that Daniel would not be back.

This was the first of my close friends to be arrested almost before my eyes.

It was also the first time I found myself under real surveillance. Every time I went to visit Larisa, I saw KGBsts around the building, and I was photographed as I went in.

I have to confess that it was very unpleasant and frightening. But once again I had to make a choice, and it was more frightening for me to contemplate the prospect of avoiding a friend, and despising myself, than to run the gauntlet of the KGB when I called on her. Gradually I lost any fear and began to brace myself for anything that might happen.

In the next few days, more and more of our friends were summoned for interrogation. Especially desperate were the women, because the KGB used even nastier tactics with them to press them, to force them to testify against Daniel, than they did with the men. Just one example of the sort of minor sadism practiced upon them was provided us by a good friend of Yuli's, a translator from the German (I won't give her name, because she is still in the Soviet Union). She gave us a harrowing description of her ten hours at KGB headquarters. "Certainly you may use the lavatory," her interrogators had replied to her request. "But *after* you have given testimony. Not before." This was at ten A.M.: she had held out stoically until she was finally released at seven, having managed to withhold any information of importance throughout that entire horrible day.

I am glad to say that only one of our acquaintances turned out to be a coward, or too anxious about hanging on to his position — which means about the same thing. This was Professor Alexander Essel from Siberia, deputy director of the medical research institute to which he was attached. That he could be induced to bear witness against a friend was not a total surprise: he was the only one among us who was a Party member. "I know what you think of my joining the Party," he had said to all of us when he took that step. "But it doesn't mean anything. I couldn't be Director of the Experimental Department without Party membership. This way I'll have a great deal more scope for my work."

The idea that one might sell one's soul to the devil has long been obsolete — the devil has ceased to exist, and so, perhaps, has the soul. But throughout my Soviet existence I was struck time and again by this same circumstance: the fate of a well-meaning man who, for very practical and logical reasons, joined the Party. The advantages were clear, and as far as he could see he harmed nobody by making such a move. The relinquishing of his principles was so slow, so gradual, that he himself wasn't aware of it until the time came (and it did, almost inevitably) when there was a confrontation between the loyalties to which he had always held and the partnership that was now absolutely essential to his career. At that point you saw a dissolution, a crumbling of the original person, a capitulation of the spirit that shocked and depressed me horribly. Observing this process, I was more than once reminded of *The Picture of Dorian Gray.*

Essel had to produce more and more "testimony" and to declare Daniel to be a person of anti-Soviet views that he was openly propagating among his friends.

As I say, none of "ours" could be induced to support these statements.

Weeks went by; all of our friends were called in for questioning; but so far I seemed to be exempt.

When the authorities at the scientific installations learned that Voronel had been taken in for interrogation, Mendeleyevo and Dubna each wanted to disclaim him as a member of their staffs. Mendeleyevo fired him from his position as director of research and reduced his status to that of senior researcher. Dubna immediately put a stop to his part-time job, and, moreover, took Voronel to court with the claim that he had no right to live in the apartment at Dubna.

I was present at this trial, which was conducted in one of the small

Moscow precinct courthouses. It was the first time I had ever been in a courtroom.

The legalities of the case were absolutely clear. Voronel's right to the apartment was indisputable. The propiska, the signatures, the seals — all were in order. Voronel acted as his own counsel. During the trial the judge made no secret of his opinion of the Dubna representatives. He openly made fun of them; he pointed out how nonsensical their claims were and how watertight Voronel's case was. The cross-examinations clearly brought out the fact that all the evidence was in Sasha's favor. When the hearing was over, the lawyer retained by Dubna immediately sat down to write a protest to the Higher Court about the rude treatment he had received in this court.

In a Soviet court of law, there is never a jury. There is only a judge, and two "people's representatives," who play a very minor role: they simply endorse the judge's decision with their signatures. Then there is a secretary, who records at his own discretion whatever aspects of the case seem important to him, and produces a précis of the arguments, seen only by the judge. There is no court stenographer; no transcript available to any interested party.

The presentation of a case is something like the formal defense of a thesis, except that at the latter proceedings a record is made of everything that is said, and the document is submitted to all concerned for verification and correction once the presentation is over. Everything is absolutely public. But in court anything in the transcript can be changed, and the defendant can do nothing about it, even if his defense has been patently altered and perverted.

Voronel's case was so open and shut that while the court was adjourned, before the verdict was announced, the secretary came up to congratulate him. We were all sure of a favorable decision, but we were too naïve. In five minutes the court returned. Everybody had to stand up. The judge read: "In the name of the Russian Soviet Socialist Republic, this court decides . . ." The court had decided that Voronel had no valid claim to his apartment and would have to vacate it forthwith.

This was a Soviet court. In the last analysis, it had to favor the interests of the large important institute over those of insignificant, wicked Voronel, however clear his rights might be, even to the judge himself.

Voronel tried to bring his case to the Higher Court, but his claim was dismissed out of hand.

* * *

September passed. October, November, and almost all of December passed, and I became almost convinced that they had decided not to call me in for questioning because they knew perfectly well that they could get no testimony from me that would be helpful to them.

But on December 30th, when I arrived at the university, I found a person waiting for me at the entrance.

"KGB," he said, pulling out his identity card. The neat dark suit, the necktie, the pale anonymous face — I knew what he was the minute I caught a glimpse of him. He produced a summons: my presence was demanded as a witness in an investigation — immediately — and he escorted me to a waiting car.

Within a short while I realized what our destination was to be. We had turned onto Energeticheskaya Street. Running along at least three long blocks on this street is the high barbed wire–topped fence surrounding the notorious Lefortovo Prison. (On the other side is the Institute of Energy; hence the street name.)

We stopped at the entrance to a two-story brick building, the first floor of which was blind, with no windows at all.

Having been transferred to the custody of a uniformed Lefortovo guard, I was taken upstairs to a large office, where I was awaited by three men who introduced themselves as KGB colonels. The spokesman told me that they were the investigators in charge of Especially Dangerous Crimes Against the State. They seated themselves at a long table and had me sit at a much smaller one in a corner of the room — an arrangement designed to make one feel small, guilty, helpless.

Before the questioning began, I was made to sign an acknowledgment stating that I had been advised of the fact that should I provide false or incomplete testimony, I was liable to prosecution under the Criminal Code. The first questions were routine, and my answers were very quick. They asked how long I had been acquainted with Daniel; what I could say about him; what sort of relations he and I had; and specifically whether there had ever been any disagreements between us — if we had ever been at odds; if anything had ever occurred that might give me grounds to believe Daniel could be hostile to me. Then I was asked if I had read *Moscow Speaking, Atonement,* and other works of Daniel's that they listed. They had all the titles.

It goes without saying that I answered I had never heard of these works. After a solid hour of interrogation, I signed an affidavit to that effect.

"You remember, Mark Yakovlevitch, that if you put your signature to false testimony you are liable to criminal charges?"

"Certainly."

"Very good."

Everything went smoothly. The officers were perfectly polite, very intelligent. After I signed, the principal among the three read over the testimony and handed it to the others.

"You know it's not too late, Mark Yakovlevitch, to reconsider this. You might think it over. You don't want to risk imprisonment for making misstatements. You can still tear this up — throw it away. You can give us the truth. Tell us what really happened. That you've really read Daniel's manuscripts." He was very kindly.

The second one took up the same tone, saying: "We all know anyone can make a mistake. Someone like yourself, a highly respected scientist, should realize that there would be no reprisals against you for having made this sort of error — if you saw fit to correct it."

Naturally, I reiterated that I was telling the absolute truth.

Next, I was asked if I was familiar with Daniel's handwriting.

"Well, yes, I think I've read some of Daniel's letters. I believe I have. But I can't be perfectly sure I could recognize his writing."

"Right," said the principal interrogator. "But we'd like you to read this excerpt from Daniel's testimony." He showed me a sheet of paper. I could read only half of it — he kept the other half covered. The document gave an account of each occasion at which Daniel had read to me from his works. There had been several subsequent to the one I mentioned, including a time when I was ill with pneumonia and he had come to Kharkov to see me. They all looked at me curiously as I finished reading.

"Now," said the senior officer, "we hope you will write the truth for us. You've been misleading us — unless you wish to claim that Daniel is not really a friend of yours at all, and *he* is lying, clearly with the intent of getting you into trouble. That's possible, of course."

Once more I answered that Daniel was my friend and that I was perfectly sure he had no intention of getting me into trouble. Meanwhile, my brain was working furiously in a vain attempt to figure out if this paper was a forgery and to guess what had happened to Daniel.

The discussion, polite but persistent, as to whether or not I was telling the truth, lasted another two hours. At the end of that time they apparently understood that I would not retract my original denial.

"Well, it's too bad," said the senior officer, with a resigned expression. "We're really sorry you can't seem to change your statement." A guard was called, and I was taken to another room, very small, with a high, barred window. There was nothing here but a bench, on which I sat and waited — without knowing what I was waiting for. I tried to use this time alone to ponder carefully everything that had happened, to disentangle in my mind every aspect of the situation, to struggle to understand what was going on. Under such circumstances I become very quiet, very slow-moving, and I attempt to eliminate any subjective emotional element from my thinking. It has always seemed to me that one can make a correct decision only when one is free from excitement, totally calm.

After an interval of thought I was ready for anything, including imprisonment. Despite the evidence of the document, I would not admit the charges; they must realize it by now, and there was nothing to stop them from treating me as a criminal.

I sat there for perhaps forty-five more minutes. At length the same guard came after me and brought me back to the room in which the questioning had taken place. One of the KGBsts asked me to sit down. Nobody said anything for a few minutes. Then the door opened — and in came Yuli Daniel.

Never in my life have I been so glad to see anybody. I sprang from my chair and ran to embrace him; we threw our arms around each other, ignoring the guards, who put a stop as soon as they could to this affectionate demonstration. To have Yuli here, within sight and reach — terribly thin and pale, older-looking as if by years rather than months; but still, thank God! here he was; still himself — was almost like seeing him risen from the dead. Neither I nor any of his other friends, nor Larisa, had had the remotest contact with him for three months.

Shortly we were each being interrogated by turns. Yuli repeated, in more detail, the statement I had already read. He urged me to corroborate what he was saying; to admit that I had heard him read from his works. "It's for my own sake that I'm asking you to admit it, Mark," he pursued. "Please believe that it would be to my advantage if you ceased to deny the facts." He even reminded me that at the time of the first reading he had requested me to give him my word that I would keep silent about it. "But now I'm asking you to forget that," he said. "You're released from that promise. It will be much better not just for you, but for me, if you tell the truth."

I said nothing.

"Are you going to refute Daniel's own statement?" asked one of the interrogators.

I tried to force myself to think. "I can't refute Daniel's statement," I finally answered. "He is my friend and a person whom I know to be incapable of lying. But about the dates: on the days those readings are supposed to have taken place, I was very ill. When he visited me in Kharkov I was in a very bad state with severe virus. Anything that happened around that time I could easily have forgotten. I was feverish for weeks and was hardly taking account of anything." I had no time to collect my thoughts. All I knew was that I didn't want to make any false or irreversible step.

The KGBsts tried hard, but still I did not retreat. The whole time they were talking to me, my mind was overcharged with unanswered questions. What was I supposed to do? What was Yuli expecting from me? Why had he expressed the wish that I should confirm this incriminating testimony? Perhaps I was making a fatal mistake, and he really did want me to retract my original statement. I had no way of knowing what would be in his best interests, and had to flounder through the interrogation guided only by a sort of instinct, which, for all I knew, was badly off course. Maybe he needed a witness to the real truth, a witness who was known to be his friend and not someone who could be suspected of being in partnership with the KGB. I might be on a totally wrong track.

It was very difficult to follow the discussion and to answer the questions while my mind was so besieged by conflict. I had never been in such a dilemma.

Finally, Yuli was dismissed. One of his guards ordered him to get up and to precede him through the doorway. We said goodbye. This time we were prevented from approaching each other, and I had to simply sit there, watching Yuli walk out, hands clasped behind his back, one guard ahead of him and the other following.

I didn't see him again for five years.

*   *   *

Yuli left, but I remained, in the same room, with the very same interrogators.

It was interesting to note what good psychologists they were. There were a few minutes after Yuli's departure when I lost confidence, wondering again if my stubbornness was to Yuli's advantage or if I might be injuring his cause.

Before, the officers had been polite and smooth; but now, sensing my momentary hesitation, they abruptly became tough and rude. They told me bluntly that I had lied to them, that I myself was liable to criminal charges.

"If you don't rewrite your testimony, you will not leave this prison," concluded the chief. "You know you're lying. We know it. You're probably worried about losing your post at the university. That's the least of your worries. You're not going to get back there. Make up your mind — you'll spend the New Year in a cell."

This sort of threat went on for five or ten minutes; but I could hardly hear their voices, I was so busy weighing in my mind which would be in

Yuli's best interests: to continue my denials or to change my testimony. It took me a while to formulate a definite policy. I decided that later on there would be nothing to stop me from doing as they said, if upon reflection I thought it would be in Yuli's best interests. If I were imprisoned today, tomorrow I could always request a second interview with these men and say, "Now I remember everything." If I escaped imprisonment, it would be only too easy to return to Lefortovo when I had thought everything over, and submit a different story. But for now, my only course was to repeat what I had said before.

The minute my resolve hardened and I felt sure of what I was going to do, they changed their behavior. No more rough words: again they were courteous and gentlemanly. But they stated very firmly that I could not leave the prison until such time as I would give an account in accord with the one they claimed they had extracted from Yuli. At this point I no longer cared for their threats. I had made up my mind.

After several more hours of hammering at me, they suddenly let me go. It was eleven P.M.

I left the prison and fled to my wife and friends, who were waiting for me in a state of mounting anxiety, more and more doubtful at that late hour as to whether I was coming back at all. While I recounted the events of the day, I drank numberless cups of coffee and ate everything I was offered; throughout those interminable hours I had been strung up at too high a pitch to think about food or drink, but now I was ravenous.

And here I have to make a very unpleasant admission. My decision, as I found later, was the right one. The absolute certainty that I was the person who could not be induced to confirm any admission of guilt he might be forced to make was what had led Daniel to devise this means of arranging a meeting with me. But the reason he wanted to was that it was vitally important for him to convey a message to other friends on the outside: from specific questions he had been asked in one of his interrogations, he had learned that these friends were under suspicion and in danger of arrest. He wanted to warn them to get rid of some contraband literature they possessed before it was too late. He had decided that for the sake of ensuring the freedom of these people, he would let me in for that heavy ordeal; he felt sure that I would be tough to the end and could not be trapped into bearing witness against him. On this point he was right, but he overestimated my cleverness. When the confrontation occurred, I was too absorbed with the question of what the right course of action would be to guess that he had engineered the interrogation and that every word he spoke was phrased so as to convey a coded warning. I should have listened carefully to each word. Yuli foresaw everything: that I wouldn't surrender, even when provided with the written testimony in his handwriting; that on account of my stubbornness the KGB would confront me with him. But he had hoped I would be smarter, and would pick up the cues he was dropping.

Years were to pass before I had a chance to hear from him what he had in mind. I went to visit him immediately upon his release, in the wretched little town of Kaluga, where he was staying, beyond the 101-kilometer distance from Moscow that ex-prisoners in his category have to maintain, and it was then that he explained his ruse to me. Luckily, word of the threat that hung over the heads of his friends came to them from another source, and disaster was headed off.

But to this day I still feel ashamed of having been so absorbed in my own maneuvers at that time that I failed to catch the hidden meaning in Yuli's words. It was a lesson to me.

The Sinyavsky-Daniel Trial

ALL THE PAPERS published articles about the traitors Daniel and Sinyavsky. They were indicted under Article 70 of the Criminal Code, which makes it a crime to spread propaganda "for the purpose of weakening or subverting the Soviet regime" or to circulate "slanderous fabrications that defame the Soviet State." They were to be tried publicly.

The trial turned out to be a turning point in Soviet domestic policy. In 'fifty-six, as we have seen, there was a slight loosening of the check-rein on freedom of expression inside the U.S.S.R., and gradually during the following eight or nine years, this liberalization expanded. The Party officials were, of course, afraid of it; and occasionally, after Brezhnev came to power, there were rumors about the rehabilitation, so to speak, of Stalin, about a movement to restore his memory in public esteem and veneration. This would have been the signal for reharnessing the creative people who were now cautiously enjoying a measure of liberty. When it looked as though this backward step might become a reality, the most eminent artists and scientists in the nation — among the latter Leontovitch, Tamm, and the then-unassailable Sakharov — fought back. They wrote a letter to the Politburo, warning against such a rehabilitation.

Now the trial, the first of its kind, would be really a sort of *ballon d'essai* sent up by the authorities. Whether writers publishing independently in the West would be viewed as traitors by the general public — and particularly by the intelligentsia — or as brave men exercising a self-evident right was a matter of crucial concern to those who wanted to crack down on the new freedoms.

It was very interesting to observe the initial reaction on the part of members of the educated classes to this trial, and I believe that this reaction influenced everything that occurred afterward on the political scene. When the indictment against Daniel and Sinyavsky was made public, Voronel and I and a few others among our friends went into action, working feverishly around the clock to arouse support for them — canvassing everyone we knew, circulating petitions to be sent to the Central Committee. We sought out people whom we knew to be fair-minded, sympathetic with liberal aims. We were taken aback by how often our pleas were rejected. "Those friends of yours may have written the truth about Soviet life," we heard from many whom we approached — intelligent, decent people — "but they're unpatriotic."

I am casting no blame upon those who raised this objection. I believe that the "crime" Yuli and Andrei had committed simply caught them unawares, mentally unprepared. This was a novel situation, and sympathetic though they might be to the ideas of both authors, they reacted with shock to the smuggling of these ideas outside national borders. They felt it was a betrayal to bring the defects of our society to the attention of foreign eyes. This concept of loyalty is in the old Russian tradition.

At the university and the institute, there were those who rejected Voronel's and my requests for support with the comment "A scientist is a scientist, and he should remain neutral in politics."

Then there was another viewpoint, expressed by an Academician, a decent and conscientious man, who, when he heard about our campaign, said: "This sort of decision should not be forced; it has to be left up to each individual for himself. This is a moral issue, a matter of one's own conscience, on which one can speak only for oneself — not as part of a group."

For one reason or another, then, more than half of the influential people among the intelligentsia kept silent about Sinyavsky and Daniel's fate. What the Party officials had in mind was achieved: even those who considered the indictment unjust were shocked by the thought of open protest. What was most painful to those of us who worked so hard to save Daniel and Sinyavsky was that not long afterward the same people who had refused to help them had a change of heart. They did become vocal partisans of the two authors — when it was too late. But in the mid-'sixties the climate of opinion was such that Voronel and I and others who fought for Sinyavsky and Daniel really had no chance of getting the indictment lifted. We could not face that fact, however, and kept right on working and hoping up until the last minute.

On February 10th, the trial began. Sasha and I and a small crowd of other supporters of the defendants arrived early at the Moscow City Courthouse.

Let me just describe what it was like to be in the vicinity of the courthouse during such a trial. Imagine the situation: you come out of the

subway station, and when you emerge onto the street, still a block away
from the courthouse, you are already surrounded by an enormous
number of policemen and plainclothes KGBsts. (Once again, you have
no trouble identifying the latter. Such an empty face, with an expression
that tries to imitate the nonchalance of all the other faces in the crowd;
such an affectation of leisure, beneath which the tension, the constant
observation of everything around is only half-concealed — you cannot
confuse these people with anyone else. Each of them looks at you, in-
vestigates, as you go by. Are you going about your own business, or are
you a friend of these condemned people in the courthouse, one who
ought to be condemned yourself?)

The nearer you approach your destination, the denser the crowd of
policemen and KGBsts becomes. By the time you are this close, they are
sure you are not just a random passerby. And now small cameras appear, and you are photographed a dozen times. The pictures will be included in many files, including, of course, the one at your place of
work. You know that any minute you may be stopped, hit with a
trumped-up charge of any crime or violation of city ordinances. You
may be taken to the police station and detained indefinitely.

If you get through this menacing sentry guard, you huddle in the
small group of your friends assembled there, completely cut off from
the anonymity of ordinary pedestrians; walled in (there is a high wall
around the entrance to the Moscow City Courthouse), and surrounded
by upwards of a hundred militiamen and plainclothesmen, who survey
you all with open hatred and contempt. These men are well trained,
thoroughly indoctrinated. And they only await the signal to close in on
you, to crush you.

On the first day of the trial I used a trick in order to enter the building: I approached one of the officers in the cordon, claiming that I had
business in the courthouse connected with another case, and showing
him my identification papers as a university professor. (They were much
more cautious during the two subsequent days of the trial; I could only
manage this once.) But once inside the building, I found that the courtroom in which Daniel and Sinyavsky were being "openly" tried was
also heavily guarded, and here no tricks could work. At least I was on
the premises, though, and would be able to find out what was going on
from Larisa when the court recessed, and could pass the news on to the
others waiting outside.

Since the court would not recess for several hours and I did not want
to hang about and attract the attention of the police guarding the door
to this particular courtroom, I walked along the vast corridor until I ar-

rived at another room where a trial was in progress. I joined the crowd of spectators filing in to observe this proceeding, and sat down.

What I had walked in on turned out to be one of the commonest of all Soviet legal actions, a divorce case. A man was suing his wife. Despite all the concerns I had on my mind, I couldn't help paying attention to this proceeding, and I can't resist giving the reader an idea of how the trial was conducted. It demonstrates very clearly the general level of public conscience in the Soviet Union.

When the sordid and pathetic accusations of each of these poor people had been made, one against the other, the judge (a woman) turned to the man and said, "You're a worthless specimen." She then addressed the wife: "What's the matter with you, wanting to hang on to an idiot like this? I can't understand it. He's no good, and he's not even good-looking. You'd be a lot better off if you got rid of him." There was a murmur of approval in the courtroom; before I left the case had simply fallen apart.

I might have been amused had I not been convinced that there is a good and profound reason for upholding the dignity of the court. The judge had nothing to offer this man except a slap in the face, nothing to offer the woman but homely sympathy. The legalities of the couple's situation were never consulted. Defying the convention that demands treating both parties with impartial courtesy, the court had simply dismissed the law. It made me realize again how slim the chances were of anyone obtaining a fair trial. Moreover, it was a revelation to see how this casual procedure was generally accepted.

I left the courtroom with less confidence than ever that impersonal, objective justice might be found in this country.

* * *

During the entire three days of the Sinyavsky-Daniel trial, all of us, all of their friends, were in an agony of suspense and apprehension. It will be remembered that the Russian press made much of the "public" nature of this trial. But the only people who favored the defendants' cause permitted into the courtroom were Larisa Daniel and Maria Sinyavsky; all the other spectators were carefully screened. The courtroom was packed; every bit of space was taken up by KGBsts or people whose antagonistic attitude toward the accused could be depended on: they had special passes. Foreign reporters were denied entry; they were simply told there was no room.

On the second day of the trial, Sasha and I received confirmation as to our guess regarding the identity of the informer. Larisa told us that

Chmielnitsky had appeared in court; he had been recalled from his post in Central Asia to provide evidence against Sinyavsky and Daniel. She said she had never seen a man so changed. In the half-year since he had left Moscow, he had become diminished somehow — pale and sallow, furtive-looking. His eyes moved slyly from face to face, and it struck Larisa that he had a particularly nasty expression when he glanced at women, as if undressing them in his fancy.

None of the rest of us saw him: evidently the KGB hustled him in and out of the courthouse by some back entrance. Here was a once lively, talented person who in any decent society would never have encountered the pressures that turned him into a coward, an object of loathing. He might even have been very successful — he was a gifted poet. But he was born in the wrong place. He had been burned by the Soviet acid test.

I never felt more desperately helpless than during these days, waiting hour after hour at the courthouse. There was no hope, even when Larisa reported a brilliant refutation brought by Yuli or Andrei to the interpretations one hostile witness or another had made of various passages from their books. "Evidence" against both authors mounted. We knew the outcome had been decided in advance. It was crushing, but no surprise, when the verdict was announced. Guilty. Sinyavsky was sentenced to seven years' imprisonment, and Daniel, in consideration of being a wounded veteran, to five. Petitions for clemency went unheeded.

*   *   *

After the trial all of us, Yuli and Andrei's friends, were absolutely exhausted. When scientists in solid state physics were invited to take part in the Winter Science School in Kaurovka, in the Urals near Sverdlovsk, Voronel and I gladly accepted the opportunity to get out of the city and have a fortnight's change of scene — we would not only participate in very interesting work in our fields; we would have a chance to ski and hike in the mountains. When we boarded the train we were much relieved at finding a coupé to ourselves. All we wanted was to rest, after what we had been through. Most of the time we just slept; we hardly even talked to each other. We had little luggage, but each of us had in his briefcase some of the material transcribed from the trial proceedings. Larisa had taken notes, and we intended to go over the case, when we were up to it, and analyze everything that had happened.

When we arrived at Sverdlovsk we were astonished to find a policeman waiting for us on the station platform.

"Citizen Azbel? Citizen Voronel?" We admitted to our identities. "You're wanted at the police office. Follow me." The police office in every city is near the railway station; we didn't have far to go.

We were terribly alarmed. If we were searched, the records of the trial would be discovered.

I realized that we must have been under close surveillance ever since we left for the Moscow-Kazansky Station; we must have been under observation while we were buying our tickets. Not only was our destination known to the police and KGB, but the exact train we would take. Although it didn't surprise us to be thoroughly checked up on in Moscow, we believed that the authorities usually lose interest in a subject once he is known to be at a safe distance, particularly in a case like this, where we were on a specific *kommandirovka* for a professional conference.

On the way to the office, we asked the policeman what the charge against us was.

"Drunk and disorderly" was the answer. The story was that we had been drinking since the start of the trip and had caused such trouble and annoyance to the other passengers that the conductor had wired a complaint ahead to the Sverdlovsk police.

We were silenced. If this childish fabrication was to be grounds for our arrest, it was easy to guess what lay ahead. A night in jail and a "routine" search of our possessions. The records of the trial would be discovered. This was a disaster, and there was no way out.

At the police station we were ushered unceremoniously into the office of the chief. He demanded to see our passports and our authorizations for travel to Kaurovka. When we produced both without hesitation, an atmosphere of confusion erupted in the room. "Just a minute, here." Police came and went, and our papers were checked over half a dozen times by different officers. "There must be some mistake." We were asked to wait in another room, but from there we could overhear a telephone conversation in the police chief's office.

"Yes. Yes, the travel certificate is in order. Yes, it's got the stamp. Yes, they each have one. Sure. Positively."

A few minutes later a gendarme came into the waiting room and told us we could go. Lightheaded with relief, we walked out of the building. On the local train that carried us to Kaurovka, we kept discussing what had happened, wondering by what magic we had been released.

It appeared that we had indeed been tailed to the station, our purchase of tickets to Sverdlovsk had been noted, and the KGB, perfectly well aware of where we were, had sent representatives to my regularly scheduled Friday lecture. Finding me absent had provided them with an excuse to make inquiries of my chairman. The chairman could provide them with no clue as to my whereabouts; he knew nothing about the note I had left Leontovitch, saying I had canceled my classes for such-and-such dates and would be away at the Winter School.

As it happened, the kommandierovka originated not from the university, but from the Institute for Theoretical Physics, which paid the expenses. However, the KGB made no further investigation, and as far as they were concerned I had left with no authorization at all. By coincidence, the check on Voronel produced the same results: they sought him only at Dubna; but having recently had his connection with that installation severed, Sasha had obtained his permit from Mendeleyevo. So it looked to the KGB as though we were both on a secret and unauthorized trip.

When the Sverdlovsk police discovered that, contrary to the information they had received, Voronel and I had perfectly valid documents proving that we had been invited to an important scientific meeting, they were at a loss as to what to do. Of course, the police chief's call had been to the KGB. Now the situation looked completely different! We were not dissidents on a clandestine mission, but eminent scientists, the invited guests of Academician Vonsovsky (Deputy of the Supreme Soviet, President of the Ural Branch of the Academy, and a host of other titles).

That was a break. But the incident revealed to us how closely we were being followed.

Of course, even to have been near the courthouse during the days of the trial was a very serious matter. I had become a bad person in the eyes of the officials. I was immediately advised that I was to be dismissed from my post at the university, and if it had not been for Rector Petrovsky, who exerted every ounce of his remaining authority on my behalf, I would indeed have been fired. Petrovsky called a Party secretary, and again I had to go through the farce of claiming that I knew nothing of the condemned writings. Petrovsky also had to back me up and vouch for the truth of everything I said.

Over the Crest

WHILE THE CONFERENCE at the Winter School was still in progress, the newspapers arrived. In *Izvestia* was the list of people eligible for the Lenin Prize. The names of those under consideration for the prize are considered at intervals. From stage to stage the candidates' merits are reviewed by the Lenin Prize Committee, and those whom they believe to be unqualified are weeded out.

I had been in the running, along with three others, all men of most distinguished reputation: we were candidates on the basis of work in the theory of metals. But after all the agitating I had done on behalf of Daniel and Sinyavsky, when the official attempt to remove me from Moscow University had been thwarted only by dint of so much effort, I assumed my chances of obtaining this award were dead. So I was perfectly astounded to find my name published in *Izvestia*. This meant that the prize was almost a certainty.

The annual presentation of the Lenin Prize is a very special event, which attracts a great deal of publicity. The Soviets are enthusiastic about heightening the prestige of their scientists, in whom they take such tremendous pride. This is not an official sentiment only: ordinary Soviet people look upon scientists as wizards who will invent ever more wonderful things, in particular weapons to insure Russia against defeat in a possible war. The presentation creates a sensation in all the news media; even acceptance into the Academy of Sciences is a lesser occasion.

I will say frankly that, although I had been sure I was no longer a candidate, I had waited for the paper impatiently and was quite elated when I saw my name. I suppose even a scientist is entitled to his vanity. Moreover, this news was very important to me because it might mean that, after all, my involvement in the trial would not hinder my further promotion. Once a Lenin laureate, it was very likely that the next step would be to become a Corresponding Member of the Academy and, in time, Academician.

An Academician is in about the most enviable position of anyone in the top echelons of Soviet society. It is not only the munificent salary, the dacha, the automobile, the easy entrée into all the most sought-after artistic and cultural events, the enormous influence, and so forth, none of which was of much interest to me, that make this so. Top-level Party members and members of the Writers' Union share these privileges and more. But the latter can never be secure. No Party official, not even the General Secretary himself, can be sure from one day to the next that he will still hold his post tomorrow — witness the case of Khrushchev, who sank like a stone in 'sixty-four and was missed by few. (It was an Olympics year, and people used to joke "Khrushchev should get the medal for the World's Record Free-Fall.") Membership in the Party renders one liable to expulsion — the most disastrous type of excommunication; you are almost unemployable thereafter. Expulsion from the Writers' Union is as bad. But membership in the Academy is permanent. Lysenko, even after being exposed as a fraud, died an Academician, and, at the opposite extreme, Sakharov's outspoken dissent against the Soviet system earned him every punishment, every condemnation, at the disposal of the authorities — but he is still an Academician. Such a position was certainly something to aspire to, and I could not be indifferent to the honor that meant it could be within my reach some time in the future.

By the beginning of April, I was already hearing advance congratulations from my senior friends at the university and the Institute for Theoretical Physics. This was a triumphant time in my life. The two physicists I had worked with looked as happy as I.

I can see myself now, in my mind's eye, on the day of the Lenin Prize awards. It is April 19th, 1966. I am in one of the large seminar rooms at the Institute for Physical Problems. All the close scientific community of the Institute for Theoretical Physics is assembled there, waiting for the representative of this institute (it was the institute that had nominated us for the prize), who was closeted with the Lenin Prize Committee. The committee is going through the last routine ceremony, the gathering of the Plenum. (The Plenum consists not only of scientists, but of artists, writers, composers, "Stakhanovite" workers and peasants, and other Soviet citizenry, all of whom have to cast their votes. For most of these electors, those who know nothing of physics or any of the other fields to whose most distinguished contributors they award the prize, this is simply a gesture, a show of "democracy." They have been told who was chosen by the scientists of the committee, and they know that should be their choice also.)

At the end of our wait, Sergei Kapitza rushed in, looking agitated. (This is Academician Kapitza's elder son, himself a physicist.)

"You didn't get it!" he said to our group — the three other nominees, and myself. "*You* got it!" he announced to three others, who had been eliminated in the finals.

I'll have to admit I was absolutely stunned. People gathered around Kapitza. "What do you mean, they didn't get it? The Prize Committee never changes the decision at this point!" A hubbub arose. "What went wrong?"

"Let me talk to them," said Sergei, and he and I with the other would-be laureates went out into the hall, where we could talk by ourselves.

The withdrawal of the prize was the consequence of an occurrence all too common in the Soviet Union, but probably unprecedented at the awarding of Lenin Prizes. Just an hour before the Plenum was to convene, an anonymous note had been dropped on the desk of Academician Mstislav Keldysh, President of the Academy of Sciences and Chairman of the Plenum. Although it is unusual for such a letter to appear at the Academy, they are delivered by the hundreds at other institutions: the Central Committee, the KGB, and the newspapers receive a great many of them every day and treat them very seriously. The letter accused me of being a close friend of Daniel and Sinyavsky and accessory to their "vicious anti-Soviet crimes." It protested the awarding of the Lenin Prize to a person of such low character.

Academician Keldysh knew as well as anyone else of my partisanship for Sinyavsky and Daniel; but since there had been no word from any source up to that time suggesting that I was thereby disqualified as a candidate for the Lenin Prize, he had naturally not concerned himself about the matter. Now, however, he was alarmed.

The timing of the delivery of this note was very precise. Had it arrived the day before, Keldysh would have had a chance to call top-level Party officials to find out what action he should take, or if he should dismiss the accusation. Two hours later, and it would have been too late; the decision about the prize would have been signed. He formally suggested to the Plenum to "postpone" the decision, as some new information had appeared and had to be checked. He didn't go into any detail.

The fact that until the last few hours I was slated for this distinguished award showed that the officials had not yet ascertained from which quarter the political wind was blowing; within a short time all such uncertainties had been resolved, and, although I did not become ineligible for prizes in the coming years, no mention of me was ever made again in the news when I did receive them. There is nothing random about recognition in the Soviet press: to attain it is a signal honor, and no one who is not in good standing with the authorities, however highly he may be regarded professionally, should hope to see his achievements cited in the papers.

There was a ripple effect from this decision. Steps of this kind very explicitly hint to the officials that the members of a group are well prepared for the ostracism of an individual who has become persona non grata. The Party bosses, who are always taking the pulse of opinion among influential people to find out how much control any specific group will stand for, pay even closer attention at any time of crisis to the relations among everyone in such groups. The unquestioning willingness of my colleagues to accept my exclusion conveyed the message "We're ready. You can take him over."

In May, the officials suggested to the Institute for Theoretical Physics that I should be eliminated from the Scientific Council there. The stated reason for this exclusion was not, of course, that I had become a man with suspect connections, on whom the KGB in all likelihood now had an active file. It was very simple: the Academy had not O.K.'d my nomination to the council.

By sheer chance the director of the institute, Khalatnikov, was on leave of absence at that time. I am sure he would have hastened to act in conformity with the first hint that there was a movement afoot to arrange for my dismissal. He lived in fear of any sort of trouble at the institute, and the faintest brush with authority, the merest breath of any sort of dissent on the part of a member of his staff, would have scared him half to death.

In Khalatnikov's absence, Lev Gorkov was acting director. He was furious when he heard I was to be let go from the council, and immediately went to the very top, the Academy vice-president, and asked indignantly just how irreversible this decision was, since the man in question really was needed on the Scientific Council. The result was very quick: I was reinstated. But if Khalatnikov had not been away, this story would have had a different ending.

*   *   *

Similar trials followed not long after the Sinyavsky-Daniel trial. Alexander Ginzburg and Yuri Golanskov were prosecuted for circulating *samizdat* material, including excerpts from the Daniel-Sinyavsky trial. As far as I was concerned at that time, the priority of my conscience was simply this: freedom of choice as to who my friends would be.

Sinyavsky and, even more, Daniel were not only men whose brilliance and courage I admired; they were people I counted among those most dear to me, who had a prime call upon my loyalties. My reasons for supporting them had much more to do with these feelings than with any political considerations. I was not among those who waited outside the court during Ginzburg and Golanskov's trial; I didn't know them. I was not yet ready to sacrifice my scientific career and dedicate my life to the fight for human rights. Shattered by what had happened to Yuli and Andrei, I withdrew into my science and continued my work on solid state physics.

The attitude of the intelligentsia toward the Ginzburg trial was very different from that which they had held toward the earlier one. Belatedly, however, people began to understand their real interests; many summoned the courage to join Sakharov in his battle to defend these men.

Not long after this trial, the mathematician-philosopher, Alexander Yesenin-Volpin* was committed to a psychiatric hospital. He was one of the first to be victimized in this way. For more than a decade he had been producing treatises that pled, with increasing urgency, for human rights and for a more equitable system of justice in Russia. Some hundreds of scientists, including many from Moscow University, signed a letter, simply expressing the hope that Yesenin-Volpin would be humanely treated and would receive careful medical diagnosis; a very innocent letter. However, the officials considered it important to demonstrate that the time of freedom was in the past. Many of those who signed it lost their jobs. Others had to condemn themselves at various meetings. Still others were condemned at meetings by their friends.

This was horrible.

When one of the most famous and talented Soviet mathematicians, an elderly man, was called before the Party committee and he was asked why he had signed this letter, he answered, "Well . . . at my age, one has to think of God." There were very few who followed his example. It was just too dangerous.

At this time the law against "parasitism" was enforced more and more often. The definition of parasitism was never really clear. When the law was first promulgated, under Khrushchev, the public was given to understand that parasites were people without visible means of support whose sources of income might very well be black-marketeering, the sale of illegally imported goods, and so forth — *spekulyanti.* But it

---

* Son of the great poet Yesenin, whose works — like those of all serious artists of the 'thirties — were suppressed soon after they appeared; but which came to light again in the 'sixties and were now widely appreciated, long after Yesenin was dead.

was explained in the newspapers (which serve as transmitters of the law and are often a citizen's only source of information as to constitutional changes and addenda) that not only the unemployed are parasites; in some cases a person *with* a job can be one — he is using his job to hide his parasitism! It became clear very early that the targets of this law were to be not shady operators in the underworld, but primarily, intellectuals.

One of the first to be charged with the new crime was the poet Yosif Brodsky. He was exiled to the North. This despite the fact that his poems had been published, his translations of foreign poetry had also been published, and there was no question at all as to his means of support. The eminent critics Chukovsky and Entin tried to protect him, but nothing could save him. By the time he came to trial, his sentence had already been determined by Party officials. The trial was no trial; only a formal denunciation.

Fortunately, by now both Brodsky and Entin are in the West, and gallant Korney Chukovsky is no longer among the living. Brodsky was a very courageous man, and his supporters were hardly less so: they knew that by coming to the poet's defense they risked, at the least, never again being published themselves. For a writer, this is death.

And now we were hearing more about parasitism, and members of the intelligentsia were again being charged with this crime.

I had little idea then, in 'sixty-seven, that this law could ever be applied to myself. At that time I was still a very prosperous scientist. But I could see that things were changing for the worse, month by month.

*   *   *

What are the reasons for these eternal and ever-renewed persecutions?

My own guess would be this: the main problem for Soviet leaders has always been simply to hold on to their power. General Secretary, President, Party Chairman — whatever the post — the incumbent must battle ceaselessly to hold it. He cannot relax his vigilance, cannot let hostile influences go undetected or opposition go unpunished, without risking dethronement. I remember a conversation among a close circle of friends about the resignation of Semychastny, the KGB chief who had to leave his post immediately upon the catastrophic exposure of the Soviet intelligence service when it failed to prevent Svetlana Stalina, Stalin's daughter, from getting to the United States. Most of us thought that Semychastny's departure was related to that incredible slip, when Stalina eluded heavy surveillance at the Soviet Embassy in New Delhi and fled to the United States Embassy. But one of my friends — very smart in politics — said: "Well, yes, that might be the reason Semychastny had to go. But it's even more likely that the sudden carelessness on the part of the intelligence service was deliberate. They let it happen on purpose, in order to create a pretext for Semychastny's resignation. It looks to me like a frame-up. Someone else is supposed to get his post. My guess is that the whole scenario was prepared well in advance." Such an intrigue struck the rest of us at first as completely unbelievable. But on consideration I admit that my friend might be right; that such maneuvers often do occur. There is a whole pattern of depositions in our history. Almost none of those who organized the Revolution survived until 1940; none of those who came to power after Stalin's death have retained their power. No one in the Soviet hierarchy can afford to ignore a challenge to the system. He feels himself to be surrounded by enemies; he must seek out every hint of opposition and quash it.

The docility of the Soviet public is ensured to a large extent by its being kept on such short rations. It is very little known in the West that the baseline used in the Soviets to gauge the growth of the gross national product (with all its exaggerated figures, as in the case of wheat) is the output of the year 1913. When as a schoolboy I encountered this fact, it struck me as perfectly natural. The Soviet economists didn't want to use as the starting point the figures that were depressed by World War I; they took care not to be accused of comparisons that would unfairly glorify Soviet accomplishments. I was mistaken about that: I discovered later that it was not the Bolshevik Revolution that brought such "prosperity" to Russia. The truth is that between 1914 and 1917 production increased considerably, despite the cataclysmic upheavals the country was going through. A comparison between the production figures during those years and the ones published during the first five Bolshevik decades would testify to the economic disaster Bolshevism brought in its wake. The 1917 agricultural output was exceeded only a few years ago.

This stunted growth obtains in what I think is the richest country in the world, with fertile soil, vast mineral resources, thousands of square miles of timberland — everything. That such a country should be reduced to so low a level of subsistence indicates a leadership far more interested in its own power than in the welfare of the people.

The majority of the populace is kept in such straitened conditions that it is hardly a figure of speech to say it is being systematically starved into submission to the will of its leaders. All the strength of the nation and of the people is concentrated on military research, on outer-space exploration, and so forth; what energy is left over goes into sport or ballet and other artistic pyrotechnics. All of Soviet wealth is poured into areas of threat or of spectacle.

And under these circumstances, the leadership assumes that persecutions are needed to keep all the people silent and obedient.

Dissent

THE FACT that I was retained at the institute proved absolutely crucial
to me, not only professionally but with regard to my own private life.
Naya and I had realized for some time that we couldn't stay together,
and early in 1967 we were divorced. (Neither of us was subjected to any
sort of judicial humiliation: an uncontested divorce is a perfectly simple
procedure, a matter of only two or three minutes in court. Except in unusual cases, custody of children is automatically assumed by the
mother.) As I mentioned before, many divorced couples are trapped
with each other, though separated by their own choice and by law, but
forced, because neither one can possibly get a propiska to live anywhere
else, to go on sharing the same cramped quarters. But when I ceded our
apartment to Naya, the institute unofficially arranged to let me have an
apartment at Chernogolovka, and when I remarried that same year, my
wife and I were able to live there.

*   *   *

My second wife is Lydia Semyonovna Warshavskaya ("Lucia" is
her name among her friends), whom I had got to know when she was
in her last year as a student in the Chemistry Department at Moscow
University.

Lucia's background was quite different from mine. Her father was a
most distinguished professor of chemistry, a Stalin and Lenin laureate, a
member in good standing of the Moscow scientific Establishment.
Lucia, at the age of twenty-five, had many of her pristine Soviet ideals
intact. "You're disillusioning me!" she used to say when we first compared our views on life in the U.S.S.R. This is not to say that she was
blind to the inequities of the system or insensitive to the destructive
elements in our society: for one thing, she had felt the effects of anti-
Semitism, of course, as much as any other Jewish Muscovite. But she
clung to the belief that these negative forces were not an inherent part
of Russian life.

Owing not only to my influence, but to the turn our lives were to take, Lucia changed her mind.

* * *

Chernogolovka was quite a change from Moscow. The whole village is a scientific settlement: there are several institutes and a number of apartment buildings, the same nine-story blocks in which most city-dwellers live, but all hidden in dense and beautiful forest. In creating these installations, the Soviet architects and planners leave standing all the trees they can, so the walk from your apartment to your institute is a very pleasant one through the woods; you can often pick berries or mushrooms on the way. In winter, you go on skis. There are various amenities: a cinema that often shows movies which never appear in town, good schools, a sports center, a polyclinic. Every attraction is offered to channel the scientists away from Moscow. A senior researcher such as I was accorded a three-room apartment, for which I paid forty roubles a month. (The size of your apartment in these scientists' villages is determined strictly according to your professional status.) We all had telephones. They were regularly bugged, by the way, because some of the institutes were doing classified work. You could hear the clicks on the line.

Everything was very convenient here, except for the provision of food. The market was pitifully ill-stocked, though lavish compared with the food stores in the villages nearby. Every time I went into Moscow, I went to a very good butcher I'd discovered — my meat "connection" — in hopes he had saved me something. Every Friday, Lucia, with the wives of other resident scientists, took the bus to Moscow to buy groceries for the week; really exhausting excursions brightened only by the occasional treasure trove — oranges, say, or fresh fish.

We were happy in Chernogolovka, although I suppose I have to admit that, like everyone else, we would have preferred to be in the capital.

* * *

In May of 1967 the newspapers were filled with editorials about the aggressive policies of Israel in the Middle East. There were innumerable articles on how, very soon, the Arabs would punish Israel; in fact, it was implied, would conquer Israel and eliminate Israel from the face of the earth.

The Six-Day War was the most exciting experience of a lifetime to thousands and thousands of Soviet Jews. None of us thought of anything but the war during that agonizing week. We hovered over our radios, hardly daring to breathe. (Sometimes the jamming was impenetrable but you could usually get the Voice of Israel, the West German broadcasts, or the BBC without too much trouble.)

Overnight, we recognized how close was the fate of Israel to our hearts. We lived in desperate fear. We knew the Arab world was totally prepared for war; that there were a hundred million Arabs and three million Jews. It seemed irrational to expect anything but disaster.

Strangely enough, the news commentary in Russian on the Voice of Israel was not very informative. We could not get a clear idea of the progress of the war, and for that reason news of the victory came as an overwhelming surprise.

The incredulity, the joy, felt by all of us is something I could never describe. Of course we couldn't express it publicly: any celebration had to be quiet and behind closed doors. We took care not to make a show of our elation.

It would be hard to convey the internal transformation that took place among Soviet Jews. They acquired a totally new outlook, a new soul; were proud for the first time in centuries of being Jews, of belonging to a people who could fight — heroically, against fantastic odds — for their own country. What a different world it became when the most notable event in one's national consciousness was not the familiar tale of persecution and defeat, but a triumph that would live in history.

Nor was it only the Jews who were deeply impressed when Israel won the war; the Russians were, too. The Soviets were not happy about the enormous military assistance they had squandered on the Arabs, with nothing to show for it. And some military personnel who had been in Egypt and other Arab countries came back hardly pleased by what they had seen there. But there was a more important change: after all the news stories about the great Arab army of one hundred million, the victory of the handful of Jews was far too stunning for the ordinary Russian man in the street to dismiss.

Before the Six-Day War, derision of the Jews for cowardice was a cliché among Russians. They were accused of having shirked military service in the Great Patriotic War: "Ivan is at the front, fighting; Avram is in Tashkent, trading." But now the popular attitude changed; a grudging respect emerged. You began to hear a new kind of joke — not, of course, pro-Jewish, but of a sort that showed a change in people's estimation of Jews. For instance: an army colonel, riding the subway, encounters a Jew and starts beating him. Other passengers ask the colonel, "What are you beating him for?" He answers, "Well! Yesterday I heard on the morning news that the Jews were approaching Gaza. Then on the evening news I hear they're approaching Cairo. And now —

today — I get on the Metro, and, my God, they're already *here!* We've got to defend ourselves!"

No pro-Israeli or pro-Jewish propaganda one may imagine could have done half as much to defeat popular anti-Semitism as this war.

But more than a year later — we were still savoring the bright reflected glory from Israel — news of a new war came over the air. Czechoslovakia was making a desperate bid for freedom. Once again we stayed close to our radios, struggling to get a clear signal, sickened by suspense, listening in hope and fear to news of Dubček's brave achievements, the valiant battles of the Czechs, and the growth of forces massed against them. There were some among us who thought the Czechs had a chance; I myself could not summon that much optimism.

When Czechoslovakia was invaded, an astounding phenomenon occurred — something that had never happened before in Soviet times: a small crowd of people conducted a protest demonstration in Moscow. Of course, it was put down almost before it began, and everyone who took part in it was arrested. But you could see that a completely new spirit was abroad in Russia. Little more than a decade before, when the Hungarian revolt took place, it never occurred to anyone, however sympathetic with the revolutionaries' cause, to make a sound. We felt very sorry for the Hungarians, but there was nobody foolhardy enough to say so.

No one in the free world can imagine how much courage it required to rally publicly against an action taken by the State. It would require an entire separate story to account for the heroism of that handful of people, to explain what gave each of them the courage to take a step that might lead to death. Two friends of ours were among them: Larisa Bogoraz-Bruchman, Yuli Daniel's wife, and Natalya Gorbanevskaya. Natalya took that enormous risk even though she had a small child at home. Both of them were badly beaten in the mêlée that erupted.

After the Czechs were crushed (and I can't describe how agonizing it was to listen to the desperate reports on the short-wave radio; we felt just like landbound people hearing an SOS call from a doomed ship), the groups who had attempted to arouse the concern of the world on their behalf were condemned. Some were exiled to Siberia; all were labeled anti-Soviet, enemies of the people, and — Jews.

To be a liberal in Russia is to be a Jew. It was announced at Party meetings, for instance, that Sakharov, who had protested the invasion, was a Jew; that his name was originally Zuckerman; that Sinyavsky was a Jew, Abram Tertz.

I had the honor of knowing Andrei Dmitrievitch Sakharov quite well.

I feel that his human stature is incomparably above that of any other person alive.

The photograph of him in this book gives only a slight impression of Sakharov's smile, his glance. His expression conveys the feeling that he is looking not only at you, but far into the distance, as well. He is slow of speech, very attentive to what others have to say; he is unwilling to interrupt anyone. In fact, it is often difficult to hear his opinion, because anyone can interrupt him and speak for him, and he will listen.

This is a man of remarkable genius. He was one of the principal inventors of the Soviet hydrogen bomb, an accomplishment that made him a member of the Academy of Sciences at once — the youngest Academician in the history of that body. Decorated three times with the Golden Star of a Hero of Socialist Labor and the Lenin Banner, Andrei Dmitrievitch received an incredible number of Lenin and Stalin Prizes and, if one adds up the emoluments that accompany these awards, he must have been the richest professional in the Soviet Union.

But Sakharov could not insulate himself from the great problems that confront modern man. He gave constant thought to the one crucial concern that confronts all of humanity equally: the danger of total annihilation through nuclear warfare. Hardly secondarily, he pondered the matter of spiritual annihilation: the suppression of human rights, particularly in the Soviet Union.

At a certain point Sakharov decided to speak his mind. No one in the Soviet Union in a position such as his could doubt that to take a dissenting stance meant to sacrifice all the rewards he had ever earned. To gain his soul meant to lose the world.

But Andrei Dmitrievitch was not at all interested in money, at least for his own use; he gave all of it, more than half a million roubles, toward the foundation of the Cancer Institute. Being at the very top of the scientific world, probably one of the most important people in the nation, he had come in for all the perquisites of the Soviet aristocracy, including a tremendous two-story dacha outside Moscow situated in a beautiful woods — for all practical purposes his private property — and so large that the mushroom crop from this single plot was enough to supply his entire household for the year. He had everything.

He gave it all up. He handed over his large house and his automobile to his stepson; made over everything he owned to others. His enormous Academician's salary went for prisoners' relief and other good causes; he kept practically nothing for himself.

In 1968 his essay "Progress, Peaceful Coexistence, and Intellectual Freedom" came into circulation. Here he presented his thoughts on the desperate need for a moratorium on the testing of nuclear weapons, and also a plea for a convergence between capitalism and Socialism.

Sakharov, despite his towering prestige, was subjected to severe official criticism after the publication of the essay. When he continued to speak out, and began to agitate publicly on behalf of those who were brought to trial for defaming the Soviet system, even he, invulnerable though he appeared to be, was toppled from his eminence. He was fired from the work in nuclear physics in which he had been engaged for twenty years and was eventually no more than a senior researcher at the Lebedyev Institute, in a department where no security clearance is required.

However painful it was to Andrei Dmitrievitch to be limited in his scientific work, he continued to dedicate all his attention — all of his life — to these two aims: to bring the great powers to their senses in regard to thermonuclear testing and the contemplation of nuclear war, and to the liberalization of Soviet internal politics. He never gave a moment's thought to the sacrifice of his own brilliant career.

When "Progress" first appeared, it was generally received as the work of a naïve idealist who had no idea of the machinery of power politics. Everybody I knew believed that, however great an intellect Sakharov might be, he was simply out of touch with reality. I shared that view myself. It seemed perfectly crazy to discuss arms limitations, the test ban, limitations of missile production, cooperation between Russia and the West in the economic support of undeveloped nations. And I lived with this impression for many years. But much later, in the mid-'seventies, I read in an introduction to a new Western edition of this work that most of the ideas about détente presently being worked between East and West, and the very concept of the nuclear test ban, were derived directly from Sakharov. Kissinger wrote that in some respects our present world is Sakharov's world.

Actually, if one lists all the more favorable trends of modern international politics, one is enumerating exactly what Sakharov set forth in his first essay.

The last time I saw Andrei Dmitrievitch, he was living in a small and dingy place, without even a propiska — legally, he has no address. With no propiska, his passport is invalid. He saw visitors in a tiny parlor or, more often, in the kitchen. His companions are his wife, Yelena Georgievna Bonner, and his very elderly mother-in-law. Yelena Georgievna suffers from injuries received during the War and is in constant danger of losing her eyesight.

When Sakharov openly expressed his sympathies for Czechoslovakia, he was subjected to severe official censure, and he and his wife both became victims of threats — including threats of physical violence — by the KGB. They have been victims of every sort of persecution since. But in spite of everything, they are incessant in their struggle with the almighty Soviet regime.

*   *   *

I thought a great deal about the workings of science and the fate of scientists in my country, and in 1968 I wrote a play, *Galileo Galilei.* Galileo's career always fascinated me, from two points of view. First, it epitomizes perfectly the entire evolutionary process of science. I was profoundly interested both by the greatness of Galileo's discoveries, and by his errors; for example, his quarrel with Kepler as to whether the earth and sun could possibly interact through empty space, or his theory of inertia, wherein he — astoundingly — predicts the law later formulated by Descartes and Newton, though he formulates it incorrectly. To me a significant part of the growth process of science or philosophy or art consists just in these inspired mistakes, which open up new avenues of exploration for subsequent generations.

Of prime interest, of course, is the dilemma of Galileo, who, in order to keep alive his chances of further scientific work, found himself forced to recant his own most important idea, and who after this recantation went on to make many discoveries. No historic event could have struck home harder to a Soviet scientist of my era.

I submitted the play to *Novy Mir,* the best literary journal in the Soviet Union. Alexander Tvardovsky, who had had the courage to publish *Ivan Denisovitch,* was shortly to leave his post as editor there; no one of his caliber could last forever in so conspicuous and sensitive a position in Russia. Even before Tvardovsky was forced to resign, he was known for his heavy and prolonged bouts of drinking. He was one of the many brilliant Russians I knew, or knew of, who could find no escape save alcohol from the intellectual prison in which he had to live. His health undermined by these excesses, he died not long after his retirement in 1970. The conflict between his longing to publish the truth and the need to stay within the good graces of the Establishment destroyed him.

The people I saw at *Novy Mir* were most appreciative in their comments about my play, but they couldn't accept it. I was told, "The time has passed when we could publish anything of this sort. You're sailing much too close to the wind." The interval of relative freedom in the arts had completed its cycle. Once again, boundaries were shrinking.

Outer Limits

I HAVE always loved to travel, and took every opportunity to do so. Travel is one of the most attractive rewards offered to scientists and to others in or near the top echelons of Soviet society. Of course, the most coveted of all prizes is a trip abroad; but my own hopes of ever going beyond the Iron Curtain were, as I have explained, almost nil. Still, I was eager to see as much as I could of the U.S.S.R. One of the scientific conferences of which I was a member took place on a steamer that went from Krasnoyarsk to Dudinka; then at Dudinka the other conference members and I went by train to Norilsk.

The trip was along the upper two-thirds of the Yenisei River, and concluded almost at its source. The Yenisei is, I would guess, two miles in width; it must be one of the broadest rivers in the world. Either shore is dense with virgin forest; the trees are perfectly huge and must be of incalculable age. This is the taiga. Once, when the ship anchored offshore, we went on land to explore. But this is no place for incursions by human beings: the minute the ship stopped moving we found ourselves surrounded by a black cloud of huge bloodthirsty mosquitoes. You could kill thousands of them with one slap.

We found the forest impassable. Over the centuries so many gigantic trees have fallen and so much underbrush has grown up everywhere that you would need a heavy woodsman's axe to make your way ten paces through the tangle. Close to, the ancient trees were even more enormous than they had looked to be when we viewed them from the deck: two or three people with arms outstretched, holding hands, could hardly have embraced one of them.

The Yenisei is quiet and peaceful-looking, but its surface is deceptive. The current is amazingly swift. When we stopped at one of the midriver islands and wanted to swim, we were warned not to venture more than a meter or two from the shore. Two of our number, excellent swimmers, went out just a fraction too far. The velocity of the river there was around twenty kilometers per hour; immediately, they were swept away by the current and carried downriver so fast that in no time at all they were out of sight. Only a motorboat could have caught up with them. Fortunately, a vessel that happened to be making its way upstream encountered them as they sped southward, and they were picked up. If it hadn't been there, they wouldn't have had a chance.

Our steamer made its way mile after mile up the Yenisei. We reached a section of the river obstructed by great rocks called the *poroghi*. Full steam ahead, the craft could have made no headway here, so strong was the current between the poroghi. At this point, the ship was hooked to an enormous steel cable, attached upriver to a powerful winch; when it wound, the steamer was pulled through the poroghi.

Finally we reached the Arctic Circle, and this was the end of our nights. The sun never dipped near the horizon. You are aware of an extraordinary sensation when night never comes: partly exhilaration and partly a constant feeling that something is strange, out of kilter. You completely lose your sense of time.

Gradually we approached still closer to the North Pole. The trees on the riverbanks changed: they became smaller and smaller, until vegetation was reduced to what appeared to be close-cropped level grass. This is the tundra. Our steamer halted a few times, and we walked around on this unfamiliar surface. When you are actually on it, you discover that the plant life is not wiregrass or moss, as you might have thought from a distance, but tiny bushes. When you study them closely you discover they are Lilliputian trees, miniatures of the forest giants we had passed farther south. Tiny little leaves; tiny roots; everything perfect, but gnarled and twisted by the wind. One of these ancient little trees — they are about one inch high, with a limb spread of perhaps two inches — is as strong as copper wire. You can't possibly break them with your hands. So they survive the gales and hurricanes that sweep across these regions.

At the very edge of the tundra is the city of Igarka, which we explored. The entire city is of wood, hauled up on barges to this area from hundreds of miles downriver. Even the streets and sidewalks are wooden. This is because until very recent times no one had devised a way of building in concrete or stone on top of the eternal frost. It is impossible to lay a foundation; you can't excavate below the frostline to pour one because the ground is frozen solid all year round for hundreds of meters down. The heat of a house without a foundation melts the ground beneath it, turns it into mud, and the building gradually sinks. People told us that the first stone buildings so designed that they would not sink were made at Norilsk; they are considered marvels of ingenuity. But in this older town these had not yet been constructed.

Walking along the wooden streets, you saw SMOKING FORBIDDEN signs everywhere. The town was a tinderbox. There were only a few locations, circles of bare earth, where you were allowed to light a match. The fears of the city authorities were only too well founded; soon after our visit, the entire place went up in flames.

In the Permafrost Research Station they had drilled a shaft, like a mineshaft, with a narrow staircase on which you can descend into the frozen earth. For the first seven meters down, it was like being in a palace of diamond dust. Everything was covered with beautiful frost crystals, incredibly white, sparkling as though lit from within. The next seven meters were different: gray, grim, and terribly cold. Looking at the walls around the bottom of the shaft, you could see that the ground was striated: a layer of iron-hard clay alternating with a layer of ice. It was a relief to return to the surface after a few minutes in that dark place.

We walked around Igarka. The town simply stops at the city limits: you just step off the edge of a wooden street and you are out on the tundra, leaving every sign of habitation behind. We strolled off for a bit and after about fifteen minutes' walk were suddenly confronted by a stretch of barbed wire. Following this fence, we encountered, here and there, scattered human bones; skulls; all that remained of thousands of *zeks* who were imprisoned there.

Farther up the Yenisei, we passed the Turukhan District and looked at the small village in which Stalin had been an exile early in his Revolutionary career. The house where he stayed is now fitted over with a glass superstructure to preserve it.

Just by chance, I once heard a firsthand account of how Stalin had spent his term of exile. An Old Bolshevik, the father of one of my friends, was there at the same time. According to him, before Stalin's arrival the exiles had constituted a very friendly community, although they were not all of the same political persuasion. There were Bolsheviks, Mensheviks, SRs — different parties — but, trapped in this icy and forbidding place, they became friendly and got along very well. They had evolved their own sociable customs: celebrated each other's birthdays, entertained when someone joined the colony or when he was released, and so forth. "Then a newcomer arrived," my friend's father told us, "a short red-faced man wearing big *sapoghi*. You wouldn't have believed the change in the atmosphere. Within a short time he had everyone turned against each other. It was no longer a community. Everybody there became an enemy to everybody else." The new arrival was Stalin, who even at that time had a genius for practicing his intrigues, sowing dissension and distrust.

* * *

Our ship went farther and farther north. Finally we arrived at Dudinka and took the one-track train for Norilsk. This was little more than a trolley, with only two cars. We stopped for a while between Dudinka and Norilsk and got out to walk over the tundra. The miniature trees were irresistible, and each of us carried back to the train a small bouquet of them.

Norilsk is one of the richest of the frontier cities in Siberia, with a big mining industry: there are several different ores to be found there. Here we saw the houses we had heard about, the ones designed so as not to sink into the earth. They are set on concrete columns, and the base of the building itself does not touch the ground. All these buildings are painted different colors to create a cheerful and picturesque effect, because it is very difficult to live in a region where half the year it is night and there is no real summer. The people here refer to the rest of Russia as "the mainland," "the continent," as if they were on an island. There is no access through the taiga except in midsummer; the rest of the year the Yenisei is frozen over. Planes are the only means of travel, besides the river boats — but one can imagine how rarely the weather permits flying in winter within the Arctic Circle.

Norilsk could not grow solely by dint of convict labor, and the State makes every attempt to attract skilled workers and technicians to this city. There is every convenience they can manage to provide, including an indoor sports center with an Olympic-size swimming pool. When the Chairman of the City Council came to show us around, there was a moment of embarrassment before we started. Staring at the little bunches of tundra plants we carried, he said: "I see that everybody here has some floral specimens. Please leave them here before we go out to tour the city — you might be attacked out there. No one in the streets will realize you've just been on the tundra, and if you pluck any foliage here in Norilsk, people react exactly as they would to a crime, just as if you had stabbed someone." Growing plants are the most precious things in people's lives in this part of the world.

Here in Norilsk, as in Igarka, you had a peculiar feeling, arriving at the edge of town. Behind you, buildings and streets; ahead of you — nothing.

This is probably the only city in the world where the major industry is fighting the snow. We were taken to see a depot full of the most monstrous plows and snow-removers — enormous machines. They have such dense blizzards here that a person can get lost on the street and die, within a step or two of his home.

I was fascinated by the beauty and severity of Northeast Siberia, but it made me shudder to think what it would be like to live in this region as a zek. No one ever escaped; it was simply quick death to attempt it. I couldn't help thinking of Korolev, the great pioneer in space research, who designed the first successful rockets and missiles. Like hundreds of other scientists, he was imprisoned in the late 'thirties; was in a camp in the taiga, and only after a long time was transferred to a *sharashka* (a research institute staffed by zeks, like the one Solzhenitsyn describes in *The First Circle*). Korolev was a man of strong and decisive character. The camp guards decided immediately to get rid of him. They had a very simple system for eliminating prisoners they didn't like. Regularly, they sent teams out to the taiga for a week, sometimes a fortnight, to fell trees and cut wood. The teams were unguarded — there was nowhere anybody could escape to — so just the team chief was boss, a convict himself, called the *bat'ka* in the zeks' jargon, the Ukrainian word for "father."

The bat'ka was usually selected from the toughest element among the prisoners, convicted killers, repeaters. Very often the team returned from the lumbering job one or two men short, because when somebody did not suit the bat'ka, he was simply murdered. At roll call the missing zek was reported as having been crushed by a falling tree, or something of the sort, and the camp bosses never checked such statements.

Nobody expected to see Korolev again when the woodcutting team went out. And when the men returned, someone was indeed missing, but it was not he; it was the bat'ka. Korolev was so strong of character, so authoritative, that, after a short spell of indecision, the team transferred their loyalty to him and turned against the chief. Korolev became the new bat'ka.

I heard this story from a film-maker who was assigned to make a movie of Korolev's life and who had spent many hours interviewing this great scientist. The incident, of course, did not appear in the film.

I feel I ought to mention something else that occurred to this extraordinary man while he was a zek, because whatever the explanation of it may be, the person to whom it happened is too significant for the event to be dismissed. Korolev told of a remarkable happening in his life that made him believe in God.

He was on a forced march, when they were transferring prisoners from one camp to another. The zeks were as usual dressed in poor clothes, quite inadequate for that climate, and were very close to starvation. Those who were not strong enough, who lagged behind or fell by the wayside, were shot. After a grueling half-day's march, Korolev felt that he had struggled as long as he could; that now his strength was gone. He knew that if he didn't get something to eat he would fail, fall to the frozen ground — and that would be the end of him.

Although a convinced atheist, like the great majority of Soviets, he was suddenly so smitten with regret for all he had not yet achieved in his life, regretted so badly the thought that his scientific and technical ideas would die with him, that unexpectedly he found himself praying, "Oh God! I am so young! I have done nothing yet! I want to do so much; I *must* do it! Save me!" He prayed with closed eyes; and when he opened them he saw ahead of him, by the side of the track, a whole loaf of bread. He couldn't believe it. He was sure it was a hallucination, because there were many men walking ahead of him — they couldn't have missed it, if it was real. Why hadn't someone noticed it and picked it up? And whence could such a treasure have come, on this frozen road of starvation? After passing the loaf by, he reconsidered. Why not try? He ran back — miraculously, he was not shot for getting out of line — grabbed the bread, and shoved it under his jacket. Bit by bit, on the rest of the march, he ate it, and survived.

I don't have any comment to make on this episode. But I thought of it often when I was in the north, and pondered the mixture of cruelty and beauty that is Siberia.

* * *

On our vacations, Lucia and I took trips together. In 1968, we went to Central Asia, to Samarkand and to Bukhara. Again, contrasts: like jewel boxes set in the midst of dirt and squalor are the medrassehs, the mosques, the palaces and tombs built by the Moslems throughout the ninth to fourteenth centuries. Many of these buildings are untouched, as pristine as if constructed yesterday. The artisans who made them had a genius for creating cool interiors: to walk off the blistering street into the palace of the Emir, with its blue-and-green-tiled halls and alabaster-framed mirrors, was as refreshing as a shower. My best memory of that area is of a day when we went hitchhiking. (In the U.S.S.R., where there are so few motor vehicles, people regularly hitchhike: you pay for the ride. Everyone does this, even in Moscow.) We were picked up by a truck, and for more than an hour the driver was lost outside the city. Not far from Bukhara, we arrived at a stretch of desert spangled all over with bits of figured ceramic tile — bright little works of art, wonderfully colorful. There were hundreds of them: we picked them up by the handful. Before we found our route, we chanced upon another marvel, a place where there was an entire clay city underground; it was absolutely preserved — there are no rains here. You would have thought it had been vacated a week before, though probably many centuries had passed since the inhabitants had left. In the time of the invasions, the populations of whole cities sometimes fled overnight, and this may have been one of those evacuated towns. There were even a few jugs and several cooking pots in one of the rooms.

These treasures and archaeological finds lie here ignored and undisturbed, still awaiting discovery by scholars who would appreciate their significance.

Other places we saw during the first years of our marriage were green, near-tropical Georgia, and then Armenia. In Armenia every square foot of arable land bears witness to centuries of hard, dedicated work: the earth there is almost all rock, and loam has been brought in, bit by bit, parcel by parcel, to create the gardens and vineyards. This was a country we loved. Everyone you met was steeped in Armenian history. In Erevan any random passerby on the sidewalk can tell you the history of whatever fortress, monument, or cathedral you may ask about. We were deeply impressed. These are a civilized, cultivated people, with a national character as different from the rigid and limited Russian personality as one can imagine. The impassable class distinctions that obtain in Russia do not exist here; no one considers himself inferior to anyone else. We were in the capital on May Day, dining in a restaurant. Having got into conversation with our waitress — an extraordinarily intelligent and charming person — we asked her to join us for a drink. Had this occurred in Moscow, she would have come up to our table and toasted the holiday standing, but here in Armenia we found that such an invitation connoted real hospitality. She drew up a chair and became our guest. The three of us couldn't have had a better time. The conversation ranged from the early ecclesiastical architecture (Armenia converted in the fourth century, and still boasts churches dating from that time) to the Armenian Holocaust of 1915 — a subject one cannot avoid here. The history of these people and that of the Jews have much in common. "We feel ourselves to be cousins of the Jews," she told us, and we heard the same statement from others in that country, too. At all events, we became great friends with this wonderful person, and she later came to visit us in Chernogolovka with her little son.

Admittedly, it was unusual for professional people to make a friend from the working classes, but in Russia, where a real caste system prevails, this friendship would have been not just unlikely, but impossible; the waitress herself would have been too uncomfortable in such an association. It was a marvelous release to our spirits to discover a country where these barriers don't exist.

However far you may travel in the U.S.S.R., however deep you may venture into the wilderness, you are inevitably brought up short and reminded of how securely you are locked in. We spent one of our vacations in the northwest, in Karelia and the Vologodsky area. This is a fantastic region, with wildlife and vegetation you could not find anywhere else in the world. There are thousands of lakes surrounded by primeval forest.

The friends in whose company we made the trip, another couple, had enough *blat* to obtain permits for all of us to enter the northern section of the Upper Kuito Lake, which is ordinarily forbidden to Russians because it is close to the Finnish border. We had already encountered the border guards at other boundaries. At the Black Sea, for instance, you cannot go for a swim after a certain hour of the evening; you would be immediately stopped. At every body of water that could provide an escape route, all around the entire map, are armed guards and rigid restrictions, from which only specially authorized people are exempted. No one at the seashore is even allowed to own one of those little inflatable rafts, to say nothing of a sailboat. Even aqualungs have to be registered; swimmers using them are supervised.

The Finnish border is particularly tight. Lucia and I and our companions had to check in to the office of a member of the border control when we were making ready to leave for a few days in a lakeside cabin in the forest there.

"Going fishing?" he asked. "Good luck. Now, probably you'll want to celebrate with a little vodka when you've caught some fish. Good! But listen: don't go rowing when you've had a drop too many. Squalls spring up from nowhere in these lakes. You could turn over before you knew what was happening, if you weren't paying attention." We were surprised: Who would expect a border guard to be so considerate of our welfare? But he had more to say. "If you drown — that's the end for you. But it's not the end for us! You'd be surprised by the trouble we have; it's a terrible job. We don't know if you've really drowned, or got across to Finland. Some people don't know that we have an extradition agreement with the Finns, and anyone who makes it over there is sent right back. Still, if someone takes a boat out and doesn't return on time, we have to send up helicopters, go out in launches, drag the lake — everything. We have to cable the relatives to come and identify the body, to make sure it's really *your* body and not somebody else's. It's a lot of trouble, a lot of unpleasantness. So be careful."

And we were reminded once more not only of our own relative confinement, but of the countless victims throughout all of our history who
spent years, lifetimes, imprisoned. After four or five days in our fishing
camp, we left for the Solovetsky Islands.

A dreamlike landscape. It was midsummer, and Solovki is very close
to the Arctic Circle, so at midnight the sun was as bright as it is in late
afternoon in Moscow at that time of year. The colors of the sea were
subtle, almost indescribable. It is called the White Sea, but it is of all
different colors — opalescent. The islands, dotted over the water, are
grassy and wooded, and sustain herds of reindeer. No one has ever been
able to explain this phenomenon, because all the other terrain that close
to the Arctic Circle is barren. It is still a mystery to naturalists how this
marvelous greenery survives here.

Nature, in that region, could not be improved upon; but the contributions of Man to the scene are chilling. We saw the ancient Solovetsky Monastery, which was used as a prison in Lenin's time. In one
small prison in the center of an island you could still see the inscriptions
scratched on the walls, messages addressed to the unknown future:
"This is where I will be for twenty years to come"; "Here we spent our
last night"; "Tell Mother I was shot"; with signatures.

The actual mechanics of long-distance travel in that huge nation can
present fearful problems. Our holiday in Uzbekistan was cut short when
Lucia contracted a high fever; no surprise, in a place where people are
totally indifferent to cleanliness. In the *chaikana,* for example, one was
served tea in cups that looked as though they had never been washed,
by a waiter whose fingernails were black with dirt. Every other person
you saw seemed to be afflicted with eye infections or some other
disease.

Having encountered bland indifference to Lucia's illness on the part
of medical officials in Tashkent, I realized we had to get back to Moscow fast. I struggled, fought, maneuvered, and bucked lines in the Tashkent airport, after having been told that there would be a five-day delay
on the first flight back we were permitted to take; and despite our having tickets and reservations on a plane that was about to leave, it was a
real feat to catch that flight.

What was amazing was that when we took off, the plane was half-
empty. Dozens of people were left behind. The reason for this is one
that Uzbeks understand even better than Russians do: at every airport,
there is a blanket reservation made in case of the unexpected arrival of
VIPs. There are no rules to cover this contingency; simply, wherever
and whenever high officials come, space must be instantly available
for them. Typically, this means ten or twenty ordinary passengers

"bumped" in advance. But in a place like Tashkent, where VIPs are accorded even more obsequious treatment, Oriental style, than they are in Russia and to which tourists and vacationers are likely to be attracted, the airport manager wants to play it safe and arrange for a great many vacancies on each flight. Relatives of officials, friends of their friends — any number of important people — may materialize at the last minute. Nobody takes a loss from flights operated on this basis; still less is anyone penalized for the inconvenience and misery inflicted upon those travelers whose trips are delayed. So this "system" is never improved upon.

Such inefficiency, such indifference to the interests of the public, surprises nobody. Everyone is used to it. No laws exist for the country's leaders, and the highest of them are above God himself. When Stalin traveled, railway service came to a halt at both ends of the line, from his starting point to his destination and at all the junctions. First a train with no passengers traversed the entire route to check the track. Then a second empty train, a "dummy," took the trip. Then a Secret Service train; finally Stalin's train, followed by another Secret Service train and, behind it, a sixth, this one empty like the first. Rail service could be held up for hours, even for a whole day. Nowadays it is a little simpler, but high officials are still accorded privileges far exceeding those enjoyed by the Imperial family in pre-Revolutionary times.

* * *

In the course of the three or four years after the Sinyavsky-Daniel trial, most of the scientists with whom I worked gradually took the view that my incriminating connection with the two writers would eventually be "forgiven."

I don't mean to say that everyone considered me an exemplary academic. My colleagues did conclude that I was not a political person, not a dissident; but some criticized me for being an eccentric. Most of them had an ingrained conviction that in order to be safe, in order to be successful, one should confine one's attention strictly to science. Any other interests they regarded as dilettantism, something too childish for a real scientist to waste time on. The head of my department, among others, frequently chided me for my interest in literature, for my participation in various discussions and gatherings with writers and artists. I remember being roundly scolded for joining a circle of cinema enthusiasts in Chernogolovka. "Why, that's ridiculous!" protested one of the physics faculty, a man to whom science was the be-all and end-all of existence. "There's nothing wrong with going to the cinema; everyone enjoys that. But what's the point of these discussions? And now on top of everything I hear that you've become interested in sociology. That's really too much! I should think you'd know that isn't a science at all. You're scattering your forces, Mark." But evidently, though I was a strange person in their view, I was not an objectionable one, so my position was increasingly secure.

My career was moving ahead in a most satisfactory way. I continued to publish papers both here and in the international journals, and *Electron Theory of Metals* by Lifshitz, Kaganov, and myself came out in England and America in 1968. I was invited for lectures and consultations increasingly often. My name was mentioned as candidate for the newly created Landau Prize, and — still more gratifying — I was included on the "primaries" list for Corresponding Member of the Academy of Sciences and accorded a large number of votes: those of almost half of the electorate.* Everything was going my way. For a while even that most desirable of rewards — a trip abroad — seemed to be within my grasp.

Once a person is felt to have earned the privilege of travel, he is usually first permitted to go as far as one of the Eastern bloc countries; then if his behavior is satisfactory, he may be allowed to go as far as the Third World — Africa or India. Finally, if he makes no mistakes, he may get to Europe or America. But he must conduct himself with the utmost propriety on his travels. Not only must his conversation be discreet and guarded at all times, his contacts strictly limited to people he is supposed to meet, and so forth, but even in his leisure time he must adhere to the strictest of Soviet conventions. (When members of my institute first began to go abroad, there was a joke on this subject. A Russian visits a cabaret in one of the African capitals, where the customers are treated to a sensational dance by a half-naked *artiste* who concludes her act by gyrating through the audience and landing on the Russian's knee. The man fails to react in any way — just sits there like a stone, without so much as a smile. The dancer is astonished. "What's the matter, are you an impotent?" she asks. "No." "Homosexual?" "No." "A pederast?" "No." "Oh — I understand! A Communist!")

In view of the heavy odds against anyone's being allowed to go to the West, and against mine in particular, as I knew from my long-ago session with the Kharkov KGB, I was incredulous when I was told by the university authorities that I might accept an invitation to a scientific

---

* Candidates for Corresponding Member are considered and reconsidered a number of times, and it is fairly easy to gauge one's chances of ultimate acceptance on the basis of the first election. Anyone receiving more than ten votes out of the fifty-odd in the first ballot is pretty nearly assured of eventual admittance.

conference in England, to be held in June of 1969. Even while I began to make preparations, I could hardly believe I would really go.

"Mark Yakovlevitch!" The Chairman of the Solid State Physics Department accosted me one day during this exciting time. "I understand you have permission to go abroad?"

"Apparently so!"

"Well, that's certainly lucky for me. I've been invited with some others from my department to go to a seminar in Trieste. There's not one in my group who's competent in theoretical physics. Don't go to England — come to Italy with us! You'd be doing me a tremendous favor."

It made little difference to me; my longing to see either of those countries was equally strong. I made the change in my application and continued with all my plans. I shouldn't have hoped.

One powerful element in the university had their reasons not to be too pleased with me. Quite a few times the suggestion had been made to me that I become a member of the Communist Party. At that time there was an unwritten system of plusses and minuses. If one was a Jew, that was a minus. If one was a full professor, that was a plus. If I became a Communist, that would be another plus, and I would be, so to say, a "positive" person. When it is suggested that one become a Communist, the officials assume that one will consider the proposal not merely as advice, but as a command. My objection to the most recent of these invitations — "It is a great honor, but I am not quite prepared for such a move" — was accepted without comment. However, it was not ignored. Nobody announced this as the reason my permission to go to the West was revoked; the alleged reason was that it was against strict regulations to change the destination of one's trip on the application form. But it was perfectly clear that this trifle had nothing to do with my case.

I had to swallow, again, the knowledge that, in the great labor camp that was my homeland, I for one would never be eligible for even a few weeks' parole.

Lodestar

In 1969, the atmosphere in the nation became increasingly tight and tense. Ever since the uprising in Czechoslovakia you could feel an increasingly oppressive weight in the very air, an unmistakable renewal of Stalinism. Censorship clamped down: nothing controversial, nothing with a liberal tinge, was published any more. Soviet people are very sensitive to these changes in policy: a casual remark dropped at a Party meeting, a two-line squib in the newspapers, the vaguest hints, may easily mean profound changes that will affect everyone's lives.

It was toward the end of this year that the Central Committee decided that the Rector of Moscow University could not be in sole authority there; that the Party chairman should have power at least equal to the rector's. This had actually been the case for some time, but now it was *de jure* as well as *de facto*. And, not by coincidence, the percentage of Jews in the university continued to drop. Over Rector Petrovsky's objections, some of the best members of his staff lost out on their promotions, but second-rate people with good Party connections moved up.

I felt the time had come for me to make a change. I would quit the university and work full time at the Landau Institute, rather than watch this process of regression and perhaps be affected by it myself. I went to talk to Rector Petrovsky, whom I found in a state of despondency.

"I've been thinking of leaving the university," I told him.

"That's a great pity, Mark Yakovlevitch" was all he could say. "But I would leave too, if I could." He could see that everything he had striven for during decades was being destroyed. His hopes of turning Moscow University into a truly great seat of learning were shattered. There was no way he could fight back. Although a distinguished Academician, a Hero of Socialist Labor, and actually a member of the Supreme Soviet, he was powerless. He was terribly depressed, and, although neither of us mentioned it, his health was obviously failing. "After what I've seen happening here, there's only one thing I can say: I wish to God I had never been born."

That was the last statement I heard from this outstanding man. Petrovsky died not very long after we had that conversation. Ironically, he received a great deal of posthumous credit, and the street on which he had lived was named after him.

*   *   *

Sergei Kapitza, hearing that I had left the university, proposed that I join his cathedra at the Moscow Physical-Technical Institute, taking a half-time position. I accepted, partly because there would be more lecturing involved, and I love to teach, and also because there was regular communication between his institute and Chernogolovka — even chauffeur service back and forth. Many of the senior scientists worked at both places.

I made a mistake in taking this position. I had been working for half a year before Sergei met me after a class to tell me that the administration, which had been furious at him for some time because of the casual way in which he ignored all official conventions and regulations, had announced that, in accordance with a recent ruling, they would accept no more part-time members on the staff. He had neglected for too long to take all the steps and go through all the channels necessary in order to regularize my job there, so I was to be let off the staff. The authorities were punishing Kapitza for going over their heads; but the victim was I.

This was quite a setback. I had been so confident that red tape would be cut sooner or later and that I would be reimbursed that I had been teaching without pay for six months. Sergei apologized profusely, but that was cold comfort to me.

The next offer I received was considerably more adventurous and rewarding. The Kalmyk University in Elista, capital of the Kalmyk Republic, offered me what was described as a half-time position, and they paid accordingly; but actually I had to spend only two fortnight-long sessions there per term, conducting very intensive courses. Nothing could have been better.

This was my first acquaintance with a small capital of a small republic, save for brief visits in the Baltic, and I was much impressed by these indomitable people.

The recent history of the Kalmyks is horrible beyond belief. The entire population was accused en masse of anti-Soviet activities under Stalin and was exiled to Siberia. The chairman of the cathedra where I worked was one of few survivors of a once large family; in fact, everyone I met had lost at least half of his family. The Kalmyks have a sort of ceremonial Eastern reserve with strangers, particularly with Russians; but when we got to know each other, they were willing to talk a little more freely than they did ordinarily with visitors from other parts of the Soviet Union.

One of my colleagues, a man of about my age, described the exile. He had been nine years old when he and all the old people, women, and children of his village (the men of military age were all in the service) were rounded up in the middle of the night by scores of Red Army soldiers with bayonets, shipped off in *teplushki* to the Tomsk region of Siberia, and actually dumped out into the wasteland. There they had to fend for themselves, beginning by building their own barracks. The survivors must have been extraordinarily tough people. They had practically no food and only such clothing as they were able to snatch up as they were being herded out of their houses. "By the time we had some kind of shelter, my sister and grandmother were dead," my colleague told me. When I tried to convey how I felt about his story, he simply observed, "We weren't the only ones." And he was right. The Chechentzy, the Balkartzy, and Crimean Tatars, the Volga Germans, and others — all were deported and their numbers decimated before 1945.

And although the other exiled nations were permitted to return after Stalin's death, the Crimean Tatars have never been restored to their homeland.

It was very gratifying to work with this man and with the others at Elista: I got much the same warm feeling I had gained years before in Kharkov, the reward of teaching people something they really wanted to learn. Some of them came later to work and consult with me in Moscow, and I was delighted to steer two of these men through their first publications, which appeared in the *Journal of Experimental and Theoretical Physics*.

*   *   *

The first time in my life it ever crossed my mind that my work in the Soviet Union might come to an end was at the very beginning of 1970.

Not too long before, the Voice of Israel had started to issue incredible reports: some Jews had come out publicly with the declaration that they wanted to leave the Soviet Union for their historic motherland, Israel.

I can't possibly explain the impact this simple statement had on the entire population of the U.S.S.R. The idea that a Soviet citizen could fail to be absolutely happy in his native land was the ultimate antipatriotic insult — unheard of. Far more serious: even the name of Israel was black anathema in Russia. Of all nations in the world none was more alien, more loathly. To broadcast the announcement "I wish to renounce the Soviet Union for Israel" at that time required courage of a high order. I just can't compare it to anything; nothing imaginable could have created the same sort of shock in the Soviet Union.

When this news first came out over the short-wave radio, some of our friends simply refused to take it at face value. To me, too, it seemed highly likely that the Soviet officials must be setting a trap. They would allow some Jews to apply for exit visas. They would permit a few of that number to obtain the visas; and then, after several dozen "turncoats" had been smoked out by this means, they would call a halt to the applications and bring charges of treason against the Jews who had been decoyed into exposing their criminally anti-Soviet intentions. The traitors would be brought to trial, and the authorities would use the trials to create a new wave of anti-Semitism, to hold up to public obloquy these Jews who were conspiring to betray their motherland and go over to the Fascist Zionist state, and at the same time, to frighten the rest of Soviet Jewry. It would be easy to convey the idea that these wicked people were responsible for the bad economic situation in the country. In short, all the classic purposes of a pogrom would be served.

I still think I may have been right. For a while it looked as though the anti-Jewish factions in the country held all the cards. But in June, something fantastic happened that made for a complete change in the outlook, in the whole consciousness, of countless Soviet Jews. No one believed it, but, according to the newspapers, eleven Jews in Leningrad had attempted to hijack a plane and escape to Sweden, whence they planned to make their way to Israel. The KGB had captured these criminals, and the date was set for their trial.

People were absolutely stunned. No one could think or talk about anything else. Nothing even remotely like it had ever happened in Soviet times. Political crimes were unheard of. The attempt was so unlikely, so completely outlandish, that everybody thought it must have been a provocation, something like the Doctors' Plot. To distinguish truth from invention in accounts of this most improbable exploit was almost impossible.

By the time the trial began, on December 15th, 1970, excitement among Jews had reached a fever pitch. There were enormous crowds outside the Leningrad Courthouse. Many of the demonstrators were arrested every day (the trial lasted three days) and, taking advantage of recent laws, the authorities sentenced those who gathered publicly for demonstrations to 15-day prison terms. It was from two of my Leningrad friends, and from the short-wave radio, that I learned the details of the proceedings: Radio Moscow and the newspapers carried nothing but vicious indictments even before the trial opened.

The originators of the hijacking plan were Mark Dymshitz and Eduard Kuznetsov. Dymshitz was forty-three, a pilot and engineer. He had distinguished himself in the air force, but during the postwar wave of anti-Semitism he found his skills and training no longer wanted. He drifted to Bukhara. Realizing after a time that he had no future there either, and that Soviet policy both internally and internationally had hardened against Jews, he applied for permission to emigrate. Years passed: nothing came of his application.

Eduard Kuznetsov had the misfortune, as a very young man, to be heard criticizing Stalin in the wrong company. The fact that he made these remarks after Khrushchev himself had just exposed Stalin's bloody tyranny and had been applauded for it made no difference. Kuznetsov was sent to prison camp. He served more than one term for such crimes: once when he was asked his occupation, he answered, "Prisoner." Who could estimate the number of Soviet citizens who have that same occupation, for similar reasons?

Another of the defendants had done a term in camp on a similar charge; he was Alexei Murzhenko. A highly gifted linguist, Murzhenko, upon his release from labor camp, had eschewed political activity altogether; his sole ambition was to be admitted to the Kiev Institute for Foreign Languages. The director there bluntly told him: "With your past, you shouldn't even dream of studying languages. You couldn't possibly become a translator or interpreter." The only work he could get, finally, was in a factory.

A third among them had also been a political prisoner, Yuri Fedorov.

But all eleven of these people, each for his own reasons, knew he could no longer survive in the Soviet Union. All had been attempting for years to obtain exit visas. The accused must have understood all along how slim their chances were of escaping the country according to their plan. They made this desperate gamble, not so much in the hope of succeeding, as to draw the attention of the world — and of world Jewry — to the fate of Soviet Jews. The idea evolved in frantic haste. That it was a sacrificial gesture rather than a cleverly worked-out scheme became perfectly clear in the course of the trial.

Because the suspects were arrested even before they passed the gates leading onto the runway, the prosecutor's entire case was based upon hypothesis. *What if* they had injured the Aeroflot pilot and the stewards of the plane they were planning to board? *What if* the getaway plane had crashed and innocent passengers were killed? (They were unarmed and had timed the takeover for an interval when there were no passengers aboard.) *What if* valuable State property had been damaged?

Dymshitz and Kuznetsov were sentenced to death; the others (one of them a woman, Kuznetsov's wife) received prison terms ranging from three to ten years. The death sentences were eventually commuted, in response to a storm of protest from all over the world; on reconsideration, the "ringleaders" were sentenced to fifteen years.* But a considerable number of their friends who had signed petitions and organized demonstrations on their behalf were brought to trial for these activities and were in prison camps for three to five years themselves.

After the sentencing, each of the prisoners was permitted to speak to the court, as is customary at Soviet trials. Dymshitz and Kuznetsov spoke movingly on behalf of their fellow-"conspirators"; all of the convicted supported each other with unshakable loyalty.

Once they had all spoken, a perfectly extraordinary event took place — something no one could have imagined happening in a Soviet courtroom. A tiny woman, wife of one of the condemned men, leaped up on a bench and called out to the prisoners: "We will wait for you! All Jews are with you; all the world is with you! We will all meet in Israel one day; we will build together our Jewish home." The families of the condemned men started to sing the *Shema Israel.* Dymshitz and the others joined in the singing, and it was five minutes before the court was brought to order.

The Leningrad Trials made clear to everyone the measure of suffering, the measure of desperation, which had brought these eleven men and this one woman to such a decision.

If the Soviet authorities hoped to find Jews silent and complaisant after the trials, the reaction that occurred must have been totally unexpected to them. Suddenly, thousands upon thousands of applications for exit visas poured into the Visa Department. With such a gallant example before them, Jews who for fear of reprisals had never dreamed of applying took new courage. If these people were willing to risk their lives, then others, too, would risk whatever they had to in order to make the attempt to get to Israel.

The applications of enormous numbers for exit visas was so unex-

* Dymshitz and Kuznetsov were not forgotten. Soviet dissenters and Jewish groups all over the world fought ceaselessly for their release until, on April 27th, 1979, they were freed, with three others, in a prisoner exchange arranged between President Carter and General Secretary Brezhnev. The five Soviet prisoners' freedom was bought by the return of two Russians convicted by the American courts of spying. It was the first instance of a prisoner exchange in which Soviet citizens were exchanged for Soviet citizens. But three of them, Yuri Fedorov, Yosif Mendelevitch, and Murzhenko, are still imprisoned at this writing.

pected that the authorities did not know how to handle them. If my own guess is correct — that the officials had been maneuvering for some time to create an impression that "Zionist plots" were afoot, which would have given them the traditional scapegoat on whom blame could be cast for everything that was going wrong in the country at that time — the idea had backfired badly. While they would have been prepared to bring to trial and imprison a dozen or so Jews and hold them up as examples to keep the rest "in their place," this was no time for the instigation of mass terror. The days of Stalin were too recent: Party bosses knew from their own experience that when mass terror begins, it cannot be ended by ukase, and often those who start it can become its victims.

Caught unawares, they could formulate no policy. What they did was to dispense exit visas to a few Jews whom they wanted to get rid of, and at the same time put a stop to any further requests by any means they could devise.

But what had emerged here in the wake of these astounding developments was — hope. And the whole spirit among Jews changed to something that had never been seen in this country in its entire history. People appeared publicly wearing their Stars of David. People appeared who defiantly declared themselves to be Jewish, and who announced their intention to emigrate to Israel.

It was unbelievable.

The thought of ever being able to escape the Soviet Union had never before entered my own mind. But when this hope arose, I had no doubt that I would be among those who made a try for it. Overnight, it became unbearable to look forward to a lifetime as a Jew in Russia, tolerated only for his talents.

I wanted to leave for my own country.

This decision was one that I had to keep to myself for a long time. In February, Lucia and I had become the parents of a daughter, Yulia, and for the time being my wife was besieged by so many new concerns that I had no intention of adding to them the prospect of those dangers and uncertainties we would confront once we applied for exit visas. So not only did I take care that none of my friends or colleagues might guess what was on my mind, but for months I kept it from Lucia. I wanted to ponder the complicated problems that lay ahead of us before I spoke to anyone.

There was no one I could consult, no one whose advice I could obtain, when it came to taking this step. The men I worked with at the Institute of Theoretical Physics were all solidly entrenched in the Soviet

Establishment — it would have been absolute madness to let any of them know that such a plan had entered my mind. There were only two people in whom I could confide, Sasha Voronel and a good friend of ours from Kharkov, Emil Luboshitz. They too were quietly hoping and planning to go to Israel.

But we were groping in the dark. It was common knowledge already that merely to make inquiries about emigration meant that you could lose your job at once. Obviously, until such time as you were ready to act it would be idiotic to betray your intentions, to become unemployed and helpless, before you had even made the first move toward an application.

The only way we could learn the complicated, obstructive mechanics of applying for an exit visa was through the *instruktzia* circulated in samizdat; earlier applicants provided this information for those who would follow after them. When we got hold of a copy of these instruktzia, we could hardly believe our eyes. The red tape is so tangled and heavy that the requirements fill twenty pages of single-spaced type.

In the Soviet Union, emigration qua emigration does not really exist. It is impossible that there could be anyone who wanted to leave that great country. A barely conceivable exception would be a person whose family is resident abroad and who wishes to be reunited with it. But even in this regard there are limitations: there is only one country in the world for which one might by an outside chance be granted a visa, and that is specifically Israel.

For over half a century a certain number of Jews, particularly in the Baltic states, had made their way to Israel. Now the Soviets at least officially recognized the right of the remaining members of these families to leave the Soviet Union for Israel in order to be reunited with their relatives. Absolutely no one wants or needs to leave the U.S.S.R. except *possibly* these Jews; so there is only this one destination for a would-be emigrant. The ruling is not for the purpose of doing Jews a favor; it is intended to make clear that only such despicable people as Jews would want to emigrate. Any Russians, Lithuanians, or others who tried to leave the country had to represent themselves as Jews even to be considered as applicants for visas.

One of the prerequisites for application demanded by the Visa Department was an invitation to the applicant from a relative in Israel. (Although the few who had succeeded in emigrating had already established a tenuous Russia-to-Israel contact, the process of locating the relatives or sponsors, advising them that one wanted to be invited, and so on, involved more detail than I can go into here.) But the invitation itself could be an advance announcement to the department that one was planning to leave; so I knew there were numerous complicated problems I had to solve before I started to set this machinery in motion.

The most serious was this: an applicant for Israel is almost certain to be kept waiting for an indefinite period (at that time, usually around three months, but it could be as long as nine) before he even learns whether or not his application has been accepted. During that interval he will be subjected to a thorough investigation. Any irregularity, any breach of the innumerable regulations in which every Soviet person is enmeshed, can be blown up into a disaster — a court case. This meant that it was urgently necessary for me to find another place to live. Lucia and I were still in Chernogolovka, but I had no propiska for the apartment. It was one of those extra-legal arrangements the institutes there often put through for top-level members of their staffs, to attract them to Chernogolovka rather than Moscow, an irregularity so common that ordinarily one would never worry about it. Now it was vital to have everything in our lives in strictest order.

Equally important, I had to have an apartment in my own name to serve as a sort of savings bank — it would constitute my "capital." It costs a great deal of money to leave the Soviet Union. Over and above the passage and freight costs, which come to more than 1000 roubles per person, there are innumerable taxes, tariffs, and fees. Just to mention two: the price of an exit visa is 400 roubles; and the price of annulling one's Soviet citizenship is 500 roubles. My salary was 500 roubles per month, but half of that went to the support of my first family. Lucia worked in the Chemistry Laboratory at the Vitamin Institute and received monthly 100 roubles, more than half of which went to pay the woman who took care of Yulia while she was at work. This meant it was almost impossible for us to save money. If I bought an apartment in a cooperative, which would cost 2000 to 3000 roubles, I would have a negotiable property. When and if I received permission to leave, I could sell it and cover the many expenses contingent upon emigrating.

But how could I obtain a Moscow propiska? I already had one — for the apartment where Naya and Vadim were living. You can't have more than one. The fact of my being divorced and remarried was of little concern to the authorities, and they told me a second apartment was out of the question.

Because I knew I would never be able to take the first step toward leaving the country until I had this second propiska, I determined to fight tooth and nail for it. For the next year and a half, I dedicated every ounce of energy toward this end. First, with the help of the powerful institute and the support of all the scientific VIPs I could involve, I obtained a document stating that it was absolutely essential for me to have a place in Moscow for my new family. Armed with this, I was able to acquire a one-room place in the city on Parkovaya Street, and, with the baby (and our cat), Lucia and I moved in.

Now that we had this foothold, I could point out to the officials that one small study was inadequate living space for a family of three; as a scientist I was entitled to a great deal more space. This was not too hard to prove, and in July of 1972 we were finally able to obtain a three-room apartment on Veshnyakovskaya Street. Nothing very splendid, but acquiring it was a triumph.

When I first mentioned this plan to Lucia, that I wanted us to try for Israel, she was assailed by doubts. The thought that we, who by ordinary Soviet standards had such a good life, should risk everything on a gamble whose outcome was so uncertain was a very difficult one for her. She wasn't so much worried by what might happen to us as about what lay ahead for our daughter.

"Mark, if it were only you and I who were concerned, you know I'd agree. But how about Yulia? She's only a baby now, but suppose they keep us waiting for years? Or suppose we never go? Imagine when she starts school: she'll be treated like the child of criminals. It will be hard enough for her to be Jewish — but to be a 'turncoat Jew,' a 'dirty Zionist!' "

"Our future may look safe now," I said, "but the situation is getting more difficult all the time. A few years from now it may be intolerable. And then . . . well, I can only say that if we stay, I can't be responsible for what happens to us or to Yulia. I just can't. Think it over." I didn't have to mention my feelings toward Irasel: the pride, the loyalty, the deep gratitude for her unconditional welcome to Soviet or any other Jews. This went without saying, and I knew that Lucia felt as I did.

For months we discussed the plan before my wife came around to my point of view; but when she did, her support was wholehearted. Having set her hand to the plow, she never for an instant looked back.

I knew, of course, that the minute one made application for an exit visa to Israel, one's status changed completely. The danger of imprisonment aside, since Lucia and I were almost certain to be fired from our jobs, the possibility of being left with no money at all was clear. We would take the chance for ourselves, but I didn't want my first family to be deprived of assistance, and I would have to confer with Naya to assure myself that she would be willing to be in a sense a partner in the risk I was taking. From the start, my earnest hope was that she, too, would take steps to emigrate to Israel with my son.

I took on all the work I could handle. I wrote night and day: the

Nauka Press had made me an offer for a popular science book of which I had given them the outline: *Through the Eyes of a Physicist.* I did a great deal of editing for the scientific journals, on top of my own papers. At the same time Lucia signed with the Mir Press to translate from the English John Ziman's *Electrons in Metals.* But with all our efforts it was still hard to get ahead. We economized on everything: clothes, meat, books. We cut every corner we could.

Hope

ON MARCH 10th and 11th, 1971, something happened that changed the face of Soviet history — something so impossible that you would not have dared even to dream of it.

Fifty-six Jews from Riga who for years had been refused permission to leave for Israel arrived in Moscow and appeared in the reception room of the Praesidium of the Supreme Soviet. Their leader handed the official at the reception desk a demand, addressed to Podgorny and Kosygin, in which they protested the contemptuous treatment they had received from the Visa Department; protested the fact that their refusals had been made orally, with nothing in writing and no reasons assigned for their detention; and announced that they would remain right there, in the Praesidium, until they received an answer. Upon delivery of this declaration, the fifty-six petitioners sat down quietly and started to wait.

Telephones began to ring; police gathered in the hall. Plain-clothesmen appeared. Behind the glass that separated the receptionist's office from the room, more police and KGBsts appeared. Finally, the secretary announced to the waiting people that they could receive the answer to their application at the Ministry of the Interior, 6 Ogaryova Street, and told them all to go there.

The Jews refused. "We've been there, and to the Visa Department, many times. We never got an answer. We won't leave the Praesidium until some competent official tells us definitely whether or not we will receive our visas."

There was more milling about, more phone calls. At noon the secretary announced that the problems of each of the applicants would be dealt with separately, and asked each person present to sign his name. This was a common tactic; the officials preferred not to approach a group but to take each individual in turn, case by case. The Jews, who were wary of being split up in this way, rejected the proposal: "As all of our signatures are on this application, we want to be treated as a group." They were then urged to select representatives, who would be allowed to confer with a member of the Praesidium. Again, the people from Riga declined, knowing perfectly well that their spokesmen would be arrested and the whole demonstration fall apart. They were warned that unless they appointed representatives, they would be seen by nobody in the Praesidium.

In answer, the Jews continued to occupy the reception room, simply sitting there in silence. After an hour, reinforcements arrived. By one P.M., there were one hundred and forty-one Jews in the hall: people from Lvov, from Vilnius, Sverdlovsk — from everywhere. They were in Moscow on separate errands, to present their individual pleas to the Visa Department. The news of the Riga contingent had spread like wildfire, and they came pouring into the Praesidium to join the demonstration.

On the heels of this crowd came several foreign correspondents. Despite the appearance of a swarm of plainclothesmen, the Riga Jews were most willing to talk to the newsmen to explain the reasons for the demonstration and recount their own particular histories. The strikers managed to convey many of their agonizing stories — familiar by now to Soviet Jews, but novel and shocking to the foreigners — before the KGBsts ordered the journalists out of the hall. At that point the demonstrators delivered a document to the officials at the reception desk, announcing that they were starting a hunger strike, in which, again, the Jews from other cities joined them.

The Western short-wave radio picked up the story by midafternoon and began to deliver bulletins on the siege every hour. People with other business at the Praesidium were absolutely astounded when they came in and saw a crowd of two hundred sitting — many of them on the floor — in the reception hall. They were rapidly ushered out, and, of course, they spread the word about the demonstration.

The Praesidium is situated in the heart of Moscow, right near the Kremlin and Red Square. The authorities were obviously reluctant to conduct mass arrests in such a public place, and there was a long interval of confusion and inaction. Not until seven-thirty did a platoon of police march in to disperse the Jews. It was the eve of Purim, and the strikers were still assembled, in the dark, listening to one of their number, who was reading and translating from Esther. The police cleared them out, but they continued their strike and demonstration at the Central Telegraph Office and returned to the Praesidium the next day.

All of Moscow was spellbound by this impossible event. Eventually, no less a personage than General Sholokov, Minister of the Interior, surrounded by his officers, came in to address the demonstrators. He could not force the group to choose a spokesman, so he finally had to address all of them.

"Zionism is Fascism!" he thundered. "No one can try to prevent the Soviets from building Communism and go unpunished." He concluded with an ominous warning: "You should not forget what we did with the Tatars!" But the people from Riga, with their reinforcements, remained silent and obdurate. And with international attention focused upon the demonstration, the authorities felt themselves prevented from using force. In the end, they had to back down. They finally offered to reconsider the entire list, as a unit, and only then did the refuseniks* leave. The majority of them got out of the country within two weeks.

*   *   *

There were repercussions from this unbelievable demonstration. Official policy toward Jews began to harden.

As of recent years, the survivors of the victims who had been killed at Babi Yar in Kiev, and at Vilnius, had established the custom of visiting these sites in early August, on the fast day that commemorates the destruction of the Temple, saying a prayer for their dead, and leaving flowers on these vast unmarked mass graves.

This year, 1971, the number of mourners increased. People were less and less inclined to suppress their Jewishness and to cooperate with the official policy, which dictated wiping out the memory of those massacres as if they had never been.† The authorities planned to put a stop to these observances. But in typical Soviet fashion they went about suppressing the pilgrimages in an "indirect" way. In Vilnius, the mourners were told that the area, a weed-grown vacant lot, was cut off to visitors because it was being used as the location for a film. In Kiev, mourners were stopped on the route with the pretext that the road was under repair. Those who walked as far as they could and then stopped to pray were arrested; some, including sick and elderly, spent fifteen days in jail. People who left their flowers on the margins of the gravesites saw them smashed, deliberately run over by police cars.

This horrible news sent a chill through all of us. It was a sign of the

---

* Those whose exit visas have been denied.

† Despite numerous petitions, there was no memorial to indicate that these were the places where hundreds of thousands of Jews had last seen the sun. A Kiev engineer, Boris Kochubiyevsky, was then serving the second year of a three-year prison sentence he received for protesting this shameful omission; his appeals were condemned as anti-Soviet agitation.

times. If I had had any doubts as to whether the Soviet Union was the nation in which I wanted my children to spend the rest of their lives, hearing of these events would have settled them forever.

By December, having waited almost an entire year for my Israeli sponsor's invitation and having sent repeated requests for it, I was not at all sure it would ever come. Possibly the letter from Israel had been intercepted. I started considering the very risky idea of receiving my letter through the Dutch Embassy, which represents Israel in the U.S.S.R., trying to obtain the invitation through that channel.

Just before the New Year, Lucia and I came home late from a concert. From force of habit rather than hope, I checked in my post box to see if there was any mail. There it was — the invitation to Israel!

I couldn't believe it. I hadn't had any idea how exciting this moment — if it ever came — would be. In a perfect frenzy, I dashed out to the Telegraph Office and sent Sasha and Nina Voronel an urgent wire: COME IMMEDIATELY. The Voronels too had been out late that night and were about to go to bed, but upon receiving the wire they hurried off and caught a cab.

"What's happened?" Sasha demanded when I opened the door. "It'd better be something pretty damn important, at this hour of the night." When they heard our news and saw the letter, they were absolutely overjoyed. They smothered us in congratulations, and the four of us stayed up until dawn, talking about everything. We speculated as to why, after such a long delay, the invitation had come through at all; what Sasha's chances were of receiving his own invitation (he had made his request earlier than I, but still had heard nothing from Israel). Did the fact that the letter had finally arrived mean that the authorities had decided to consent to my application? Had Sasha's letter been deliberately held up? This seemed possible. Sasha, much to the alarm of all his friends, had become openly involved with some groups of would-be emigrants, and it didn't seem fanciful to me to imagine that the KGB might be punishing him in this way. Would it ever come, and, if so, when? Could we really hope that we might some day be rid of the shackles of Soviet Russia?

It was cause for another celebration when Voronel received his invitation as well, which happened soon afterward.

These letters did not, of course, mean that we could immediately apply; they simply enabled us to take the first of the innumerable steps that were necessary to start the process in motion.

At this point I should outline the preliminary moves one has to make toward emigration from the Soviet Union.

First, you have to have the invitation from Israel, witnessed by a notary. In addition to this letter you have to bring to the Visa Department a character reference, or recommendation, from your place of work. (This makes absolutely no sense; everybody knows that at the same time your superiors have to send a confidential recommendation to the same department.) Further, you must provide a certificate from the House Committee of the building where you live, merely attesting to the fact that the address you claim really is your residence. Your passport, your I.D. card at work, your Labor Book (the record of employment everyone has to have), and your propiska already provide this information. The aim of these requirements is simply to isolate the applicant, put stumbling blocks in his way, and train a spotlight on him. For obvious reasons no one wants to broadcast his intention of emigrating until he has to; but to obtain this certificate of residence is to announce your plans to hundreds of people, to everyone in your apartment building. Since it is known that an applicant may be kept waiting for months or years before his fate is decided — if it ever is — the prospect of this long-term notoriety is daunting. It prevents a great many desperate people from ever trying to apply.

It is not always possible to obtain the reference from one's chairman or boss; he is not legally obliged to provide it. But the next set of papers demanded is almost certain to involve trouble. You have to bring in documents signed by all of your next of kin, releasing you from any financial obligations. In this context those standing in this relation to you are not only your mother and father, husband or wife, mother- and father-in-law, but, in the event of a divorce, your *former* spouse. These permits are the most senseless of all the requirements made. Parents in the Soviet Union cannot be considered dependents, since by law all retired people are entitled to a pension. But many old people are simply too frightened to sign this release. As for the ex-spouse, the obstructive intention of demanding such permissions is obvious, and there are many real tragedies in cases of divorced couples. Not everyone can divorce and maintain amicable relations. Let's say the former wife is receiving child support, which she may until the child is eighteen. She is now entitled to demand the support money in a lump sum. But what she considers satisfactory compensation is absolutely at her discretion — there is no set limit to the amount she may demand. And it happens quite often that a wife or husband who did not want the divorce, who is angry with the former partner or is simply vindictive, just refuses to sign the release on any consideration.

The application itself, therefore, quite frequently turns into an incredibly tangled problem, because it involves and threatens such a number of people.

In my own case, only one of these obstacles was really serious. My first family raised no objections; after some hesitation Naya too made plans to apply for Israel. I went to Kharkov to ask my father for his release, and, dismayed though he was by the possibility of our separation, he had no fears for himself and signed the paper for me. The real difficulty was this: Lucia's father, some of whose work in chemistry had been classified, believed that if he gave us the release, he might lose his position and bring down trouble on the heads of the rest of his family. He unconditionally refused us his permission.

Of course, at the time I received the letter from Israel, I couldn't foresee this problem, nor all of the others that lay ahead. I was filled with optimism.

*   *   *

New Year's Eve of 1972 was a time of extreme tension and excitement for me and for my friends. About ten or fifteen of us gathered at Anatoly Rabinkin's in Chernogolovka to celebrate, and none of us could stop discussing emigration to Israel. I remember someone there telling the joke that was currently going the rounds: Brezhnev's mistress says to him, "Why don't you permit free emigration?" "Well," he asks, "wouldn't you be lonely — with no one around except for the two of us?" She replies, "Lonely? Not a bit. Of course it might be a little lonely for *you* — being left in this country all by yourself." We laughed uproariously, but couldn't be distracted for long from the real situation that was on our minds. We talked about the timing of people's applications and of what their chances actually were of being let go; of the likelihood of their being detained indefinitely or imprisoned here. Not one of us, even in this close circle of friends, was rash enough to come out and announce his own plans.

Out of that company everybody has now left, after waiting for periods that ranged between one and five years. Everybody — with two exceptions. These are Victor Brailovsky, a computer scientist whose good humor and faith in the future spread over all of us at the party, and his wife, Irina, a gifted mathematician. No one there was more hopeful on behalf of the people who were trying to leave, or more convinced of their right to make this decision. The Brailovskys applied, with their son and Irina's elderly mother, in October, 1972. In 1980 they are still waiting. The Brailovskys played a tremendous part in the lives of all of us who worked and waited together during the next half-decade; they will reappear in these pages.

Among the other people still in the Soviet Union whom I met and with whom I fought are:

Anatoly Shcharansky, who was three times identified in condemnatory articles in *Izvestia* together with me, and who was sentenced in 1978 to thirteen years of imprisonment.

Vladimir Slepak, mentioned in the same articles and who, also in 1978, was sentenced to five years of exile.

Alexander Lerner, whose name also appeared in the same articles. Professor Lerner is in his sixties, very ill, and is waiting out his ninth year since he applied for his visa.

Yuri Orlov, recently sentenced to seven years of imprisonment, to be followed by five years of exile. (He, of course, is a Russian.)

Ida Nudel, an engineer, who had waited for six years when she was sentenced to four years of exile.

Yosif Begun, who, after seven years of waiting, two of which were spent in exile, has been sentenced to three more years.

There is no end to the list of these people. At this point I have to deeply apologize to those whose names are absent here: those who applied around the same time I did, or a little earlier, but with whom I did not happen to be acquainted, and those who were imprisoned. I bow to their courage. I want them to forgive me for omitting their names, and to understand that I cannot attempt to write a history here. I have to write only what I knew from my own experience.

* * *

There was some important work I wanted to complete before the time came when I declared myself, when very probably all the scientific journals in the country would be closed to me.

Just in 1971, I had entered a new avenue in my scientific life.

A theoretical physicist applies the rigorous mathematical approach to any problem that may arise in science. This has the advantage that one can work at one time in hydrodynamics, at another time in cosmology, then work in solid state physics, switch to biophysics, and so forth. It is really a matter of one's own choice. And at this time, I became much interested in the DNA molecule.

DNA is a very specific and unique molecule — you might call it the czar among molecules. This is the molecule responsible for all of our inherited characteristics — the size of each of our eyelashes, the age at which we will cut our teeth, the shape and size of our fingers — literally everything. This is the molecule that summarizes, so to speak, in each of our cells, a huge book — actually a whole vast library — containing all the information about us. A typical DNA molecule is so long that the total DNA in one human cell adds up to about 1.8 meters — but so thin that a billion of these molecules, closely packed, would be just one millimeter in breadth.

We don't yet know the language and the grammar of the DNA book, but we know the sequence for four of the simplest living beings: three bacteriophages and one virus. The number of known sequences increases all the time. We know which part of the molecule is responsible for each quality in these entities. This means that for the first time people can, at least in principle, create living beings that never existed on earth before; beings that can be designed according to our own plan. Incredibly, the first partially manmade bacteria have already been created: Professor Walter Gilbert brought into being a creature, his own "artifact," the bacterium that manufactures insulin. This bacterium has no need for insulin — but we do. And recently an oil-consuming bacterium was created; its creator received the first American patent for an artificial living being.

The perils of research in this area are formidable: hypothetically, a new virus may come into existence that could destroy all life on earth. It could be a virus that thrives on antibiotics, and, as it had never existed before, no creature in the world could have built up an immunity to it. Investigations into new recombinant DNAs have to be conducted under the most tightly restricted conditions; the precautions surrounding experiments in this field are the most demanding applied to any sort of scientific research. There are those who decry this work on grounds of the terrible danger. But in my opinion, to curtail exploration cannot be justified. To accept the intellectual death of humanity for fear of physical death seems to me a pusillanimous choice. I cannot condemn Prometheus, who brought us fire, though many people have met their death by fire.

I had certain ideas about the problems of DNA, and while I was still awaiting my invitation from Israel I had started working out elucidations related to them. I didn't want to make my application, and thus possibly be shut out of science for an indefinite time, before my idea on the physical approach to DNA study was published. I planned to present it to the International Biophysical Congress, to be held in Moscow in August, 1972. This meant that we could not apply at the same time as the Voronels, and Sasha and Nina requested their visas on May 12th. But the delay could not be helped. I knew I absolutely had to make this contribution, which might be the last piece of work that I would be able to bring to the attention of the scientific world for months or years. I thought it to be my most important paper.

Courage and Cowardice

THE FIRST very well-known professor to request an exit visa was Alexander Lerner, in December of 1971. Professor Lerner was one of the most successful scientists in the country. Although not a member of the Academy, he was the deputy director of a large scientific institute. He was frequently consulted on scientific matters by the Central Committee of the Communist Party. He was allowed to travel abroad; he was very prominent in Russia in cybernetics, a field that was attracting an increasing number of gifted people. The fact that such a person was trying to leave the country was electrifying.

I suppose I need hardly repeat that people were very circumspect about discussing news of this kind, which never appeared in the papers, on the Soviet radio, or on TV. Officially, it hadn't happened. Until a much later date, there wasn't a word in the news media about the Jews who were emigrating, or trying to emigrate, and certainly nothing about this eminent scientist among them. But Professor Lerner's application was widely known almost as soon as he made it. The scientific community officially kept silent about it, but excitement and alarm were in the air.

Alexander Lerner was not motivated to take this step by fears as to his own future in Russia; he could hardly have been more secure. It was on behalf of his son and daughter (born late, when he and his wife were almost middle-aged, and a tremendous blessing to them because they had lost their two first sons in the War) that he wanted to leave. Professor Lerner knew much more than most people did about the renewed threats to Jews that were now gathering momentum in the provinces, and how bad the situation was becoming; he was a member of the small top-echelon rank permitted access to real news sources. He felt that things could only get worse, and he could not be sure of what would happen to his children when he was gone, when they no longer had his prestige for their protection. So, although both of his children were doctoral candidates at the time, the whole family decided to risk everything and apply for their visas.

Then in March of 1972 Veniamin Levitch, Corresponding Member of the Academy of Sciences, put in his application. This event caused an even more explosive effect than the news about Professor Lerner, and fortified the intentions of many who had been undecided. Clearly, if eminent men like Lerner and Levitch felt it wise to attempt to obtain their exit visas, one should follow them. They were certainly clever enough to make the right decision.

My own consciousness of haste redoubled. One couldn't tell what the future might bring. The punitive measures being taken against Jews who were trying to emigrate increased in frequency and severity. You began to hear more about people being hauled in and subjected to interrogations by the KGB; about arrests and imprisonments. And now, suppose the authorities closed the door to the outside world once and for all? What if the Visa Department were simply shut down, and the fragile hopes upon which we lived were totally extinguished? This worry was particularly agonizing in my own case because my research and conclusions on my paper were still not complete. I was working around the clock, and not until quite near the date of the International Biophysical Conference was I actually able to finish it.

I rather looked forward to the conference, and when the time came read my paper,* I had every expectation of arousing a considerable stir.

During my entire professional life I had been most fortunate with regard to attaining recognition for the ideas I presented. Only once had I been challenged, and that was in 1956, when Landau had misunderstood my electron theory — the occasion that culminated with the vindication of my approach, and quite a triumphant entry into the wider sphere of Soviet and international science. From that day to this, I had become accustomed to audiences that not only credited my views but which were usually very much interested in them. But to my dismay, today there were no comments, no questions. I was totally bewildered by my audience's indifference: I was positive that — my solution aside — the very problem I was attacking was too exciting not to attract serious attention. The reason for this cold reception dawned on me only much later, and I will return to the subject in due course. At the time, I was baffled and disappointed.

During a break from the meetings, while we were all moving around

* "Inverse Problems for DNA."

and making one another's acquaintance, an American scientist came up to me and introduced himself. "I wonder if I could talk to you for a minute," he said. "Could we step outside and take a walk before the conference starts up again?" In the Soviet Union, where "the walls have ears," this is an invitation you hear very often — but hardly from a Western scientist! I accepted, and we left the building. When it was possible to talk without being overheard, he began with a question that simply astounded me.

"Is it true that you want to go to Israel?" I was really amazed, because I had told no one of my intentions. But I decided not to lie about it, and said yes.

"Well, I'm a friend of Veniamin Levitch. I know that you and he are very close. He's told me a lot about you." Once more I was astonished, because Professor Levitch and I didn't know each other particularly well. But I didn't want to let Levitch down: maybe now that he had applied for his visa, he needed all the support he could get from other scientists, and he may have had some very good reason for mentioning me to this man. So again I said yes.

"What I wanted to ask you is this," said the American. "Do you have any suggestions to offer as to how someone like myself could help? What can we do to assist the people who are trying to get to Israel?"

I had a great many ideas; I had thought about it constantly for an entire year. Nothing could have been more encouraging than this question. Because the Soviets valued their international scientific contacts and presumably would not want seriously to alienate scientists from other countries, I felt that concern on the part of friends from abroad was a tremendous asset to those of us who were trying to emigrate. Here was someone who evidently was willing, not only to interest himself in the trials faced by beleaguered fellow-scientists, but to take some risks on their behalf. I was very grateful to have met him. We conferred for a couple of hours.

It was more than a year before I discovered why this man had sought me out. When he heard my name and ascertained that I was a friend of Professor Levitch, he concluded it would be most unlikely that there were two Professors Azbel, both of whom knew Levitch, and both of whom were hoping to leave for Israel. So he believed I was the man about whom he had heard. This was a mistake. There was another Azbel, David, who had recently applied for his exit visa, had been refused, and who at that time — although a man over sixty years of age — was about to start the battle on behalf of Soviet Jews for which he later became so well known. I didn't know David Azbel then, but later, when we were fighting on the same front we became well acquainted.

* * *

Here I have to interrupt my narrative and say something about the story of David Azbel. It is actually a saga. I can give only a brief sketch of it — a full account would require another book.

David told me once that reading *The Gulag Archipelago* had made only a faint impression on him, because what Solzhenitsyn had witnessed and experienced was so much less frightful than what he had undergone himself.

Azbel's life started very auspiciously. He displayed talent and ability from the start; he was extraordinarily bright and able in school, went on to the university, and advanced rapidly in his chosen field, chemistry. He had been working on his candidacy for two years when, at the beginning of the 'thirties, he was arrested and indicted under the "conspiracy" charge upon which so many hundreds and thousands were imprisoned in Stalin's time. He was convicted and sentenced to five years. A five-year sentence, it was universally recognized (even by the OGPU), meant that the person was completely innocent of any crime at all.

Azbel's enormous strength of will and courage were evident from the start of his term. He refused to accede to any demands he knew to be unconstitutional and, as a result, was subjected to daily beatings and to being locked in the *kartzer*. (The kartzer is the punishment cell, a vertical coffin-shaped slot cut into the wall of the sub-basement of the prison, with this disadvantage to the prisoner over being shut into a real coffin: that one can neither lie down nor sit in it.) After a few days of being entombed in this manner for nine hours at a stretch, David decided to refuse to leave the kartzer. He would not move when his guards came to march him back upstairs to his cell, two floors above. The only way they could handle him was either to kill him or to drag him bodily through the corridors and up two flights of stairs. It was not in their instructions to kill him; so they were forced to carry him. The first such experience turned out to be the last — they never took him back to the kartzer. But they redoubled the beatings and took away his clothes, leaving him naked in the freezing cell. He was now the object of all the guards' resentment and hatred: they even brought their degenerate mistresses into the prison to witness this rebel in his extremity. David, uncowed, greeted the women with an obscene gesture — whereupon he was beaten into unconsciousness.

After the five years of his sentence were up, David was still in the prison. Two more years went by; there was no explanation for his continued incarceration. To protest the illegal prolongation of his imprisonment, he finally went on a dry hunger strike. When, within a few days, he was urinating blood and was obviously close to death, he was hospitalized, resuscitated, and then brought to trial again, this time on charges of anti-Soviet activity. That was how they designated the hunger strike. He was sentenced to ten more years of solitary confinement — a year for each day that he had fasted.

But some time before that term was up, the State evolved the institution of the sharashka, the prison research institute where scientists, technicians, and experts in almost every field could be held and where they worked incredible hours at almost no expense to the government. David Azbel was transferred to a sharashka and started to work there in chemistry.

After the War, everyone in the institution was offered immediate release if he would transfer to the Uranium Works and do research there; the Soviets were now planning to produce atomic weapons. David refused to consider the offer and was too decent a person to keep his reasons to himself. He told all his colleagues that he did not believe anyone who went to the Uranium Works would ever come out alive. (He was absolutely right. At the time there were not even the most rudimentary safety precautions at the Uranium Works, and of those who made this bid for freedom there was not one survivor at the end of two years.)

A *stukatch* among the inmates told the authorities the name of the man who had warned against accepting this tempting proposal, and David Azbel was removed from the institute and spent half a year on death row in the most notorious of all Soviet prisons, Butyrki. He fully expected the predictable outcome of this stay, but instead was transferred in a transport to Kem, the seaport whence convict ships sail over the North Sea to one or another of the unspeakable labor camps in the farthest outposts of Siberia. Kem is one of the ports created by Peter the Great. That Czar deliberately founded it as a hell for convicts and exiles; when he was asked what it should be named, Peter just answered, "K em!" "To ———!" — a very bad Russian curse.

David found himself in a gang composed mostly of habitual criminals, incorrigibles who for all practical purposes had been condemned to death, and in this company he embarked.

Very, very few people have survived to tell about these prison ships. The hold of the ship was built up with a gridwork of planks, on which the prisoners lay. There were no sanitary facilities of any sort; by the end of the voyage men on the lower rows actually suffocated in the excrement of the people above. To send somebody "down" was to issue a death sentence.

The bosses of this nightmare world were the *retsidivisti*, the recidivists — men who by all odds must be the toughest criminals in Russia; all of them ready to kill upon the slightest provocation, or on no provocation at all, and every one of them a long-term veteran of conditions almost as bad as this. The prisoners' food rations were not distributed individually; they were simply thrown down the hatchway to the hold, where the most powerful zeks took care of handing them out. So the bosses were never hungry. But others died of starvation.

There were other ways of dying, besides hunger and suffocation. The criminals played cards, and for lack of money used human lives as their chips. The man who drew low card paid his forfeit by killing a victim who had been selected in advance.

David survived by means of the same talent that had kept Academician Obreimov alive in the labor camp: he was very good at telling stories, and in that loathsome nether world this gift was a godsend. Early on in the voyage he was "brought up," that is, rescued from the lower planks.

Once the chiefs among the criminals learned what David's profession was, they became greatly excited. After a few days of conferring together, they came to him with a proposition.

"Look here, Engineer" (that was what they called him; in their view any scientist was by definition an engineer), "we're going to take this ship over. You must know something about navigation; your job is to get us out of here and over to America." These men were inhumanly tough, and David didn't doubt for a minute that they would be able to kill the ship's crew and captain, heavily armed though the latter were. But he knew the plot wouldn't work: when the ship-to-shore radio signals changed or failed, the coast guard would immediately know what had happened and would solve the problem as they had more than once before: they would send up a plane to bomb the ship out of the water. Such was the Soviet response to prison-ship mutinies: he had heard about it from a fellow-prisoner, a former coast guard pilot who was in the same convoy as his on the way to Kem. It took David a long time to persuade the desperate zeks to abandon their plan.

The trip took weeks. Once arrived on the barren shore, where, although summer was not yet over, heavy snow was already falling, the prisoners were divided up into brigades. The guards had a simple system for identifying the toughest element: anyone wearing reasonably warm clothing, after that trip in the ninth circle, had obviously robbed the others. It was easy to distinguish the strong from the weak. The most vicious of the criminals were herded off to a high-security barracks. The administration was well aware of the threat these men posed, and would deal with them separately from the others. Unfortunately, David, who had privileges among these ruthless people because of his gift as entertainer, was still wearing the clothes in which he had embarked: he had been protected from robbery by the convict bosses. So he was locked in with the worst of the criminals. He knew his days were numbered: for one thing, these quarters were unheated.

The first guard who ventured into their barracks was brutally murdered, clubbed to death with a slat ripped out of one of the wooden struts. The camp authorities would not be likely to let this dangerous mob last very long.

The crowd of prisoners in that consignment was enormous, over five thousand men, and all had to be registered. The job of registrar and bookkeeper was ordinarily handed over to some of the educated prisoners from the medium-security barracks; but all this lot consisted of "career" criminals, completely illiterate. After a fruitless search for someone qualified to do this work, the guards checked even the segregated barracks. David, the only person among those thousands who could do it, got the job as bookkeeper. He knew he was living on borrowed time and that once the zeks had all been registered, he would be returned to the company of the doomed retsidivisti.

On almost the last day of his bookkeeping job, a ferocious blizzard swept down from the Arctic. David summoned all his courage and edged toward the door. Despite the presence at the entrance to the administration barracks of several guards, he threw himself out into the storm. It was not at all difficult to get away. No one attempted to capture him. He heard a few rifle shots behind him, but that was all. They knew nobody could survive long on the tundra.

Of course, David had no intention of trying to get to Central Russia. After much thought and many calculations as to the route the ship had taken, he had deduced that they must be in the vicinity of the new convict-built emplacement in the far northeast of Siberia, the city of Norilsk — the very city I visited some twenty-five years later. It was known that there were several sharashkas in the town. His aim was to reach one of these institutes. He knew it was a perfectly crazy hope, seeking such a place in the midst of a blizzard, but his chances of survival in the zek gang were even less.

(Once more, life confirmed his calculations. Not a single member of the brigade to which he was attached was alive two months later. Nobody killed them, but there was no one to rob in their segregated barracks; their means of survival was gone. They were marched every day up a steep hill, where they spent twelve to sixteen hours in construction work, with no protection from the razor-sharp Siberian wind. The rations were the same as those given the other prisoners on lighter work — practically nothing. Even the strongest of them was dead within eight weeks.)

Impossible though it would seem, by some blind instinct David Azbel did find a sharashka. The entrance was unguarded — who in God's name would attempt to escape during a Siberian blizzard? — and I will never forget his description of how he materialized like an apparition from another world into the midst of the scientist zeks who were working in the place. They surrounded him excitedly: Who was he? How the hell did he get there? But — most urgent of all — *What was the news from Moscow?* Most of them were Muscovites, and to many of these homesick people the feat that Azbel had performed paled in interest beside the hope of hearing news from the capital. (It was seven years and more since David had been a free man in Moscow, but he dredged up what he could remember having heard from more recently arrested zeks.)

He had to leave the warm building and go back out into the same gale that had been raging when he arrived, taking with him the sharashka scientists' promise that they would try to have him drafted into their institute. His fantastic luck held, and he found his way back to the labor camp. Early in the morning, the guards there were totally at a loss: they knew that someone had escaped the night before, but at head count everybody was there.

Shortly, he was transferred to the sharshka, and this saved his life. At the time of the Khrushchev amnesty, he was freed. He spent a year in exile, during which time he met and married his wife. After being "rehabilitated," he returned to Moscow; the couple had a son.

David Azbel's career thereafter was almost meteoric. This amazingly talented man, after a life of such horrors as would have incapacitated most people for any kind of future, managed to complete the requirements for his candidate's degree within a year, although his field had changed almost out of recognition during his imprisonment, and went straight on to achieve his doctorate. He became a professor.

In 1970, he was already past middle age. Nevertheless, the dream of real freedom was so strong in him that he decided to cast away everything he had fought for so hard since his release. He applied for his visa.

When I consider the roster of the valiant people I knew who applied for visas in full knowledge of the dangers this step might bring, I cannot think of one more intrepid than David Azbel. After so many years of intolerable misery, and then of superhuman struggle to recover the lost ground in science, he had earned the right to decline any more challenges that life might present to him. He could have rested on his laurels and spent his last years enjoying all the advantages of his position as a highly respected scientist, a member of the Soviet aristocracy.

But he cannot live in the gilded cage.

When his application for a visa was denied, he refused to be intimidated. He fought incessantly. In 1974, he began what he declared would be his last hunger strike. He didn't eat for eighteen days. Thank God, he was finally given permission to emigrate. He is now in Israel.

That is the story of the person for whom I was mistaken at the International Biophysical Congress in Moscow.

*   *   *

I don't think any professor was permitted to leave the country until October of 1972. But then finally a cyberneticist, Dr. Rutman, and an economist, Dr. Moishezen, received their exit visas. This was the first indication that it might be possible for a scientist to get out of the country.

I could not wait any longer. I had no patience left. We had our foothold by this time, the flat on Veshnyakovskaya Street. We had saved enough money to survive for a year or so. I had managed to complete and publish in the *Journal of Experimental and Theoretical Physics Letters* a paper on DNA, and to send a second one to the American journal *Biopolymers*.

I have always hated to leave anything unfinished, and there was still a great deal to be done. I was correcting my book, which was scheduled for publication later in the year. I had been forced to chop and change the original design of this book; the editor at Nauka made me cut out everything that was not related specifically to physics. "Your views on the other sciences, on aesthetics, on philosophic questions — they're very interesting," he told me, "but we can't afford to try anything novel here. Stick to physics." This is a quintessentially Soviet viewpoint: a member of one discipline is not entitled even to have thoughts in any other area. Every field is tightly compartmentalized. At all events, if I wanted to publish I had to make these cuts, and, however reluctantly, I was doing it.

Writing is a highly lucrative profession in Russia. You are paid by the unit of a signature, sixteen printed pages; the price differs according to subject matter and, of course, is relative to the author's stature and popularity — a well-known writer can come close to being a millionaire.

The proceeds I was to receive on this book, 200 roubles per signature, I hoped would be our principal source of support for a considerable time after my application for Israel rendered me unemployable.

I knew in December that if I applied for an exit visa now, prior to publication, the book would be buried. (I was right. Nauka shrank in patriotic horror at the prospect of publishing the work of a would-be emigrant. When they heard of my application they hastily canceled all their plans.) But the news of the two scientists who had made their escape so greatly intensified the sense of haste that had been driving me for so long that I had to risk my book's being aborted. If those men could make it, so might I, and I should strike while the iron was hot.

Perhaps no incident had been more decisive to me in the last year than having been requested by my director to tell a gifted student of physics who had written his candidate's thesis under my tutelage, and whom we were about to take on in my department, that he could not be accepted at the institute after all. "You can see my position," Khalatnikov explained. "I simply cannot take another Jew into the department. We've already accepted one Jew this year; the best qualified of all the applicants." It made me bitter to remember my own rejections, over and over, from the institutes at Kharkov years ago. Now this young man would have the same experience I'd had, and here it was *I* who had to say "I'm sorry — the institute's situation has changed — there is no room in the department for a Jew." This student's chances of eventual success would be incomparably slighter than mine had been.

It was becoming more and more impossible to live in the prison of the Soviet Union.

Nobody at the Institute for Theoretical Physics had any idea that I was planning to apply for my exit visa; in fact, just a week before my application Professor Khalatnikov declared, "Well, if I'm sure about *anyone* here, positive that he'll never apply, it's Azbel." He couldn't imagine that anyone with such favorable prospects would be willing to throw them away. I had kept this secret from everybody, except — undoubtedly — the KGB, which must have been aware of the invitation from Israel. I remember standing by a window at the institute one day, staring out, thinking, when in walked the executive director. He was also chief of the Party organization, a retired colonel, and very probably one of the KGBsts at the institute. He just casually said to me, "Ah there, Mark Yakovlevitch! You're thinking: 'To go, or not to go' . . . Aren't you?" And he left without waiting for my answer.

There were the last days of planning my departure from Soviet life. Several impediments yet stood in the way of applying for our exit visas. First, we still did not have the required release for emigration from Lucia's parents. Second, I was anxious not to cause any trouble for my institute, toward which I felt a strong loyalty. The Institute of Theoretical Physics is a very powerful organization. With about half a dozen members of the Academy of Sciences on its staff, and as many Stalin or Lenin laureates, it is hardly vulnerable to any sort of official interference or criticism. But even so, I did not want to subject it to the embarrassment of having a "defector" on the staff. I decided to take a leave of absence, during which I would make all my final arrangements, make my application at the Visa Department, and, before the end of my time off, send in a letter of resignation. With the same idea in mind, Lucia had already quietly resigned from her laboratory, telling them that it was too difficult to commute to Chernogolovka from Moscow.

At that time I had not had a vacation in three years, so there was almost five months' paid leave owed to me.

On December 2nd, 1972, after a meeting of the Scientific Council, I approached Isaak Khalatnikov. I'll just say here that we were *na ty,* which means we addressed each other informally in the second person singular. In Russia this means very close relations between the speakers.

He was startled by my request. "Five months, Mark! What do you need it for?" The question was perfectly reasonable. As a matter of fact, the senior collaborators at the institute were absolutely free. If I wanted to take off, say, three or four weeks for a skiing vacation, it was easy to arrange. But this came as a surprise. "Five months! That's certainly a long leave of absence, especially beginning at this time of year!" I started to talk about the book I was revising and how I needed time, but he was as experienced as I at this sort of work and found it hard to believe I would need so many months to do the job. "No, I cannot give you five months. I'll give you two months, for this year." That was not quite what I wanted, but after trying a little longer to press my point, I had to yield. Taking with me Khalatnikov's signature on a leave-of-absence for December and January, I left.

But evidently Khalatnikov couldn't stop thinking of my strange request, and when I got home from the library the next evening Lucia told me that his chauffeur had come over with a message that I call him immediately. Within an hour or so I was in his Moscow apartment. Khalatnikov received me in his study, just the two of us.

"Mark," he said, "look. I'm not interested in your private affairs. You may have any number of reasons for asking for a leave of absence, and you know I'm always willing to do anything I can for you." This was true: if Khalatnikov was sure he wouldn't run into any difficulties (he always steered clear of confrontations with those in authority over him), he always let his collaborators do pretty much what they wanted. "But let me ask you to answer just one question for me. If your answer is no, then that's the end of our conversation — and perhaps you would join us for dinner. You're not intending to apply for Israel?"

He knew that if asked, I would answer the truth.

I asked him a question in my turn. "Let me put it this way. Right now you don't know anything. I think it would be better for you if things stayed that way. Do you really want to know the answer?" Of course this was an implicit answer.

Khalatnikov was terrified by the bare idea that someone at *his* institute — the institute where *he* was director — would apply for emigration. It was an unreasonable fright, all out of proportion: he had little to fear. But he wanted to appear in the eyes of the world 100 percent pro-Soviet, totally beyond the shadow of a doubt. He said, "Yes, I do want to know the truth."

"I intend to apply for Israel."

"You're *crazy!*" For a moment I could see that he was on the point of flying into a rage. Then he made an effort and pulled himself together, evidently realizing that if he became excited, if he started shouting at me, he might lose his chance of keeping abreast of my plans. *"But!* . . . all right." For the time being he would put up an unruffled front. "And — do you intend to do it soon?"

"Yes."

"Very soon?"

"Yes."

"That is — in the next few days?"

"Yes."

"Then before you apply I want you to hand in your resignation from the institute. I want you to resign voluntarily. You can't go ahead with this and make trouble for us. You *must* not!"

"Isaak," I said, "I'm ready to send you a letter of resignation as soon as I find some sort of employment, some means of support to keep my family going while we're waiting for permission to leave. But just the fact of your being scared is not a good enough reason for me to quit right away. I can't simply let my wife and daughter starve. If you have any sort of trouble, of course I'll resign at once. But I don't see why you should."

"Very good," he said. "And suppose I find you a position elsewhere? Naturally the salary wouldn't be nearly as high as what you are receiving here, as director of a department in an institute of the first class."

(There are three classes of institute, and the higher the class, the higher the salary of the staff.) "Now, if I do that, will you hand in your resignation immediately?"

"Yes."

"All right. But I would much prefer it if you left the institute as of now."

"Let me bring something to your attention, Isaak. You're frightened. But you'll lose face before the senior scientists if you get rid of me that way."

"Would you be interested in their opinions?" he asked.

"Yes, I would."

"Whose views do you want to hear?" I mentioned the names of several of my colleagues.

"I'll make a note of that," he said. "But before anything happens I want to give you some advice: for God's sake, drop the whole idea. Just drop it. I'll forget you ever mentioned it." I made no reply. "And if not, I want your guarantee that you'll leave the institute at once. I'll try to find you some sort of reasonable position."

The idea of dinner had evaporated, and I left.

The next day, as I knew, the regular seminar at the institute was scheduled. I didn't attend, being on leave of absence; but I knew that Khalatnikov would discuss my conversation with other members of the senior staff.

The day after that was Soviet Constitution Day, December 5th. This is a national holiday, so I was surprised to hear a ring at my door very early in the morning. When I opened, there were two of my colleagues: Corresponding Member of the Academy Lev Gorkov and Professor Larkin. Although taken aback by their visit at such a time, I invited them in. They must have risen very early to get here at this hour and had made quite an effort to arrive at a time when I was sure to be in. They didn't greet my wife, who was in the living room, but hastened unceremoniously into my study.

"We've come to talk about your application for Israel," Gorkov began. "We've all discussed the situation. We want you to leave the institute." He said nothing at all about my being placed in a position somewhere else.

"Well," I said, "and what about my family? How am I supposed to support them? People sometimes wait years for their visas. You know that."

"That's your business," answered Gorkov.

"But you know as well as I do what I'd be in for. Suppose I were charged with parasitism? It must be clear to you that I'm perfectly willing to resign at once if the institute has any problems about it; I told Khalatnikov that."

"We can't wait for problems," said Gorkov. "We don't want to wait for problems. We want you to leave the institute."

I turned to Larkin for his opinion.

"I think if you were all exiled to Northeast Siberia, it couldn't matter less," he pronounced. "What matters is the institute. Having someone who's applying for Israel on the staff would be a black eye for us. Suppose they react by canceling permission for some of us to go abroad for a conference or seminar, for example? That's the kind of thing that could happen, or worse. We can't justify keeping you on another minute."

I should like to stress that Larkin was not a cruel person; no more callous by nature than most. He was simply a perverted person; perverted by the specifics of the Soviet regime. A psychiatrist friend of mine once told me that under Stalin new forms of psychopathology emerged in the Soviet population. (Among women who suffered from delusions, by far the commonest was the belief that the victim was Stalin's wife or mistress.) It struck me that among men, scientists, deprived as so many were of any kind of emotional rewards save those derived from their profession, were similarly liable to espouse an irrational conviction: that science took priority over everything else in life. Larkin was a not at all unusual adherent to this faith. In his eyes, human lives — in this instance the lives of my wife, my daughter, and myself — were as nothing, if our interest conflicted with the smooth workings of his scientific institute. This was a person who was probably the best teacher of young scientists at the institute and who had more of a following among them than any other professor there. He was very effective and good with people who were even more talented than he, and he was quite talented himself. However, it suddenly came to me that perhaps he really would be capable of letting us all be killed if it meant retaining freedom of action in anything that related to science.

I really hadn't expected this, but now, out of a sort of curiosity, I wanted to see how far they would go. Larkin had already made his position perfectly clear, but I turned back to Gorkov. Gorkov and I were close colleagues. Over the years we had accumulated a good many mutual obligations. I have told how he saved me from being dropped by the Scientific Council. In my turn, I had done everything I could for him whenever the opportunity arose. At one time he had gone through a serious crisis, when his little son was ill and he had been unable to obtain the services of an eminent physician, the only specialist in the child's disease in whom he had any faith. The man was besieged by patients, but as I had the luck to be acquainted with him, I was able to persuade him to take on this one additional case. The outcome was successful. The child recovered, and since then Gorkov had often mentioned what a tremendous debt he felt he owed me. So — just experimentally — I addressed him again.

"I understand what Larkin is saying," I said. "But Lev: how would you feel about hiring me pro forma as your secretary, just as protection before the law?" I was only interested in what he would say: I happened to know that such a procedure would be very hard to put through, because not long before I had planned to do the same thing for Voronel when he had applied for his visa, and thus eliminate the danger of parasitism charges against him when he lost his job. But I found that I would need a certificate from my institute to present to the Union for Domestics, Chauffeurs, and Secretaries, attesting that I needed a secretary; and I knew my Khalatnikov too well to pursue the matter further. He would have asked why I needed an employee in that capacity, and who it was. On learning it was Voronel, whose application for an exit visa was known to everybody, he would have put a stop to the plan before it was started.

Gorkov was caught off balance; it took him a while to answer. Finally he said, "I don't think I could do that. I don't like any kind of tricks."

It had never occurred to me that so cordial a relationship could possibly be severed in this way.

I asked him another favor — not an experimental one. "All right, Lev, I'm resigning as of now," I said. "But I have five months' leave pay coming to me. Now that I'm out, I don't care to go to the institute again. Would you take care of this payment for me?" Obviously relieved at being asked to perform a business errand that didn't involve any special commitment, he agreed.

A week later I was told that the institute would pay me only for two of the five months I was owed. I consulted a lawyer, who advised me that the law would be on my side in this issue; that he would take the case if I wanted to bring it to court.

I called the scientist secretary of the institute, Lev Aslamasov (a dark little man, who subsequently — but only for a year — was Khalatnikov's son-in-law) and told him I was planning to challenge the legality of the institute's withholding these funds. He sounded nervous and conciliatory, and shortly afterward I received the money. Khalatnikov must have decided that a lawsuit, no matter what the outcome, would be damaging to the institute.

When I next saw Gorkov, I asked him, "Was that your idea of taking care of my salary?"

"Well, I did what I could. The Accounting Department told me you were entitled to only two months' pay."

"Couldn't you have checked with the Academy lawyer?"

"I did my best," said Gorkov. It was a long time before he and I spoke to each other again.

The Visa Department

I HAD originally planned to send all my documents to the Supreme Soviet, with a letter requesting exemption from the requirement for a release from my wife's parents. Since my hand was forced by the premature loss of my institute job, I no longer felt I had the time to go by this circuitous route. Besides, it was too tempting to make a try at putting in an application directly. Who could tell? A miracle might happen. So I collected all my papers, including a petition to be permitted to apply for the exit visa without the release from Lucia's parents; and, on the day after my resignation, December 8th, I went to the Moscow Visa Department in Kolpachny Lane.

Ironically, all the offices that deal with emigration, and with Jews or other "dangerous elements," are right off Bogdan Chmielnitsky Street. Chmielnitsky was the notorious seventeenth-century Ukrainian commander who betrayed his country and, further, murdered almost a million Jews. The pogrom he initiated was the worst in history until the Nazi Holocaust.

I don't think it is by chance that those who killed the helpless met an unhappy fate. The Ukrainians exterminated Jews with fire and sword; but when it came to doing battle with any except the unarmed, this nation surrendered supinely, though richer and more populous than Poland and Turkey combined. She had no idea then of defending herself against invaders, but simply thought over the choice: Who would be her master? Whose mistress would she be?

I am positive that those who oppress unprotected people are sentenced to a miserable fate. The same weakness that motivated these persecutions brought on abnegation and defeat.

It was only too appropriate that to pass from the Visa Department to the Central Committee, where one may enter pleas, to the Ministry of the Interior, where one can try to enter further appeals, to the Praesidium of the Supreme Soviet, and, nearby, the KGB — which takes care of those who enter pleas — one finds oneself over and over again on Bogdan Chmielnitsky Street. Now for the first time in my life (but not for the last; I would many times have to follow this route, and often under police escort) I made my way along this street so ominously named.

The woman official in the Visa Department was tall, formidable, handsome in a tough, forbidding style. I was sitting across from her on an old and creaky chair — the office was shabbily furnished — and jokingly I inquired, "Why do you have such broken-down chairs here? This one feels as if it might collapse at any minute."

"And so?"

"Well, you know — suppose someone broke his neck, got killed, if one of these things fell apart?"

"It's possible," she answered, without smiling. "And it wouldn't bother me at all." I was punished for trying to joke with the enemy. It was a humiliation.

She went through my papers, and when she came to the application for a permit to apply without providing the release from my parents-in-law, she said, "This I have to discuss with the deputy chairman." She left the office, and in a few minutes came back and told me that the deputy refused to accept my documents without this release, so I couldn't apply for my exit visa.

"Where can I enter an appeal?" I asked.

"Well, you may go to the All-Union Visa Department, in the Ministry of Internal Affairs," she replied. (The officials there — KGB, in fact — had the authority as to who could leave and who could not.) There was no encouragement in the woman's tone; I could tell she felt she was sending me off on a perfectly useless quest.

When I came to the Ministry of Internal Affairs, which is on Ogaryova Street near the Central Post Office, and filled in a card with my name and address, profession, age, and my reason for being there, I was informed that I couldn't be received at the Visa Department that day. There was a large delegation of Leningrad refuseniks who had come to appeal their cases, and the Department would be tied up all day. Nobody was in a hurry.

Wanting time to think everything over, I went out into the corridor and sat down. I considered what I ought to do next. Meanwhile, the group of refuseniks came out of the office where they had been consulting with the emigration officials; it was the lunch hour. However, at this moment a uniformed man emerged from the same doorway and called out in a loud voice, "Anyone here named Azbel?"

"I am Azbel," I answered.

"You're to be admitted to the Visa Department directly."

Only later did I realize why I had been admitted. When the visa officials were handed the card with my name on it, their curiosity — pure human curiosity — was too strong to permit them to turn me away. They had already had a great deal of trouble with Professor David Azbel, who had been waiting for his visa for almost a year now and had been repeatedly refused. He was not the sort of person to take this senseless injustice lying down: he had joined protest demonstrations and had several times come to the Praesidium of the Supreme Soviet with other refuseniks to demand their release from the country. He had been arrested many times and was well known to the authorities. When they saw the name of another Professor Azbel, they could not resist checking into this new phenomenon right away.

The interviewers were three colonels. They started asking the usual questions: who I was, where I had been educated, where I had received my doctorate, and so forth. Finally we came to the purpose of my visit.

When they learned that I wanted to apply for my visa without the consent of my parents-in-law, they at once declared that this was impossible, and produced all the nonsensical arguments that were supposed to back up this ruling: the parents were elderly; they might become incapacitated; might be in need of help; one never knew what might happen . . . They knew as well as I did that this line of reasoning was ridiculous: that the pension of a retired professor, a Stalin and Lenin laureate, was high enough so that my father-in-law could never possibly be in need of financial assistance, particularly not from a person who had just been fired and had no income, no means of support, himself.

Eventually this meaningless discussion bored even the KGBsts. They had been through it all too many times. They abruptly switched to another subject, which evidently was of real interest to them: what made me want to apply for emigration.

"You can't deny that you've done very well for yourself," one of them challenged me.

I knew they had heard all the rhetoric on this point from other applicants. They had heard over and over about the historic Jewish motherland, about the Jewish centuries, about the applicants' love for Israel. But nothing could be unlikelier than for a KGB colonel to understand what these people were talking about; they had no common frame of reference. It is useless to explain to a blind man how marvelous colors are; he may believe you or not; he can't sense it. And I was tired of the idiotic conversation we had been having. I couldn't tell these men all the elements that had gone into my decision; but, having been a lecturer for twenty years, I was accustomed to presenting quite a number of essential ideas in a form that was at once true and clear enough for the understanding of a general audience.

My idea was very simple.

The situation of Jews in Russia is, in fact, insoluble, given the culture and mentality of the population. On the one hand, any anti-Semitic actions, any discrimination, cannot be legally justified and are not only very unpleasant for Jews but arouse the indignation and contempt of the civilized world.

Now: despite barriers erected in their way, Jews, because of their own intellectual priorities and because of their centuries-old inclination to engage in abstract thought, are very apt at science and medicine. That is why, obstacles notwithstanding, a very high percentage of the top positions in the Academy of Sciences and in the medical sphere are held by Jews. This disproportionate representation in these areas cannot be made acceptable to the majority of the people. In a hypothetical Russia with no State anti-Semitism — if one could start the entire nation over with a clean slate — an attempt to create equal opportunities would be not only unrealistic but in a sense undemocratic, because it would lead to Jews holding an even more significant percentage of prestigious positions than they do at present. That in itself would result in a re-emergence of anti-Semitism. Therefore, there is no chance of resolving this dilemma inside the country. The only solution is to allow those Jews who prefer to leave the country to do so, rather than to confine them within its borders and restrict their possibilities with "quota systems" and other fetters.

I really think that this is the only possible solution, because the anti-Semitism that has existed for centuries, and inheres almost like an instinct among the simple people, cannot be excised within a generation or two, nor can it be simply ignored.

This idea was absolutely novel to the three men sitting before me. But it made perfect sense to them — indeed, it was their own feeling. They themselves, Russians, were anti-Semitic. No one knew better than they how offensive it was to see a Jew in the enviable position of university professor. And to add insult to injury, this damn Jew wanted to leave the country. No one was more adamantly opposed than they to any "equal opportunities." No one worked harder than they did to reduce the percentage of Jews in the universities to as close to zero as possible.

Something rather strange happened: for a moment they forgot that here was a Jew, an enemy. For a moment there was a certain human contact between us. Probably for the first time during their work with people who were trying to emigrate, they heard statements which they did not consider to be Jewish demagoguery, but something real. It appeared that our approaches had something in common — of course, nothing that they would express aloud — but in essence, there it was.

When I had finished, they were not inclined to resume the tired and specious arguments with which they had started out. They might be hard men, they might be cruel, but they had red blood in their veins; and we had reached a point where we were discussing things on a purely human level.

"Now," I concluded, "should I be prevented from leaving by some foolish regulations? Let me tell you something. I know that my position in the West will be much lower than the one I hold here. This won't be a step up in the world, it will be several steps down. But to stay here, at the top of my profession, and to be forced to keep other Jews out of it — I can't live that way. Do you really think I should be hindered by the parents, who are declining to sign my release only because they are afraid of you?"

There must have been a moment when the senior of the three interviewers thought, "Why not make just one exception?" He picked up the telephone and called the Deputy Chairman of the Moscow Visa Department.

While waiting for the connection to be put through — it was quite a long interval — I suppose his ordinary habits of mind reasserted themselves. What was happening — that *he* should be simplifying, should be expediting, the visa application of a Jew?

In short order this man, a KGBst of many years' standing, found a way out of so unlikely a role. While still talking to the deputy chairman, he started riffling through my papers to check as to whether they were all completely in order. The deputy, who had seen all my papers only an hour before, must have said: "Yes, with the exception of the father-in-law's release, they're all in order." The conversation went on for some ten minutes before the deputy chairman at the other end of the line apparently began to understand what was required of him; and with a sigh of relief the colonel hung up the receiver and said, "Look here: you didn't bring the recommendation from your place of employment."

I explained to him that I had left the job deliberately in order not to create any problems for the institute. (Everyone knew by this time that such a procedure was fairly common. There was an almost unwritten agreement between the authorities and the applicants not to bother too much with the requirement for a character reference from one's superior if the applicant had resigned.)

"When did you resign?"

"December seventh."

"Oh, well! If it had been a year ago, or six months, that would be something different! But if you've only just left, we'll have to have the reference."

At this juncture I understood that there would be no escape from these entanglements; that the colonel would never allow me to submit my application without the recommendation. I thought everything over and finally concluded that of the two impossible tasks it would be easier to force Khalatnikov to give me a character reference than to fight with my father-in-law, who was immovable in his refusal to give us the release.

"All right," I said, "I'll attend to the recommendation. But it will take a while. By the time I have it, the deputy chairman may have forgotten that in my particular case he was willing to waive the requirement for a release from the parents. Would you please make a note on my application to the effect that the documents will be accepted without the parents' release?" Again, this was an occasion when the colonel did not want to make an about-face and retract a decision he had made himself. So after a moment's hesitation he took his pen and wrote on my application: "Application for visa to be accepted provided all documents are in order, with the exception of the wife's parents' consent, which will be waived in this instance."

This was better than nothing, and I left the office clutching the precious piece of paper, but still acutely aware of how difficult it would be to deal with Khalatnikov.

All this happened on December 8th, and it was not until quite a while later that I heard I would be permitted no contact at all with Khalatnikov. But I already knew that now he had got rid of me, he would do everything in his power to avoid taking any action on my behalf.

Outside on Ogaryova Street, having stopped to think everything over, it suddenly occurred to me that obviously the recommendation from one's chief at work really was of no importance; the woman official at the Moscow Visa Department, who had checked all my papers, had said nothing about it, nor had the deputy chairman when she consulted him. The only stumbling block he had presented me with was the missing release from my in-laws. (This shows, by the way, the arbitrariness of the requirements covering emigration, which is one reason we all had such tremendous difficulty ascertaining what the rules actually were. As time went by it became increasingly clear that if the authorities were willing to let you go, one or two missing documents didn't matter too much. If they wanted to keep you, there was no end to the number of regulations upon which they could draw.)

I decided to make an experiment. I went back to the Moscow Visa

Department. When the official saw me, she could hardly speak from astonishment. Having sent me to the All-Union Visa Department, perfectly confident that my application would be rejected there, she really couldn't believe her eyes when I reappeared only an hour later.

"Yes — what now?" she asked.

"I brought you the permission to file my visa application," I answered. She gasped.

"Is that Colonel *Danilov's* signature?" she asked, unbelievingly. As I hadn't noted the name of the KGBst with whom I had been speaking, I simply pushed the paper closer to her and said, "You know best." The fact was, as I found out later, this was the famous Colonel Danilov who never before or after in his career as an emigration official had made one single concession of any kind to any Jew. Seeing his signature, the woman was astounded. I don't know what she thought — maybe that I was an illegitimate nephew of Brezhnev! Whatever she may have surmised to be the explanation for this unprecedented waiver, she at once became very polite and said, "Of course I'll accept your documents. I'll file them right away."

Thus I became one of the very few who managed to apply for a visa in just one day. Typically, people are sent to and fro, from office to office. They lose weeks, frequently months, simply completing the process of entering the application.

When I came home and told Lucia, she couldn't believe it.

And I have to say that despite all the horrors that we knew might lie ahead of us, for the first time in our lives we felt ourselves to be free people. We had nothing to lose any more. We had declared ourselves apart from the Soviet community; we had become outsiders. This meant that there was no longer anything we had to conceal. We had joined the very few who could say what they thought — and who could think about anything they wanted to.

I cannot describe this incredible feeling of inner freedom. All the fears that had encumbered me were lifted — gone. I wasn't afraid of being fired — I had been fired. I wasn't afraid of losing my position in the hierarchy — I had already lost it. I wasn't worried about my professional future — I no longer had one. The heavy Soviet gravitation no longer weighed me down, and I felt released, as if I could fly if I wanted to.

Knowing Soviet officialdom, I had told my wife beforehand that we had to be prepared for anything. As I had what now seemed the rather bad luck to be high in their regard as a scientist, it could well be three years before we obtained our release; it was already clear that the chances of being let go without too much delay were in inverse ratio to one's professional importance. I was preparing Lucia for the worst, but my hope was very different. I had thought over all the factors that could work in my favor. First, never in my career had I worked on anything that required a security clearance. Second, I had never tried for promotion above the lowest level compatible with whatever research or teaching I was engaged in. I had never tried for an administrative position; never aimed to become chairman of any department I worked in and had accepted the chairmanship of the Department of Electron Theory of Metals at the institute only because they couldn't have obtained the permission necessary to hire me part-time in any lesser post. And I now saw it as a stroke of luck that I had lost the Lenin Prize. Third, I had bowed out of the institute without stirring up any trouble for anyone there. So why should the officials detain me? It would only be a waste of time and effort for them. In the depths of my soul, I felt my release would come soon; perhaps a delay of only a year would suffice them to demonstrate their toughness.

Two weeks after I applied, Naya too made application for herself and Vadim.

Greeting the New Year of 'seventy-three was very special. The Rabinkins, who had been our hosts the previous year, came to us from Chernogolovka to celebrate. They knew we had applied, and they were considering what the best time would be for them to take the same step themselves.

This was an occasion unique in all our lives. We were free, and almost crazy with hope and optimism. We wished each other *"L'shana haba'a b'Yerushalaim"* (Next year in Jerusalem), and we really believed it might come true.

*   *   *

It was to be a long, long time before any of us experienced again even an echo of that same euphoria. A new existence began, a harried and nervous life wherein day after day we trod the minefield laid out for those betrayers who proclaimed their intention to transfer allegiance from the Soviet motherland to malign and sinister Zion.

But this might be the place to say that after our battle was over, and I looked back over those years of agonizing suspense and struggle, I realized I was grateful to Fate that I had not been allowed to leave at once. I consider the experience I gained of incalculable value. In retrospect, I believe that if in 'seventy-three I had been endowed with the gift of prophecy, had been able to foresee those years of trouble, and had been magically permitted to choose between living them through or emigrating at once without having to fight, I would have chosen the struggle. Not only because it constituted a test of oneself, a test whereby you could gauge the limits of your strength; your powers of consistency; could measure your self-respect; could look into the eyes of your children knowing that they could not be ashamed of their father for any reason; but more than that.

Ordinary life is pretty much of a routine. Things change very slowly, infinitesimal step by infinitesimal step. Everything is predictable, and the whole interlocking mechanism of human relations is established. You depend on certain people; other people depend on you. Anyone who meets you knows from the start what your position is; this knowledge influences his behavior toward you. You are respected not for your immediate achievements, but for the whole construct of your life.

But after a citizen of the Soviet Union has applied for his exit visa, he immediately finds himself in a different sphere. The feeling of weightlessness that buoyed me up during those first days was not totally illusory: the stresses, and more significantly the supports, that surround a member in good standing of society are abruptly removed, and one finds oneself free-floating in a completely unfamiliar medium.

In the group of would-be emigrants in which we found ourselves, nobody had reason to consider anyone else more important or more knowledgeable than himself. No one could claim more expertise at managing this new life than anyone else. No one depended upon another for his thinking; everyone could have his own opinion. This was a kind of pure democracy. Each of us — even a teen-age kid — could challenge someone else's proposals. If a random assemblage of soldiers suddenly had to strip naked and swim through a rapids, no one would care who was a general and who a private; what would matter would be who swam the best and who was most intelligent at helping the others to safety. Our rank, and our insignia of rank, were gone.

I think our situation was very similar to the conditions that arise after a great revolution, where there is no privilege carried over from previous times. I was at the epicenter of such a revolution, infinitely smaller as to the number of participants than those we read about in history, but no less dangerous and no less exciting.

Of course, people remained themselves. They might not always be good or kind or decent, so if you felt a responsibility toward them you had to think over not only what was the best course to take along the perilous route we were all treading, but also of a way in which they could be persuaded to take it. A decision that is second-best, but is accepted by the majority, is much more important under these circumstances than a decision that is in fact the best but is not accepted.

Perhaps what I am saying is perfectly obvious to Western perceptions, but the understanding of these processes is hardly possible to a Soviet person. The people among whom Lucia and I found ourselves after our application, and we ourselves, learned democracy — both its best and worst — by trial and error.

As I say, I moved into a second life, outside the Soviet system I had always known. And I feel at present, after my long term in the embattled nucleus within the vast labor camp where I was born, like a person who has actually led three lives, because here I am now, a citizen in the free world, after having been successively a member of the Soviet Establishment and an outsider in Soviet society.

I am an Odysseus who heard the Sirens and remained alive.

I am very grateful to the destiny that gave me this chance.

BOOK II

Confessions

FOR A LONG TIME to come, the only occasions on which I met my former colleagues were at scientific seminars. When I walked into the first one I attended after my application for Israel, I found myself an object of fear. All but one or two of the scientists removed themselves from my vicinity. They were afraid to look at me. Purely accidentally, everyone happened to turn in another direction when I passed by. Purely accidentally, if I was near they were so interested in what was being written on the blackboard that they were simply oblivious of their surroundings. They were afraid to show any signs that they hadn't forgotten me.

At the end of the seminar Lev Aslamasov came up to me and said: "Professor Khalatnikov has asked me to tell you that if you have anything to talk to him about, don't call him — don't come here to see him — but convey it to me, if you please. I'll handle any messages you may have for him, and I'll let you know what his answers are. Any contacts between you are supposed to go through me." Khalatnikov and I had known each other for twenty years.

Many, many months passed before I came to a seminar again; and when I did, it was for the sake of science — not for the sake of the scientists.

I received another shock when I went to Kharkov for the first time after applying for my exit visa. Having lived in Kharkov half my life, I knew almost everybody there. The group that comprises the Kharkov intelligentsia is a very close one; we were all acquainted. On all my previous returns I was stopped in the street a dozen times on my way to my father's place by someone who wanted to welcome me, to hear my news, and tell me his. These genial reunions were a great part of what I looked forward to on a visit home.

Now that I had applied for Israel, I found myself walking through a dead city. I didn't see a single familiar face, because when anyone caught sight of me, he changed his course — he suddenly had an urgent errand that took him in another direction. This was incomparably worse than Moscow, where friends outside the institute saw no reason to avoid me.

On the very evening of my arrival, however, after supper, the same people who had failed to recognize me in public came crowding in to visit. In fact, my poor father, who had hoped for a private family gathering, was upset by the number of guests, and couldn't help complaining during the rest of my stay that he had expected to have at least some chance to talk to me alone.

"You may not know what's been happening since you were last here," one of my friends explained. (Again, I am not giving the names of the people I was close to in private life whom I left behind in the U.S.S.R.) "Quite a few of us have been hauled in to the Big House for questioning about you. Before they let us go, they warned us you were a dangerous Zionist, an agent of the Israeli intelligence." (Zionism is not simply evil: since the 'twenties it has been outlawed as a crime, and one of the most serious.)

Only two of my Kharkov acquaintances really turned their backs on me. One was a man who had defied the authorities once too often and now had been scared into opting for a life of safety and full cooperation with the Soviet regime; and the other was a chemical engineer, our neighbor in the apartment house. He and I had often argued when I was a teen-ager; he had considered me a know-it-all brat, and must have harbored a hostility that I wouldn't have guessed at. According to the others, it was he who had told the KGB that I was a lifelong Zionist and undoubtedly a spy for Jewish and American interests.

The rest of these people, although they could not afford to recognize me openly, took a considerable risk by making the effort to see me at home; and when I became aware of the situation here, I was overwhelmed by the loyalty and bravery of almost everybody I knew. They stuck by me in the hardest time of my life.

*   *   *

A new, many-sided, and very busy life began. A great many tasks lay before me, and I couldn't exclude a single one of them.

I worked on my science as before, only now with much more strain. In the past, although I am by nature a person who works quite rapidly, I had never felt hurried. I was always fairly self-confident; never bothered, for example, by fears that someone else would solve the problem in which I was interested before I had done it myself. That had never happened, and I moved ahead at my own speed.

Now everything changed. I was pursued by the many ideas I wanted to realize, without knowing how much time I might have. I could be imprisoned at any moment; already I had noticed I was under heavy surveillance. Sometimes for days in succession, whenever I left my building a Volga parked nearby would start up and inch past me, and I would see the same car everywhere I went. I desperately wanted to complete and publish the works I had in mind before I could be prevented from doing so. It took time, and I was exasperated when I found that the desire to rush was not enough to increase the limit of speed at which a man can work.

This urgent haste, which is so uncongenial to a scientist, had become necessary more than a year before, at the time I began looking into DNA, when I knew I would apply for my visa. Then I was slowed by various new vexing problems having to do simply with the mechanics of writing and publishing a paper abroad. Previously, I had written in Russian; the piece was translated into English by a professional at the institute and then it went to the typist. Afterward it was sent out to the censor at the Academy of Sciences; then to the State censor. The institute handled the whole thing for me, including submission to foreign journals.

Now all this was impossible. I had to translate my papers myself, and because I was not perfect in English, the results were rather rough. It is certainly not customary to submit to the journals pieces in need of editorial work with respect to correctness of the language! Moreover, because we had very little money, I had to be my own typist. The typewriter I bought was not secondhand but tenth-hand, an antique that dated from the beginning of the century, and it must have weighed nearly forty pounds. It was not a very good machine; even if it had been, my beginner's attempts at typing produced pages (turned out at the rate of one per hour) that were studded with mistakes. The end results bore no resemblance to the neat, well-organized manuscripts the scientific journals were used to seeing. I can smile about it now, but at the time, when to continue publishing was in a very real sense a matter of life and death, the investment of so many weeks' awkward effort was torture.

When the first paper was in as good shape as I could manage, I came up against a brick wall. Without the State censor's O.K., it would never cross the borders of the Soviet Union by post. There was only one way of getting it out of the country, and that was to contact some Western tourist, preferably a scientist, who would take the paper back with him and send it to the journal to which I wanted it submitted. (The reader will undoubtedly understand my reasons for not going into detail as to each of the people whom I found to perform this kindness.) I typed the piece on both sides of the thinnest onionskin paper so that my "courier" would not be inconvenienced.

I knew that this procedure entailed a tremendous risk. If discovered, I would certainly be charged with an attempt to smuggle "classified" information outside the Soviet Union. (It goes without saying that the contents of the paper were not secret and, under the circumstances, could not be.) If that happened, nobody could help me.

Then, if the paper did reach the journal, the referees' comments couldn't be mailed back to me. All my correspondence from abroad was cut off soon after my application for Israel. Hundreds of letters were sent to me during those suspended years, but it was a long, long time before a single one from a foreign country arrived. I had to wait, often for months, before another visitor could bring me the referees' queries; and then my answers could not reach them for many more months. Again, this created almost insoluble problems: no journal in the world could be expected to accommodate routinely to such a situation, where contact between contributor and publisher was so slow and undependable.

For many reasons, then, to continue my work was both dangerous and difficult. But I had no choice. I could not simply stop living until such time as the KGB allowed me to leave and start life again. The things I considered to be of vital importance I did, and I was willing to face any consequences. If the officials wanted to set the precedent of punishing a scientist for publication of his scientific papers, all right. I would go to prison, but this would provide the Western scientists with a much clearer idea of what was going on in the Soviet Union than they could have at present and might arouse increased concern as to the status of Soviet refusenik scientists.

As it turned out, this, my first year of waiting, was an auspicious one. The editor-in-chief of the American journal *Biopolymers,* Professor Murray Goodman, took care of all the shortcomings in my manuscript both as to language and as to the technical presentation, and the paper was published. I will always be grateful to Professor Goodman. The next paper, which went to the most prestigious American journal, *Physical Review Letters,* met with the same success: editors Ulenbeck and Trigg were not put off by the terrible condition of the manuscript. What is more, when I was unable to respond to the referees' suggestions for an expanded treatment of the point I was making, they did me the favor of going to press with it at once, just as it was.

But these labors were only a fraction of what I had to do.

Voronel, who had made his application a few months before I made mine, had given a great deal of thought to the most urgent of the professional problems that scientists in our position would face once they were excluded from their laboratories and institutes: the loss of contact with their fields. Scientific ideas evolve so rapidly and are fed by so many currents of new discoveries, new solutions, that to be cut off from this mainstream for any length of time means actual intellectual starvation. It was essential to keep open any lines of communication that we could. Voronel decided to initiate a seminar for those of us who had applied for Israel and were barred from officially recognized institutions.

By this time about ten of the scientists we knew had applied for exit visas and had either been already refused for an indefinite period, or were very nearly certain they would be. When Voronel first proposed these conferences to them, by no means all of the refuseniks saw the value of his proposal. "We are struggling for our freedom" was the objection. "There are groups organizing protest demonstrations, sending petitions to international bodies — fighting to get out. It's impossible to suspend everything and simply discuss physics at a time like this." But Voronel and I and a few others wanted both to keep ourselves alive professionally and to join battle as a unit, maintaining contact, if we could, with colleagues in other countries and — we hoped — engaging their support. He organized a seminar to meet every Sunday noon at his apartment.

The Seminar itself was devoted solely to the reading of papers and the discussion of our scientific ideas.

At first, these meetings were attended by only eight or nine members: Voronel and I, Victor and Irina Brailovsky, Doctors Dan Roginsky and Victor Mandelzweig; Professors Moishe Giterman and Veniamin Fain; occasionally Dr. Yevgeny Levitch, Professors Alexander Lerner and the very distinguished Veniamin Levitch. But the gatherings increased in size, and in time over twenty scientists were in regular attendance. The Seminar, so tentatively initiated, is at present a strong and vital organization.

Assisting Voronel, who was chairman, with the planning and procedures of these meetings involved a considerable amount of my time.

Another significant venture that Sasha started at the same time and that is also still very much alive was the samizdat journal *Jews in the U.S.S.R.* This was the first publication of its kind to appear in the Soviet Union since the 'twenties; also, it was I believe the first samizdat periodical to include a masthead, with the names and addresses of its editorial staff. This was such a bold challenge to the authorities that they were caught off guard, and, having concluded that a seminar and a journal so scrupulously nonpolitical (the journal carried articles on such subjects as the origins of the Yiddish language, medieval Jewish scholarship, and similar topics), were fairly innocuous and might indeed distract the refuseniks from more dangerous enterprises, they refrained from interfering. They must have later regretted keeping hands off.

I worked hard on *Jews in the U.S.S.R.* and with the Seminar; but what absorbed the largest proportion of my time was being what you might call a consultant to people who were hoping to apply for their exit visas. In those days the Voice of Israel announced the names of people who had made application. Others who wanted to take the same step but had no idea of how to go about it, of what the Visa Department would demand of them, or — most essential — how they could manage to survive during the interval before permission was granted, when in all likelihood they would be thrown out of work — were anxious for advice, particularly from someone whose name was known and whose judgment was respected. Voronel had for some time been conferring with prospective emigrants, and now they started coming to me as well. Within a month or so I was receiving ten or twelve visitors a day; quite frequently a crowd would be waiting in one of our rooms while I took each of them in turn into my study. We couldn't arrange to talk as a group: usually these were people who had separate problems and questions of their own and who wanted to clarify them and get my opinion; they didn't want to share all their personal concerns with strangers.

Within a short time after my application I found that my apartment was bugged. Every time a new person arrived, I greeted him with the words: "Don't say anything here that you wouldn't say in the reception room of the KGB." These people either posed their questions to me in writing, or else we went outside to talk. (I got one of the first indications that the KGB was listening in after a scientist from Moscow University came to discuss his hopes of emigration. He expressed the very reasonable fear that if he was refused an exit visa, he would lose touch with his profession. I told him about the Seminar and mentioned that we received all the important scientific journals from the West — colleagues of ours in foreign countries, once aware of our plight, had arranged to have the American *Physical Review, Physical Review Letters, Chemical and Engineering News,* and the British *Physics Bulletin,* and other publications sent to me. Immediately after I told the man about these subscriptions — we were speaking in the privacy of my study, and he was a person I could absolutely trust — the journals stopped coming.)

Surprising though it may seem, we were in telephone communication with Israel at that time. Some of those who were among the first to emigrate had set up a schedule of telephone calls back to the Soviet Union. Thus, when my applicants asked about jobs, housing, care for the aged, and so forth, I was able to make inquiries of our contacts on the other side and provide substantial information.

Almost everyone who came to me was a perfect stranger, someone I was seeing for the first time. Glad though I was to help anyone who sought assistance, the interviews were a drain on me emotionally. People were very different — not all of them wholly pleasant. Some had questions related to their future financial prospects, or to the situation in Israel with respect to their particular demands, their expectations, and requirements. Others wanted to leave without their children or without their wives! The majority, of course, were very decent, willing to shoulder responsibility and grapple with problems; but this was, overall, a most varied cross section of humanity. I couldn't allow myself to pass judgment on them or to show irritation, no matter how bizarre their particular plans might be. Tired and impatient though I sometimes was, astounded by the fantastic schemes or the trivia presented for my consideration, I tried to retain my equanimity. I felt it was my obligation to remain calm and cooperative and simply to explain — for the hundredth time in a month — how one applies for a visa: what documents are necessary, the recommendation from one's place of employment, the release from one's parents — and all the details. I had to present in advance an excuse for the fears of the old people, since it was almost always true that the parents refused to sign the release. I would urge the applicants not to be too indignant, and suggest that they explain to the family the strategy the authorities were using to force the elderly parents to serve as stumbling blocks on the route to freedom for their children.

Sometimes Russians came; and then I had to outline the means by which they too could apply. (As I have mentioned, they had to find Jewish relatives in Israel.) I had to hear all these people's troubles, and I couldn't tell them that most of the Jews who were waiting for their exit visas were in a much worse situation than what they themselves complained of. I'll never forget how I felt listening to one of these applicants, a Lithuanian, who told me how lucky I was to be a prominent Jew! Years went by and I was still trapped, while he had received his exit visa almost at once.

Those years of consultations served as very useful experience. Never under any other circumstances could I have found myself "confessor" to so many people, and such varied ones. They had to be totally open with me; they had come for advice and could not afford to conceal any of their plans or problems.

I was often astounded by the selflessness and generosity of the people who were trying to leave. For instance, there was a doctor who had elderly parents, parents-in-law, and two very old aunts, one of them almost blind. He had to consider carefully the difficulties these fragile old people would have, undergoing the unaccustomed trials of air travel, the discomforts of the long stopover in Vienna, and the uncertainties as to how they would manage once they arrived in Israel. It would never have crossed this kindly man's mind to make plans that did not include all these members of his family. He was typical of many.

Some of the problems presented to us were heartbreaking. One would-be emigrant, Dr. Tiomkin, was divorced, and had custody of his daughter, who wanted to go with him to Israel. Their exit visas were forthcoming soon after his application — a rare stroke of luck — and it looked as though everything would work out satisfactorily. Both Voronel and I urged him to leave immediately, not to delay a minute by fussing with the disposition of his possessions.

"For God's sake, don't bother with all your things," we advised. "You've got your visas — go as fast as you can. Don't you know they've stopped people even at the airport? Don't give them time to reconsider." Several people had been detained at the last minute, and had spent months or years as stateless people, citizens of no country in the world, because when you receive your exit visa you have to relinquish your Soviet passport. "Get out while the going is good!"

But Dr. Tiomkin was much concerned with packing his precious books. To take any book published before 1947 out of the Soviet Union requires a special permit from the Lenin Library, and to obtain such a permit naturally takes up a great deal of time. Day after day he was at the library, obtaining, or attempting to obtain, these permits. We begged him to forget it all and get out of the country as soon as he could. It was not only the books that delayed him. In the Soviet Union there are no services one can hire to assist with moving; everyone has to attend to the boxing of all his possessions unassisted, and one can imagine what a huge job this can be, particularly since one can't do it in advance. There is no way of knowing how long the wait will be between applying for a visa and receiving it; the permission to leave may never come at all. One cannot pack up everything and wait indefinitely, with absolutely no idea of when, or whether, one will go. Many people left their things and decamped as fast as they could when they got the visa, but Dr. Tiomkin was one who found it hard to abandon everything that he owned. He could not understand our urgency; he was entitled to these weeks in which to make his preparations for the move, and there was a lot he had to do.

While he was winding up his affairs and crating his things, something horrible happened. His daughter's visa was withdrawn. And soon afterward, the child disappeared. After several weeks, which Tiomkin spent in a desperate panic, he received a letter from her. She had been picked up by a couple of strangers — KGBsts — and had been conveyed to a Pioneer camp thousands of miles away, in the south. She wrote her father repeatedly, begging to be released, while Tiomkin went from government agency to government agency, pleading for her return. Meanwhile, the KGB persuaded Tiomkin's ex-wife to take legal steps to regain custody of the girl, and this change of guardianship was accomplished without a hitch. The anguished father, now a man without a country (his visa had expired), stayed for several more years in the Soviet Union, making every attempt to recover his daughter; but in vain. Finally, he reapplied for a visa and went to Israel, hoping his protests might be more effectual if they came from outside the Soviet Union. That is where he is now, in Israel, writing, agitating, organizing demonstrations; still battling for his daughter. But it is perfectly possible they will never see each other again.

Hardly anyone had a more difficult time than those who were deliberately detained by a former wife or husband. One friend, a woman with three children, had been divorced for years from an alcoholic who had never seen his family since the separation. This man refused to sign his wife's release, on grounds that it would be destructive to his family ties for his children to be taken away from him! He claimed he *might*, at any time, wish to renew relations with them.

Sometimes there was nothing I could do in such a case except advise the applicant to offer the former spouse an outright bribe. One man who came to me had been married to a Russian woman, who, since the divorce, had become a vicious anti-Semite. They had not seen each other for a very long time. There was no question of child support — there were no children — but she refused to give her ex-husband the release purely out of spite. He had almost no money — he was a junior collaborator at one of the institutes, and this is a very ill-paid position — so he took a tremendous chance, sold everything he owned, and offered her the proceeds. He was doubly lucky in that she accepted this payment for her signature, and that the Visa Department let him go. He could have been like so many others kept waiting indefinitely, with no salary and no belongings — not even a table or chair.

Some of my visitors had no feeling at all of obligation toward others who were in the same position as they — no feeling of community — because in the Soviet Union there has never existed any community. One of the most striking examples of this "every-man-for-himself" viewpoint was provided by a person whom I had known for quite a while, an economist, who came to consult me. Aron was fat, soft, very sweet, and a person notable for the extreme caution with which he made any statement. He would never say, "It's a nice day, isn't it?" He would say, "It seems to me — though I am in no case prepared to insist upon it — that the weather is good today. However, I assume that there may be different opinions: it may be too hot for some, or possibly too dry for others. Yet I just want to say that in my personal opinion this is reasonably good weather." This was the furthest extent to which he would commit himself.

Aron told me with disarming frankness that he was not a brave man; that he was terribly afraid of the KGB. He wanted to leave the country but would do anything to manage it quietly without stirring up any trouble. I tried to convey a sympathetic attitude, and gave him credit for being so honest. As things worked out, he was able to obtain an exit visa with very little delay.

When, years later, I was in America, I kept hearing from many people that this same man was telling everyone who would listen that no one was refused an exit visa in the Soviet Union except those who had been in top-secret military work. When this report reached me, I naturally assumed that here was one of those common misunderstandings that crop up all the time when former Soviet citizens speak to Western people. I had noted that several times already. Because of the differences in mentalities, in frames of reference, it can be difficult for Western listeners to understand everything a Soviet person is trying to say. I was anxious to warn Aron to be more cautious in expressing himself before his new audience. For the Soviets to refuse exit visas to scientists or engineers who had held classified jobs obviously would make a certain amount of sense in the middle of an arms race: it would be hard to condemn such a restriction out of hand. If sympathizers outside Russia were to become convinced of the fiction that only those in top-secret work were prevented from emigrating, the entire fragile network of support so essential to the desperate people we had left behind would collapse.

When I met Aron and brought the subject up, he stoutly said, "Yes, of course I made that statement. I'm positive of it. Only people with a security clearance are detained." It was totally unlike him to take such a definite stand, one so damaging to so many people.

"My God! You know that isn't true! How about me? How about Voronel and Giterman? Aren't we fair examples of scientists who were in fields completely outside of classified work? And we were detained for years!"

"Well, of course I only saw you at the Institute for Theoretical Physics," he said. "But how do I know what other work you might have been doing?"

I could hardly speak for a minute. "Let me mention one important point, Aron," I finally answered. "When you make a statement like that, you may easily be destroying the lives of a great number of people. You know how many thousands there are waiting for release — praying for release. We have no way of gauging how much foreign opinion weighs in the decisions made by the Soviets, but it's pretty obvious that protests and appeals sent from the West have actually rescued a great many refuseniks. When you back up the Soviets in their excuse for preventing Jews from leaving the country, you may be cutting off the only hope of a great many unhappy people. If the sympathies of Westerners cool — what will those people have to hang on to?"

"I am just expressing my opinion," he replied stubbornly.

This was *not* his opinion, and it was not his manner of expressing an opinion. My guess is that disseminating this idea is his payment for the extraordinary dispatch with which he received his release from the Soviet Union. Ever since then, I haven't been able to shake the feeling that probably more people remain slaves in the West than I could ever have imagined when I first left Russia.

It happened to be this same man who early in 1973 introduced me to a professor of psychiatry by the name of B——. Aron told me, in his customary noncommittal way, that he could not really vouch for this man; that he didn't know him too well; he would leave it up to me to find out what kind of person B—— was; he couldn't actually recommend him.

This man was an interesting type. He had a long thin face and quick eyes, wore a triangular beard, and presented a rather Mephistophelian appearance, except that he had the pear-shaped figure of a very sedentary man. His career was a peculiar one: he had been medical supervisor of prison camps in Siberia. He had a wide acquaintance among top officials. He appeared to be very well-off. His manner was genial and ingratiating.

Dr. B—— had a daughter, and also an almost-grown stepdaughter by his second wife. His plans were very sophisticated and devious: he would try to obtain exit visas for one member of the family after another, and they would emigrate inconspicuously, at intervals. He started conferring with me about these visas when we first met. But at this writing, he is still in Moscow. He has not applied to go. He will certainly never leave, and I don't think he ever intended to. He did successfully manage the departure of his wife's daughter: he maintained that she had gone ahead to prepare the way for the rest of the family, to find them a place to settle. But as far as I can see, what he really wanted — and achieved — was simply to get rid of his stepdaughter.

One wonders, now, why he saw so much of the man who introduced us, and why he was so intensely interested in refuseniks. He spent a lot of time with us.

I suppose part of the attraction we held for some doubtful elements was that, having made public our intention of emancipating ourselves from the Soviet power, we had a certain amount of power ourselves. Soviet people are trained from infancy to know that silent obedience to authority is the only way to ensure one's safety. But a person who decides he is indifferent to safety, who is willing at any risk to speak his mind, need obey no dictates save those of his own conscience. In that sense, he has acquired power. He owns himself. The fact that we were in telephone contact with the outside world, too, fascinated other peripheral people. The international lines were not yet disconnected, and anyone interested in our cause was able to call and (for a while) to receive calls from us. The charges were paid at the Israeli end with contributions sent by concerned people from many different countries.

These calls constituted a lifeline. They were the only evidence we had that we were not alone; that we had a certain support in the outside world. I am not able to explain how vital such contact was. Across those vast distances, we became part of the Israeli community.

The calls came in at Victor Brailovsky's apartment, usually twice a week. Because of the number of people who were often waiting on the same line, and because of interference by the KGB, the conversations took up many, many hours. Usually I went to the Brailovskys' at six or seven in the evening; quite often got home at three A.M. or even later. The talks principally concerned the fates of the various refuseniks here. Their friends who had made it to Israel were desperately anxious to know what was happening to those who remained; to know about the refuseniks who were being tried, imprisoned, or exiled. The callers wanted to provide what help they could to those who needed it most. On the Moscow end we asked for news, too — news of those few who were starting their lives over in Israel, and also news of the world, which ordinarily came to us here in such distorted form.

One of these telephone calls was from the President of Tel Aviv University, Professor Yuval Ne'eman, among the most distinguished scientists in the world. He proposed to me a professorship at Tel Aviv University. Needless to say, I considered this offer a great honor and immediately accepted. Almost at the same time, the same offer was made to Voronel, and Weizmann Institute at Rehovot made similar proposals to Professors Levitch and Lerner. So within a few months of the first call there were, of all improbabilities, four professors in Moscow attached to Israeli institutions of higher education!

Professor Ne'eman did one more thing that lifted our spirits as nothing else imaginable could have: knowing that we had no positions, no lectures, he proposed that we dictate lectures over the telephone to Israel where they would be tape-recorded. He also initiated a series of scientific conferences over the wire with our colleagues in Israel, Professors Deutcher, Imry, Aharony, and others.

We were most gratified but thought the idea a perfectly natural one. Insulated from the realities of the outside world as we were, we had no conception of what sacrifices these arrangements entailed. We did not know that the technical work on these tapes — editing, amplifying, and so forth — demanded a great deal of time, expense, and effort. And we were completely ignorant of the fact that each telephone call of two lectures' length ran up a bill corresponding to almost a month's salary for a professor. It was terribly expensive, and Tel Aviv University is not rich. Nor is Israel a rich country, and it has many other needs. Nevertheless, not once was it hinted to us that we should cut down on the length of our lectures. What is more, not a single person in the university had a word to say against this expenditure. Everyone knows how careful all institutes and universities are of the money they allocate for research purposes; how important every dollar is for them. But no one at Tel Aviv — literally no one — made any objection to this huge outlay of money. The generosity of the university and everyone connected with it was inexhaustible. The positions offered to us, which were confirmed by the university Senate, were kept open year after year.

The most pressing concern of all of those who consulted Voronel and myself was how they could live and provide for their families in the months or years between requesting a visa and receiving it. Very nearly all the applicants lost their jobs within days of applying to emigrate, if they hadn't accepted the inevitable and resigned beforehand. We became a sort of information exchange between Soviet Jews who were trying to emigrate and the many people abroad who wanted to contribute to their support. Our sponsors sent gifts of money or brought in negotiable objects, such as Western clothes, tape-recorders, phonograph records, and other items. (I might mention that what became the most prized of these gifts was children's vitamin pills manufactured in the shape of cartoon figures. It was against regulations to send pills to inmates of labor camps; but these vitamins in the guise of sweets could get through the parcel checks.)

There is an anomalous system in the Soviet Union covering the merchandising of foreign luxury goods. The many laws regulating the sale of imported items are suspended for various categories of retail outlets. Besides regular stores, there is a whole range of shops for the use of different classes of privileged customers. (Some of these places are for the exclusive use of the Party elite, and in them the prices are one-tenth to one-twentieth of what is charged elsewhere.) For our own purposes, there were the *beryozki,* the shops for those who pay in foreign currency. The State permits the existence of these concerns for the benefit of the elite, who may earn dollars, pounds, yen. Of course, much of this payment goes to the government in duties and taxes. What remains does not come to the individual who earned it in the original foreign currency; possession of a single American dollar, for example, is a serious criminal offense — under some circumstances it may be a capital crime. But the State itself is eager to get hold of foreign currency. The payee receives approximately fifty kopeks on the dollar, after a thirty-kopek tax is deducted; and the foreign money can be changed not into ordinary roubles and kopeks but into the coveted "certificate money," vouchers that are honored at these special stores. That is the medium in which those of us who received royalties for foreign publications were paid. This was so also, of course, in the case of musicians, performers, and poets who gave readings.

In the beryozki one can find everything from Japanese transistors to American blue jeans. One certificate rouble here has the buying power of around eight roubles elsewhere. The recipient of the foreign money would buy these items, and then resell them. By practicing the strictest economy, a family could live on $100 for two or three months.

Though all this was absolutely legal, Voronel and I could not explain the details of these transactions, nor the sources of the money, to everyone who came to us for advice. Most of them were total strangers, and since the authorities took every opportunity to cut off sources of supply to the refuseniks, we could not afford to explain the details to people whose bona fides we had no way of checking. We could only assure the applicant that if he did apply for a visa he would not starve, and that whatever happened he would not be alone.*

* * *

The kind of activity in which I was involved could not go on for long without interference from the police or the KGB. Over the years after I applied for our visas, the police appeared so frequently, at such unpredictable times of the night or day, that our little daughter often went to Lucia to ask "Mama, why are the police here all the time?" However often we tried to allay her fears, Yulia's life was much more difficult than that of an ordinary Soviet child of an educated family, which is difficult enough. On the one hand children are told: "The Soviet system is the best in the world; the Russians are the best people in the world"; and on the other, they are cautioned that they should never repeat what they hear at home; they should be silent outside. Yulia was beginning to sense the same mysterious obstacle that I had become aware of at her age, but for her it was more serious. There was something amiss about her parents, though she could not analyze what it was. What was the matter? She knew her life was not an ordinary one. She never had the security of knowing that she was a normal child, with normal parents, who lived like everyone else, had jobs, and were respected in the community, until we were in Israel. And then you could see the change in her — a real transformation.

To know that all my conversations at home were bugged and that I was under close observation much of the time became a familiar fact of life. I almost got used to the nervous strain, just as you might to the symptoms of a chronic disease. Even now, when I step out the entrance of my apartment building in Tel Aviv and happen to see a passing car slow up and stop right beside me, it takes quite a few seconds before I realize I am no longer in the Soviet Union. My first reaction is sudden: my insides contract, and I brace myself. Will the door open; will the man inside ask me to step in; will I be driven to police or KGB headquarters for an interrogation that may culminate in a prison term? For years, I had to be prepared for arrest at any time. Wherever I went, I carried in my briefcase all the things I would need in case I should be imprisoned without warning. All of us who were active in the refusenik cause did the same.

---

* The reader will note that I am really providing here only an indication of the sources of this support, and will I hope understand my reasons for omitting the names of most of our benefactors.

But once more I want to stress that, as of December 8th, 1972, precisely because I was always ready to be arrested, I was free. I was prepared for anything and had nothing to lose. I had shed the caution and wariness that are second nature to a Soviet person the moment I walked out of the Visa Department. In spite of everything, I was happy. I never lost the sense of being unburdened, of having shed handcuffs and leg irons. Since my former colleagues, the State, and the KGB all knew exactly where I stood, I could openly say everything I thought.

It is ironic to contemplate what a high percentage of Russians' taxes go toward defraying the expense of having themselves spied upon. If the life of a person who is not suspected of any wrongdoing is under the close scrutiny I have described — the passport, the difficulties of travel within the country, the registration at one's address, the strictures when it comes to moving from one place to another — one can imagine the thoroughness of the surveillance over someone who is felt to be dangerous to the State. I have heard that at times the number of KGBsts who followed Solzhenitsyn was about five hundred. They had to trace him and his visitors everywhere they went. When he went down into the Metro, someone had to be in readiness for him there if he took the train in one direction; there had to be others waiting to follow him if he went in the other direction; and still others if he changed his mind and didn't go anywhere. Any friends or acquaintances or chance contacts he met during the day had to be traced, and a tail was put on anyone *they* saw or met. Due to all the chance ramifications both as to people and places, Solzhenitsyn's movements required espionage by a small army.

Even I, at times, required the services of dozens of KGBsts. Whoever came to see me was checked. If it was a friend, he was not in any particular danger. But if it was someone who had not been to my place before, the question arose as to what his purpose might be in visiting me. Most of my first-time visitors were known to be applicants for exit visas or refuseniks seeking advice. On occasion callers who were not in that category and not my ordinary friends were summoned to headquarters the minute they left my apartment, shown the photograph that had been taken of them when they entered, and advised that I was a suspect person whose company it would be better to avoid.

Obviously, this supervision must cost the Soviet State a tremendous amount of money. But here is one area in which they don't care to economize. I've heard that one single day of the sort of heavy supervision I was occasionally under costs 1000 roubles, almost a year's salary for an average person. The KGBsts have ordinary cars, and in addition, taxis driven by their men (if a dissident, a suspect person, finds a cab in

Moscow within a five- or ten-minute delay, he would probably be right if he guessed it was driven by one of them). Not to mention the men on foot, the cameras, the electronic equipment, tips to informers, and other necessities for surveillance.

*　　*　　*

Only one thing really bothered me, and now I feel I can confess I was really scared: the minute I applied to leave, I had hanging over my head the possibility of a charge of parasitism.

I knew several highly trained professionals who were punished for this "crime"; they were assigned an assembly-line job at some very remote factory. It was not the work at such a place that frightened me, but the fact that it would consume ten to twelve hours of my day, and I would have very little chance of working on physics. This would be a disaster. As a scientist, I would soon be dead.

If I were imprisoned, it would arouse the indignation of our supporters abroad. But to be forced into some kind of time-consuming labor would not engender the same sympathy. And the concern of our foreign colleagues was our only hope; without it, few of us had a chance of freedom. So I dreaded charges of parasitism more than anything else that might lie ahead for me.

My first thought after being fired from the Institute of Theoretical Physics was to apply to Kapitza, who had so often been my mainstay in time of trouble. I wrote, asking him if there was any chance of my being taken on at his institute, even in the capacity of the most junior collaborator; I couldn't afford to care about the position. Kapitza sent me back a very kind answer, saying he would be able to take me on, but only if he could be absolutely sure that I wouldn't take part in any refusenik activity and would refrain from any special attempts to obtain my exit visa. This could have meant a total reversal of all my plans, and I couldn't accept these conditions.

I tried other avenues. Before too long, to my surprise, a physicist who worked at the Institute for Scientific and Technical Information — a man I hardly knew, not a Jew but a courageous and generous Russian who was ashamed to witness the sort of treatment applicants for Israel were receiving — offered me work for his institute. Of course it was not a tenure-track job; it was only temporary work. I received scientific papers, usually in English, and condensed them for the journal *Fizika* (*Physics*).

About two months after obtaining these assignments I heard the first of those long, aggressive rings at my doorbell which were to become so

familiar, so easy to identify, during the following years. It was a policeman, who told me my presence was demanded at the Regional Police
Headquarters.

Arriving at this headquarters, I was questioned by a major of police.
He advised me that charges of parasitism were to be brought against
me.

"This is definitely a mistake," I told him. "I am publishing regularly
in my field. Furthermore, I am working for the journal *Fizika*. According to international regulations of which you are no doubt aware, a scientist is not supposed to be drafted into compulsory labor. I wish to file
a complaint that I am being threatened with illegal prosecution."

They let me go; but I knew that I was not out of danger. One's
employment could be cut off at any time: once the authorities found
you did have a source of support, they put a stop to it. Some of my
refusenik friends became *dvorniks,* elevator operator, janitors, and so
forth; but only until such time as the KGB learned about it. Then they
were fired straight off.

I was glad I had not mentioned the job at Elista to the major of
police: that I was still scheduled to teach there was overlooked for a
while, and the post was not sabotaged until the summer of 1973.

*   *   *

On April 12th, 1973, my former wife and my son received their exit
visas. It was a tremendous relief to know that their wait was over, but
at the same time it was a terrible feeling not to know when I would see
them again.

The fact that Vadim's and Naya's visas had come in became known
everywhere within a matter of hours. Everyone assumed that this meant
I, too, would soon be allowed to go. Two of my former colleagues at
the Institute for Theoretical Problems jumped up and rushed out of the
middle of a seminar, caught a taxi, and got to my place as fast as they
could. All of a sudden — after five months — they were concerned
about me and came to ask if I needed any help. Maybe I could use some
money? They would be glad to contribute to my support. I was not particularly gratified by this abrupt reappearance of friends whose memory
of my very existence depended on the KGB's granting exit visas to my
first family. Perhaps I was not so deep in trouble after all. And who
knows? Having a friend who was almost on his way to Israel might
have its advantages for them. I had little to say to my visitors except
"Thanks — but no thanks."

Deadlock

I CANNOT put into words what I felt when I took Naya and Vadim to the airport and saw them off to Israel. I watched Vadim walk past the opening in the exit ramp, the section that we called the Bridge. He turned around to wave goodbye — perhaps for the last time. Suddenly he called, "Daddy!" and I saw that he was tossing something to me. I caught it — a little plastic boat, his farewell present. The officials, outraged that this toy had trespassed on the no man's land between us, hustled him past the opening. He was gone. He was just twelve years old. Less than three months before we had celebrated his birthday.

At all events, he and his mother were out of danger.

A month after Naya and Vadim left, I received a postcard in the mail requesting me to call at the Visa Department. This was very bad news. I knew that the notification sent to those whose exit visas had been granted was usually delivered, by hand, by the police, and always requested the addressee's presence at the Visa Department "urgently." There was nothing urgent about the communication I got: this was the card they sent when permission was going to be refused.

The disappointment sank into me, a heavy, heavy weight. I couldn't even talk to anyone for a while. When Sasha Voronel (who had been advised of his refusal some time before) came over to confer about the next Sunday's Seminar, I just handed him the card.

"So they're refusing me too," I finally said. "It was to be expected. The hell with them." I had tried not to believe in my hopes so as not to be hit too hard if I was mistaken. But everything had looked so auspicious. They had let my son and Naya go; people around us were excited and were almost sure we would be next; my case had been under investigation for half a year rather than the three months that was the ordinary waiting interval at that time. "I can't see any reason for going over to the Visa Department. They don't have anything more to tell me."

"If I were you, Mark, I would do what they ask you," said Voronel.

"What for? They can't give me any sort of reason for the refusal. I have nothing to talk to them about."

"You ought to go."

"Why?"

"I'll tell you. People in our position ought to keep everything very clear. You want to be able to say you have been officially refused, rather than that you just assume it." He emphasized and re-emphasized this point, but it was not until late in the afternoon that I was finally persuaded to go to the Visa Department.

The official there appeared astonished by my casual and nonchalant manner when I approached her: I got the feeling she would have enjoyed it had I appeared crushed and miserable. I would have hated to give her that satisfaction. Without wasting any time, I simply asked her to tell me the reason I was denied a visa.

"The State considers it undesirable for you to leave the country."

"Is the Visa Department aware that I have never been in work that required a military security clearance?"

"Of course."

That was it. I left, knowing little more than when I came. The Visa Department never explains anything and never puts anything in writing.

*   *   *

What was the reason for my refusal?

Let me try to clarify, if I can, the guiding principles behind the granting and withholding of exit visas in the Soviet Union.

In my own case, two reasons were obvious, one personal and the other a general one. But both serve to illustrate the factors and motivations that held me, and hold people in similar situations, for such long months and years.

The personal element had to do with my former director, Khalatnikov. My application for Israel actually terrified him. He could not distance himself fast enough and far enough from me, and he was determined to make it clear to the other scientists at the institute that it was absolutely disastrous to apply for a visa. Khalatnikov knew what he was doing, and it was he who decided from the very beginning that an example should be made of me. Not only did he decline to give me the standard letter of recommendation, but, as I gathered from the line of questioning in some of the KGB interrogations I underwent during the next few years, he must have warned the authorities that, although I had never actually been in work that required a security clearance, I was a man of such wide-ranging interests, with such a large circle of acquaintances among other scientists, that it was perfectly possible I could have acquired secret information from others who were in classified research — a perfectly ridiculous idea. Khalatnikov wanted to set me up in the role of outcast and keep me dangling. The worse things were for me, the more prolonged my uncertainty, the clearer the object lesson for the rest of his staff. I served the same purpose as the thief chained to the pillory in the public square of a medieval town. While he is on view, other would-be criminals are deterred from their crimes; the longer he stays there, the clearer the point. On the other side of the coin: soon after I applied for Israel, members of the Institute for Theoretical Physics began to receive quite a shower of blessings. First of all came better apartments and permits for trips abroad. The punishment for defecting was horrible; the rewards for loyalty, lavish.

The plans of the State coincided with those of the institute, but the authorities had broader issues in mind. Soviet officials very frequently state for the benefit of the Western press that they allow for very nearly free emigration; that the number of those who are refused or detained is no more than 1 percent of the applicants; that no one is refused save those who have been involved in classified military research; and that even their cases are regularly reviewed. They claim that these people are released when their expertise is no longer dangerous to the State; in other words, when the secret information they have is obsolete.

This 1 percent is very far from the truth. It is computed in accordance with a typical Soviet trick. While it is true that around 200,000 Soviet citizens have left the Soviet Union — admittedly an impressive number — it is much more difficult to estimate the number of those who apply to leave but cannot. When they publish the figure of all who left, they include the number released during the years of significant *aliyah*,* but when they indicate the figures on those who have been refused, they provide only the percentage of those who have been denied visas at the very moment the statistics are being compiled. So the "1 percent" may actually be correct at a given moment, but this does not take into account the ever-growing backlog of refuseniks. Let's say that during a certain time-span one hundred people apply and one is refused. That one may stay in Russia for a decade, but at the next count of refuseniks he will be excluded — he has already been counted.

More important: there is no way of estimating the number of those who would apply if they were not terrified by the horrible examples they know of. They see jobless people, deprived of their civil rights; those under such close supervision by the police and KGB that they can hardly breathe; those with no visas, no passports; and, finally, those

* The *aliyah* is the body of Jews who return (or intend to return) to Israel.

sent to prison or exile. It takes little imagination to understand the many deaths among refuseniks: to these sufferers, every other route out of the Soviet Union appears to be closed.

The statistics describing the ratio of refuseniks to emigrants offered by the Soviets for the inspection of the outside world are deceptive in another way, too. If you are a retired pensioner from one of the Baltic states, a Ukrainian housewife, or, let's say, a day laborer, and apply to leave the country, your chances of obtaining permission will be nearly 100 percent: the Soviets put little value on the contributions such people make to their society. On the other hand, if you are a Muscovite, a Leningrader, an intellectual, a professional of any sort, your chances of getting out are perhaps one in three. There will be no time limit to your detention. I was approached for advice by people who had applied for emigration, veterans of the Great Patriotic War, who are still waiting. The grounds for refusal were that they served in the armed forces and might be in possession of military secrets! Among people of higher education, too, there is a sliding scale. A mathematician has a better chance of being released than a physicist, since people like Academicians Vinogradov and Pontryagin have announced that "Soviet mathematics doesn't need Jews — they have made no important contribution to that science."

Generally speaking, however, the Soviets feel keenly the disadvantage and humiliation of losing prominent figures in the sciences and the arts. To tighten the fetters on the intelligentsia, the State came up several years ago with an education tax imposed on those with university educations. There was absolutely no way for an ordinary Russian professional to raise this ransom, unless it was sent to him from abroad. The demand constituted a very nearly impassable barrier to emigration on the part of a member of the educated classes. Pablo Picasso bought the art critic Golomshtock's freedom for the price of about $20,000, before the Jackson Amendment forced the Soviets to abandon the scheme for the time being. But this tax can be reimposed at any time: the law that put it through was ratified by the Soviet Council of Ministers.

The central problem is that there are so many millions in the Soviet Union, particularly among the nationalities other than Great Russian, who would leave if they could that the Soviets have to put every imaginable obstacle in the way of emigration, even of the nationality they most despise. The U.S.S.R. will probably not hermetically seal its borders and thus make it clear to the world that the entire nation is a labor camp. But by keeping a large number of applicants for visas in a constant state of imbalance, of apprehension, insecurity, and actual fear for their lives, they will stem the outward-going tide.

Hunger Strike

In 1973, we were still very optimistic. My hopes were not all dashed, and I started to turn over in my mind what means I could possibly invent to find a way out.

The first thing I did was to write a letter to one of the best and oldest British scientific journals, *Nature,* with an appeal to scientists throughout the world, urging them to support us in our struggle. (*Nature* and several other professional journals, including *Physics Today* and *Chemical and Engineering News,* took up our banner and became invaluable partisans and allies. Beginning in August of 1973, they published reports continuously about what was happening to scientist refuseniks, and I will be grateful all the rest of my life for the moral support they provided and the actual, tangible support — the rescues — for which they must take a great deal of the credit.)

Upon being definitely informed that I would not be allowed an exit visa, I felt the time had come to let the Soviets know that I, and many of the other scientists "in refusal," as we termed it, were ready to fight for our freedom. Seven of us, all members of the Seminar, all refuseniks, got together after one of the sessions on a Sunday in May to plan a decisive protest, something the authorities could not ignore. We were Sasha Voronel; Victor Brailovsky, who became my closest friend during our later years in refusal; Alexander Lunts, a computer scientist; Dan Roginsky, a high-energy physicist; Anatoly Libgober, also a mathematician, still in his twenties; Moishe Giterman, whom Sasha and I had known for years; and myself.

All of us were determined to take a stubborn and highly visible stand. At first we had differing ideas as to what this stand should be. Voronel and I believed that the most rational policy for scientists to pursue was to appeal specifically to the scientific community, and to enter the struggle from the base of our identity and status as scientists. Lunts was in favor of such methods as joining the demonstrations that protesters were then beginning to conduct, or engaging in other sorts of active protests. My own idea — backed by Voronel and Giterman from the first — was to stage a hunger strike. After considerable discussion, everyone else agreed that this might well be the most effective of all the plans we had considered.

We gathered (of course in the streets, out of reach of the bugging) quite a few times during the weeks that followed to confer about our strike, but we carefully kept the idea to ourselves. The authorities could easily have sabotaged the plan by putting one or all of us under house arrest in advance of the date scheduled for the start of the strike, preventing us from assembling under one roof. It was very important to be together: a handful of individuals, at a distance from one another and out of contact, could hardly sustain a united demonstration.

We discussed where to hold the strike. Obviously, the more crowded and public the location, the more impressive it would be. For instance, nothing could have been better than the middle of Red Square, where thousands of witnesses would be sure that we had no access to any food — that the fast was conducted in good faith. But naturally we would have been arrested within minutes. So we wanted to hold our strike in an apartment, a place with a telephone so that we could keep in touch with the outside world; and a place not occupied by anyone who wasn't taking part in the strike, because we didn't want even a grain of food on the premises. Furthermore, it had to be easy of access to all comers: we wanted to see anyone and everyone who cared to visit us. We wanted to be in a position to say to the most random and unexpected guest: "Come on in. Everything here is open to inspection. Please look around, anywhere."

We finally settled on the Luntses' three-room apartment as being the most convenient.

Our second problem was something on which we had to take a chance. Although we were all in fairly good condition, most of us were not too young; all but Anatoly Libgober were around forty. And having spent all our lives in the Soviet Union, growing up with the wartime and postwar shortages, which took their inevitable toll physically, we all bore witness one way or another to the austerity of those years. Giterman, a tall thin man, very quick at everything he does, expending a lot of nervous energy every minute, had not a spare pound of fat on him. Brailovsky had liver trouble. I was subject to occasional gall-bladder attacks and had a minor form of hypoglycemia. People with this disease are liable to spells of abnormal hunger, and if there is nothing to eat or drink, they break out into a sweat and may almost lose consciousness. When our wives learned of our decision — we had postponed telling them about it, to avoid extra discussion — all of them were extremely apprehensive.

"Two or three weeks of fasting, perhaps more!" Lucia exclaimed. "Why, Mark, you'll kill yourself! What will you do if something goes wrong? Can you get a doctor?" We had several doctors among our acquaintance, and one of them was an elderly man I had known for years. But he was a veteran of troubled times and had spent a term in prison during the Stalin era. He admitted to me that, at his age and after all he had been through, he was afraid to help anyone who was planning a protest against the regime. After thinking it over, we realized that, failing this old friend, we could ask only some of the junior physicians among "our own" to come in and check us if they got the chance.

We would have had no trouble recruiting as many participants as we wanted. There were already over twenty refuseniks among scientists, and many of them were as determined as we were to try anything to bring public attention to our situation. But we were limited in our numbers by the size of the apartment we had to choose; for even as few as seven people, the project involved a considerable amount of deliberation and planning. But finally everyone was convinced of the usefulness of this particular sort of strike — even our wives — and we made all the final decisions. The date was set: June 10th, 1973.

The time was not chosen by chance. General Secretary Brezhnev was about to leave for the United States, and we wanted to ensure that he would be met with as many difficult questions as possible.

Our friend Emil Luboshitz had just received his exit visa and would be in Israel by the 10th. We had talked over with him the entire maneuver, and he was supposed to be our chief representative, so to say, in the free world. We arranged the timing of our strike with Emil. He would contact the press and spread the news of what we were doing among those who would understand the significance of the demonstration; first of all to Professor Yuval Ne'eman. It was very brave of Emil to take on this role, because he was as yet quite unknown as a Jewish activist; moreover, he was fluent in no other language but Russian. But he felt very strongly about our cause, and nerved himself to demand the attention of people who had never heard his name. He anxiously reviewed our plans down to the minute so that he could synchronize his announcement of our hunger strike with the exact time at which we would start.

The strike was supposed to begin in the evening (the evening, according to Jewish law, is when the new day begins). At midday on June 10th we had our last luncheon; and at six o'clock, Voronel, Giterman, and I arrived at the Luntses' apartment.

A half-hour passed — nobody else arrived. "What's holding them up?" I started pacing the floor, stopping at the window every time I passed it to look out onto the street. Lunts's wife was still in the apartment, waiting to say goodbye to her husband before she left for the Brailovskys' flat. She and Lucia and Irina Brailovsky, our children and Victor's mother-in-law, were to spend the time of our hunger strike together there. They wanted each other's protection and support.

She finally had to tell us the truth. "Do you know about the silent demonstration today at the Arbat?" she asked us.

"Yes. What about it?"

"Well, the others wanted to go over there and join them for a few minutes."

"Good God! When was that?"

"About four or four-thirty."

We were beside ourselves. Even the most inconspicuous of silent demonstrations nearly always culminated in police action. If Lunts, Brailovsky, Libgober, and Roginsky were delayed or arrested, what were we supposed to do? The whole strike, so long and carefully thought out, would fall through.

Minutes passed by. "Do you know what's going on in Jerusalem right now?" I demanded desperately, looking at my watch. "Luboshitz has just announced that the hunger strike is starting. More than half the strikers aren't here! I never could have imagined such a disaster!" We were expecting the first call from Luboshitz, when he would convey the initial statement we were to make about our strike directly from ourselves to anyone who was interested, at nine o'clock. What in hell had happened to the others?

With only an hour to spare before the call — and by that time Giterman and Voronel and I were beside ourselves — Lunts and the other strikers arrived. They had indeed appeared at the silent demonstration, where there was a small group assembled in the Arbat, holding up placards reading LET US GO. The police reacted — predictably — as if to a rioting mob. Everyone present was arrested and brought to the police station, where they were questioned for two hours before being released. Had the incident occurred a few days later, our friends might not have been so lucky: the routine sentence for demonstrators became a minimum of fifteen days *imprisonment*.

But by the time the telephone call from Emil came in, we were all together: we were in a position to say that the hunger strike had started, and that we hoped it would be successful; that is, that it would attract the attention of the outside world, particularly the attention of scientists, to the obstacles preventing emigration from the U.S.S.R. We didn't tell Luboshitz about those harrowing two hours, when each minute was like days to us, because we ourselves didn't know whether or not that close call was an augury of disaster.

Since we had told nobody at all of the hunger strike, it came as an absolute surprise to the KGB. They had no time to take any measures to suppress this action. The KGB is very effective when it is carrying out scheduled plans, but if anything unexpected happens, if there is any element of surprise, it requires an interval before it can react. Everyone in that cumbersome organization has to await orders from the top echelon; no one in the ranks wants to risk his position by taking unauthorized responsibility or making a move without specific instructions. So, for a while, the authorities refrained from interfering with us.

Our life, what you might call our regular routine, began. We divided the rooms. A large room with two beds and a metal folding cot was occupied by Brailovsky, Voronel, and myself. Lunts and Roginsky were in another small room, and in the third were Giterman and Libgober. The most notable feature in all the rooms was row upon row of large bottles of mineral water, the only sustenance we permitted ourselves. We had discussed at length the rules of our fast and had considered whether it might be fair to drink fruit juices, or to take some kind of vitamins. But we concluded that nothing except water would be appropriate. I have to say that obtaining the mineral water turned out to be easier said than done: our wives and our friends ran all over Moscow to find the brands that had been recommended to us by our doctor friends, and to find enough of it to keep us supplied.

We were not idle for a moment throughout the hunger strike; as a matter of fact we had almost no rest at all. I think that this made the fast much more bearable than if we had just sat back and contemplated the passage of time. We were too busy to think about how we felt, about our central problem, or even about how hungry we were.

In the first place, not wanting to get completely out of condition as the result of such a long confinement, we decided to start our day with setting-up exercises. One could hardly call them gymnastics — within a few days we were too weak for anything very strenuous — but we went through the motions and tried to maintain a certain amount of muscle tone. We wanted to make a point of keeping in the best shape we could, and we even took the trouble of shaving every day. Also, we took "walks." We were afraid to leave the apartment — for obvious reasons. It was always locked, and we never opened to a visitor before we had checked his identity; there was one of those glass bull's-eyes in the door, through which we could find out who was calling. Though we couldn't go out, luckily there was a large balcony off one of the rooms, which we paced, and having traversed it a few times we would give ourselves credit for having gone on a good long hike! It was no surprise to us, by the way, to note, after the first day or so of our confinement, three or four KGBsts on the street every time we looked down from the balcony.

Since we could consume nothing but mineral water, we had to enjoy it. Now and then, when one of us opened a bottle he proposed a toast to the company, after which we might find ourselves talking about the wonderful things we would eat when the fast was over.

That was only the background to our life. Each of us had brought his work. Voronel was writing a long article for the *Review of Modern Physics*. I was working on a paper for the *Physical Review*. The others all had their various jobs, and we didn't allow ourselves to lose a single day, though I have to confess that after the hunger strike was over and we checked through the work we had done at that time, we were amazed at the number of misspellings and other mistakes we had made. When one doesn't eat, one's head doesn't work too well!

During the hunger strike, we continued to deliver our lectures over the telephone to Tel Aviv. Many of our friends urged that we discontinue them for the duration of the fast, but we did not want to give up any work that we felt we could possibly manage, so we ignored their advice and went on lecturing. This was a considerable effort, particularly toward the end: these were two-hour lectures.

The most essential and most time-consuming of our activities was to answer the hundreds of telephone calls that poured in on us from all over the world. We had several days of calls before the KGB actually realized what was happening, whereupon our line went dead. But after only about an hour, during which the constant ringing stopped, it started up again. We heard that so many of our callers from abroad had expressed furious indignation at this suspension of our service that the authorities had felt it politic to reconnect the line. An astounding victory!

We allowed ourselves a rest from the calls only late at night. We switched off the phone from one A.M. to seven A.M.; the rest of the time we took turns answering. There was not a ten-minute break. I am very sorry the ledger in which we made a note of each of these calls will never leave the Soviet Union, because they were all most interesting. On the wire were senators and housewives, spokesmen for Jewish communities, scientists. The calls were from America, Australia, from Israel, France, Italy, from England, from all over the world. Hearing from these faraway partisans filled us with hope. We felt sustained by an enormous support. And though none of the literally thousands of cables that were sent to us from everywhere in the world was delivered, we knew from those who got through to us on the telephone that they had been sent.

Very moving were the calls from the Jewish community of Sheffield; from the British physicist Professor Ziman; from the American senators Jackson, Ribicoff, and Javits. Some of the callers urged us not to risk our health, our lives, in this way: they counseled us to stop the hunger strike. It goes without saying that we could not consider these suggestions. Only once did we have a difficult time in that regard. On about the seventh day of our strike, most of us were working in our "big" room when Dan Roginsky dashed in from the adjoining room, where he had been taking his shift at manning the telephone, and announced excitedly that the present caller was Rabbi Goren, Chief Rabbi of Israel. "Rabbi Goren sends his congratulations on our fight; but he says that since the Sabbath begins this evening, we will have to break our fast! He says it's a violation of the Sabbath to fast on the holy day."

Rabbi Goren was one of those who fought at the Western Wall in Jerusalem; famous as a hero of the Six-Day War and also as a devout and scholarly man of God. His opinions necessarily carried much weight with all of us, and with no one more than Dan Roginsky himself. Roginsky had become a practicing Jew at the time he applied for his visa; had taken the Hebrew name of Dan (he was originally Vladimir) and made every effort to observe the precepts of his faith. Roginsky was faced with an insoluble conflict. Of course he could not agree to the rabbi's proposal, nor could he speak on behalf of the rest of us; but just as obviously, he could not reject what the rabbi said.

"I asked him to wait just a minute so that I could let you all know his opinion."

Everyone started talking at once. "Wait!" Victor Brailovsky interrupted. "We'll really have to discuss the problem. Dan, ask the rabbi if he could call us back." Roginsky went back to the telephone and returned with the message that Rabbi Goren agreed to call again, but warned us that evening was approaching and it would soon be the Sabbath. He would talk to us in two hours exactly.

We immediately dropped everything we were doing and got together to confer about this new problem. To stop the hunger strike, even for a day, would be to cancel out the entire demonstration; that was perfectly clear. But to defy the explicit instructions of the Chief Rabbi of Israel was out of the question.

"It's obvious that Rabbi Goren is on our side," I said. "It's just a matter of convincing him that what we're doing is right."

"That may not be possible," answered Roginsky. "If it's a violation of the Sabbath to fast on that day, there's nothing we can do about it. We are Jews; and it is *as* Jews, who are fighting for the right to be allowed to go to our own homeland, that we're acting. What could be more incongruous than for us to gather here and publicly defy an injunction of our faith?"

"Rabbi Goren may exempt us from this obligation in view of the circumstances," I said.

"I doubt it. He sounded very serious. It would be *hillul haShabbat* — breaking the Sabbath."

"When he calls back, let Mark talk to him," suggested Brailovsky.

At the precise time agreed upon, the telephone rang. Rabbi Goren and I talked for quite a while, but the essence of the conversation that had to do with suspending the hunger strike was rather short. (Incidentally, we had to speak in English; I knew no Hebrew at that time.)

At the start, the rabbi repeated what he had told Dan: it would be a desecration of the Sabbath to fast for the coming twenty-four hours. On Friday evening, when the first star appears, one lights the Sabbath candles, blesses the wine, and then partakes of a ceremonial dinner. The Sabbath continues through the next day, until sundown on Saturday.

"Rabbi Goren!" I said. "I am sure that you were not under an obligation to drop your arms and observe the Sabbath during the Six-Day War."

"That's a very different situation," he answered. "We were fighting for Jerusalem. We were fighting for human souls. In such a case, it is permissible not to observe the Sabbath."

"So are we," I answered. "We too are fighting for human souls. And not only for our own. Because every time we make our protest against the obstacles to emigration from the Soviet Union heard, it affects thousands upon thousands of people here. We have much the same reason you did to pursue our course without interruption, even on the Sabbath."

"That's perfectly true," he agreed. "However, you can easily imagine — we could not risk losing a war for the sake of religious observances. But you can stop a hunger strike and then resume it again."

"Yes, we can," I answered, "and we are ready to do it, if you suggest it. But all medical opinion would be against such a procedure. All the physicians we've talked to have told us that to interrupt a fast for a day, and then to start it again, is a very dangerous thing to do." More than one of the doctors we had sounded out mentioned the dangers of breaking a fast and then resuming it. To eat after abstaining from food for a long interval is a shock to the system; and to compound the shock by fasting again is something that one does only at one's peril. "But we're certainly not thinking primarily of our health. If you feel that we should observe the Sabbath by partaking of food, why of course we'll do it." Rabbi Goren had no intention of making a suggestion that would be detrimental to our health, and he found our arguments absolutely convincing.

"You're right," he conceded. "Go ahead. You have my blessing. And on the Sabbath, all of Israel will pray for you."

We were profoundly touched by his words, and celebrated the continuation of our hunger strike with — an additional bottle of mineral water!

The concern and support of thousands of people all over the world moved us tremendously. Israel was not the only country where people prayed for us, nor was it only Jews who did so. We learned that congregations prayed for us in English, American, French, and Italian churches.

The entire strike was quite a severe trial of our good will and our courage; it was not easy to go through with it. There were times when each of us felt terrible, but nobody wanted to admit it to the others. There was no turning back — the strike could not be called off — so we hid our distress as best we could. After it was all over, we compared notes and realized that each of us had experienced the same feelings: when one's heart stopped for an interval, or suddenly started to beat desperately fast; or when one almost blacked out for a while. We had to call upon all our strength. Often, it would have been a vast relief just to lie on the bed and forget everything. But all the time we had visitors. These were both friends and strangers: people who had applied for exit visas who wanted to encourage us or to ask us for advice, and, as always, the varied assortment of worried people — ranging from scientists to cab drivers — who were still trying to summon the courage to apply. There were others who had reason to know they could never leave the country: we were a magnet even to them, because we had a direct line to the West. After suffering in silence for many years, they suddenly had a chance to make their voices heard. It was extremely important to make the most of this rare opportunity to let the outside world know what was going on in the Soviet Union; we couldn't say, "Excuse us, we're not feeling too well; please come back later." We couldn't postpone transmitting this information even for an hour or two.

We also had Western journalists who came to interview us. These interviews were not always clear sailing. To this day I remember one of them very well, with Theodore Shabad, correspondent of *The New York Times*. Although he listened to what we had to say, Mr. Shabad at first evidently misunderstood our point. When one of our callers in New York read his published piece to us over the telephone, we realized that it was clearly susceptible to misinterpretation: it read as though we had stated that our detention in the Soviet Union was on valid grounds of national security; that we had all been in classified work. We had tried to explain to him that, although the authorities claimed this was the reason we were not permitted to emigrate, the claim was false: none of the seven of us had ever been in secret work. We immediately called up Mr. Shabad and asked him to come back for a second interview, which he did, and the next day the *Times* published our correction of his original statements.

This event really consumed our energy. It was not too easy to talk to a person at length, to go over the same ground twice, when to us the point we were making was so painfully clear. But Mr. Shabad was punctilious about giving us a second hearing, and despite the fact that at that time Soviet-American relations were particularly uneasy, all the further coverage we received in the American press was most sympathetic. (Of cource, the American papers are nowhere available to ordinary citizens in the U.S.S.R. save under very exceptional circumstances, and at the beginning we had no clear idea of what sort of press we were getting.)

During the hunger strike, we even gave a party. My wife's birthday, June 18th, fell during the fast. We rose to the occasion: we made comic cards dedicated to her; we presented her with flowers, which friends were kind enough to get for us; all of us signed the congratulations and plastered the walls with slogans in her honor. We proposed numerous toasts to Lucia — and drank them, of course, in mineral water.

Our principal entertainment during those fifteen extraordinary days was to listen to the short-wave radio, on which our hunger strike was mentioned frequently. There was a great deal of publicity about it abroad (naturally, not one word about us in the Soviet Union), in particular because of Brezhnev's visit to the States. Soviet authorities were peppered with challenging questions by the American press and by congressmen and senators; their reply (that we were an irrelevant "tiny bunch of intellectuals") evidently convinced nobody. We really began to feel that our hope of drawing the attention of the world to what was happening to refusenik scientists was being achieved. Most encouraging to us were the messages we received from our own colleagues in other countries.

Western scientists are a very powerful influence in the Soviet Union. The President of the United States depends on votes, and can extend support or withdraw it from any group according to his estimation of which move will meet with more approval from the electorate. Scientists have no such motive for changing their allegiances, and the knowledge that they were concerned about us and would speak out on our behalf was our most valuable reward.

A Victory

WHEN THE STRIKE had been in progress for twelve days and news items about it were pouring out of the radio every hour, the telephone ringing constantly, and our friends coming and going in a state of mounting excitement, a caller arrived with unexpected news. This was Anatoly Libgober's mother. She had run over in such haste that she was completely out of breath.

"They've requested Anatoly to go to the Visa Department," she announced.

"What? Are you sure?"

"Positive. Anatoly is advised to appear at the Visa Department without delay."

"I don't like the idea of anyone leaving the apartment," said Giterman. "It's obvious this might be a trap. Anatoly could be arrested the minute he walked out onto the street."

"Yes, we'd better talk it over," said Anatoly. Almost every day we deliberately got together for a conference, because we felt ourselves obliged to go on record with our reaction to any arrests, any harassments of refuseniks that came to public attention during our strike, or any other such events, and we felt that we had to present a common opinion. From the very beginning we had decided that we could not make any statement that was not unanimous. Naturally, our views, the policies each of us favored, were often very different, so it took a lot of time and discussion and strength to work out these compromises.

From the time our demonstration began, scientists had become more than ever a suspect category of professional, and many of our refusenik colleagues were now being tailed by the KGB. A number of them were arrested and interrogated. The right course for Anatoly to take was extremely hard to decide. It looked very possible that he was being decoyed out of the apartment and that once he left that would be it — we need not expect him back. However, after long consideration we decided that on the off chance the implied offer of an exit visa might be the real thing, he ought to go. He couldn't be expected to miss such an opportunity. But he would not break the hunger strike; he would go to the Visa Department fasting.

We went through several hours of horrible suspense before Anatoly returned. He slumped exhausted into a chair — strong though he was, the fast had taken its toll and the trip to Kolpachny Lane had been hard for him.

"What happened?"

It turned out that he had been received by none other than the KGB general. The general had been very polite and kind to him, and told him that they would reconsider his visa application if he stopped the hunger strike. Anatoly was courageous enough to reject this proposal. Even before the start of our demonstration, we had decided that the only thing that could or would make one of us halt the strike was the offer of an exit visa; no lesser promise, however enticing, would be acceptable. Further, we had planned that if one of us should receive his visa, he would leave the Soviet Union immediately, to prove that we had no other aim whatsoever than to get out of the country.

We were impressed by Anatoly's nerve; and his response turned out to be very effective. Two days later, he was officially informed that he was granted permission to leave. Before the hunger strike was over, Anatoly Libgober was no longer a citizen of the Soviet Union.

Even if this, the release of one of the seven, had been the only result of the strike, we would have felt that we had achieved a tremendous success. We were absolutely happy and, as to those of us who were left behind, considerably more hopeful. But Anatoly's release was not the sole advantage gained by our demonstration: several other scientists got their visas. This was a breakthrough: for over a year prior to our strike, almost no scientists had been allowed to leave.

The strike had not been easy. As the days passed, we lost our strength and our kilograms. All of us became much thinner. When Brezhnev returned to the Soviet Union and the summer vacation began, the time came to conclude our demonstration. We felt we had fulfilled our task, and that it had been even more effective than our most optimistic forecasts.

On June 25th, fifteen days were up. We packed and got ready to leave the Luntses' apartment. We embraced each other and planned that within a month, by which time we should presumably be able to eat normally again, we would celebrate our strike.

It was rather difficult for me to take the first steps out onto the street, where a taxi Lucia had hailed was already waiting. I found that I couldn't even pick up my briefcase, in which I had my clothes. They were winter clothes: although the June weather was pleasantly warm, from time to time all of us had had spells of feeling frozen. We had used up any extra calories stored in our systems. I had lost about thirty-five pounds.

When we arrived home, Lucia got out of the cab carrying my briefcase, and then suddenly dropped it when she turned around and saw that I was about to fall. While she was running back to grab my arm, the cab without warning reversed and ran over my briefcase. To this day we don't know whether this was an accident or done on purpose. It may have been a mean joke by way of a little revenge for the troubles we had brought down on the heads of the KGB. During the years that followed we were occasionally subjected to strange pranks as well as serious harassments, and it became hard to distinguish which minor accidents were fortuitous and which deliberate. As I mentioned before, a certain percentage of Moscow cabs are KGB-operated.

I took the elevator, though our apartment was only one flight up; I couldn't possibly have managed the stairs.

This was the first evening in fifteen days when I could eat. The word "eat" is putting it too strongly: all I was permitted was twenty-five grams (less than an ounce) of carrot juice, mixed with the same quantity of water. That was all. However, I will bear witness that never in my life have I tasted anything so good, anything more delicious, than this innocent concoction. I drank it drop by drop. I had been advised to drink it slowly, but I would have done so anyway: I wanted to prolong this pleasure as much as possible.

After that banquet I went to sleep. When I woke in the morning I got straight up, as had been my habit during all those days of the fast; but I found I could not stand, and fell back onto the bed. I was perfectly astonished, and tried again. With a great deal of difficulty I finally managed to remain upright, and started to make my way into the kitchen, where Lucia was making the tea. I had to support myself with my hands against the wall as I walked, though it was only a few steps from the bedroom to the kitchen. I found myself weaving uncontrollably, like someone who is almost dead drunk. By the time I made it to the kitchen I could barely move, and I fell onto the chair. The next thing I saw was my wife's face. She was staring at me. She had gone perfectly white — as white as the wall. What was it? I asked her for the mirror, and when I looked into it, I saw what had terrified her so. The face of a dead man looked back at me. It was yellow-green, and a stream of dried blood leaked from lips to chin. When I opened my mouth, there was blood inside.

What astonished me was the effect of those two spoonfuls of soft juice. The entire body, which had become accustomed to living without food, was renewing all its functions and reacting belatedly to the fortnight of starvation. The result was incredible. I felt a thousand times worse than during the hunger strike. During the strike I could do exercises, however perfunctorily. I moved; I talked. But now, and for the next several days, I was immobile, and silent, in bed. To walk four or five feet was a problem. Lucia put a row of chairs on the route to the bathroom so that after I had crawled a foot or two I could sit down and rest.

Later, I heard that all of the other strikers had had the same experience of losing strength altogether, and they were as surprised as I. Also all of us, having come to the end of our extraordinarily heavy schedule of activities, felt the most overwhelming sensation, not only of fatigue, but of hunger all the time. We could have eaten almost anything. But on medical advice we were hardly allowed to eat at all — just infants' food.

Not until two weeks had passed could I go down the street. Those of our neighbors who didn't know about the hunger strike took one look at me and assumed I had been very ill and had spent those weeks in the hospital. I have a vivid memory of looking at the benches in the courtyard, which were about seventy or eighty feet from our entrance, and thinking, "My God, will I ever be able to cross that distance?" I felt as if the benches were fifty miles from me. It was quite a while before I could reach them. My recovery was slow and difficult.

Within a month, I could walk about half a mile. We celebrated the "anniversary" of the end of the strike on August 24th. We were not yet allowed to eat roast meat or anything like that, but at least we had graduated from strained food.

Each of us had a little certificate money still laid by. This currency we had never spent before on anything we consumed ourselves; it was too precious — actually our principal means of survival. But this once we splurged at the beryozka, and we had a real feast: smoked salmon, herring in sour cream, everything we could think of, with Swiss chocolate and other foreign sweets for dessert. We spent three roubles apiece! This was about the first and last time we ever ate the food that only the elite have in Russia; food that in much of the rest of the world people take for granted. We were very festive and gay, buoyed up by hope.

Invitations

THE SUMMER of 1973 was the first in my life as an unemployed person. Before my application, Lucia and I usually spent our vacations in travel, except when there was a small baby in the family. After Yulia arrived we used to go to a seaside resort, to the Black or the Baltic Sea. I had not yet risen so high in the ranks that we were able to stay in one of the resort sanatoria, which are really first-class hotels; we "roughed it" in one or two rented rooms in a private house.

But this summer (quite warm but never unbearable; it never gets very humid in Moscow) we spent in the city, and it turned out to be rather pleasant. The lectures on physics to Tel Aviv University continued. I enjoyed going over to the Brailovskys' apartment and spending several hours there, once or twice a fortnight. These were cozy and genial occasions: we all sat and talked while waiting for the phone to ring, and not only were the Brailovskys the soul of hospitality, but Irina's mother too was extraordinarily good company. She was Fanya Moiseyevna, a rather elderly person but very active, very entertaining to talk to; we were great friends.

Those overseas lectures were widely reported in American and European scientific journals, and we received coverage in American and British papers and weeklies such as *Newsweek*. Of course we never laid eyes on these articles. The censors saw to it that professional journals which mentioned the refusenik scientists never appeared in the libraries. *Nature*, for example, was now almost always unavailable. As for a foreign paper or news magazine — we never saw one.

In early summer all of us in our Seminar learned that there was to be an International Magnetic Conference held in Moscow in August. We received an invitation from the organizers of the conference — one of whom was Professor Eugene Stanley of M.I.T. — to participate in it and to present our papers. This was the first such proposal we had received since our visa refusals.

The three among us who had been involved in work on various magnetic problems, Voronel, Giterman, and I, started to prepare our lectures, and dictated the abstracts, which were to appear in the conference bulletin, over the telephone to Israel, whence they were transmitted to the program's sponsors. This was the only way they could be sent.

August came. We received a message from Professor Edward Stern, of the University of Washington in Seattle, asking us to come over to the Hotel Rossiya to meet him and the other visiting members of the conference. We were glad to accept.

Voronel and Giterman and I had barely started out for the hotel before we became aware of the inevitable shadows behind us. That was a strange day. In fact, it was a strange week, because we were invited back to the Rossiya several times to discuss science with our foreign colleagues, and we were tailed the entire time by KGBsts. Also, we could not doubt that our conversations were bugged. It was not only making these visits that was nerve-wracking, but the knowledge that if our families happened to be out of the apartments at the same time we were, our homes would be searched in our absence. Twice as I was returning to Veshnyakovskaya Street I saw the light go off in our windows before I entered the building, and Voronel and Giterman had the same experience. There is nothing unusual about these proceedings. By law an investigator is required to obtain a search warrant and to perform the search in the presence of the suspect; he also has to summon a witness. But the authorities routinely ignore these formalities, and, of course, the neighbors, should they observe what is going on, keep silent about it.

The conference visitors (there were several hundred of them, principally Americans but also Canadians and a few Britons) had all heard about what was happening to us, but they told us they couldn't really believe it until they saw it with their own eyes.

"Are all those men detectives? You're really being followed wherever you go!" one of the Englishmen commented in amazement when we joined the conference members in their suite. They had noticed the KGBsts in the lobby, in the elevators, everywhere.

"Yes, they are."

"And is it true that people are being arrested simply for trying to emigrate? That some refuseniks are in prison?"

"Yes, it is." But we did not pursue the subject; we were here to discuss physics and knew that it might be a fatal mistake to say much about the perils of our situation. They could see it for themselves, and they understood without further explanation. A great many scientists there expressed a wish to help us in any way they could. There was only one favor we could ask, but a very important one: to convey our papers to the various journals for which they were intended.

"You realize we're not permitted to attend the conference," Voronel said at our first meeting with Professor Stanley.

"So I've heard," he answered. "I've asked to see someone on the Organizing Committee to find out if we can't change that."

The visitors did everything they could to lift the ban on our presence at the conference. First they tried to persuade the Soviet officials who were making the arrangements to allow us to attend only long enough to deliver our papers; that would be the extent of our participation. They offered to provide any guarantees demanded that we would just present the scientific papers; that there would be no other sort of discussion involved. They couldn't understand that in the eyes of the authorities, this was the most serious of threats. If we had utilized the opportunity of appearing at a public forum to explain the problems of emigration, so much the better: our statements could be labeled overt anti-Soviet propaganda, and we would be open to criminal charges. But to present scientific papers, without a word on the subject of our thwarted attempts to leave the country, would prove that everything said about us was slander; that we were in actual fact working scientists who were being deliberately excluded from our science.

The Americans were advised in no uncertain terms that we could not attend the conference. We were not too surprised by this blank refusal, and we came up with an alternative: Could we invite the visitors to an extra session, which we would hold at the Voronels' apartment, where our Seminar was regularly held? The three of us would deliver our papers there. The visitors accepted without hesitation.

We didn't know at the time what our foreign colleagues were planning, but discovered shortly that they put up an announcement of this forthcoming *ex cathedra* session of the International Magnetic Conference on the bulletin blackboard at Moscow University. The Soviet officials were astounded. They were even more shocked when one of the American chairmen rose to his feet at the session to which we had been denied entry and mentioned our program for the benefit of anyone who might have missed the bulletin: "Professors Azbel, Voronel, and Giterman will deliver their papers at the apartment of Professor Voronel." He then gave Voronel's Narodnovo Opolcheniya Street address, instructions as how to get there by subway, and the date and hour.

The problem of scientists ostracized from science became one of the major topics discussed by the visitors. The authorities were totally unprepared for this furor, and made a typically threatening response. They multiplied the number of plainclothesmen to a point where, on the morning we arrived at the Rossiya to meet our guests and escort them to the Voronels', the hotel public rooms, the streets, the entire area was simply swarming with them — hundreds. But once again, there was one of those delayed reactions: no decision to arrest us had actually been made. The foreigners' outraged reaction to our situation had stunned the officials, and now no one was prepared to take any concrete action: if they had wanted to arrest us, they had waited too long.

We, of course, had no way of knowing at the time that we might not be hauled in at any moment, and to make our way through that gray army was extremely unpleasant. By the time we were all assembled at the Voronels' apartment, there were twenty of us — the refusenik scientists — and, incredibly, forty of the visitors! This was an enormous crowd in so small an apartment. We had to put down a rug and let almost everybody sit on the floor, or just stand.

When we were all settled, the forty-first guest arrived. This was Professor Eugene Stanley. "I apologize for being late," he said. "Let me tell you what held me up."

Just five minutes before Professor Stanley was to leave for our session, he had a caller at his hotel room, a Soviet scientist who told him that Academician Vonsovsky, Chairman of the International Organizing Committee, wanted to see him immediately on a matter of importance. Professor Stanley told the man who brought the message that he could not see Vonsovsky right then; he was on his way to the session of lectures by the excluded scientists. "Oh, don't worry!" was the answer. "We'll get you there in the conference car . . . if you still want to go. You'll hardly be delayed at all." Stanley agreed, and left for the ill-timed interview.

Vonsovsky greeted him effusively and launched into an explanation of what was "really" going on. "These are very subversive people," he began. "All of them — they're only pretending to be scientists. Their real aim is to play a certain political game."

"Is that true?" asked Professor Stanley. "But I still can't see why you didn't allow them to deliver their papers. We guaranteed that it would be only a scientific talk; that otherwise we would immediately stop it. As a matter of fact, the only politics I have heard here is from the officially approved scientists. Not a single one of these other men ever once tried to broach the subject of politics with me."

"But you can see how irregular all this is!" answered Vonsovsky. "What are they doing, organizing a seminar in a private apartment?"

"That's right; that's just what I've been wondering!" said Stanley. "Why don't you reserve an auditorium at Moscow University for their talks?"

Vonsovsky was not prepared for this. "Professor Stanley! — You can't imagine how expensive it is to rent an auditorium at the university. It's unbelievable! We don't have the spare funds."

"Oh, I'm sorry, I didn't realize that. Here — I'm more than willing to pay the rent myself." And Stanley took out his checkbook. "Just tell me: how much will that be?"

"No, no," said Vonsovsky. "It's much too late to make new arrangements." He was having a hard time trying to manage everything according to the suggestions of the KGB.

"Oh, if that's the case we have no alternative. I have to leave for the seminar directly. And — how about the car? I believe I was told I would be driven over there in the conference car."

There was no escape. The Soviets valued Professor Stanley too much to risk offending him further. But when he left he was not alone: there were two representatives of the Soviet Organizing Committee with him: one of them Professor Borovik-Romanov, now an Academician and the Deputy Director of the Institute for Physical Problems, and another self-styled physicist — it was doubtful if he was involved in science at all, since not one of us knew him. And there was also the official interpreter.

Thus Professor Stanley was the last to arrive, with his uninvited companions.

We delivered our talks. The physicists from the Soviet Organizing Committee felt they could not afford to be among the audience; they went into the kitchen and drank coffee, which Nina very politely provided. The interpreter sat with us for only twenty minutes and then blankly announced, "There is nothing interesting for me here." And that was true, because nothing interesting to the KGB could happen in this room, except for things they already knew. As we all knew, the room was thoroughly bugged.

The session lasted for the regular two hours and, again, received much attention in the Western press. The visiting scientists expressed considerable astonishment that we could persist in our work despite the mechanisms used to silence us, and despite the poisoned atmosphere in which we had to pursue our research. By the time they left we had many more friends in the West, none more partisan than Professor Stanley and Professor Edward Stern. Ever since that time, they have always kept us in mind. Ed Stern took care of our scientific publications in America, and he was one of the organizers of our system of scientific communications with the West. He devoted an enormous amount of time to our interests, and we all consider him to be very nearly a saint.

But this was not the only result of our maverick international session.

Apart from foreign scientists, some of the Establishment Soviet scientists were so interested in what we had to say that they came to listen to our talks. Among them were Dr. Yesilevsky, who worked at the Institute of Solid State Physics; Drs. Rabinkin and Fain, from the Institute for Chemical Physics; and Dr. Privorotsky, from my former Institute for Theoretical Physics. Possibly because of the "umbrella" provided by the Americans, no reprisals were taken against these scientists — except in one case. Khalatnikov wanted to be more Catholic than the Pope — more pro-Soviet than the KGB, and when he learned that Privorotsky had attended our session, he fired him.

Privorotsky, a short, dark, solid man, an acquaintance of mine of long standing (I knew him in Kharkov when he was a student), was a man of strong and decent principle; he did not intend to take this punishment lying down. He applied to the Soviet Court, charging Khalatnikov with having taken illegal and unjustified action in his case. It is interesting to note that the case was so clear-cut, the rights and wrongs so completely beyond dispute even by the KGB's standards of that time, that the Soviet Court (which undoubtedly consulted the KGB and the Party Committee before handing down their decision) saw fit to decide in Privorotsky's favor. He was reinstated.

Khalatnikov didn't learn anything from this experience; he stirred up every kind of trouble a director can invent with which to plague a subordinate, and it was he who drove Privorotsky to the only decision he could possibly make — to apply for an exit visa. Privorotsky probably would have applied sooner or later, but Khalatnikov harried him to such an extent that he could not delay. He made his application soon after his reinstatement.

Partings

UNTIL THAT SUMMER, almost no one I knew had left, except for my own first family. The only farewell party I had been to so far was Golomshtock's in 1972. With the few of Picasso's roubles he had left over after paying the education tax, he had bought at the beryozka every delicacy he could afford and invited all his friends over to say goodbye. It was a very moving occasion. There he was, with his wife and baby, in their one-room apartment; the three of them on their way to a different world. The table was laden with marvelous *zakuski* and with every kind of rare drink, including whiskey and gin, which many of us had never tasted before. Everyone was deeply touched by the Golomshtocks' extraordinary hospitality, and late into the night we were still there. We couldn't stop talking — we didn't know when we would have a chance to talk together again. It was hard to suppress a feeling of absolute finality at such a time. As a matter of fact, when one of us was released, all the rest who stayed behind automatically and unconsciously spoke of him in the past tense, just as if he had died.

Soon afterward, Dan Roginsky, who had been waiting for his exit visa for two years, received it. He was the second of those who had participated in the hunger strike to be allowed to go. The day after Roginsky left, Moishe Giterman got his permission. For the second time in two weeks we were at the Sheremetyevo Airport — a large crowd, fifty or sixty people. These farewells were terribly hard. One last toast, one last embrace; then our friend was gone. We saw him once again, when he waved one last goodbye from the Bridge. This was the worst part for those of us who were left behind. But we were full of hope. We who had conducted the hunger strike and were still in Russia — Voronel, Brailovsky, Lunts and I — were sure that, one by one, we too would very soon ascend that ramp and in our turn would take off for the country that we now considered home.

Just after Giterman left, the Yom Kippur War started, and the issuing of visas almost came to a stop. We lived, with all our feelings, in Israel. The retreat of the Israeli army we at first considered to be a military ploy, a trick. Only later did we begin to understand that the situation was mortally serious; that this war had found Israel unprepared; that the Israelis had not anticipated the possibility of a war so shortly after the last one; and that the nation would survive against the hundred-million strong Arab army only through the incredible heroism of its population of three million.

We spent sleepless nights and anxious days the whole time the war was in progress. Once more, we listened constantly to the short-wave radio. Once more, what rejoicing on the day of victory!

When the New Year came, although visas were being issued again, we were still in Russia. For the New Year's vacation — which is the principal holiday in the Soviet Union, being the only one throughout the year unconnected with Soviet history or politics — my family and the Rabinkins and some of our friends who had not yet applied borrowed a cottage in the countryside about forty miles outside Moscow and left together for a long house-party weekend. This was the second New Year's Eve we would celebrate as people who were really outside the Soviet system.

It was a wonderful place; a small house — actually just one big room — hidden in a lovely snowbound forest. The winter in Russia (and to me, every season there) is extremely beautiful. I loved the sight of the evergreens under their huge caps of snow. The skiing was very good, and there was a great deal of entertaining going on: dances, parties, and excursions over the hills. We spent three days there, but I was so worn out from the alternation of hope and disappointment, from agonizing worry over the war, and from the innumerable conferences with people applying for their visas, that I slept the entire time, except for New Year's Eve itself. The others were amazed, because I lay there like the dead almost without interruption, except for really important conversations, for seventy-two hours. The one big room was full of guests, everybody going in and out — talking, someone strumming the guitar, children playing — but I slept through it all save for an occasional hour when one of the couples who were seriously discussing the pros and cons of applying for an exit visa woke me up to ask my advice.

That long sleep stood me in good stead. I needed every ounce of strength for what awaited me in the following years, which proved far more difficult than the one just past.

Once again at midnight we raised a toast and fervently hoped to meet "next year in Jerusalem."

* * *

In January, 1974, there was an increase in the number of silent demonstrations by Jews in Moscow and Leningrad. These were completely nonviolent assemblies: the participants did nothing more threatening than stand together and try to hold up their placards on which were written pleas for their release. But that was enough. In the city centers, there is a policeman stationed at intervals of every 100 feet, and the number of KGBsts in any crowd is hard to compute. It never took more than a few seconds before the protesters' signs were torn away from them, and members of these groups, apparently chosen at random, were imprisoned. It was no longer a matter of a few hours' questioning in the police station: the authorities were now determined to halt all these activities for good.

The mathematician Dmitri Ram and three or four others of my Seminar colleagues, enraged by these horrible reprisals, asked me to join a group of refuseniks who were planning to convene at the Central Committee to present an appeal on behalf of the victims. I can't say I was really in favor of this idea — I didn't think it would have any effect — but since we had decided to stick together in whatever action we took, I agreed to go.

We all knew what would be the probable result of such an action. On the day we planned to meet I packed a toothbrush, razor, and other necessities in my briefcase, and dressed in several layers of warm clothes. It was very cold, and if we wound up in a prison cell I knew I would be glad to have them.

We were supposed to meet at ten A.M. in the reception room of the Central Committee, which occupies an enormous gray office building in Old Square. But I was held up and couldn't get there until almost eleven. I didn't worry about the time too much, since Soviet officialdom always keeps people waiting for endless hours; whatever might happen (including the likeliest eventuality — the arrest of all of us) I thought was sure to be long delayed.

But when I got to the Central Committee Building, I was alarmed to realize that I might have come too late. I went up the steps and into the huge reception hall unhindered. There was a considerable number of people there, but my friends were not among them. I came out again, ran to the telephone booth at the Metro entrance, and called Dmitri Ram's wife. We had all agreed to check in with her by phone and let her know if we were safe.

"Bella! Has Dmitri called?"

"No. I haven't heard anything; where are you? At the Central Committee? And none of the others are there? No — no one has called." We both knew that almost certainly they had been arrested, and here I was, perfectly safe, while all the people I had promised to be with had been taken off God knows where. I started sweating, both from anxiety and from my several layers of woolen clothes. I never felt worse. What would they think of me? I had let them down.

For a while longer I searched futilely around Old Square near the building, and then went back to the reception room. Finally, knowing what an irrational thing it was to do, I approached the officer at the desk.

"I was supposed to meet some people here at ten," I said, "but I was late and now they're not here. I'd like to ask . . ."

Before I had finished my query, a KGBst materialized at my side, beckoned to two policemen, and within less than a minute I had been escorted out onto the street and into the back of a truck. Six or seven policemen got in with me. The truck started off and I found myself on my way somewhere — I didn't know where.

We went through a section of the city that was not familiar to me, and after about half an hour stopped at a large gray building. Under escort by the policemen, I was marched inside and up two flights of stairs. On the landing, I passed people in white coats — evidently doctors and medical workers. Possibly I was in a mental hospital!

A thrill of real terror went through me. I valued my brain, and knew that the "treatments" used in this sort of place can turn a normal person into someone very far from normal.

They led me along a corridor, past a row of locked doors. Finally, the last door was unlocked by an attendant and I was ushered into a small and terribly overcrowded cell.

"There's Mark!" said a voice. It was Dmitri. He and the other friends I was to meet at the Central Committee were here; all told, there were about twenty of us.

"Oh, my God, I'm glad to see you!" I exclaimed. Despite my fears, I was wonderfully relieved. Now, whatever might happen to us, at least we were together.

"We saw you dashing to the telephone and running around looking for us," said Voronel. "You looked absolutely distracted; we couldn't help laughing."

"Where were you?"

"Didn't you see the bus in the rear courtyard? They herded all of us into it, and we waited at least twenty minutes before they drove us here."

The cell, with three iron-barred windows, was just big enough to hold eight bare metal cots. This was the *vitrezvitel'* — the drunk tank. Drunkards so far gone that they cannot move are picked up off the streets by police and dumped here overnight to sleep it off; the next morning they are fined and let go. At present the whole vitrezvitel' was occupied by refuseniks: about a hundred of us were jammed into the half-dozen cells — everyone who had been to the Central Committee for the presentation of the petition.

In that vitrezvitel' I saw quite a few people who had been in refusal longer than we had, and whom I knew very well by now. Among them was a man in his sixties, short, a little stout but well-built, with short dark hair; clean-shaven, rather handsome, with an unusually persuasive voice and manner. This was Professor Alexander Lerner, who had requested his exit visa in December, 1971. By this time he had been waiting three years for it. David Azbel was there, too; this was the first time he and I had had a chance to talk.

Also in the cell was Professor Veniamin Fain. Then there was the mathematician Elias Essas, who became an observant Jew at the time he made his application. He is still in the Soviet Union at this writing. Felix Kandel was there, too, the creator of the famous animated cartoon series "Nu, Pogodi!" ("Just Wait!"), about the wily hare who repeatedly eludes the wolf who is trying to catch him. His movies are distributed all over the world, and he had won many film festival awards. Kandel had been told by the authorities, simply, that a man as famous as himself would not be allowed to emigrate from the country.

Anatoly Shcharansky was another one of the inmates of the vitrezvitel'. He was a short, stooped man, still in his thirties; energetic, fast-talking, and possessing the advantage of a very good command of the English language. He was almost the first of the activists to make contact with the foreign journalists and bring the plight of the refuseniks to the attention of the Western press. He was a friend of many dissidents, including Academician Sakharov.

Soon after I made Anatoly's acquaintance, he married a girl who was also awaiting her exit visa. When she obtained it, confident that Anatoly too would be let go within a short time, she left for Israel. They could not foresee that Anatoly would wait and hope for three more years, and at the end of that time be convicted of treason and sent to prison camp in Siberia to serve a term of thirteen years.

Colonel Lev Ovsishcher was there, one of the three "Minsk Colonels" famous among Jews. All of these men were conspicuous for their heroism in the War. All of them had been decorated with numerous high Soviet orders; all had been front-line officers. Not only were they refused exit visas but, immediately upon their applications, they were broken to the rank of private and deprived of their veterans' pensions.

Of the three, only two are now alive. The third, Colonel Yefim Davidovitch, had a bad heart: he suffered several coronary attacks. Day-to-day existence in refusal is extremely difficult for anyone who is not in good health: the relentless strain, the suspense, the awareness that not Israel, but prison or exile, may be one's destination — this creates a stress that is hard on the toughest constitution. When this courageous man suffered a fourth heart attack, all the refuseniks applied to the Soviet government, pleading that a person who had given his whole life, his heart's blood, in the war to defend Russia, should be allowed to spend his last months — or maybe days — in freedom. This request was denied, and Colonel Davidovitch died not in his ancestral homeland but in Minsk. He was surrounded at the last by many, many friends.

Colonel Ovsishcher, who was in my cell and who had come from Minsk to join us at the Central Committee, is still in the Soviet Union. Only one of the Minsk Colonels, Colonel Alshansky, is in Israel.

Very naturally, the primary concern of the family men among us was our children. Alexander Lerner was still in terrible suspense as to whether his son and daughter would be released. (The daughter eventually did receive her visa, but at this writing Professor Lerner and his wife and son have awaited theirs for nine years.) Felix Kandel lived in fear for his two boys, the eldest of whom was of draft age. (This meant three years in the service, and an indefinite period thereafter of detention, on grounds of being "privy to military secrets." The alternative — if the boy evaded the draft — was three years in prison.) Kandel suffered most on behalf of his younger son, who at an impressionable age had been forced to witness night searches of his home by the KGB. These events were turning his childhood into a real-life nightmare. There were also new families now, in which the children had been born in refusal. The Brailovskys had an infant daughter; Elias Essas had just become a father.

None of us knew what would happen next. Being locked in here could be the first stage of a long imprisonment: perhaps we were being held pending a move to a far worse place. Fortunately, we all found a great deal to discuss: physics, religion, philosophy, politics — everything. We knew we were being bugged, but were perfectly indifferent to it. Living as we did then on the edge of the precipice, we never knew how much time we had left to talk about the things that really mattered to us, so every minute was precious.

There were only two in the cell who failed to join in our conversations. They sat apart, on the very edge of one of the metal bunks, and stared at all of us in terror. Finally the younger of the two men ventured to ask what we were here for; what had happened.

"We're refuseniks. We were on our way to the Central Committee to present an appeal for exit visas." The man told us he was a correspondent for the Vladimir newspaper; he had just arrived in Moscow to see some people at *Pravda,* and it was purely by chance that he was in the vicinity of the Central Committee at the time of the mass arrest. He had heard very little about refuseniks, and absolutely nothing about the sentencing of any of them. (I should mention again that there had been nothing about Jewish emigration in the papers, on the radio, or TV, for years — since the late 'sixties, when there was an official denial that any Jews were being hindered from leaving the country.)

The other, older man had also been hauled in with us by accident; he was a plasterer, working on a building in Old Square, out on his lunch hour. The KGB, in its zeal to pick up all the activists who were gathering to present the appeal, had cast its dragnet a little too wide, and anyone in the vicinity who *looked* Jewish was rounded up. The workman was not a Jew at all. The poor man never did recover from his fright. He couldn't shake his impression that he had been arrested along with a dangerous criminal gang, and he wouldn't speak a word to us. But the journalist from Vladimir talked to everyone and became really interested in our cause.

In the afternoon each of us was summoned separately to an office downstairs, where a KGBst interrogated us and delivered a warning: *"Don't do it again!"* He didn't specify *what* we shouldn't do; we were supposed to understand that without explanation.

About nine P.M. one of us was called out and didn't come back. Then a second was summoned, a third, a fourth, one after the other. No one bothered to tell those who remained behind what happened once one had left the cell: everybody had to find out for himself.

I was one of the last to be called. We were being let go. A policeman escorted me to the exit, and then kept me under guard for several blocks along the street, thus preventing me from catching up with any of my friends who had gone ahead or from waiting for the few who would follow me. It was around ten when he released me from custody and eleven when I got home, where my worried wife was waiting. Before I could even talk to Lucia, I had to strip off two or three layers of outer clothing: once the fear of a long-term imprisonment was past (at least for the time being) and my mind was free to register other sensations, I realized I'd never spent such a sweltering day!

*   *   *

Three days later, on March 4th, I was ordered to appear at the Regional Police Headquarters. Once again I was warned that I would be prosecuted for parasitism. I told the major of police again that I was working for the journal *Fizika*.

That was the end of my job. My friend at the journal, the man who had arranged for me to take on this work, told me what happened. Within a day after my appearance at the police station, two plain-clothesmen appeared at the office, inquired if they had a collaborator named Azbel in their employ, demanded to see my registration card, and took it with them when they left. In parting, they warned the editorial staff that once my present assignments were completed, I was not to receive any more. No one was to make out another registration card for me.

Thus I was punished for taking part in the gathering at the Central Committee.

I am glad to say, however, that to many others there were rewards for that attempt to enter a plea and from the other demonstrations that were conducted around the same time, however quickly the protests were extinguished. Almost all of us who were active on behalf of people trying to emigrate found it practically impossible to leave the country ourselves; at the time of which I am writing it was hard to believe that we would ever go. But it looked very much as if it was the activities of the vocal refuseniks that cracked open the gates for the second, enormous wave of applicants. With very little publicity — almost unnoticed — they started pouring out of the country. The attention of the outside world had been attracted to the plight of these trapped people; when the Jackson Amendment was passed, the Soviets could no longer ignore the pressures of international opinion. Within the year, about thirty-five thousand people emigrated from the Soviet Union, a historic event, because during the previous forty years only about three thousand Soviet citizens had been allowed to leave. We were overjoyed at this exodus. But we ourselves continued to be held as hostages, object lessons for other Jews who, despite having achieved public distinction and having reaped their Soviet rewards, might want to leave for freedom too.

Among those accorded permissions in 'seventy-four there were, for the first time, veterans of the War, some of whom had been waiting quietly for many years. Their release only made more agonizing the detention of others to whom the Soviet Union owed so deep a debt. The Minsk Colonels were not the only heroes ungratefully treated by a state whose very existence had once depended upon the valor of such men. One whom we came to know well was Fayermark, from Kharkov.

Fayermark's military career was legendary. When, during the War, the Soviets planned to recapture the Kerch Peninsula in the Crimea, he was one of a thousand men ordered to take part in a false maneuver to distract the enemy and make them concentrate their armaments at a particular location. In fact, a massive attack was planned from the opposite side of the peninsula. It was hoped that these forces could take the Germans by surprise while they were directing their fire at the decoy troops, and wipe them out. Eighteen-year-old Fayermark was one of the only three of this thousand who survived the battle. He was so badly wounded that when he was carried into the field hospital no one thought he had a chance to survive. But eight months later he was back in the front lines.

Fayermark was decorated with the highest military award one can earn: Hero of the Soviet Union. He fought up to the last day of the War and earned numerous other awards and medals. He was one of the most admired War veterans in Kharkov, one of the city's very few Heroes of the Soviet Union. In 1974, Fayermark applied for his visa. The authorities were profoundly shocked that a much-decorated patriot, a well-known and universally respected veteran of the Great Patriotic War, should choose to join the despised ranks who transferred their allegiance to the Israeli flag, and he was refused. He spent almost a year pondering his situation and finally made a decision: he went to the Veterans' Office in Kiev.

"I am returning these," he said, handing the official his Golden Star, the Hero of the Soviet Union Medal, and the Order of Lenin that accompanies it.

"You're giving up the decorations?"

"Yes."

"Why?"

"Because I am beginning to understand that a Hero of the Soviet Union will never be allowed to emigrate."

"Right." The man picked up the medals. "And now you can go." Fayermark expected that, at the very least, these cherished awards would be handled respectfully and that he would have to sign a document of some sort verifying that he had relinquished them. He had earned them with his blood. But the official simply picked up the Golden Star and the Order of Lenin and threw them in the drawer.

Traps

When Emil Luboshitz left for Israel in May of 1973, he took with him something of utmost importance — though of no weight. This was our plan for the hunger strike and his mission to organize support for it. And when Moishe Giterman left for Israel in September of that year, he took with him another idea of ours.

We planned to hold an International Scientific Symposium on the base of our regular Sunday Seminar. We would invite physicists from the West, as well as from other parts of the U.S.S.R., who we thought would care to contribute papers. This session would be held the following July. The idea was so unprecedented that I myself felt it to be something almost crazy. By this time the reader will undoubtedly understand that, though an action may be perfectly permissible according to Soviet law, it may at the same time be so far removed from the norm imposed by authority, so alien to policy and custom, that it has all the impact of a crime.

Most Russians, responsive to lifelong training — like the burned child who fears fire — avoid transgressing any of the unwritten laws. But we, who no longer felt ourselves to be part of the system, determined to pursue our science just as we wanted. We had learned much, and I believe contributed something of value, in our meetings with the scientists who were in Moscow for the Magnetic Conference. If we couldn't accept the Westerners' invitations to international conferences nor attend the Moscow sessions, why shouldn't we schedule our own conference, maintain our contacts with these colleagues from abroad, and thus keep abreast of new thinking in our fields?

The session we planned was to be completely free of political tinge. No one would talk about emigration. Talks in any area other than phenomena in physics and their application in various other fields of science would not be accepted. We certainly weren't naïve enough to think that this strict adherence to our scholarly concerns would exempt us from official reprisals. But we could only brace ourselves for whatever might come.

As of January, Sasha Voronel, Victor Brailovsky, and I began to dedicate all our energies to the planning of this symposium. At the first of the year we announced the dates on which it would be held: July 1st through 5th, 1974. An International Organizing Committee for the symposium was set up in various countries. The secretaries for the committee were, in America, Professor Edward Stern; in England, Professor Norman Chigier; in Israel, Professor Raymond Orbach. The seminar was to be multidisciplinary, and the Board of Sponsors included a remarkable number of very well-known scientists and experts in related fields. There were Nobel laureates, members of the Royal Academy of Science, many members of the National Academy of Science and of other academies. To give a random sampling: Kenneth Arrow, Rodney Porter, Hans Bethe, and Yuval Ne'eman were among them.

Making contact with all these people was very hard. About two months before, the inevitable had happened — the KGB had cut off the Brailovskys' telephone. That was the end of our lectures. The communications between people planning to emigrate and their friends, relatives, or news contacts in Israel were broken; and perhaps worst of all was the loss of that warmth and encouragement which had sustained us so tremendously.

One of the other Moscow refuseniks, Yevgeny Yakir, was receiving overseas calls, and we dictated the bulletin for our conference over his line. But shortly afterward, his phone went dead, too. After that, the chances of hearing from the West became rarer and rarer. Now and then one of our friends offered us the use of a telephone, but we stopped accepting this hospitality when the subscribers immediately found their own service cut off, as ours had been. (Coin-operated telephones in the Soviet Union do not take incoming calls, and by that time for us to attempt a call out to Israel was impossible.) But Sasha, Victor, and I had managed to get all the announcements of schedules through in time, and we went ahead with our plans.

In April the authorities made their reaction known. Two of the most widely distributed national papers, *Trud* and *Sovietskaya Rossiya*, carried an item reading: "Information has been received that Tel Aviv University [sic!] is planning to hold a session in Moscow. The Soviet Academy of Sciences reports that it knows nothing about such a session, and the Competent Organs [this term is used to denote the KGB] state that such a session could not be permitted in Moscow. Obviously it is not for Tel Aviv University to plan any sessions in the U.S.S.R." This was a warning to us, a very clear threat. Of course, we had seen it coming, and we followed the only course possible to us: we ignored it. (Incidentally, we were not surprised that the Academy denied all knowledge of the conference, though we had sent an invitation to them, and also to the Committee on Science and Technology.)

The next news we heard gave us pause. To our dismay, it appeared that President Nixon was scheduled to visit Moscow at the exact time of our proposed International Scientific Symposium! This was a dangerous complication. It was perfectly obvious that our action, inflammatory as it would be at any time, would now look like a deliberate protest, a provocation. We argued the question: to postpone the date of our symposium, or to press ahead with the original plan. We finally decided that it would be out of the question to ask busy American and European scientists to switch their long-range plans because of this unfortunate coincidence in dates, and we would have to go through with it as it was now arranged.

The projected session was attracting wide attention. Quite a few Western newsmen called on us for interviews; articles on our situation appeared in all the British and American papers. It was at this time that Voronel, Brailovsky, and I began seeing a great deal of Hedrick Smith of *The New York Times,* a most interested and I would say sympathetic observer of our world, and author of *The Russians,* the best and most accurate study of the U.S.S.R. I have ever read. Another *Times* writer with whom we kept in close touch as of that hectic summer was Christopher Wren.

We began to hope that the accidental timing of our conference with Nixon's visit might possibly be an advantage. Just perhaps, the authorities might not want to interfere excessively with our symposium and display their repressive policies right under the eyes of foreign observers, although I must say that I personally put little faith in Nixon's own concern for human rights.

In May and June, we watched while Moscow underwent an astounding transformation. Everything was done to impress the Americans with the great advances made by the Soviet people. Miles of streets, long stretches of highway, were widened and repaved; the job was done in feverish haste. Buildings were renovated; trees were planted. The routes the President would take on his visit were mapped out in advance. All this work was done only in places he would see, but everything "behind the scenes" would, of course, remain unchanged. Millions of roubles were spent, but little of permanent value was constructed. The original Potemkin villages, built over two hundred years ago, at least had the advantage of being very sound structures. In Kharkov there were still standing until recently two houses that were put up to make a good impression on Catherine the Great on her royal progress, and when one of them was demolished to make way for apartment buildings, it proved so solid that the workmen had to use dynamite to raze it. The "improvements" made in 'seventy-four were mostly façade.

Toward the middle of June, the Soviets renewed their attack upon us, this time in earnest. The organizers of our symposium were now accused of "inciting international and interracial hatreds," a serious crime in the Soviet Union, covered by Article 60 of the Criminal Code. To find oneself specifically indicted in the Russian newspapers is a curious and frightening experience. Since the press is the official, acknowledged mouthpiece for the Competent Organs, there is a perfectly good chance that you will be arrested on the charges cited; tried, convicted, and imprisoned. Alternatively — this usually is in response to strenuous international protests — the issue may evaporate, although no one who has been condemned in this way will ever be safe again from some sort of repetition of the charges, and sooner or later the net is almost sure to close on him.

We knew that some or all of us were in very real danger of arrest. Victor Brailovsky and I decided that if we wanted to be free at the time of our conference, we had better get out of Moscow right now, and time our return to the city so close to the start of the session that the authorities could take no action against us without the knowledge of our guests from abroad. A friend of ours offered to lend us his dacha in Saltikovka, one of the villages outside of the city, and we thought it would be worth a try to see if we could elude surveillance long enough to go out there and "lie low" until July 1st. We would take our work with us and try to get something done during the fortnight we spent there.

Of course, if the KGB had already planted a stakeout on us, this plan would have been unworkable. Although we knew that when the time approached for our symposium they would begin to close in, we hoped that this far in advance of the session we would not be under particularly close checks. It was worth taking a chance. Carrying our briefcases and my incredibly heavy old Remington, we left Moscow in the dead of night: Victor and I, with Lucia and Yulia. The four of us walked several blocks along Veshnyakovskaya Street before hailing a cab to drive out to Saltikovka. (We didn't want to take the train, where we would have been more liable to observation.) Irina Brailovsky could not come; she had her new baby to take care of and had decided it would be easier for her to stay with Fanya Moiseyevna in Moscow.

I was certainly not in a very good humor. I had just received, for the first time in my entire career, a letter from the *Physical Review Letters* rejecting my paper on DNA. Having published with no trouble at all over a hundred papers in the best Soviet journals and everything I had ever submitted in the Western ones, I was, to put it mildly, taken aback. Most discouraging to me was the referee's comment, which indicated that he actually did not recognize the topic of the paper. It appeared to me that he had misunderstood even the title.

Since it had required four months for the paper to arrive at the *Physical Review Letters,* and six more months passed before I received the answer, I was in a state of real distress. I would undoubtedly be imprisoned before long. Would I have time to reply to the comments and clarify the theory I was trying to convey? I knew that I had some competitors embarked in the same field. Because I had spent much time and much strength struggling to work on this theory — forcing myself to concentrate despite summonses and threats from police and KGB, despite the taxing hours spent with visa applicants and desperate people in refusal — I could not view this rejection as anything less than a disaster. The frustrating part was that I knew the results I had obtained were valid and were of real interest. After two decades of work in physics, I could evaluate the significance of what I had accomplished. But before I could revise and clarify, very probably either someone else would come up with the same solutions, or I would be silenced by the grim machinery of the Soviet system.

Had I known what the next few years would hold, I would have been much more despondent than I was. Several more papers were to be rejected, and I never understood the reasons until I finally left the Soviet Union and had a chance to address all my attention to this problem and analyze what had gone wrong. When at last this opportunity came, I was able to make just a few changes in my presentations. These papers not only were accepted by the journals that had previously rejected them, but gave rise to an overwhelming response. I received an enormous number of requests for reprints, and was invited to speak at an international conference on DNA. But that was not something I could foresee in 1974.

What I had come up against was a sort of Iron Curtain that separates the Soviet and Western conventions of scientific writing. Anyone would think that the language of science was an international one; but this is not quite the case. I was astonished after my release to discover how relatively little known Soviet science is in the West. It is respected, but from quite a distance. It came to my notice not long ago that several scientific discoveries made both in Britain and America, which were hailed as very significant ones, had, as a matter of fact, been anticipated in Soviet journals. This was certainly not a matter of plagiarism: the authors of the Western papers had simply not had the time nor the patience to comprehend the Russian prototypes. For the first time I understood why references to Soviet papers are so relatively rare in the Western literature — a source of frustration to Soviet authors, which gives rise to the idea of Western prejudices and even unfairness.

The Soviet style is much more elitist than the Western. It presupposes a reader who is willing to grapple with a great number of statements fused into the shortest possible space; the presentation is highly condensed — to a foreign eye, almost to the point of incomprehensibility. Further, in Western theses the author usually starts out with the particular, and only at the end permits himself the generalities that are the core of his presentation. Soviet scientific writers do the opposite. These differences in approach, trivial though they may appear, are quite profound. It is not easy for a person whose entire training and experience has been shaped by one method to switch to the other.

The *Electron Theory of Metals* and the papers on resonance must have presented much the same challenge to the foreign editors as this recent work on DNA; but since they came from recognized Soviet physicists, were submitted by a famous institute, and the field with which they dealt was perfectly familiar to the referees, the latter managed to get through what may have seemed to them a thicket of abstractions. The work on DNA, on the other hand, in a new and, for me, untried area, and employing an approach which was not at that time in the mainstream, met with total incomprehension.

I was in no position to take these factors into account in 1974, and the first rejection of my life hit me very hard. Brailovsky and Voronel and the other scientists among us were just as dismayed as I was by my bad news. We spent hours in vain speculation as to what was wrong, surmising, among other things, that the problem lay simply in my no longer being affiliated with the institute. The others felt that if I couldn't publish abroad, they too would be cut off.

My frame of mind while I was revising the paper, fighting to concentrate on my work and ignore the danger of arrest, which I knew was growing closer, was a black one. But I couldn't drop my science — I was married to it. As it always has, even at this time of tension and defeat, my work (which at this time was on DNA heat denaturation) provided me satisfaction and excitement. Victor Brailovsky was also working on a paper. He is a computer specialist, and had embarked on some interesting new ideas.

After our hours of work, we would often take walks through Saltikovka, in the beautiful Central Russian summer. Our wooden dacha overlooked a small forest of transparent young green trees, intersected by a path that led down to a lovely brook. There was a lake nearby. Very quiet. Very lazy. It was refreshing to be out of the city, in the wooded silence. We broke up our sessions at the typewriter by long hikes in the countryside or an occasional swim. We talked about science, and about everything else, as if we had nothing to worry about. We were almost happy. My family looked forward to two pleasant weeks before we had to return to the very nearly intolerable pressure and tension of Moscow.

On June 18th with some of our "legitimate" friends (refuseniks didn't come to visit us, so as not to attract KGB tails and expose our hideaway) we celebrated Lucia's birthday, picnicking outside in the garden in front of the house and offering her toasts in Georgian red wine. It was fun, although Lucia said toward the end of the party: "You know, I've become superstitious about my birthday. It was strange last year to be celebrating during the hunger strike, when you might have been arrested at any moment or . . . something even worse could have happened. And now — I can't help being scared. Perhaps it's a bad-luck day for me." We were practically sure that the interval we were enjoying at that moment couldn't last much longer.

The next day all of our friends except Victor left, and at midday Lucia and I set off for the bazaar — there was just about nothing to eat in the house, after the party — leaving our daughter in Victor's company. It was a clear sunny day, and walking along the unpaved narrow road in the chequered shade of assorted birches, oak, and pines was a real pleasure for us. We hadn't gone far before we ran across a small hedgehog on the side of the road, the most endearing little animal imaginable. He wasn't shy of us in the least.

"Yulia would *love* him!" said Lucia. "We've just go to take him to her." We hurried back to the dacha with the hedgehog, and our daughter was in raptures from the moment she saw him.

We resumed our walk, and when we arrived at the village discovered that we were in luck: unexpectedly there was actually some fresh fruit at the bazaar. We stood in a long line, and finally started back home with our find.

We were near the house when I suddenly caught sight of two men in city clothes emerging from the shrubbery at the end of the road. Irrationally hoping not to frighten Lucia, I said nothing to her when I saw them but simply kept on walking at the same brisk pace as before, just as I would have when encountering any ordinary vacationers in that place. The men approached.

"Are you Mark Yakovlevitch Azbel?"

I couldn't tell for a moment whether the man who accosted me was

KGB or a police detective, but the role of the person with him was easy to guess. He was an oversized, muscle-bound creature with the empty, inhuman face of a hired killer, evidently included on this mission in case I should attempt resistance.

As they closed in on me, an old gray Pobeda drove up and stopped next to us; there were two more plainclothesmen inside, who got out and surrounded me. The KGB usually drive a Volga; this car, a relatively large sedan of obsolete manufacture, was by way of camouflage. (The number of cars in and around Soviet cities driven by police or KGB, and identifiable as such because of license plates whose numbers are preceded by the letters MAC, MOC, or MOy, is incredible — probably 20 percent of the traffic in Moscow. If in addition to them you count the limousines, the taxis, and the sinister little double-motor coupés also operated by the KGB, you realize that probably almost 30 percent of the automobiles to be seen on the streets are being driven by these operatives.)

The first man, who had to play the role of boss in this group, presented me with a police detective's I.D. This is an ordinary procedure: the KGB is reluctant to expose itself and often uses the police for "cover." They very seldom deliver a warrant or produce their own cards of identity. If the charges being brought are not to be made public, they stage what looks like the police arrest of a suspect of a common crime. This officer simply told me I was under arrest — he produced no warrant.

I managed to smile and tried to calm my wife's fears. "There's nothing to worry about, Lucia!" I spoke in a loud voice, hoping that Victor would hear me from within the house and would have a chance to escape by the back door. The officer and the KGBsts smiled back at me.

"Dr. Brailovsky isn't there," said the first man. "He's already left, in another car."

"That's right," another one of them joked. "He was the first to go, so he got the first choice of cars. He's in a much better one than this wagon."

"And where is my daughter?"

"Oh, she's all right. She's out in back, in the yard."

I didn't want Yulia to understand that I was being arrested. I called to her, and when she appeared, assumed a cheerful air.

"My hedgehog drank some milk and then went to sleep," she told me. "What's the matter, Daddy? Are you going away?"

"I'll be back, dear; these are some colleagues of mine who want me to go to a conference in Moscow." Fortunately, my daughter was only four years old then, and it didn't occur to her to question this unex-

The Jubilee Seminar*
May 1977

I open the Jubilee Seminar. Seated on the right, half-hidden, wearing spectacles, is Sakharov, flanked by Dina Belin and Elias Essas. Immediately to my left are Professor Naum Meiman and Victor Brailovsky. Standing at left in the rear is Grigori Rosenstein. (*Courtesy Fayerman*)

*In the final photograph of this group, one person's identity has been obscured to avoid reprisals.

Academician Sakharov between Elias Essas and Professor Yakov Alpert. Veniamin Fain at far right. (*Courtesy Fayerman*)

Sakharov, Veniamin Fain, myself, and Veniamin Levitch. Back to camera: Naum Meiman. (*Courtesy Fayerman*)

Max Gottesman of the National Institutes of Health. (*Courtesy Fayerman*)

Professor Naum Meiman speaks. In front of bookcase: Larisa Vilenskaya, an engineer, and Vladimir Slepak (now in exile). (*Courtesy Fayerman*)

Professor James Langer of Carnegie-Mellon. (*Courtesy Fayerman*)

Kenneth Wilson of Cornell. (*Courtesy Fayerman*)

Mario Grossi at the blackboard. (*Courtesy Fayerman*)

At our farewell party, July 1977: Rune Torwald, Swedish M.P., Yevgeny Yakir, Lucia, and myself. (*Courtesy Roland Loefler, Idé & Media, Stockholm, Sweden*)

Our farewell party. Vladimir Prestin stands second from left; next are Veniamin Fain, A. Tsinober, Grigori Rosenstein, X———, Rune Torwald, Alexander Lerner, myself; Yuri Golfand and Vladimir Slepak, with Father and Pavel Abramovitch half-hidden behind them; Victor Brailovsky, Khait, and a Western guest. The women are, from far left, Mrs. Essas, Larisa Vilenskaya, my wife, Irina Brailovsky, and a Western guest. At left front is Lainer.

pected circumstance. My wife only looked at me with an attempt at a smile. She wasn't surprised. This was her birthday present from the KGB.

Three KGBsts remained in the garden while the police officer and another KGBst accompanied us into the house. Lucia and I went into our room, where my briefcase was, as always packed and ready. The man stayed close, and while I checked to see if there was anything I had forgotten, it occurred to Lucia that my notebooks were in the top drawer of the bureau and could easily be found in case of a search. She instantly decided to find a better place to hide them, and asked the man to step out of the room for a moment, saying she had to change her clothes.

"That's all right with me," he answered. "Either you change with me right here, or you don't change; you can wait. I'm not leaving the room."

In five minutes I was ready. I tried to make my preparations as fast as possible, because I felt that Lucia was getting more and more nervous, and her fears would be communicated to Yulia if I didn't go soon. I kissed her hurriedly, saying nothing but "Good luck! Don't worry!" and got into the car with my escorts.

* * *

I was driven to Moscow, to the 46th Precinct Headquarters, where I was escorted into a small room with one barred window. There I was told to wait. I wasn't left alone: one of the men who had arrested me remained with me in this cell.

There would have been no point in my asking the man anything about what was happening: he wouldn't have answered me, and probably knew nothing himself.

I sat on a wooden bench against one wall, opened my briefcase, took out the book I had had the foresight to toss in before we left, and started to read. Since Victor had been arrested before I was, I guessed that he was being interrogated right now, and I would have to wait until whoever was in charge had finished with him. His fate would be decided before they took up my case.

From time to time I got up and looked out the window at the asphalt yard. On the edge of it there was a small tree, very graceful and in full leaf. I didn't know how long it might be before I saw a tree again; I tried to commit it to memory.

An hour passed. The door opened, and I was transferred from the custody of the plainclothesman to that of a uniformed officer, who asked me to precede him down the long wide corridor. This led to a big

room with large windows, furnished with the now-familiar long conference table, a couple of ashtrays, and some pens. Seated at this table and
facing the solitary chair designated for me were four men, one in the
uniform of a colonel of police, the others in civilian clothes. One of the
latter, a stout, unpleasant-looking man whose bearing led me to assume
that he outranked the others, directed at me a threatening stare as I followed the order to sit down facing them. I felt sure he was trying to intimidate me by this unblinking, angry look.

"So, Mark Yakovlevitch," he began. "We here represent all the authorities." He made what you might call an introduction of everyone
there. "We" — meaning himself and the fat red-faced man beside him
who was leafing through some papers with his short, repellent
fingers — "represent the KGB." He gave me their names, which I don't
remember; their rank was general and colonel. Next to the colonel was
an older man, nervous-looking, with a receding chin: he turned out to
be the Prosecutor-General of Moscow. The fourth man, impressively
uniformed, was the Deputy Chief of the Moscow Police.

"We all want you to realize that what happens to you now depends
only on yourself," said the general. He reached across to the other
KGBst, who handed him the papers; then turned again to me. "Have
you read this article in *Trud,* or the copy in *Sovietskaya Rossiya?*" He
placed in front of me photocopies of the piece claiming that Tel Aviv
University had announced plans for a session in Moscow, and the official denials.

"Yes, I have."

"In that case, you know why you're here. The Soviet press never
lies." (This is an oft-repeated slogan.) "The Academy of Sciences and
the Competent Organs gave you a warning. You didn't pay attention to
it. Now — this is your last chance. If you value your freedom, if you expect to get back to your wife and daughter, you'll want to sign this document." He handed me another paper.

"I, Mark Yakovlevitch Azbel, hereby attest that I will not participate
in the organization of the so-called International Scientific Symposium.
Further, I will refrain from any other anti-Soviet activity." There was a
place for my signature.

"You must understand," the KGBst continued, "that we're perfectly
well aware that you are one of the main organizers of the symposium.
You should understand, moreover, that whereas others may not be considered instigators of this plan, *you* will not escape responsibility unless
you sign."

"Let me make one point," I answered. "This document implies that I have already taken part in anti-Soviet activity. If I signed, that would be an admission of guilt. I would be liable to prosecution."

"Don't worry about that," he snapped. "You did participate in anti-Soviet activity — but this isn't the time to discuss that. You'd better sign. It's your only chance. Also, you'll have to account for the fact that on your organizing committee you've got a so-called professor, Yuval Ne'eman, who is known to be an Israeli intelligence officer."

This was typical of the paranoid, ignorant thinking of the KGB. Yuval Ne'eman was not only a professor of physics, but a member of the Israeli Academy, the National Academy of Science in America, and a number of other academies, and the winner of several international prizes. The list of his honorary titles and scientific degrees fills almost a page in *Who's Who*. What is most extraordinary about his life is that he was unable to embark on the study of physics until after the 1948 Israeli War of Independence: he served as a colonel in the army and couldn't enter his chosen field until long past the age at which most physicists are in midcareer. Despite this delay, and notwithstanding the later interruption of his work when he fought in the Six-Day War in 1967, he earned a reputation as one of the most distinguished physicists of the century, one of those who determined the direction and development of modern physics. And this KGB general referred to that uniquely gifted man as an "intelligence officer," a spy; stripping Professor Ne'eman of his world renown, his degrees, his honors, with a contemptuous word. I started to take issue with his ridiculous statements, but he interrupted me at once.

"We didn't come here to discuss the Israeli intelligence network. We came to decide what is going to happen to you. Are you going to sign this paper or not?"

"If that is the only question, my answer is no. I will never sign such a document."

"Maybe you will be able to persuade him," he said, addressing the Prosecutor-General of Moscow. I could see the prosecutor grow pale. It looked to me as though his hands were trembling. Evidently he was desperately afraid of the KGB chief. He spoke with difficulty, stammering from time to time, and constantly glancing over at the other man as if to check that he was saying the right thing. The general nodded encouragingly every time their eyes met.

The older man attacked me with alternating inducements and threats. "You had better think about your wife and your daughter. You want to get back to your science, don't you? It will never happen if you continue with your anti-Soviet activities. And you can't hope to succeed with them. I'll tell you right now . . . you'll be crushed. Your friends will escape, but you won't." (Later I learned that the other organizers and participants in our group were told by this same tribunal: "Of course, the eminent scientists with big reputations — Azbel and Voronel — will get off scot-free. They're just using you for their own advantage. They won't be bothered much, but *you* will spend years in prison.")

Once it started, I could not stem the flow of frightened eloquence from the prosecutor. When he finally came to an end, the KGB chief took over again, this time — abruptly — in a kindly, fatherly role.

It was obvious that they wanted very badly to find some one of the organizers of the seminar who would surrender, who would yield to them.

Although I knew that there had been considerable publicity in the outside world concerning our projected session, I suppose it was not until this confrontation with such a formidable array of top-ranking authorities that I fully realized what a threat we posed to them. How this general must have longed for the days of Stalin — when men like Voronel and Brailovsky and myself could have been permanently silenced in the cellars of Lubyanka without the knowledge of a single living soul; without a whisper of protest from anyone in the nation, much less a voice from abroad. Times had changed; they had to use a certain amount of caution and tread warily.

Because it was difficult to listen carefully to arguments that couldn't possibly persuade me, my attention wandered to the contemplation of these officials. I looked from one to the other of their tense, angry faces. The curious thought occurred to me even then that this powerful group was less free than I, who sat before them.

After a long hour, during which one after another of them explained the advantages of signing the paper and, without being absolutely specific indicated the disastrous consequences if I declined, the general became aware that what they were saying was taking no effect. He interrupted the deputy chief of police, who was giving me his own version of the arguments that had gone before.

"Well, I don't think we need to discuss this any more. We have here a criminal who refuses to benefit from the leniency of the law by confessing his crime. We have tried to save him. There is nothing further we can do. We'll call the guard."

The guard appeared and conducted me back to the cell in which I had been kept waiting before. Here I sat in silence for another hour. Perhaps they still had an idea that left alone, hungry, filled with mounting fears about what was to happen to me, I might surrender.

At the end of that interval, two guards opened the door and escorted me along the same wide corridor I had traversed before. We left the building. At the entrance a plain black Volga was waiting; this time there was no need for camouflage. I was ordered into the car and was accompanied by four plainclothes KGBsts, not the same men who had been with me on the way to the city.

We drove through all of Moscow and at the edge of town turned off onto a highway I had not traveled before.

"Where are you taking me?" I asked. My escorts were silent — they had not spoken a word as we drove through the city. "Obviously I'll know where we are when we get there," I pointed out. "Why are you so afraid to answer a simple question? Am I that dangerous a character? I'm alone, and there are four of you here. What's the matter — are you scared of me?" This was a bald insult, and one of them, the chief, didn't want me to get away with any more.

"You're going to Serpukhov Prison," he said.

"Is that right? So you wouldn't feel safe, just jailing me in Moscow. You have to take me a hundred miles away." They couldn't answer, because they *were* afraid to leave me in Moscow. They couldn't predict what kind of uproar the imprisonment of the organizers of the International Scientific Symposium might cause. Who knew what kind of questions journalists might ask, at this hour so crucial for the future of détente, with Nixon himself soon to arrive in the capital? It was better not only to shut us up in jail, but to make doubly sure that our whereabouts would be unknown to anyone interested in our cause, that contacts with any of them would be impossible, and that there was no chance of demonstrations outside the prison.

We passed picturesque landscapes: woods in the height of their summer foliage, and small villages. I tried to eliminate the thousand fears and speculations as to Lucia and Yulia's situation, and to my own future, that crowded into my mind. I made a conscious effort and actually enjoyed the scenes we drove through.

We arrived at Serpukhov late in the evening. The prison was at the very far end of the quaint and ancient town, whose winding roadways still run through some indestructible remains of early medieval walls and towers. Serpukhov is more famous now for its high-energy accelerator and for its Physics Center than for its monastery, but centuries ago it was renowned as a holy place. The old brick monastery walls are worn but fantastically solid: three or four feet thick, and twelve feet high, they were impregnable to attack. The heavy iron gates were new, as was the barbed wire on top of the walls. The gates swung open, and we drove into the court.

The moment we drove inside, a Soviet law was broken. According to the Constitution, one cannot be imprisoned without prior sentencing by the court, except if one is awaiting trial for a serious offense, in which case one is officially committed, after a hearing, to a special place of preliminary detention. There has to be a writ of detention under these circumstances, and the prisoner must receive a copy of it.

Technically, it was the Warden of Serpukhov Prison who had committed the crime of depriving a citizen of liberty without due process. But he took only the smallest of risks by responding to one of those orders from above, which come in — always — by telephone, rather than by any documented order as demanded by the law. It would have been easy enough for the authorities to arrange for my appearance in court and for the provision of the required papers. The reason for omitting these formalities in my case, and in the similar ones that came up at the same time, was to provide the people on top with an "out" in the event that things went wrong. If a real protest should be raised on behalf of a prisoner illegally detained, the higher authorities could always claim that an error was made at a lower level of the hierarchy. They could agree that the prisoner had indeed been wrongfully detained, and could make a show of punishing the warden or other official "responsible" for the false arrest. However, the chances of such an eventuality were close to zero, and I wasn't the first prisoner — nor certainly the last — to be admitted in this extra-legal way.

Stone Walls and Iron Bars

THE RECEIVING OFFICER at Serpukhov was surprisingly courteous. I realized almost at once that not only were the legal requirements as to the taking of a prisoner being suspended in my case, but, once I was inside, the routines to which a new inmate is ordinarily subjected were being suspended also. They didn't perform a body search. They did ask me to open my briefcase and checked through the contents; but despite all the strict prison regulations, they left me my pills (I carried medication for occasional gallstone attacks), my razor, my fountain pen, paper, and the book. They took nothing but my watch and even left me my money, some fifty roubles. As I was escorted to the cell, we passed a small group of women — I suppose they were servants to the official staff of the prison — who opened their eyes wide as I went by. "Look — there goes a general!" I heard one of them exclaim. "They've let him keep his briefcase! Probably a top-level spy!"

Two officers escorted me through a long, chill stone corridor, separated into sections by solid iron partitions. One of the officers carried keys, and we had to stop at intervals while he unlocked the doors between these sections; once we passed through the door he locked it again behind us. We went through ten or twelve of these partitions before we arrived at an L-shaped jog in the corridor, at the corner of which was a door. This door — also iron, and six inches thick — was opened. For the first time in my life I entered a prison cell.

My initial reaction was completely unexpected: relief and pleasure. The young man sitting on the iron bench in this cramped airless place looked up as I walked in and I recognized him immediately as one of "ours," although we had never actually met. He was Tsipin, among the earliest refusenik activists, who in 1971 was one of the principal signers of the first public declarations of intent to emigrate, with a demand for permission to do so. I had heard his name mentioned in connection with the group jokingly nicknamed the "Hunvebins," after the Chinese youths who fomented disorders during the Cultural Revolution. These were the young protesters who had organized the original silent demonstrations.

Of course, it was not by chance that we were both in the same prison. Evidently this was the place designated for the "preventive arrest" of people who might make trouble during Nixon's visit. There was certainly no need for the officials to make a distinction between the seminar group, which was inviting scientists to a scientific meeting, and those who were planning demonstrations during Nixon's visit. They would simply lump us all together as a dangerous element and announce that we were all in custody for security reasons.

This was the first time Tsipin and I had ever had a chance to talk. He was a short, slight man, still in his early twenties, with deep-set brown eyes, wearing a thick dark beard. He had been a first-year medical student when he originally applied for his visa: he was immediately expelled from the university. Three years had passed since then, and much of that time he had spent in prison — far too long for such a young guy.

This was the cell about which I had the nightmare when I was in Israel, which I described at the beginning of my story. It was supposed to accommodate four people, but at this time there were only two of us in it. In every other respect it was exactly as I described it, with only one square foot of floor space, only one very small window set high into the wall and equipped with a metal awning so that you never saw the sky.

"I haven't had anything to eat all day," I said to Tsipin after we had exchanged introductions. I opened my briefcase. "And what's more, I forgot to pack my cigarettes in here."

"I haven't eaten either; I arrived only about an hour ago, too late for the food," said Tsipin. "And I'd offer you a cigarette, only I ran out myself this morning." I checked through the contents of my briefcase. I had nothing to read; I had finished my only book.

"Let's try to get a few supplies in here." I had seen an electric button by the door: I pressed it. No one came. I went on ringing. Finally, the guard's eye appeared at the glass porthole, and the small iron aperture set into the cell door clicked ajar.

"What do you want?"

"I want to see the warden."

"You want to see the *warden!* He should come down here, at your service, whenever you suddenly have a desire to see him? That's something new. I'll give him the message." Actually, perhaps just for a joke, the guard did put in a call for the warden and told him that the newly arrived prisoner in the farthest cell block had requested to talk to him.

No one could have looked more astounded than the guard himself when, fifteen minutes later, the warden appeared outside our cell. He was an imposing figure in his major's uniform, striped and epauletted.

According to regulations, when any of the prison authorities enter a cell, inmates rise to their feet and stand at attention, with their hands clasped behind their backs. However, I didn't feel myself to be a criminal, nor did Tsipin; so we omitted these formalities, remained seated, and invited the warden to sit down also.

The guard has to keep the inmates under constant observation through the spyhole when they are being interviewed by an official, and this time, because it was the warden himself who was our visitor, the man went so far as to keep the door open while we were talking. We could not help noticing the curiosity and stunned amazement on his face when this august personage did in fact accept our invitation: sat down on the iron bench and asked us what we wanted.

I set about explaining what we had in mind. "Comrade Tsipin and I both realize there are no writs for our detention," I began. The major nodded politely while I was speaking. "We are perfectly well aware that you are not in a position to handle the situation at your own discretion," I went on. "We know that of course our committal here was not under your personal authorization, but under orders from Moscow." The major, as if activated by inertia, could not stop nodding agreement. "But as your instructions are limited to holding us in the prison — presumably no corrective or punitive measures are to be taken against us — I can see no advantage to you if we are subjected to excessive deprivations. We feel entitled to make a few minimal requests. First, we want something to eat. Second, we want a chess set. Moreover, we need cigarettes and we need books. I think you can see the point of complying with our requests: obviously we are not serving life sentences here, and I don't want to conceal from you that all our experiences in Serpukhov will be made public."

The major was in a vulnerable spot. That he had been maneuvered into taking us into custody in the absence of the writ required by law, and now this evidence that I was not at all afraid of him, must have suggested to him that this was a very unusual case and that he had better be careful not to make any mistakes. It was pretty clear that he had been given no orders of any sort with reference to us, aside from instructions to receive us into the prison, and his response to my remarks made it clearer. He evidently made up his mind to use his own judgment; that is, to concede every point I made.

"In this particular case there is no reason to deprive you or Citizen Tsipin of whatever may make your term here reasonably tolerable," he said. "I regret that at this hour of the night it will be impossible to obtain the regular supper for you, but I'll do what I can to provide something to eat. About the cigarettes — again, it's too late to buy any, but I'll make inquiries among the staff to see if I can get you a pack. If not, I believe I have a supply of *makhorka* [rough, locally-grown tobacco], which might be better than nothing, to tide you over until tomorrow."

"Very good," I said. "And one more thing: I'd appreciate it if you'd let your staff know that we have no intention of observing the prison regulations. We don't intend to stand at attention for any of these guards or officers. And we don't wish to retire at ten P.M. or rise at six. We mean to keep our own hours; kindly remember that. We are not here because we are criminals, but because we are Jews."

I can't really explain how, after years of dreading this very fate, once it overtook me and I was completely at the mercy of a crude and unpredictable tyranny, I somehow could not metamorphose into a convict. Looking back, I myself am surprised that the very walls, thick and ancient and oppressive, horribly close, did not by their sheer weight crush us into servility and obedience. At the time I was drawing on nerve I didn't know I had, and it seemed perfectly natural to stand up for such rights as any person innocent of a crime would know he was entitled to.

The galley was closed, but they sent us several pounds of bread — very acceptable under the circumstances; we were terribly hungry. The makhorka came too, delivered by the guard — he was still speechless from surprise.

The next day we were permitted access to the *laryok,* the prison commissary, where we could buy any tobacco, milk, and sweets, we might want, without any limit on how much we could spend (ordinarily, a prisoner is allowed to spend only four roubles per month at the laryok). Luckily, I had money on me; enough to keep us both in supplies. The chess set came: a brand-new one, with the pieces still in their cellophane wrappers. We were given books.

Oddly enough, our insistence upon living like free people gained us respect, rather than outrage, on the part of the guard in our corridor. Very soon word got around among the other guards about these prisoners who answered every regulation demand with the assertion: "We are Jews — not criminals. We refuse to obey." They watched us when the officials came in to interview us, saw us sitting or standing like free men rather than snapping to attention, and they listened while we insisted upon our rights. They were full of admiration.

"That's rather strange, isn't it?" I remarked to Tsipin. "You'd think they would be resentful when we ignore the rules. They're subject to so

many regulations themselves." He said no; that he had observed this
same response before when he was in Matroskaya Tishina, one of the
largest prisons in Moscow, not too long before. "I was brought in there
with a group who had been arrested at a silent demonstration," he said.
"The situation was a lot worse than ours here: we had been tried on
charges of hooliganism, were convicted, of course, and got fifteen days.
When we were hauled in, you should have heard the wardens and the
other prisoners: 'Death to the Jews! Death to the zhids! God-damn
Jews!' " But, he went on, when everyone saw the way these Jews be-
haved — their courage, their refusal to knuckle under, their spirit — it
was impressive to see how people's attitudes toward them changed.
"We simply would not behave like convicts. It took a lot of guts to
stand on your dignity in that place: the officials were really tough. But
we just wouldn't crack. The other inmates began to feel respect and
sympathy for us. If one of the Jews wound up in the 'hole' — and that
happened all the time — when he came back to his cell, very often the
guy in the cell above would try to send him some cigarettes or bread;
he'd lower them down on a string outside so that they could be pulled
in through the window. And the guards shut their eyes to it. Our whole
crowd was incredibly brave; even the worst anti-Semites couldn't help
admiring them."

"How about the officers?"

"Oh, they didn't change. They loathed the Jews. Jews were in punishment cells more than anyone else. You've never seen one of those holes,
have you? Well, you can't sit or stand. And for extra punishment they
handcuff you: the handcuffs are made so that they tighten against every
move you make . . . I won't describe it."

Here at Serpukhov, very few of the officers were as amenable as the
warden. They were infuriated by what they considered our privileged
circumstances and arrogant attitude. One of them, a real Gestapo type,
turned livid with rage when he came in on his first round of inspection
and we refused to observe the humiliating courtesies demanded of convicts. To be unable to punish us for our stubbornness was a terrible
frustration to him, and he avoided our cell on future rounds.

Under these circumstances our days were not quite the same as those
of the other prisoners, but naturally we were perfectly aware of the kind
of life they led. We knew what a thin line separated us from them, and
how heavy were the odds that we might find ourselves in their shoes, or
worse, at any time. Moreover Serpukhov was considered a fairly "easy"
prison; I would hate to find out at first hand what a "hard" one was
like. In the cell block adjoining ours there were not only women but
small children, living in horrible dim squalor and misery. The children

had no food other than the tasteless and meager prison rations — no real meat, no vegetables, nothing.

Our day started at six A.M. Tsipin and I were exempt from reveille, but no one could have slept through it; the loud obscene curses of the guards at the door of the cell farthest from ours on the block were the first sounds we heard in the morning, and then more of the same as they came closer and closer to ours, where they stopped. It was a horrible way to wake up.

At six-thirty the slot in our door was opened and they shoved in two mugs of black tea; on the next round, we were given a bowl of kasha. After this sparse meal, I did setting-up exercises and then shaved. This was not my daily routine at home: I got plenty of exercise in my everyday life. As to shaving, I have a light beard and don't have to bother about it more than once every two or three days. But here in Serpukhov it was a matter of pride, even if there were no witnesses besides the ignorant guards, to keep up appearances and avoid the dishevelment of a depressed, defeated convict. The first time I wanted to shave, it created a problem. As prisoners are not allowed to have in their possession nor to use any sort of utensils, they have to wait for the services of the prison barber. I had an electric razor, but there was no outlet in the cell. I called the officer, and the warden himself was presented with this dilemma, which he solved by permitting me to walk to the end of the corridor, under escort by the guard, and use the electric outlet there. The immobility and confinement of the hours in the cell weighed so heavily that this daily trip became rather fun; a change of scene.

By way of lavatory facilities, there was a cold water tap and a toilet — not enclosed — in the cell; and once a week we had access to the communal *banya,* where we washed as best we could with small slivers of very bad soap.

After breakfast and the shave, we usually lay on the bunks and read for a while. It was against the regulations to lie down at any time between six A.M. and ten P.M., but we had made our protest. After a day or two of being cursed out by the guard, we were left alone. Very little light came from the window; we read by the dim light of the 60-watt bulb in the ceiling, and used the top bunks so as to be closer to it. The bulb never went off: it was kept on all night. This was unpleasant when one was trying to sleep. Also it was startling and very annoying to be suddenly awakened by the guard and ordered to keep one's hands outside the covers: the rules demanded that the prisoners' hands be visible to the man doing the inspection rounds, at all times. We ignored the guards' commands, and after the first night they left us alone.

Around nine-thirty every morning I set to work, revising and expanding the paper on DNA. Not for the first time in my life was I grateful to Fate that I had chosen a profession that permitted me to work with nothing but paper and pen. A great many of my friends who spent time in Soviet jails and prisons suffered as much from being deprived of the laboratories and equipment required by their particular areas of science as they did from being deprived of liberty. I worked until one P.M., when, usually, we were taken for a "walk" in the "fresh air."

When I first heard this would be part of our routine, I imagined that we would be taken out to a yard; that there would be some space in which to walk and look around. Of course, I was wrong. We left our cell, under guard; we were led past all the partitions, at each of which we had to stop while the door was unlocked. Escorted through the yard, we were then locked into a stone enclosure at the end of it. The walls were ten feet high and topped by a dome of barbed wire. We never saw the sky except through a cross-hatchwork of this wire. Above us, we could see a guard looking down into these open cells. There were about ten or fifteen of these pens, of varying sizes, each corresponding to a particular cell within the prison buildings. They were divided by thick, solid walls, so there could be no communication between the inmates of different cells. These roofless boxes ranged from four feet in diameter to probably twenty, the latter accommodating twenty, thirty, or forty people, who were all confined together. On our way to these enclosures, arrangements were carefully made so that we would not pass any other prisoners going for their walks or returning from them. Very strict measures were taken to isolate the inmates of each cell from those in any others.

We were lucky. There were only two of us, and sometimes we chanced to be locked into one of the boxes designed to accommodate all the inmates of one of the biggest cells. But we had just one hour of this walk on the concrete flooring of the exercise space. There wasn't a blade of grass or the smallest creeper growing through the rough wall. There was nothing your eye could rest upon that didn't announce the fact that you were in prison.

I intended to keep myself physically fit, and even attempted to do some jogging. But it was impossible even in the largest of those enclosures: you would get dizzy almost at once. The door was of solid iron, painted black. It was all covered with inscriptions. Evidently other inmates had taken note of times when the overhead guard was observing a different cell and, before his attention returned to this one, had scrawled their names and the terms of their sentences on its surface. We learned the knack of predicting the moment when the guard would be looking elsewhere — not at all easy, as he was very conscientious at his job — and we drew a Star of David, using a broken spoon handle for a stylus, and signed our names. On that same door we read the name of Alexander Lunts, one of the members of our seminar and an organizer of the international meeting; also that of our colleague Lev Gindin. So they were in Serpukhov too!

At two o'clock we were returned to our cell, and dinner was served. (In Russia the principal meal is eaten around the middle of the day; breakfast and supper are less substantial.) Our dinner started with "soup": nothing but warm water with only the remotest suggestion of any other ingredients — possibly a bit of rotten potato or a cabbage leaf. It never contained meat. The second course consisted typically of potato again, and a small amount of very bad herring. Dessert was the same tea we got at breakfast, or *kisel* (a fruit jelly) — at least so they called it; it was simply warm water with only a faint taste of anything else in it. Supper, which came at six P.M., consisted of a small amount of kasha. And that was all. Without the laryok, we would have starved.

Now and then I played chess with Tsipin. We called our one-man teams the Seminarists and the Demonstrators. At ten P.M. the whole prison was supposed to go to sleep. Nobody was allowed to sit up on his bunk, to read, even to keep his eyes open. Once again, however, we were exempt, and the guards simply joked as they went by our cell — "Good night! It's bedtime!" — instead of cursing us, as they did the other inmates. We slept when we wanted to.

Planning the Sunday Seminar activities, working on science, reading and thinking about further possible ways to keep our science alive, about future contacts with Western scientists, took up nearly all my time. I couldn't talk over many of these ideas with Tsipin. I sensed certain limitations in his outlook. His approach to the problems that faced all of us in refusal was too rigid, too tough. I had an uneasy feeling about him: it seemed to me that a person with such a stubborn one-track mind would find himself totally at a loss if the strategy he was pursuing turned out to be a dead end.

On July 3rd, Tsipin and I were playing chess when, without any warning, the door opened and the warden walked in. "Take your belongings and come with me," he said to Tsipin. Tsipin, who had hoped for his release around this time — Nixon's visit was to end the next day, so the authorities' fears as to his attracting the visitors' attention to his cause would be over — rapidly collected his things and shoved them into his bag. While he was packing I said to the warden, "Isn't it true that solitary confinement is a special punishment? When Tsipin leaves, I will be in solitary confinement."

"Don't worry," he said, "you won't be alone for long." Tsipin was ready to go.

"Best of luck."

"Thanks." Tsipin and I had arranged that whichever of us was released first would contact the other's family, explain what had happened, and bring the encouraging news that it appeared we were being held only temporarily. I was extremely glad to see him go and know that some of Lucia's fears would soon be allayed. Knowing how anxious she must be was the only real torture I was suffering here.

I sat down on the bench and lit a cigarette. I was in a state of some trepidation, wondering who my next cellmate might be. It didn't seem too likely that the warden would provide me with an ordinary criminal for a partner, because I knew that the authorities were afraid of the contagion of ideas spread by refuseniks. We had already aroused a great deal too much sympathy among the general population; I doubted that they would take the slightest chance of increasing the scope of this support. But I couldn't be sure.

My speculations didn't last long. That evening the door opened, and there before me stood Dmitri Ram and Sasha Voronel! We embraced one another, overwhelmed with relief and joy. They had been arrested forty-eight hours after I was, and had been here since, in another cell block.

Dmitri Ram is a large, stout man with strikingly dark, round, humorous eyes. He was one of the most indefatigable of the activists. He was a little lame at the time of which I am writing, because not many months before he had been set upon and severely beaten in a busy section of midtown Moscow. As I mentioned before, there are always hundreds of policemen everywhere in the capital, and although his attackers were supposedly an ordinary gang of hooligans, one could hardly doubt that they were KGBsts in rather unconvincing disguise: the police simply stood by without interfering. Dmitri was in pain for a long time after his beating — his leg had been broken and badly set, and the doctors had to rebreak and reset it before they were through. By the time he arrived at Serpukhov he was walking almost normally again.

My life in prison became really interesting, because now we all had a chance to discuss together not only plans for the future of our seminar group, but our own current work — everything we were thinking of. The chess set was forgotten.

Two days later the warden came back. This time it was my turn to collect my belongings and follow him. I embraced my friends.

"If they're letting me go, you two will be next," I said, picking up my briefcase.

"Tell Nina I'm all right, and not to worry," was Sasha's last request.

"I'll do that before anything else."

I followed the warden through the many locked partitions. In the reception room my watch was returned to me. When we came out into the courtyard, and I stepped outside the heavy monastery walls, I felt almost dizzy. I assumed they would simply let me go to find my own way back to Moscow; but no, there awaiting me were two plainclothes KGBsts, who instructed me to get into the black Volga that was parked in the courtyard. The huge prison gates opened, and we drove back to Moscow.

"Where are we going?" I asked as the car turned off the highway into the city.

"To the Seventeenth Precinct. You're to be questioned."

"By the police?"

"By the KGB."

What in God's name awaited me now, I wondered. For a while I had thought I was free.

What happened next was the damnedest thing, and I will never understand it. We drove directly to the Police Headquarters. It had been rather a long drive, and when the car stopped I announced that I wished to use the men's room.

"Oh, don't bother. The questioning won't take more than ten or fifteen minutes," said the chief of my two escorts.

"The hell with that. I will remain perfectly silent; I will not utter one word. I refuse to cooperate in any way unless I get to the men's room first."

"We're late enough as it is! Well, all right, if you absolutely insist." We walked into the building and up two flights of stairs.

When I came out of the lavatory, I felt ready for anything. We walked down the stairs to the ground floor again, and to my amazement, they escorted me out the front door, onto the street.

"Where am I supposed to go now?"

"Wherever you want," answered the chief KGBst. I was bewildered.

"Well — I want to go home."

"That's up to you," he said. "You're free. Good luck. And let's hope that next time we meet, it will be under more favorable circumstances."

What was the point of that game? I couldn't figure it out (I still can't), but I didn't wait for the next proposal. I hastened off to the subway.

I wasn't sure where to go now. My family would probably still be in

Saltikovka, but since my Moscow apartment was near a stop on the same line that led out to the village, I decided to drop by at home on my way and see if there were any messages for me. I ran up the single flight of stairs and, just in case, rang the doorbell while I was searching for my key. The door opened. It was Lucia.

Never, since the day we met, have we been so glad to see each other.

"I can't believe it — can't believe it," Lucia kept saying when we were finally able to talk coherently. "They said you'd be released, but I knew I'd never be sure until I saw you with my own eyes. What happened? Where were you?"

"Didn't Tsipin give you my message?"

"Tsipin? No, what message?" This was strange, that Tsipin should have failed to perform this errand. To convey messages, particularly from a prison, was the most essential service any of us in refusal could do for one another. It lodged a doubt in my mind as to his dependability. But I had no time to think about it; I was impatient to see my daughter.

"Where is Yulia?"

"Everything's all right, Mark! Don't look so scared! She's staying in the country with a friend of the Schwartzes. She's fine. I'll tell you about what's been going on when we have a minute. Let's hurry; we ought to go over to the Voronels' right away." We both knew that Irina Brailovsky, Nina Voronel, Bella Ram, and the other wives of imprisoned men would be in a perfect agony of suspense until they heard their husbands' release was imminent.

On the way, Lucia told me what had been happening in Moscow while I was in Serpukhov. Not only Sasha and Dmitri, Lunts and Gindin, but all the organizers of our Seminar had been imprisoned just before Nixon's arrival; also dozens of other activists and dissenters. The KGB had made a clean sweep of "troublemakers." Nearly all of the would-be participants in our International Scientific Symposium had been alerted to the situation and had stayed away, with the exception of two who were arrested the minute they arrived at the Voronels' apartment building. It was quite a scene, because there was a crowd outside of the building, Western correspondents among them, watching everything.

"How about our visitors from abroad?" I asked. Our invitations had been accepted by over thirty scientists: Americans, Canadians, British, even Israelis.

"They didn't come. Someone found out that they had all been denied entry visas. They weren't allowed into the country."

"Why, that couldn't be true!" I said. "Most of them were supposed to attend the great jubilee at the Academy!" The Academy of Sciences was to celebrate the two hundred and fiftieth anniversary of its founding early in July.

"The jubilee was canceled."

"*What?*"

"The whole celebration was called off."

I was astounded to hear that this very important ceremonial occasion hadn't taken place. Was it possible that the authorities' fear of contacts between Western scientists and our Seminar-in-exile could be the reason for this awkward change of plans that had been months, perhaps years, in the making? If that was the case (and I was not the only one to whom this conjecture occurred; it turned out that many of my colleagues and also some of the American journalists came to the same conclusion), then we were a more dangerous element than we had thought. Correspondingly, we were in even more danger than we had thought ourselves to be.

Within a few minutes of our arrival at Oktyabraskoye Polye, Bella Ram was there, and Irina Brailovsky and nine or ten other wives or relatives of the people who had been arrested at the same time I was. They had a grapevine system whereby they could contact each other immediately, and they all gathered together in an amazingly short time. I was inundated with anxious questions. I reassured them; told them everything I had seen; said we had not been treated badly at all; and predicted that their husbands would be out within two days, which they were.

The basis for my confidence was the knowledge that we had the attention of the Western press. Our arrests (or "disappearances") had been reported in all the principal papers abroad. If they had not been, who is to say that we would not be in Serpukhov still, or somewhere much worse?

Lucia

LUCIA AND I didn't get much chance to talk alone until very late on the night of my release, when, after I had spent many hours trying to allay the fears of the wives of the other arrested men, we finally got back home. I couldn't wait to hear how she had got through her fortnight as a prisoner's wife.

"When you were driven away," she told me, "I went back into the house and sat down and gave up. I couldn't even move. I've never felt so alone in my life. I kept thinking: Was there anything I could have done? What would have been the point in screaming at them and telling them you were innocent? It wouldn't have made any difference. There was literally nothing I could do. I've never felt so helpless."

The next thing she knew, Yulia came in, looking dreadfully pale, and said, "Mama, I've got a terrible stomach ache." She must have caught some kind of intestinal flu; during the next couple of hours she had several bouts of diarrhea, and it seemed ages before she was able to lie down and start dozing off. "Whenever she was asleep I tried to decide what I ought to do," Lucia said, "but my mind was paralyzed. You were gone; Yulia was sick; I was in someone else's home. I realized that you might be gone for a day . . . or it might be years and years. How could I manage? I couldn't get a job. I kept thinking: Mark is forty-two. Perhaps he will be fifty-two, or nearer sixty, before I see him again. I knew it didn't make sense to let all these thoughts take over; I should be trying to find a way out of there. But I couldn't do anything without help, and there was no one in Saltikovka I could go to."

Suddenly it occurred to her that Irina didn't know Victor and I had been arrested. She knew she had to call her at once. She went over to the cot and looked at Yulia, who opened her eyes.

"Now I don't want you to worry, dear," she said, "but I have to be out for a few minutes. You try to sleep. There's tea on the table, and the chamber pot is right under the bed. I'll be back in no time."

Once outside, Lucia shut the door and looked nervously around. She walked cautiously past the clump of bushes at the end of the path, and then started to run. None of the nearby cottages had telephones: the nearest phones were in the village, at the bus station. Lucia ran as fast as she could the mile to the bus stop, managed to catch the bus to Saltikovka without too long a wait, and dashed from the village square down to the station. She tried the telephones one after the other, and only after the last one proved to be dead did she realize that all the lines had been disconnected.

It wasn't hard to guess what had happened. The KGB will occasionally cut off all the telephone service in an area where there is someone whom they want to keep incommunicado. In Moscow, where there are public phone booths on every block, you will sometimes have to try ten or fifteen of them before you get outside one of these blacked-out areas. It is typical of the KGB's heavy-handed methods that they don't hesitate to inconvenience or endanger huge segments of the population in order to silence one or two people.

Lucia was in a frenzy. She knew it was highly dangerous if any of us dropped out of sight unnoticed; she absolutely had to get the news out. "I almost went crazy," she told me. "For a moment I even thought of taking the train to Moscow — but how could I let Yulia stay alone all that time?" She decided to try the telephones at the post office.

Again, she ran — it was almost another mile to the post office from the bus station. But the phones there were dead, too.

"I begged the girls at the desk to let me call from the postmaster's phone; I told them it was an emergency, that my husband had suddenly been taken very ill and was being driven by ambulance to Moscow. I had to get a message to someone to meet him there." This fiction was one that we had all settled upon in advance in the event any of us were arrested: one could hardly announce in public, "My husband is in prison."

The clerks were not anxious to help. "You'll have to get permission from the postmaster," they told her. Luckily, he was in his office, and, seeing an obviously desperate woman in a real crisis, he told Lucia she might put through the call.

Of course, the Brailovskys' line had been cut quite a while before; but some friends of ours, the Kraskos, who had not yet decided to apply for emigration but were completely in sympathy with us and often conveyed our messages regardless of the risk to themselves, would take the call. (I can refer to these people by their real names because fortunately, they are now in Israel.)

By lucky coincidence, Irina happened to be at the Kraskos' when the call went through. When she heard that I had fallen ill and had been taken to the hospital, and that Victor had caught the infection from me and was probably hospitalized also, she understood at once; but assuming that Lucia was at an ordinary pay phone, dropped the "code" and said: "What time were they arrested? Are they together? For God's sake let me have the details." It was horrible, because the postmaster, sitting just two feet from Lucia, was listening in on the parallel telephone and heard everything. Without a second's delay, the line clicked off. Lucia jumped up. "Thank you so much!" She ran out of the office, followed by the astonished and angry stares of the postmaster and the workers at the desk.

By the time she got back to the dacha, around eight o'clock, Lucia was so exhausted and distraught that even our little daughter — only four years old, and still feeling very ill — noticed her appearance.

"Mama! What's the matter with you? Are you sick too?"

"No, no, I'm fine. Just a little tired. Go back to sleep, darling." Lucia lay down on the sofa. But then she sprang up, with the sudden thought that, of course, the place might be searched. She opened the drawer and grabbed my notebook, my most precious possession, in which the most important among other memoranda were hundreds of addresses of refuseniks, of would-be applicants for visas, of friends in Israel, in America, in England — everywhere.

"I wanted to hide it. And I knew that here I was in this cottage, no curtains on the windows — if there was anyone outside he could see me perfectly easily. I might as well be on a stage. He could watch me while I thought I was hiding it." It was a nightmarish feeling. She was so harried that for a minute her mind refused to work. She looked everywhere — where and how could she get the book out of sight? She finally decided to shove it under Yulia's mattress. When that was done, she sat down again to think.

What to do next? How could she stay at this dacha, completely alone, with a sick child? The KGB could appear at any minute. And she was totally cut off from everyone. "I've never felt so lost in my whole life. I simply *dreamed* that someone, anyone, would come to the rescue; but I knew there wasn't a chance: nobody knew you'd been arrested except for Irina, and she couldn't possibly leave the baby to come here." Her thoughts raced in a circle, but she could see no way out of this trap. She kept glancing out the window (it was still light outside), fancying that she saw something move in the clump of bushes at the end of the path. Her nerves were strung up to the snapping point. Suddenly — it was not her imagination — there *was* someone outside, approaching the house.

Just before he got to the door, Lucia recognized him. Pale, frightened, glancing all around as he walked — it was Tolya.

The name is changed. Tolya is a close friend of ours. Not one of those who applied to emigrate, not a dissenter; just an ordinary Soviet citizen and one of the nicest guys I know. For him to appear at our place at that time was an act of pure heroism. He knew perfectly well that the dacha might be under surveillance by the KGB and that if he were caught assisting us it might mean the loss of his job — he had a family to support — and he could be threatened with any sort of prosecution.

It was only owing to such friends that we were able to survive during those years: to Tolya, to other courageous people all over the country, to friends known and unknown abroad.

Lucia could hardly believe her eyes. They couldn't say much to each other because of the likelihood that the place was bugged. Almost immediately, Tolya suggested that they go for a walk. As they were leaving, Yulia piped up. "Guess what, Tolya? We had a guest today."

Lucia stood at the doorway, petrified. A guest! What guest? What could have happened while she was out?

"You did?" Tolya asked, turning paler.

"Yes! A hedgehog! He came to visit and spent a while with us, and then went away."

Almost faint with relief, Lucia and Tolya went out for their walk.

"What in the world made you come?" Lucia asked. "I've never been so grateful to see anyone in my life."

Tolya and his family spent the summers with his aunt, who had a dacha nearby. That evening, returning from his daily commute to Moscow, he heard from the aunt that some people who looked like plainclothesmen had driven up to her place and asked if Azbel and Brailovsky were staying there. It was obvious to Tolya what was happening. It wasn't until much later that we discovered the KGB must have completely lost track of us when we left Moscow. A real dragnet had been cast not only in Saltikovka but at all the suburban villages. Also at the railway stations and the airport, everywhere on that date, there were KGBsts with photographs of myself and Brailovsky.

Tolya and his family took Lucia and Yulia to stay with them until the child was well. Meanwhile, he contacted Irina in Moscow and brought Lucia two messages from her: first, reassurance — she had gotten word to Chris Wren and other newsmen about Victor's and my arrest, which meant we would have whatever protection could be provided by the attention of the outside world; second, an invitation to stay with her for the duration of our imprisonment.

Despite her relief when she joined Irina in Moscow, Lucia felt that her situation was becoming worse hour by hour. She just felt it. She was worried inside, filled with mounting anxiety. Now that Victor and I had been arrested, she and Irina might be picked up as well — and then what would happen to Yulia?

Again, the same fates that intervened on our behalf so often during those harrowing years came to the rescue, this time in the person not of a friend of long standing but of someone who was almost a stranger. An elderly woman who had heard much about our struggle, and who learned from mutual acquaintances of my arrest and Lucia's fears, took Yulia for a visit at her country dacha until this crisis was over. The offer of shelter came like the answer to a prayer; in the days that followed Lucia had occasion to thank God a hundred times that our daughter was spared the tension and humiliation in which she and Irina's whole household were enmeshed.

Immediately after she returned from settling Yulia at the old lady's place, Lucia went with Irina to call on Professor Alexander Lerner. Professor Lerner was a member of our Seminar, but not one of its organizers; not an activist in it. Nonetheless, it appeared that he was under house arrest. The two women were detained by the policemen posted outside of his apartment and taken in for five hours of questioning by the KGB.

Thereafter, Irina and Lucia were under house arrest themselves. For fifteen days neither of them could step out the building without finding a KGBst at their side — not shadowing, not tailing, but shoulder to shoulder, like the best of friends. Over those next weeks, the constant presence of these agents (one of them was assigned to Irina's mother, too, and another to Leonid, her teen-age son) became like a Chinese torture to everyone in the apartment.

On the first day of this supervision, Lucia and Irina astounded their escorts by going straight to 24 Kuznetsky Most, the central Moscow office of the KGB. There they met Nina Voronel, who was being shadowed as they were. All three demanded an audience with the top officials, whom they asked where their husbands were and how long they were to be detained. The officials would not tell them what prison we were in, but they did say how long we were to be held: fifteen days. This news was a relief; but for all of them, the weeks under this close surveillance were a terrible strain. They could never be sure that they too would not be jailed.

Lucia's KGBst introduced himself at their first meeting, "Georgi Borisovitch." (These agents do not customarily mention their family names; and even the first name and patronymic are likely to be aliases.) Georgi

Borisovitch became an all-too-familiar figure in our lives during the years that followed: he had been assigned to us from the start, but now that he was out in the open, so to speak, his subsequent appearances signaled bad trouble.

After several days of accompanying Lucia everywhere, he could not refrain from a few attempts at conversation, in the course of which he blurted out information about the KGB that his superiors would undoubtedly have preferred not be known.

"Here we are, going on errands together," he said once, "and everyone passing us assumes we're just friends. You might be surprised if you knew how many of the couples and groups you see around Moscow are the same sort of friends." Although we had always been aware that "they" were all about us, this was the first time Lucia had absorbed the idea that of any group you might observe walking together in the streets, there was a measurable possibility that some of them might be guarding the others. Soviet law makes no provision for this sort of arrest.

On another occasion, when they were on a bus, Georgi Borisovitch commented: "A bus is certainly a good safe place to be. Now occasionally, in the case of someone who is, shall we say, not good enough for us — if he was in a car, there might be an accident."

"So that's how you murder people!" Lucia exclaimed.

"Oh, just joking!" he retracted hastily.

The day before my release, the house arrest at the Brailovskys' was finally lifted, and Lucia went home, feeling, without Georgi Borisovitch's company, as though an incubus had been lifted from her back.

When she entered our courtyard she looked around to make sure there were none of "them" around. The courtyard was empty, but when she walked into the entryway she came across one of our neighbors. This woman, catching sight of her, turned pale.

"Quick! Lucia! What are you doing here? Hurry! Come on into my place; run!"

"What's the matter?" asked Lucia, dodging after her into the apartment.

"Why, ever since you've been gone this place has been surrounded! They've been everywhere; the entrance hall has been crowded with them, and your door has been guarded night and day. You shouldn't have come back! You're going to be arrested. Everyone who's come to the house has been taken in for interrogation."

Just two hours before, the woman said, a man wearing dark glasses had come into the courtyard, sat for a while on the bench, and conferred with each of the KGBsts there.

"Don't worry," said Lucia. "I know him. That was Georgi Boriso-vitch, who's been guarding me all this time. He must have been there to tell them it's all over; to give them orders to go."

That evening this woman and all the other neighbors called on Lucia and listened breathlessly to her description of the last two weeks. They were heartily sympathetic; they repeatedly asked what they could do to help her.

Here I ought to say something about these neighbors. They were all different sorts of people, from working-class to professionals — in Moscow until recently there was no segregation as to where one lived; no "Park Avenue" or "Harlem." We were all distributed fairly randomly in these huge many-entried nine-story apartment blocks. Not only classes, but nationalities were scattered, so very few of our neighbors were Jewish. But even at those times when we were being hunted like hares by hounds, our casual acquaintances in Entry 1 were much more likely to protect us than to betray us. Even when I was at the peak of my notoriety as an activist, we never had any evidence that our neighbors were against us. I have to make one exception: a woman who lived on the same floor as we did, and who seemed to keep track of our comings and goings with such extraordinary accuracy that we did think she must be a *stukatch*. But as far as everyone else was concerned, we actually felt a certain amount of tacit support. There were some who quietly offered assistance of all kinds; they carried messages for us and took the risk of letting us use their telephones.

Friends and Enemies

The day after my return, Lucia and I took the train out to the country to fetch Yulia, and then returned to our borrowed dacha in Saltikovka. I hoped to rest for a while, but a day or so later when I came into Moscow for a few hours and stopped by at our apartment to pick up some books, I found in the mail a summons to the "Ispolkom," the City Hall Executive Committee. I was advised that if I did not respond to the summons, I would be liable to penalties under the Criminal Code. This meant that the threat of prosecution for parasitism was coming dangerously close.

However hopeless my outlook appeared to be — the work at Elista had terminated, and the editing job for *Fizika* had been cut off entirely — I would have to concentrate all my forces on an attempt to find a job, absolutely any kind of job: dvornik, elevator operator, delivery man — anything. Even if the authorities discovered and put a stop to whatever employment I could find, I might gain a breathing space of a few weeks.

This job-seeking turned out to be a very unusual experience. Even before the officials would have had time to interfere, I found myself absolutely in a vise. I understand that in many parts of the West, people of education may work, if need be, as cab drivers, waiters, janitors, and so on, and that they don't feel particularly demeaned by doing this work; any employment is considered to be respectable. In the Soviet Union, where class divisions are extremely rigid, for a university professor to look for menial work astounds and shocks people as much as it would have, a century ago, had a grand duke tried to get a job as a stable boy. Because there is such a heavy demand in almost every sphere for educated people, not only is a university graduate without an appropriate position considered by everyone to have something wrong with him, but there are official regulations that force him to take the work for which he was trained. As for the possessor of a doctorate — there simply does not exist a single Ph.D. without a post, except for those few who were in the same position I was.

If I had been younger, if I had been in a junior post, perhaps I could have passed myself off as someone who wanted a temporary change of occupation, who wanted to do manual labor for reasons of health — something like that. Had it been possible to avoid producing my Labor Book, I could have concealed my occupation. Labor Books are issued to everyone, and it is just about impossible to find employment without showing one's record to a prospective employer. There it was in black and white — full professor at Moscow University and chairman of a department at the Landau Institute for Theoretical Physics. There were nothing but encomiums, signed by various academic dignitaries, in the section for "Appraisals." Naturally, in this record, it was indicated that I had left these positions voluntarily. Anywhere I applied for work, suspicion would be aroused. What was the problem? Why had I left the university and the Landau Institute? If I wasn't satisfied with my posts, why wasn't I looking for something else of the same sort? And, of course, at each of the places where I asked for work there was an official who was linked to the KGB. This person would inevitably call my previous place of employment. After he learned that I had resigned when I applied for Israel — that was it. I would be shown the door.

For three solid weeks I left the dacha early in the morning and never got home until so late at night that Lucia had started to worry in earnest. After I had been job-hunting for a few days, she no longer asked me what the news was when I got home. She could see by my face that nothing good had happened. Now and then my hopes were raised. Friends introduced me to managers of bookstores, for example, who considered hiring me in the capacity of delivery man or stock man. But then the moment arrived — inevitably — when I had to produce my Labor Book. Their eyes widened when they looked through it. Even those who could see I was a decent person, and who could guess in part my situation, had to turn me down. "Professor of physics! I would get into real trouble, Professor, if I didn't call in and make inquiries about this . . ." That would be the end of that.

I felt like a rat in a maze. It was time to reconsider, to try some other avenue.

The idea of becoming secretary to a scientist on my own level was, as I knew, a hopeless ambition. But suppose I changed policy and applied to a person of very high status, who was as nearly immune to the pressures the authorities could apply as anyone in this country could be?

I telephoned Academician Alexander Mikhailovitch Leontovitch, the very eminent scientist to whose cathedra I had·belonged at the university. I mentioned before that he was often referred to as "the conscience of the Soviet Academy of Sciences"; a person of absolute integrity. When he heard who was calling, he cordially invited me to come over to his apartment and tell him what was going on. When I got there, I explained the trap I was in and made my request. I could see he was very unhappy.

"Mark, you know I want to help you, very badly," he began. "What bothers me most is realizing that if it were I who had applied for Israel, being older, and being an Academician, I wouldn't have been subjected to the same sort of retaliations that you have. It's terribly unfair. But here's my situation. I don't know if you've heard, but my wife is very ill. I have to have access to the best doctors, and she has some special prescriptions. God forbid, she may have to be hospitalized before long. I have to be able to get her into the Kremlin Hospital, if the need arises. I am getting medicines there right now, and she is taking special treatments that are unavailable anywhere else.

"I hope you know how I feel about you. Under any other circumstances I would hire you at once. But as it is — you understand me."

Of course I understood, very well. For Academician Leontovitch to have access to the best medical care for his wife was not a right, but a privilege, one that he might lose. In this instance, to act according to his own wishes and convictions might easily be to risk the life of his beloved companion of forty years. The authorities could threaten him with the only weapon in the world that could intimidate so courageous a man. He knew they wouldn't hesitate to use it.

I expressed my concern for his wife, apologized for having troubled him, and I started to look for other possibilities. One of my friends suggested that I apply to an author we both knew who might be able to take me on as secretary; but it happened that the man already had one, a dissenter who had been in danger of prosecution himself. I began thinking of other writers of my acquaintance and went from one to another of them. (Writers, in that country where the written word is so powerful — and so dangerous — are the super-elite.)

I discovered that quite a few writers, like the first man I saw, were already providing protection for dissenters in this same way. No one could hire a second secretary. To hire me, the prospective employer would have had to apply to a top official in the Union of Writers, General Ilyin — a former KGB general. Since the applicant would have had to supply my name, it is no great wonder that I was repeatedly turned down. A number of others to whom I appealed, having served prison sentences under Stalin, were still, although "rehabilitated," in too insecure a position to offer shelter to anyone else.

It was still summer, and almost all the people I wanted to see were on vacation out of town. I remember those travels: the train rides to various Moscow suburbs. I can see in my mind's eye a montage of the many faces — old and young, bearded and clean-shaven — and hear over again the many kindly phrases that all, however sympathetically, conveyed the inevitable "No."

                              *   *   *

On one Sunday morning I had an unexpected visitor at the dacha. A big man, black-eyed, exuberant — this was Ernst Neizvestny, by far the most famous sculptor in the U.S.S.R. I was much surprised to see him there (we had met only occasionally) and to discover that he had come to discuss his own plan for applying for an exit visa.

If public recognition, wealth, and success were the only requirements to assure a satisfactory life for an artist, nothing could have influenced Neizvestny to emigrate. His career was spectacular. His art aside, this man would always have been venerated in the Soviet Union. He was a much-decorated veteran of the War, wounded when reconnoitering a nest of German artillery. He still has a ghastly scar, actually a hole, in his back. He had already gained a great reputation as an artist by the late 'fifties, when he astounded everyone by shouting down Khrushchev's criticisms of modern art. This dangerous confrontation actually increased Neizvestny's fame and popularity; he was always flooded with more commissions than he could handle, principally portrait busts and monumental sculpture.*

But Neizvestny had far bolder and more creative plans for his work than any sculptor would be permitted to realize in the Soviet Union. He had to be free, at whatever cost. Although he could hardly have anticipated it at the time, he was to be cruelly punished for applying to leave the country. One of his studios was vandalized after he made application, and all the work in it crushed.

After we had talked over his situation, which certainly presented problems — the Soviets would not be likely to release so excellent and so famous an artist without a fight — I told Ernst about the plight I was in myself, and how desperate I was to find someone who would hire me. He was ready to take action at once.

"Why, I'll hire you as my secretary!" he announced. "Give me a day

---

*I mentioned earlier that the most unexpected order he ever received was from Khrushchev's widow, to design the memorial over his grave. I have seen it, and it is an impressive piece: Khrushchev's head — atop a black-and-white marble column; the black, so the artist explained, to symbolize Khrushchev's failings and mistakes, and the white to commemorate what was fair about him: his generosity; the amnesty for Stalin's prisoners.

or two so I can find out how to get around the union regulations; I'm sure I can arrange it!" When we met in Moscow a couple of days later, he was not quite so confident. "I've been looking into the requirements for hiring someone, and the papers we'd both have to file are just impossible. We couldn't get away with it. But I'm trying a different tack now; don't give up hope! I've talked to some people who think they know of a way to manage it." And so it went for several days in succession: Neizvestny tried everything he could think of to provide me with a job, or at least with the semblance of one; but he had no luck and finally had to give up. (We met on street corners: my home, where I might be awaited by summonses or by the police, was off-bounds until this dilemma was resolved.) At one of our meetings, Ernst told me something rather revealing: he had just run across an acquaintance in the subway, a poet popular not only in the U.S.S.R. but in dozens of countries all over the world, nearly a rival to Yevtushenko. Audiences flock to hear his readings, to admire his verse and his courage as well: the poet has a reputation for "flying in the face" of the Soviet regime. "I said I was going to see Mark Azbel," said Ernst, "and asked if he wanted to come along. I've never seen anyone disappear so fast. He turned pale, and vanished into the crowd like magic."

* * *

Autumn came. We were still at our dacha. The Moscow police and the KGB would not be likely to follow up the summons I had received as long as I was not at my permanent address. They could wait. I couldn't.

The weather turned cold. There was no heat in the cottage except for a small wood stove; we walked in the forest and picked up fallen branches for firewood. Like very nearly all these dachas, the house was not insulated, and I became apprehensive as time went by. It would be very tough to be trapped there once the snow flew.

The village of Saltikovka was by now almost deserted. It was a beautiful fall, unusually dry. A pale sun shone almost every day through the thinning foliage. The dachas there are very close to one another; there are usually quite a lot of people around. But now, this late in the season, we had practically the whole district to ourselves — a novel pleasure.

I had little chance to enjoy it. I spent more and more of my time job-hunting and had very nearly lost hope.

At last, without a shred of optimism, I went to see a scientist whom I hardly knew, a man I had only met once or twice. He is not Jewish; he is a Russian, someone with no reason for feeling any particular concern for refuseniks. Within less than twenty-four hours I had a job.

When he and I went to the union office to file the notice, the woman official there told him that he would need an affidavit from his director stating that it was essential for him to have a secretary. He calmly advised her that as a Lenin laureate (which he is) he had no need for such a document. He was so suavely authoritative that the woman backed down. He invented cover-ups for me: told the official that I was a scientist on leave for reasons of health; that I had lost my Labor Book. He managed to stampede her into filing the appropriate papers, and before an hour was up, I was in his employ. The position, of course, existed only on paper. I didn't actually work for him, nor was I paid, but this legal fiction might mean my freedom. Naturally I planned to say nothing at all about the job unless I was actually brought to trial.

I think of that courageous man often, and devoutly hope that he never had any trouble on my account after I left. I much regret being unable to put into this record the name of such a noble person; I can only say that for the rest of my life I will always feel deeply indebted to him.

It was a tremendous relief to move Lucia and Yulia back to the warmth of our own home. And very shortly, word of my return got around among the people who needed advice on emigration. Once again my "clients" were in and out of the apartment all day.

In Search of Cover

THE EVENTS of the last few months had a cumulative effect on me.
Soon after we returned to Moscow I suffered increasingly from gallstone attacks. Within a few days I found myself in the hospital.

This was not a special institution for the privileged classes, such as I
had been in once or twice before in Moscow, but an ordinary general
hospital. Now it was my turn to find out at firsthand what medical care
is like for the majority of Soviet people: to be at the mercy of incompetent and callous *sanitarkas;* to spend days and nights in such close prox-
imity to five other very sick people that it was hard to breathe.

But I certainly cannot criticize the doctors at that place. They worked
the same incredibly long hours that my parents had, and however vari-
able the level of expertise among them, no one could doubt their dedication. When I declined to be operated on, they tried a series of dietary
regimens and medications until, eventually, the symptoms disappeared.

I had plenty of visitors, and the hospital staff too had an occasional
caller — the KGB. The latter were interested to know if I was feigning
the illness, using the hospital as a cover from which I might suddenly
emerge. At that time a Soviet-American scientific conference was in
progress, and the authorities were anxious to keep me away from it.
They must have been delighted to find me really ill.

Some of the American scientists had announced that they would boy-
cott the meeting if I were prevented from attending. When they were
told I was not being deliberately kept away but was sick in the hospital,
they were suspicious of the story. Two of them, very well-known physicists, Bertram Halperin and Walter Kohn, came to see me to check if
what they had been told was true.

I was tremendously touched and very glad to see them. We had an interesting visit: they discussed what was going on at the conference and
asked for all my news: how I had fared in Serpukhov and afterward.
When I told them about the threat of legal action against me for parasitism, they were outraged. By the time I recovered, the danger of being

taken to court on these charges, and having to use my last powder and
shot — the "job" with my scientist acquaintance, a defense that might
buy me only a short-term immunity — was eliminated, at least for the
time being. Walter Kohn got in touch with the American Physical Society. Its then president, Professor Wolfgang Panofsky, one of the leading
physicists of the world, advised the Soviet Academy that if these charges
were pressed, it might go badly for Soviet-American cooperation in
physics.

I was deeply grateful for this defense.

In May I had to go to the Regional Police Headquarters to have my
passport renewed.* I refused to produce my Labor Book. (The police
routinely demand to see it, but since there is no regulation requiring a
passport applicant to provide this record, I stood on my rights and
declined.) The colonel in charge said, "I'll have to make inquiries about
this," and left the office. He didn't come back for a long time. When he
returned there was another man with him — suave, well dressed, with a
self-assured manner — a KGBst of the upper echelon. The colonel left
us alone.

"I want to make you a proposition, Mark Yakovlevitch," said this
man. "And before I make it, I wish to assure you that I will back it with
any guarantees you may request, from any source you may request. —
We're asking you to withdraw your application for an exit visa. Once
you've done so, you'll find every obstacle removed in your road back to
Soviet science. Moreover, it won't be long before you're Corresponding
Member of the Academy. And Academician."

I suppose I shouldn't have been surprised by the effrontery of this
offer. The assumption that every man has his price — that I would be
willing to betray my friends and my cause if the rewards were great
enough — was a natural one to the KGB.

"I am perfectly satisfied with the present course of my scientific career," I answered.

"Give it time! Perhaps you will reconsider," he urged.

"I can definitely say I won't."

Probably owing to the intervention of Professor Panofsky, they did
issue me a new passport. It didn't look anything like the ones I had
carried before; it had a different set of numbers and code symbols. I
suppose I was now on file as having moved into a new, near-criminal
category of Soviet citizen.

*   *   *

* A passport had to be renewed every five years until the holder was forty; the one
issued to a citizen between the ages of forty and forty-five was valid for life.

Meanwhile, other events happened in the world of refuseniks. The first trials against draft evaders began.

In 1972, when applicants for Israel protested their draft calls because they would soon be citizens of another country, the authorities left them alone. But now, two years later, these grounds for refusing to serve were no longer accepted. In Russia you are ordinarily liable to the draft between the ages of eighteen and forty. If your status in the reserves is above a certain rank, you can be recalled even up to the age of fifty or over.

Refuseniks in the service have an extremely tough time, because one of the most insistent themes stressed by army propaganda is that Israel is a Fascist state, an enemy of Socialism. The officers make a point of letting the troops know which among them are applicants for exit visas. One can imagine the treatment accorded these men by their fellow-soldiers: the brutal insults, the beatings.

Once the serviceman's stint is up, as I mentioned, he is ineligible for emigration, because he is "possessed of military secrets." So it may be years before he has any chance at all of leaving.

Men who applied for Israel and resisted their draft calls were now being sent to prison for three years. Nevertheless, the number of requests for exit visas increased, particularly in the Ukrainian cities, where Jews, having in recent years acquired a renewed pride in their national origin and a corresponding willingness to take a stand publicly as Jews, were persecuted more severely all the time.

The KGB fought with these people. Agents in the guise of street rowdies attacked some of them, beat them, and arranged for their arrests on charges of hooliganism. The most severe punishments were reserved for those who made pilgrimages to the places where, under the Germans, countless Jews had been murdered. More and more of the mourners who tried to pay these annual respects to their dead received prison sentences; the State was determined to erase the memory of the slaughters.

The city government of Kiev went so far as to plan the construction of a recreation park — a stadium and dance platform — on the actual site of Babi Yar. Probably Nature herself could not tolerate such a desecration. The autumn rains came just as the ground over which the foundation for the stadium was to be set had been dug out and loosened. The location was on the crest of the hill, and this high ground began to move. A landslide — or rather a mudslide — poured down onto the heavily populated section of the city at the foot of the hill — the lowest part of Kiev, called the Podol. The disaster occurred very rapidly. Without warning, mud, filled with human skulls and bones, inundated the Podol, and dozens of people in the streets and on trams were mired and smothered to death under this moving graveyard.

Many of the plain people of Kiev raised an outcry, saying that this was God's vengeance against those who would make a playground of a place where people had been slaughtered. The city had to call a halt to the plans for building on that site. Only recently, a piece of memorial sculpture was finally put up at Babi Yar, but the inscription on it makes no mention of the fact that the hundreds of thousands of Soviet people who were killed there were Jews. And up to now there is still not even a marker in Kharkov; inasfar as possible, the memory of what happened at the Tractor Works is obliterated.

Nothing remains. Not only is the recent memory of the slaughtered Jews wiped out, but of the many centuries of Jewish culture in that country nothing remains. No museums, no documents, no objects of art, not a photograph. It would be much harder to restore this culture in Russia than to reconstruct the culture of Ancient Egypt or Greece or the Mayan people.

* * *

The officials who interrogated us in June had repeatedly mentioned that it was only when we invited foreign participants to our Seminar that we broke the laws against "fomenting international and interracial hatreds" (sic), against Zionism and "incendiarism"; but for the ordinary weekly meetings, they had no objection. However, now all the excitement surrounding the failed International Scientific Seminar made the authorities realize that, after all, even our weekly meetings could not be ignored. When Western scientists of the stature of Albert Szent-Gyorgyi, Julius Axelrod, Arthur Kornberg, and George Wald — to name but a few — had been willing to serve on our Board of Sponsors and had become active and concerned about scientist refuseniks, the officials concluded it was high time to shut down our Seminar completely. Of course, they approached the problem in a roundabout way.

Sasha Voronel was summoned to appear in police court on charges of parasitism.

"Parasites" can not only be forced into factory jobs; some are exiled. The famous poet Brodsky was exiled for parasitism, despite the fact that he supported himself by his writing, and that Korney Chukovsky, the critic Edkin, and even Dmitri Shostakovitch wrote to the court in his defense. Here I feel that perhaps I should explain what this punishment really means.

The very concept of exile has to do with the geographical hierarchy in Russia. To be trapped in a place of exile means, as well as a bitter unremitting struggle just to obtain the essentials for survival, total deprivation of any cultural life at all. All one's connections with the outside world are cut off. As for human contacts, the villagers are the same "dark people" they were described to be a hundred years ago: ignorant, miserable, many of them congenitally defective as the results of generations of alcoholism. To these people an outsider is someone to be avoided, suspected, hated; if he is a Jew, he should be attacked and beaten. The implication behind this specific sentence is that the majority of Soviet citizens are born, live, and die in exile, in conditions considered horribly punitive by anyone who lives in the central cities. And this is the actual fact.

Voronel now, in his turn, was in danger of a sentence second in degree only to a term in hard-labor camp — some people considered it just as bad or worse. He had found a "legal" job: he had been appointed to the editorial board of the international *Journal of Statistical Physics,* published in the United States. But this work, of course, would not protect him if he were indicted as a parasite.

What could he do? "If I'm exiled, that will prove in no uncertain terms to everyone who's been concerned with us exactly what's going on in this country," he said. But the rest of us couldn't bear the prospect of his undergoing this punishment. He had already waited an eternity to leave the Soviet Union; as a convicted criminal he would have three more hard years — at the least — added to his term in purgatory.

"Don't just walk into the trap," I said. "Get out of the city, as far as you can. You have friends in the Crimea — go and stay with them. Things may cool off after a while. If we can keep the Seminar going without you, that will show the KGB that, as far as we're concerned, they can't 'divide and conquer.'" After long deliberation, Sasha and Nina finally decided to leave.

At the next meeting of the Seminar, Brailovsky, I, and the other participants met as usual at Sasha's apartment, but we found that the key didn't work! The lock had been broken. Just as it became obvious what had happened, we heard footsteps on the stairs and a captain of police appeared.

"What's going on here?" he demanded. "There's been a robbery in this apartment. It's under investigation right now. If you all don't clear out of here immediately, you'll be taken in as suspects."

We had no choice but to go, but we had no intention of canceling the Seminar. After a little discussion we accepted Victor Brailovsky's kind and courageous invitation to hold it at his apartment.

The Brailovskys had three tiny rooms, two of them connecting. There were five people living there: Victor and Irina; their teen-age son, Leonid; the baby, Dahlia; and Fanya Moiseyevna, Victor's mother-in-law. They invited all of us (the Seminar in full complement numbered up to thirty people) to this twenty-square-meter space. We were absolutely packed in: sitting or standing, we jammed the two little rooms. While the meetings were taking place, Irina's mother, the baby, and Leonid were trapped in the third room. We were such a solid crowd that we blocked it off.

In Sasha's absence I was chairman, a position I assumed with considerable trepidation. Sasha was the founder of the Seminar, and he was the heart of the organization. It was not at all easy for anyone else to deal with so many diverse personalities, most of whom were eminent authorities in their fields, much more accustomed to chairing meetings themselves than to following procedures suggested by others. I described earlier the way Landau's seminars were conducted: this is the classic Soviet method. If a speaker did not meet the highly critical standards and the exacting expectations of the senior scientists present, his talk was interrupted and he was dismissed, within minutes. This tradition did not obtain, naturally enough, among us; still, it was a problem in diplomacy — since many of us were of roughly equal stature in the scientific world — to avoid offending or alienating eminent professionals who were not accustomed to the different procedure. Moreover, the fact that we were trying to branch out and deal with not just one science but several — physics, mathematics, cybernetics, computer sciences, and others — meant that many of our listeners were at first unfamiliar with the material being discussed, and all the more likely to betray impatient reactions to the presentations.

That Sasha Voronel maintained unity, enthusiasm, and a real sense of the benefits each member of this group was receiving from the others was a great credit to his remarkable tact and thoughtfulness. He is an amazingly gifted person. I certainly didn't believe I could step into his shoes; all I could do was try. Sunday after Sunday, the meetings continued. We had a great deal to give each other; and by means of this vital interaction, we kept our science growing.

In the late fall, Sasha decided that after such a long interval it might be safe to leave the Crimea and return to Moscow. He had been away for over two months and would take the chance of coming back. He and Nina and two of their friends who were also returning to Moscow managed to get a coupé to themselves on the train. When we finally saw each other, Sasha described the trip.

When they boarded, Sasha saw that the two compartments adjoining his were filled to the doors with KGB agents. Apparently he was to be under heavy guard for the entire journey, and it was not clear what they had in mind for him when he reached Moscow. Sasha is not the kind of person to sink back and accept defeat under such circumstances. While the train was approaching Kharkov, he got up and went into the dining car. When the train stopped at the station, he simply stepped off. The KGBsts, who had of course seen him pass by their compartment on his way to the diner without his wife or friends, carrying no coat or bag, assumed that he was simply on his way to fetch a beer; they didn't even bother to follow him. Not until an hour later did they realize that he hadn't returned to this car. In a perfect fury, they searched every inch of the train from van to caboose. It was too late. They had missed him.

I don't know whether these men knew that Kharkov was the city where Sasha had grown up, where he might find friends to take him in, but I very much doubt it. The run-of-the-mill agent who follows a subject generally knows nothing about his quarry, not even what sort of crime he is suspected of. They are simply ordered to shadow him, and they shadow him — that's all.

When Sasha described this evasion, I was struck for the hundredth time by the inefficiency of the KGB's methods. The organization operates by a sort of saturation technique, evidently valuing quantity over any other factor in its lower-level manpower. Often you might be inclined to laugh at their clumsy ways — until you heard of nighttime raids and searches of people's homes; of arrests that are actually kidnappings; of horrible beatings; unexplained accidents and fatalities. Sasha's story is the only instance I know of when someone has actually shaken the agents who are tailing him, whether at close range or concealed at a distance. Cumbersome though their methods sometimes are, they usually work.

The frustrated KGBsts redoubled their surveillance over Nina and followed her night and day all over Moscow, hoping to catch her making contact with Sasha. But within a few days — unpredictably as always — they seemed to vanish. By the time Sasha ventured to leave Kharkov and come home (he had been sheltered by various friends, more or less in rotation), the hunt was off. The authorities must have been adopting new tactics. His movements were still being checked, but no longer at close range. To be spied upon from a distance was something to which we were now all accustomed; we considered it just routine. Of course, they could close in at any minute; but one cannot remain at a peak of apprehension all the time, and unless we were at very close quarters with the KGB we went about our business in an almost ordinary way.

Actually, even the most inoffensive of Russians live under such a constant strain that it casts a stamp on their faces. We have often had foreign visitors exclaim: "Everyone I pass in the street knows I'm not a

Russian! People come up to me and start a conversation in English or German or French. How can they tell I'm a foreigner?" It is perfectly easy: the look of confidence that other nationalities wear sets them quite apart from the Soviet people. They don't share the fear, the stress, the insecurity, that cramps a Russian's expression and his whole bearing. This wariness is observable in people of every age and every class — there is no position in the hierarchy so safe that the holder of it can move about without fear. Even children have a look of excessive caution. Our little daughter, after only a year in Israel, appears at the age of eight very different from the way she did at seven. Relatives in Moscow, upon receiving recent photographs of her, wrote us, "Yulia no longer has the look of a Soviet child." The strain, the tension, in her face is gone.

We never knew exactly why the authorities ceased their threats to prosecute Voronel. Not having access to the foreign press, we could not tell whether some specific protest had been raised in the West on his behalf or whether the changes in the international situation generally had suggested to the Competent Organs the advisability of suspending their plans for him. But although the KGB continued to spy upon him, Sasha was no longer harried and driven to take flight.

So we proceeded with our seminars. We continued to meet at Victor Brailovsky's for a while, not wanting to focus the authorities' attention back on Voronel at that time.

It was at Victor's apartment that we received our first visit in a long time from one of the Western scientists whose support had meant so much to us. This was Professor Gregg Dash, of the University of Washington at Seattle. It had been months and months since we had had any evidence that we were not forgotten; that our colleagues outside the country were aware of what was happening to us and were concerned with our battle. Hardly anyone could have been a more welcome guest.

Gregg came in bringing with him a present, a Magic Slate, one of those boards on which you can write and then peel back the cellophane cover to make the words disappear. Other American friends who had been with us before had described the heavy surveillance under which we lived, and he had the good idea of providing us with this means of exchanging messages that not only couldn't be overheard but that left no evidence.

The Magic Slate turned out to be a godsend. It wasn't always easy to get out of earshot of the bugs by going out for a walk, particularly in the Russian winter. Nothing could have served our purposes better than this device.

We all talked with Gregg for hours. He brought us encouraging messages from Ed Stern, and renewed the invitations to lecture for the Physics Department that the University of Washington had extended to both Voronel and me. He told us that they were waiting for us there, and also at the University of Pennsylvania.

At our Seminar, Gregg Dash gave a talk. This was one of the first opportunities we had had in years to catch up with what was going on in American science. He described his own researches in solid state physics and on rare gas–absorbed layers on graphite, and also demonstrated for us one of the earliest portable computers. We were fascinated: these machines were unknown in the Soviet Union at that time. His visit recharged us with new thoughts, new hopes.

Another Farewell

I CANNOT REMEMBER ever having been so happy at hearing the news that one of us would finally make good his escape as on that December 7th when Sasha Voronel received his exit visa. We could hardly believe it. More than two long years had passed — thirty months since he began his fight. Some of his best friends had been released long since; even his son and his parents were in Israel. But his and Nina's prospects never seemed to change, except for what appeared to be the worse.

By that time, when so much communication with the West had been cut off, if one of the activists in the aliyah received permission to emigrate, he spent his last days in the Soviet Union besieged by people who urgently needed to send their messages to the outside world. Not dozens, but hundreds of those who were left behind had information to be conveyed to friends, supporters, and relatives in Israel. From the minute the word was out that the Voronels would be allowed to go, their place swarmed with people, night and day. None were more desperate than those who had waited so long for their invitations from Israel that they realized the authorities here had interfered and prevented the delivery of their letters. They hoped their would-be sponsors would renew the invitations — perhaps a second or a third would get through. Voronel had to commit to memory countless names, petitions, and protests, as well as urgent pieces of news. Most of the talks took place in the bathroom, where he ran the water in the tub so that the noise would drown out voices and nothing would be picked up by the bugs.

The Visa Department gave the emigrant a definite interval, ordinarily about two weeks, during which he was to make preparations for his departure; at the end of that time he was supposed to go. But Sasha's schedule was so jammed — he had to confer with all these refuseniks, make arrangements for the continuation of the Seminar, and hand over to others his editorial duties on *Jews in the U.S.S.R.* — that he couldn't possibly fit everything into a fortnight. He made arrangements to leave on December 26th.

"Don't be a fool, Sasha. You've got to go right now," I urged him. "Don't take chances! You've seen what's happened to people who delayed. This is awfully risky."

"No need to worry! I'm a privileged person now. They treated me very politely at the Visa Department; they've made all kinds of concessions, suspended a lot of the regulations for me. I've got my visa — nobody's going to take it away."

"A thousand things can go wrong," I warned. But Sasha had a very strong feeling of responsibility toward those he would leave behind. He felt he was no longer a private person; he had to bend every effort to help the refuseniks, and he would work for them incessantly, struggling to do his utmost, right up to the moment he left. There was so much he had to do for those others who were attempting to get out of the country that in the end he was unable to make time even to say goodbye to his own relatives.

This frenzy of activity had descended upon each of our group who received his or her permissions. Usually by the end of the two weeks the person who was leaving was on the verge of collapse, having spent almost the entire time without sleep, his brain filled with the messages and requests, the sorrows and hopes of so many people. For Sasha, who had been in the forefront of the battle, the work was double or triple what it had been for most of the others.

At first everything went very smoothly. In official eyes, Voronel's status had changed completely: he was no longer a refusenik, but an eminent scientist — a Western scientist — to be accorded the same courtesies due a distinguished visitor in the country. He received the best possible treatment, as did Nina. Nina had to attend to all the packing and to the disposition of what they couldn't take with them, and also had to fill out the endless forms demanded by the Emigration Department; but at least she was able to perform these chores without hindrance. Usually the officials would not permit a man's wife to do all the paperwork: the head of the household had to appear himself at the Visa Office. For Voronel, they suspended this rule and many of the others that routinely applied to emigrating Jews. Red tape was cut for him; things were easy, and his feeling that he need not worry about minor problems such as planning his departure a few days later than the date specified seemed reasonable.

On December 20th I arrived at the Voronels' door, my briefcase heavier than usual with a lot of material, including the latest issue, No. XVII, of *Jews in the U.S.S.R.* I rang the doorbell (in Moscow the entryways are left unlocked: you just ring and walk up to your host's apartment. There are no speaking-tubes or lock buzzers downstairs). When the person who opened to me turned out to be someone I didn't know, it was no surprise. Most of the crowd I saw there every day, patiently queuing outside the bathroom where the tap ran almost uninterruptedly, were unfamiliar faces. Automatically, I shook hands with the man who had let me in and edged through the group standing near the doorway.

On the instant, I realized whom I had shaken hands with. In the living room, the Voronels' books and papers were scattered all over the floor. It was a search. Not only were the Voronels' belongings thoroughly rifled, but shortly my briefcase, and everything belonging to his other guests, was searched too.

The alleged reason for this investigation was to seek evidence related to the trial of the writer Maramzin, which was then taking place in Leningrad. Among the hundreds of pounds of books, typescripts, and notes that the KGBsts put into sacks and hauled away with them when they left, there was not a word connected with Maramzin. All the material they confiscated was connected with Jewish interests; even novels and plays published during the 'twenties and 'thirties. There were books on Judaism, on Jewish art — they were dumped into the sacks. Every copy of *Jews in the U.S.S.R.* was taken, including the current issue, which I had brought in my briefcase.

While they were rummaging through all the Voronels' things, it occurred to me that three or four of the KGBsts who were doing the job seemed more cheerful, less businesslike than they ordinarily do. Finally, one of them turned to Sasha and Nina and the guests who had been entrapped as I had — we were standing at the doorway, watching with helpless fury as they shoved their finds into containers — "Have you read the papers today? Here — take a look." With an expression of triumph on his face, he handed us a copy of that day's *Pravda.*

The lead article announced that the Soviets did not intend to observe the conditions demanded by the Jackson Amendment, and that therefore they would not sign the Soviet-American trade agreement. This was very serious. News of the passage of the Jackson Amendment had astounded and deeply impressed us. Who would have thought it possible that one of the great superpowers would take serious economic risks for the sake of a disinterested ideal? Our hopes had soared: we were practically positive that now the emigration would be much simplified.

What made things go wrong, in my opinion, was the glare of publicity surrounding the whole event. This backed the Soviet leaders into a position where they would lose face by an obedient change of their emigration system. If they had not confronted directly the humiliation of being brought to their knees before the entire world, it would have been easier for them to change their policy on the issue of permitting Jews to leave the country. Their condemnation at the time of the Jackson Amendment meant that the Soviets had decided to demonstrate to the West that they could not be forced to knuckle under, and they were willing to risk billions of dollars in possible loans from the United States in order to prove this point.

After several hours, the KGBsts left, taking with them almost all of Voronel's papers and many of his books. Sasha himself was ordered to appear immediately at headquarters for interrogation.

Nina and I waited anxiously hour after hour while he was gone. "If he doesn't give them any testimony on the manuscripts they took, they won't let us leave!" said Nina, in anguish. She kept exclaiming: "We should have gone! We should have gone last week! I knew it; I should have insisted. It was a mistake to delay!" She was terribly frightened. She hadn't seen her son for a year, and aside from all the other reasons they had for rejoicing when their visas came through, naturally the prospect of being reunited with him was what mattered most to her. Now she was crushed. She paced the floor and berated herself. "I should have told Sasha we *had* to go. I knew something would happen!" I tried to encourage her, but I was very nervous myself. The possibilities opened up by that day's news were very dark.

We were tremendously relieved when Sasha walked in, but we couldn't tell what the further plans of the KGB might be. We could only be glad Voronel was not in prison at that very moment. Despite amounting anxieties, Voronel proceeded just as before to confer with the dozens of people who flooded him with their requests, their pleas for help — quite as if he had no doubts at all that he was really going to go.

On the 22nd, it was time for Sasha to have those of his belongings which were to be sent by surface freight taken to the Customs Office. He would have to spend the day watching officials pull apart everything it had taken weeks to pack, leaving it all in random heaps for him to struggle with when they had finished; he would have to produce the many permits required that authorized him to take his remaining books and papers out of the country; he would have to use persuasion and bribes to prevent the confiscation of all his family pictures. We had heard all about these brutal procedures from others who had gone before. While he was at customs, I spent the day planning for tomorrow's Seminar — the last one at which Voronel would be present, if all went well — and for the farewell party Lucia and I were to give him.

We expected Sasha to join us early in the afternoon, but he didn't arrive until about six. When he walked in, we both noticed that he looked strange. He came up to Lucia, took her hands in his, and kissed each of them, saying: "Yes! That's it! That's it!" He appeared off balance, weaving.

"What's the matter, Sasha? Are you drunk?"

"Well . . ." he said slowly, "just two hours ago I thought I had seen the last of my chances of getting to Israel, and said goodbye to my freedom. But here I am, still at large. I'm not in prison — not yet, anyway."

Sasha was indeed drunk, but not from alcohol. Having spent the last two days strung up to an impossible pitch of apprehension, he had undergone a shock at the Customs Office from which he was barely recovering. At the end of the day, while he was hurriedly finishing the repacking of his disordered belongings and closing his trunks, a man suddenly materialized at his side. Voronel glanced at him — and froze.

It was "Pirozhok," as we all called him, the KGBst regularly assigned to Voronel, as Georgi Borisovitch was assigned to us. (*Pirozhok* means "bun"; the man always wore a hat in the shape of one, and in fact there was something repellently bun-like about his whole appearance.) What in God's name was he doing here? Voronel could only believe that at this late date he was to be arrested.

The KGBst's unexpected appearance at the Customs Office, and the quiet purposeful way he approached, drove Sasha almost out of his mind. Now that I think of it, I believe that the sole point of Pirozhok's errand was to force Voronel to leave immediately, on the next plane out. After he had tailed him for so many months and compiled so much evidence against him, which, had the authorities wished, would have put Voronel away for years, the agent probably hated to see his elusive victim freely going about his business, taking his own time. He simply wanted to exert power over Voronel this one last time.

The next two days were wonderful and terrible. The Seminar was transferred to my apartment, and I was formally installed as chairman. I had taken on this role pro tem while Sasha was in the Crimea, but now that it was to be permanent I felt a great responsibility and concern. I have always tended to work on my own; I never thought I was very diplomatic or talented as a leader.

Concern as to my own shortcomings aside, this last meeting of the Seminar for Voronel was very hard on me. He and I had been the best of friends since we were sixteen and seventeen years old. We corresponded during all the years when we were in different parts of the country. We saw each other all the time after I came to Moscow. The crisis of Daniel and Sinyavsky's trial brought us even closer. We were together constantly in the aliyah. Now we had to part, no one knew for how long — perhaps forever.

Today, no matter how I felt, I couldn't permit these thoughts to surface in my mind; they had to remain somewhere deep in my soul. After the lecture — Dr. Shepelev spoke on polymers — I took the floor and announced that the second part of the Seminar would consist of another talk, which I would give myself.

The Seminar was attended by almost double the regular number of people. Despite the overcrowding, Lucia and I managed to thread the entire space with ribbon, hung with dozens of pictures of Voronel and his family, cartoons and photographs, with humorous inscriptions. I recapitulated the story of his life while the company roared with laughter and passed the pictures from hand to hand. We could not afford to cry at such a time, so we laughed instead.

The celebration of Sasha and Nina's leavetaking resumed two evenings later. Throughout our three small rooms, in our kitchen, in the corridor, on the stairs leading up from the entryway, even in the bathroom, at least a hundred people were jammed. The mountain of overcoats in Yulia's room was so huge that no one could get past it. The only way to get across the room was to climb up and slide down. It was impossible to provide drinks and *zakuski* for such an enormous crowd, but Lucia and I and the many friends who helped us did our best. No one could sit down; the place was like the Metro at the rush hour, with everybody cheek by jowl — with the difference that the atmosphere was highly festive. If ten people left, a dozen replaced them.

We didn't know every single one of the company and, as it turned out, neither did the Voronels. A certain percentage of the guests didn't look quite right — but you can't tell a person who may, after all, have been invited by somebody there, to get out of the house because he looks like a plainclothesman!

The party lasted until four A.M.

But this was not the same sort of unfeigned cheer that we had felt at earlier farewell parties, such as Giterman's or Emil Luboschitz', two years before. In those days Lucia and I and almost everyone else had thought that, in all probability, this was only a temporary goodbye. But by now, some of us were far from positive that we would ever see Sasha again.

Yosif Begun, Vladimir Slepak and his wife, Anatoly Shcharansky, and Ida Nudel were at that party. So was Yuri Orlov, who was a participant and lecturer at our Seminar. They are all in prison or in exile at this writing. Others who were celebrating, perhaps still hoping that, after Sasha, they might be the next to go, were Alexander Lerner, Vladimir Prestin, and Pavel Abramovitch. Professor Lerner has been waiting since 1971; the two others since 1970.

Battle Fatigue

Even then, at the turn of the New Year of 1975, when the majority of our group had been waiting for only two years or a little more, there was an undercurrent of uncertainty, a loss of hope. The moment we had initiated the request for an invitation from Israel, our entire lives had been cut in two. I kept thinking of Kipling's lines: "If you can make one heap of all your winnings, / And risk it on one turn of pitch-and-toss . . ."

That is what nearly all the refuseniks had done. They had made a heap of all their winnings, and they lost it when they applied for permission to go to Israel. They lost their jobs, their privileges, their contacts and communications — everything. They became people outside the law. Like plague victims, they lost all but the most loyal and devoted of their friends.

This is a terribly difficult situation for everybody, but particularly for children. When we applied, our children — mine, the Voronels', the Brailovskys', and those of most of our other close friends — were either old enough to realize what we were doing, and to bear the brunt of rejection by their classmates, accounting it as the price they paid for their freedom; or infants, who, we assumed, would be in Israel before they could be affected by the atmosphere around them. But the children were getting older. The psychological effects of constant insecurity, of seeing one's parents weighed down by anxiety and apprehension (however carefully they tried to conceal it), of moving from one place to another for no reason that the child could see, could hardly fail to be damaging. Yulia was two when we applied for our visa. Now she was four and a half. If over three more years went by this way, she would be destined to a pariah's life in school. Her schoolmates, her teachers, would not let her long remain in ignorance that her parents were wicked Zionists. What she would face would make my own childhood injuries look like pinpricks by comparison.

The Brailovskys' daughter, Dahlia, was born at the very beginning of

1974. At that time, thinking that their permission might come at any minute, Victor and Irina were terribly worried that she might arrive aboard the plane to Israel. Now she was a year old, and nobody could say whether she would see all the horrors and humiliations of life as a refusenik. I find it unbearable to realize that, while I am writing this book, Dahlia is six years old. All her life has been spent in refusal. She has already witnessed a night search and the arrest of her father. These are not the sort of shocks from which it is very easy for a small child to recover.

Victor's son was just twelve when they applied for their visa, in 1972. Now he is nineteen.

It was for these children and youths in refusal for whom I felt the strongest sympathy. If they are still in school, they cannot leave; it is against the law, so they have to stay and face insults and beatings. Afterward they cannot enter the universities, which is the natural expectation of children of this class. If they are already university students at the time their families apply, they will be expelled immediately. They don't have any real life. They can't work, because ordinarily they will not be accepted even at a low-level job. All the teen-agers around them move in the ordinary sphere, where duties and expectations are absolutely predictable: everyone else is working toward a goal and has something definite in the near future to look forward to. But as for the refusenik youths — nothing depends on them. They live, so to say, in their suitcases; they live at the railway station. Many of the best years of their lives are spent simply waiting. They live on money they cannot earn: philanthropy from the West. Tourists bring in blue jeans (almost the most valuable commodity of all in the Soviet Union), tape-recorders, records, or other things that they can sell, and so survive. But each year their waiting becomes more difficult.

For strong young people to live on charity is humiliating. At the same time, they are distinguished from others of the same age, not by shabbiness, but sometimes, on the contrary, by appearing more prosperous than their contemporaries. They are far better dressed. No refusenik could afford to replace his children's outgrown clothes with new clothes at Soviet prices; once the authorities put a stop to financial contributions from the West, it was terribly hard to find the money even to eat. The kids wore clothes that had been donated from abroad, and good foreign clothes became almost an insignia of the outcasts. Nothing hurt me more than to see these youths — idle, aimless, grim with disappointment.

In my telephone contacts with Israel I often had to be the bearer of bad tidings, but I never felt worse in this role than when I was obliged to report the death of one of these youngsters. His parents were friends of ours, so we knew the boy; a bright, sensitive kid. He had been brought up (as few children of the intelligentsia were) in full awareness of his family's views on the Soviet system, and he knew they had applied for Israel. Halfway through the school year when he was in the sixth grade, he heard from his parents that they had been summoned for an urgent meeting with the principal of his school. What could have gone wrong? He was an excellent student, exemplary in his behavior. He suddenly realized what must have happened: a paper he had written about Brezhnev — composed simply to relieve his own mind; it was intended for his journal — had got mixed in with the homework he'd handed in the day before.

The boy knew what would be in store for his family if it was discovered that he could write such an essay — or entertain such ideas — with impunity.

When the mother and father came home on the eve of the scheduled interview at the school, they found their son dead. He had hanged himself. The poor boy, probably afraid that he might cry out involuntarily before he quite lost consciousness, had sealed his mouth with adhesive tape before he jumped.

"Tell them he was murdered!" his grieving mother demanded of me before the call from Israel came through.

There were other such tragedies, though none in which the victim was so young.

As time passed, families were broken to pieces. Couples were separated. More than once the spouse who had gone ahead to Israel despaired of ever being reunited with the one left behind, and married someone else.

Month by month, things were getting tougher. The Soviets, belatedly reacting to public opinion abroad, were evolving subtler techniques of harassment, methods that would not necessarily draw the attention of the rest of the world. No one in the West could be expected to react strongly to news of increased draft calls, for example. Here was a nation with a standing army and the universal draft — what was so cruel about young people doing a stint in the service? As for the punishments inflicted upon refusenik activists — the authorities mounted a real campaign to represent these people as individuals who, long prior to their attempts to emigrate, were known for their bad characters. Scandals were concocted about them; they were publicly slandered and vilified; they became victims of yellow journalism.

Most frustrating of all to the "old refuseniks" like ourselves, who had now been waiting long years, was to see others, who had never thought of going to Israel until a few weeks before, impulsively applying to emigrate and being released with no trouble. They poured out of the country by tens, by hundreds, by thousands: quiet people, provincials, people whose contributions to society the Soviets did not particularly value. Meanwhile, Muscovites, Leningraders, members of the educated classes found it harder than ever to get visas. As to the more conspicuous activists — very nearly all of us, maybe 99 percent, were refused, time and again. We who had applied around the turn of the decade or before, who were vocal in our protests at being denied permission to go, had served, I believe, as battering rams. We breached an opening in the prison wall. Glad though we were to see others escape, it was hard to accept the fact that we ourselves would be left behind.

Not long before Voronel left, I remember Lucia observing one day, "You know, it seems to me there are fewer people here all the time coming around to consult with you and Sasha." We thought about it, and realized that she was right. Although our friends and acquaintances who planned to emigrate still hastened to ask our advice when they came to the point of applying for visas, the flood of strangers had noticeably diminished. They probably feared a sort of contamination from such long-term refuseniks; it seemed safer to them to learn the ropes unassisted, or to pick up from less conspicuous sources information as to how to manage their lives once they had lost their employment.

So, stranded behind the outgoing tide of emigrants, we found ourselves in an increasingly vulnerable position. Brailovsky, I, and the others found it more and more difficult to get through each day, to keep on working and planning, under the weight of such heavy discouragement.

*   *   *

The fact that Lenin * spoke out strongly against anti-Semitism (and this accounts for the enthusiasm with which many Jews initially welcomed

---

* The story went around Moscow some time ago that the devout Communist historian Marietta Shaghanian, one of the few scholars in Russia permitted access to the vast unpublished files stored under the Lenin Museum, once came across an unexpected find in her researches: a letter addressed to the Czar Alexander I, requesting permission for the writer to take the Czar's name as his own Christian name. For a Jew to file this plea if he wished to assume the Czar's name upon conversion was compulsory at the time. Attached to it is the reply, signed by the Czar's secretary, acceding to this request. The man who wrote the appeal was a certain Blank, Lenin's maternal grandfather. These papers disclosing Lenin's tainted ancestry were hidden away again with all speed, but evidently the historian could not resist mentioning her discovery to someone, because eventually everybody heard about it. This may explain why there is absolutely nothing at all about Lenin's forebears in the displays at the Lenin Museum: almost no pictures and no memorabilia of any sort dating from before his parents' time.

the Revolution) introduced a schizophrenic element into the position on Jews that the Soviets could publicly assume. A Russian has to hate Jews; moreover, anti-Semitism is a wonderfully convenient weapon with which to manipulate people, to deflect blame for political or economic disasters away from the country's leaders in time of need. But according to Lenin, a true Communist cannot be an anti-Semite. The press wrestled with this contradiction for years. While "International Jewry" might "conspire for world domination," and Zionists might be excoriated without apology, specific attacks on Soviet Jewry as a whole were by convention a little oblique. One knew that Cosmopolites were Jews specifically because they had Jewish names. The "poisoners" who were supposed to have devised the Doctors' Plot also had to be listed by name to ensure that the public understood the point of that horrible story. However simple the deduction (Soviet people easily and automatically separate Jewish from Gentile names), some elementary thought-processes had to be employed in order to absorb the propaganda.

But by the 'seventies these subtleties had gone by the board. The publication of *Invasion Without Arms, Zionism Unmasked,* and dozens of other such books signaled the end of all restraints on this subject. It is an indication of the official opinion of the Russian mentality that anti-Semitic tracts of such low quality, irrational tone, and poor scholarship could be approved for publication in the U.S.S.R. ("Approved" is hardly the right word: the former was published in a first edition of 350,000 copies and sold for thirty-five kopeks!) Not only is *Invasion Without Arms* quite as hysterical, quite as shrill as the *Protocols of the Elders of Zion,* the notorious hoax published three generations ago, but much of it is actually plagiarized from that earlier work.

Early in 'seventy-five, I began to get occasional messages from former colleagues. "So-and-so sends you his regards"; "So-and-so wants to be remembered to you." These greetings always presaged a visit from the person who had sent them; he too wanted to apply for an exit visa and wanted to find out how to go about it. More than once I happened to see the man in question on his way over to my place: my study window gave out onto the courtyard, and I could see the people passing back and forth across the areaway. I was always struck by the furtive appearance of such a visitor. You could see even from a distance, by his walk, by his whole bearing, how frightened he was. Some of these people had fought heroically in the War; some were known for their extraordinary courage in dangerous sports — one, I remember, was a famous alpinist. But to consult someone about applying to emigrate from the U.S.S.R. was to brave a different danger from the sort that he had challenged before. He suddenly felt himself a tiny creature, trying to nerve himself for the ordeal of opposing a superpower.

Around this time the emigration reached such proportions that popular attention was drawn to the whole phenomenon, and it was no longer only the people directly concerned who were aware of the tens of thousands who had left the country, and the reprisals carried out against so many of those who were held here. The situation had become common knowledge, and I believe the Soviets may for a while actually have feared an upsurge of popular support and admiration for these Jews.

Because our Sunday Seminar served not only as a forum for scientific exchange, but as an increasingly important rallying point for refuseniks and their supporters abroad, I felt we should expand the scope of our discussions. Up to now, the Seminars had been concerned only with the exact sciences. But there was such a growing interest on the part of our members in history, religion, and the humanities that Victor Brailovsky and I decided to devote one seminar in four to sessions dealing with these fields. This would allow us to invite refusenik scholars in other disciplines, and Western scholars as well, who could provide a linkage that we, cut off from everything, so desperately wanted with the whole, broad, free world. They could bring us knowledge in the humanities that we lacked and for which we were thirsted. That this knowledge was out of our reach made our thirst for it all the sharper.

The decision to open the doors of our Seminar to fields other than science was not an easy one to make, since even the scientific sessions were now considered subversive. It was absolutely intolerable to the KGB that a group of scientists who were supposed to be dead as scientists were continuing their work. And now we were aiming at the international contacts that were considered a rare privilege in the Soviet Union, to be permitted only to the most reliable and pro-Soviet people.

But more than that: if the Seminar became more than a scientific meeting ground, if it was a full cultural center, a place where people were free to discuss any kind of social or intellectual problem, we would have started something unheard of throughout the entire Soviet regime: an institution in which the exercise of intellectual freedom was possible.

Once again, we avoided politics altogether. But we knew that the very idea of free thought, of a genuine philosophy, was alien and terrifying to the Soviets. It meant the uniting of all the strands of intellectual society. It was not by chance that when these seminars were organized, among those who attended were not only refusenik scholars, but members of the establishment — people who had no intention of trying to leave the country. They were willing to take the risk of being ostracized or fired; like ourselves, they had been hampered too long by the rigid and stratified confines of Soviet culture. Frustrated by the blacked-out areas, the blank spaces in all the historic, sociological and literary resources available to Soviet academia, they were as much in need of these cross-currents of information as we were.

Ordinarily we had between twenty-five and forty people at our scientific gatherings. When we began the broad-range seminars, the number of participants more than doubled. It was astounding that such a crowd could manage to squeeze into our apartment. They came despite the obvious risks. Our speakers discussed in particular Jewish history, religion, and literature — highly dangerous subjects. All of us knew that at the Second Leningrad Trials seven men were condemned to long prison sentences for teaching the Hebrew language and culture. We knew that others from Riga, from Leningrad, Odessa, Kishinev, and elsewhere were at that time in labor camps for "anti-Soviet activity" ranging from reading the early Zionist classics to studying the Bible. But people were really desperate to learn about their cultural heritage, and I couldn't have changed my plans for the Seminar without losing my self-respect.

During the years that followed, we were kept supplied with books brought in to us by visiting scientists and tourists. I couldn't possibly list the hundreds of individuals who provided them; I can only say that I hope they know how grateful we were, and how many, many people read the books. Not all of them were scientific or scholarly works. One of the most widely appreciated was *Ninety Minutes at Entebbe*. Lucia could not resist the temptation to translate this heroic account, and there was such a long waiting list for the issues of *Jews in the U.S.S.R.* in which it was published that the last readers had a delay of several months before they could get hold of a copy.

Despite the danger, once the Seminar started to cover these different fields there was a permanent flow of lecturers and visitors to our sessions, from all over the country, not just Moscow and Leningrad. I remember Dr. Zlobinsky and Dr. Kislik, from Kiev; Dr. Gurfel, from Riga; other scholars from Kishinev, from Vladimir, from everywhere.

One of the first meetings I chaired when we had lecturers from abroad turned out by sheer chance to be very luckily timed.

The guests were a Dutch scholar, an Englishman, and an American. The Dutchman spoke first, but before his talk was fairly started we heard the loud pounding of boots coming up the stairs. There was no knock — the door burst open — and in came a police officer and a plainclothes KGBst. I had seen the officer before; he had been one of my interrogators at the Regional Police Headquarters when I was called in to answer parasitism charges.

I faced the intruders and braced myself to protect the visitors: my first thought was, of course, that the KGB knew that the foreigners were here.

"What are you doing in my apartment?" I demanded.

"We got a complaint from the neighbors — noise and disturbance," said the officer.

"Where is your warrant?" asked Lucia.

"I happened to leave it at headquarters," the man answered with a smile. "But no problem — we saw your sign on the door: 'Welcome. Come Right In.'"

He turned back to me. "We have already warned you, Mark Yakov-levitch, about the charges of parasitism that will be brought against you. Now it looks as though even more serious charges may be preferred. Who are all these people? What sort of meeting is this?"

"These are my guests. We are conducting a scientific meeting," I replied.

"I'll want you to give me the names of everybody present," said the plainclothesman.

At that point I realized I had guessed wrong: the authorities didn't know about the foreign visitors, and the fact that the raid occurred while they were here was just coincidence.

"You can take the names of my guests if you wish — there's no way I can stop you," I said. "And I can't make you give us *your* names. But your superiors will have no trouble finding out exactly who conducted this raid, and they may not be very happy about it. Three of my guests are distinguished scholars visiting from the West. The Soviet Union may have trouble getting Western scientists to accept invitations to this country if they learn that they might be subjected to unannounced intrusions by the KGB. If there are any kind of international problems as a result of this action, you two will be responsible." I looked at my watch. "You have exactly two minutes to get out of here. If you stay any longer, I will consider that this meeting has been broken up."

The two men paled, and the KGBst's eyes darted around the room.

"You have visitors from abroad?"

"Yes. Invited to this country by the Soviet Academy of Sciences . . . One minute is up."

They turned on their heels and left. "We'll talk to you again," was the parting shot from the KGBst.

A few days later I was on my way to join a group of refuseniks who were planning to present a petition to the Central Committee, when a black Volga edged out of the traffic and crept along beside me. The car stopped; a policeman stepped out and requested me to get in. There is no use trying to resist this kind of arrest. I entered the car and was driven to the Regional Police Headquarters. There I was led into an empty room and left sitting by the desk, alone, for two hours.

A KGBst came in, settled into place before me — by now, the very gestures of these people had become familiar to me — and launched into the attack. He told me that the Seminar was operating under orders from foreigners who were pretending to be scientists, and that the Competent Organs knew it was an anti-Soviet organization.

Because I knew that the decision as to whether or not I was to be imprisoned must have been made already, I answered him rather quietly. I said that an attempt to halt the Seminar would violate basic scientific priorities and would give rise to an overwhelming reaction abroad. I pointed out that it was much better for recognized Soviet scientists to have international contacts simultaneously with our Seminar than to endanger it.

Certainly I had no hope that this KGBst was a person who could make any decision with reference to our case. I was using him just as a microphone, to convey my answers to his superiors.

Fortunately, after he had delivered his quota of threats, I was allowed to leave. That night I spent at home.

I was particularly glad to be at large at that time, because shortly afterward we had one of the most interesting lectures we ever sponsored, a talk by Ernst Neizvestny.

Neizvestny laughingly referred to himself as "the wealthiest dissident in the country." At that time he had no problems in the Soviet Union as to the recognition of his extraordinary talents, but he told us how hard it was not to be free as an artist. "I am condemned to a lifetime of taking commissions from Party officials. The work I'm dreaming of would never be approved in the Soviet Union." And he enthusiastically described for us the massive piece he was planning, his *Tree of Life,* a huge sectioned edifice with compartments in which statuary and paintings would be displayed. He showed us all the designs for this marvelous work, a diagram of the entire structure — 150 meters in height — and hundreds of sketches of each of the sections. He had it all worked out down to the last detail, even to the special composition walkway leading up to the monument, in which the footprints of the visitors would be impressed.

His lecture drew an enormous crowd. People were fascinated by the project, and quite a few of them took photographs. The one reproduced in this book was taken by Fayerman.

I hope that now that Neizvestny has finally fought his way out of the Soviet Union — he is living in America — he will be able to realize this beautiful and spectacular work.

Including the arts and humanities turned out to be a most sucessful innovation, and general interest in our Seminar increased tremendously. But science, of course, continued to be our primary resource.

Some of the scholars who attended the meetings for the first time told me later that they had come reluctantly, unable to believe that seminars conducted under these strange circumstances could be of such high scientific caliber as they had heard they were. Apparently people were really surprised by what they witnessed here, and the prestige and reputation of our small institution grew to a degree unexpected even to ourselves. Among the scientists who came that year and who expressed the warmest appreciation of our Seminar were Herman Cummins, Distinguished Professor of Physics at the City University of New York, and Professor Peter Pershan of Harvard, who, with seven or eight other American physicists, appeared and spoke at an extra session we held in the summer. They later published an account of our "determined efforts to remain intellectually alive," and they contributed much to our ability to do so.

The first Nobel laureate to participate in the Seminar was Professor Howard Temin. He arrived in the Soviet Union just at the time that two of our group, good friends and frequent visitors to our Seminar, were arrested: Boris Chernobilsky and Dr. Yosif As.

Yosif As and Boris Chernobilsky had joined a refusenik group that was planning to go, again, to the Praesidium of the Soviet Union to present a group petition. Dozens of people assembled there, and this time the authorities, rather than rounding them up and taking them off the premises for twelve hours in jail or in the drunk tank, herded them into buses, drove them far out into the countryside miles from town, dumped them in a remote woods, and left them there. It took them the entire night to walk back to Moscow. They were told that this was only a warning: if they tried to repeat their attempts, things would go much worse for them.

Undaunted, this entire group of refuseniks went to the Praesidium again the next day. This time they were not only rounded up and driven out of Moscow, but when they got off the bus they were heavily beaten. All of us in the Seminar were terribly distressed by news of these events, but there was nothing we could do at present except carry on.

That Sunday the lecture was delivered by Dr. Temin. He spoke on the
nature of cancer. What he had to say was so extremely interesting that
we all urged him to continue the talk the next day. He agreed, and we
arranged another special session of the Seminar, to be held at six in the
evening after the speaker had made his scheduled visits to various official institutions.

On Monday morning, I set off for the Praesidium; this time I was to
join the protest group. I took with me as usual the briefcase with supplies I would need in the event of being imprisoned. With me was Dr.
Gherman Shapiro, who had come to Moscow from the Baltic expressly
for the purpose of making this visit to the Praesidium.

Immediately upon ascending from the subway station, we found ourselves in an enormous crowd of policemen. Without a moment's delay — we hadn't taken a step in any direction — two of them accosted
us, and we were straightaway escorted to a bus parked near the Praesidium Building. It turned out that we were to be the only civilian passengers aboard; the rest of the bus was packed with policemen. Under this
incredibly heavy escort, we were driven off. Naturally, no one told us
where we were going.

During this trip, I described to Dr. Shapiro (who is a physician) the
lecture we had heard from Dr. Temin the day before. He listened with
the greatest interest. There was something funny about discussing the
intricacies of cell structure and other technicalities with an audience of
one educated person and about twenty-four policemen! They were listening, too; they made no conversation among themselves.

I recognized the route after a while. We were on our way to the same
vitrezvitel' to which I had been taken before. Dr. Shapiro and I were
ushered up the same flight of stairs I remembered from my previous imprisonment here, and once again I found myself in the same cell I had
been in before, where the other prisoners were almost all the same people I had seen there on that previous occasion. It was certainly a strange
crowd to be found in a Moscow drunk tank: I should say there were
about ten professors, most of them people of the highest distinction in
the country. There were Stalin laureates in this cell; Professor Naum
Meiman, for example, was among us.

As before, the inmates of the *vitrezvitel'* ignored their worries and
plunged into discussion. Of course we had no way of knowing whether
this time we might not be in for a long-term imprisonment. We were
like victims of sadistic practical jokes — we never knew whether it was
safe to smile, to dismiss the inconvenience, or to brace ourselves for real
danger.

I made the experiment of trying to explain to the guards that my friends and I absolutely had to leave, because an important foreign professor would be waiting for us; just as one could have predicted, this was in vain and it was not until ten P.M. that I left the cell. As before, we were each called one by one and could not tell what had happened to those who preceded us, or what was in store for ourselves. Only when I had been called, had been subjected to another round of threats from three KGB officers, and had been escorted several blocks away from the *vitresvitel'* by a policeman, was I able to leave for home.

Lucia told me that Temin had come and gone, and had left a message that he would go to Academician Sakharov's. I went straight out and telephoned to Sakharov's apartment, and spoke to Yelena Georgievna, Sakharov's wife, who asked me to come over right away.

When I arrived, Temin and Valeri Turchin were there. I told them everything I knew about the arrests, but none of us knew at the time that some of the women, including Ida Nudel, had been arrested and fined. Worse: Drs. As and Chernobilsky had been charged with malicious hooliganism and were at that very moment in the notorious Matroskaya Tishina prison. We found that out only the next day, whereupon Sakharov and Temin entered angry protests with the authorities. They were ignored. After many complaints and appeals, and after some of us formed a defense committee that sent an account of their imprisonment (without a trial) to colleagues in the West, were As and Chernobilsky released.

For Howard Temin, this scientific mission to Russia must have been a strange and alarming experience. But he didn't hesitate an instant to take up our cause, and we were well aware that we were very fortunate in having him with us at that time.

Flight and Close Pursuit

OBVIOUSLY the KGB could hardly have been pleased at having been forced to suspend their actions against members of our group when scientists from other countries took up cudgels on our behalf. They could be expected to devise a new means of attack, something well within the law which would be beyond criticism from anyone outside of the Soviet Union.

We in the Seminar went about our business — as we had to, if we were to survive as an entity — as if the KGB didn't exist. Victor Brailovsky and I were working now on the plans for a jubilee session of the Seminar to celebrate the fiftieth anniversary of Hebrew University in Jerusalem. The lecturers who were to appear at this three-day meeting would be the most distinguished scholars in Judaic studies ever to assemble in Soviet times. It was a most exciting prospect. The Western reader can hardly imagine how eager we were to learn of our past, of our culture and history — simply buried alive more than half a century ago. We were working out the speakers' schedule, and I was completing the outline of the talk I myself was to deliver at this session, when something occurred to change all my plans. It was a nasty blow.

An army officer appeared at my door and delivered a summons into my hand. It was not the first time I had been requested to report to the military, but the previous summonses had come in the mail. If need be, I could have claimed that they had been lost or misdirected. This time there was no way out: I had to sign a paper acknowledging that I had received the order and had been apprised that unless I complied with it I would be charged with violation of the appropriate article of the Criminal Code. For the first time in all these years of struggle, I was seized with a feeling of hopelessness. The army was the one captor it would be impossible to elude.

When I came to the Military Department, I pointed out to the colonel in charge of my case that I was automatically exempt from recall into the service, since I was over forty.

"A lieutenant is in the reserves until the age of forty-five," he said.

"I know that. But my rank is *second* lieutenant. I can't be drafted after forty."

"You've been promoted, Mark Yakovlevitch. You're a first lieutenant. You'll be in the reserves until nineteen seventy-seven."

"Ridiculous! How could that happen without my knowing it?" He handed across the desk a document confirming the promotion of Second Lieutenant Mark Yakovlevitch Azbel to full lieutenant. It was dated December 2nd, 1972 — within days of my application for an exit visa. This weapon had been held in readiness for a long time.

"You're to report to the Medical Committee, at once."

I went home, too stunned to think. I had fought without let-up for three years. Now I was confronted by ignominious defeat. This time, it would be much harder to call upon help from abroad. Our foreign colleagues could sustain us, could protest when the conventions of the academic community were flouted, or when grave injustices were committed against us. But what defense could they provide against a law that all citizens of this country had to accept?

"The Medical Committee may find you unfit," said Lucia when I told her of my orders. "The hospital has your record." She was clutching at a straw.

"The Medical Committee will find me fit for any service the KGB thinks suitable. There's just no way out of this," I answered. "Whatever comes — let it come." I slumped into an armchair and just sat there, silent. I couldn't move.

Lucia never told me until long afterward how disheartening it was for her to see me defeated; she had been sustained all along by the conviction that no matter what happened I would come up fighting. At that juncture I saw no means of escape, and I couldn't force myself to put up a front of optimism and spirit any longer. The noose was tightening around my neck. There was nothing more I could do.

Victor Brailovsky and a few of my other friends arrived soon afterward to help me with the final arrangements for the anniversary seminar. They were seriously alarmed by my news.

"Look, Mark, there's only one thing you can do," said Victor, "and you've got to hurry. Get out of here. Get under cover for a while. Try a delaying action; gain some time."

The others agreed. After considerable discussion, I decided to take their advice.

It is not so easy to get "under cover" in Moscow. I left home at three

A.M. the next morning, carrying nothing with me, not even my briefcase. Taking two or three successive cabs in order to shake possible surveillance, I went to the apartment of some friends who, although not refuseniks themselves, were totally in sympathy with our battle. They offered me shelter the minute they found me at the door. Not wanting to attract attention as an unregistered guest, nor to endanger my host, I moved from one such friend's place to another's during the next five days. These again are people whose names I won't cite, but whom I will never forget. I must say those were strange days. To be hiding out this way like a gunman in a Mafia war, to be a "fugitive from justice," was something I had never imagined in my whole life.

During that time, Lucia and I could communicate for the most part only through a series of intermediaries, though once or twice when I was staying at the apartment of someone who had an "innocent" telephone, the number was relayed to her via grapevine and she called me from a pay station. She told me that military personnel were constantly appearing at our place in search of me, and that members of the Seminar also were subjected to numerous inquiries about me by military police. All my friends sent messages urging that I leave Moscow: "Go somewhere; go south; get out of the city at least for the time being" was the advice I heard from all sides. I had never missed a single meeting of the Seminar before, and I was extremely reluctant to be away for this special session in April; but it looked as though I had no choice. I let Lucia know that we had better go.

Lucia had to make all the arrangements. Two days after we had decided to leave Moscow, she and I met at the corner of Moskvina and Tchaikovskaya streets at seven in the morning. She and Yulia arrived in a cab according to the schedule she had conveyed to me by our messengers. With me was my host of the night before, Boris, who had insisted upon seeing us off. We were more acutely aware than ever of the risks entailed by going anywhere without a witness to the departure.

"Daddy! Boris! We're going to Odessa!" Yulia announced enthusiastically as we got into the taxi. "Mama thought it would be fun to take a trip! We only just decided this minute; we didn't even pack. Look — we have nothing but this shopping bag!" For fear of the bugs, Lucia had not said a word about the trip until she had coaxed Yulia out of our apartment for an "early walk." Of course, Yulia was delighted by this sudden plan.

At the Kiev Station, we walked warily through the crowd, Lucia keeping an eye on everyone around us, glancing from left to right, left to right. It seemed to us that we had never seen so many policemen. There was one every few meters.

Suddenly one of them came up to us.

"Let's see your papers." There was nothing we could do; we produced our passports. Having checked them, he said: "Right. And now your tickets."

"What do you need to see them for?" demanded Lucia. Our daughter, terrified, all at once started to scream. "You're frightening my child! What do you think you're doing?"

"I have to see those tickets," he insisted, raising his voice to be heard over Yulia's cries.

"What's the reason for this?" Lucia repeated furiously.

"There's been a robbery; the station lockers have been robbed. You're suspects."

"Oh, my God, how ridiculous!" she snapped. "And if I won't let you have the tickets?"

"You'll be detained. You'll miss the train."

Lucia finally produced the tickets, though she would not surrender them into his hands. He calmly made a note of the destination printed on them, the number of the car, and the seat numbers. "That's all right, then," he said, and let us go. We left for the train, perfectly well aware that from now on we would be under unremitting observation. Even before we boarded, we were surrounded by a swarm of KGBsts.

When we got to the coupé in which we had reservations, we were very glad to see that the fourth passenger in it was a perfectly ordinary middle-aged man, with none of the earmarks of a KGBst. But our relief was short-lived. Soon after the train started, the conductress came into our compartment and requested that our traveling companion move to a seat in another section. From the tone of her voice he understood at once that this was an official demand and got up to leave, casting a curious glance at us as he went.

The seat was taken by a younger man in tie and sports jacket, one of those we had seen on the platform. We saw that we would not be able to draw a breath in privacy for this entire journey. I remembered Voronel's escape in Kharkov and realized that the KGB remembered it too; they were not going to allow anything of the kind to happen again.

The strain of being under this man's eye was horribly annoying — we couldn't talk at all. Lucia in particular was irritated beyond endurance. We went into the corridor for a while, but the KGBsts posted there actually huddled around us.

"Get back! Get back!" Lucia suddenly burst out. "Your orders are to check on us — not to smother us!" Astonished, they did move back a step or two, but we were no better off than we had been in the compartment.

We went back in and sat down. The first man, of course, was still sitting there; beside him on the seat was a copy of Lenin — evidently he carried the book with him everywhere. After an hour's silence, Lucia couldn't stand it any more. To the KGBst's surprise, she opened a conversation with him. She introduced herself. He had to reciprocate: Andrei Petrovitch.

"What sort of work are you in?" she asked politely.

"I attend the Highest Party School." The Highest Party School is a very special institution where people are trained for Party service, not only for the Soviet Union but for the Eastern democracies; there are even some students from African countries. People are accepted there only on the recommendation of the senior authorities of their City or District Party Committees. This elite is comprised of those who will be the future leaders of Russia or of their several nations. They study the workings of government, international affairs, and, of course, Marxism-Leninism.

"Oh, I feel so lucky to have met you!" exclaimed Lucia. "I've always had so many questions in my mind about Lenin's writings, and here I find a real expert! What a wonderful chance!" The man at once became extremely uncomfortable.

"Well," he said, "you undoubtedly know a great deal yourself, and I can't call myself an expert on any problems to be found in Lenin." He was actually frightened. Nobody is supposed to ask any questions on the so-called classics of Marxism-Leninism. Every word in them is Holy Writ and beyond discussion or dispute. Teachers of Marxism-Leninism answer the rare, rash questions on their subject simply with the words: "So . . . aren't you expressing anti-Soviet ideas?"

Trapped by Lucia, the young man was evidently very nervous. He was used to playing a predictable sort of game. Ordinarily he would, so to say, *pretend* to explain everything to a person who wanted elucidation on the subject, and the other player would *pretend* to understand, and to be satisfied with the explanation. But he must have known enough about us to realize there was no guarantee Lucia would observe these conventions. He knew that we were taking risks much more serious than those involved in asking the wrong questions about Lenin. Further, to judge by his very jumpy manner, it was obvious that our conversation was being overheard.

Lucia leaned forward and gestured toward his book. "Please," she said, "could you hand me your Lenin?" Andrei Petrovitch reacted with shock. Nobody is supposed to say *"your* Lenin"; it is *"our* Lenin"; everybody's Lenin. But he could not protest; he had to pass the book over. Lucia opened it to the first page, and initiated the attack.

"Here it says," she began, "that it is the workers who should order the State; that any kitchen maid is perfectly able to run the State. What does that mean? Take me: for all practical purposes, I'm a kitchen maid myself. I am a housewife. Am I qualified to order the State?"

"Well, Lydia Semyonovna! In the first place, you're not a kitchen maid," Andrei Petrovitch riposted weakly.

"Well, I am. I'm not a worker; I spend all my time in the kitchen. I understand nothing about the machinery of the State. And do the workers understand it? In Lenin's time, the workers were illiterate. Even now they don't know much about how the government operates. How can they run the State? Do you find any workers in the Central Committee? You'll spend many years in the Highest Party School, learning all this. How could all the complexities of a bureaucracy be learned by a kitchen maid? Do you know of a single kitchen maid in government?"

The man cleared his throat nervously. He had to make the right answer. "Well, of course the workers should run the State," he answered, "because by definition they're the most progressive element in society."

"I don't understand. Lenin was certainly not a worker himself, and who in the government when he was in power *was* a worker?"

The man turned bright red. "Well, you should think it through," he advised.

"Good heavens! You *have* thought it through; why don't you explain it to me? This is such a wonderful chance for me, to have all these things I've never understood explained."

At this point he apprehensively cast his eyes around him as if *he* were the culprit who might be close to arrest, rather than ourselves; abruptly said, "Oh, excuse me! There's something I'm supposed to attend to right now! I'll be back — we'll discuss it later"; and hastened out of our coupé. The minute the door shut, Lucia grabbed the book and leafed through it rapidly to find more ammunition, but she had put the man to flight: we had the coupé to ourselves until late that night.

That didn't mean the corridors were empty of agents. After we had got Yulia into bed and left her for a while so that she could drift off, we were under close observation. The doors of the two compartments on either side of ours were open, and at the entry of each were four agents. We were tailed everywhere we went: one of the men accompanied me even to the lavatory. Never, even in prison, have I been so irritated and uncomfortable.

Once settled in the berth that night, I ran my situation over in my mind. My apprehensions had been increased by observing a police officer, the sole occupant of a coupé at the rear of our car. There would be a stopover in Kiev. If he was aboard for the purpose of making my arrest, I could be removed from the train at that station, when hardly anyone would know about it. Such a maneuver, carried out with a minimum of witnesses, exactly suits the KGB. So it wasn't easy to turn off my thoughts. But knowing I might well need all the rest I could store up, I made myself sleep.

Lucia, too, had seen the policeman and had come to the same conclusion as I about what would happen in Kiev. She couldn't close her eyes. At one A.M. she was startled to hear Andrei Petrovitch climb down from his berth; she felt sure her fears were to be realized. Absolutely involuntarily, "Where are *you* going?" she demanded when he started to leave the compartment. (She had to smile when she told me about that later.) He didn't answer, naturally; simply left and closed the door. But he didn't come back. We stopped at Kiev; Lucia held her breath; no one came in; and after an interval the train started off again. She knew nothing would happen that night, and finally she got to sleep herself.

The next morning, illogically, we felt rather revived and cheerful. Lucia and I were astounded, and laughed very heartily, when at breakfast Yulia suddenly said: "Mama! You told me not to tell anyone where we're going; that I should just say we're taking a trip south. Shouldn't I say that we're going to Israel?"

This shows you how observant children are. For obvious reasons, we hadn't told our daughter that we had applied for Israel, and our friends were warned not to mention it in her hearing. Actually, it seemed to us that we had hardly ever pronounced the word "Israel" in front of her. But evidently, ever since we had applied, she had sensed a journey in the air and felt that by no matter how many detours, we had started on our way somewhere. Despite our cautious silence on the subject, she knew by now that it was Israel. She understood our plans, and we stood corrected, if we thought we could hope to conceal anything from our bright little darling.

That day our KGB guards relaxed their vigilance a little: the trip was coming to an end, and they hadn't lost me. As a matter of fact, I have the impression that all these KGBsts were so bewildered by everything that happened among the refuseniks that they evolved a superstitious feeling about us — anything could happen, with these damn Jews. Once, at the end of an interrogation, a KGB chief said to me sourly: "Well, we know that even before you leave this room, the news of your detention and everything we said here will be broadcast." And it was almost true. When you have supporters everywhere, all over the world; when a whole people sympathizes with you; when your friends never relax their vigilance, nothing is impossible. Even when a blow descends seemingly unobserved, there are always eyes that follow you with con-

cern and love. In the depths of my soul there was always an almost sub-
conscious awarenesss of this constant defense; and in a very real sense,
that is what kept me alive throughout those hard years.

When we got to Chernovtsy in the West Ukraine, where we had been
invited to make a stopover and visit our great friend Fanya Gokhberg,
the KGBsts performed their familiar trick: they disappeared immediately. They have some professional knack of simply dissolving into thin
air; I've never understood it. Within a couple of minutes there was not a
single one left in sight; presumably the Chernovtsy KGB was checking
us, but now the interval of stiflingly close supervision was over. They
knew we had adhered to our travel plan — not backtracked to Moscow
or taken any other unexpected route — and for the time being that was
all they wanted to make sure of.

A day or so later, we proceeded to Odessa. Lucia had made plans for
us to stay in the dacha of some acquaintances of ours, Isaak L——,
Anna Y——, and their grandson Sasha. We didn't have to worry too
much about endangering them by our presence, because Odessa is a
resort town and almost everyone takes in lodgers. If they came under
scrutiny by the police, our hosts would have little trouble dissociating
themselves from us.

The first Moscow news we heard at the end of this trip filled us with
such a strange mixture of terror and pride that I cannot say which feeling predominated. Victor Brailovsky and our friend Professor Ilya Piatetsky-Shapiro were apprehended conducting a demonstration on the
steps of the Lenin Library. With a small crowd of other courageous
people, they were protesting the exile of Mark Nashpitz and Boris
Tsitlyonok, two activists who had recently been brought to trial for a
silent, nonviolent demonstration on behalf of the imprisoned "hijack-
ers."

We were profoundly impressed, Professor Piatetsky-Shapiro, a man
who lived for science and had hitherto kept out of politics, with this
brave action entered the fray in the front lines. For twenty-four hours I
was in anguish, perfectly sure that he and Victor would both follow
Nashpitz and Tsitlyonok into exile — they must have expected it themselves — but the Soviets' wrath proved unpredictable again: it was announced the next evening over the short wave that, after being interrogated, all of our friends had been freed — thank God!

*   *   *

That spring the Crimea was unusually cool but sunny. For a few days
we enjoyed a strangely peaceful interval. We wandered about the town

and by the docksides, and went to the beach, where there was not much of a crowd. I worked on my paper and — for the first time — took a rest from any refusenik activities.

I was in no position then to understand the sudden silence of the Military Department in my case. Our place of refuge was certainly no secret, but so far the army appeared to be leaving me alone. I knew my recall orders had been no mere scare tactic — they had been closing in. Now, mysteriously, days went by without my being called up or arrested. I simply had to summon 'faith that somehow, for some reason, the attack had been diverted.

It was a very long time before I learned why this change came about. Professor Eugene Stanley, upon hearing of my draft call, had sent a furious letter to Academician Keldysh, President of the Academy of Sciences, and strongly suggested that if the Soviets pursued this sort of persecution against me, it might well jeopardize Soviet-American scientific exchanges. Of course I couldn't possibly know of Stanley's championship at the time: all I knew was that there was nothing logical, nothing predictable, in my fate. I could arm myself for battle — and the enemy disappeared. Conversely, I could relax my guard — and out of nowhere a new threat, worse than any I had encountered before, would suddenly confront me.

At all events, I now decided that it might be fairly safe to go back to Moscow; I was willing to take almost any risk in order to participate in the special session of the Seminar, scheduled to begin on April 3rd.

Lucia and I were actually at the ticket booth — I had pulled out my wallet and was counting out our fare — when a KGBst materialized at my elbow.

"You're planning to go to Moscow, Mark Yakovlevitch?"

"Yes."

"Let's just say you've given it a good try." We couldn't go.

We had been in Odessa about two weeks when we got a cable from Fanya Gokhberg. Fanya announced that she and her family had received their permission to leave. I caught the next train back to Chernovtsy, eager to say goodbye to her and also desperate — as everyone is when a friend leaves for Israel — to convey through her as many messages for friends in that country as she could possibly hold in her head.

No one prevented me from going to Chernovtsy, but I hadn't been there long before I received a cable from Lucia, which, although coded in circumlocutions ("Aesopian" language, as we called it) was obviously an urgent appeal for my return. I acted upon it at once. Lucia was on the platform to meet me. "What happened? Police? KGB?"

"Worse." Apparently just as Lucia was seeing me off on the trip for Chernovtsy, the police had come to our rooms. "The minute I got back to the dacha, Anna Y—— told me they had been there, looking for you," Lucia said. "I decided not to let you know right off — I thought you should have a chance to say goodbye to Fanya before you had something else to worry about. But the next morning, I was sorry I hadn't cabled. I was wakened by a knock on the door — it was Isaak, saying: 'Someone is here for you, Lydia Semyonovna.' I could tell by his voice whom he meant, and I was terrified. I only prayed that when I was taken, he and Anna Y—— would take care of Yulia. If they didn't, what in God's name would become of her?" Lucia tried to pull herself together, got dressed, combed her hair, put on lipstick, and went out to meet the foe.

The little dacha was surrounded by a fence. Lucia went to the gate. Our nervous hosts were already there. These people were very sympathetic toward us; they liked us. But if Lucia were arrested, sorry though they might be, they wouldn't embrace her or wish her good luck. They couldn't afford to. They were a quiet retired couple in their sixties. Why should they risk interrogations, surveillance, and troubles with their neighbors that might last the rest of their lives? Although they were present, and very curious to find out what was going on, Lucia knew she could not lean on them at all.

A man awaited her at the entry. "Alexander Ivanovitch Tikhonov," he introduced himself brusquely. "Senior Investigator of the Moscow City Prosecutor's Office. I'm here to see Mark Yakovlevitch Azbel — at once." For a second Lucia was too scared to answer. But somehow the years spent outside the Soviet system had created in her a kind of self-respect, a dignity, that no conventional Russian citizen could maintain. Ironically, we, the refuseniks, the pariahs, were freer in some ways than anyone in the highest echelons of the Establishment. Lucia drew herself up.

"If you address me in that tone, I will not stay here. I will not answer anything."

He was astounded. "Would you tell me, please," he began in a much more courteous style, "where I may find Mark Yakovlevitch Azbel?"

"I don't know. He is away."

"And where?"

"I don't know."

"You're his wife, aren't you? And you don't know where he is?"

"That's right."

Tikhonov looked furious. "He is wanted by the Prosecutor's Office, on charges connected with the publication of a subversive journal. Tell him when he returns to report to me immediately." And he presented her with a summons.

She wouldn't touch it. "He will not report to you," answered Lucia. "If you want to see him, you'll have to serve *him* with a summons."

"And how can I do that, when I haven't been told where he is or when he will be back?"

"That's your business," said Lucia.

The investigator left, in a rage.

Our hosts could hardly wait until his car drove off before they turned to Lucia with open-mouthed astonishment. "How could you possibly speak to the investigator like that? Where did you get the nerve?" asked Anna Y——.

"I couldn't believe my ears," her husband said. Their fifteen-year-old grandson was simply overwhelmed. Never in his life had he imagined a person standing up for his rights before an official.

When we got back to the dacha, I saw that Lucia hadn't exaggerated: Anna Y—— and Isaak L—— really did regard her with absolute awe. And the boy, wide-eyed, assured me that my wife was the bravest person he had ever heard of.

On our way back to our place, we had stopped at the telegraph office and cabled the Brailovskys, asking them to come to Odessa to get Yulia if they failed to hear from us at stated intervals. We used our code; we knew they would understand at once.

Now that we had made sure our daughter was safe, we cautiously began to enjoy our stay in Odessa. We simply had to force ourselves at times to forget our fears, no matter how pressing they were — otherwise we couldn't have held on to our sanity. Would the investigator come back? We made up our minds not to speculate about this prospect. Day after day went by, and he didn't return.

But if I thought Tikhonov had dropped my case, I was wrong.

Arsenal

IT WAS A WHILE before we became aware of the new menace that was gathering force in this part of the Soviet world. We first learned of it when a funny story started circulating around Odessa; fantastically unlikely, but apparently true.

Three KGB agents had recently visited a factory in Odessa; walked into the director's office and demanded to see the Party chairman and the trade union chairman, who of course made their appearance at once. One of the KGBsts opened his briefcase, took out a small metal six-pointed star, and threw it on the desk.

"What is that object, would you tell me, please?

The factory director and the two other bosses turned pale and remained silent.

"What is it? We're asking you!"

The Party chairman, who was supposed to be responsible for all ideological concerns at the works, finally replied, in an almost inaudible stammer, "Well — a — that looks like a — a Star of David . . . the Jewish symbol."

"Right!" said the KGBst. "And this Jewish symbol is being manufactured right here, in this factory!"

"Why, that's impossible!" protested the trade union chairman.

"Impossible, yes; but let's go and see what's going on in the factory," said the agent.

The six men moved through the plant, passing from machine to machine, until one of them suddenly turned and stopped. "Look at this!" In front of him, a worker was operating a sheet-metal punch. From the die, one after another, dozens of Stars of David were pouring out.

After a moment of silent shock, the trade union boss slapped his forehead. "Oh, of course!" he said. He ran over to a nearby lathe that was being operated by a woman and, without waiting for her permission, grabbed her handbag, which was standing on the floor beside her. "Let me show you!" He hurried back to the KGBsts, opened the bag, and snapped it shut two or three times. "You see? Here. The star is a component of the clasp. It's the spring." He showed them the devices that locked the bag: two flat metal cups, inside of which were springs — little hexagonal stars. Quite an ingenious design.

When it became clear that the factory was not turning out Zionist symbols, all six sighed with relief, and the chief KGBst dismissed the trouble by saying, "Well! This isn't *our* problem! It's a problem for the O.B. Ch. S.S. [the department that checks on illegal productions]. It's up to you to report it there."

This was amusing. But a few days after I heard the story, I realized it was a portent of something really serious. When I picked up a copy of the newspaper *Vechernyaya Odessa*, I found on the front page an article on the emergence of vicious anti-Soviet Zionists, Enemies of the People, fomentors of interracial hatreds, with a specific denunciation of one criminal in particular — Lev Reutberg. He was a prominent refusenik who for years had been fighting the same battle here in Odessa as I had in Moscow. I felt sick.

Worse was to come. Day after day, the same paper carried lead articles so hysterical, so irrational in tone and content, that I doubt any Black Hundreds* propaganda could have matched it. Suddenly the poison started flooding in from all sides. A movie, *Tainoye i Yavnoye (Secret and Open)* was shown locally. It was filled with sensational "revelations" about incidents of Jewish treachery in Soviet history. This documentary-style film presented one crazy passage after another, culminating with the disclosure that there had been a link between international Zionism and *Adolf Hitler!* Zionists had inspired and financed World War II and the slaughter of six million of their own people!

This venom, originating in the provinces and destined to pour over the Soviet public — the majority of whom, little literate in history and deep-dyed with a superstitious fear of Jews going back a thousand years — was terrifying. To convince the Russians that Jews were responsible for the War could result in actions against them more violent than any yet seen even in this bloodstained land.

I talked to Victor on the telephone and described the situation here. We both understood that this was an experiment: the authorities were

---

* "Black Hundreds" was the popular designation for the so-called League of the Russian People, a sort of Ku Klux Klan, founded in 1904. The organization was chiefly responsible for the sweeping massacres and pogroms that occurred between that date and 1917. It was heavily supported by Czar Nicholas II.

"trying it out" in the province. If the public would swallow it in Odessa, perhaps the whole nation was ready for this sort of hatred.

I had read anti-Semitic news items ever since I was fourteen or fifteen years old. These articles always opened the way to arrests, to firings, to hostile charges and accusations of every kind. They always heralded the deterioration of the situation of Soviet Jewry as a whole. Of course every Jew felt such attacks as a personal threat, because no matter how high one might be in the hierarchy, one could never be secure. No marshal, no general, could be positive that the Party leaders might not suddenly decide it was for the best to imprison him or kill him.

At present these articles and this film came closer to my own life than any that had gone before. The first victims of the new change for the worse would be the refuseniks — the people who had openly declared that they didn't want to live in Soviet Russia; those who rejected Soviet citizenship.

Had all this happened twenty years before, it would have been the end for Soviet Jewry. Under Stalin, the exile of whole peoples, the existence of millions of people imprisoned and exiled — the whole Gulag Archipelago — remained almost unknown to the entire outside world. Within this nation, nobody protested. Nobody spoke about it. Only a few rumors leaked beyond the borders. Now that there was a chink in the Iron Curtain, world opinion could modify the course of such an onslaught.

Before leaving Moscow, I had got wind of the fact that during this summer of 1975 a number of important Americans were planning to visit the Soviet Union, among them a group of senators who had requested an opportunity to confer with the refuseniks. I had very much hoped for the chance to talk with them. Now with the explosion of threats against Jews, I knew I *had* to be there. For the West to know what was brewing here might be the only hope of safety for hundreds and thousands of people. Without witnesses, a reign of terror actually might be on the way.

I collected the series of articles from the *Vechernyaya Odessa* and set myself to wait for the first possible chance to get back to the capital.

I had another reason, too, for wanting to make American contacts. At that time my mind was teeming with thoughts on the further development of the theory of certain transitions in DNA. Although I had been hit very hard by the rejection of my last paper, I knew that the points I was proving were valid. I simply had to summon confidence from nowhere and continue to write. The work I had in progress at the time was a major piece intended for the American *Journal of Chemical*

Physics. I hoped to get it to the States with one of my American colleagues who was expected to visit in early fall.

* * *

I wasn't prevented from taking the train back to Moscow, for no reason that I can positively identify, though it may have been connected with the forthcoming visit of the American senators, two of whom had called me before telephone contacts were broken. The authorities may not have wanted to be embarrassed by questions as to why I wasn't in Moscow, and the KGB and the military kept at arm's length for a while. Lev Reutberg was also going to Moscow but planned to take the plane. I heard to my horror soon after my arrival in the capital that he was stopped at the airport by police, taken to prison on trumped-up charges of malicious hooliganism, tried, and sentenced to three years. (At this writing, Reutberg has served his sentence but has still not received his exit visa. In the early days of emigration, a Jew who had served a prison sentence on this sort of charge would ordinarily be allowed to leave for Israel when his term was up. This convention no longer obtains. Now there is absolutely no way of predicting when, or if, an applicant will receive his visa, even if he has "paid his debt to society.")

Checking into my mailbox upon my arrival, I saw at once that, though I had not been prevented from returning to Moscow, the authorities would be only too glad if I turned right around and left the city again. There were two summonses awaiting me (both of them brand new — dated the day of my arrival), one to the Military Department and another to police court. Immediately, a third arrived: my presence was demanded at the Division for the Investigation of Most Dangerous Crimes at the Office of the Prosecutor in Moscow. (This corresponds to the Attorney General's Office in the United States.)

I had no time to worry about these warnings. I hurried over to Victor Brailovsky's, where I found a considerable number of our friends. They told me that the senators would be expecting us the next day but one at the Sovietskaya Hotel. We all conferred about what we would discuss with them — if this meeting actually came off. I showed Victor the articles from the Odessa paper; until he saw them with his own eyes he found it hard to believe that such ravings were in print. He agreed that nothing was more urgent than to let the Americans know about this fantastic new threat. We also had to plan details, such as the various routes each of us would take on his way to the hotel, so that if some of us were arrested there might be other "survivors" who would keep the appointment.

On the day in question, I arrived at the suite to which the senators had invited us after a Metro trip on which I would say one in ten of my fellow-passengers was a KGBst; at the Dynamo Station, where I got out, perhaps one in five.

It was quite an event, meeting the Americans. Here were Senators Ribicoff, Javits, Humphrey, Leahy, and quite a few others, whose names were less familiar to me. What an amazing joke the fates were playing in arranging this unlikely conjunction of people! Here was a group of men, among the most powerful individuals in the most powerful country in the world. As important guests of the Soviet Union they were accorded red-carpet treatment: the best suites in the most elegant hotel, every luxury, every service imaginable. They had been welcomed two days before by Leonid Brezhnev. Now, in accordance with their own request, they were to confer about the future of Soviet-American relations with the outcasts, the pariahs of the Soviet world: hunted, jobless, disgraced refuseniks. The Competent Organs had to tolerate this meeting; but they were not likely to forget it.

We practically overflowed the big salon: there were about twenty-five of us, and a dozen of the Americans. No journalists were present: this had been announced as an unofficial meeting, and they had been asked to wait outside.

With few preliminaries, the senators began to question us about the position of Soviet Jews since the breakdown of the trade agreement. We told them what was going on, and I described in particular the sudden outburst of hate propaganda originating in the south.

"My God, that's unbelievable! Tell me, do you think we'll make things worse by taking such a hard line with the Soviets?" one senator asked.

"We certainly do not," I answered. Victor Brailovsky, Professor Fain, Professor Lerner, and all the rest expressed complete concurrence with that opinion. "We're speaking for all refuseniks when we say that we believe economic pressures are the only means the United States can use to improve this situation. We support the policy of America's holding this line, not retreating a single step. While she continues to withhold most-favored-nation status from the Soviet Union until barriers to emigration are lifted, there's hope for us." But we added that, however tough a stance the United States would adopt, we felt it was important for the Americans to convey their decision in the most tactful terms possible. The U.S.S.R. would never jeopardize its authority and prestige by openly bowing to foreign demands. They had to be given every opportunity to change their policies inconspicuously, without being forced to make public the reversal of their plans, or the reason for it. If the Americans emphasized the point that the Jackson Amendment was not something directed specifically toward the Soviet Union, but was an expression of the general American position on human rights, the Russians would feel less resentment and would be more inclined to accept its conditions.

Of course we were not so naïve as to think that the American senators waited for our suggestions before deciding what to do on this issue. But it meant a great deal to us that they expressed the wish to hear our ideas, and that they appeared really interested in the insights we could offer as to dealing with Russian psychology.

After the conference — we talked for about two hours — the newsmen poured in to interview all of us. I remember one correspondent asking me if I didn't fear that the refuseniks would be in even greater danger if the papers made public the names and histories of people who were being harassed, fired, falsely accused of crimes, and otherwise persecuted. Most of us had heard this question before, and we all felt strongly about the answer. "Our only chance of survival lies in being known," I said. "Once we are forgotten, it will really be the end of us."

We left the hotel filled with new hope. This was the first face-to-face interview we had ever had with such a number of important representatives of the American government. It was wonderful for our spirits to see the interest and respect they showed toward our organization.

We were disturbed later to hear that one of the reports on our meeting, Robert Toth's in the Los Angeles *Times,* suggested there were two factions, with differing policies, among the refusenik scientists: Professor Lerner's and Professor Azbel's. We had always worked as a unit, and absolutely nothing mattered to us as much as the cohesion and mutuality we maintained among ourselves. But I suppose there is little interesting or newsworthy in the description of a united front.

Questions

It was only the next day that I found myself in the Prosecutor's Office, having been subpoenaed as a witness for the preparation of charges to be brought in a case the nature of which was not cited.

The scene in which the questioning was to take place was by now a familiar one: the barred windows, the table, the straight chair for my use, armchairs for the interrogators. The senior interrogator was Kudryavtsev, whose name I had heard.

After the usual preliminaries, the duel began. Kudryavtsev started by questioning me about the Seminar. Who conducted it? Who participated in it? What subjects did the lectures cover? How had the Western scientists heard of it? I answered that I had no intention of providing information that was presumably being compiled on a case the nature of which had not been specified.

"The charges that will be brought are against the anti-Soviet activities in general of a certain group in Moscow. We have reason to believe that the Seminar is one of the manifestations of this anti-Soviet activity."

This put me in a bad position.

"I can't give any testimony as to the Seminar. If the Seminar is charged with anti-Soviet activity, then I, as chairman, am charged with the same. That makes me not a witness, but a suspect, in which case I don't have to say anything that might tend to incriminate myself."

One of the officials wrote on the protocol of the interrogation that I had been subpoenaed in the capacity of a witness and noted that I had repeatedly refused to give testimony. This was a criminal offense, and he warned me that I was now subject to prosecution for my silence.

Thereupon I was put through one of those senseless but horribly nerve-wracking sessions of threats and menaces that are a regular part of Soviet legal routine. This one lasted eight hours — eight hours during which Kudryavtsev tried to crush my will and force me to give him the facts about the Seminar. I had to keep silent about everything, even about trivial details undoubtedly known to the KGB. Any one minor bit of information, such as the name of even one participant in the Seminar (and owing to the "bugs" they must have known them all perfectly well), could have been used as an opening wedge for a case to be built up against us.

It is strange that, taking into account the elasticity and irrationality of the Soviet judicial system, such extreme pressure should be applied in order to obtain signed testimony. The authorities will spare no effort to obtain it. Such a document is regarded as an invincible weapon in court even if, as sometimes happens, the signer may repudiate his testimony, claiming that it was obtained under duress. Since in some instances people are imprisoned without warrants and without charges, it seems inconsistent that in others the law should try so hard to obtain written evidence on which to base a process. I assume that it is when an investigation or trial is planned which is bound to attract public attention that the prosecutor goes to so much trouble to observe the letter of the law.

I made my way home that evening hungry, thirsty, and utterly worn out. I was glad to leave Kudryavtsev without an iota of ammunition against the Seminar, but I knew that it was too early to think nothing else would happen. And indeed, only a few days passed before I was summoned again to the Prosecutor's Office. This time the interrogator was none other than Alexander Ivanovitch Tikhonov, whom Lucia had confronted in Odessa. I almost smiled when I caught his name, remembering Lucia's account of how she had stood up to him. But I was not smiling by the end of that session, another day of relentless, uninterrupted probing. I answered only "I don't know," or "I can't remember."

For the time being, that was the end of the interrogations. But we knew that now the Seminar was in real danger. It had evolved into something that cannot be tolerated in the Soviet Union: a free institution.

A few days after the interview with Tikhonov, I was called — for the first time since my application — to the Visa Department, where Colonel Fadeyev, chief of the department, had requested to see me.

He informed me that I was again to be refused permission to go to Israel.

"For what reason?"

"Your security clearance."

"I never had a security clearance," I replied. "My work has never been in an area that required one. And the Visa Department knows it, unless they've forgotten. I was advised here in May of 'seventy-three that the department was aware I had never been in classified work. They told me then that the reason I couldn't obtain permission to leave was a policy against releasing scientists at my level. How could I have received a security clearance since then, when for the last three years I've been in refusal and not attached to any official institution?"

"I'm only telling you what we have been told by the officials of the Academy of Sciences," was the answer. "They know best — I'm not an expert on physics," he added with a smile. It was obvious that the "officials" to whom the colonel referred were not the scientists, but the KGB. There was no point in disputing the matter further.

Just out of curiosity as to how he would answer, I asked Fadeyev how long this new reason for my detention would be in force.

"I can't tell you," he said. "All I know is that you will not be allowed to leave at present, and certainly not this year."

Speaking from my own experience, I would say that a human being is a very funny creature, because this conversation filled me with hope. The very mention of a time limit — that I would *not* be permitted to go this year — created the thought that perhaps I was not actually trapped here forever. I was so cheered that I could not wait for Lucia's return from Odessa — I expected her within a few days — but ran to the telegraph office and wired her the news. I was really excited, more so than if Fadeyev had said, "You'll get your visa next year." Professor Levitch, for one, had heard that promise over and over, and his permission had as of that time been postponed three times in three successive years.

A day or so after Lucia's return we were going through the mail when she encountered something surprising.

"Read this, Mark." She passed me a letter written in a hand I didn't recognize, which began: "Dear Lydia: Reluctant though I am to write on this subject, I feel that we women owe a loyalty to one another, and that it is my duty, however painful, to let you know about your husband's recent behavior . . ." There followed a catalogue of clandestine love affairs, in which I was alleged to be involved, that would have amazed a Don Juan! This missive was signed "A Friend." We burst out laughing. Because my wife's nickname among her friends has always been Lucia, it was obvious from the first that the writer was no one who really knew her. By a simple process of elimination we immediately guessed who had concocted this ridiculous letter.

"The KGBst! Georgi Borisovitch!" we exclaimed, almost simultaneously.

"I just *know* this is his style," Lucia added, reading it over appreciatively.

Due, I believe, to the high fidelity of the "bugs" in our apartment, we never received another such letter. Thereafter our code name for Georgi Borisovitch was "We Women."

During the next six weeks, two incredibly lucky breaks occurred for me. In late August we had an extraordinary session of the Seminar, attended by several American geneticists who had come to Moscow for a Soviet-American Symposium on Biochemistry. Among them were David Baltimore, who soon afterward received the Nobel Prize; Walter Gilbert, from Harvard; Henry Sobel; and Max Gottesman. They gave several talks, which were of the greatest interest to all of us and particularly to me.

Because it was so difficult to gain access to Western scientific literature — all the publications in which any refusenik's work appeared were either unavailable or hopelessly out of date by the time I saw them, and the issues of journals that carried articles about us also were stopped — I had not seen the first DNA sequences obtained by biochemists. The information only started to appear at the time I made my application. This meant I was, in a sense, working in the dark. So the information I gained from these lectures was crucial and timely. Fortunately — or perhaps I should say miraculously — one of our lecturers, Professor Gilbert, the author of a very powerful new method of DNA sequencing, told us about part of one of the DNA sequences obtained by this method. This was very exciting; it meant that for the first time I might have a chance to make a check of the ideas on which I had been working.

I immediately started to study this sequence from the mathematical, or more precisely, from the statistical-physical viewpoint, using my approach. What I had in mind was to develop a method that permitted the learning of information about the DNA sequence from the study of its physical properties. Such a method could be checked only if someone would make the experiment I indicated, with a known DNA sequence. According to a certain model, I could predict the results of the experiment of a certain sequence. Then I could *forget* that I knew them, apply my theory to the results of the calculation, and finally compare them to the sequences Professor Gilbert had provided.

This was not an easy task, because I had to perform by hand certain calculations that involved large numbers and do a series of operations with them. Such figuring takes an enormous amount of time: the work that could have been done by a simple pocket calculator in a few minutes took me several days and gave only the roughest results, very inaccurate. I started to dream of a calculator. Without one it would be almost impossible to make much progress in verifying my theory.

Very soon after this session with the geneticists, there took place in

Moscow a Soviet-American symposium on the problems of solid state physics. This is a field in which I had been much involved, so it was natural that the participants in this symposium made contact with us, and came to our Seminar to deliver their talks. Among them were Professors Joseph Birman and Herman Cummins, from C.U.N.Y., who brought me a present, by far the most wonderful gift I ever received in my life and exactly what I had been longing for: a pocket calculator. This was not so sophisticated a model as to give me definitive answers to my questions, but it was certainly good enough for the preliminary calculations.

I was so happy that nothing bothered me, and I hardly worried when, the day after I acquired my marvelous machine, I received a summons to appear at 24 Kuznetsky Most — the Central U.S.S.R. KGB Headquarters.

I was taken to the office of two high-ranking KGBsts, who delivered to me an ultimatum: if I didn't call a halt to the Seminar immediately, I would be subject to charges of espionage.

When I told Joe Birman of this threat, he was terribly alarmed. "My God!" he exclaimed. "What do you advise us to do? Wouldn't it be safer for you if we didn't return?"

"On the contrary. The only protection we have is to go ahead with our plans. If we surrender, the Seminar will simply cease to exist. They will have crushed us. As far as I personally am concerned — it's the existence of the Seminar that is keeping me out of prison right now." He understood. For the entire remainder of their visit, the American scientists went out of their way to demonstrate their support. The night before their departure they very hospitably invited me out to dinner.

The only thing that saddened me at that party was something that always made my heart sink when I was in the company of foreigners: this was to hear their casual references to their travels. Someone had gone through England on his way from the United States; someone else was going to Japan; still another planned to spend a month in Italy. To be almost perfectly sure that you, yourself, will never leave Russia, never see any part of the world outside of the Iron Curtain, is a singularly forlorn conviction. And by that time, despite all my efforts, a part of my consciousness was quite, quite sure that I was here forever.

We made fast friends with our American colleagues; we felt more stranded than ever when they were gone.

Bad News

OVER THE COURSE of the last year, our group had had a growing concern on our minds: the "drop-outs," the emigrants who were leaving the Soviets, not for Israel but for other countries, principally the United States.

It was not compliance with the legal fiction of application for a visa to Israel while intending a different destination that we found shameful; every emigrant had to do that, be he Russian, German, Lithuanian, or any other nationality. The problem was with reference to those refuseniks who had expressed a fervent loyalty to Israel, a great devotion to the ancestral motherland; those who claimed that this was their sole reason for wishing to transfer allegiance from the Soviet Union. They said they longed to partake of Jewish culture, to work for Israel, to contribute their talents to her.

When people who expressed these strong patriotic sentiments turned out to have America or England or Western Europe as their destination, we were not only disillusioned; we were humiliated. The very possibility of anyone leaving the Soviet Union was due to the heroic efforts of Jews who dreamed of Israel, who sacrificed their liberty, and in some cases their lives, to build the road to freedom. In our opinion, those who rejected Israel cast shame and mockery upon the memory of these people. We couldn't forget that it was Israel — and Israel alone — that had aroused the world's sympathy on behalf of Soviet Jews.

I don't want to discuss the Jews who left Russia for Germany and did everything possible to prove that they were true bearers of German culture, or that Germany should be held responsible for their existence because their mothers had been raped by German troops. I cannot blame individual Germans for what happened in the War, but for a Jew to leave the Soviet Union and pray for a visa to Germany — that was beneath contempt.

Yet this was not the whole problem. If Israel were a prosperous,

flourishing country — if she were a rich nation like Switzerland, for example — I wouldn't feel so strongly about the people who, after loudly
protesting their patriotism, chose to turn around and leave her, to
make their lives elsewhere. But Israel, which is constantly in danger,
desperately needs all the helping hands that are offered. She waited for
the Russian aliyah as for a life-giving transfusion.

Nothing vexed me more than hearing people in our position talk
about what was wrong with Israel: material shortcomings, inefficiency
of one sort or another. We knew Israel was not perfect. We knew that
not every Israeli was an idealist or a hero. Our nation had innumerable
very serious problems, but it seemed clear to me that for this very
reason it devolved upon us to try to alleviate those troubles. To abandon our country in favor of another that offered more goods, more
choices — I couldn't stop feeling ashamed of the people who made this
choice. These same people would run to Israel if the need arose, and if
Israel should ever be annihilated again, the rest of the world would
despise the Jews who let it happen. And they would be right.

We had one other reason for worrying about drop-outs. The Soviet
regime can tolerate emigration when it comes to Jews, but not when it
comes to the other nationalities. If it turned out that many Jews were
leaving for the prosperous United States rather than for troubled Israel,
then all the other Soviet minorities, and even Russians, might claim that
this was not solely a matter connected with the unenviable aliyah, but a
right that applied to everyone. This the Soviets would not stand for.
We were afraid that Jews who left in search not of a decent life but of
a better life might indirectly be the cause of an eventual total ban on
emigration. Circumventing the intention of the laws that cover emigration, they might slam the door behind them on the rest of us.

* * *

To manufacture cheer at the New Year of 1976 required quite an effort.
"Next year in Jerusalem" seemed a dream further out of reach than
ever before.

This year, the authorities evidently decided that the whole Russian
public was ready for the sort of infection they had tested out in Odessa
and other provincial cities. The film *Secret and Open* was shown on na-
tionwide television.

During the previous decade, not one single news item had come out
in any of the media about emigrant Jews. But now stories about them
appeared on TV: of course they were shown as evil people abandoning
the motherland that had nurtured and favored them. These films were
always concluded by an interview with some "tame Jew," as we called

them, usually an artist or performer, well known to the public, who repudiated the traitors and described how happy he was to be in the Soviet Union.

More and more twisted, paranoid propaganda began to pour out of the air waves. The papers devoted lead columns to the "history" of Zionist treachery. Now the entire U.S.S.R. was barraged with pieces on how it was Jewish machinations that brought about the War. The public was asked to believe that it was not so much to imprison and kill Jews that the Nazi concentration camps were built; the principal victims were Communists, Slavs. Zionists had financed Hitler. Zionism and Fascism were essentially the same thing. And, for the first time, we were told that there were Zionists not only in the Western world but here in Russia, in Moscow.

The threat was coming closer. I can't describe the sinking sensation we felt when, one evening while we were watching the news, the faces of two of our friends, Vladimir Slepak and Yosif Begun, flashed up on the screen. The announcer identified them as Zionists bent on the destruction of the Soviet regime and as Enemies of the People. ("Enemy of the People" is not simply a general condemnation: this is a specific category of criminal — the most dangerous, the most despised.) At this writing, both of those gallant men are still in exile.

News articles began to appear, exposing the criminals, traitors, who wanted to leave not for Israel, where they had in fact no relatives, but for the United States, where they wanted to make a lot of money. They didn't care about democracy or humanity or ideals; they were just liars. Everyone who had applied for a visa was affected by the condemnation of the drop-outs, because, as Jews discovered centuries ago, "If Ivan steals, Ivan is a thief; if Abram steals, all Jews are thieves."

Not long afterward, anti-Semitic diatribes began to appear in the samizdat as well as in official publications. This was historically a novel phenomenon. The underground press had never been anti-Semitic, either in Czarist times or in our own. Now there appeared such writings as those of Yemelianov, who was one of the lecturers of the Znania Society, in which he described the Jewish plot that aimed at the domination of the whole world, particularly Russia. Among his claims was the statement that all the American leaders, including the Presidents, were either Jews or Masons who were taking their orders from Jews. He propounded the question "Which will survive, Israel or Russia?" because, he said, the Zionists planned to crush Russia before the year 2000.

That was the extreme right. But even among a large section of the intelligentsia made up by the Slavophiles, you will find an undercurrent of these same thoughts, however modified. In their view, the West is identified with evil. And since they consider Jews to be the bearers and apostles of the Western spirit, they regard Jews as a menace to the true Russian life. They want to get rid of them; if they can't throw them out, they will annihilate them.

The mutual exclusiveness between Russians and Jews makes a certain sense, if you take into account the strangely divided Russian mentality. Two opinions conflict but somehow coexist: on the one hand, Russia is culturally way behind the West. On the other, she has a special spirituality, a depth of faith to be found in no other nation of the world. This conviction of superiority is not an idea imposed by Communism: it is unmistakable in the works of Tolstoi and Dostoievski, and at present of such dissident writers as Solzhenitsyn and Corresponding Member of the Academy Shafarevich, the mathematician. It runs through all strata of society; the theme is reinforced throughout one's Soviet education, where one finds all of Russian history deformed to prove the point.

As the Russians wanted to feel themselves singled out above all others, they were in a kind of rivalry with the nationality declared in the sacred texts of their own faith to be the Chosen People. The Christian philosopher Shimanov actually urges his disciples to reject the Old Testament on those very grounds. Those of Shimanov's persuasion are so desperate to stake a claim to superiority that they are willing to cancel out a great deal of the Christian Scriptures. And such ideas were maintained by a large part of the Russian intelligentsia. This was also natural: to reject any challenge to its own pre-eminence is a survival mechanism for any chauvinistic culture.

To use the language of physics: I would say that Russia is in a certain meta-stable state; that is, a state that is not the optimum but that is very difficult to leave. You might compare it to a powerful human brain, so locked in conflict between beneficent and destructive impulses that it cannot ratiocinate; or better, to the state of a turtle, which is well protected by its shell from all the dangers with which Nature might confront it. But this armor prevents it from evolving. It cannot drop it and start to run: it would lose the protective advantage of the shell and be eaten by others.

Russian literature has always been partly hortatory, didactic. Even the most supremely gifted of Russian writers of the nineteenth century considered themselves to be not only artists, but to some extent teachers, prophets, critics, advisers. In our own time many of the dissenting writers who have come to the West (with the notable exception of Sinyavsky) remain inside Russia in mind and spirit. Many of the Russian-language journals and papers that appear in the West implicitly

represent different parties, some of which hold that Solzhenitsyn is
the prophet, *the* beautiful personality, absolutely beyond criticism.
Subscribers to this faith hold that one cannot find fault with Slavophile
ideas, nor with any sort of dissident. There exists an unspoken party
discipline, in the sense that no ideas outside these schema will ever be
printed in these publications. No other viewpoints will ever be considered. This literature rejects pluralism in favor of a very special, rigidly
delimited approach.

It seems to me significant that these most courageous people, who
deserve the utmost respect — they risked their lives by opposing the Soviet system — have become close to the approach of that very system,
through the absence of democracy; through the absence of pluralism.
By their indifference to the West, by the rejection even of the European
languages, they have voluntarily erected an Iron Curtain around themselves.

This hermetic sealing-off of themselves by some émigré dissidents
from the perfectly accessible world around them strongly suggests that
the intellectual insulation against foreign influences within Russia itself
is not entirely imposed from above. That Russians, even when trans-
planted, even when perfectly free, may create in microcosm a new totalitarianism, with a new prophetic czar, provides us with an insight into
one of the dominant features of the Russian people. This is the belief that
the Truth is unique. When this belief obtains, then this truth must be
imposed on everybody. *How* it should be imposed is a secondary problem. And this is the start of any dictatorship.

In essence, both Solzhenitsyn and the Soviet officials were actually
presenting as an ideal variant kinds of authoritarian states. The great
difference, of course, is that Solzhenitsyn, Shafarevich, and others of
the same mind are absolutely honest. But I think that in their discussions
they do not take into account the real ways of history and of revolution.
They cannot, because as Russians they have been deprived of any kind
of political experience or participation in free political life. One should
not forget: some of the Communists at the beginning of the century
were also men of courage, honor, and self-sacrifice. But the road to hell
is paved with good intentions.

It took two centuries of bloodshed and upheaval before Europe finally became democratic and developed democratic institutions. Russia
never had any experience — except for some short months in 1917 — of
any such political or social experiment; of the need for compromises; of
the necessity for thinking of the consequences of various actions.

That openness to Western ideas, Cosmopolitanism, liberal thinking,
should be considered criminal by the Soviet Establishment was no dis-

covery to us. But that some Russian dissent should share this view was not so easy to accept. Except in the work of Sakharov and a few others, the all-too-familiar xenophobia often seems to re-emerge.

* * *

The television productions were followed by new measures against the refuseniks. For one thing, the use of certificate money was now forbidden. A dollar no longer had the buying power of about four roubles, which it did when changed to certificate currency; it was now worth about fifty kopeks. Families who had survived on fifty dollars a month — with difficulty — were now reduced to penury. The refusenik community, then numbering around three thousand, was confronted by a real threat of starvation. This led to a wave of demoralization; naturally many would-be applicants for exit visas changed their minds.

This problem was especially difficult outside Moscow. It was terribly hard to get help to the refuseniks who were at a distance; all of us who were concerned with their fates had to redouble our efforts.

This was an unexpected drawback. The Soviets, despise us though they might, had at first not despised our money. But now they decided to emulate Catherine the Great: they wanted no profit from the nasty Jews, and they were willing to deprive us even of our means of survival.

This reduction in our resources was not, of course, accompanied by any reduction in the levies imposed upon emigrating Jews: an exit visa still cost 400 roubles; cancellation of one's Soviet citizenship cost 500 roubles. Air fare, including freight charges and various taxes, never came to much less than 500 roubles per person.

Such were the legal costs. But there were other damages, much more vicious. Strange events began to occur; sinister happenings reminiscent of former days in Russian history. An activist named Rubinstein who was planning to attend a refusenik demonstration in Leningrad received a summons to the Visa Department. When he arrived he was met not by emigration officials, but by two KGBsts. They took him into a room apart and sat down with him for a conference.

"We strongly urge that you absent yourself from the demonstration," they said. "We suggest that you change your plans." Rubinstein said he had no intention of following their suggestion; he was definitely going to be present at the demonstration. "Think it over for a while," they said, and left him for half an hour. When, upon their return, he told them he had not changed his mind, they quietly ushered him out.

At the very threshold of the Visa Department, he collapsed. After a few minutes he gathered his forces, rose to his feet, and staggered home. Having been wounded in the War, he had access to the Veterans' Hospital, and he was taken there by ambulance. The doctors who examined him were astonished and baffled: how could Rubinstein have been poisoned? His buttocks and the backs of his legs showed evidence of poison of the ipric type. Soon a couple of plainclothesmen appeared at the hospital, and after a conference with them the doctors changed their diagnosis: Rubinstein was a victim of some rare infection.

I heard about this from Rubinstein himself.

In 1976 news of several other similar events began to circulate among us. I am confining myself here to what I saw myself.

Ilya Levin, another Leningrad activist, a man known to be in close contact with Western newsmen, fell very ill and was hospitalized with a disease none of the doctors could diagnose. At first, they urged him to confess to some strange addiction — his system was full of a chemical that defied analysis. It was months before he could walk again.

The dissident novelist Vladimir Voinovitch, after a conference with the KGB (he had been called in to discuss "the possibility of a lightening of censorship" — and was naïve enough to accept that invitation), was horribly stricken after his interview. No one ever knew what had happened to him. It was evidently not poison, but, to judge by the description he gave us of his symptoms, he might have been subjected to a high-frequency ultrasonic radiation.

Broader Horizons

OTHER SEMINARS besides ours came into being, in various fields. There was one on history and philosophy that was chaired first by Vitali Rubin and the cartoon scenarist Felix Kandel, and later by Arkady Mai. There was also a very active seminar in Riga conducted by Dr. Gurfel and Professor Tsinober, and another in Kiev by Dr. Kislik. The authorities directed their tactics against these groups as they did against ours, but the others proved to be as stubborn as we were.

Just recently the Kiev paper had charged Dr. Kislik with espionage. The publication by refuseniks of scientific papers abroad, which at first went unpunished, could now be a very serious offense.

Any of us might become the next target, and we lived under almost intolerable pressures all the time. But there was nothing we could do except go on with our work; and I continued to do my research on DNA sequencing.

The general outlines of the problem on which I was working became clear by means of the little calculator I had been given, but the time came when I needed a real computer. One of my physicist friends — a man who had not applied for an exit visa — was willing to perform these calculations for me on the machine available to him at his institute. I owe him infinite gratitude.

I worked feverishly, trying to check my theory, and, as usually happens when such an experiment is made for the first time, many obstacles cropped up. Still, it was very exciting to perform this imaginary experiment; I felt increasingly hopeful that I would be able to validate my theory. These were most interesting days for me.

At the same time, our Seminar attracted more and more foreign guests. These visitors were very varied. I can give the reader only a most fragmentary idea of who came and what they talked about — it would require an entire catalogue to cover everyone.

One was the writer Herbert Tarr, a best-selling author and a rabbi who had been a chaplain in the American army, who read us excerpts from his autobiography. This was, on the surface, a humorous book. But when he had read us a few pages, he was astonished by our silence. Nobody even smiled. The passage he had chosen was about the bar mitzvah of a very retiring boy, almost pathologically shy, who was so smitten by stage fright at the prospect of standing up before the congregation that the ceremony looms up ahead of him as the most terrifying ordeal imaginable. In the coaching sessions, the rabbi offers to make it easier: he will omit the requirement of a speech; all the boy has to do is read this portion of the Prophets. But the child, although almost paralyzed with fear, insists upon taking on the challengely entirely. When the time comes, the whole synagogue, aware of the young speaker's difficulties, listens with strained attention and utmost sympathy as the boy, standing before them, grapples with this important rite of passage. No one will permit anything to interrupt his talk; not a whisper nor a laugh can be heard throughout the building. Even when one of the listeners breaks a string of pearls, which roll in every direction all over the floor, no one will stoop to pick them up. Supported by the kindly concern of every person in the congregation, the boy triumphs over his handicaps and becomes a successful bar mitzvah.

We were so touched by the description of these people's support of the painfully shy boy that we simply couldn't respond to the comic bits in the story. In our Soviet experience, we had never seen this kind of generous attention paid to a person who deviates from the norm. In Russia, no one who differs from others is allowed to forget it for a minute, even if the difference is a trivial one. Starting from your earliest days, when you are tightly swaddled, you are bound in every way throughout your life. If, for instance, a child is left-handed, no matter how much of a torture it may be for him, he will be taught and chastised and mocked until he becomes right-handed. Children who have physical or mental problems of any kind are simply out of luck. No one will tolerate their differences.

So we listened to Rabbi Tarr's account as seriously as if we were hearing about a sort of miracle. It gave us a feeling of hope, because we thought that if such people as these were fighting for us, we could not lose our battle.

Another Seminar meeting that made a profound impression on us was the one at which the speaker was Dr. Irving Greenberg, American scholar of Jewish history and philosophy. He gave us a talk on the philosophical and perhaps even the mystical meaning of modern Hebrew history. He felt that the events of the past thirty years had in a way recapitulated, encapsulated, all of Jewish history. The Holocaust could be compared in the magnitude of its horror only with the destruction of the Temple. But the very same generation that survived it saw the miracle that Jews had dreamed of for two thousand years: the creation of Israel. And now, we are witnessing the return of the Jews to Israel, and — though coincident with the assimilation, and the abandonment of their Jewishness, by hundreds of thousands — the revival among countless others of the Jewish spirit. Dr. Greenberg pointed out to us how extraordinary it was to behold and to be, in however minuscule form — like drops of water reflecting the sun — part of this miracle.

I remember too the visit of Chaim and Yaffa Gunner from Massachusetts. They stayed for dinner after their talk. Lucia and I were fascinated by their discussions of problems incredibly foreign to our experience, most notably the American movement for women's liberation. Yaffa Gunner was an enthusiastic feminist — the first I had ever met. In the Soviet Union, although the very topmost stratum of the political, military, and professional hierarchies is a man's world, throughout almost the entire rest of society I saw no sex discrimination in the work force. It astonished us particularly to hear that in America women were agitating to be accepted in heavy and dangerous occupations. Here, no employment — including any kind of construction work, road work, and so on — was considered too tough for women. For many decades women had been under the double burden of holding down these heavy jobs and maintaining their family life. Most of them dreamed of a time when they might be able to bring up their children, run their households, and perhaps have enough leisure so as not to lose their youth and looks prematurely from constant overwork. Russia has a long-term inoculation against this aspect of the feminist movement. But even so, it was very interesting to hear about what was going on in the United States and to marvel at the chasm between our two societies.

Other visitors were Dr. Jeremy Stone and his wife. Jeremy is the Director of the American Federation of Scientists, and he told us about the structure of that organization. He ventured little comment on our Seminar, and we had no way of knowing what he thought of us until, after his return to America, we found he had energetically taken up our cause and become one of our most effective supporters.

Not all of our guests were important or influential. There were students, travelers, and people who just dropped in to ask if there was anything they could do to help us. I hope they have some idea of how glad we were to welcome them. One of the first of these, a man whom I will never forget, was a young Frenchman, Alfred Ramani, just beginning his doctoral studies in physics. He called upon us several evenings in succession in 1976, and we talked about everything. When he heard that almost no mail addressed to me from abroad had been delivered since my application for an exit visa, he offered to put into effect a scheme by which he might force the resumption of this service.

When he returned to France, Alfred set himself to write me a spate of very innocuous letters — seven or more a week. He mailed them registered, special delivery, with a return receipt requested. When he had mailed about fifty letters, he went to see the postal authorities in Paris to complain about the absence of receipts. After many objections and delays, they paid him compensation, half of which was provided by the French post and half by the Soviet, in accordance with the international regulations. After this process had been repeated several times, I began to receive his letters. Being forced to disburse, the Soviet post had very probably brought the matter to the attention of higher officials. Threatened by this unwelcome attention (not to mention the expense), they evidently thought it best to permit the delivery of at least these particular letters. My censor must have been reprimanded: later, a trickle of foreign mail began to come in.

Alfred got in touch with French scientists, and it was owing to his efforts that many of them first heard about our situation and began to interest themselves in our struggle.

Of course, not the seminars nor our work nor our frustrations and longings were the sole business of our lives. We had our joys as well. One high point that year was the marvelous occasion when another of our lecturers, a rabbi from New York, performed the Jewish wedding ceremony for Yuli Kosharovsky, one of the longest-term refuseniks we knew. Kosharovsky had applied in 1970, left Sverdlovsk for Moscow in hopes that his chances of obtaining an exit visa would be better here, had fallen in love, and wanted to be married in the Jewish faith. This was one of the most joyful weddings I ever attended in my life. It took place in Yuli's one-room apartment, packed with all his friends.

I had never actually been to a Jewish wedding before. We all sang Jewish songs, and danced. The rabbi spoke of the special circumstances of this wedding; and when, according to tradition, the wine glass was crushed underfoot as a reminder, I was told, of the destruction of the Temple, no one there could remain unmoved. We all thought of the Jerusalem where we hoped to be together again some day. We felt closer than any family.

Yuli and his wife, now the parents of a small baby, are still in the Soviet Union.

* * *

In the early autumn of 'seventy-six, Victor Brailovsky and I began to make plans for a special seminar we would conduct in March of the following year. This would be the fifth anniversary of the beginning of our Sunday Seminar, and we decided to make it an international occasion. Because of the fiasco that had occurred in 1974, we agreed that this time we would not publicize our plans in advance. We would invite Western scientists but not announce anything special about the actual date until the time came. We started preparing our abstracts and papers, and began to devise routes through which we would send out our invitations.

At about the same time, Veniamin Fain, who had always felt very strongly about the suppression of Jewish identity in this country, began to organize an International Symposium on Jewish Culture, to be held in December. Professor Fain's plan attracted a great deal of interest on the part of the Jewish intelligentsia all over the country, and before the entire agenda was completed he had on his organizing committee not only all the people regularly involved in our Seminar and at least ten other notable Moscow refuseniks, but scholars from Leningrad, from Riga, from Vilnius, Minsk, Kiev, Tbilisi, and other cities. Invitations to take part in the symposium were accepted also by a tremendously impressive list of scholars, clerical and public figures abroad, among them Elie Wiesel, Charles Liebman, Telford Taylor (the chief prosecutor at the Nuremberg Trials), and the historian Shmuel Ettinger.

The subjects to be covered at this session were strictly limited to Jewish culture and tradition. Papers were accepted on languages and dialects, on the spiritual and cultural influences affecting Soviet-Israeli Jews and Western Jews, on the role of the family in the maintenance of national traditions, and so forth. Seventy-seven papers were eventually accepted. These were scholarly, sociological, historical in character — scrupulously nonpolitical.

I have to admit that, although of course I joined the organizing committee for this symposium, I was very doubtful as to its chances of actually coming off at that tense and hostile time. Although the government was by now willing to make a few perfunctory gestures about admitting that Soviet Jews really did exist, and had permitted visitors' visas to a few foreign rabbis, all of us saw these courtesies as token attempts to make a favorable impression abroad. The great majority of Soviet Jews were still terrified of becoming involved with the resuscitation of Jewish tradition in this country, fearing the familiar reprisals and repressions.

In June, while we were in the midst of all our plans for both of these conferences, Victor Brailovsky's work was abruptly interrupted for a day.

He was on his way to my place one morning when he was picked up by a police car, driven to headquarters, and told by an officer there that he was among the suspects in a case where one member of a crowd conducting a refusenik demonstration had insulted, struck, and spat upon a policeman.

"The policeman will be here shortly to make identification," he was told. There was no line-up: Victor was the only civilian in the office. He was kept waiting for three hours, during all of which time he was interrogated about his connections with the Seminar and with *Jews in the U.S.S.R.* Naturally, he answered next to nothing. Then he was driven to another police station and made to wait two more hours. Finally, the man whom he was suspected of attacking arrived to make the identification.

"You wouldn't have believed it, Mark," Victor said. "The policeman was almost a foot taller than I am — an absolute monster. It's just impossible to imagine anyone asking for trouble from that man." After studying Victor conscientiously for several long minutes, the giant smiled. "No, that's not the guy," he said, and they let Brailovsky go.

The circumstances of Victor's arrest that time were rather more bizarre than usual, but I could never enumerate the many episodes of a similar sort that occurred to all of us: incidents that constantly impeded our lives; that turned each hour into a nerve-wracking game of hide and seek. You couldn't shrug off this sort of harassment, because there was no telling when a grotesque annoyance might turn into something a thousand times worse. You couldn't predict such a happening, nor could you foresee the outcome: Would you be back on the street at the end of the day — or in Lefortovo? I might just mention that, after our first year or two in refusal, many of us had aged in appearance far beyond our chronological ages. Western correspondents in their news reports often commented on how much older we looked than we were. To be on one's guard night and day, never knowing what trip-wire might lie in one's path ahead, took a great deal out of us. I remember hearing that during the Great Purge, the victims' first sensation upon being arrested was one of tremendous relief; and I had had the same feeling myself when I was taken in 1974. There is no worse strain than to be constantly aware that it *might* happen; that it probably *will* happen — but not to know when.

Within about forty-eight hours of his day-long detention, Victor was summoned to the Visa Department. I waited for him all day, completely unable to concentrate on anything. What would the emigration officials have to say to him? I longed to hear good news. What a tremendous joy it would be to know that everyone in that family, from Irina Moiseyevna to little Dahlia, was finally safe! But I couldn't help dreading the prospect of their departure, too. Voronel was gone; if Brailovsky left as well, my remaining friends and I would feel more than ever like castaways watching the rescue ship depart, leaving us behind. Victor and I had become the closest of friends. Moreover, I couldn't imagine anyone else with whom I could work so harmoniously.

When at last I saw him, I found him pale, ashen.

"What did they say?"

"They gave me permission to go. I may have my exit visa."

"Thank God!"

"But not Irina."

I was perfectly stunned. "What reason did they give you for that?"

"Her security clearance." Irina was in the same position as I: she had been given a fictitious security clearance, subsequent to applying for her visa.

"And Leonid?" Victor's son was by now very close to draft age.

"He'd be permitted to go with me. But I haven't any intention of going without Irina."

We all discussed the situation from every angle during the next few days. I urged Victor to go: in Israel he would have more leverage with which to fight for Irina's release than if he stayed here and continued struggling from within the trap. It was a cruel choice for them to have to make, but in the end Victor adhered to his original intention.

He remained. At this writing, he and his family are still in Moscow.

What was the meaning of these two successive tortures, the latter so profoundly agonizing? Perhaps the authorities wanted a record on the police blotter that Brailovsky had been detained for a day. Perhaps the Visa Department wanted to be able to say that Brailovsky had been offered the chance to emigrate and had declined it. Probably we'll never know.

*　*　*

The summer of 'seventy-seven came. Our plans for the Fifth Anniversary session of the Seminar were coming along very well, and many

Western scientists had accepted our invitations. To free my mind for an interval and to give myself time to work on my calculations, I planned to go with my family to Odessa again for a vacation. Actually, while I was in refusal, the summers were almost the only time in which I could do my own work. The conferences with people considering emigration, the work on the Seminar, assembling material for *Jews in the U.S.S.R.*; fighting for our own release and for that of other refuseniks, from September through June, left me very little time for science. I treasured the short summer months.

But I now felt more rushed than ever. If our plans to conduct an international Seminar, or indeed, if Professor Fain's proposed Symposium on Jewish Culture, were to be sabotaged, I might never be able to complete the series of formulations I was evolving. In view of these two oncoming events the danger of being arrested was much greater than ever.

That summer I hardly saw the sea in Odessa. Victor had received a second and more sophisticated computer, a Hewlett-Packard 67, from one of the delegations that visited us late in the winter. Then Voronel handed over to me a long-awaited Texas Instruments 52. I was working constantly on the computers. I learned them perfectly, and I forced the TI52 to work for six or seven hours, without a break, on the program that I inserted into it. I utilized its possibilities by 200 percent! — making it perform way above and beyond the capacities described in the manual that came with it.

By the end of the summer, after many frustrations, I began to see that the predictions of my theory were in numerical correspondence with the results of the computer. It was great fun and a great satisfaction. Now I was able to start writing my paper on this development.

* * *

Just before we left Odessa, we heard news of the Helsinki Agreement.

We were very skeptical, but still ventured to think that, as this agreement was signed by the Soviet Union and published in the newspapers here, it might help our cases at least a little bit. One of the stipulations concerned the right of people to join their families. Since I in particular had a son in Israel, I felt Lucia and I had new grounds for hope.

(Despite the KGB's having cut off all the telephones on which we had made contact with Israel, we had evolved a system by which we could, just occasionally, still receive calls on "innocent" phones. I will not go into detail as to how we managed this, whose phones we used, or how we conveyed their numbers to the callers, but two or three times during the past year I had talked to Vadim. It was a milestone in my term of refusal to recognize from the timbre of his voice that I was now talking not to a small boy, but to someone in early manhood. A strange and sad feeling, to have your son go through these decisive years and to have no part in his life.)

*   *   *

When we arrived in Moscow, my friends and I formed a delegation of refuseniks to storm the citadel of the Central Committee once again. This time we wrote a request in advance for a hearing by someone in authority to whom we could present our specific complaints as to the prerequisites for emigration demanded by the Visa Department, which were impossible to fulfill. Also, we wanted to inquire whether our status might not have changed, in view of the Helsinki Agreement.

To our astonishment, this time we walked into the building — about sixty of us — unhindered. This was something new and encouraged us to hope that official policy toward us might have changed. Rather than finding ourselves rounded up and imprisoned, we were told that we would be received by the Chief of the Administrative Department of the Central Committee, Comrade Albert Ivanov. They ushered a few of us, the spokesmen whom the whole group of refuseniks selected to take part in this interview, upstairs to a large conference room, where we were met by Colonel Obidin, then Chairman of the Visa Department of the Soviet Union, as well as by Comrade Ivanov.

We were Victor Brailovsky, Yuli Kosharovsky, Vitali Rubin, Vladimir Slepak, Alexander Lerner, and myself.

Ivanov was a stout and ruddy person, genial in appearance, with a permanent smile on his face. Obidin made quite a contrast: thin, angular, with sharp narrow eyes, which he raised only occasionally from the sheaf of papers on the table before him, to cast a calculating glance at each of us.

We made the most of this rare opportunity to present our grievances to someone in power. But when the two officials rejected all our observations and protests one after the other — perfectly politely, but blankly indifferent to the reasoning behind our claims — we began to realize that this reception was nothing but a pro forma gesture, probably conceded for the benefit of the Western press, which was interested in the fate of our delegation. Obidin told us that the provisions in the Helsinki Agreement referring to the reuniting of families actually *narrowed* our chances of emigration, rather than broadening them; the Soviets insisted that "family" comprised absolutely no one but next of kin. This interpretation of that section of the agreement nullified the claims of many, many applicants.

Not yet willing to accept the real nature of this interview, I brought up another urgent problem.

"Quite a few of us have been advised that we have security clearances, about which we knew nothing until after we made application for Israel. We would like to know who makes decisions on this point, and to request a chance to speak with them."

"Nobody will be allowed to see the committee that made these decisions," said Ivanov. "It would be unthinkable to dispute a policy determined by one of our Soviet scientific institutes. Moreover, the reasons for establishing such a policy are always confidential."

Silenced on this issue, we brought up another.

"The requirements made by the Visa Department as to the consent of parents, or of former spouses, is an extremely critical one," said Slepak. "Very obviously, the old people may withhold consent because of fear. A divorced person may do the same from motives of revenge, even if he or she is financially independent of the person who's trying to emigrate."

"Why, we understand that," answered Ivanov, smiling more genially than ever. "But that's your own private business! Why should we *help* you leave the Soviet Union? Certainly we demand the consent of these family members. We will continue to demand it."

In short, absolutely nothing came of our meeting. "I suggest that the members of the delegation you represent send in to the Visa Department requests for the reconsideration of their applications" were the only encouraging words we heard from Ivanov. I, at least, put little stock in that invitation.

We were met outside the building by our refusenik friends and by a group of correspondents from Western newspapers; I think I remember Robert Kaiser, among others, in the crowd. We all moved a few blocks away, to a nearby square where the memorial to the soldiers who were killed a century ago at Shipka, in Bulgaria, stands. We gathered at the benches there and began to describe to everyone all the details of this meeting.

As a matter of fact, just this gathering in the square was a completely novel occurrence in Moscow. Although the Soviet Constitution provides for the right of peaceful assembly, this right is never exercised with impunity. There were plainclothesmen all around the fringes of our group; but since there were a great many people present, and many of them foreign newsmen, we ignored the KGBsts. We plunged in and started to discuss all our next moves.

Many of those who were there immediately decided to resubmit their applications for visas. I had felt that this idea was merely a talking point — something to keep us quiet for a while — and I didn't attend to it myself until some weeks later, when a friend of mine told me that the day he appeared at the Visa Department with his own renewed request, the officials there asked him why Professor Azbel hadn't reapplied.

At this news I have to confess that something inside me stopped for a minute. Long-suppressed hopes were awakened, and I thought: Maybe that's a sort of hint; maybe this time the application will lead to permission. I mention this just to show how desperate I was at the time. I wanted to believe something I knew I shouldn't believe, something that was sure to be just another mockery the officials had concocted with which to plague us. But, like the others, I submitted my new application.

Nothing came of it.

Under Fire

W HEN AUTUMN CAME, the International Symposium on Jewish Culture and the jubilee session of the Seminar were approaching. Official attempts to abort both of these events started almost simultaneously.

On November 22nd, *Izvestia* published an article entitled "The Formula of Treachery." This was the story of a scientist turned traitor to science and to the Soviet Union: Alexander Voronel. It told how he had started a subversive political organization, using science as a "front" or "cover"; made an attempt in 1974 to attract international membership and support; failed dismally; and went to Israel. This heavy-handed warning to our Seminar must have baffled many of the paper's readers. If the organization in question had been forced to disband two and a half years ago, and the villain of the piece had left the country in defeat, what was the relevance of this news item now? The story would have been incomprehensible to anyone other than the refusenik scientists and their associates.

Then on November 23rd, the KGB started vicious attacks on the forthcoming Jewish symposium. Almost all those connected with it were raided; their apartments were searched, and their precious books were confiscated. The next day many of our friends were mourning their treasures: the works of Martin Buber, Cecil Roth's *History of the Jews,* Einstein's *My People,* Hebrew textbooks and grammars.

All this gave rise to a great deal of adverse publicity in the Western press. Shortly, the Russian papers suddenly put on a campaign, attempting to convey the idea that Jewish culture was flourishing in the Soviet Union. But at the very same time, there was an increasing number of interrogations in the Prosecutor's Office and by the KGB. Dozens of people who were associated with Professor Fain's symposium or with *Jews in the U.S.S.R.* were hauled in and threatened with long-term imprisonment.

By mid-December, many of the people from Riga, Leningrad, and other places who tried to get to Moscow to attend the symposium were rounded up on various charges and put under house arrest. The prospective foreign visitors were notified that they would not receive entry visas.

Life Sentence

I COULD FEEL the net closing in, and I started to work more feverishly than ever on my unfinished paper; I would have hated to be arrested before I had completed this work. I spent several days on end at my desk, refusing to answer the door or permit any sort of interruption. On December 16th, at around ten in the morning, my doorbell started to ring, over and over. Lucia and my daughter were out for the day. I let it ring and went on writing. The bell became more and more insistent, and finally sounded uninterruptedly for minutes on end. It was obviously the KGB, but if I answered it after such a long interval, I felt I would put myself in the wrong. I stubbornly refused to open. Finally, heavy footsteps pounded up the stairs and there was a loud knocking on the door across the hall. I heard the voice of our neighbor, the woman whom Lucia and I suspected of being an informer.

She answered the inquiries. "Professor Azbel? No, I haven't heard him go out. He must be at home." At once, there was a prolonged banging at my door. My back was up. Nothing would have made me open it.

The siege went on without let-up almost all day. Such persistence is unusual for the KGB; they usually operate more patiently, knowing it will be easy enough to pick up their quarry sooner or later.

In the evening, when it was finally quiet and I had finished that day's quota of work, I decided to go out. When I opened my door, I found a perfectly enormous summons tacked to it. I hadn't realized these documents were printed in different sizes — this one could be read a block away!

The following morning, feeling that I might as well respond to the summons by myself as under police escort, I made my way to KGB Headquarters at Kuznetsky Most. At the entrance to the building I was met by a broad, round-faced man wearing a "pirozhka" hat.

"Good morning, Mark Yakovlevitch," he greeted me. Noting my

blank expression, he identified himself. "Don't you know me? I am Georgi Borisovitch." This was the man who had shadowed Lucia while I was in prison in 1974. I couldn't help being amused: he looked almost offended. For a moment he hadn't taken into account that his only association with me over the years had been to tail me from a distance, so that whereas I was perfectly familiar to him, he was not to me. "Very nice of you to come," he said, and ushered me through the huge felt-covered doors of an office I had not seen before.

The man who met me in this office was evidently someone in very high authority. Georgi Borisovitch did not step over the threshold when I went in, but bowed politely to this august personage without raising his eyes. I heard later that the man who interviewed me was the chief liaison between the KGB and the Central Committee. He was a tall, slender, mustached man with long, elegant hands — completely unlike any KGBst I had ever seen before. I would have taken him for a professional of some sort, perhaps an academic; he had absolutely no resemblance to the gray robots with whom I had previously had dealings.

The double doors closed silently.

There were two massive desks arranged so as to form a T. On the bigger desk was a row of telephones. He introduced himself with a polite bow: "Sergei Ivanovitch Gavrilov." He urged me to take off my coat and to be seated in one of the comfortable armchairs. Noticing my briefcase, and immediately realizing the reason I had it with me, he reproached me.

"You're a great deal too cautious, Mark Yakovlevitch! I'm surprised. We're here for a conference." He paused. "Now let me ask: Would you like to have an official talk, or would you prefer an unofficial discussion?"

"Well, as I don't know exactly what we're going to talk about, I can't answer that question."

"I suggest we make it unofficial, in any case," he said. To demonstrate the informality of the occasion, he sat not at the head of the huge desk, but right across from me, in another armchair. He must have made arrangements for us to talk without interruption, because during the entire interview all the telephones were silent, and no one came to the door.

"If we're supposed to have an unofficial discussion" — I made caveat — "I'll assume that you will spare me the demagoguery I usually have to hear in these offices. I hope I won't have to be told that our science Seminar is a group of subversives, or that our meetings are just camouflage for anti-Soviet activity, and so forth."

Sergei Ivanovitch smiled. "Very well, I'll accept your suggestion. Now let's begin. I want to inform you first that your case has been very thoroughly gone into; carefully and attentively considered. I ought to let you know before we go any further that you will never be allowed to leave the Soviet Union."

Occasionally during the past four years I had been submerged by the fear that I might never leave Russia. But to have this foreboding confirmed by an official whose authority I could hardly doubt stunned me for a long, horrible minute.

I drew a breath and tried to rally. "I hope you're aware that my work has never required a security clearance," I said. "Everything I've written is in the open literature. I've never been involved in classified work. You know that?" He didn't even try to back up the fiction that the Visa Department had concocted for me.

"Yes, certainly, I know that."

"Then why should I be detained?"

"Well, Mark Yakovlevitch, you should understand the real situation. We've inquired about you among the scientists whose opinions count. All of them spoke very highly of you and of your scientific activity — too highly for your present purposes. You're now only forty-four years old; you're in a period of very considerable productivity. We know about your publications." (He was referring to the papers in *Biopolymers,* the *Physical Review Letters,* and the *Journal of Chemical Physics;* no subsequent work of mine was yet in print.) "We cannot allow a scientist of your standing to leave the country. It's time for you to face the fact that you're not going to go." For a moment I couldn't answer. "You should adjust yourself to that prospect," he continued. "We don't intend to bother you unless you put us in a position where we have to. You should be reasonable. You should begin to sever some of your contacts. Quite a few of your present associates are nothing but hooligans — just kids."

"You're talking about my friends."

"Not really! Not really! I know who your real friends are, and I'm not referring to them. I mean the crowd who are always organizing demonstrations, always making trouble for us. Actually — what do you have in common with these people? No, Mark Yakovlevitch! They're not your friends. And in any case that's not the point. Now let me explain why I wanted to see you. I feel we could come to a sort of gentlemen's agreement," he said.

Without a moment's hesitation, I concurred. "All right. I assume we might have a gentlemen's agreement." It was fun to observe the interest and surprise of this self-possessed person at what he obviously felt to be my quick capitulation. He hadn't expected it. He was certainly a very intelligent man: this was the first time I'd had an opponent in these offices with whom it was worthwhile to make contest. I lit a cigarette, and gave myself a minute in which to gather my forces.

"Our agreement will be as follows," I said. "Up to now, I have taken part only in those activities from which I could not refrain, on principle; in activities that I considered absolutely essential. My own priority, as you certainly know, is science. And I have been deprived of my work. I have not been able to pursue my science. When I applied for my exit visa, I was willing to lose the possibility of free work in science for several years. I knew you wouldn't let me go without using my case to scare my colleagues, but I hoped it wouldn't be for more than three years. I thought that after the hunger strike, after the imprisonment, and after everything else that happened, you would feel that those who could be scared by my example *would* be scared, and that I had served your purpose. So I assumed you would let me go. I've been waiting over four years. Now you tell me that my detention will be lifelong. I can assure you that I won't remain in Moscow for more than a year."

"What do you mean?" asked Sergei Ivanovitch. "I don't think your plans are independent of us."

"Indeed they are," I answered. "I started out by accepting your offer of a gentlemen's agreement. But the agreement I have in mind is rather a one-sided one. From the very beginning of my struggle for an exit visa I made up my mind that the outside limit for waiting would be five years. That leaves me about a year to go. During this time, I won't increase my activity. However, I won't change the nature of what I am doing. But when my deadline is up, I'll consider that there remains no possibility of returning to real science any more. Therefore, I'll have nothing to lose. I'll become an extremist of a sort you haven't dealt with before. You'll encounter some new troubles, which, I assure you, you don't anticipate. Either you'll have to let me go, or you'll have to imprison me for a long term; you won't have any other choice.

"You seem to know a lot about me, Sergei Ivanovitch. You probably realize that I'm not lying. Obviously I have no desire to spend a long time in prison, but still less do I desire to spend the rest of my life the way I do now. So there are the alternatives for you. Which do you prefer: simply to let me go, or to create another martyr to arouse the sympathies of the scientific community? It seems to me that in this case our interests coincide."

He raised his eyebrows. "In exactly what sense is this a gentlemen's agreement?" he asked.

"I will pursue exactly the same activity I'm working on now — nothing less but nothing more — and you will refrain from creating interference."

"What do you mean by interference?"

"I mean anything that takes me away from my science. I'll go my regular way for eight months. After that — or before that, if I'm harassed and deprived of my working time — I'll take extreme measures. You mentioned the people who organize demonstrations; you say they're just kids. Well, I'll be much more of an extremist than they are, and I'm not a kid . . . Just think it over."

It was not a poker game; he could see I meant it and that I was desperate. He stared at me for a while, without saying anything. "All right," he answered finally. "I think I understand you. But meanwhile, Mark Yakovlevitch — you should be reasonable. For instance: about this Jewish symposium. If you dissociate yourself from it, that will simplify our decision. As to the international session of the Seminar: cancel it. At least get out of the active organizing." His voice took on a very emphatic tone as he assured me: "You'll never regret it. Disentangle yourself from those causes. You don't have to do it overnight. But get out of everything — gradually."

I sighed. "Sergei Ivanovitch, do I look to you like a fool?"

"Not at all. Why do you say that?"

"Well, you're proposing that I abandon my friends, lose them — not to mention what else I would lose — and cooperate with you. But have I passed all this way in order to be linked with you? What would I do it for? Why did I lose everything? Certainly not in order to find myself in the end — one of your people."

"That's not what I'm proposing," he protested.

"No, not in so many words. But once I followed your suggestions, I would have no choice." He was silent for a while.

"Let's get back to the here and now," he said. "I ought to tell you straight off that we're going to do anything we have to do in order to prevent Professor Fain's Symposium on Jewish Culture and your international scientific meeting. They will never take place."

"I know you have all the power," I answered. "You can do whatever you wish. It will mean only that you bring about the alternative I mentioned, earlier than I expected. It's up to you."

Georgi Borisovitch ushered me out. Again I was aware of how overawed he was by Gavrilov's high station: the official's prestige had evidently rubbed off onto me, since I'd had the distinction of being received by him, and I was escorted to the door with courtesy and deference very unusual on the part of a KGBst. Within an hour I was at home.

Lucia was terribly upset when I recounted the interview, but neither of us had time to contemplate our bleak prospects. The cultural symposium was only four days off.

During those four days the number of searches, of interrogations, of raids and arrests — not only in Moscow, but in all the other cities where there were people who were planning to attend the symposium — increased to epidemic proportions.

The night before the symposium was scheduled to take place, December 20th, there was a beautiful snowfall, and, looking out the window, I said to Lucia, "Let's go out for a walk." I didn't have to say that it might be my last chance to walk in the snow for an indefinite time to come; that the probability of my being arrested by tomorrow was very high.

"I'll just see if Yulia's asleep," she said. I went down to the street ahead of her and waited at the entrance. Late though it was, a young couple came strolling past the building, and the man stopped to ask me for a match; then they walked on past.

The street and the sidewalk were empty; nothing was to be heard and little to be seen, except the falling snow. But "I can just *sense* them, all around," said Lucia; so could I. "Let's make an experiment!" she suddenly suggested; and, without changing pace until the last second, we ducked into a narrow opening between two buildings and ran up a short flight of stairs. In no time, we heard footsteps — dozens of footsteps — hurrying back and forth on the sidewalk just outside our hiding place. We went down a couple of steps, and peered out. The street was simply swarming with KGBsts — including my young couple — fanning out in all directions, searching frantically. They had materialized out of nowhere. We hid until we were tired of the game, and then Lucia called out loudly, "Here we are, you can stop looking!" We emerged, and resumed our walk. From that point on, there was actually a crowd following behind us.

* * *

The next morning, all the participants in the symposium were supposed to meet by ten A.M. in front of the synagogue at Arkhipova Street. (The refuseniks met there as a rule every Saturday; it was our regular place to foregather and exchange the essential news of our community.) Not until then would we be notified of the address where the symposium was to be held. It was clear that the authorities would put a complete stop to the meeting if they could, and its location was to be kept secret until the last minute.

At nine, I left my apartment — not without my briefcase. I had only just emerged from the courtyard when a man wearing a pirozhok appeared by my side.

"Good morning, Mark Yakovlevitch." It was Georgi Borisovitch. The inevitable had happened.

"Well — where am I going?" I asked.

"As far as I know, you're going to the *universam* [the supermarket]," he answered. I had indeed been thinking of buying some groceries, if I could, after the meeting at Arkhipova Street. The bug in our apartment had evidently picked up Lucia's and my conversation at breakfast. The man knew my itinerary.

"All right. Let's go to the market," I said. "Unfortunately, I don't have a shopping bag."

"Oh! Well, you have your briefcase. Luckily I have an *avos'ka* with me." (*Avos'ka* means "in case"; people often carry around in their pockets a rolled-up string bag that they can pull out *in case* they run across something they need to buy.)

"I don't need the avos'ka," I said, feeling the joke had gone far enough. "Let's go." I was much surprised to see no car. Every other time I had been arrested, I'd been hustled into a car and driven to the police station or KGB office; as I said, the authorities much prefer an inconspicuous arrest to one that attracts attention.

We walked to the trolley line, waited for the trolley, and rode it to the stop nearest the local police headquarters. But once on foot, we didn't turn off toward the station; instead, we marched to the universam. What in hell was going on? I stopped still.

"Georgi Borisovitch!" I demanded, "what are we going here for?"

"Why, I thought you wanted to get your groceries!" Only then did I understand that it was not a joke. I was really supposed to do my shopping, with Georgi Borisovitch at my side. I was astonished. But since I really did need to get some supplies — New Year's Eve was approaching — I thought, Well, why not?

"In that case, I have to go back home."

"Why?"

"I don't have the shopping bags." So back we went. Lucia, of course, was much surprised when I walked into the apartment, because she had been looking out the window when I left and had seen my arrest. She was just going out to telephone our friends — including some correspondents on foreign newspapers — to tell them I had been picked up. I asked her to bring the bags and explained that I was allowed to go shopping.

Ordinarily when I went for groceries I took both a rucksack and one of those big, wheeled carrying-carts; that way I could do a whole week's shopping, if I was lucky in finding what we wanted, in one single trip. But somehow I didn't like the idea of trudging the streets, loaded like a horse, with Georgi Borisovitch at my elbow — so I only took a few string bags along.

Back to the market! I bought my supplies, and the KGBst guarded me the whole time. I tried to figure out the reason for this semi-arrest. What had kept them from using the ordinary means of putting a person out of circulation for a while? The only guess I could come up with was this: that Sergei Ivanovitch's conversation with me had been entirely a test, to check my reaction. Maybe I would be scared. Maybe I would be willing to make unexpected concessions. Or — maybe — it would be a good idea if I decided the KGB was not so bad after all.

When I came to the cashier to pay for what I had bought, I found I wouldn't be allowed to keep the wine and vodka I had selected for our New Year's Eve party. It was not yet eleven A.M., and you can't buy alcohol before that hour.

"We'll have to come back," I said to Georgi Borisovitch. He didn't look too happy at the prospect of a third trip to the universam. We struggled back to Veshnyakovskaya Street. I declined his offer to help carry the bundles.

On my way into the courtyard, I saw people walking by with New Year's trees. These are always hard to find, and my eyes lit up when I saw them. Yulia would be terribly disappointed to have her New Year's Eve without a tree. I asked one of the passersby where he had got his tree, and he told me where they were on sale. I said to Georgi Borisovitch, "I don't know what your plans are, but I'm going to bring my groceries home and then try to get one of those trees. After that I'll go back to the store for my wine and vodka." Willy-nilly, he had to go with me to the fir-tree bazaar. There was a long queue there, and the temperature was about zero.

It was hours before I got home, laden with my liquor supply and with the tree. I left the miserable, freezing Georgi Borisovitch at the entry door to my building. I almost felt sorry for him!

When I decided to go out again a little later, and opened the door of my apartment, I found a group of policemen, with walkie-talkies, and several KGBsts on the landing. They informed me that I would not be allowed to leave my apartment.

That was the beginning of my house arrest. I went back in and told Lucia that I couldn't leave the building.

We spent the rest of the day on tenterhooks, wondering what had happened to the other people involved with the symposium. If I was being held this way, Professor Fain must certainly be under arrest as well; probably also the other organizers of the event. In the evening Lucia (who was not confined to the building and who was followed by KGBsts only at a distance) went out to try to telephone various friends who had been planning to attend. We wanted to learn their fate.

An hour later I heard her footsteps running lightly up to the second floor. There was a KGBst posted right outside our door. Before she came in, I heard her voice addressing him jubilantly.

"They did it! They did it!"

"Did what?" the guard asked.

"They held the Symposium on Jewish Culture!"

"Oh, for God's sake!" he exclaimed angrily. (This man happened to be almost the only one among the KGBsts around us who would have known what Lucia was talking about. The others were simply under orders to keep visitors out and to keep me under very close surveillance. As usual, they were not told anything about the "crimes" their presence prevented me from committing.)

Lucia ran in, radiant and triumphant.

"What happened?" I demanded.

At ten o'clock that morning, about a hundred refuseniks and others who planned to attend the cultural symposium — among them was Academician Sakharov and a crowd of Western news correspondents — had gathered outside the synagogue. It didn't take them long to realize that something had gone wrong: Professor Fain wasn't there. Nor were Yosif Begun, Vladimir Prestin, Pavel Abramovitch, Victor Brailovsky, and Vladimir Lazaris. None of the conference organizers was there. It was obvious to everyone that we were all under arrest.

There was an interval of confusion. No one knew what to do. But shortly, Natasha Rosenstein (she and her husband, Grigori, were in the forefront among dedicated activists) passed a note through the crowd, inviting everyone to her apartment. This was an extremely courageous action on her part. She is an extraordinarily brave person, one of the few we knew who had the courage to bring up her children as observant Jews. She knew perfectly well what the consequences of her invitation might be.

Of course, the crowd around the synagogue was completely hemmed in by plainclothesmen. But a certain amount of protection was afforded by the foreign newsmen. Furthermore, as I have mentioned before, the

KGB does not make the most trifling move without orders. They were unprepared to make any more arrests, and could do nothing but follow the crowd over to Natasha's apartment.

When the company was assembled in the Rosensteins' small rooms, they realized that none of the scheduled speakers was there. All of the lecturers had been arrested.

"We'll conduct the symposium anyway," announced Natasha. "We have some of the papers here." Before they could begin, there was loud knocking at the door.

"We're not going to open! I'm not letting anyone in! If you insist upon entering, you can just break the door down!" Natasha called out. The banging ceased.

The symposium began, under the chairmanship of Professor Naum Meiman. There were about sixty people there, not counting the journalists. Seven papers were read — of course, not by their authors, who were in police courts or under house arrest. At four in the afternoon when the symposium adjourned (naturally, they had to limit it to that one day), everyone present, including Natasha Rosenstein and her small sons, left the apartment under cover of the foreign journalists.

However different the symposium turned out from the way it was originally scheduled, it was a victory.

* * *

The symposium had been planned to take place over three days, but the organizers' house arrest was not lifted until the end of that entire week, December 23rd. I was finally allowed out for walks, but not without a very close escort. Whenever I went out of the building with one of these plainclothesmen, I would give myself the satisfaction of explaining to him the reason we were under surveillance, and from what activity we were being prevented. Also, when we were listening to the news accounts of our situation that were broadcast in Russian on the BBC or the Voice of America, we opened the apartment door so that our guards could hear the programs. I don't believe these men had ever encountered such opposition before on the part of the people they guarded.

Being under this sort of arrest imposed on us a relentless strain. It was horribly annoying, and for Yulia really terrifying, to find a silent figure posted by the doorway every time one went out, and policemen and strangers swarming about our home. I had insisted that the guard outside our apartment move up on the staircase — with the threat that I would get word out to the foreign press that the KGB kept children under arrest — but even so, Yulia was terribly nervous, not really herself, during the seven days of our arrest. I found there was no way of shaking the KGBst who went with me when I took a walk, nor even of keeping him more than a few inches from my side. Only one thing frightened these men, and that was a camera. When Lucia tried to photograph me on the sidewalk, my escort abruptly moved out of range; nothing else could make him budge. As a matter of fact, she did manage once to get a shot of me with Georgi Borisovitch, but that picture disappeared from our effects within the year.

I was anxious to get word from Professor Fain, Professor Lerner, Victor, and the others; and Lucia tried to get in touch with anyone she could by telephone — but all the phones in our vicinity were "out of order." We were pretty much incommunicado. People did try to visit us, but they were turned away by the police and plainclothesmen who surrounded the building; all of them were photographed. I had only two contacts during that time with the outside world. One was a wire that somehow slipped through, from Vladimir Lazaris, saying that he was "ill" and was worried that I might have come down with the same illness. So Vladimir was under arrest, too.

The other occasion was when Valeri Fayerman infiltrated the building. He came in on skis (not an easy feat for him, since, being a southerner, he was a complete novice at skiing) in hopes of being mistaken for a resident of the building returning from an hour's exercise. He casually propped the skis in the entryway, ran briskly up the stairs past the KGBst posted there, and rang our bell. He got in before the guards could react. (They had no search warrants or other legal means of entering our apartment.)

From Valeri we learned that our friends were having a much worse time than we were. Professor Fain's apartment had been raided and searched; valuable books and papers were confiscated. The same thing had happened at the Brailovskys', and Victor had been subjected to three full days of grilling by the Prosecutor's Office. These official reprisals were not confined to Moscow. In every city of the Soviet Union where there were any groups that had been in contact with Professor Fain, raids, detentions, and interrogations were going on.

When the week was up, all these retaliatory measures ceased. Professor Fain was in no mood to consider the issue closed. But for the bravery of one woman, his long-cherished plan would have come to nothing, and, as it was, all of the scheduled speakers had been forcibly prevented from appearing. He and Yosif Begun made an appointment with an American official at the United States Embassy to discuss the aborted symposium and the violation of the would-be participants' rights, in terms of the Helsinki Agreement.

As they approached the embassy they were rushed by a group of plainclothesmen and hauled into a waiting police car. When the official the two refuseniks were to see, the one who had witnessed the arrest, tried to protest, he was told that these were dangerous criminals. Professor Fain and Dr. Begun were driven to police headquarters and held there for eighteen hours; all the documents they had with them, including correspondence relative to the symposium, and the papers that were to have been read, were confiscated. They were not released until late at night.

Shortly afterward, Yosif Begun was tried on charges of parasitism and exiled to the northeast of Siberia.

A Life Split in Two

WRITING about that time, when a handful of helpless people stubbornly pursued their plans to foregather and hold scholarly discourse, against the will of one of the most powerful states in the world, fills me with double feelings, as if I lived at the same time in two different worlds. On the one hand, here I am, free, able to go almost anywhere on earth that I care to. I can express any ideas I wish, political or religious; I can publicly join the company of others and express these ideas, and learn theirs. But I spent forty-five years in a place where people are willing to risk their lives for a fraction of such freedom. Half my heart and half my soul are still there, with my friends.

* * *

I interrupted the writing of this chapter to put through a call to Moscow. It took two hours before the operator could break through a busy signal. I knew perfectly well that it was impossible for the line to be engaged; Victor Brailovsky, to whom I was trying to speak, would have hung up immediately on any call other than the one from me. The Israeli overseas operator — by now the operators know about these calls and are willing to keep trying, no matter what sort of interference they encounter — finally put the connection through, and, although when Victor answered his voice was almost inaudible, I managed to make out what he was saying.

That very day, December 21st, 1978 (the anniversary of Stalin's birth, ninety-nine years before), the Brailovskys and three other friends of ours had been subjected to KGB searches. It was horrible to hear about. Dahlia had been terrified by the invasion of a crowd of strange men who, she could not but realize, were her parents' enemies. What was most chilling to Victor and Irina was that Dahlia had simply retreated, crouching in a corner with her head in a pillow. She didn't even ask what these men were doing here, why they were going through every-

one's belongings — even through the clothes of her invalid grandmother. She withdrew into herself.

The KGB left after eight hours, taking with them all the records of
the Seminar, taking Victor's pass to the Lenin Library, taking all typed
or handwritten manuscripts and, most destructive of all, the mathematical papers on which Victor had been working for two years. Evidently,
the KGB was more determined than ever to put a stop to the Seminar.
They served a summons on Victor and Irina before they departed. On
the following day, the Brailovskys would have to appear at the Office of
the Prosecutor for an interrogation. God knows what lies ahead.

* * *

Nineteen seventy-seven arrived: the start of my fifth year in refusal. Our
prospects looked grimmer than ever. I felt I was approaching the
crossroads closer and closer. The Soviets would get rid of me soon, but,
whereas a year or so earlier I had still been reasonably confident that
my route of departure would lead to Israel, now after such a long wait
it looked a great deal more likely that a prison term lay before me.

It is interesting to note that among the people I saw casually every
day, there was less and less fear of contamination from me. Somehow,
everyone had become accustomed to thinking of me and of some of the
other refusenik scientists as people who, although living in Moscow,
were in a sense stateless — men without a country, but not necessarily
enemy aliens. The same people who early in 'seventy-three had so
pointedly eschewed my society at the Thursday seminars of the Institute
for Theoretical Physics were less afraid now to claim acquaintance with
me. A few of them, and some of the scientists at the other institutes, had
also applied for exit visas during the ensuing years: the ice was, to a certain extent, broken. During the last couple of years, I occasionally attended a seminar at the institute, if the topic under discussion was one
of particular interest to me. After a while everybody had thawed toward
me a little.

There were just two exceptions. One was Professor Lev Gorkov, who
had been furious to hear from Western scientists that the role he played
in firing me from the institute was known to them. I have no idea why
he thought I was under any obligation to keep the fact of his visit to me
at that time confidential. Actually, it had been quite a long time before I
mentioned it to anyone, but that was because of my deep feeling of offense at his cancellation of our friendship.

The other was Professor Isaak Khalatnikov. The minute he caught
sight of me, he simply froze. He changed his glance in any direction to
avoid meeting my eyes; he attended to the lecturer as if hypnotized. Ob-

viously, no one "from above" had advised him what attitude he should take toward such a pariah, but he was taking no chances. Only once did he make the concession of saying "good morning" when he encountered me without warning in the hall. But Gorkov never spoke to me again.

January 13th, 1977, was the sixtieth birthday of Professor Ilya Lifshitz, who had inherited Landau's chair at the Institute for Theoretical Physics. The celebration was to be held at the Scientific Council of the Institute for Physical Problems. I hesitated for quite a while before I decided to go. I felt that I couldn't pass up this jubilee of my teacher, a man of whom I was so fond and to whom I owed so much. Professor Lifshitz had deplored my plan to leave for Israel; he felt it was a great mistake with regard to my career. "Isn't it a strange idea to go off into the unknown, Mark, when you've got such solid prospects ahead of you here?" he had asked me. "You've had your ups and downs — you certainly haven't been very cautious in the choice of your friends — but you can see as well as anyone else what sort of future you have." Notwithstanding the fact that I hadn't taken his advice, Professor Lifshitz, who is not the sort of person to follow the lead of others in making his judgments, maintained relations with me.

Except at Landau's jubilee, I have never seen so many people in that lecture hall. There were physicists from every corner of the country. As is the tradition at the institute, the lectures were witty and amusing rather than pompous, and Professor Lifshitz appeared to be quite overwhelmed by the enthusiasm of everyone there.

When the talks were concluded, the guests moved into the reception hall, where drinks were being served. The unofficial part of the evening began. As far as I myself was concerned, the occasion was a perfectly astounding one. I never would have imagined it, but I was accorded an extremely warm, hearty welcome. People I hadn't seen for years crowded around me. Aside from Gorkov and Khalatnikov, there was hardly a single physicist present who didn't come over to greet me, to ask how my life was going, to drink a toast to my success. These were physicists from all over, not just Muscovites — some of them men I hardly knew.

It was clear that my position in the eyes of my colleagues had changed completely. The hostility and contempt I had faced when I was first in refusal had reversed itself: I was conscious of a real concern and respect. I was quite stunned. It was not only my science for which they respected me, but for my activity in dissent and Zionism.

Because dissent in the Soviet Union is not directed against rational legislation and democratic government, but is rather the open presentation of the ideas that all thoughtful intelligent people in the country share but are afraid to express in public, a dissenter actually has the sympathy of a great many people. They feel him to be their representative, someone who is willing to take the risk of fighting on their behalf.

Officially, there is absolutely no public news on the activities of dissenters and refuseniks, aside from the occasional bombshell exposé of a "Zionist plot" or anti-Soviet crime. But during the half-decade just past, enough news of our struggle had emerged, mostly over the short-wave radio from abroad, so that everyone — certainly every Jew — knew what we were doing. I have mentioned how numerous were the occasions when a perfect stranger surfaced into our lives, lent a lifesaving helping hand, and disappeared without waiting to be thanked; how this support, somehow always there when we needed it most, kept us going through the darkest times. It was these kindnesses, ranging from a generous gesture to a dangerous risk or sacrifice, that made me realize time and again that our struggle did not go unrecognized.

Now it appeared that a great number of Establishment scientists, not only refuseniks and their well-wishers, were on my side. I had not at all expected this backing from my fellow-physicists, and I was very much touched. No one actually said it, but the toasts to my "success" meant to my eventual escape.

*   *   *

On March 5th, 1977 (the twenty-fourth anniversary of Stalin's death), an article appeared in *Izvestia* by one Sanya Lipavsky, a refusenik who announced that he had withdrawn his application for an exit visa. Lipavsky claimed to have been an informer for the CIA, and listed others who had been similarly "linked with the CIA," with whom he had "been in contact." Among those named, some, thank God, were no longer endangered by this sort of attack, because they had left the Soviet Union: David Azbel, Vitali Rubin, and several more. The remaining "spies" and associates he mentioned, however, were still in Moscow: some Western diplomats and correspondents; Anatoly Shcharansky, Professor Alexander Lerner, Vladimir Slepak, and myself.

I would find it hard to describe the sensation that went through me when I read my name and those of my friends in this list of traitors. I immediately thought of the Doctors' Plot and understood a bit how the targets of that cruel slander must have felt in that long-ago January. After all these years, that same terror was loosed upon us again, and this time I was among the malefactors. This article, and the one accompanying it, which consisted of outraged commentary on the activities of the refusenik spies, was a frightful blow to us who were accused, to every Jew and every thinking person in the Soviet Union. We had seen it all twenty-five years ago, but, despite the anti-Zionist propaganda of the last few years, no one had anticipated this brutal revival of the Stalin spirit. If history was to repeat itself further, we were lost. The "doctors-poisoners" had been imprisoned and tortured for months; only the miracle of Stalin's death saved them.

Lipavsky merely listed his "fellow-spies" without specifying exactly what they were supposed to have done. The only acts of espionage he actually described were his own, and these were fanciful to a degree: cloak-and-dagger exploits of the most unlikely kind. He claimed to have buried stolen documents in woods outside Moscow, arranged midnight rendezvous with CIA agents, and so on — activities no refusenik activist could possibly get away with unobserved. There is no category of people in the Soviet Union under heavier surveillance than the activists. But it would be hard to strain the credulity of the ordinary Russian reading public. They had been prepared to swallow the story of the gang of poisoners in 'fifty-three, and probably would be quite as ready now to accept this shocking news.

Very shortly, we heard on the BBC the State Department's denial that the CIA had any contact with anyone named in the article — except for the author himself. It certainly suggested poor judgment on the part of the CIA that they should make use of a refusenik; but of course the man may have been a double agent, which would explain a great deal.

Soon after the publication of these articles, closed Party meetings were held everywhere: at institutions, work places, even apartment buildings. A closed meeting excludes all non-Party members, and the assumption is made that what is discussed there is confidential. The entire agenda is "secret," but, inevitably, the policies formulated, the decisions made, at these special meetings leak out as rumors — always unofficial, never documented. No source can be identified. It was thus that Khrushchev's speech on Stalin, to give a most notable example, was disseminated.

Word got around that the closed meetings were called to denounce Soviet Zionists. The way was evidently being prepared for "spontaneous" anti-Semitic activity. Immediately, horrible incidents began to occur. One of my refusenik friends, Veniamin Bogomolny, was beaten by a gang of toughs on a Moscow street. When a policeman tried to interfere, the attackers simply showed him their KGB I.D.s, and resumed beating Bogomolny.

Another refusenik, the well-known construction engineer Professor Wolf Grigorievitch Chudnovsky, soon after being told that he was permanently ineligible for an exit visa, was assaulted while walking near his home. His wife was with him: she also was beaten. They both had to be hospitalized, Professor Chudnovsky with a broken leg, and his wife with a concussion. They were in their seventies.

News of these incredible outrages stunned us all. I felt increasingly certain that my own turn would come soon, and now had real fears for Lucia and Yulia as well. We could not lead charmed lives forever.

Within days, the KGB closed in on Anatoly Shcharansky. He was closely followed everywhere he went by plainclothesmen, both on foot and in cars. On March 14th he was able to get news of his plight out to Israel and to the West, but in this case the Soviets showed themselves unaware of the bad publicity that would arise from his further persecution. He was arrested on the 15th. It was obvious to the rest of us that Shcharansky's today could be our tomorrow.

Time was growing short. We had planned an International Seminar on Collective Phenomena in Physics, scheduled to begin on April 17th. To judge by the events surrounding previous attempts to hold a seminar to which foreigners specifically were invited, and by everything that was happening right now, nothing could be anticipated but more arrests.

It was at this time that the Brailovskys decided they had to get their son out of this horrible country, whatever the cost. Victor let the Visa Department know that he had reconsidered. He received no answer at all.

The atmosphere of tension and fear thickened by the minute. I lived in fear of going to prison, leaving my manuscript on DNA unfinished. I had a rough draft completed; with the results I had obtained by computer, this had turned into quite a massive paper, about a hundred pages. A friend of ours in Leningrad, a woman with a very good command of English, had offered to type it for me. I wanted also to finish the work on the current edition of *Jews in the U.S.S.R.* and to consult with one of our Leningrad editors, Emilia Sotnikova. With both of these concerns in mind, I planned a quick trip to Leningrad.

On the evening of my departure, my doorbell rang. I opened to find Georgi Borisovitch. He handed me an official summons to appear the next morning at 24 Kuznetsky Most, at the office of Sergei Ivanovitch Gavrilov.

"I'm on my way to Leningrad," I told him. "I can't come now. Of course you can arrest me, but otherwise I plan to meet my schedule." He left, and for the remaining hours I was not at all sure I wouldn't be taken in to headquarters. But I boarded the night train without hindrance.

I had arranged for telephone contact with Lucia while I was away through Oleg, a resident in our building. He had no connection with any of the dissenting groups but was willing to let us use his phone and to take messages for us.

In the midst of my business in Leningrad, new blows descended. An article appeared in the *Literaturnaya Gazeta* by a man named Petrov-Agapov, a former dissident, who, like Lipavsky, had recanted his heresies and now exposed the "anti-Soviet" activities of the dissidents. His article denounced the group that was monitoring Soviet adherence to the Helsinki Agreement and named Professor Yuri Orlov, Alexander Ginzburg, Vladimir Slepak, and Anatoly Shcharansky as members. Soon after the story appeared, Professor Orlov followed Anatoly Shcharansky to prison.

On top of that, an article appeared in the *Verchernyaya Moskva*, condemning Shcharansky, Slepak, Professor Lerner, and some others for "vicious and criminal activities financed by the CIA." The piece was signed by Leonid Tsipin, the man who had shared my cell at Serpukhov.

All these arrests put me into a frenzy of anxiety about Lucia. For twenty-four terrible hours I couldn't reach her on the telephone. When I returned home, my first words to her were: "For God's sake, are you all right? Where have you been? I was worried sick!"

"I couldn't come home," she answered. "I was in exile for twenty-four hours." She gave me an account of what had happened — what she called "a day in the life of a refusenik housewife!"

Having spent an extra hour at the universam late on Thursday afternoon — a consignment of oranges had come in, and Lucia joined the enormous queue, having no intention of letting such an opportunity pass — she trudged home in the dark, laden with all the week's groceries. Approaching our apartment building, she saw a black Volga with four men in it parked out in front. Even without its identifying plates, she would have known whose car this was, and since there was no one else in our building subject to visits by the KGB, she realized at once that it was we who were the object of the stakeout and that we were in for a search. Owing to the interest of the Western newsmen and others in the activities of refuseniks, we were by now so conspicuous that the KGB didn't want to conduct a clandestine raid. They would have to go through the procedure according to regulation, with a householder on the premises. They were waiting for Lucia's return — possibly, they were taking advantage of my absence and hoping Lucia would make less trouble for them than I would have.

We had a great deal of "contraband" literature in our rooms, including some valuable Judaica, a file of issues of *Jews in the U.S.S.R.*, and our *Ninety Minutes at Entebbe*. Lucia knew there was only one way to forestall the search and prevent the confiscation of these materials, and that was to stay away from the apartment so that there would be no way the agents could raid the place legally.

Still carrying the heavy bags, she went to pick up Yulia at her nursery school, about four blocks away. "Yulia! You know what? I'm in the mood to visit people!" she greeted our daughter. "Let's go and see the Makonovitskys! You can play with Grisha." Yulia, who is very sociable, was at first delighted with the idea. When they arrived at the Makonovitskys' (the names here, of course, are changed), they found that by mischance these friends were not at home.

"So our wanderings began. It was just dreadful. Yulia started to cough and sniffle, I was simply worn out lugging those shopping bags, and it was getting colder by the minute. Of course I had to put up a front. 'Let's go to Rachel's. Wouldn't that be fun?' I said, but poor Yulia was dragging her feet. She kept saying, 'Let's go home, Mama. I've changed my mind; I don't want to visit anyone! And I need to go to the bathroom!' It all turned into a nightmare." They went on foot and by bus from one place to another. Everywhere they went, the friends who would have rescued them were out. "You wouldn't have believed the run of bad luck. It must have been eight o'clock before we got to the Levins' — thank God they were there — and you can imagine how kind they were to us. Poor Yulia was crying by that time, and I was almost in tears myself." True to our native Russian tradition of hospitality, Tolya and Marina Levin plied them with food and urged Lucia to stay as long as she needed to.

After Yulia was asleep, they all conferred about what Lucia should do next.

"They'll lift the stakeout when they realize you're out for the night," said Tolya. "I shouldn't think they'd wait for you much after midnight. Let's get hold of Rafa: he and I can go over there with you and take the books out; bring them here."

They put this plan into action, but not without one very bad moment. When they arrived at Veshnyakovskaya Street, around one A.M., they found they were a minute too early. The Volga was only just leaving. "There I was, a sitting target, right in the courtyard, while they were driving out," said Lucia. "The car stopped. I thought: They've seen me! But it wasn't that: they were stuck. The driveway hadn't been shoveled." It seemed to her that hours passed before the Volga, after much backing and filling, moved out onto the street; she stayed behind a snowbank until it was gone.

Like burglars, Lucia and our two friends crept silently into the apartment. She didn't turn on the lights, but groped through the rooms, found the books in their various hiding places, packed them in three suitcases, and with her confederates made a quick getaway.

"Bravo, Lucia!" I exclaimed. "I can hardly believe it! But they didn't come back on Friday? We weren't searched, after all?"

"No, and I'm pretty sure why not. When we got out of the building, just as we were turning the corner, we saw a couple of kids, teen-agers — very late for them to be out walking! They looked at us hard when we walked by and then started running. We were sure they were *stukatches*. I suppose they reported having seen us, carrying big val-ises." Having lost Lucia's trail, and knowing that wherever she was she evidently had the contraband with her, the KGB — which never con-ducts a search without reason to believe they will find what they're looking for — must have postponed or abandoned their plan.

That was a very close call.

* * *

I fully expected to be summoned to 24 Kuznetsky Most upon my return to Moscow; but a day passed, then two days, and nothing happened.

On my third evening at home, Lucia went out to her Ulpan, her un-derground school of Hebrew, leaving me to look after Yulia and put her to bed. At around eight o'clock I had guests: an American couple, tourists. They were among the many generous people who had heard our names through organizations such as Save Soviet Jewry, and whose company was always as welcome to us as any prison-visitors' to a zek. I can never be able to put into words how much solace and hope they brought us.

I gave my guests tea and told them about Shcharansky's arrest and about the other recent disasters. When we had been talking for a while, I heard someone at the door. It was Oleg, the neighbor who let us use his telephone, saying there was a call for me. Alarmed — everyone we knew was aware that we hated to impose on Oleg's kindness, and no one called me unless it was very urgent — I excused myself and ran up-stairs.

"Good evening, Mark Yakovlevitch," said a familiar voice. "Georgi Borisovitch here. I called to say that Sergei Ivanovitch would like to see you. He'll be waiting for you at nine-thirty at his office." This was in-credible.

"Sorry," I said. "I don't have any friend by the name of Sergei Ivano-vitch. If this is an official request for my presence, it's certainly a strange hour and a strange way to convey it. I'm astonished that you would call me to someone else's telephone. Sorry. I won't come."

"Well, Mark Yakovlevitch! If you won't come, I'll have to go there and fetch you."

"If you have a summons, there's nothing I can do about it. But unless I'm served with one, I'm not going anywhere. That's that."

"All right, Mark Yakovlevitch," he answered. "See you soon." I returned to my guests. It was unfortunate that this had happened when Lucia was out; I was upset at the thought of leaving our daughter alone.

"Let us help," the Americans urged when I explained what the call was. "We'll stay until your wife gets home." Once again — out of the blue — a bad situation was saved by beautiful friends who an hour ago had been strangers. I accepted with thanks. When the doorbell rang, I went in to kiss Yulia goodnight and wrote a note for Lucia, trying to adopt a lighthearted tone: " 'We Women' picked me up. Have gone to see Sergei Ivanovitch. Back soon. Don't worry." Georgi Borisovitch was right there at my door; he handed me a summons and ushered me into a waiting car.

This was an extraordinary event: the working day was over, and it was an unusual time to start an interrogation. I tried not to speculate about what might be ahead of me. Meanwhile, my attention was distracted in any case by being driven so fast. I've never known anything like it. We went through all the lights, sped across crossings, and forced any traffic we encountered to scatter. We were at Kuznetsky Most in minutes.

I found Sergei Ivanovitch in a different office from the enormous one in which I had previously been received; this was a very small room with nothing impressive about it. Once he started speaking, it occurred to me that the change to this little office had probably been made because it was more favorable acoustically for bugging. He spoke as if for the benefit of another listener — certainly not me. There was something markedly different about his manner; he no longer created the impression of absolute autonomy that he had before. I can't imagine what had caused this apparent diminution in his status. It looked as though someone of still more authority had stepped into the case, someone to whom Sergei Ivanovitch had to report.

Sergei Ivanovitch launched immediately into remarks of a kind familiar to me on the part of all the other KGBsts who had spoken to me in these offices, but not at all the sort of thing I'd heard from him before.

"We know everything about your activity," he began. "We know it is very vicious and very harmful. We are aware that you are still associated with the journal *Jews in the U.S.S.R.*, and that you recently took a trip to Leningrad to work on it. We know that you're the prin-

cipal organizer of the espionage ring, your scientific Seminar. You have
been warned, but you have not responded to the warnings." This time
he was not a human being, but a machine that did nothing but repro-
duce the words it had been programmed to say. I settled back in my
chair, preparing myself for an endless harangue.

"To get down to specifics," he said: "about the so-called International Seminar . . ."

"Excuse me, Sergei Ivanovitch," said a voice at the door. It was the
guard, who showed every sign of embarrassment and hesitation. "You
are wanted on the telephone." I was astonished. At my last conference
with Gavrilov, not once had a telephone rung or any other interruption
occurred; and at ten P.M. such an interruption was doubly unlikely.
Sergei Ivanovitch rose, the guard whispered something to him, and he
disappeared for five minutes.

On his return, he sat down again. "To resume what I was saying," he
said. "As to the anniversary Seminar you've been planning, I am free to
tell you that, although I can't be a hundred percent positive, it looks as
though this *particular* session . . . will be permitted to take place."

In none of my dealings with any other KGBst had I ever been surprised, but if Sergei Ivanovitch intended to keep me off balance, he certainly succeeded. In both my first interview with this official and in my
second, he thoroughly astounded me. The first time it was because of
the complete independence of his attitude; he was the only KGB official
I had ever met who could, apparently, make his own decisions. I'd had
a distinct impression that he was no longer in charge at this second conference, but now he amazed me again, by pronouncing this go-ahead
for our Seminar. Certainly what he had been saying a few minutes
before had not prepared me for the news that they might tolerate the international session. I was too wary to really believe it. "I assume there
will be no anti-Soviet activity during the anniversary Seminar," he went
on. This was a ridiculous caution: I had always skirted political issues
with the greatest care, not wanting to put any weapons into the authorities' hands with which they might crush our Seminar. He knew it, too.

Once Sergei Ivanovitch had made this completely unexpected concession — or prediction — I waited to hear what quid pro quo he expected
from me. But there was none. "That's all I wanted to tell you," he said.
I couldn't conceal my surprise.

"Does that mean I may leave?"

"Yes, of course." He smiled. "I know your wife is worried. Certainly — you may go." When I left the office, Sergei Ivanovitch accompanied me to the door, where we were joined by Georgi Borisovitch,
who had been waiting in the reception room. All three of us went out

onto the street. Why were they still with me? Had I misunderstood the permission to leave? Was some sort of trap being laid for me?

"Just a little way down to our right is the jail," said Sergei Ivanovitch, jokingly. "Very convenient." My apprehension mounted. With Georgi Borisovitch still at my elbow, Gavrilov accompanied me to the waiting Volga and asked me to step in. I did so, and my escort said something to the driver, then shut the door, and I was driven off, unaccompanied. There was no use asking the chauffeur what was happening or where I was going.

We drove again at breakneck speed — I had to brace myself at the turns — and within a few minutes we were on Veshnyakovskaya Street. The car turned in to the courtyard of my own building, stopped, and the chauffeur courteously got out, held the door for me, and bade me goodnight. I hurried to my apartment.

The entire episode made no sense. No matter how hard I tried, I couldn't guess the reasons for this interview. Perhaps he realized that if at some point I announced to my friends that the KGB was going to prevent our anniversary Seminar, there would be even more publicity abroad than if the officials unexpectedly chose to ignore the occasion — to pull out the rug from under us as we made our protests. Or perhaps they wanted to disarm us, to postpone their preventive measures until the last minute, so that, if they wanted, they could catch unsuspecting participants all in one net. Or — one further speculation: they may have made the mistake of thinking that I would keep quiet about this late-evening visit to Kuznetsky Most, and then when news of it leaked out, they could make it look as though I had connections with the KGB. I just don't know.

When I walked into our apartment Lucia said, "There you are, Mark! So Sergei Ivanovitch kept his word!"

"What do you mean?"

"Well, when I came in and found the nice American couple — you can imagine how surprised I was — and they gave me your note and told me about your being called out, naturally I thought you'd really been arrested. I tried to make polite conversation with them as long as I could, but finally I couldn't stand it any more and went up to Oleg's and called the KGB."

"You *what?*" I was perfectly stunned.

"I called Sergei Ivanovitch. I still have the telephone number at Kuznetsky Most; Irina and I got it when you were in prison."

I certainly can't think of many people in the Soviet Union who would have made that call, at that time, under those circumstances.

"Well, what did you say?"

"A man answered; I asked to speak to Sergei Ivanovitch. He sounded very doubtful. He asked twice who was calling, and then I had to wait quite a while before Sergei Ivanovitch came on the line. I said to him. 'I want to know where my husband is!' He told me that you were right there, and that you were almost finished with your conversation. I asked what was going to happen to you next — were you going to be arrested? — and he said not to worry, that you'd be home within the hour."

I could hardly believe it. For the rest of the evening, in the midst of my conversation with the Americans, whom we persuaded to extend their visit for an hour or so, I kept bursting into laughter at intervals every time I thought of Lucia's call.

* * *

The air was electric with excitement and apprehension as the date approached for the International Seminar on Collective Phenomena in Physics, our anniversary meeting. It was certainly a strange sensation, for all of us, to be constantly aware that a few days hence we would either be hosts at an unprecedented landmark occasion in the area of international scientific exchanges — or prisoners. This was the Soviet Union: we knew there was no third possibility. This time, as we knew from the fates of Shcharansky, Orlov, and Ginzburg, if the authorities decided upon the second alternative, it wouldn't be a matter of house arrests. We would be in Lefortovo.

On the Saturday before the Seminar was to begin, I left my desk for a while and started out for Arkhipova Street, to attend the regular weekly gathering of refuseniks in front of the synagogue. I was swamped with work, being in the middle of all my preparations for the next day, but thought I had better make an appearance anyway. At that tense time, all of us worried terribly if someone was absent from these meetings, and I didn't want to alarm my friends.

When I emerged from the Metro and took the turn down toward the synagogue, I saw a familiar figure in a pirozhok cap, waiting for me at the corner.

"Good morning, Mark Yakovlevitch!" It was Georgi Borisovitch.

"Well, what now?"

"I have a message for you from Sergei Ivanovitch. He asked me to tell you — this is strictly official — that if you stay away from the synagogue today, your Seminar will take place as planned, without any trouble."

"What? But he must know there's nothing special going on at the synagogue. This is just our ordinary Saturday gathering."

"I'm only giving you the message," he answered. "Sergei Ivanovitch says if you do go to the synagogue, he cannot guarantee you anything."

I stopped to think. This was a strange request. I had no pressing reason for joining the assemblage, but couldn't understand being offered such a disproportionate reward for obedience to so trivial a demand. What was the idea? My presence or absence at Arkhipova Street could hardly be a matter of concern to the officials.

This might be some sort of psychological experiment. At this eleventh hour, perhaps they wanted to exert a certain degree of control over my actions. If I obeyed this prohibition, they might feel reassured that I would be able to prevent the Seminar from becoming a forum for politics despite any pressures. I hadn't needed that warning; I was certainly not willing to play into their hands by giving them legal grounds for destroying the Seminar. But if it would allay their fears for me to make this meaningless concession, I would do it. It would have been hard to see the work and plans of an entire year coming to naught over such a trifle.

I caught sight of Victor Brailovsky and Professor Fain, who were on their way to the synagogue, so I went across the street to tell them that I wouldn't be there and to explain why. Professor Fain regarded yielding to any sort of request from the KGB as something unforgivable, and told me so. In this case I felt it wouldn't make sense to ignore such an insignificant demand; I couldn't take the responsibility for providing the authorities with a pretext to destroy our session.

I went back to my apartment. It was very lucky I did, because some of the scientists who were expected at the Seminar had paid us an advance visit; I would have hated not being there to greet them. They were Kenneth Wilson from Cornell, Max Gottesman of the National Institutes of Health, and Mario Grossi, a radiophysicist and astronomer attached to the Center for Astrophysics in Cambridge, Massachusetts.

Like everybody else in my field, I had heard a great deal about Professor Wilson, and I had always hoped for a chance to talk to him. (We never knew in advance who would be able to visit us, so I was far from certain that this opportunity would ever arise.) He is a round-faced man of medium stature, very silent. He talks little and doesn't like to write; even putting down the results of his own research is an ordeal for him. He occupies a unique place in academic history: he was the first person ever to be granted tenure at Cornell University, with a full professorship, despite the fact that during the previous two years he hadn't published a single paper. This exception to the rules showed Cornell's good judgment. When Professor Wilson's basic results were eventually published, all the other great universities in the United States and many all over the world offered him choice posts on any conditions he would care to mention. He rejected them all; his first loyalty was toward Cornell.

We all sat down and had a very informal lunch, which Lucia somehow put together, and started talking about the difficulties some of the guests we had invited had experienced in attempting to enter the country. It was the French scientists whose efforts to join us were most uncompromisingly rejected. Professor Minko Balkansky, the famous mathematician Loren Schwartz, and the Nobel laureate physicist-philosopher Alfred Kastler, who had applied at the Soviet Foreign Ministry in Paris and specifically stated that their reason for making the trip was to attend the Moscow Seminar on Collective Phenomena in Physics, had been turned down point-blank.

"George Wald was prevented from coming, too," Mario Grossi told us. Professor Wald had been with Robert Goldberger, of the National Institutes of Health, in Leningrad two days before, and they were planning to travel from there to Moscow to attend our session. Professor Wald made no secret of his sympathies: he is extremely active on behalf of human rights and of the scientific rights of his colleagues. He has always been vocal in his concern for justice; he cannot be indifferent toward the suppression of freedom. He was so infuriated by the situation of dissidents and Zionists in Russia that he decided to hold a rally in Red Square. He had conducted demonstrations for similar causes in other capitals of the world, and now was perfectly prepared to agitate in the heart of the Soviet Union, as well. He would do the same in Chile or Argentina or wherever he considered that a protest against injustice was in order. The reader can easily imagine the reaction of the authorities when this plan came to their attention. Naturally, they couldn't arrest a man who is one of the best known of all American scientists; but neither could they tolerate a freedom rally in Red Square.

"I saw him at Kennedy Airport when we were leaving," said Mario. "He was just getting off the plane from Helsinki, and he told me how they had kept him out of Moscow." The Intourist officials had caught up with Professor Wald just as he and Professor Goldberger were making arrangements to leave Leningrad, and had informed them that, owing to some unfortunate mix-up in reservations, there was not one single hotel room free in Moscow. "A terrible mistake!" the agent apologized. "You may be sure that the people who mismanaged the reservations so stupidly will be punished! But you won't be able to go to Moscow." They hustled both professors off to Helsinki, where, they assured them, there was plenty of room in the most splendid hotels. From there, George Wald flew back to America.

Others among our prospective visitors had encountered difficulties. An extraordinarily talented professor of physics from Harvard University, Bert Halperin (the same person who had come to see me in the hospital in 1974), and another very prominent physicist, James Langer, were detained at customs for five or six hours. They were finally told that they would be allowed to enter Moscow, but if they tried to attend the Seminar they would be forthwith expelled from the Soviet Union. Ken Wilson said that he too had been detained, though not for so long a time.

"I didn't have that sort of trouble myself," said Mario, "but I can't believe the number of plainclothesmen following us. Even on the subway, on our way over here — we saw them everywhere. We haven't taken a step without someone shadowing us. It's suffocating. Is it always this bad? It must be horrible for you." He told us how, as a very young man, he had joined the partisans in Italy, and risked his life day after day for over a year during the German occupation, carrying leaflets and occasionally grenades through the streets of Rome. "For years and years after the War was over, even after I left Italy and moved to America, I felt anxious whenever I was walking somewhere and heard footsteps behind me. I couldn't stand it. If somone just happened to be in back of me, walking in the same direction, I had to turn, or stop and wait till he'd passed by. Being here makes it all come back to me."

That night, which I had been so nearly sure I would spend in prison — and God knows how many days and nights thereafter — I stayed awake for hours, wondering what would happen the next day. I could hardly believe it when April 17th dawned, a bright and beautiful spring morning. Here I was, still in my own home, making everything ready for the lectures.

It was early when we all set to work: Lucia washing the breakfast dishes and tidying the rooms; Yulia performing her regular Sunday job of cleaning our worn-out lecturers' blackboard; and I, moving all our chairs into the small living room, which was our lecture hall. I taped the bolt on the door so that it didn't have to be unlocked every time someone came in; typed up the list of scheduled speakers, in Russian and English, and posted it on the bulletin board. There were quite a few of these routine procedures to be done, and there was something unreal about going through them this time.

Now and then I looked out the window, where, ever since eight A.M., a huge closed van had stood, parked directly under us, and where KGBsts swarmed in ever-increasing numbers. From the roof of the van, believe it or not, sprouted a network of antennae. We were bugged from all sides — the entire area was bugged.

On the stroke of twelve, the people began to arrive. The very first —
a signal honor — was Andrei Dmitrievitch Sakharov. Close on his heels
was Professor Eric Fawcett of Toronto. This was not our first meeting:
we had seen each other at one of the International Conferences on Low-
Temperature Physics in Moscow. Even before that, we were acquainted
by reputation, as early as 1955, when I developed a theory that predicted a certain kind of resonance in metals under conditions close to
absolute zero, and a little later, independently, Eric Fawcett was the
first person to observe this phenomenon experimentally and to confirm
the predictions of the theory.

Jim Langer and Bert Halperin arrived safely, despite the threats delivered to them at customs, and with them, Mario Grossi. Just after
them came Professor Max Gottesman, one of the most distinguished
researchers in the world in the field of viruses and the molecular structure of phages.

Obviously, I can't mention all the visitors who came from abroad,
but I was profoundly impressed by the courage of each person who
came to us. We were in a dangerous position, but once we had made
the decision to leave this country, we had no choice as to the risks we
were taking; they were absolutely unavoidable. Our guests, however,
did have a choice. It would have been not only easy for them to ignore
our existence, but very understandable. Nevertheless, here they were —
not at the Academy of Sciences, which awaited them, but crowded into
our shabby rooms. They were taking their chances in order to throw us
the precious lifeline of support and friendship. There were only too
many means by which their hosts might retaliate against them for such a
breach of Soviet convention.

We eventually comprised a crowd of between fifty and sixty people.
Of course all the regular members of the Seminar were present: Victor
and Irina Brailovsky, Yevgeny and Rimma Yakir, Professors Yuri Golfand, Naum Meiman, Alexander Lerner, Veniamin Fain, Veniamin
Levitch, Yakov Alpert, and dozens of others.

It was just incredible to me that our faint hope of a jubilee session to
celebrate the fifth anniversary of our unauthorized existence was actually coming true. Incredible. I was in a state of considerable euphoria
when I stood up to welcome everybody and to present a brief account
of our Seminar and its struggle. I could still hardly believe that these visitors were really here: free Western scientists, famous in their fields,
honored guests of the very Soviet Union that had pushed us into our no
man's land. Underneath the triumph was a feeling of painful distress.
Here we were, hosts to this distinguished company, while Anatoly
Shcharansky and Yuri Orlov were in Lefortovo Prison, and Yosif Begun

in his exile. I couldn't think of them without anguish nor without a stab of fear for ourselves.

It was not particularly novel to us, but it must have been very strange for our foreign guests, to be so totally surrounded and besieged. During the entire course of the Seminar, KGBsts overran the courtyard; there were several in all the entries to the building. They took photographs of everyone who went in. They were in the street, on the sidewalk, in the alleys between the buildings. There were several cars parked outside all the time, and the van with its antennae never moved. We were in the dead center of the enemy camp.

The Soviet people present were able quietly to pursue their discussions: we were, so to speak, hardened to surveillance. The foreigners, too, managed after a while to adopt our nonchalant attitude, but it couldn't have been easy for them. I later read accounts of our meetings in various Western publications (Robert Coleman from *Newsweek,* for one, joined us for a day), in which the nervous strain of the situation was vividly described. I remember the expression of sudden relief on each face as the guests arrived, having successfully passed through that human barricade.

Once the talks began, however, none of us paid attention to the activities of the plainclothesmen outside. We refuseniks were absolutely fascinated by our guests' presentations — to be updated in current science was manna to the starving. Nothing we heard was more dramatic than Mario Grossi's lecture on the vehicles that had been landed in Mars. He showed us the first slides that had ever been taken on that planet — pictures that were as yet unpublished; we were almost the first audience in the world to see them. Mario was one of the principal researchers whose work enabled spacecraft to make that incredible voyage, and there is a plaque on Mars with his name on it.

Everyone there was both impressed and very much touched when Professor Golfand read the paper on wave logic by the absent Yuri Orlov.

Those were four highly emotional days for all of us. We were prisoners, reaching out desperately to grasp the hands of friends in the free world. And to our infinite gratitude, these emissaries from the outside seemed to share our feelings. At the end of every day, some of them stayed and we talked for hours. I remember walking mile after mile around Moscow with Mario Grossi and Eric Fawcett, trudging through the chilly spring night until almost dawn. We talked and talked; we just couldn't go our separate ways when all of us knew the time for such conversations was so short and the future so uncertain. We all became fast friends; it was Mario who, later, encouraged me to write this book.

Eric Fawcett gave me two presents, the first a five-dollar Olympic

Jubilee coin bearing a representation of the Marathon runner. It symbolized the marathon I was running, though I didn't know the distance or the time or whether I would ever cross the finish line. The other was one that expressed our situation only too well: a splendid edition of *Alice in Wonderland*!

Before the end of the Seminar, we asked all the visiting participants to join us for lunch at a restaurant not far from our neighborhood, the Kazakhstan. This entertainment turned out to have a distinctly *Alice in Wonderland* aspect.

We all walked in, about forty of us, and I asked the hostess if we could please all sit together. There were practically no other patrons in the place. It was more or less a workingman's restaurant, and most of their custom came in after five o'clock. The woman asked us to wait, and we were all talking so hard and fast that it was about half an hour before it occurred to me that there was quite a delay here. Why hadn't we been seated? Finally, several tables were pushed together, and we all settled down and picked up our menus.

There was something strange. Not the menus, which, as everywhere in Moscow, were beautifully printed on glossy paper, page after page of Lucullan dishes — but the fact that the entrées we ordered actually were available! Ordinarily in such a place you are told that they have "run out" of almost anything you may request, and you are lucky to get some simple-minded Russian steak dish (*"bifshteks"* or *"antrecot"*) and cabbage, no matter what the menu may advertise. Here were not only tomatoes and cucumbers — absolute treasures, even in Moscow — but salmon and caviar! What's more, a trio of waiters appeared, and the service was quick and excellent. Ordinarily, a single waitress — none too competent — would have been the sole person serving in such a restaurant.

There was a prolonged dispute after luncheon as to who was to pick up the check. Mario, Jim, Eric, and the rest suspected that our treating them to this meal meant that a few of us would have to sell another table or lamp; but they eventually realized how much it meant to us to be their hosts, and they let us handle the bill.

The Soviet diners at this party were so stunned by the appearance of the salad — we hadn't seen a single tomato for months — that we held back, wanting to be sure that our guests would get enough. As a result, when we were finished there was quite a lot left over. Lucia, in agonies at seeing these wonderful things go to waste, slipped up to me and whispered, "I'm going to do something terrible" — whereupon she approached one of the waiters and asked if she could wrap up these leftovers and take them along. One can imagine with what disdain this request would be met by a well-trained waiter in a fashionable restaurant.

"Certainly, madam, let me attend to it," he answered. While he was packaging the salad, he commented to Lucia, "I see you are entertaining physicists from the United States! And how interesting: no one could stop talking physics, even at dinner."

"Why, that's extraordinary, that you understand English!" Lucia exclaimed.

The man looked confused, caught out. "Oh, well, no; just a couple of words. I worked once for a short while at the Rus." And he didn't say another word. At that point the mystery of our wonderful feast became clear to Lucia — as it had been to some of us from the start. The reason our service had been delayed so long was that we were awaiting the arrival of these waiters and of the special food. And the man's remark made the situation even clearer: the very elegant Rus is the "show" restaurant of Moscow, where important foreigners are entertained by Party bosses. The staff there speaks several languages, and reports to the KGB.

After one more day of intense exchange of information (we maintained a tough schedule, and packed an enormous amount of work into those four days), Lucia and I gave another dinner, this time at home, before we saw our visitors off.

This Seminar left me with one of the best memories in my life and, I am positive, in the lives of the other refuseniks as well. It was an absolute triumph.

On the Rack

THE FACT that the anniversary session had been such a success put me in a new position. If our group had been a thorn in the side of the Soviet body politic before, now it was a serious threat. We were recognized and respected as an organization by important American, Canadian, and Western European scientists with whom the Soviets were most anxious to be on cordial terms.

What could they do with me now? They could hardly let me stay and arrange a repetition of this extraordinary occasion, which had given rise to a great deal of sympathetic comment in the Western press. The KGB would have to make its choice soon: to get me out of the country, or into prison or exile.

For a week or ten days after the conference, nothing happened. The plainclothesmen vanished, the stakeouts disappeared; we had space to breathe.

Of course, this couldn't last. At the end of that quiet interval, a new front-page "exposé" of the espionage and treachery of Anatoly Shcharansky, Alexander Lerner, Vladimir Slepak, and "one Azbel" appeared in *Izvestia*. My first name and patronymic were omitted in the piece, and the writer combined the story of David Azbel's dissident activities with an account of my subversive Seminar. David was already in Israel, but the ordinary reader would not know that. The journalist, capitalizing on my namesake's notoriety, was blackening me with two brushes.

Immediately after the publication of this article, while I was at home trying to enjoy the peace of a pleasant spring evening, I had an unwelcome visit from Georgi Borisovitch, who handed me a special summons to Lefortovo Prison, where I was to appear at nine A.M. on the following Tuesday, May 10th, in the Chief KGB Interrogator's Office, as witness for the investigation of the case against Anatoly Shcharansky.

I hadn't expected this at all. The KGB knew everything about us, and must have been aware that I was not very well acquainted with Shcharansky. He is a much younger man than I; and, as it happened, he and I, though fighting the same war, had been on different fronts. I had not been with the group that monitored Soviet adherence to the Helsinki Agreement, and he had had little contact with the Seminar. We respected and liked each other, but our paths didn't cross very frequently.

My colleagues, when I told them about the summons at our next Sunday Seminar, were very much surprised and naturally extremely apprehensive.

Once at the Chief Interrogator's Office — this was in the same building where I had spent a horrible day before Yuli Daniel's trial — I had to wait, sitting on a hard chair in a dimly lit room filled with other people, also waiting. The atmosphere in that room was heavy with fear; it was indescribably unpleasant.

After half an hour I was called by the duty officer, who conducted me to a hall, where he stopped in front of an iron door and pushed a button. The door opened, we walked through, and it silently closed behind us. A second KGBst, who sat there on duty, took my passport and conducted me up a flight of stairs; we then marched through a corridor lined with closed doors, installed in which were small red electric bulbs. Some of these were lit, probably indicating that the rooms were in use for an interrogation. I was ushered into one of the last rooms, a small office with a barred window, furnished with the familiar table and telephone, the smaller table for the witness, two chairs, and an iron safe in the corner. The interrogator was a colorless bespectacled man. By now almost all of these people seemed interchangeable to me; I can hardly remember their faces.

The questioning started, as so often, innocuously, almost conversationally. I was asked if I knew Shcharansky. Yes. How long had we known each other? I couldn't say. Was he present at the meeting with the American senators? I refused to say whether or not I had been there myself. Had he and I signed some letters of appeal sent to the American Congress? I said I could not remember.

At the beginning of this interrogation, I had announced that I wished to put the answers to all questions in writing, myself. The official said I might do so, but first I must make the answers orally.

He grilled me for about two hours, and, as I always had under these circumstances, I avoided making any sort of definite statement. The official could not maneuver me into saying anything more concrete about Shcharansky than that I was acquainted with him. Oddly enough, the man didn't try very hard to force any real information out of me. He repeated his questions in a perfunctory tone, almost as if he were as tired of the whole senseless conversation as I was.

At length he pressed a button, whereupon a plainclothesman came in; he was left to guard me while the official went out of the room. Ten minutes later he returned, bringing with him a typed paper.

"All right," he said, "will you please sign this?"

When I read it, I was so furious, I could hardly control myself. The text ran: "I, Mark Yakovlevitch Azbel, wish to inform the Office of Interrogation of the KGB of the following facts: I have known Anatoly Shcharansky for a considerable time, although I cannot specify exactly how long. Our acquaintance was the result of our both making applications for exit visas, and of our joint appeals to Western organizations, in particular to the Congress of the United States. I was present at the meeting with American senators at the Sovietskaya Hotel, where Shcharansky served as interpreter." And so forth. Answers I had specifically withheld were all here, in the affirmative. It was a bald denunciation of Shcharansky and, moreover, was presented in the form of a gratuitous deposition to the KGB.

It took me a minute to take myself in hand so as not to start shouting with rage — that would have opened me to a charge of "resisting the authorities." When I could bring myself to speak, I said, in what seemed to me an ordinary quiet voice, "No. I won't sign this paper."

"But why not?"

"Because I did not say this. I didn't 'wish to inform' you of anything."

"Oh. Well, if there are any inaccuracies, here's a pen. You can just cross out any errors."

"It's not the details that are wrong. It's the entire text. I didn't say I had joined in any activity whatsoever with Shcharansky. Actually, I didn't make any of the statements that are indicated here."

"Well, Mark Yakovlevitch! I'm afraid you don't understand the situation. We know you're guilty on the same count as Shcharansky; at least implicated with him. You'd better not try to be so tough with us. You *have* to sign this protocol. You're allowed to change anything you want. In fact, if you insist, you can write just below your signature, 'I retract my testimony,' and sign it again."

It was a very rough game. If I *retracted* the testimony, this would be an admission that I had produced it. I explained this point to the official, but obviously it was not logic that mattered in this case.

He hammered and hammered at me, applying the crudest psychological pressure, saying in almost so many words that if I knew what was good for me, I would try to avoid changing my status from that of witness to that of accused.

At two P.M. he announced that I could take a break for dinner (something that had never occurred in my previous experience at this sort of session). They would keep my passport while I was out of the building.

I went out to a telephone booth and called a friend who had offered to serve as contact when he heard I had been ordered to appear at Lefortovo, so that he could let Lucia and the others know what was happening — if I got the chance to get through to him. (This was not Oleg, of course. I didn't want to endanger him.) I told him about the false protocol and the hours of verbal bludgeoning that I had been subjected to in an attempt to make me sign it.

Then, although I was not hungry, I decided I had better have something to eat. I didn't know any restaurants in that vicinity, so I went across the road to the Institute of Energy, to the students' dining room. For some reason the heat in that place, the borscht and the revolting macaroni dish, which was the only food they were serving, the horrible overcrowding — hundreds of students, thousands of flies — the whole scene, remains acutely vivid in my memory of that excruciating day.

Upon my return to Lefortovo I found, not surprisingly, that the interrogator knew of my telephone call. "You know you are forbidden to divulge anything about an interrogation, without the written permission of the prosecutor," he said. "The proceedings of an interrogation are confidential prior to the trial. This warning is just so that you won't be able later to plead ignorance of the law — though we know perfectly well you were not ignorant of it."

He resumed his efforts to make me sign the paper. After a few more grueling hours, another officer came into the room, evidently higher-ranking than the man who had been dealing with me up to now. They were pulling out the big guns.

"We are not playing games here," said the second man. "You'll have to sign. We have ways of seeing to it that you sign. The sooner you do it, the better for you."

By eight in the evening, when I was finally released, I was as exhausted by this struggle as if I had been beaten. The loud implacable voices, repeating over and over the same threats, and the sound of my own voice persistently pronouncing the same counterarguments, had eventually become a physical torture.

As I left, I was presented with a summons to return at nine A.M. the following morning.

The trip home was interminable — to get from Lefortovo Prison to

Veshnyakovskaya Street takes over an hour by bus — and I was almost too tired to move. All I could think of was how I would tell Lucia and Victor what I had been through; how it looked to me as if the KGB hoped to maneuver me into the same trap in which Shcharansky was caught; and then I would fall into bed to store up my strength for the next day's test of endurance.

But when I got home, I found we had a visitor! It was my father, who had arrived unexpectedly. I had completely forgotten it, but the day after tomorrow was my forty-fifth birthday, and he had come from Kharkov to celebrate.

It was a considerable effort to smile, to embrace my father, to convey enthusiasm and hospitality, at a time like that. I had to brush off the events of the day: "It was nothing, just one of those routine interviews; not worth discussing. How wonderful that you're here! Yes, I have to go back tomorrow, but don't worry."

After a few minutes I excused myself, saying I needed a breath of fresh air after being inside all day, and Lucia and I went out to walk. Victor, whom Lucia had alerted via two or three messengers when I got home, joined us on the street, and I gave him an account of the interrogation.

My father waited up for us. When we returned he looked at my face and said, "You'd better get some sleep; you've got to rest up for tomorrow."

Throughout the years of refusal, I had tried to conceal from Father as much as I could about what we were undergoing. Although he had known all along that I was not having an easy life, this was the first time he had seen the situation as it really was. No matter how cheerfully I tried to minimize his fears, it was obvious to him that I was in serious trouble.

"When you applied, my only hope was that you wouldn't leave too soon," he told me. "I knew how much I would miss you, and I hated the thought of seeing you go. Now I have only one desire: I want you to *leave, to go!* For God's sake — when will you be out of this?"

The next morning I was back at the Interrogator's Office. This time they made me wait, in that dim hall filled with anxious people, for two solid hours.

I always had an escape hatch from this pressure: my unsolved scientific problems, which were very exciting to me. I was always able to fill intervals of enforced leisure by working these problems out; I became absorbed in my science and was able to shut off the outside world.

But at this particular time I have to admit that to take this mental route was very difficult. Shortly before this interrogation I had learned that the paper submitted on my behalf to the *Proceedings of the Royal Society* and to *Nature* by Professor Ziman had been rejected. To have my work consistently declined — something that had never once happened to me when I was part of the Soviet scientific Establishment — undermined the sense of my efforts. I had to force myself to forget about it in order to continue producing. It would have been wonderful for my morale if I had known then what sort of reception these same results would achieve later, after I had familiarized myself with the Western style.

Also, it would have made a world of difference to me if I had been aware of the battle being fought on my behalf by people outside of the Soviet Union. I had no idea that at almost the very same hour that I was sitting in a dim room full of frightened people on our way to hours and days of KGB interrogations, which would conclude for some of us with years in labor camps, Professor Minko Balkansky in Paris was initiating a very strong action on my behalf. He collected hundreds of signatures of prominent French writers, scientists, painters — including those of Ionesco, of Simone de Beauvoir, of Professors Kastler, Schwartz, and many, many others — on a petition for my release.

I heard about this much later, from Professor Minko Balkansky himself. "Professor Kastler and I planned to present the petition to Brezhnev — he was in France on a state visit at the time, as you probably know. But the whole idea fell through. We were sent away from the Soviet Embassy to a Russian official's residence in the suburbs, where nobody would receive us — and there we were again dismissed. We didn't see anyone but a rather stupid butler, who asked us several times who we were and what was the point of these signatures, and then showed us out."

The two professors were much discouraged by their failure to fulfill their mission. However, knowing Soviet methods as I do, I cannot doubt that the entire interview with the "butler" — who had them repeat their names and describe their errand, over and over — was recorded; and that the man himself was not at all the simpleton whose part he played, but an agent who was doing his job of obtaining exact information as to the visitors and to the contents of the large volume they carried with them. I am certain that this attempt materially increased the odds in favor of my release.

That second day, the interrogator tried something new. He conceded without argument my right to read each question, which he transcribed, and to answer it in my own hand (a right guaranteed by the Criminal Code). But the questions took a new turn. They were all specifically concerned with documents Shcharansky and I might have signed

together. He produced several of these: completely innocuous letters
(typewritten, and with our signatures in type), which no prosecutor
would bother to magnify into "anti-Soviet propaganda" unless he had
absolutely no other materials available, such as greetings to the Israeli
people on Hanukkah or Rosh Hashana.

This was like the opening move in chess. It was clear to me that if I
let them capture this one insignificant pawn — that is, the admission
that I had signed anything that also bore Shcharansky's signature — it
would be almost impossible to·retain my position, which was based
upon my consistently denying any memory of ever having signed even
one of these letters.

"Well, there's certainly nothing compromising or criminal here," the
interrogator insisted. "I can't see what objection you might have to
agreeing that you were among those sending New Year's greetings to
Israel! What's so important about that? You know, I am actually trying
to improve your situation. You're aware that your exit visa depends on
us. I want you at least to make a gesture of cooperation."

"I can't remember signing anything you've got here. Moreover, I was
called in as a witness — no charges have been brought against me, so I
am not obliged to answer any questions concerning myself. As to
Shcharansky, I have no idea. I don't know what he's signed or hasn't
signed." I braced myself to repeat this whatever might happen, whatever damning evidence might be produced.

Because everyone knows that an interrogation is not an investigation
but a means of collecting material that can support the prosecutor, all
of us, the refuseniks, adopted this same stubborn stance under these circumstances. To admit to the most innocent of actions, even to confirm a
statement known to be true, is to provide the Prosecutor with ammunition that will be used against the defendant, or against you, the minute
you pass the fine line that divides a witness from a person under indictment. The interrogator's role was to apply every incentive possible, positive or negative, to make me cross that line. I had to attempt to stand
stock-still.

He barraged me with all sorts of written "evidence," including small
fragments from depositions (referring again to ceremonious messages to
Israel) that, he claimed, were made by Shcharansky. He offered me absolutely no proof of the authorship of these documents. (Of course,
even if he had, I knew perfectly well that the methods used with
Shcharansky would have been incomparably crueler than the battering I
was undergoing — there was little reason to doubt that he could have
been subjected to pressures nobody could withstand.)

The interrogator kept warning me that I was making myself increasingly liable to prosecution on grounds of withholding testimony. The entire day was spent in this way, except for the dinner break, when, ignoring the ban on calls, I telephoned again to the friend who was serving us as messenger.

"I suppose I have to tell you right now," he said, "Victor has been served with the same summons as yours. He has to be at that office tomorrow."

This was really bad. They might be getting ready to use this investigation as an excuse for the harassment of any number of refuseniks: Victor knew Anatoly no better than I did.

When I left for home that night I carried with me another summons, not for the next day but for May 13th, which meant that I would be free at least for my birthday.

Upon my arrival at the apartment, again, I had time to say only a word to Father before hurrying out. I went to Victor Brailovsky's to bring him up to date on the events of that day.

My birthday was hardly a festive one. My father's spirits were much depressed by the realization of how much danger I was in; Lucia was very anxious; and even our Yulia, usually so gay and talkative, was silenced by the gloom that affected us.

We had invited Irina and Victor to come over when the Prosecutor's Office was finished interrogating him. When eight-thirty arrived, then nine, and they still hadn't appeared, we began to worry. At ten we were still sitting around the table, too nervous to eat or to put up any pretense of celebrating. Even at eleven, we had heard nothing. Not until midnight, after I had run outside the twentieth time to telephone the friend who took our calls, did I get news: "Victor is on his way home from Lefortovo. He couldn't tell me anything over the phone."

Lucia and I leaped up from the table and went down the street to hail a cab. When we arrived at the Brailovskys', we could see at once that Victor was not only exhausted but really sick. He had been held at Lefortovo until almost eleven — for all practical purposes not as a witness, but as a suspect. The interrogation had been prolonged six hours after the working day.

"We'll go outside," he said. His apartment, like mine, was bugged all the time. Once on the street, he told us about the fourteen hours of torture he had been through. The interrogator was a Ukrainian, a brutal personality without the mask of manners or persuasiveness that most such functionaries know how to assume when it suits their purposes.

"You're going to be sent up on the same rap as Shcharansky," he told Victor, pounding the desk with a clenched fist. "And let me tell you something: you may imagine you'll get two or three years in camp, and then be released and go to Israel. Don't fool yourself. Where you're going, people like you don't last more than a year." He attacked Victor all day and half the night. There was no midday break; not a moment's relief.

"They're probably just trying to terrorize you," I said. "They'll give up soon." But I was not at all sure of what I was saying. The treatment inflicted on Victor was a great deal tougher than what I had got, and the weapon with which he was menaced was far more dangerous than the letters to Israel to which I was supposed to admit authorship. This was a letter to President Carter, sent to him at the time of his inauguration, urging him to make free emigration a prerequisite for granting Most Favored Nation trade status to any nation in question, not only with reference to the Soviet Union, but to other countries, as well. The KGB claimed it was sent by the Moscow Jewish activists and that Brailovsky had composed it.

Victor, who was feeling ill (he is subject to liver attacks), finally decided he would risk everything. To the last round of questions he no longer answered, "I don't remember." He announced that he would refuse to testify. The interrogator was startled. It was the first time he displayed any reaction to anything Victor said.

"You can get a prison term for refusing to serve as witness," he pronounced.

"I know it. But I refuse."

"You had better think it over. I assume you will have changed your mind by tomorrow." He handed Victor a summons for nine A.M.

This was the beginning of a black interlude in our lives, and also in that of Veniamin Fain, although once Professor Fain refused to give testimony, they let up on him. But day after day, Victor and I left home every morning before eight o'clock, exactly like people going to their jobs, to arrive at Lefortovo by nine. We got home between eight and midnight, speechless with fatigue. There were stakeouts in front of our apartments all the time; we were followed everywhere. Once on a weekend, when I was calling on one of the editors of *Jews in the U.S.S.R.,** my host's apartment was raided and everyone present was subjected to a personal search. They took my notebook — the most precious object I owned — and all back copies of the journal.

Soon afterward, the KGB interrogations were alternated with sessions at the Moscow Prosecutor's Office in Novokuznetsk Street. These latter interrogations were positively a rest cure, compared to the ones at Lefortovo. I was not locked in; the place was not connected to a prison.

---

* Under KGB pressure, publication was stopped in the summer of 1979.

The sessions were probably supposed to increase the tension, but they had the opposite effect; I felt them to be a respite from those days in the Lefortovo offices.

Days and days went by this way, a round of threats and warnings at one of the institutions or the other. It became just about impossible to look cheerful when I got home at night; to keep up a front for Lucia's benefit and — particularly — for Yulia's. I could not sustain such an effort indefinitely.

"We can't go on like this," I said at last to Lucia. "You'll have to send for your own separate invitation from Israel. Yulia can't stand much more; she's miserable. Don't wait any longer. She's got to get out of this place and out of this country. We can't subject a child to such a life. You and Yulia are like people living under a curse."

Lucia protested vehemently. "We won't go until you do!" she said, leaving unspoken the thought that, if they actually could receive visas and emigrate ahead of me, we might never see each other again. "Besides, everything's sure to turn out all right! There are so many people fighting for you, Mark!" (Not long before, we had got word of Save Azbel demonstrations at American universities, notably the University of Pennsylvania, and a Committee for Azbel, Lerner and Levitch at the Massachusetts Institute of Technology. My gratitude for these efforts was limitless, but by now my hopes were extinguished.)

It took a long time before I could get Lucia to say that if my situation had not changed by autumn she would reconsider, and that meanwhile she would at least send for her invitation to Israel. I did manage to persuade her to take our daughter out of the city, to visit friends of ours in the resort town of Koktebel, in the Crimea.

When they had gone it was actually a relief to come home after my horrible day's "work" to the empty apartment; not to have to smile nor to summon one last ounce of mental energy with which to invent some way of assuaging the fear so clearly written on their faces. The only person I communicated with much at that time was Victor.

At the end of three weeks I was summoned (again by Georgi Borisovitch) to an interview at Kuznetsky Most with the same Sergei Ivanovitch Gavrilov to whom I had presented a sort of ultimatum the previous December. This time, Sergei Ivanovitch adopted a fatherly pose.

"Mark Yakovlevitch! I've thought over everything we talked about when we last saw each other, and do you know, I've become almost convinced that you were right. I have even approached the highest authorities with the suggestion that you should receive your exit visa. They are in agreement." I remained silent. He went on: "But it's only natural that they should want your testimony on Shcharansky before you leave." He gave me a minute to let that sink in. "Now look. What are they asking you about? Just some minor details. Small, simple things that are of no importance to anybody! But I hear that you behave as an enemy. That you don't want to answer these questions. That you won't cooperate on even the most trivial points."

As Sergei Ivanovitch talked, it crossed my mind that Tsipin, and the other defectors from the aliyah, might have been entrapped exactly in this way. Perhaps they had taken that first small step on the route which had led — not to the freedom for which they fought so long — but to moral suicide. Permission for Israel was so close! — right within your grasp. To reach it, you had to make only one tiny concession. And then another little concession would follow, and then another — until in the end you found yourself a spokesman for the KGB.

Sergei Ivanovitch pursued his argument.

"You know that the Prosecutor's Office and the Interrogator's Office are absolutely independent. I cannot give orders for them: no one can, not even the highest authorities. *I* cannot let you go — unless you give me this testimony. And they've started to feel doubtful. They say that if you are such a stubborn and open enemy . . ." He left the sentence unfinished. "They cannot allow an avowed enemy to leave for the West. Why shouldn't you be just a *little* cooperative?"

I heard myself reiterate the same improbable explanations on which I had fallen back so many times before: that I would be glad to give any testimony within my powers, but that I didn't want to lie. I realized it must sound unlikely that I had such a poor memory, but what could I do? My memory was absolutely perfect when it came to physics, but my science demanded all of that faculty, and there were no powers left over for the things they were asking me about. "How can I lie?" I protested. "If I start to lie, to say that I remember this or that, I'll be lost. Pretty soon I'll have to invent more and more details — after that I'll be caught out; it will be obvious that I'm lying. And I'll lay myself open to charges of giving false testimony. Then I really would be guilty. I'd have no escape, and as you said, Sergei Ivanovitch, our courts are independent even of the highest authorities. Rather than be given my exit visa, I'll be sentenced. So I cannot possibly change my attitude." Then, still polite and "reasonable," I went on the offensive.

"What bothers me," I said, "is that these interrogations are not going smoothly at all. There's something wrong with them, you know? I am very worried by the pressure there. I'm being subjected to threats! And I don't understand the problem. You know very well that neither I nor Victor Brailovsky can give any information about Shcharansky. We know him, but we aren't particularly close friends of his. Brailovsky was told a year ago that he could get his permission to go. He recently reapplied and received no answer. So something is going wrong."

Sergei Ivanovitch answered brusquely, "If Brailovsky produces proper testimony on Shcharansky, he'll get his visa. If not, he won't. And the same conditions may apply to you!" But then his voice became sympathetic, almost wheedling. "You're so close to your permission! Why should you delay it? Who knows how long you may be held if you can't just remember one or two trivial things?"

The second interrogation after my meeting with Sergei Ivanovitch took place on the 10th of June. This time I was to be questioned by Comrade Chernykh — not the same man who had been battering me all these weeks, but his superior. The appointment was, again, for nine A.M., and, again, I was kept waiting, first in the room full of frightened people and then, after an hour or so, in a separate room, where two KGBsts sat with me, reading newspapers, until early afternoon. Only then was I conducted to Chernykh's office. He was a short, broad man with coal-black eyes, piercing and intense.

Chernykh greeted me like an old friend. He apologized for the long delay. "But," he said, "I am sure you'll understand. What happened was that Anatoly Shcharansky asked for an interview with me, and of course the person in trouble has to be considered first. So I had to talk to him before I could see you, and that's why you had to wait. Once again, I'm very sorry. Since you've been held up for such a long time, maybe you'd like a cup of coffee?"

"Thank you, no." I didn't know what might be in the coffee, for one thing; even if I'd been positive there was nothing in it, I wouldn't accept the hospitality of the KGB.

"First I want to ask you," he began, "do you have any complaints about your previous interrogator? As supervisor of the interrogatory corps, I have to check the methods of the men under me. I have to make sure they fulfill all the requirements of Soviet law." I answered that they frequently violated the law, which, if I understood it correctly, made very specific distinctions between the questions that may be addressed to a witness in a criminal investigation, and to a suspect; that also prohibited threatening and intimidating a witness.

"I'm very sorry to hear that," he said. "Of course, some of these men are young and inexperienced — they will learn. There has been a real change in investigatory methods in recent years. We no longer approve of an adversary relationship between interrogator and witness or, for that matter, even between ourselves and criminal suspects."

Of course this conversation was just the preliminaries, and all my forces were concentrated for what was to come once this senseless and time-consuming chatter was dispensed with. I understood that it would not be wise to show irritation or boredom: Chernykh was observing me closely, trying to gauge my frame of mind and how nervous I might be.

At two o'clock he dismissed me for an hour's dinner break, overriding my suggestion that to save time we might skip the break. When I returned, the interrogation proper began.

It was different from those I had undergone before. There was no grilling; there were no threats. He simply watched me write my invariable "I don't know" or "I don't remember," and went on to the next question. After an interval he told me that I might condense my answers and simply sign a blanket statement referring to all the documents with which I had been presented, saying that I could not remember whether or not I had ever cosigned any letter with Shcharansky. I wrote a line to that effect and signed it.

Chernykh put his signature to my pass, and the interrogation — a model interrogation in the "new style" — was over. I received no fresh summons when I left, but he politely advised me not to leave town over the weekend (it was Friday).

I was almost positive that this was it. By Monday, they would have decided whether I would get my visa, or go up on whatever charges they might fabricate, and I would have an indefinite future in a prison within the prison that was my native country.

It goes without saying that, although I gave an account of this interview to all my friends, I mentioned to no one except Victor how sure I felt that the authorities' decision was actually at hand. I didn't wire Lucia to tell her — I didn't want either to scare her or to raise false hopes.

When I came home, late on Sunday evening, I found a post card from the Visa Department. I was advised to call there. The name of the specific inspector I should speak to was provided.

My heart pounded. A post card always meant refusal. None of the activists I knew who had received his permission had been notified by mail, but, as I mentioned before, by a policeman who called at the applicant's residence and delivered to him by hand a request that he go to the Visa Department, at a stated day and hour.

This, then, could be a final refusal. However, the card said it was "urgent" for me to call — I had never seen the word "urgent" on a message that portended refusal.

I have to admit that I couldn't shut my eyes all night. Release; refusal. Which would it be? I was sure they would let me go; for the next minute I was positive they never would; and these conclusions alternated back and forth in my mind until morning.

On the stroke of nine I was in a telephone booth, dialing the number on the card.

"The inspector you wish to speak to is not in her office yet; she will be delayed this morning." My nerves almost snapped when I heard those words.

I couldn't get the connection until eleven: those were the two longest hours I ever spent in my life. At long last, the inspector came on the line.

I gave my name. "I was supposed to call this office," I said. "What is the problem?"

"Well — your problem is solved," she said.

"And by that you mean . . . ?"

"You are allowed to leave the Soviet Union."

Epilogue

My LAST DAYS in the Soviet Union remain a chaotic blur in my mind's eye. I never slept more than two or three hours out of the twenty-four: most of my time was spent trying to commit to memory the messages dictated to me by the enormous number of refuseniks who, immediately upon hearing that we were to be released, poured into our apartment in an endless stream, desperate to grasp at this rare opportunity of making contact with their families and friends who had preceded them to Israel; also of people who wanted to find sponsors. All overseas mail was censored; all legal telephone connections were severed. Pleas for help, plans for the future, instructions of every kind, private "codes" for correspondence — the messages of hundreds of people — all had to be conveyed out of the country in my head. I had to force my memory as I had never forced it in my life before. I used all my experience, all the methods that I knew, to imprint these reams of words on my brain — just to hold them until such time as I could commit them to paper, which I would do the instant I was out of the country. I had seen Voronel go through this unbelievable test of mental and physical stamina, and now my turn had come.

Throughout all the years of refusal I had always promised myself, and had persuaded Lucia to promise, that if our permission ever came we would not risk waiting an extra hour. We had suffered so much anguish on behalf of friends who delayed — it was only too easy to be trapped again in the interval when one was no longer a Soviet citizen but was still within Soviet borders. Whoever it was among the top Party officials that had authorized our release might fall from power — these changes occurred all the time. An overnight switch in policy toward the emigrants, a change in relations with the United States, or a mere remark made by an American congressman at which the Soviets took offense, could reverse our situation without warning. When the gate to freedom opened, we would make a run for it. We wouldn't stay one minute beyond the interval that would be required to pack our most essential belongings and fulfill all the legal and financial demands made by the government of people leaving the country.

When the time came, I found I could not go this way. I didn't have it in me to drop silently out of our close refusenik company without taking these last words that my friends — also hundreds of strangers — longed so terribly to convey to the outside world. What's more, I discovered I could not leave the country forever without saying certain farewells. To mention two of them: I knew it would be impossible to go without a last goodbye to Andrei Dmitrievitch Sakharov. And it would be impossible to embark on this new life without making the trip to Kharkov for one final visit to my mother's grave.

When the Visa Department suddenly offered me every courtesy — my status changed abruptly from something very close to that of wanted criminal to exactly that of distinguished foreign scientist — and, among other privileges, offered me a choice of dates for my departure, I took not the eight or ten days, which would have been just sufficient to rush through all the preparations, but — though I knew perfectly well how reckless it was — the maximum: three weeks. July 5th was our deadline.

I couldn't possibly sort out in my memory the details of those frantic days and nights. I had to cope with an unbelievable amount of red tape. I had often accompanied friends who were leaving Russia on their races through Moscow from bureau to department, from ministry to embassy, from bank to customs, where the emigrants had to fill out forms, obtain affidavits, make any number of payments (both legal and bribes); seek officials' signatures, countersignatures, seals, and stamps; produce the enormous sheaf of documents a Soviet citizen has to accumulate — but not until my own permission came did I know what it was like, to spend so many of my waking hours performing this staggering number of final duties. Everywhere I went, I was surrounded by a sort of rotating guard of refusenik friends; some just wanting to be with me for these last days; others seeking advice; still others entrusting their messages for Israel to my memory.

Only a few scenes from those weeks come back to me now.

I wonder if any slave ever felt as happy buying his own person from his owner as I felt in the *sberegatelnaya kassa* (savings bank), paying out 800 roubles for our exit visas: two small documents, printed on flimsy yellow paper. (The price for Jewish souls had gone way up since the start of the emigration: the authorities hadn't originally realized that not just a trickle, but tens of thousands of people, would want to leave the country, and that a very profitable business could be made of this exodus.) After I'd got them, I couldn't refrain from pulling the visas out of my wallet every ten minutes to marvel at them and make sure they were really there. And I never could have imagined being so glad to be robbed and defrauded as I was when paying over almost half the proceeds from the sale of our apartment, a thousand roubles, for the cancellation of our Soviet citizenships.

Then I remember sitting with Academician Sakharov and Yelena Bonner in their small kitchen, all of us making a rather futile effort to look cheerful. We were painfully aware that the circle of Andrei Dmitrievitch's dissenter and refusenik acquaintances was diminishing: some were emigrating; others were in exile. As a parting gift I gave Sakharov the Olympic Marathon coin that had been presented to me. His own marathon is unending.

Another scene from those feverish days comes back to me. I went over to the Institute for Physical Problems with all my scientific *archiv* — reprints and preprints of everything I had published, and also works in progress — to have them verified as nonclassified materials so that I might take them with me out of the country. (This was an unusual concession on the part of the authorities. Often an institute will blankly refuse even to touch the documents of an emigrant scientist; he cannot take a single paper with him, so he will never have access to his own body of work again, save what has appeared in the literature. Artists cannot take out their own works if the art is considered "important to the Soviet State.")

As I was going out of the institute, I met one of my colleagues, a professor of physics, now Corresponding Member of the Soviet Academy. He smiled genially when he saw me.

"Is it true that you've got your visa?"

"Yes, it is."

"Well — to be frank, I didn't believe they'd let you go. But I'm very glad for you. Where will you be settling? M.I.T.? California Institute of Technology?"

"But I don't intend to go to the States."

"No?" He was obviously interested. "Do you really think that England or Western Europe would suit you better? Why do you think so? It seems like a mistake to me. You should look into it more carefully when you're out of the Soviet Union."

"But I'm not going to Europe. I'm leaving for Israel."

"Oh, come on! Of course you have to *declare* you're going to Israel, but good heavens, we've known each other for almost twenty-five years. Don't keep it up for my benefit! I won't mention your plans to anyone, and anyway, at this point it doesn't make any difference."

"But I really am going to Israel."

"To *Israel!* Why on earth? We've all heard that you've received offers from universities in the States!"

"It's not concern about finding a position that keeps me from going there," I said. "I *want* to go to Israel."

The expression on his face clearly showed that there would be no sense in trying to explain anything to him. He shrugged his shoulders; this gesture meant: "Well, you know my good opinion of you as a scientist, but there's no doubt about it — you always were a strange person."

We were sorry for each other. I was sorry for him: half-Jewish; a very decent man, but without any idea that in a person's life there might exist emotions or any kind of social or national feelings. If he hadn't known me for years he would have assumed I was simply deceiving him. As it was, he pitied me as a foolish idealist.

Lucia, too, was breathlessly busy during those days. She handled more than her share of the paperwork, making duplicates of all our documents and spending literally days with the notary public. He was one of the many functionaries we both dealt with at that time who made no secret of their loathing for Jews and of their rage at seeing us make good our escape. He forced her to obtain extra signatures on everything, to verify and reverify each and every paper, and he refused to place his seal on my certificates of scientific discoveries.

"They were notarized once before," Lucia said. (We had had it done when we first applied for our visas, never thinking we would be detained all those years.)

"Oh, we used to make that mistake" was the answer, "but now the regulations are tougher. You Jews won't find it so easy to get out as you did before."

She coped with all the packing: clothes, chinaware, books. I do remember one moment of "comic relief" during that time: a friend of ours, Lyalya, had come from Kharkov to help with the work, and she went out with Lucia one day to beg, borrow, or steal some cardboard cartons, which are almost unobtainable in Moscow. By the end of their excursion they were both weighed down with these boxes — neither of them had a hand free. But they passed by a store where, *mirabile dictu,* toilet paper was on sale! Lyalya stopped in her tracks, robbed Lucia of her last roubles, and joined the queue. Even at such a critical time, she insisted on getting toilet paper to bring home to friends in Kharkov, where it is in even shorter supply than in the capital. She would have stopped to buy it if Moscow had been burning down.

"We can't carry it," objected Lucia.

"I have some twine," Lyalya informed her. She bought twenty-four rolls of the paper and strung it in a triple row around her neck. "Let's go!" They picked up the cartons and hurried home, attracting the stares of passersby on their way. "That's some necklace, lady," commented a truck driver who watched the festooned Lyalya crossing the street, "but no woman who needs that much toilet paper could ever catch a man!"

Crowds of our other friends were in the apartment almost around the clock, helping us to pack as well as seeking these last conferences. Every evening when we got home Lucia and I would describe to each other the hectic events of our day, while everyone listened with wry amusement. Over and over, we each had the same experience: one of us would walk into an office where we had business and would be brutally insulted by some clerk or minor official who had not been alerted to the fact that the Soviets intended to smooth our path and provide us with VIP treatment during these last days. Seeing a Jew, and obviously not an Establishment Jew, who was making inquiries concerned with his forthcoming emigration, they reacted instinctively. "I haven't got time for you now. Come back in . . . oh, six weeks." "We can't be bothered here with you damn Jews running off to your filthy Fascist Israel!" And then, when we made use of the telephone number I had been given by the Chairman of the Visa Department "just in case of any trouble," and the message "from above" was phoned in as to the reception we were supposed to be accorded — what an about-face! The very same clerk, now frightened almost out of his wits, was ready not to be more than polite; he would grovel. It is of such defective personalities — at once bully and lickspittle — that a huge segment of the Soviet population is made up: the petty bureaucrats. How glad we would be to see the last of them! Our old-refusenik friends, upon hearing the anecdotes we gleaned daily in our hurried rounds, laughed and commented ironically, "Inoculation against homesickness."

Thus, despite our sudden elevated status (and did the Soviets think that these unexpected amenities would wipe the last five years out of our minds, and turn us overnight into propagandists for the fairness and kindness of Russia toward emigrants?), what most of those who had gone ahead to Israel had been subjected to on their way out was certainly no secret.

My dealings with the section of the Customs Department that handles surface freight did not take very long, partly because of my newly acquired "protectors" and partly because we had so few possessions left. There were some restrictions, however, that I could not get around. I have a photograph of my mother, into the frame of which was set the

Swiss watch that Father gave her for a wedding present. The watch was stopped forever at the hour of her death.

"You can't take out such jewelry," the man at customs told me. I had hardly considered a plain inexpensive Swiss watch to be jewelry, but he was adamant. I still feel a deep sense of loss, a permanent resentment, whenever I look at the frame with the empty round space. We emigrants were stripped of everything on our way out. Things of no value to anyone but the owner — one's files, one's letters, one's diaries — could not be taken. To be robbed of your money and valuables was one thing; to be robbed of your memories, a bitter blow.

I am glad to say that I rescued a good part of my library. I would have hated never to see my books again — none more precious than the copy of *Theoretical Physics* by Landau and Lifshitz, with Landau's inscription on the front page: "To my dear Mark," and his signature — just *Dau.*

* * *

I went to Arkhipova Street for the last time, to the synagogue, where an excited group surrounded me and announced that Professor Fain, too, had received his exit visa. My cup ran over.

"That means Victor will be next," I predicted. We three scientists had been those interrogated in the Shcharansky investigation; our cases were evidently linked; and if two of us were to be freed, why not the third? This marvelous news removed a weight from my spirit, a weight that returned all the more heavily when hope for the Brailovskys began to fade.

When I returned to Moscow after my brief, sad visit to Kharkov, I found the refusenik world in a state of terrible turmoil. This time, literally dozens of people who knew Shcharansky — even those who barely had a nodding acquaintance with him — were being summoned for interrogation. The trial was in full preparation.

By that time I could hardly absorb anything that was going on around me. My mental capacities were totally occupied by just one thing: keeping the messages I had been given, and was still receiving, in my memory. The most valuable benefit I could perform for the hundreds of friends I was leaving behind was to preserve their urgent words intact until I could deliver them in the West, and addressing myself to this task left me barely able to assimilate other concerns. When I look back on that last week I find a blank.

We were given not one, but a succession of farewell parties; the last one, as was customary, we gave ourselves on the eve of departure, in our almost-bare apartment. If it weren't for the photograph (which shows only a fraction of the people who were there) I would have to say — with painful regret — that I could hardly remember our party at all. Trying to relive that occasion, I can feel only the tremendous warmth of feeling in the crowd around us, and my own desperate hope that these friends would soon follow. A few of the people I most longed to say goodbye to weren't there — they were in prison or exile. Had this celebration taken place a year later, there would have been many others absent for the same reason, including Vladimir Slepak.

The last of our guests left after three A.M., except for two who were going to accompany us to the airport. We slept (on the floor — the beds were gone) until four. We had to be at Sheremetyevo by six.

It was early dawn when we climbed into our taxi. We had nothing with us but my valise, some briefcases, and the carrying box in which Tyopa, our cat, was riding. The sun had not yet risen when we arrived at the airport, but Sheremetyevo was already crowded with dozens of our friends who had got there ahead of us, having come to see us off. Victor and Irina were already there. So were Grigori and Natasha Rosenstein; Vladimir Slepak and his wife, Maria; the Levitches; Naum Meiman — everyone. We joined them to drink a last toast to our future meeting in Israel — *"L'shana haba'a b'Yerushalaim"* — before we went into customs.

I didn't have much trouble in customs, except that they wouldn't let me take the scientific papers on which I was currently working — no manuscripts could go — despite the O.K. I had received from the institute. I was beyond caring; I wanted only to move on.

We went up the enclosed staircase and arrived finally at the Bridge, where we stood — at midpoint between East and West — looking down at the sixty or seventy friends who waited below to watch us pass. How many times had we waited there, looking up with yearning and envy, and love, at one of our own who was on the way to freedom. What a strange sensation it was to be here ourselves, after all these years of diminishing hopes.

The moment was brief: I was ushered along to the Passport Control booth, where I handed in our visas. Usually the Passport Control takes just a couple of minutes; but ten minutes went by, then fifteen, and I started to feel somewhat nervous. It was only the previous day that I'd heard about the arrest of Valeri Turchin, representative of Amnesty International. Moreover, there were rumors that Brezhnev was ill. Either one or both of these events could affect my situation. The decision to let me go still might be revoked. I had made a conscious effort not to think about those two items of news after I'd heard them — to force them aside in my mind, since nothing I could do would have any effect on my prospects. Now, inevitably, the fear came flooding back in.

Nothing changed during the next half-hour. I rejoined Lucia and Yulia on the Bridge. Never in all our own experience of seeing people off here had we witnessed travelers pass beyond this opening and then return. I could see that Lucia also was worried, but we just stood there, saying nothing to one another.

Suddenly, threading his way through the crowd below, his eyes ahead of him — not glancing at us — there was Georgi Borisovitch.

Time passed. Flight time was approaching: 10:45. By now we were the only passengers left at the Bridge. I went back to Passport Control and asked one of the border guards what was going on; what was the reason for the delay?

"Your visas aren't here; they took them to another office. Some technical problem."

Again I thought of Turchin's arrest. What could this "technical problem" be, save that our release was being reconsidered?

At this eleventh hour, it looked as though once again my fate was in the balance. If I was right about that, if they were now thinking over the pros and cons of letting us go, there would be consultations all the way up the line. Soviet officials are always reluctant to assume final responsibility for any action without a directive "from above." If new orders were neeeded, they would have to come from the very top.

I knew that if I were sent back to Moscow right now, I would not be the first Jew to be so served at almost this same juncture; and if my next destination was a prison camp — well, this would be just another roll of the dice for an old refusenik.

I couldn't keep our friends in the dark much longer. They were still assembled in the huge hall below, looking up at us, bewildered as to why we were hovering here when all the other people had long since gone off to board the plane.

"What's going on?" shouted Ilya Essas.

"Something's happened," I called back. "Our visas are gone. They've been taken." Even from that distance I could see the shock on their faces, and hear a chorus, a multiple sigh, of disappointment and alarm.

At this moment a uniformed woman, one of the customs inspectors, briskly walked past us and then turned back in astonishment.

"What are you doing here? The plane leaves in ten minutes!"

"We were told to wait. We asked why, and how long, but nobody knows."

"Well! That's nonsense! I'll find out what's going on." She took up the speaker of a sort of walkie-talkie she carried around with her.

"Dusia!" she called into it. "I have passengers here for the Vienna plane! Hold up the flight a minute." She disappeared. Within a short while, she came back.

"Where are your tickets?"

"Right here."

"All right." She took them. "I'm canceling your reservations. I'm having them take off your luggage. The plane can't wait any longer."

"But what's the matter?"

"I don't know anything!" she exclaimed in an injured tone of voice, as if all this confusion was our fault. "You can't board the plane now."

"But — what should we do?"

"I don't know! If you *are* allowed to leave, you'll pay a fine for the flight's being held up."

We just stood there. We didn't have our visas, we didn't have our tickets, and the plane would go without us. Now we had nothing in the Soviet Union. We had no passports, no belongings at all. We had no place to live.

We tried to console our daughter, who was bravely struggling to hold back tears, but there was nothing Lucia and I could say to each other. We were smitten much too hard for words. Neither could blame the other for our delay in leaving the country — for obtaining the longest possible interval in which to make our preparations and last farewells. We had treasured those extra days. And now we found ourselves without so much as twenty-four hours' grace during which we still might hope for another chance at another flight: our visas expired after July 5th. Tomorrow they would be worthless bits of paper.

Our cat, the only one of us who could express her feelings, cried continuously in her box. We went on waiting — but for what? I became more and more convinced that I was awaiting arrest. Evidently our friends had the same idea, because when we went back to the Bridge and looked down, everyone was still there: Professor Fain, Pavel Abramovitch, Yevgeny and Rimma Yakir — everyone.

I hardly have to explain how courageous it was of all of them, particularly those among them who were not involved in the emigration, to remain. But there they were, making common cause with refuseniks, right under the eyes of the KGB, as the minutes ticked on — another half-hour, then an hour. By that time all of us could only wonder when the police, the border guards, or the KGB would arrive.

After another interval, the guards at the Passport Control booth suddenly announced: "Here are your visas. Hurry!" I grabbed my briefcase and the cat's carrying-box, Lucia and Yulia picked up their things, and we ran past Passport Control. We kept on running, through the second waiting hall for the use of departing passengers only, and were confronted by several ramps. No one would explain to us which one led to the exit. After several fase starts we found it for ourselves. We were already, in principle, on the other side of the border. We raced toward the door.

"Stop! Where are you running?"

"To the Vienna plane."

"Stop! You have to go through the security control!" We knew nothing about that — they don't have these securi controls at national airports within the Soviet Union — but we backtı cked, went through the checkpoint, and started running again, along a very extensive glassed-in corridor. Through the glass we could see our friends, who had rushed to the place outside the building whence this corridor could be seen. Alexander Lerner caught sight of us, waved encouragingly, we signaled back, and they all waved as we sped desperately by.

We were headed toward the gates that led out to the runway, where the bus that took passengers to the plane was waiting. When we got there, we were stopped by a border guard.

"What's the matter?" I asked.

"First, let's see your visas." They took the visas, examined them attentively, checked our faces carefully against the photographs.

"Now — sit down. You'll have to wait."

"For what?"

"You just have to wait."

"But what's going on? We're supposed to be on the Vienna plane. Will you tell us, please, what's the matter? If it's taken off, we ought to go back to the building and try to do something. If it's still here — we've got to hurry."

"Sit down and wait. That's all."

There was no possibility of changing anything, so we sat down; there was a bench by the gates. We both had the same idea: the reason we had been decoyed to the gates was to separate us from our friends, who had last seen us actually on our way. They would imagine that by now we had boarded the plane, and they would all disperse and go home. Thus we could be arrested with no witnesses.

Fifteen minutes passed. Lucia finally couldn't stand it: she jumped to her feet and went over to the officer who had checked our visas.

"What are you tormenting us for? Has the plane actually left or not?" He looked at her, thought for a while, and slowly answered, "Wait. They'll be coming soon."

"*Who* will be coming?" Again he was silent. Finally he said, "The passengers."

"What do you mean?"

"Well . . . the weather is bad. We're grounded. You should go to the waiting hall."

"But will the other passengers come there too?"

"Yes. Just wait."

"Are you sure?" It was a naïve question. But in any case, we were absolutely helpless.

"M'yes," he said unconvincingly. "Go on. Go back to the waiting hall." And so we proceeded back through the same corridor. We saw that it was sprinkling rain, but even through the dead weight of my fatigue I was able to think a little, and reflect that I had never heard of a jet flight being delayed by a summer shower.

Behind the fence of iron bars we could see dozens of umbrellas. These were the umbrellas of our friends, who hadn't left during these interminable hours, who patiently, stubbornly waited to see what would happen to us. This silent loyalty, this indomitable unity with us, gave us a new measure of strength.

We returned to the waiting hall. We saw with our practiced eyes a large number of plainclothesmen, interspersed throughout the crowd.

We sat on our chairs, silent, numb. After a while I decided to check my documents, and, looking through them, I received a shock.

"I've lost my tickets," I told Lucia.

"Oh, of course you haven't — don't worry — look through the papers again!"

"But Lucia, you remember: I was worried about being so tired and absent-minded that I might lose them, so I carefully kept everything in this." I had a transparent plastic holder. "Now look! Here are the visas. Here's the vaccination certificate for the cat. Here are the customs slips. Everything is here! Except for the flight tickets."

"Well, they couldn't just disappear."

I searched frantically again — with no results.

Finally Lucia said, "Look, if they're going to let us go — they'll let us go, even without the tickets." But of course this was only a shaky assurance to me. "Here's what you ought to do," she added. "Go to the Inquiries Office; maybe somebody's found them."

The woman at the Inquiries Office blankly refused to offer any assistance whatsoever toward finding the tickets. For a long time I tried to persuade her to help us — she could announce the loss over the public-address system — but she brushed me aside. Finally another woman who was sitting in the same office with her, listening indifferently to our conversation, spoke up.

"Why didn't you come for them right at the beginning?" she asked.

And belatedly I recognized her: this was the woman who had taken our tickets in order to have our reservations canceled. She could have easily got hold of us and returned them. But she didn't care. We were Jews; we were emigrants; we were the enemy.

By the time I got them back and had reassembled all my papers, I no longer had a shred of hope left that we were going to go. It was afternoon. We still didn't know what had happened to our flight. At last — more than three hours after we had gone to the Passport Control — we heard the announcement: "Passengers for Vienna should proceed to Exit Nineteen."

Again we walked down the glassed-in corridor. Again we saw our friends waiting — the umbrellas were gone; the shower was over. They were still there; they waved and smiled. Again we came to the border guards, but this time they allowed us to pass through the doors and mount the bus that was to take us across to the runway. It was driven over and stopped by the Red Star Aeroflot jet. The doors of the bus didn't open.

"What's holding us up?" asked one of the passengers near the entrance.

"We're waiting for the commander of the border guard." It was obvious that the driver and the stewardess themselves were astonished by this unaccustomed delay.

It was twenty minutes before the commander arrived. The doors opened and the passengers filed out: he checked the documents of each person separately as we went by. When he had finished, we were almost surprised to be permitted to board the plane.

Now we dared to believe that this was the end of our story, but we were wrong. For almost an hour, we sat in the plane. The engines were silent.

"Sorry," said a woman's voice from near the captain's cabin. "Very sorry — it's never happened before — but you'll all have to leave the plane."

"Why?" demanded one of the passengers.

"Don't ask me — I don't know. I don't understand, but you have to leave the plane." We went back down the steps, got into the bus, and were driven to the same door from which we had left. We marched back through the now-familiar corridor. There again, outside, penned behind the bars, were our friends. They hadn't gone — all of them were still there.

It was past three in the afternoon. Our daughter was exhausted and starving. Yulia was only seven years old; she had endured a night with almost no sleep, and had had hardly a bite to eat since yesterday's very light supper. Here we were, with no money to pay for a restaurant meal: I had of course distributed my last roubles among our friends.

"You've got those souvenir jubilee coins," Lucia reminded me. We had been allowed to take three of them with us: coins minted for the fiftieth anniversary of the Revolution.

"Oh, yes! Thank God!" We moved into the restaurant to try to get something to eat. Probably our faces — particularly Yulia's — were too eloquent to ignore, so instead of making us undergo the usual hour's wait for service, a kindly waitress brought us food immediately.

We had barely started to eat when the loudspeaker went on: "Flight for Vienna, now boarding." We hastily folded our scrambled eggs in the bread — the poor cat resumed her howling — and hastened back the way we had come. All our friends were still there at the barrier. They watched our odyssey resume. Like actors going through another rehearsal, we repeated the same procedures as before: the bus ride, the wait for the commander of the border guard, the thorough checks of our documents, the boarding of the jet.

We could not credit our senses when the same stewardess reappeared and enunciated her plaintive "Sorry!" But this time, we were not asked to disembark. She was announcing a further wait before takeoff: the plane's food supplies, which had been removed an hour before when the decision had been made to cancel the flight (and this was the first we had heard that the flight had actually been canceled), were to be brought back aboard.

It was six hours past the scheduled time when at last the engines started to roar and we began crawling down the runway. When we made a forty-five-degree turn before lift-off, we could catch one last glimpse of the barrier. There, still standing behind the row of iron bars, were our friends. The last faces I could make out were Vladimir Prestin's, the Beilins', Ilya Essas', the Yakirs', and the Brailovskys'.*

When at last we were airborne, all the passengers began to discuss the bad weather conditions over Vienna, which was the explanation they had been given for the delay. "Extraordinary! In July!"

* * *

When that evening we got out of the plane and set foot on Austrian soil, we were barely conscious. But still, we were absolutely happy.

We were free.

* In November of 1980, Victor Brailovsky was arrested for "defamation of the Soviet state" and was sent to Butyrskaya Prison. Irina still bravely carries on.

A man emerged from the crowd that was awaiting incoming passengers, approached us, and embraced us. "I'm from the Israeli Consulate. I have a car waiting for you. What happened? We've all had a terribly anxious day — this flight is never off schedule."

We could hardly relate to him at that point everything we had been through, but we gave him some idea of our long agony, and concluded by mentioning what we had heard about weather conditions over Vienna.

"Why, there hasn't been a cloud! We've had a perfectly beautiful day."

A day and a half later, we were in Israel. We had come home.

But I have a strong feeling that had it not been for my friends, my brothers and sisters who — prisoners themselves — stood by and waited, staunchly refusing to move until they had seen with their own eyes that we were gone, the gates to freedom would have closed on us forever.

It is to those brave, indomitable people, and to all the Soviet *aliyah,* that I dedicate this book.

— Mark Ya. Azbel
Tel Aviv University
1980

Index

Index